What everyone should know about the Bible

What everyone should know about the Bible

V. GILBERT BEERS

Tyndale House Publishers, Inc.
Carol Stream, Illinois

To *Arlie,* *my bride of fifty-six years,*

who has daily given me, our children, and our grandchildren,

a desire for the Word of God.

Visit Tyndale's exciting Web site at www.tyndale.com

TYNDALE and Tyndale's quill logo are registered trademarks of Tyndale House Publishers, Inc.

What Everyone Should Know about the Bible

Copyright © 2007 by V. Gilbert Beers. All rights reserved.

Cover photo of woman reading copyright © by IZA Stock/Getty Images. All rights reserved.

Cover photo of woman smiling copyright © by Art Vandalay/Getty Images. All rights reserved.

Cover photo of man on rock copyright © by Wilfried Kricichwost/Getty Images. All rights reserved.

Cover photo of senior man copyright © by Paul Thomas/Getty Images. All rights reserved.

Cover photo of man lying on blanket copyright © by Nick Clements/Getty Images. All rights reserved.

Author photo copyright © by Lewek Photography. All rights reserved.

Designed by Timothy R. Botts

Edited by Linda Schlafer

Unless otherwise indicated, all Scripture quotations are taken from the *Holy Bible,* New Living Translation, copyright © 1996, 2004. Used by permission of Tyndale House Publishers, Inc., Carol Stream, Illinois 60188. All rights reserved.

Scripture quotations marked "NKJV™" are taken from the New King James Version®. Copyright © 1982 by Thomas Nelson, Inc. Used by permission. All rights reserved.

Library of Congress Cataloging-in-Publication Data

Beers, V. Gilbert (Victor Gilbert), date.
  What everyone should know about the Bible / V. Gilbert Beers.
    p. cm.
  Includes bibliographical references and index.
  ISBN-13: 978-0-8423-5307-6 (sc)
  ISBN-10: 0-8423-5307-0 (sc)
  1. Bible—Introductions. 2. Bible—Miscellanea. I. Title.
  BS475.3.B44 2007
  220.6′1—dc22   2006033641

Printed in United States of America

13	12	11	10	09	08	07
7	6	5	4	3	2	

CONTENTS

Finding Your Purpose in Life

1 Creation is "what" and the Creator is "who." We know the Creator is there because we see his fingerprints and footprints everywhere. It is impossible to have fingerprints and footprints without someone to make them. We are thankful for the "who" as well as the "what," but we worship only the Creator, not his creation. *Creation: Genesis 1:1–2:3 / pages 10–12*

2 There are things we do not, should not, and cannot know about God, for they are too majestic for human understanding. But there are other things we must know, for they are too significant for us not to understand them. *Creation: Genesis 1:1–2:3 / pages 10–12*

3 Satan *cannot* steal your soul. He will have it only if you give it to him. Jesus *will not* steal your soul. He will have it only if you give it to him. The choice of who has your soul is yours alone. *Temptation and Fall: Genesis 3 / pages 13–14*

4 The best gifts given without a giver's heart are unacceptable gifts. The smallest, most humble gifts, with a giver's heart, are acceptable to the Lord. Cain's gift was an acceptable gift from an unacceptable heart, which made it an unacceptable gift. Abel's gift was an acceptable gift from the acceptable heart of a giver, which made it acceptable. *Cain Kills Abel: Genesis 4:1-16 / pages 14–15*

5 Obeying God is for our benefit more than for God's benefit. What if Noah had refused to build the ark? God would have lost Noah and the animals, but Noah would have lost everything. *Noah and the Great Flood: Genesis 6:9–9:19 / pages 28–29*

6 Half lies do not produce half consequences. Abraham's half lies about his half sister and wife Sarah brought full consequences. Half sins are full sins, with full consequences. *Abraham and Sarah Visit Egypt: Genesis 12:10-20 / page 36*

7 Since God made you, God can fix you. Sarah's God was, in her mind, too small, too limited, too incapable. She knew that God had made her, but she thought he couldn't fix her or give her a son in her old age. God can do anything, so if he doesn't work a miracle in our lives we should not build fences around him. *Abraham Is Visited by Strangers: Genesis 18:1-15 / pages 37–38*

8 The road to glory is paved with service. Before Rebekah could become Isaac's wife and thus the mother of all further covenant children, she had to first water the camels of Abraham's servant. No work, no glory. The crown never precedes the cross. The reward comes only after the victory, and that is achieved through dedicated effort. *A Bride for Isaac: Genesis 24 / pages 39–40*

9 God does not always want what he permits. He does not always will what he allows to happen. God did not want Job to suffer, but he permitted it so that generations of people could see what true faithfulness is. God does not want the suffering and deaths that come from hurricanes, tornadoes, fires, and other tragedies. He permits these things for reasons beyond our grasp and beyond the moment. *The Book of Job / pages 45–46*

10 Everyone wants to be desired, wanted, and loved for who he or she is. Poor Leah! Her father didn't want to keep her around the house, so he secretly forced a marriage. Her husband didn't want her, for he had worked seven years for another bride. Her younger sister certainly didn't want her as her husband's other wife, with all the complications that brought. Leah was "the unwanted one," but she had six of Jacob's twelve sons,

viii

>

What
Everyone
Should
Know
about
the

Bible

including Levi, through whose tribe Moses and all other Levites of the priestly clan came. Also through Leah came the line of Judah (son of Jacob), from whom King David, King Solomon, and Jesus' earthly heritage came. To be undesired does not mean being unproductive or unblessed. *Jacob Marries Leah and Rachel: Genesis 29:14-30 / page 42*

11 "Why?" is often a valid question, but it is seldom an answerable question. Joseph must have asked why when his brothers sold him as a slave, when Potiphar's wife lied about him and had him thrown into prison, and when Pharaoh's cup-bearer forgot about him for two years. After Joseph had been elevated to the role of ruler over Egypt, he could understand the whys more clearly. *The Story of Joseph: Genesis 37–41 / pages 43–45*

12 A year of service may demand two years of training or preparation. Moses trained for eighty years for a work that took only forty years. The more significant the work, the more demanding the training may be. *The Story of Moses: Exodus, Leviticus, Numbers, Deuteronomy / pages 76–77*

13 "From" may be less significant than "to." The Hebrews escaped from life-threatening slavery to a life-threatening wilderness, where they were transformed from a band of slaves into a great nation. *Exodus from Egypt: Exodus 12:37–13:16 / pages 78–80*

14 All food is God's gift. The Israelites had daily manna in the wilderness, a food that God miraculously gave them. You and I also have daily manna, for God miraculously gives us our daily food. Of course, we work to earn it, but it is no less God's miraculous provision for us. Starving people in other places would gladly work hard for food if it were available. Never take tomorrow's food for granted; it is daily manna from heaven. Tomorrow's clothing, shelter, and other necessities are also daily gifts from God. *Food in the Wilderness: Exodus 16 / page 80*

15 Delegate to others what they can do so you will be able to do what you need to do. This was Jethro's advice to Moses, and Moses listened to him. *Jethro's Visit: Exodus 18 / page 81*

16 Abundant receiving should stir abundant giving. We should give to God so abundantly that someone must tell us to stop. The Israelites had received vast treasures from the Egyptians. When the opportunity came to give, they gave so much for the Tabernacle that Moses had to tell them to stop. *The People Give Gifts for the Tabernacle: Exodus 35:1–36:7 / page 82*

17 The Lord will lead us to the doorstep, but he won't force us through the door. We must do that ourselves, often as a step of faith. The Lord led the Israelites to the doorstep of the Promised Land at Kadesh in the wilderness of Paran, but the Israelites had to choose to go in. They chose not to do it, which kept them in the wilderness for another thirty-eight years. *Israel at Kadesh-barnea: Numbers 13–14 / pages 98–99*

18 We shouldn't assume that we can see everything with our natural eyes. Balaam's donkey saw the angel in the road, but Balaam the prophet didn't. Balaam's donkey was more spiritually perceptive than the prophet was. When a little child knows and loves God more than we do, it's time to work on our spiritual maturity. *The Story of Balaam and Balak: Numbers 22–24 / pages 100–101*

19 Don't ask a statesman to do a general's job or a general to do a statesman's job. Moses was the right person to lead the new nation through the wilderness, but he was the wrong one to lead the conquest of the land. Joshua was unprepared to do Moses' work, and Moses was not prepared to do Joshua's work. God chooses his leaders wisely, and they must choose wisely to follow God so they can lead wisely for God. *God Appoints Joshua as Moses' Successor: Numbers 27:12-23 / pages 101–103*

20 God sometimes uses ungodly instruments for godly purposes. Rahab the prostitute was an essential instrument in helping the Israelites conquer Jericho. Do not despise unholy instruments if God uses them for holy purposes. You and I are also unholy instruments, but we trust God to use us for holy purposes. *Visit to Rahab's House: Joshua 2 / pages 116–117*

21 We may lose, even when the scoreboard of life says that we've won. Or we may win, even when the scoreboard of life

x

>

What
Everyone
Should
Know
about
the

Bible

says that we lost. The Israelites won militarily in Canaan, but the conquered Canaanites won culturally by infecting their conquerors with a pagan lifestyle. Military conquest was overshadowed by cultural defeat. *Incomplete Conquest: Judges 1:19–3:6 / pages 117–118*

22 Beware of the cycles of life: Prosperity begets complacency; complacency begets spiritual weakness; spiritual weakness begets oppression from the enemy; oppression from the enemy causes us to cry out to the Lord for mercy. The Lord hears and rescues us; in him we again become prosperous; prosperity begets complacency; and the cycle repeats itself. *The Book of Judges / page 128*

23 Weakness with faithfulness, as in Ruth, shines brighter than strength with unfaithfulness, as with Samson. The driving force of the moment may be lost to the quiet lingering record of simple submission. *The Story of Ruth: The Book of Ruth; The Story of Samson: Judges 13–16 / pages 132–133*

24 People give preference to appearance. God gives preference to the heart, and God's way works better than our way. When Samuel looked at Jesse's sons to anoint one as Israel's next king, even this godly man assumed that the tallest, most handsome son would be God's choice, not the youngest and smallest. *Samuel Anoints David: 1 Samuel 16:1-13 / pages 152–153*

25 A slingshot with God is greater than an arsenal without God. David had a slingshot and five stones, with God. Goliath had state-of-the-art weaponry, without God. David won. Goliath learned an important lesson as he fell to his death. *David Conquers Goliath: 1 Samuel 17 / pages 153–154*

26 Never harm the Lord's anointed. Despite Saul's insane jealousy and his persistent efforts to murder David, David remained loyal to God's anointed king as long as Saul lived. David's reason for not harming Saul was, "I must not harm the Lord's anointed." Be careful not to tear down someone who has been called to serve God, no matter how much you disagree with, or dislike, that person. *David Respects the Lord's Anointed: Excerpts from 1 & 2 Samuel and 1 Chronicles / pages 154–158*

27 Materialism produces the bitter fruit of too much of the things that matter least and too little of what matters most. In the end, materialism, as described by Solomon in Ecclesiastes, is "empty," "vain," and "meaningless." *Solomon's Regrets: The Book of Ecclesiastes / pages 206–207, 209–210, 214–215*

28 Husbands and wives need to refresh their marital commitment, and at the same time refresh their marital romance and passion for each other. Such freshness and passion is what we see in the Song of Songs. *The Song of Songs (also known as the Song of Solomon) / pages 215–216*

29 Never mortgage or leverage the best to gain the worst. Solomon neglected what he requested from God—wisdom—and focused on the things he did not request—wealth, power, and fame. It is foolish to buy security with the currency of destruction. Solomon secured his kingdom by marrying foreign princesses and importing their pagan gods, and he did this at the high cost of destroying his kingdom. Sometimes the cost of peace is greater than the cost of war. Look at the price tag before you buy the easier way. *Solomon Turns from God: 1 Kings 11:1-25 / pages 206–207, 209–210*

30 Easy come, easy go. The kingdom came to David through great military sacrifice, with constant threat to his life. His son Solomon squandered his inheritance spiritually even as he built it economically. David's grandson, Solomon's son, quickly squandered the entire kingdom with a selfish momentary decision. *The Kingdom Divides: 1 Kings 12:1-24; 2 Chronicles 10:1–11:4 / pages 219–224*

31 Golden opportunities can become lost opportunities. Gold offered is not gold received. Gold that remains at arm's length is worthless. Opportunities are golden only when they are accepted and redeemed. Both Jeroboam and Rehoboam had golden opportunities to obey the Lord, prosper, and build a great kingdom. Each squandered those opportunities and their gold turned to ashes. *The Kingdom Divides: 1 Kings 12:1-24; 2 Chronicles 10:1–11:4; Jeroboam and the Golden Calves: 1 Kings 12:25-33 / pages 219–224, 226–227*

xii

>

What
Everyone
Should
Know
about
the

Bible

32 God's most powerful revelations may come as a gentle whisper. Elijah expected God in a mighty wind, a great earthquake, and a roaring fire, but instead he came in a gentle whisper. Look for God in the silences of life as much as in the visible and audible signs, even if they are dramatic. *Elijah and the Still, Small Voice: 1 Kings 19:1-18 / page 231*

33 It is not so much what we have as how we get what we have and what we do with it. This is the message of 2 Kings. Having much that we cannot use is less significant than having a little that we can use. Much without God is less than a little with God. *The Book of 2 Kings / pages 245–246*

34 It is hard to pray to God when you are running away from God. How can you be running away if he is close enough to hear you pray? If you try to run away from God, you may actually run into his open arms. You may think you are escaping from God when you are actually escaping to God. Jonah learned this lesson as he tried to run away from God, but he discovered that God was already there ahead of him. You can't hide from God, for he is everywhere. *Jonah and the Great Fish: Jonah 1–2 / pages 246–247*

35 Even a fish's belly can be a great classroom if the Lord is the teacher. Ask Jonah! In the belly of the fish, Jonah took a crash course in Obedience 101. You may not like the classroom of life, but if God is your teacher, listen to him. *Jonah and the Great Fish: Jonah 1–2 / pages 246–247*

36 Loving a lovely person makes sense. Loving an unlovely person defies human logic. From a human perspective, we can love only the lovely. From God's perspective, we must love the unlovely also, for he loves both, and so must we if we want to be like him. *The Book of Hosea / pages 248–249*

37 Never laugh at or mock God's people or cheer when they fall. When God is grieving, who are we to cheer? This is the message of Obadiah. *The Book of Obadiah / pages 272–273*

38 God is with his faithful people—in a fiery furnace or a den of hungry lions. Daniel and his friends discovered that. If you are in a fiery furnace or a den of hungry lions today, be faithful to God and he will be with you. *The Fiery Furnace; Daniel in a Lions' Den: Daniel 3, 6 / pages 294, 296–297*

39 Without the cradle there would not have been the cross. Without the birth of Jesus, there would not have been the sacrifice of Jesus for our sins. To die, Jesus first had to be born. To shed his blood for our sins, he first had to have a body with blood. *Jesus Is Born: Luke 2:1-7 / pages 324–325*

40 Life is in the blood. For us to have everlasting life, a blood sacrifice has to be made. Jesus' sacrifice is the only one sufficient to cover the sins of the world. The bloodline that led to the cross, where Jesus shed his blood for us, came through a woman. That lineage was filled with sinful people just like us. *Jesus' Genealogy and Birth: Matthew 1:1-17; Luke 2:1-7; 3:23-38 / pages 309–312*

41 Food without labor; fame without effort; power without service—we are all tempted with the same three temptations that Satan threw at Jesus. Temptation is most vicious when we are most vulnerable. Satan works with weakness to further weaken us. God works with weakness to further strengthen us. *Jesus Is Tempted: Matthew 4:1-11; Mark 1:12-13; Luke 4:1-13 / page 334*

42 Jesus has no racial prejudice. In his time, racial prejudice was focused mostly against the Samaritans, the mixed race that settled in ancient northern Israel. Jesus showed that he loves all people, regardless of their race. *Jesus and the Woman at the Well: John 4:4-42 / pages 340–341*

43 Honor the prophet next door. The people of Nazareth had the awesome privilege of living with the Messiah, but this became their downfall. They couldn't accept the man next door as the Messiah. *Jesus at the Nazareth Synagogue: Luke 4:16-30 / pages 348–349*

44 Evil forces can recognize good, but they cannot accept it. Good forces can see evil and accept it. The demons usually recognized Jesus as the Messiah, but they refused to accept him. The Pharisees usually did not recognize Jesus as the Messiah. Though they were supposedly good and even godly people, they made plans to murder him. Beware of seeing evil and considering it good, and of seeing good and regarding it as evil. *Jesus Heals a Man with an Unclean Spirit: Mark 1:21-28; Luke 4:31-37 / pages 349, 381*

xiv

>

What
Everyone
Should
Know
about
the

Bible

45 Yesterday's scoundrel may become tomorrow's saint. Ask Matthew, who was once a hated tax collector but became one of the Twelve and the author of our first New Testament book. Jesus changed him, and that is what makes the difference for us, too. *Jesus Calls Matthew: Matthew 9:9; Mark 2:13-14; Luke 5:27-28 / pages 350–351*

46 Our Lord may choose ordinary persons for extraordinary purposes. He chose twelve ordinary men to be his apostles. James, John, Peter, and Andrew were ordinary fishermen. For those of us who consider ourselves ordinary, this is a great comfort. *Jesus Chooses Twelve Apostles: Mark 3:13-19; Luke 6:12-16 / pages 358–361*

47 Our Lord permits evil and good to coexist until he judges evil. When Jesus chose the Twelve, he chose Judas Iscariot, even though he could see the future clearly and he knew that Judas would betray him. If you wonder why evil works side by side with your good work, remember Judas. There will come a time of accounting. *Jesus Chooses Twelve Apostles: Mark 3:13-19; Luke 6:12-16 / pages 358, 428, 435–436*

48 Authoritative teaching comes from authorized teachers. God authorized Jesus to teach, so his teaching was authoritative. *The Sermon on the Mount: Matthew 5–7; Luke 6:17-49 / pages 358–359*

49 We are either for or against Jesus. That's what Jesus said. We cannot be neutral, for to be neutral to Jesus is to actually be against Jesus. *The Sermon on the Mount: Matthew 5–7, especially the conclusion in 7:21-27; Luke 6:17-49, especially the conclusion in verses 46-49 / pages 358–359*

50 If we seek unlimited forgiveness, we must give unlimited forgiveness. As we forgive others, God will forgive us. *The Sermon on the Mount: Matthew 5–7; Luke 6:17-49 / pages 358–359*

51 As we receive much from Jesus, we should give much to Jesus. Some women who traveled with Jesus and the Twelve had been healed or had demons driven from them, so they helped support Jesus' ministry. "When someone has been given much, much will be required in return" (Luke 12:48). *Women Help Jesus in His Work: Luke 8:1-3 / page 367*

52 Great truths often come in simple packages. So it was with Jesus' parables. He taught the most profound truths with simple stories. Truth bathed in profundity may sink into obscurity, drowned in a sea of words. *The Parables of Jesus: Matthew 13; Mark 4; Luke 11–15 / pages 370–372*

53 If even the demons recognize Jesus as the Son of God, how can we as religious people not recognize who he is? *Jesus Heals Many: Matthew 8:28-34; Mark 5:1-20; Luke 8:43-48 / pages 374–375, 381*

54 Hunger for God should always be greater than hunger for bread. The people who saw the miracle of the loaves and fishes should have learned that. *Jesus Feeds 5,000: Matthew 14:13-21; Mark 6:30-44; Luke 9:10-17; John 6:1-15 / pages 377–378*

55 The identity of the Son of God can be lost in a basket of bread. For many who enjoyed the bread at the feeding of the five thousand, Jesus was no more than a food source, so they looked to him for more food. They lost the greater message that only the Son of God could perform such a miracle. Be careful when you pray that you are not consumed with what you want God to give you rather than with who God is. *Jesus Feeds 5,000: Matthew 14:13-21; Mark 6:30-44; Luke 9:10-17; John 6:1-15 / pages 377–378*

56 Only God the Son, the Creator, could work the miracles that he worked, for only the Creator could supersede creation. The miracles of Jesus are evidence that he is truly God the Son. *Jesus Walks on Water: Matthew 14:22-33; Mark 6:45-56 / pages 374–379*

57 Those closest to us may also be farthest from us. In his childhood, Jesus' brothers lived in the same household and shared the same dinner table with him. Until he rose from the dead, they could not believe that he was the Messiah. After the Resurrection, when he was distanced from them, they believed. *Jesus' Brothers: John 7:1-9 / page 392*

58 Return love for hatred. The Good Samaritan was hated by the Jewish people because he was a Samaritan, but he returned love to the wounded Jewish man because he was in need. *The Parable of the Good Samaritan: Luke 10:25-37 / pages 400–401*

xvi

>

What
Everyone
Should
Know
about
the

Bible

59 Our best work may be to sit and listen. There is a time to rush ahead and a time to sit quietly and listen to God. Jesus commended Mary for skipping the frantic meal preparations for a quiet time with him. *Jesus Visits Mary and Martha: Luke 10:38-42 / page 401*

60 Prayer is a multifaceted jewel. In Jesus' prayer, he prayed for food, gave praise to God, asked forgiveness for sins, sought God's will, and made other requests. Prayer is not just getting, but giving; not just asking, but praising; not just seeking my will, but seeking God's will. *Jesus Teaches His Disciples to Pray: Luke 11:1-13 / page 401*

61 The currency of heaven buys more and lasts longer than the currency of earth. The rich fool spent all his time and effort to gain riches that he couldn't take with him, and neglected to gain the riches he could send on ahead. A fool hoards riches that he can spend only on earth and neglects riches he can spend only in heaven. *Parable of the Rich Fool: Luke 12:13-34 / page 402*

62 Pride can bring great shame, and humility can bring great honor. A proud person who seeks first place is shamed when put into last place. A humble person who seeks last place is honored when put into first place. *Parable of a Seat at a Wedding Feast: Luke 14:7-14 / page 407*

63 There is greater joy in finding something lost than in keeping something and never losing it. Even the angels have a party in heaven when a lost soul comes to God. *Parable of the Lost Coin: Luke 15:8-10 / pages 407–408*

64 Perseverance in prayer pays off. God encourages persistent prayer. Jesus said so in his parable about the persistent widow who was seeking justice. If something is worth praying for, pray for it with perseverance. *Parable of the Widow Who Kept Asking: Luke 18:1-8 / page 414*

65 Prayer and pride do not mix. Prayer is not the time for pride, as with the Pharisee who was proud of his false godliness, but for humility, as with the tax collector who was humbled by his ungodliness. *Parable of the Pharisee and the Tax Collector: Luke 18:9-14 / pages 414–415*

66 Fairness is giving people what they deserve, no more and no less. Generosity is giving people more than they deserve. Mercy is refraining from giving people what they deserve, such as punishment. *Parable of the Laborers in the Vineyard: Matthew 20:1-16 / pages 415–416*

67 Things that seem important here, or people who seem important here, may be unimportant in heaven. Things or people who seem unimportant here may be important in heaven. God's values are not the world's values, and the world's values are not God's values. *James and John Want to Sit at Jesus' Right Hand: Matthew 20:20-28; Mark 10:35-45 / page 416*

68 Obedience is more than talking; obedience is doing. Saying yes to God is not enough, for we must do what we say. *Parable of the Two Sons: Matthew 21:28-32 / page 419*

69 Give Caesar what belongs to Caesar, and give God what belongs to God. Taxes are important for the work of the government; gifts to God are important for the work of God. *Pharisees Try to Trick Jesus: Matthew 22:15-22; Mark 12:13-17; Luke 20:20-26 / page 420*

70 A small gift with a giving heart is much more significant than a large gift with a grudging heart. *The Widow's Offering: Mark 12:41-44; Luke 21:1-4 / page 420*

71 Too late is sometimes too late. There comes a time when there is no second opportunity. The five foolish bridesmaids learned that they were too late for the wedding feast, and they could not get in. If we are too late in making a decision to accept Jesus, we will not be able to go to his home. *Parable of the Ten Bridesmaids: Matthew 25:1-13 / page 427*

72 More is given to those who are faithful with time, talents, and treasure; and more is taken from those who are unfaithful in their use. Use them or lose them, and invest personal time, talents, and treasure wisely. Don't dig a hole and bury your personal resources. *Parable of the Three Servants: Matthew 25:14-30 / page 427*

73 We don't get to heaven by doing good things for needy people, but by becoming godly people. That happens when we

xviii

>

What
Everyone
Should
Know
about
the

Bible

accept Jesus as our Savior. When we have accepted him and have become godly people in Christ Jesus, we are expected to do good things for needy people. *Parable of the Sheep and Goats: Matthew 25:31-46 / page 430*

74 Godly events are not occasions for ungodly conduct. It was inappropriate for the disciples to argue at the Last Supper, of all times and places. This should remind us to avoid church arguments. *The Last Supper: Matthew 26:20-30; Mark 14:17-26; Luke 22:14-30; John 13:1-30 / pages 432–434*

75 A servant is not greater than his master, as Jesus told the disciples. Think of every humble act that Jesus did. How can we strive for pride when we think of him? *The Last Supper: Matthew 26:20-30; Mark 14:17-26; Luke 22:14-30; John 13:1-30 / pages 432–434*

76 Never betray Jesus with a kiss of affection or a false show of love. Never pretend that you love him while you are doing unloving things against him. *Judas Betrays Jesus with a Kiss: Matthew 26:47-56; Mark 14:43-52; Luke 22:47-53; John 18:2-11 / pages 437, 440*

77 There are times for guardian angels to stay away. Jesus had at least seventy-two thousand guardian angels ready to rescue him from his passion, but he would not let one of them help him. *Judas Betrays Jesus with a Kiss: Matthew 26:47-56; Mark 14:43-52; Luke 22:47-53; John 18:2-11 / page 440*

78 The religious leaders condemned the Son of God because he told the truth about who he was. If Jesus claimed to be God's Son, but wasn't, it would have been blasphemy. Since Jesus claimed to be God's Son, and was, the religious leaders committed blasphemy against God when they rejected and crucified his Son. They condemned him for the "sin" of telling the truth. *Jesus before Annas, Caiaphas, and the Sanhedrin: Matthew 26:57-68; Mark 14:53-65; Luke 22:66-71; John 18:12-14, 19-24 / pages 440–442*

79 What enormous price must be paid for the sins of the whole world? All the riches of the world are not enough. Only the blood of God's Son was sufficient. *Jesus on the Cross: Matthew 27:32-56; Mark 15:21-41; Luke 23:26-49; John 19:16-37 / pages 443–445*

80 The Resurrection distinguishes Christianity from all other religions. We have hope for our life beyond the grave because Jesus conquered death by rising from the dead. *The Resurrection: Matthew 28:1-10; Mark 16:1-8; Luke 24:1-12 / pages 450–454*

81 The Ascension, with witnesses to that event, proves that Jesus is in heaven, where he is preparing his eternal home for us. How could we expect to go to heaven if he were not already there? *Jesus Ascends into Heaven: Mark 16:19-20; Luke 24:50-53; Acts 1:9-11 / page 454*

82 Jesus' scars are marks of honor. To Thomas, they turned doubt into faith and hope. In heaven, they will probably remain on Jesus as evidence of his great sacrifice for us. Revelation 5:5-6 says that the Lamb who was killed is worthy to open the seals. That will be Jesus, the wounded Lamb of God. *Jesus on the Cross: Matthew 27:32-56; Mark 15:21-41; Luke 23:26-49; John 19:16-37 / page 457*

83 The school of suffering in which we are the teachers may become the school of suffering in which we are the students. Saul inflicted suffering on believers, but the Lord said that Saul would suffer much for him as a believer. *Saul Persecutes the Christians: Acts 8:1-3 / page 474*

84 Some people come to Jesus like Saul—in a blinding moment. Some are nurtured through childhood to love Jesus. *Saul's Conversion: Acts 9:1-9 / pages 474–475*

85 The worst may become the best, with Jesus' help. Saul the mass murderer was one of the worst enemies of Christians, but he became Paul the great apostle and missionary. Pray for those that you think are hopeless so that they may have hope and bring hope. *Saul's Conversion: Acts 9:1-19 / pages 474–475*

86 If you claim the name, live up to the name. Christians should be Christlike because we bear the name of Christ. Barnabas, the "Son of Encouragement," lived up to his name by encouraging the Jerusalem believers to trust Saul and by encouraging Saul as a new believer. *Barnabas Helps Paul at Jerusalem: Acts 9:26-27 / page 476*

xx

>

What
Everyone
Should
Know
about
the

Bible

87 Never reject what God calls acceptable. That was God's message to Peter. Likewise, never accept what God has called unacceptable. *Cornelius and Peter's Vision of Unclean Animals: Acts 10 / pages 483–484*

88 If you pray, expect answers. Otherwise, why pray? Peter's friends prayed fervently for him when he was in prison but did not believe that their prayers would be answered. They did not believe it even when their prayers were answered. *Peter Released from Prison: Acts 12:6-19 / pages 485–486*

89 Jealousy is a fire that consumes reason. The Jewish religious leaders in the towns that Paul and Barnabas visited were offered the greatest gift of all time—salvation through Jesus. The Bible tells us that it was jealousy, not logic or reason, that motivated them to reject this great gift and want to destroy the messengers. Evil seeks to destroy the messenger and the message. *Paul and Barnabas at Pisidian Antioch: Acts 13:42-45 / pages 493–494*

90 Some doors may close so that others may open. Doors may close to one opportunity so that they can open to another. When you find doors closing to something you want, perhaps you should ask which doors may be opening. Likewise, some doors may open so that others may close. *Paul's Macedonian Vision: Acts 16:6-10 / pages 502–503*

91 God specializes in the impossible. There was no possible way for people to escape from a dungeon when their hands and feet were bound in stocks. God can do anything, and he freed Paul and Silas. *Paul and Silas in the Philippian Jail: Acts 16:16-40 / pages 503–504*

92 How do we get to heaven? "Believe in the Lord Jesus and you will be saved"(Acts 16:31). This was Paul and Silas's message to the Philippian jailor, and the message is the same today. *Paul and Silas in the Philippian Jail: Acts 16:16-40 / pages 503–504*

93 The road to the mountaintop may lead through the valley. To reach Rome, where he longed to witness, Paul first had to be imprisoned for two years in Caesarea. Paul's "pulpit" in Rome was preceded by Paul's prison in Caesarea. *Paul Appeals to Caesar: Acts 25:1-12 / pages 524–527*

94 The power of presence is the greatest gift of love at a time of need. Paul needed encouragement as he entered Rome as a prisoner. Fellow believers publicly risked their lives to meet with him personally and encourage him. *Paul at Rome: Acts 28:11-31 / page 535*

95 Prejudice breeds prejudice, racism breeds racism, and religious activism breeds religious activism. The Jewish believers and the Gentile believers of Paul's time allowed their prejudice against each other to breed further prejudice. *The Book of Ephesians / page 541*

96 Joy is too good to hoard. If we have it, we must share it. Paul had the joy of Jesus, and even though he was imprisoned in Rome, he had to share it with his friends at Philippi. *The Book of Philippians / page 541*

97 Walk the talk and talk the walk. In serving as a godly person and a godly leader, both are essential. *The Book of Titus / page 547*

98 Threats from within are often more dangerous than threats from without. The threat of our choices for pagan ways may be more ominous than the threat of external persecution. *The Book of Jude / page 554*

99 The family glue that binds us together is intimately related to the glue that binds together the family of God. Love God first, and love others, including your family, as you love yourself. When we have our love relationship with God intact, we can build a proper love relationship with one another. *The Book of 1 John / page 555*

xxii

>

What
Everyone
Should
Know
about
the

100 The Creator of the universe yearns for us to live in his home in heaven if we choose to do so. His love for us restrains him from forcing us to go there. Love is not love if it is forced, and choice is not choice if it is mandated. Love is love when it is a choice. The best alternatives are motivated by love. *The Entire Bible Message / page 564*

Several years ago, in an adult Sunday school class at our church, the teacher asked us to put four names in chronological order: Moses, Joseph, David, and Nehemiah. Most of the class flunked. We considered ourselves a church in the center of Bible learning, not on the fringes. But most of the class didn't know this simple Bible information.

How would you do with that test? The name Moses sounds older than Joseph, doesn't it? But the kid with the colorful cloak came on the scene hundreds of years before the man who led Israel through the Exodus. What about Nehemiah and David? The boy who battled Goliath and later became Israel's second king was centuries older than the man who led a group of exiles back to Jerusalem to rebuild the city's walls.

Suppose someone asked you to list ten important Bible stories. How would you do? Can you name all twelve of Jesus' disciples? How about the names of the Minor Prophets? Do you know the name of Abraham's wife? Could you outline the entire panorama of God's plans through the ages, with all of the principal events and people involved? That would be quite a challenge, of course. But that is what we will do here.

So who cares about all this? Why spend time on this information? Does it matter if we know that there are only two Bible books named for women? Is it important if we can't name the twelve tribes of Israel or recite the Ten Commandments?

A recent survey by a research group showed that 12 percent of Americans believe that Joan of Arc was Noah's wife. Sorry, wrong ark. Does that matter? The right Bible information will not see you through a fractured marriage or the death of a loved one, but if so many people know so little about the Bible, it makes us wonder how many other misconceptions about the Bible are out there, especially about doctrines and teachings that do matter. You would be embarrassed to tell someone that Noah's wife was Joan of Arc, wouldn't you? You would also be embarrassed to tell someone that the epistles were female apostles, or that the birth of Jesus is recorded in the book of Exodus. Of course Bible knowledge is important.

Bible information alone won't help you endure the extra mile in your journey when life hurts. Knowing the names of the twelve tribes of Israel won't give you great comfort when you've just been diagnosed with cancer. But the more you know the Bible message and its people, its panorama and purposes, the more you will relate to the God of the Bible, his plans for your life, and how he will make the difference when you hurt. When you know more of God's book, you understand more of the God of the book, and that makes all the difference in the world.

What Everyone Should Know about the Bible will help you to see and understand the panorama of God's plan for the ages, the Big Story, and how this comes to focus on God's plans and purposes for your life, today and every day yet to come.

At first glance, the Bible may seem like a dusty book about people of long ago and far away, imbedded in a culture radically different from ours and written in a language far different from ours. That first impression fades quickly when you look more carefully and discover that the Bible is the greatest adventure story of all times. The Big Story is a tapestry woven from the threads of many Bible stories and events that reveal the people with whom God worked through the ages.

With a closer look, you will discover that the Bible is an autobiography of God, who has the lead role in the drama of the ages. It is God's story. That closer look will also reveal the powerful truth that this is your story, too. The stories of long ago may be about Abraham, Isaac, Ruth, and Nehemiah. The Big Story is about God and you. The Big Story is about God at work through the ages, creating and managing the great epochs of time. It is also the story of God's plans and purposes for you and me—yesterday, today, and tomorrow.

The Bible may seem ancient, but it is as contemporary as your last heartbeat. It may seem distant, but it is as near as your next breath. It may seem far away, but it can speak to you with a life-changing power that is spiritual dynamite. It is about your concerns, fears, needs, desires, and ambitions, and your plans and purposes for tomorrow. The Bible is the Handbook of Purpose for your life, for there you will find your purposes clearly presented.

God and you, you and God. That is the essence of the Big Story of the Bible. It is important to grasp the wholeness of the panoramic plan of God so it can shape the wholeness of the rest of your life. *What Everyone Should Know about the Bible* presents the Big Story of God at work in his universe *as it happened historically,* not as it is presented in the sequence of Bible books, for as you know, Bible books do not strictly

xxiv
>
What
Everyone
Should
Know
about
the
Bible

follow the timeline of history. It is vital that you see the panoramic plan of God arranged sequentially through the ages, starting with that timeless time before time began.

The bottom line of the Big Story is Your Story—what this panoramic plan of God means to you and how his plan of the ages will shape your purposes today. Since God's Big Story is ultimately Your Story, it is vital that you discover the purposes God has for your life. That is truly a Big Story.

As with any book that seeks to tell you "everything you need to know," you will get the most from this volume if you first discover how best to use it. In that light, consider this your brief owner's manual.

Discovering the purpose of *What Everyone Should Know about the Bible*

This book comprises interlocking purposes: (1) to help you see God's panoramic plan throughout the ages, the "drama" of God at work among us. This drama is divided into forty-nine "scenes"; (2) to help you discover your purpose in life from each scene; and (3) to introduce you to Bible enrichment material that will help you understand the Bible story as presented in each scene—important events, dates when things happened, what you should know about the books of the Bible, and questions you may ask. To capture the purpose in a phrase, we might say, "Discovering your purpose in life from God's panoramic plan of the ages."

God's panoramic plan

If you want an overview of the entire drama of God at work, read The Big Story from scene to scene, skipping over the support material. This will give you a sense of the Bible as it unfolds chronologically. For example, you'll encounter the story of Job where he likely appeared historically, about the time of Abraham. You will read about the "silent scenes" between Genesis and Exodus, and again between the close of the Old Testament and the beginning of the New Testament. You will see the narrative harmonized in six Old Testament books that cover the same time periods—1 and 2 Samuel, 1 and 2 Kings, and 1 and 2 Chronicles— and again in the life of Jesus, as seen in the four Gospels. You will also see how Ezra, Nehemiah, and Esther fit together historically.

Discovering your purpose in life from God's panoramic plan

Another approach is to read The Big Story from scene to scene and discover how your own life fits into God's panoramic plan by reading "Discovering My Purpose from God's Plan" at the end of each scene.

Start at the beginning, and . . .

Another way to read this book, of course, is straight through from start to finish. If you do, you'll soon recognize the other features within each scene: Questions You May Be Asking (clarifying things that need it); Great Events of This Scene (a list of stories within The Big Story); Significant Dates of This Scene (a Bible time line); Heroes and Villains (the stars of this scene); Did You Know? (high-interest information from the scene); and What Everyone Should Know about . . . each book of the Bible.

If you use this book as intended, you will soon understand "what every-one should know about the Bible."

Before Time Began

The Heavens Before Creation

Characters:
Angels; God the Father, God the Son, God the Holy Spirit; morning stars; Satan

Time Period:
The time of mystery before Creation

Dates:
Before time began, so there were no dates

Where Scene 1 of the Big Story Can Be Found:
Genesis 21:33; Exodus 33:20; 34:29-30; Deuteronomy 33:27; 1 Chronicles 28:2; Job 38:4-7; Psalm 68:19; 102:24, 26; 110:1; Proverbs 8:22-26; Isaiah 9:6-7; 14:12-15; 66:1; Ezekiel 43:7; Matthew 8:11; John 1:1-4; 10:30; Acts 7:49; Philippians 4:18; 1 Timothy 3:6; Hebrews 1:13; 10:13; 1 Peter 3:12; and Revelation 22:16

In Scene 1, Find the Answers to These Questions:
What happened before Creation? What was God doing all that time?
How old is God?
What does God look like?
Did Jesus live before he was born at Bethlehem?

Look for this in Scene 1
> The morning stars may have been angelic beings.
> God has eyes and ears.
> Satan was once an angel.

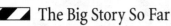

The Big Story So Far

The time before time began, the vast, sweeping eternity before Creation, is often a mystery to us. We have many questions about this timeless time, and the Bible doesn't tell us much about it. Is pre-Creation a biblical secret? Actually, the Bible tells us more than we realize, but we must look for it.

It is important to understand something of this time, for our understanding reveals the nature of God and what he may have been doing during these eons of timeless time.

Questions You May Be Asking

Where did God come from? How old is he? When did he begin?
How long did God live before he created the universe? When was he born? How did God get started?

Some scientists say that the universe is from four billion to twelve billion years old. If that is true, and we don't know that it is, God has been around infinitely longer than those billions of years. God was already present, long before Creation. Does the Bible tell us how old God is? Is there any hint?

The Bible has significant things to say about this, but not in the opening story in Genesis. In Psalm 102:24, the psalmist, inspired by God, writes, "My God, who lives forever." Note that it does not say "My God who *will* live forever," which would suggest future eternity but not past eternity.

"Lives forever" means that God had no beginning and will have no end. He has lived from forever, lives now, and will continue to live forever. He was never born and he will never die. He always was and he always will be. That's what the word *forever* means. It is mind-boggling because our minds are finite and we can't grasp something infinite.

Genesis 21:33 and Deuteronomy 33:27 speak of "the Eternal God" who always was and always will be. Psalm 102:26 addresses God, saying, "You remain forever," and 102:27 continues, "You are always the same; you will live forever." The God who has no end also had no beginning. He always was. He has always existed. Eternal and forever speak of no beginning and no end. God always was and always will be. This is hard for our limited human minds to grasp, but it is not too hard for our trusting souls to accept.

What about Jesus? He was born in Bethlehem about 4 B.C., wasn't he? If he was God, how could he be born, and if he was born, how could he be God?
It's very hard for us as human beings to grasp the Trinity, the Triune God—Father, Son, and Holy Spirit. The Bible teaches us that God is

2

\>

What
Everyone
Should
Know
about
the

Bible

one God, but three persons. We will fully understand it when we go to be with him. Until then, we have to settle for more faith based on less knowledge than we would like, but the Bible does tell us some important facts.

John 1:1-4 tells us, "In the beginning the Word [Jesus] already existed. The Word was with God, and the Word was God. He existed in the beginning with God. God created everything through him, and nothing was created except through him. The Word gave life to everything that was created, and his life brought light to everyone." This is a profound and clear statement about Jesus before Creation, and Jesus as God, the Creator of the universe.

Hundreds of years before Jesus came to Bethlehem, Isaiah spoke of him as the coming Messiah. "For a child is born to us, a son is given to us. The government will rest on his shoulders. And he will be called: Wonderful Counselor, Mighty God, Everlasting Father, Prince of Peace" (Isaiah 9:6).

Jesus has always been God—God the Son, one person of the Trinity. He always has been and still is the second person of the Trinity. He was there at Creation and long before Creation, and he is the Creator. He is not only called Prince of Peace, but Mighty God and Everlasting Father. Jesus said, "The Father and I are one" (John 10:30).

Jesus' birth at Bethlehem was God coming into a tiny human body that would one day be offered as the ultimate sacrifice for our sins. We sometimes call this birth at Bethlehem the Incarnation—God in human form. To die on the cross for our sins required a body, and Jesus came into that body that night in Bethlehem.

What does God look like?

The Bible uses terms for God's appearance that are also used for our own appearance. Does God look like us, or do we look like God? Surely that is unlikely, because he is a spirit who is everywhere at once. So when the Bible speaks of the face of God, the hands of God, or the feet of God, attributes that we have, these are more likely functional attributes rather than physical attributes. However, it is interesting to note how many attributes are common to God and us.

God has a face, but because he is truly holy, we human beings cannot look at his face now. The brilliance of God's face is so intense that we could not bear it. God said this to Moses when Moses went up Mount Sinai, "You may not look directly at my face, for no one may see me and live" (Exodus 33:20).

God permitted Moses to see his reflected glory, and even that was so brilliant that when Moses went down from the mountain, his own face glowed so much that the people were afraid to come near him (Exodus

34:29-30) and Moses had to put a veil over his face. We would not dare to look at the sun, which is God's creation, for more than a fleeting moment. If we cannot bear to look at one small part of Creation, how could we look directly at the face of God that is infinitely more glorious than the sun?

Does God have hands? God says that he has hands. He said to Moses, "I will . . . cover you with my hand," so that Moses would not die by looking into the face of God (Exodus 33:22).

What about feet? God told Ezekiel that he had feet. Ezekiel 43:7 says, "The LORD said to me, 'Son of man, this is the place of my throne and the place where I will rest my feet.'" (Ezekiel 43:7). God also refers to his footstool, which presupposes feet, several times (1 Chronicles 28:2; Psalm 110:1; Isaiah 66:1; Acts 7:49; Hebrews 1:13; 10:13).

The Bible tells us that God's "everlasting arms" are under us (Deuteronomy 33:27). Other Bible references talk about God's arms, such as Psalm 68:19 and Isaiah 40:11.

Does God have eyes and ears? 1 Peter 3:12 tells us that "The eyes of the Lord watch over those who do right, and his ears are open to their prayers." So the Bible tells us that God has eyes and ears, to keep watch over us and to hear us pray. Dozens of Scriptures tell us that our God listens to us.

Can God speak audibly? Most of the time, even in Bible times, he spoke to his people through Scripture or through his prophets. Today, most of us have never heard an audible voice from God. We rely on God's Word in the Bible to hear him speak to us.

However, many times throughout the Bible we read that God spoke audibly to his people. This presupposes a mouth and whatever else it takes for God to talk.

What about a nose or a sense of smell? What about taste? The Bible speaks of "a sweet-smelling sacrifice that is acceptable and pleasing to God" (Philippians 4:18). That tells us that God has a sense of smell, which suggests a nose.

God prepares feasts in heaven for his people, so we assume that he will dine with us (Matthew 8:11: "Many Gentiles will come from all over the world—from east and west—and sit down . . . at the feast in the Kingdom of Heaven."). If so, God eats, and even feasts. Jesus, God the Son, ate after he arose from the dead, as well as before his crucifixion (Luke 24:41-42).

4

>

What
Everyone
Should
Know
about
the

Bible

Does God look like us? Do we look like him?

Although we are made "in the image of God" (Genesis 1:26-27), we probably do not look exactly like God, and possibly do not look in any way like God. He has our five senses—touch, taste, smell, hearing, and sight—

but he surely has many more than just five senses. He may have five hundred or five thousand senses, or even more. We, of course, will also have many more than five senses when we go to live with God some day in heaven. Heaven will not be limited to our five senses, for there is much more there to sense and experience. God is all-knowing (omniscient), all-powerful (omnipotent), and present everywhere (omnipresent).

What was God doing before he created the universe?

Have you ever wondered what God was doing through the long stretch of timeless time before he created our universe? I have. What was he thinking? What was he planning? How long did it take? The Bible opens with the Creation story, but much had already happened before then. God had been busy long, long, long before that. Creation is merely the beginning of the story of our universe and the people who are unique parts of that universe.

How long did it take for God to plan his Creation? Could it have taken millions, or even billions of years?

How long would it take for you to design one snowflake? How about one billion of them, or a billion times a billion? We're told that no two snowflakes are alike, yet there must be multibillions in one acre of snowfall. How about all the snowflakes on the thousands of acres on one mountain? Multiply those billions times all the snow in the world for one day, or for one winter—then for thousands of winters. The number would be staggering. Trillions times trillions times trillions. Yet no two snowflakes are alike! How long would it take to plan countless snowflakes with no two alike?

Let's think next about a sunrise or sunset. I like to photograph them. But I'm standing in one small place at one moment of time in a very large world. Sunrises and sunsets are perpetual—one is happening somewhere in the world at every moment. The sun is always rising and always setting, painting literally billions of sunrise or sunset pictures each day. Multiply that times thousands of years. God is quite an artist, isn't he? How long would it take to plan all of these glorious paintings?

Think of the intricacies of other parts of Creation. Think of the planning needed for every leaf and for the design in each one. What about the billions of flowers and flowering bushes and trees? A billion times a billion leaves or flowers. How long to design each one?

Then, of course, there are stars, planets, and galaxies. Can you imagine planning for a trillion worlds or more? Each has its own unique features. Each needed intricate planning. Have you considered that our vast, seemingly endless universe may be only one small part of God's greater domain?

What about the design of every animal, every butterfly, every seashell? Was God planning all this marvelous stuff for eons of time before he said, "Let it now happen?" Of course he was. God obviously must have had awesome plans before he set to work creating our world. Creating a universe with such intricate uniqueness everywhere is one type of creativity—planning it all is a different type of creativity. The two fit hand in glove.

Then we come to the most complex, intricate marvel of all Creation—you, and billions of others like you. Each of us is different. There are about six billion people in the world today, and about 160 million more are added each year. By the year 2025, it is projected that there will be more than eight billion people alive on earth. How many people have lived since the days of Adam? Would it be safe to estimate twenty to twenty-five billion? That is a large number of unique Creations!

Each of us has a highly complex body, with miles of nerves and blood vessels, a heart that keeps on beating for almost a century, and more intricate design than the finest anatomy book can possibly explain. What about the DNA, the lifemap for each one of us? DNA is different in each one of us. How long would it take to design billions upon billions of unique DNA maps, unique sets of fingerprints, and unique iris prints for each of us?

How do we know God did his planning before Creation began? The Bible tells us that he did. For example, Proverbs 8:22-26 says, "The LORD formed me [wisdom] from the beginning, before he created anything else. I [wisdom] was appointed in ages past, at the very first, before the earth began. I was born before the oceans were created, before the springs bubbled forth their waters. Before the mountains were formed, before the hills, I was born—before he had made the earth and fields and the first handfuls of soil."

The plans of God are intimately associated with the wisdom of God, whether plans for the Creation of the universe and us or the daily sustaining of our lives. That wisdom, and those plans, were already there at Creation. So is it unreasonable to think that in God's infinite wisdom and planning, he knew your name and your entire lifemap even before he created the world?

When we come to the last scene and move from the course of the world's history into that timeless time beyond our time, the forever yet to come, we will look back and say, "All we have done here on earth is nothing compared to the infinite detail of the heavens and the new earth." Before the dawn of Creation, God was planning all that, too.

Of course, God had other things to do before the Creation of the

6

>

What
Everyone
Should
Know
about
the

Bible

world, such as creating millions of angels and looking after all the other celestial beings that we may not yet know about.

Were there any other heavenly creatures there with God before Creation?
In Job 38:4-7, where God speaks of creating the world, he asks Job, "Where were you when I laid the foundations of the earth? . . . as the morning stars sang together and all the angels shouted for joy?" What morning stars? What were they?

The morning stars are possibly other celestial beings. They were present when God created the universe, and they celebrated Creation with the angels. What were these morning stars, the celestial beings, like? Why were they created? What is their purpose?

In Revelation 22:16, Jesus calls himself the morning star. This would suggest that the morning stars may be Christlike beings, like *the* morning star, though of course much lesser beings than God the Son. They are angelic in nature, but perhaps not angels—Christlike in nature, but not Christ.

Angels were also in the cheering section as God created the universe. They were shouting, perhaps singing, for joy. This wasn't Job speaking. It was God speaking to and through Job, revealing startling truths to Job and to us. There will be more about this celestial cheering section when we get to the time of Creation.

Another being was present in the timeless time before Creation. Satan was the first visitor in Eden, and the first to meet with Adam and Eve. He was on the sidelines when God created the universe, but he wasn't cheering. He was plotting how he might destroy this beautiful work.

Where did Satan come from? Did God create this evil being?
God is a holy God, so he could not and would not create evil or an evil being. Scripture suggests that at first, Satan was one of the angelic heavenly beings created a long time before our universe, but then he rebelled against God and was cast out of heaven.

Many believe that Isaiah 14:12-15 speaks of Satan and his fall. Others believe that these verses are only about the king of Babylon: "How you are fallen from heaven, O shining star, son of the morning! You have been thrown down to the earth, you who destroyed the nations of the world. For you said to yourself, 'I will ascend to heaven and set my throne above God's stars. I will preside on the mountain of the gods far away in the north. I will climb to the highest heavens and be like the Most High.' Instead, you will be brought down to the place of the dead, down to its lowest depths." Was Satan one of the original morning stars or some other angelic being? God called him "O shining star, son of the morning." Is that another way of saying "morning star"?

This passage from Isaiah sounds much more like a description of Satan than merely of the king of Babylon, doesn't it? First Timothy 3:6 adds only a fleeting possible commentary on this: "An elder must not be a new believer, because he might become proud, and the devil would cause him to fall," which could also be translated "he [the elder] might fall into the same judgment as the devil." This alternate translation suggests that the devil was cast down from heaven because of pride, which harmonizes with the passage from Isaiah.

What was the celebration of angels and "morning stars" like?

As God prepares to open the curtain of human drama by creating the earthly stage for it, let's try to picture the pre-Creation celestial drama. For this, we must use our imaginations, working from what little we know.

In the dark shadows, perhaps somewhere in that primordial earth described in Genesis 1:2, as "formless and empty, and darkness covered the deep waters," Satan lurks, fallen from heaven and plotting how he might destroy the glorious work God is ready to begin. Since Satan had once been in God's presence, he knows about God's majestic plans for the universe. He is waiting . . . waiting . . . waiting to get even, or to try to do so. He will do everything possible to frustrate or even destroy God's beautiful plans—plans that could have taken billions of years of careful planning.

At the same time, a magnificent choir of angels and "morning stars," those other nameless, indescribable celestial beings, gather in the bleachers or ramparts of heaven to observe the most incredible act ever performed and eager to celebrate the majesty and glory the Creator had been planning for ageless ages.

Discovering My Purpose from God's Plan

1. *The time before Creation reveals the "who" of Creation but not the "what" of Creation, while God's handiwork reveals both the "who" and the "what" of Creation.* We worship the "who" of Creation, but not the "what" of Creation. We give thanksgiving for the "what."

2. *There are things we do not, should not, and cannot know about God, for they are too majestic for human understanding.* But there are things we should know, and they are too significant for us to ignore.

3. *Satan lurks in the shadows of your life as he lurked in the shadows of Creation, seeking to frustrate and destroy the glorious work God is doing in your life.* Resist him!

Everything from Nothing

God Creates the Universe

Characters:
Abel; Adam; Angels; Cain; Eve; God the Father, God the Son, God the Holy Spirit; morning stars; Satan

Time Period:
The time of Creation

Dates:
Dates begin, but no one knows when

Where Scene 2 of the Big Story Can Be Found:
Genesis 1:1–4:26

In Scene 2, Find the Answers to These Questions:
How many angels were there when the world was created?
Who was in the cheering section when God created the universe?
When was the world made?

Look for this in Scene 2
> Eve was a 10!
> One man had thousands of children and grandchildren alive during his lifetime.
> We know of only two trees that were named in Eden.
> The Garden of Eden may have been in modern-day Iraq.

The Big Story So Far

Where did all of this incredible Creation come from, this Creation with such wonderful design and order? Every thinking person has thought about Creation—the awesome works he or she sees each day. How did it happen? How long did it take? How could all this wonderful stuff come about?

The time of Creation is a mystery to us. We who believe the Scriptures believe that God created the heavens and the earth. We can't fudge one inch on the "who" of Creation: God made everything. But even the most devout believers have differences of opinions about the "how" and the "when" of Creation.

The Bible tells us that God had plans for Creation eons before he said, "Let it be." He even planned you and me long before the dawn of Creation. So when he said, "Let it be," Creation took place according to plans that had been carefully laid over vast stretches of eternity.

At last the appointed time came for God to create. His plans were carefully laid for every leaf, sunset, flower, animal, and person. According to the Scriptures, he then spoke Creation into existence. He said, "Let it be," and it was so.

Questions You May Be Asking

How long did it take God to create the universe?

There is divided opinion about this even among evangelical Christians. Some believe in a young earth and think that God created the universe in six twenty-four-hour days and rested on the seventh day. Could he have done that? Of course he could. Would he? Why not? Some have said that Creation took place a little more than four thousand years before Jesus came.

Others believe in an old earth, and think that God created the universe in six epochs of time that were possibly millions or billions of years each. Could God have done this? Of course he could. Would he? Why not? This view reconciles with the view of many astronomers today who hold to the "big bang" theory. Some say that all the matter that "banged" was originally about the size of a basketball, while others say it was the size of a marble. From that came all of the worlds—stars, planets, and galaxies rushing from their source faster and faster toward their destiny, whatever that destiny may be. Based on their research, some astronomers claim that the expansion from the marble-size bit of matter to all of space took place in less than a second. Something that instantaneous must surely have been engineered by the Creator. It is impossible that it just happened.

10

>

What
Everyone
Should
Know
about
the

Bible

The question that troubles many who hold the big bang theory is simple—where did the marble- or basketball-sized core of energy come from? Since it wasn't God, it had to be created! Someone had to make it, and that someone had to be God, so God enters the stage of timeless time either way, with a young earth or an old earth. The "who" of Creation seems beyond rational debate. The "when" and "how" of Creation are still subject to debate, even among devout Christians.

This divided opinion generates considerable passion. Old earth believers see it as a flaw in the young earth theory that the sun, moon, and stars, which govern a twenty-four-hour day, were not created until the fourth day. How could days one through three have been twenty-four-hour days, managed by a time-governing and season-governing solar system that was not yet created?

The young earth believers think that specific Bible words are compromised when we call a "day" a long epoch of time. If the word chosen is "day," then they believe that it is a day as we know it.

How long did Creation take? It took as long as God wanted and needed—no more and no less. The debate concerning the length of time is not the purpose of this book, beyond the casual mention above.

The creation of the universe is wrapped up in the first two chapters of Genesis. So much happened in such a short Bible account—the creation of the far-flung heavens, the earth and all that is in it, all plant and animal life, the seasons and the food supply for all God's creatures, and, of course, our first ancestors.

Was anyone there except God?

We often assume that all Creation was accomplished by God the Father, in a lonely work done by a God who lived alone in the heavens. That's not what the Bible says.

The Bible tells us that the triune God—the three persons of the Godhead, God the Father, God the Son, and God the Holy Spirit—were not only at Creation, but were actually engaged in creating.

Genesis 1:2 says that the Holy Spirit was there, hovering over the emerging Creation. John 1:1-4 tells us that Jesus, God the Son, was there. He was not clothed in the human body he took upon himself at Bethlehem, but he was present, creating the universe. No wonder he could do the miracles that he did on earth. The one who made the wind and waves can surely order them to be still. He who created life can surely cause Jairus's daughter, Lazarus, and the widow of Nain's son to live again after they had died. This is a minor detail for the Creator.

Let's go now to the grandstands, the bleachers of heaven, and see the celestial beings called "morning stars" and the great angelic choir celebrating Creation with song and praise. You never have heard such a worship service and never will on this earth.

How many angels were in this choir celebrating Creation?

Revelation 9:16 gives us an indirect hint. In the timeless time after time has ceased, there will be an angel army of two hundred million mounted on horses with heads like lions, with fire, smoke, and sulfur coming from their mouths. Try to picture that scene in your imagination! How would Hollywood depict it?

The angels of Revelation 9:16 will be armed for war, for they are the armies of heaven. These were likely the same angels who appeared to the shepherds when God the Son was born in Bethlehem. We often miss the fact that the angels who appeared to the shepherds were part of the "vast host" of the angel army, perhaps the same two hundred million angels who will go to war against Satan. Revelation 5:11 also affirms the vast host of angels in heaven.

Luke 2:13, the story of angels appearing to the Bethlehem shepherds to announce Jesus' birth, says, "Suddenly, the angel was joined by a vast host of others—the armies of heaven—praising God." These are probably the armies of heaven that Michael will command to conquer Satan and his fallen angels (Revelation 12:7). They are probably also the angelic army host that celebrated Creation as two hundred million of them sang together in one magnificent, glorious choir of choirs.

Let your imagination run wild as you try to grasp a choir of at least two hundred million angels and a vast host of "morning star" celestial beings, cheering, singing, applauding, and celebrating as God brings his plans, formed over eons of timeless time, to reality—those plans for which he has been planning for countless ageless ages. How Satan must have gnashed his teeth in the dark background!

Were Adam and Eve real people?

Adam and Eve were as real as you and I. They ate fruit, walked in the Garden, made love, had children, made enormous mistakes, sinned, repented, felt sorrow and pain, and after Eden, scratched out a living with hard work in the dirt.

Eve got pregnant, had children, and raised them, struggling with the same issues of motherhood that many today struggle with. Evidently Adam and Eve were both successful and dismal failures in parenting, as is so often our situation. Abel modeled their godly qualities, while Cain broke their hearts. Yes, they were people just like you and me, and

12

>

What
Everyone
Should
Know
about
the

Bible

very real indeed. You might have enjoyed having them over for Sunday dinner, as long as they left Cain at home.

What did Adam and Eve look like?

When Eve was freshly created, she was a perfect 10 who could have won any beauty contest forever after. Adam was whatever the male equivalent of a 10 would be. These people were God's direct handiwork, and they lived in a paradise that was the foretaste of heaven. They had it made. Their lifestyle was about as spotless as could be until Satan destroyed it all. They must have been models that would have dazzled us if we looked at them.

Then sin came, and they were expelled from Paradise. Eve had children, probably many, many children. Scratching out a living in middle-eastern soil was tough work, and life became subject to sweat, pain, childbirth, earning a living, and the heartbreak of one son who murdered another son.

Where was the Garden of Eden?

The description given in the Bible doesn't exactly fit anything we know today. It speaks of a river flowing from Eden that branched into four other rivers—the Pishon, the Gihon, the Tigris, and the Euphrates. No one knows where the Pishon and Gihon were. Some think the Flood altered the flow of these two. If we start with the place where the Tigris and Euphrates rivers join today, we are near Basra in southern Iraq, about fifty miles northwest of the Persian Gulf, and about two hundred miles southeast of ancient Ur, where Abraham was born and lived for the first seventy years of his life.

What was the tree of the knowledge of good and evil?

The Lord put many fruit trees in Eden, but two were unusual, one never again to be seen outside of Eden and the other to be seen again only in heaven. The tree of life (Genesis 3:22) permitted a person to live forever. The tree of the knowledge of good and evil (Genesis 2:17) permitted a person to discern good and evil in a godlike fashion, except that it would give that person the option of sinning.

The Lord did not forbid Adam and Eve from eating fruit from the tree of life. If they had eaten this fruit only, they could have lived forever in the heavenly state of Eden. Because they ate from the tree of the knowledge of good and evil first, they suddenly had the choice of sinning. The Lord could not permit Adam and Eve to live forever in a sinful state, for that would not be heaven or Eden but an endless state of condemnation and judgment (Genesis 3:22). Banishing Adam and Eve from Eden prevented them from eating of the tree of life and living forever in a sinful condition.

What does *begat* mean?

Some Bible versions use the word *begat* to indicate birth. As you look closely at the context of this word use, you will see that it does not always mean that someone was born from that person, but sometimes means that he or she descended from that person. *Begat* may mean children, grandchildren, or any other lineal descendants. This is important when working with the chronology of the Bible.

Why did the Lord reject Cain's offering?

It certainly wasn't because it was a grain offering, for the Lord later commanded offerings of the firstfruits of grain harvests. The problem was not *what* Cain gave, but *how* he gave it—grudgingly, angrily, with a heart not right toward God. The best gifts given without a giver's heart are unacceptable gifts. The smallest, most humble gifts, offered with a giver's heart, are acceptable to the Lord.

Sometimes Satan is called Satan, and at other times he is called the devil. Which is correct?

Both are correct, but it's more complicated than that. Satan has at least a dozen names in Scripture:

1. Satan
2. the devil
3. dragon (thirteen times in Revelation)
4. the serpent (Genesis 3:4, 13-15)
5. angel of the bottomless pit (Revelation 9:11)
6. ruler of this world (John 12:31; 14:30; 16:11)
7. commander of the powers in the unseen world (Ephesians 2:2)
8. the god of this world (2 Corinthians 4:4)
9. *Apollyon* (Revelation 9:11)
10. *Abaddon* (Revelation 9:11)
11. Belial, translated as scoundrel or troublemaker (fourteen times in the Old Testament)
12. prince of demons or Beelzebub (seven times in the New Testament)

Great Events of This Time

1. **God undertakes Creation** (Genesis 1:1–2:3).
2. **God makes Adam and Eve** (Genesis 2:7-25).
3. **Temptation and Fall occur** (Genesis 3).
4. **Cain kills Abel** (Genesis 4:1-16).

Heroes and Villains: The Stars in Scene 2

You will notice many heroes and villains throughout the Bible, but some are more heroic and some are more villainous than others. Most

14

>

What
Everyone
Should
Know
about
the

Bible

Bible people, though not all, are partly heroes and partly villains. Adam and Eve had heroic qualities, but they also failed miserably in resisting temptation and in raising their son Cain. God used three murderers, the stuff of villains—Moses, David, and Paul the apostle—in wonderful ministry. Some, like Ahab and Jezebel, were so incredibly evil that it is hard to find any good quality in them, and they certainly are not heroic.

If you want to say, "I'm not a hero, and I'm not a villain," join the crowd of most Bible people. They were neither heroes nor villains, yet to some extent they were both heroic and villainous.

Here are the most notable Bible people of this time. There were others, of course, such as Cain and Abel, the sons of Adam and Eve. Abel pleased the Lord, so Cain murdered Abel.

ADAM

God created Adam from the dust of the ground and breathed his breath into this first man to give him life. Adam was placed over Eden to care for it. He could use the Garden freely, except that he was not to eat the fruit of the tree of the knowledge of good and evil.

God created Eve from Adam's rib. The two of them submitted to Satan's temptation and ate fruit from the one forbidden tree in Eden. For this disobedience to God, they were driven from the Garden and were forced to work the land.

Bible events in Adam's life
1. God creates him.
2. God places him in the Garden of Eden.
3. He names all the animals and birds.
4. He sins when tempted.
5. God punishes him.
6. God sends him out of the Garden of Eden.
7. Cain and Abel are born to him and Eve.
8. Seth is born to him and Eve.

EVE

Like Adam, Eve was not born. God formed her from a rib in Adam's side, and she thus became the only person on earth to come directly from a man. All others, except Adam, have been born of women. Adam and Eve were the only two human beings who began life as adults. Eve lived in the Garden of Eden with Adam until Satan tempted her to eat the forbidden fruit of the tree of the knowledge of good and evil. With that disobedience to God, Eve and Adam were forced to leave Eden to work the fields.

Bible events in Eve's life
1. God creates her from one of Adam's ribs.
2. She sins when tempted by Satan.
3. God punishes her.
4. God sends her out of the Garden of Eden.
5. Cain and Abel are born to her and Adam.
6. Seth is born to her and Adam.

What everyone should know about the book of Genesis
THE STORY OF NEW BEGINNINGS

The book of Genesis presents the story of Creation, the beginning of all things on our earth. It is the book about other beginnings—the beginning of temptation, sin, and forgiveness, the beginning of God's covenant with people, and the beginning of the family with which God made that covenant.

Moses was the author of Genesis, and he probably wrote it during the time of the wilderness wanderings, between 1450 B.C. and 1410 B.C. He had time to write during the forty years in the wilderness. Where did he get all this information? Some of the story line was passed on to him through preceding generations. Much was given to him by inspiration directly from God. The heartbeat of Genesis is its story of newness, of beginnings.

Our quest for newness leads us down good roads and bad roads. The daily grind, the same old thing, the repetitive routines and burdens, the same old sameness all lead people to want a new beginning, a fresh start. Some seek newness by abandoning the old rather than seeking something new. They jump ship, not because the ship is bad, but because the trip is boring. They often discover that a boring ship is better than a stormy ocean with no ship. They have escaped the undesirable for something even more undesirable. They have escaped a boring or monotonous known for a high-risk unknown.

Jumping ship may be leaving a good job for a lesser one, leaving a mate and children for loneliness, leaving home for homelessness. Before long, the luster of newness fades and becomes merely the other side of the same old coin, but with more tarnish. The quest for newness often means abandoning a boring encounter with good for a fresh encounter with the not-so-good.

Some seek newness by a fresh start with what they already have. Their newness keeps the best of the old, but freshens it with God's help. A new attitude, for example, may make the same old job look quite fresh. A new attitude may also make the "same old mate" look quite good.

If you want to encounter newness and pursue new beginnings, read Genesis. The first new beginning was the dawn of everything, the sunrise on God's handiwork called Creation. God spoke and new worlds, new people, new creatures called animals and birds and fish appeared, new marvels called plants emerged, and a new garden called Eden grew, bathed in honeymoon freshness. There were even new creatures called man and woman in this garden.

16
>

What
Everyone
Should
Know
about
the

Bible

Something new called sin also appeared in this garden with an encounter with a serpent. With sin came the newness of choice—a God-given gift to choose good or evil, love or hate, joy or sorrow, heaven or hell, God or Satan.

Genesis is the story of something new called generations, embracing the love of a husband and wife for each other, the gift of children and grandchildren and great-grandchildren, to many generations. It is the story of our choice to leave godly or ungodly footprints on our future generations. For the most part, Genesis is the story of Abraham and Sarah and their future generations, with their successes and failures. More specifically, it is the story of the generations of Jacob and his sons. It is the story of heroes and villains who left footprints in the sands of time and allow us to follow in the footprints of our choice.

So many of the beginnings in Genesis promise a better tomorrow. Many end in the disappointment of a bitter yesterday. I can't think of one Bible character in Genesis who, at the end, could have been fully satisfied. Every one, including the greatest, Abraham, Isaac, and Jacob, must have longed to erase some stains of the past and have another new beginning. The ultimate message of the Bible is that there still *is* a new beginning in Christ, even when we have botched the first, second, or tenth opportunity. That is called hope.

Did You Know?

Cain was first of several things He was the first baby ever born, the first child to grow up, the first person to commit murder, the first person whose offering was rejected by the Lord, and the first person to be alienated from his family. Cain's list of firsts is not exactly first class.

Would you like to meet a cherub? Cherubs sound cute and cuddly, like a little baby or a small angel. Sometimes a parent will call his or her little one, "My little cherub." But no thinking parent would want a child to look like a cherub from the Bible.

The biblical description of the cherubim (the plural of cherub) sets aside that babylike innocence associated with cherubs and puts a more mysterious or even frightening face on this heavenly creature. So what are the cherubim? What do they look like?

In many places throughout the Bible, the Lord mentions heavenly creatures that he created. Some call all of these heavenly beings forms of angels. But the Bible distinguishes among angels, the Angel of the Lord, archangels, cherubim and seraphim, morning stars, demons, and Satan, which are all "other-worldly" or spiritual beings.

We'll talk about angels, archangels, and the Angel of the Lord later in this book. Certainly all of them are angelic beings, with archangels being a higher rank of angel. Michael and Gabriel are archangels. Some think that the Angel of the Lord is the Lord himself.

When Adam and Eve were expelled from Eden, the Lord sent cherubim to guard the gateway with swords so our first parents could never return.

Ezekiel 10 speaks of cherubim at length. Here are some of their characteristics, according to Ezekiel: (1) The moving wings of the cherubim sound like the voice of God Almighty, and in Ezekiel's vision they could be heard clearly in the outer courtyard of the Temple (Ezekiel 10:5). (2) The cherubim can move forward in any of the four directions they face. They go straight in the direction in which their heads are turned, without turning aside (v. 11). (3) They are covered with eyes all over their bodies, including their hands, backs, and wings (v. 12). (4) Each cherub has four faces—of an ox, a human, a lion, and an eagle (v. 14). (5) Each has four wings and what looks like human hands under its wings (vv. 20-21).

Ezekiel 1 adds more description of cherubim: (1) The four wings are two pairs of wings (v. 6). (2) One pair of wings stretches out to touch the wings of other cherubim, and the other pair of wings covers their body (v. 11). (3) Their legs are straight like human legs, but their feet are split like calves' feet and shine like burnished bronze (v. 7). (4) Beneath each of their wings are human hands (v. 8). (5) They look like bright coals of fire or brilliant torches, as though lightning is flashing back and forth among them (v. 13). (6) They dart back and forth among each other like flashes of lightning (v. 14). (7) As they fly, their wings roar like waves crashing against a shore or like the voice of the Almighty (v. 24). (8) When they stop, they lower their wings (v. 24).

If you read Revelation 4:6-11, you will find similar heavenly beings, but not the same as the cherubim of Ezekiel 1 and 10. The heavenly beings of Revelation 4 have six wings, not four, as in Ezekiel. They are also covered with eyes and appear similar to, though different from, the cherubim Ezekiel described. Each creature in Revelation has a single face, not four faces, although among them, they have the same four faces as the cherubim, but not on the same body, as the cherubim do.

How would you like your "little cherub" to look like a real cherub? There were artistic renderings of cherubim in the Tabernacle and Temple. Descriptions of the cherubim in the Tabernacle may be found in Exodus 25:17-22. There were two golden cherubim, one on each end of the lid of the Ark of the Covenant. Each seemed to have two wings, but these were only artistic representations and not necessarily a documented portrait. In 1 Kings 6:23-28, we find the same type of cherubim decorating the inner sanctuary of the Temple. These were made of olive wood covered with gold. Their wings were outstretched fifteen feet, and they stood fifteen feet high.

18

>

What
Everyone
Should
Know
about
the

Bible

What about seraphim? We must go to Isaiah 6 for some description of them: (1) They are called mighty (Isaiah 6:2). (2) Each has six wings (v. 2). (3) With two wings they cover their faces, with two wings they cover their feet, and with two wings they fly (v. 2). (4) They were mighty singers, so powerful that their glorious singing shook the foundations of the Temple and filled it with smoke (vv. 3-4). (5) One seraph picked up a live coal with tongs and cauterized Isaiah's lips (vv. 6-7).

It would seem from all of this that cherubim, seraphim, morning stars, and angels are each different types of created heavenly beings.

Adam's big family The question is often asked, "Where did Adam's children and grandchildren get their mates?" The answer is simple. Adam lived 930 years and had "other sons and daughters" (Genesis 5:4). How many? Perhaps hundreds of children and thousands of descendants lived during his lifetime.

Let's say that Adam and his wife had a new baby every three years for nine hundred years. That's three hundred children. But during those nine hundred years, each generation had another generation. If we figure one generation each twenty-five years, that's thirty-six generations of offspring while Adam was still alive. Before he died, Adam may have seen thousands of offspring! Did Adam have other wives in addition to Eve? We don't know. If so, this scene could multiply greatly. Think of wrapping Christmas gifts or baking birthday cakes for a family that large!

Discovering My Purpose from God's Plan

1. *Satan cannot steal your soul.* He can have it only if you give it to him. Jesus *will not* steal your soul. He will have it only if you give it to him.

2. *Footprints and fingerprints are convincing evidence that someone with feet and fingers was here.* The footprints and fingerprints of Creation are convincing evidence that a Creator was here. Otherwise, where did those prints come from?

3. *Creation stirs celebration.* Celebrate the Creator and his Creation!

4. *Our words are often too small to express our ideas.* So it is when we try to fully describe Creation. If we use "magnificent," "the best," and "awesome" to describe toothpaste and soap, what words do we have left to describe the handiwork of the Almighty?

5. *The Creator created something from nothing.* You and I must be careful not to take that something and reduce it to nothing.

6. *We are made in the image of God, but we cannot emulate the person of God.* We can reflect his qualities, but we cannot fully exhibit his personhood. You and I can be godly, but only God can be God!

7. *Adam and Eve should have known today's dietary slogan, "You are what you eat."*
8. *The best gifts given without a giver's heart are unacceptable.* The smallest, most humble gifts presented with a giver's heart are acceptable to the Lord. Cain's gift was acceptable, but his ungenerous heart made it unacceptable. Abel's gift was an acceptable gift from a giver's heart, so God received it.

The Time
of the
Ancients

From
Adam
to Noah

Characters:
Adam; Enoch; Enosh; Eve; Jared; Kenan; Mahalalel;
Methuselah; Noah; Seth

Time Period:
From Adam to Noah

Dates:
No dates known

Where Scene 3 of the Big Story Can Be Found:
Genesis 5:1–9:17

In Scene 3, Find the Answers to These Questions:
Could there really have been a time of "middle earth"?
What two people were never born?
Which man never died?

Look for this in Scene 3
> Children hundreds of years old—did it ever happen?
> Seven men lived nine hundred years—can you name two
  of them?
> Noah's ark was bigger than a football field.

◢◣◢◣ The Big Story So Far

The time of the ancients is one of the most mysterious periods of the Bible. Things were so different then from how they are today. People lived for hundreds of years—some of them almost a thousand years. There were also, according to the Bible, "giant Nephilites [living] on the earth . . . who became the heroes and famous warriors of ancient times" (Genesis 6:4). This tantalizing Bible window gives us just a peek into an era of great mystery. If we wanted to write a story about "middle earth" or some fictitious culture or kingdom, we could surely put it within this time of the ancients. We could let our imaginations run wild in that fiction and perhaps be on target as to how things actually were.

This time of the ancients was also a time of great wickedness. The giants, heroes, and famous warriors of ancient times weren't godly; they were villains. In fact, they became so wicked that God ultimately decided to wipe out his human creation and start over again with one man, Noah, and his family.

◢◣◢◣ Questions You May Be Asking

Why did these people live so long?

The ancients lived for hundreds of years. Imagine doing laundry and getting meals for nine hundred years without washing machines, dryers, electric stoves, or other appliances. It's enough to make an ancient wife weep.

Genesis 5:1-32 is the record of the oldest of the oldies. Methuselah beat them all by living 969 years, just a little short of one thousand years. The Bible suggests that he and the other ancients were having children throughout most of those years. Think about nine hundred years of parenting! Imagine having children who were nine hundred or more years old! What was said of Adam's large family applies even more to Methuselah.

If he started having children at age twenty, Methuselah could have had several hundred children. His children could each have had hundreds of children. And their children, and the children after them, would have multiplied many times over. Methuselah could have started his own village, and perhaps he did. Like Adam, Methuselah could have seen thousands of offspring before he died. That was called having a tribe.

Don't picture thousands of little children running around the tent. These "kids" were of all ages from birth to hundreds of years old. Before Methuselah died, there were children and spouses, grandchildren and spouses, and great-grandchildren to the forty-fifth generation of "great." How would you like to invite the whole family for Sunday dinner?

22

>

What
Everyone
Should
Know
about
the

Bible

Such ultralong lives suggest the absence of disease and sickness, and they probably had much healthier diets than ours. That would make a long, long life more acceptable, wouldn't it?

Where did the "heroes and famous warriors of ancient times" come from?

There seem to have been two dominant strains of people during those days—the godly descendants of Seth, and the ungodly descendants of Cain, who murdered his brother Abel. The Sethites, who may have been called the "sons of God," or godly ones, were obviously not all perfect, either. As in any godly family, there are some who stray, and so it was with the Sethites.

Not surprisingly, some Sethites married "outside the faith." Many began to marry the Cainites who seem to have had more than their share of beautiful girls (Genesis 6:2). This intermarriage may have been what brought giants and great "heroes and famous warriors of ancient times" (Genesis 6:4). The old legends have been lost, of course, but what legends they must have been!

The intermarriage of Sethites and Cainites also brought great evil. Wickedness spread throughout this age until the time of Noah, when things became so bad that God was grieved that he had made these people. He decided to wipe out all humanity and start over with the one remaining godly family—the family of Noah.

God also decided that he would not permit people to live as long after that (Genesis 6:3). From this time forward, the human lifespan diminished, so that by the time of Abraham, it was reduced to about two hundred years or less. By the time of David, seventy was considered old.

Noah and his family were at the end of the age of the ancients who lived many hundreds of years. We don't know how long this age of the ancients lasted. It could have been a couple of thousand years or many thousands of years.

Did You Know?

There were seven men who lived more than nine hundred years Genesis names seven of them (5:3-27; 9:29):

1. Adam, 930 years
2. Seth, 912 years
3. Enosh, 905 years
4. Kenan, 910 years
5. Jared, 962 years
6. Methuselah, 969 years
7. Noah, 950 years

Mahalalel almost made it to nine hundred; he was 895 years old when he died (Genesis 5:17). Were there other ancient "ancients"? There were probably hundreds who lived more than nine hundred years, but the Bible does not tell us who they were. It is interesting to note that the next list of men with long lives records the descendants of Shem, Noah's son. They averaged between four hundred and six hundred years in age, much less than their ancestors. Ages are not given for the descendants of Ham and Japheth (Genesis 11:10-26).

One of the ancients never died Enoch, like the prophet Elijah many years later (848 B.C.; see 2 Kings 2:1-12), was taken up into heaven without dying (Genesis 5:23-24).

The size of Noah's ark The ark was 450 feet long, 45 feet high, and 75 feet wide. Let's compare its length to a football field. A football field is one hundred yards, or three hundred feet, long. The ark was one and a half times as long as a football field. It was higher than two ranch houses and one-fourth as wide as a football field is long. That was one big boat—all made by hand with handmade tools—and it had to float for fourteen months.

The water of the Great Flood Where did all that water come from? It was partly from rain—incessant rain for forty days and forty nights. But more water may have come from below than from above, as "the underground waters erupted from the earth" (Genesis 7:11).

The length of time of the Flood From the time the ark was finished until Noah and his family left the ark on dry land, more than fourteen months passed. That's a long time to be cooped up with all the living animals and birds of the world! It's also a lot of feeding and cleaning. Think about that the next time you grumble over taking care of your pet.

The people aboard the ark There were only eight—Noah, his wife, their three sons, and their wives. No children are mentioned in the Bible. For some reason the Bible does not tell us the name of Noah's wife.

How old was Noah when his children were born? The Bible says, "By the time Noah was five hundred years old, he was the father of Shem, Ham, and Japheth" (Genesis 5:32). We don't know how old Noah was when the first of his three sons was born, but this verse suggests that he was almost five hundred when the last son was born. If he was so old, why did he have only three children? This is one of those fascinating silent mysteries in the Bible. We don't know the answer. Apparently, he had only three children during his entire lifetime of more than nine hundred years.

24

>

What
Everyone
Should
Know
about
the

Bible

Discovering My Purpose from God's Plan

1. *Some secrets belong to God, so recorded history cannot claim them.* In the time of the ancients, many of God's secrets were hidden from curious eyes. History can't help us, so perhaps imagination can.

2. *Heroes are not always godly heroes.* Sometimes their heroic deeds are undesirable, though impressive. So it was with the ancients.

3. *God knows the unknown future, for he controls it.* It's a good idea to follow God obediently. You can't see your next footstep, but God can.

The Time of Dispersion

From Noah to Abraham

Characters:
Abraham; Noah; Noah's wife (unnamed); Shem, Ham, and Japheth (Noah's three sons); the wives of Shem, Ham, and Japheth (not named)

Time Period:
From Noah to Abraham

Dates:
No date is known for Noah. Abraham was born about 2166 B.C.

Where Scene 4 of the Big Story Can Be Found:
Genesis 9:18–11:32

In Scene 4, Find the Answers to These Questions:
Was there ever a time when everyone spoke the same language?
Did Noah have any children after the Flood?

Look for this in Scene 4
> The Great Flood was not all rain. Where did the other water come from?
> It seems that the last of Noah's three children was born when he was about five hundred years old and that he had no other children before or after this time.

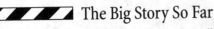

The Big Story So Far

An old man and his impossible boat

From the time of Noah until the time of Abraham is the time of dispersion. When this time begins, we see only one man, his three sons, and their wives as the future population of the entire earth. All other people were drowned in the Great Flood that God sent. Among the ancients, Noah alone pleased and obeyed God (Genesis 6:9).

When Noah was 480, God commanded him to make an ark. It took the next 120 years for Noah to complete it. Noah became a father some time before the age of five hundred, and had three sons named Shem, Ham, and Japheth. He was six hundred when the Flood ended. Shem turned one hundred years old two years after the Flood (Genesis 11:10).

After the Flood purified the earth, Noah lived another 350 years. During this time, the age of dispersion began.

Shem became the father of the Semites, which included Abraham and his descendants through Isaac. Judaism, Christianity, and Islam all have Semitic roots.

Ham became the father of some dark-skinned races, including the Egyptians, Ethiopians, Libyans, and Canaanites.

From Japheth descended the Indo-European family of nations that stretched from the south coasts of Europe to Persia and included the more white-skinned races.

From one language to six thousand languages

The nations dispersed, but they all spoke the same language until the event at the tower of Babel. Their dispersion was not only by tribe and nation, but also by language. A visit to the United Nations reminds us of the diversity of languages in the world today, which began at Babel.

The World Almanac lists 197 nations at this time. There are approximately six thousand languages in the world, and many thousands of dialects. We have come a long way since the tower of Babel.

Genesis 10 is a preview of the many tribes, nations, and peoples who would come from the dispersion. Notice the names, such as the Ludites, Anamites, Lehabites, Naphtuhites, Pathrusites, Casluhites, and Caphtorites (Genesis 10:13-14). Anyone who has studied the Old Testament has encountered dozens of these strange names. This was the age of scattering, or dispersion.

Questions You May Be Asking

Did the Great Flood purify the whole world of sin? Did it keep people from sinning after that?

Not really. One of the great lessons of Scripture is the flawed condition of all people—sin. You would think that Noah and his family, having experienced the direct hand of God in sending the Great Flood, would have been models of godly behavior.

However, it wasn't long after the Flood that Noah laid down in his tent, naked and drunk. The problem was compounded when Noah's son Ham, and possibly Ham's son Canaan, saw him and invited Ham's brothers to take a peek at their naked father, probably snickering disrespectfully as they did so. Noah's other two sons didn't share in this event. Shem and Japheth backed into the tent with some cloth to cover their father's shame without looking at him. Ham's disrespect for his father earned his father's curse.

Flash forward many years to the time of Moses and Joshua. Ham's descendants, the Canaanites, are an ungodly people occupying the Promised Land. Shem's descendants, the Israelites, are invading the land to claim it as their own. The Israelites won militarily. The Canaanites won socially and morally by infecting their new conquerors with a pagan lifestyle. History repeats itself. The descendants of Japheth, commonly thought to include the Gentiles surrounding the northern coasts of the Mediterranean Sea, would become the people evangelized by Paul, also a descendant of Shem.

Was there really a time when everyone spoke the same language?

"At one time all the people of the world spoke the same language and used the same words" (Genesis 11:1). This same-language people multiplied in numbers and in paganism. The world before the Flood repeated itself until sin reached pandemic proportions.

The story of mankind comes to a crossroad at ancient Babylon, called Babel in the Bible story. There the people proposed building a city with a giant, stepped tower called a ziggurat, a common form of temple building in ancient Mesopotamia. Ziggurats often had seven color-coded levels, leading from a large base to a small top. Each level was connected with a stairway.

The tower of Babel was unusual in its size and height—possibly as much as three hundred feet along each of its four sides, or the length of a regulation football field. Thus, the tower was more than twice the size of a football field, an enormous structure that required many thousands of mud bricks or stones. Some think that the color coding of the levels from bottom to top was black, orange, red, yellow, green, blue, and white.

The tower of Babel was a work of enormous pride of the kind that sets itself and its people apart from God, or even against God. It's the kind of pride that makes people think not only that they don't need God but that they *are* God.

God was displeased; he scattered the people and confused their language. It was the decisive beginning of multiple languages and dialects. The world would never be the same after this. With the beginning of many languages and dialects also came the widening differences among many nations, peoples, and cultures. Since that time, the great problem has been to reconcile people, tribes, nations, and cultures that are separated mostly by language, but also by cultural distinctions.

What is the earliest recorded history of this period?

The archaeology of Mesopotamia has unearthed remains of people who some believe lived as early as 10,000 B.C. Mesopotamian *recorded* history stretches back as far as 6000 B.C. Should we assume that the people who lived in 10,000 B.C. or even in 6000 B.C. came before the Flood or after the Flood? If they lived before the Flood, we don't have an accurate timetable for this period. If they lived after the Flood, there must have been a vast stretch of time between Noah and Abraham. On the surface, this seems to conflict with Genesis 11:10-26.

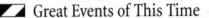

Great Events of This Time

1. **Noah builds the ark** (Genesis 6:1–7:10).
2. **The Great Flood occurs** (Genesis 7:11–9:19).
3. **Canaan is cursed and Shem is blessed** (Genesis 9:20-29).
4. **Proud people build the tower of Babel** (Genesis 11:1-9).

Significant Dates of This Time

Circa 6000 B.C., the earliest Mesopotamian recorded cultures appear.
Circa 2166 B.C., Abraham is born.
No other dates from this time are known.

Heroes and Villains: The Stars in Scene 4

NOAH

In the days of Noah, people were exceedingly evil. God searched for a godly person and found only Noah and his family. God planned for a great flood to destroy the earth and commanded Noah to build an ark, a large boat that would help him and his family survive the Flood. With some of each species of animal and bird on board, God closed the ark and Noah and his family survived. They landed on Mount Ararat, in what is now eastern Turkey.

Was Noah a hero or a villain? Certainly he was godly, or the Lord would not have spared him from the Flood. He was heroic, exhibiting patience and persistence in building the ark in desertlike surroundings,

30

>

What
Everyone
Should
Know
about
the

Bible

undoubtedly suffering taunts and insults from his unbelieving neighbors. He showed a bit of villainy after the Flood as he lay naked, drunk, and exposed to his family. Few Bible heroes escape some villainous behavior.

Bible events in Noah's life
1. He pleases God.
2. He has three sons: Shem, Ham, and Japheth.
3. God instructs him to build an ark.
4. He obeys and builds the ark.
5. He takes animals and birds into the ark.
6. He goes into the ark with his wife and family.
7. He and his family are safe in the ark during the Flood.
8. He leaves the ark after the Flood.
9. He builds an altar to the Lord after the Flood.
10. God makes a covenant with him after the Flood.
11. He dies at the age of 950.

Discovering My Purpose from God's Plan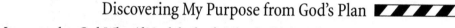

1. *It pays to obey God.* What if Noah had refused to build the ark?
2. *Even godly people have their flaws.* Noah drank too much wine and got drunk.
3. *God's ways transcend our ways.* In a world with only one language, who would have thought that pride would be the catalyst to create hundreds of languages?

Friends of God
The Time of the Patriarchs

Characters:
Abimelech (Philistine king); Abraham (Abram); Abraham's unnamed servant who arranged for the marriage of Isaac and Rebekah; Asenath (Joseph's wife); Asher (son of Jacob and Zilpah, Leah's maid); Ben-ammi (son of Lot and his daughter; the Ammonites' forefather); Benjamin (son of Jacob and Rachel); Bildad the Shuhite (friend of Job); Bilhah (Rachel's maid); Dan (son of Jacob and Bilhah, Rachel's maid); Dinah (daughter of Jacob and Leah); Edom (son of Lot and his daughter; the Edomites' forefather); Elihu son of Barakel the Buzite (friend of Job); Eliphaz the Temanite (friend of Job); Ephraim (son of Joseph and Asenath); Esau (son of Isaac and Rebekah); Gad (son of Jacob and Zilpah, Leah's maid); Hagar (Sarah's maid); Isaac (son of Abraham and Sarah); Ishmael (son of Abraham and Sarah's maid Hagar); Issachar (son of Jacob and Leah); Jacob (son of Isaac and Rebekah); Job; Joseph (son of Jacob and Rachel); Judah (son of Jacob and Leah); Kedorlaomer (a pagan king); Laban (Rebekah's brother; Jacob's father-in-law and uncle); Leah (Laban's daughter, Jacob's wife); Levi (son of Jacob and Leah); Lot (Abraham's nephew); Lot's wife (not named); Manasseh (son of Joseph and Asenath); Naphtali (son of Jacob and Bilhah, Rachel's maid); Pharaoh (king of Egypt); Potiphar (Pharaoh's official); Potiphar's wife (not named); Rachel (Laban's daughter, Jacob's wife); Rebekah (Laban's sister, Isaac's wife); Reuben (son of Jacob and Leah); Sarah (Sarai, Abraham's wife and half sister); Simeon (son of Jacob and Leah); Tamar (Judah's daughter-in-law); Zebulun (son of Jacob and Leah); Zilpah (Leah's maid); Zophar the Naamathite (friend of Job)

Time Period:
From the birth of Abraham until the death of Joseph

Dates:
2166 B.C. to 1805 B.C.

Where Scene 5 of the Big Story Can Be Found:
Genesis 12–50 and the book of Job

In Scene 5, Find the Answers to These Questions:
Abraham was one hundred years old when his son Isaac was
    born. How old was Sarah?
Did Job and Abraham ever meet?
Why did a woman become a pillar of salt?
Why did Jacob marry four women when he wanted only one?
The Ishmaelite traders who sold Joseph were his relatives. How
    were they related?

Look for this in Scene 5
> The story of the patriarchs begins, not in Israel, but in a
    Sumerian city.
> None of the patriarchs had even one verse of our Bible.
> Sarah was almost ninety when a Philistine king wanted to add
    her to his harem.

The Big Story So Far

The story of the patriarchs and Israel begins in a Sumerian city, the
ancient city of Ur, located in southern Mesopotamia. Abram (who
would later be called Abraham) lived there with his father, Terah, his
wife Sarai (who would later be called Sarah), and his nephew Lot.
Abram's brother Haran had died and Abram was taking care of Haran's
son Lot. Abram was born in Ur, a prosperous city with a large library,
and had lived there for seventy years.

Ur was like many other cities. It was wealthy and prosperous. It had
gained the world but lost its soul. Excavations of the royal cemetery at Ur
gave a portrait of life in Ur about three hundred years before Abraham.
They revealed beautiful jewelry, treasures, magnificent harps or lyres,
golden daggers, golden helmets, and other works of gold. There were
even chariots filled with treasures buried in these tombs. Ur was a cultural center with a large library of clay tablet books, like little clay pillows
the size of your hand. They were written in cuneiform, with little wedge-
shaped characters stamped into the clay when it was still soft. Ur was
also the pagan center for the worship of the moon god Nanna.

34

> **Why would Abraham want to leave such a city? He had lived there
for seventy years. Why leave?**

What
Everyone
Should
Know
about
the

On a human level, Abraham and his family faced three conflicting
pressures—the changing political scene in Ur, the Semitic religion he
embraced instead of worshiping the moon god, and pressures of the
wealthy Sumerian culture. The real reason for his leaving, however, was

Bible

a direct command from God, as seen in Acts 7:2-4: "Our glorious God appeared to our ancestor Abraham in Mesopotamia before he settled in Haran. God told him, 'Leave your native land and your relatives, and come into the land that I will show you.' So Abraham left the land of the Chaldeans and lived in Haran until his father died. Then God brought him here to the land where you now live."

The first leg of the journey to the land of promise
Abraham's family migrated from southern Mesopotamia to northern Mesopotamia, stopping in a town named Haran, named for Abraham's dead brother. The intent was to move on to Canaan, but apparently Abraham's father, Terah, was not able to travel, probably because of deteriorating health. He died in Haran.

Onward to Canaan
Abraham would become head of the tribe, for he was the older of two living brothers. At God's command, he gave that tribal leadership to his younger brother, Nahor, and moved on to Canaan. God promised that he would make Abraham the father of a great nation and a blessing to many. Abraham was now seventy-five years old (Genesis 12:1-2, 4).

How did a lonely old shepherd become a friend of God?
As a shepherd, Abraham spent many nights under the canopy of the stars. He had no Bible, no church, no fellowship with other believers, no books to guide his spiritual life, and no conferences—nothing but the stars, skies, trees, and animals.

So where did Abraham get his knowledge of and fervent passion for God? The explanation comes two thousand years later in the book of Romans, "They know the truth about God because he has made it obvious to them. For ever since the world was created, people have seen the earth and sky. Through everything God made, they can clearly see his invisible qualities—his eternal power and divine nature. So they have no excuse for not knowing God" (Romans 1:19-20).

Abraham had what every other person in the history of the world has had—the evidence of Creation, the fingerprints and footprints of the Creator all around him, the convincing proof that someone has made it all. Abraham responded to what he saw. He recognized that Creation can come only from a Creator, and majestic Creation can come only from a majestic Creator. He formed a heart-to-heart, mind-to-mind friendship with that Creator. Any other person could have done the same. Most didn't, for they chose to ignore the convincing evidence that they saw. Abraham knew God because he responded to God's handiwork and saw the One behind the work.

Abraham also had a unique personal relationship with God, for God spoke to him audibly, person-to-person, heart-to-heart, mind-to-mind, in very specific conversations. Only a few Bible people had this special privilege of conversations with the Creator.

Abraham wasn't perfect

As Abraham and his family camped at Shechem, in Canaan, God talked with him again. God promised to give the surrounding land to Abraham's descendants. Abraham had formed such a friendship with God that God actually talked with him.

From Shechem, Abraham moved southward toward the Negev. There was a famine in the land, so Abraham took his family to Egypt to wait it out. As he entered Egypt, he had a growing fear. His wife Sarah was exceptionally beautiful. Perhaps Pharaoh would want her in his harem and would kill Abraham to get her. Abraham concocted a devious plan. He would tell the Egyptians that Sarah was his sister (which was half true, for she was his half sister). Abraham and Sarah shared the same father but had different mothers. He would not tell them that she was also his wife, which was a silent lie, sometimes called a half lie, and a blatant deception.

Sure enough, the Egyptians saw this beautiful woman and told Pharaoh about her. Before long, she was in Pharaoh's harem, and Abraham was rich with gifts from Pharaoh. Suddenly, he was cattle rich but wife poor.

The Lord sent a terrible plague to Pharaoh's household. The truth came out, and Pharaoh was furious. Pharaoh sent Abraham, Sarah, and their possessions out of the land with an armed guard. Never again could they return to Egypt.

Too much stuff–too much strife

Suddenly Abraham was a rich man, living again in the Negev. He had evidently shared his riches with his adopted son and nephew, Lot, for he was also rich. Both of them had their wealth in livestock. Too much stuff led to too much strife between Lot's shepherds and Abraham's shepherds because there was not enough pastureland for both and they were crowding each other. To keep peace in the family, Abraham offered Lot the best land, and Lot took it. He moved toward Sodom, which at that time was a very fertile area—the best grazing land in the region.

Lot soon got into trouble. A petty king named Kedorlaomer (or Chedorlaomer) battled against some of the cities of the region, captured Sodom, plundered its riches, and took Lot prisoner. Abraham soon heard the news and mobilized his own fighting men, attacked Kedorlaomer by night, caught him by surprise, and defeated him. Lot was free—his uncle Abraham had helped him again.

36

>

What
Everyone
Should
Know
about
the

Bible

A canopy of stars—a promise from the Creator

God appeared again to Abraham, perhaps as Abraham took care of his sheep under the canopy of the stars. There were no modern city lights to dim his view of the night sky, so it must have been a dazzling display of thousands of stars. This time God promised Abraham a son and descendants as plentiful as the night stars. Abraham must have smiled as he looked at those thousands of stars shining in the dark sky.

God continued his conversation with Abraham later the same night and entered into a covenant with him. From that time on, Abraham and his descendants would be covenant people through Abraham's promised son.

Time passed, and the promised son did not arrive. Abraham and Sarah were now much too old to have children. Sarah began to doubt that God would fulfill his promise through her. She concocted a devious plan, which was socially acceptable then but showed a great lack of faith in God's promises. She gave her Egyptian maid, Hagar, to Abraham as a wife. Hagar's son would be Sarah's son. That son was Ishmael, whose birth would devastate the relationships in this family.

A covenant with God

When Abraham was ninety-nine, the Lord appeared to him again and renewed his covenant with him. "Serve me faithfully and live a blameless life. I will make a covenant with you, by which I will guarantee to give you countless descendants" (Genesis 17:1-2). At that time, God changed Abram's name to Abraham, and his wife's name from Sarai to Sarah.

This covenant is the foundation of the entire Old Testament. God continued, "I will confirm my covenant with you and your descendants after you, from generation to generation. This is the everlasting covenant: I will always be your God and the God of your descendants after you. And I will give the entire land of Canaan, where you now live as a foreigner, to you and your descendants. It will be their possession forever, and I will be their God" (Genesis 17:7-8).

Then God said to Abraham, "Your responsibility is to obey the terms of the covenant. You and all your descendants have this continual responsibility" (Genesis 17:9).

While Abraham and his family camped at Mamre, near modern Hebron, three men visited him one day. One was the Lord, in human form. He promised that Sarah would have a baby within the year. Sarah, who was almost ninety, laughed and doubted God. How could a ninety-year-old woman have a baby? Impossible! The Lord scolded Sarah for her laughter and reaffirmed that she would indeed have a child.

Bargaining with God—a challenging prayer

Before leaving Abraham, the Lord told him of his plans to destroy the wicked city of Sodom, where Lot lived. Abraham entered into a challenging prayer of negotiation with the Lord, seeking mercy for Sodom. Would the Lord destroy Sodom if he found fifty innocent people? The Lord said he would not. Abraham gradually lowered the number until at last he asked if the Lord would destroy Sodom if ten innocent people were found. The Lord promised that he would not.

However, the Lord did not find even ten innocent people in this wicked city, so he determined to destroy the city by fire from heaven.

Two angels visited Sodom and almost forcibly removed Lot, his wife, and his daughters. They had all grown to love the lifestyle of this evil city and were reluctant to leave it, even with the angels urging them. The angels persisted and dragged them from the city, but Lot's wife looked back longingly and was turned into a pillar of salt as God rained fire and brimstone upon Sodom and Gomorrah. Abraham must have wept as he saw the flames and smoke rise from the condemned cities.

Incest in a lonely cave

Lot and his two grown daughters were alone now, living in a cave in the mountains. Lot's wife was a pillar of salt. The daughters' fiancés had refused to leave Sodom, so they were destroyed with the city. The daughters hatched a devious plan. Since they had no one to marry, and thus would never have children, their father was their only hope for getting pregnant. One night they got Lot drunk, and one daughter had sex with him without his knowledge. Another night they got Lot drunk again, and the other daughter had sex with him, but he was unaware of it. At last both girls were pregnant, and in time each had a baby.

The older daughter named her son Moab. His descendants were the Moabites. Most of them were enemies of Israel. The one beautiful exception was Ruth, who became the great-grandmother of King David, the ancestor of Jesus. So Jesus' bloodline came in part from this incestuous birth. The younger daughter named her son Ben-ammi, and he became the ancestor of the Ammonites. They, too, were later enemies of Israel. These two births brought enormous sorrow and hurt to the descendants of Abraham.

Ungodly lies from a godly man

Abraham had not learned his lesson when he lied to Pharoah in Egypt. He did the same thing again to a local Philistine king, Abimelech, by telling his neighbors that Sarah was his sister. Abimelech took her to his palace to make her one of his wives, but God warned Abimelech in a dream not to touch Sarah. The angry Abimelech returned Sarah to

What
Everyone
Should
Know
about
the

Bible

Abraham with a thousand pieces of silver and riches in livestock. Once more, Abraham's lies had made him rich.

Sarah must have remained an unusually beautiful and youthful woman into old age. She was almost ninety when Abimelech tried to add her to his harem—not something many kings would want to do!

The miracle baby

The year passed, and Sarah had the promised baby. Abraham and Sarah named him Isaac. Ishmael had been the heir to the family fortune for several years. Sarah wanted Isaac, not Hagar's Ishmael, to be that heir, and her jealousy boiled over. She demanded that Abraham send Hagar and Ishmael away into the wilderness, hoping that they would die there. Abraham reluctantly agreed to do it, so Hagar and Ishmael were on their own in the wilderness. This event would come back to haunt Abraham's great-grandson Joseph, for Ishmael's descendants would sell him into slavery in Egypt.

Isaac grew to be a strong young man. He was on target to be the heir of the family fortune and the covenant, too. Then one day God asked the impossible of Abraham. "Take your son, your only son—yes, Isaac, whom you love so much—and go to the land of Moriah. Go and sacrifice him as a burnt offering" (Genesis 22:2).

Abraham was dazed. How could God ask such a thing? But Abraham obeyed. As he made the journey with his beloved son, he must have asked why a hundred times. Why would God ask him to do such a terrible thing? How could he have descendants as plentiful as the stars if he killed his only son?

At last, on the mountain, as Abraham lifted the knife to plunge it into Isaac, God stopped him and provided a ram for the sacrifice. Abraham had passed God's supreme test of obedience and showed that he would sacrifice his only son if God told him to.

On that mountain, many years later, King David bought Araunah's threshing floor. That mountain became the Temple Mount, where David's son Solomon built the Temple. Today, the Dome of the Rock stands on that mountain.

Arranged marriage

The years passed, and Sarah died. Isaac was not yet married, although he was about forty years old. Abraham was growing older and was concerned for his son. Isaac was the heir to the covenant, but for future generations to come, Isaac needed a wife. Of course Isaac could not marry a local pagan girl. The mother of the covenant people must be a godly and worthy ancestor like her husband. Abraham sent his servant to Haran to find a bride for Isaac among his relatives.

At the well of Haran, just outside town, Abraham's servant prayed for God's direction. The servant would ask a young woman for a drink of water. If she also volunteered to water his camels, he would know that she was the right woman to become Isaac's wife. Before he had finished praying, Rebekah came to the well carrying her water jug. Abraham's servant asked her for a drink, and she volunteered to water his camels also. Rebekah had a servant's heart, for a thirsty camel could drink twenty to thirty gallons of water, and the man had ten of them. He was also a stranger.

Rebekah was the daughter of Bethuel, son of Nahor, Abraham's brother. The servant told Rebekah's father and brother why he had come, and they all agreed that Rebekah could return with Abraham's servant and marry Isaac.

Things did not go so well with Isaac and Rebekah, however. They begged God for a child. They were getting a late start because Isaac was forty when he married. Twenty more childless years went by. During this time, Abraham married Keturah, and they had six sons. One of them was Midian, who became the ancestor of Moses' wife Zipporah and her father, Jethro. At last Abraham died, at the age of 175.

The battle of the birthright

When Isaac was sixty, God sent twins to Isaac and Rebekah. The first-born, Esau, was red and hairy at birth. They named the second son Jacob; he was born grasping Esau's heel.

Esau was the older son, so the birthright belonged to him, but the Lord had told Rebekah when she was pregnant that the older son's descendants would serve the younger son's descendants. Jacob would inherit the covenant, not Esau.

As the boys grew up, Esau became a skilled hunter, and Jacob stayed around the house. Because Esau brought home such savory wild game, Isaac loved him the most. Jacob was his mother's favorite—not a happy family situation!

One day Esau went hunting but found nothing, while Jacob stayed home and made a big pot of lentil stew. When Esau returned, he was desperately hungry, so he asked for some lentil stew. Jacob offered it to him in exchange for his birthright, so Esau agreed and swore to Jacob that the birthright was his.

Water in the wilderness

Isaac became a "cattle rich" man, wealthy in animals, which brought tension and jealousy from the nearby Philistines. Each time Isaac dug a well, the Philistines stole it from him. Isaac refused to fight for these wells, so at last the Philistines left him alone and even made a treaty with him. Isaac named the final well that he could keep "Oath," and the

40

>

What
Everyone
Should
Know
about
the

Bible

place became known as the "well of the oath," or Beersheba. It is still called that today.

When twins were torn apart

Isaac grew old and blind. One day he sent his son Esau to hunt so he could eat his favorite meat, before giving him the family blessing. This was strange, for Esau had married Hittite wives, who made life miserable for Isaac and Rebekah. Hittite wives could not possibly make good mothers of the covenant people. Isaac knew in his heart that this was true, but he still favored Esau and his tasty meat. Now we see one major flaw in old Isaac. His belly prevailed over his brain.

While Esau was hunting, Rebekah hatched a dangerous plan. She would cook a young goat, and Jacob, pretending to be Esau, would take the meat to his blind father. Since Esau was hairy, Rebekah put Esau's clothing on Jacob and made gloves from the hairy skin of young goats for Jacob to wear. Then she sent him to Isaac to trick him.

Isaac was suspicious, but he was deceived when he smelled Esau's clothing on Jacob and felt the hairy gloves. He believed that this was truly Esau and gave him the blessing. Jacob was now heir to the family fortune and the covenant.

Before long, Esau appeared with his wild game. When he learned what Jacob had done, he was furious and threatened to kill Jacob when his father died. He begged Isaac for a blessing, but Isaac had given it all to Jacob.

Jacob had no choice. Rebekah urged him to run away to Haran to find a safe haven with Rebekah's family. Rebekah paved the way by pressuring Isaac to send Jacob to find a bride among her family, so he went with Isaac's blessing and a charge to marry a wife within the faith and within the family.

Stairway to heaven

That night, as Jacob slept under the stars near Bethel, he had a dramatic dream. A stairway or ladder reached up from Bethel to heaven, and angels of God went up and down on the ladder. Then God spoke to Jacob from heaven and reaffirmed that the covenant was truly through him and not through Esau.

Meeting at the well of Haran

When Jacob arrived at Haran, his first stop was the well—probably the same well where Abraham's servant had met Jacob's mother, Rebekah. Before long, Rachel appeared with her father's flocks to get water from the well. Jacob, dazzled by her beauty, rolled the stone away from the well and watered her sheep. Then he kissed her and told her that he was her cousin.

Rachel ran home to find her father, Laban, who welcomed his nephew, son of his sister Rebekah who had left home many years before. Jacob began immediately to work for Laban without pay. After a month, Laban talked about wages. Jacob must have surprised him. "I will work without pay for you for seven years if I can marry your daughter Rachel," he promised. What a bargain for Laban! Of course he agreed.

Switched brides

Seven years passed, and there was a big wedding. On the wedding night, when it was time for Jacob to make love to his new bride, Laban somehow switched brides. Jacob made love to Rachel's older sister Leah, thinking it was Rachel.

In the morning he was furious. Laban's excuse? We don't marry off the younger daughter first. If you agree to work another seven years without pay, you can marry Rachel this week. Jacob was trapped, so he agreed.

The years with Laban were not happy years for Jacob. Laban was a cheat, a thief, and a deceiver. He tried every way possible to cheat his nephew and son-in-law, but the Lord was with Jacob, and his flocks and herds grew faster and stronger than Laban's. This bred jealousy, not only from Laban, but from Laban's sons.

Contest of jealous sisters

During these years, Rachel and Leah were very jealous of each other. This was not surprising since the two sisters were married to the same man, and he obviously loved the bride of his choice, not the bride thrust upon him. Their jealousy spawned a contest to see who could have the most children. They even gave their servant girls to Jacob as surrogate wives to produce children for them. At last there were twelve sons and one daughter.

This was not a happy family situation, especially in the relationship with Laban and his sons. Jacob plotted with his two wives to run away from Laban, taking only what belonged to them. The wives agreed, for not only had Laban cheated his son-in-law, he had also cheated his daughters.

Laban, of course, caught up with them, and after heated conversations agreed that they should part in peace. As far as we know, Laban never saw his daughters, son-in-law, or grandchildren again. The fruit of dishonesty had rotted on his family tree. Perhaps Laban didn't realize it, but his dishonesty with his loved ones had driven them from home. He was a loser in many ways.

42

>

What
Everyone
Should
Know
about
the

Homeward bound—but to what?

Jacob was headed home now, but he was seriously worried about Esau. When Jacob had left twenty years earlier, Esau had sworn that he would kill him.

Bible

Soon word came that Esau was headed toward Jacob with four hundred men. To appease Esau's anger, Jacob sent gifts of animals ahead of him. Throughout that night, Jacob wrestled with an angel of God until dawn. Just before dawn, the angel put Jacob's hip out of joint, so that Jacob limped for the rest of his life. Then the angel blessed Jacob, renamed him Israel, and left.

The next day was the dreaded confrontation with Esau, but Esau was forgiving, so he and Jacob moved back toward home. Jacob settled for a while in Shechem, then at Bethel, then went on to Bethlehem. When they reached Bethlehem, Rachel gave birth to her second son, Benjamin, but died in childbirth. At last, Jacob returned to Mamre and his father, Isaac. His mother, Rebekah, had evidently died during his absence. Before long, Isaac also died, and Jacob and Esau buried him. Esau moved away to the east, and his descendants became the Edomites, longtime enemies of Jacob's descendants, the Israelites.

Playing favorites

Jacob had twelve sons and one daughter. His favorite son was Joseph, the older son of his beloved Rachel. He showed favoritism without hesitation or shame, which created enormous jealousy among Joseph's half brothers. The jealousy and anger increased when Jacob gave Joseph a "coat of many colors" to show his special favor. It intensified more when Joseph had dreams that suggested his brothers would one day bow before him. Foolishly, Joseph told his half brothers and his father about those dreams.

One day when Joseph was seventeen years old, Jacob sent him to check up on his brothers, who were taking care of the sheep in the fields. When they saw Joseph coming, the brothers' anger and jealousy boiled over, and they made plans to kill him. When a band of Ishmaelite traders came by, they decided to sell Joseph as a slave instead of killing him.

Remember Ishmael, the son of Hagar, whom Abraham sent into the wilderness to die? These Ishmaelites were great-grandsons, or possibly great-great-grandsons, of Abraham. They may have remembered their ancestor Ishmael and the way Joseph's great-grandfather had sent Ishmael into the wilderness to die so that Joseph's grandfather Isaac would be the sole heir. What a delight to sell this heir of Isaac's as a slave! They took Joseph to Egypt and sold him to an Egyptian official named Potiphar.

Lust for a slave

Potiphar liked Joseph and saw immediately what a fine slave he had bought. Before long, he put Joseph in charge of his entire household. Potiphar's wife also noticed Joseph and kept pressing him each day to have sex with her. When Joseph refused, Potiphar's wife was angry, and one day she lied and told her husband that Joseph had tried to rape her.

Potiphar had no choice but to put Joseph in prison, but even there the Lord prospered Joseph, and he was soon put in charge of all the prisoners.

Strange dreams

One day, two of Pharaoh's servants were put into the same prison as Joseph. One was Pharaoh's baker, the other Pharaoh's cup-bearer. Each had a dream, and Joseph told them what their dreams meant. The baker would be put to death, and the cup-bearer would be restored to Pharaoh's service. Everything happened the way Joseph said it would.

Two years went by, and the cup-bearer forgot about Joseph. Then one night Pharaoh had two strange dreams. In one dream, seven fat cows came up from the Nile River, followed by seven lean cows that ate the seven fat cows. In the other dream, seven plump healthy heads of grain were eaten up by seven withered heads of grain.

Pharaoh was troubled by these dreams. They were very vivid, and he was sure they meant something significant. His wise men and magicians could not help him, as they did not understand the dreams. Then the cup-bearer remembered Joseph, and before long, Joseph stood before Pharaoh and his highest officials.

Joseph had a choice. He could brag about his ability to interpret dreams and make himself look important, or he could give God the credit. He gave God the credit. It was a dangerous thing to do, for Pharaoh was considered a god, and Joseph could be put to death for such heresy. But Pharaoh was anxious to know the meaning of the dreams and did not put Joseph to death.

Joseph told Pharaoh the meaning of the two dreams, for both dreams had the same meaning. During the next seven years Egypt would have plentiful grain. These years of superabundance would then be followed by seven years of intense famine.

Before Pharaoh could think about what to do, Joseph volunteered a plan. Pharaoh should appoint a wise man to manage Egypt's grain program and store vast amounts of grain during the years of plenty. This would put Egypt in a position of leadership during the years of famine.

>

What
Everyone
Should
Know
about
the

Bible

From a prison to a palace—the same day

Pharaoh and his officials were so impressed with Joseph that they unanimously gave him the management of the grain program. Pharaoh went one step further and made Joseph ruler of all of Egypt, subject only to Pharaoh.

During the next seven years, Joseph stored vast quantities of grain. People must have wondered why this young governor was storing so much grain. Why would anyone want storehouses filled with grain when there was so much? When the famine came, Egypt had plenty, though the neighboring nations were starving.

A dreaded trip to Egypt—with a happy ending

Back home, Jacob and his family were going hungry, so Jacob sent his sons to Egypt to buy grain. They may have feared seeing Joseph as a slave in some Egyptian field, but they told themselves that he must be dead by this time.

To buy the grain, Joseph's brothers had to appear before the ruler of Egypt. They did not imagine that this was their brother Joseph, of course. Joseph put the brothers through several tests to be sure that they had repented of their foul deed of selling him. When he was convinced that they had repented, he told them who he was. Imagine their surprise and terror when they learned that this powerful ruler of all Egypt was none other than their kid brother, Joseph, whom they had sold as a slave.

Joseph sent wagons home with his brothers and moved his entire family to Egypt. There the family had plenty of food and pasture for their flocks. Joseph had not only saved Egypt but had saved his family as well.

The story of the patriarchs and of the book of Genesis ends with the death and burial of Joseph.

Questions You May Be Asking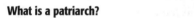

What is a patriarch?

In the Bible, a patriarch is the head or founder of a tribe, the one at the top because he is the oldest of the clan and the father of them all. Even today, we speak of a father figure in a family as the patriarch.

The Bible record focuses mostly on three patriarchs—Abraham, his son Isaac, and Isaac's son Jacob, whom God renamed Israel. As the Bible story came to a focus many years before on the one man Noah, and all descendants of the world thereafter would come from him, so now it refocused on Abraham. God's covenant people would follow after one man and his descendants. Abraham was father of all covenant people who accepted God's covenant and lived by it.

Another patriarch who lived during this time was named Job. He probably lived in northern Mesopotamia. He was the head of his family, tribe, or clan, but he was not a patriarch in the lineage of God's covenant people.

Why is Job's story inserted here?

Most Bible scholars believe that Job lived during the time of the patriarchs. Bible books are not all arranged chronologically. If they were, Job would interrupt the Genesis story and probably appear about the time of Abraham's story.

Did Job and Abraham ever meet?
It could be. Job probably lived in northern Mesopotamia, perhaps not far from Haran, where Abraham (Abram at that time) and his family settled. As prosperous shepherds, they might have met and talked about the God they both loved. The Bible is silent about that, so we just don't know. There is no Bible evidence to support the idea, but isn't it fun to think of Abraham and Job talking about the God who meant so much to both of them?

What does Job have to do with me today? If Job isn't part of the covenant story, why put his story in the Bible?
Job's story is about human suffering and misery, and devotion to God through it all. When suffering comes, as it will come, what will we do with it? How will we handle it? Job is a model for us. No matter what came his way, Job remained faithful to the Lord. He refused to turn away from God during tough times.

Why was Abraham such an important person?
Abraham was a Semite, a descendant of Noah's son Shem. He and his family lived in the Sumerian city of Ur. At that time, the region's political power was shifting, so Abraham lived under three undesirable forces: Sumerian culture, unstable political power, and the local worship of the pagan moon god, Nanna, which threatened Semitic spirituality. These three forces were troubling. He and his family were apparently the only godly people in this prosperous pagan city.

Abraham and his family finally left at the direct command of the Lord. Perhaps the pressures of the heathen religion and culture, and the uncertain political powers, did not offer a fertile ground for their godly lives. They migrated to the north and settled in northern Mesopotamia in a town called Haran. There Abraham's father, Terah, died and Abraham became the heir and the head of the tribe.

God had other plans and called Abraham to leave Haran with his immediate family and travel southwest to Canaan, where the Lord entered into a covenant with Abraham. He would be Abraham's God and Abraham would be his follower. The spiritual heritage of all future generations would flow through Abraham and his descendants.

Why did Sarah tell her husband to get another woman pregnant?
God promised a son to Abraham and Sarah, but they were old, too old to have a baby. God's covenant would flow through this son, so the son would perpetuate not only their family but God's covenant.

Ten years passed, and there was still no baby. At last Sarah decided

46

\>

What
Everyone
Should
Know
about
the

Bible

to solve the problem her way. She gave her Egyptian servant, Hagar, to Abraham to be a surrogate mother. The son of Abraham and Hagar would legally be Sarah's son.

When Abraham was eighty-six, Hagar had a son, and Abraham named him Ishmael. This birth brought enormous tension between Hagar and the barren Sarah. When Abraham was ninety-nine and Sarah was eighty-nine, God renewed his covenant to give Abraham and Sarah a son. He changed their names at this point from Abram and Sarai to Abraham and Sarah. The next year, Abraham and Sarah had a baby boy and named him Isaac.

How did the quarrel between Sarah and Hagar help to send Joseph to Egypt seventy years later?

Abraham and Sarah had their promised son at last. Abraham was one hundred and Sarah was ninety. Then tensions escalated between Sarah and her Egyptian servant, Hagar, so much so that she demanded that Abraham send them away from the tribe. Grieved, Abraham sent his seventeen-year-old son, and his mother, Hagar, into the desert, possibly to die. They would forever be separated from the tribe.

Flash forward almost seventy years. We see ten of Abraham's great-grandsons, sons of Jacob, selling their brother Joseph to be a slave. Who bought this young man and took him to Egypt to die as a slave? A band of Ishmaelite traders—probably great-grandsons, or possibly great-great-grandsons, of Joseph's great-grandfather Abraham (Genesis 37:25).

These Ishmaelite traders surely knew the story of how their great-grandfather Ishmael was sent into the wilderness to die so that Joseph's grandfather Isaac could rule the tribe. It is very possible that they knew this was Isaac's heir. What sweet revenge to sell him as a slave in Egypt!

It is generally accepted that many modern Arabs are descended from Abraham through Ishmael, and most modern Israelites or Jewish people are descended from Abraham through Isaac. The descendants of Ishmael and Isaac are still engaged in bitter conflict today.

Why did Abraham try to kill his son Isaac?

For more than twenty-five years, Abraham and Sarah had waited for God to give them the baby he had promised. Through this baby, God's covenant and Abraham's tribe would be perpetuated. At last the baby came, when Abraham was one hundred and Sarah was ninety, and they named him Isaac. After Sarah nagged Abraham, probably with great passion, Abraham sent his older son, Ishmael, and Ishmael's mother, Hagar, into the wilderness, perhaps to die, to give this favored son, Isaac, leadership of the tribe and make him heir to God's covenant.

One day God spoke to Abraham and commanded him to offer his

beloved son as a burnt offering on a lonely mountain called Moriah. Abraham must have wept bitter tears. How could God ask him to sacrifice his only covenant son? But Abraham obeyed, and at the very last moment, God stopped Abraham from killing young Isaac for the sacrifice. It was a powerful test. Would Abraham, father of the Old Testament covenant, obey God at all cost? Would he sacrifice his beloved son, as God would later sacrifice his Son on the cross?

What is significant about the mountain where Abraham almost sacrificed Isaac?
This was Mount Moriah, where Solomon later built his Temple. Today, the Dome of the Rock dominates the top of this mountain. Only a few hundred feet northwest is Golgotha, the hill where God's Son was sacrificed. The custodian of the Old Testament covenant almost sacrificed his son a short distance from the place where God the Father sacrificed his Son, as the basis of the New Testament covenant.

Why did Isaac marry his cousin? Weren't there other acceptable girls around?
Isaac grew to manhood, and before long, it was time for him to get married. Abraham was concerned that his son not marry a pagan neighbor girl. There were many other girls nearby, but they were all from pagan tribes. As surely as Isaac would be the father of covenant people ever after, his wife would be the mother of covenant people. She simply could not be a pagan.

Abraham sent his servant to Abraham's relatives in Haran to find a bride for Isaac. There the servant met Rebekah, a daughter of Abraham's nephew Bethuel. Today not many people would marry their father's nephew's daughter, but it was vitally important for the custodian of God's covenant to have a godly wife, for his descendants would also be her descendants. A godly father and an ungodly mother would not make good ancestors for covenant people.

How long did it take for Isaac and Rebekah to have children?
Isaac married Rebekah when he was forty (Genesis 25:20). For twenty years, he and Rebekah pleaded with God to give them a child. Finally, when Isaac was sixty, he and Rebekah had twin sons, Jacob and Esau. Esau was born moments before Jacob, so he was heir to the covenant blessing—not only his father's wealth, but also the line through which God would carry his covenant to future generations.

Esau was frivolous with his birthright and sold it to Jacob one day for a bowl of lentil stew. Esau also married two Canaanite wives, ungodly women who would have marred his covenant lineage. Old Isaac should have known better, but in his old age, he still favored Esau, the son who cooked his favorite meat for him.

When Isaac was old and blind, Jacob tricked his father into giving

What
Everyone
Should
Know
about
the

Bible

him the blessing, which included his father's inheritance, leadership of the tribe, and his right to be the one through whom God's covenant would pass.

What was that mysterious ladder to heaven that Jacob saw?

When Esau learned that Jacob had tricked their father, he was furious and threatened to kill Jacob. Fearing for his life, Jacob ran away from home and headed toward Haran to hide out with his distant relatives.

Along the way, Jacob had a powerful dream. A ladder stretched from his campsite at Bethel all the way to heaven. Angels went up and down on this ladder. God spoke to Jacob and reaffirmed him as the rightful owner of the covenant.

Why did Jacob marry four women when he wanted only one?

At Haran, Jacob met Rachel, probably at the same well where Abraham's servant had met Jacob's mother, Rebekah, years before. He fell in love with his first cousin and bargained with her father, Jacob's uncle Laban, to marry her. He would work without pay for seven years for this right. But at the end of the seven years, Laban switched brides, and on his wedding night, Jacob unwittingly made love to Rachel's older sister, Leah. Morning revealed the switch, but it was too late. Jacob had consummated his marriage with Leah, not Rachel.

Jacob was furious with Laban. Why had he switched girls? Laban's excuse was that in his culture, the older sister must marry first, so if Jacob wanted the younger sister, Rachel, he must first marry her older sister, Leah. The father forced his unwanted daughter onto Jacob, and suddenly he had two wives.

These two jealous, competitive sisters entered into a contest to see who could have the most children with Jacob. When their own fertility slowed down, they gave their servant girls, Bilhah and Zilpah, to Jacob as surrogate wives, to bear children for them. Altogether Jacob had two wives, two surrogate wives, twelve sons, and one daughter, Dinah. You can only imagine the family tension with such complex relationships and competitive spirits.

How did the twelve sons of Jacob become heads of the twelve tribes of Israel?

In time, Jacob no longer wanted to work for his dishonest Uncle Laban, so he secretly headed home with his enormous family and his wealth in cattle. He was a rich man now, but he had to deal with his twin brother, Esau, who had sworn years previously that he would kill Jacob.

The night before his dramatic meeting with Esau, Jacob wrestled with God and prevailed, but God caused him to limp from that time on. He also gave Jacob a new name, Israel. Thus, Jacob's sons would become the heads of the twelve tribes of Israel. This is jumping ahead of the story a little, but there was no tribe of Joseph, only the two half tribes of Ephraim and Manasseh, Joseph's two sons by his Egyptian wife Asenath.

Did Jacob and Esau ever become reconciled? Did it last?

They did, but it was more like an agreement not to bother one another than it was brotherly love. Esau graciously forgave Jacob and went his way. Jacob went back home and managed his wealth at the old home place at Mamre, modern Hebron, with a brief stop at Shechem and Bethel. After their father died, Esau moved to Edom, in the city we know today as Petra, for there was not enough pasture for his flocks and Jacob's flocks around Hebron.

In the years ahead, the Israelite sons of Jacob and the Edomite sons of Esau were often in conflict with each other, still fighting it out. Hundreds of years later, when the Israelites escaped from Egypt and headed toward the Promised Land, they asked permission to travel peacefully through Edom, but the Edomites refused and met them with an army. Rather than fight their distant relatives, the Israelites took a longer route (Numbers 20:14-21).

Many years after this incident, King Saul fought the Edomites and was victorious (1 Samuel 14:47). Still later, King David killed almost every male in Edom (1 Kings 11:15), but a few leaders escaped and became Israel's bitter enemies for many years, especially against David's son Solomon (1 Kings 11:25).

Why did Joseph's half brothers hate him so much? Why did they want to kill him?

The story of Joseph opens with Jacob playing favorites with this son. That's because Joseph was the older son of his beloved Rachel, who died giving birth to Benjamin. Joseph had also been born in Jacob's older age, which added to Jacob's favoritism.

All of Joseph's ten half brothers were sons of Rachel's sister, Leah, and the servant girls Bilhah and Zilpah. The ten were all sons of Jacob, but with three different mothers, which is why they were Joseph's half brothers. Many of them were also half brothers to each other. Joseph had one younger full brother, son of Jacob and Rachel, whose name was Benjamin.

It was all too obvious to the half brothers that Jacob favored the beloved son of the wife he loved the most, the wife for whom he had worked for fourteen years. The last straw for the half brothers was the richly ornamented robe, or cloak of many colors, that Jacob gave to Joseph. Some have said this robe was a symbol of Jacob's favoritism, even suggesting that Joseph could be his heir, leaping over all ten of his half brothers. This only aggravated the hatred his half brothers had for him.

To add more fuel to the flames of hatred, Joseph had some dreams

50

>

What
Everyone
Should
Know
about
the

Bible

and told them to his half brothers. In one dream, the brothers' sheaves of wheat bowed down to his sheaf. In another dream, the sun, moon, and eleven stars bowed before Joseph. The message was obvious—not only the brothers but his father and his father's wives would bow someday to Joseph. It was too much. The half brothers' hatred was rapidly coming to a boiling point.

The opportunity for revenge came when Jacob sent Joseph to check on his half brothers, who were tending sheep near Dothan. They captured him and sold him to Ishmaelite traders, who took Joseph to Egypt and sold him as a slave. To all involved, this was Joseph's death warrant, for he would probably die in slavery, working under the blazing Egyptian sun. These Ishmaelite traders might have been grandsons or great-grandsons of Ishmael, Abraham's son who was sent to the wilderness to die so that Joseph's grandfather Isaac could be Abraham's heir. Revenge was sweet as they sold Joseph in Egypt. He would surely die soon doing the brutal work of an Egyptian slave.

How did God take special care of Joseph in Egypt?

Joseph didn't die. An Egyptian high official named Potiphar, a member of Pharaoh's staff, bought this handsome young slave. Potiphar was kind to Joseph and Joseph served him so well that Potiphar put him in charge of his entire household.

Potiphar's wife also noticed Joseph and lusted after this handsome, talented young man. Perhaps her husband was much older and undesirable. She made every effort to seduce Joseph, and when that failed, she lied about him to Potiphar, telling him that Joseph had tried to rape her. For that, Joseph was thrown into prison.

Even in prison Joseph served well, and the head of the prison soon put him in charge of the other prisoners and the prison work.

One day, two of Pharaoh's staff members were thrown into this same prison. One was the king's baker, the other the king's cup-bearer, who not only served the king's wine to him but tasted it to be sure it wasn't poisoned. If he didn't die, Pharaoh knew it wasn't poisoned and that it was safe to drink.

These two officials each had a dream one night. Joseph interpreted their dreams, and when they were released from prison, things happened the way Joseph had said. The baker was impaled on a pole, and the cup-bearer was restored to Pharaoh's service. For two years, the cup-bearer forgot about Joseph, so Joseph continued to suffer in the harsh Egyptian prison.

How could a slave-prisoner become ruler of all the land of Egypt in one day?

It was a God thing. No one could do that on his own. This is how it happened. One night, Pharaoh had two dreams. In one dream, seven fat, healthy cows came from the Nile River, but soon seven ugly and gaunt cows ate the seven healthy cows.

In the other dream, seven healthy, plump heads of grain grew on one stalk. Soon seven shriveled and withered heads of grain swallowed the seven plump heads.

Pharaoh was deeply disturbed by these dreams and asked his magicians and wise men for their meaning, but no one could help him. Then the cup-bearer remembered that Joseph had told him the meaning of his dream.

Pharaoh called for Joseph and asked for the meaning of the dreams. Joseph was very courageous in telling Pharaoh that he personally could not do it but that his God would do it through him. For that, Joseph could have been instantly put to death. But Pharaoh wanted answers, so Joseph lived, and God told Joseph about the coming seven years of plenty and the seven years of famine.

Pharaoh and his officials recognized something very special in Joseph and his God, so Pharaoh put him in charge of the whole land, mostly to store grain during the years of plenty so that they would have food during the years of famine.

Why would an Egyptian king give so much power to an Israelite slave, a foreigner?

The Pharaoh in power at this time saw clearly that Egypt could rise or fall within the next fourteen years if Joseph's interpretations were correct. Skilled management of grain storage during the next seven years, and a skilled distribution of that grain during the subsequent seven years, would put Egypt in a position of world leadership when the coming famine swept over that part of the world and reduced its neighbors to poverty.

Without that, Egypt could fall with its neighbors, a poor victim of seven straight years of famine. Joseph stood before Pharaoh at a decisive moment for the future of Egypt, perhaps for generations to come. Pharaoh and his officials were unanimously convinced that Joseph was the man for the job of managing the grain storage program. God had revealed this mystery to Joseph alone. Wasn't it likely that this same God would reveal many other things to Joseph along the way? All Egypt was in his hands.

What
Everyone
Should
Know
about
the

How did Joseph's siblings connect with their long-lost brother?

The half brothers thought that Joseph must be dead by now. He couldn't possibly live this long as an Egyptian slave. When famine swept over their land, they came to Egypt to buy grain, never expecting to see Joseph alive.

Unknown to them, when they talked with Egypt's ruler, they were talking with their long-lost brother. Joseph put them to some tests to be sure they had repented of their evil deed of selling him as a slave. At last he was sure they had repented, so he revealed himself as their brother and moved the entire family to Egypt so he could take care of them as long as he lived.

Genesis ends with the family of Joseph living comfortably in Egypt and with the death of Joseph.

Great Events of This Time

1. **Abraham journeys to Haran** (Genesis 11:27-32).
2. **Abraham journeys to Canaan** (Genesis 12:1-9).
3. **Abraham and Sarah visit Egypt** (Genesis 12:10-20).
4. **Abraham and Lot part** (Genesis 13).
5. **Lot is captured and rescued** (Genesis 14).
6. **God makes a covenant with Abraham** (Genesis 15).
7. **Ishmael is born and Sarah is jealous** (Genesis 16).
8. **God renews his covenant with Abraham and Isaac is promised** (Genesis 17).
9. **Abraham is visited by strangers** (Genesis 18:1-15).
10. **Abraham bargains for Sodom** (Genesis 18:16-33).
11. **Sodom is destroyed** (Genesis 19:1-29).
12. **Lot is deceived by his daughters** (Genesis 19:30-38).
13. **Abraham deceives Abimelech** (Genesis 20).
14. **Isaac is born** (Genesis 21:1-7).
15. **Hagar is sent away into the wilderness** (Genesis 21:8-21).
16. **Abraham and Abimelech make an agreement** (Genesis 21:22-34).
17. **Abraham offers Isaac** (Genesis 22:1-19).
18. **Sarah dies and is buried in the cave of Machpelah** (Genesis 23).
19. **Isaac gets a bride** (Genesis 24).
20. **Abraham remarries, then dies and is buried** (Genesis 25:1-11).
21. **Esau and Jacob are born** (Genesis 25:19-26).
22. **Esau sells his birthright** (Genesis 25:27-34).
23. **Isaac deceives Abimelech at Gerar** (Genesis 26:1-11).
24. **Isaac refuses to fight for some wells** (Genesis 26:12-33).
25. **Jacob tricks Isaac and gets his father's blessing** (Genesis 27:1–28:9).
26. **Jacob dreams of a ladder to heaven** (Genesis 28:10-22).
27. **Jacob meets Rachel** (Genesis 29:1-14).
28. **Jacob marries Leah and Rachel** (Genesis 29:14-30).
29. **Jacob has children** (Genesis 29:31–30:24).
30. **Jacob works for Laban** (Genesis 30:25-43).
31. **Jacob and his family leave Laban** (Genesis 31).

32. Jacob wrestles with an angel (Genesis 32:22-32).
33. Jacob meets Esau, who forgives him (Genesis 33).
34. Dinah is dishonored and there is a massacre at Shechem (Genesis 34).
35. Jacob and his people give up idols and renew the covenant with God at Bethel (Genesis 35:1-15).
36. Benjamin is born and Rachel dies in childbirth (Genesis 35:16-20).
37. Isaac dies and Esau moves away from Jacob (Genesis 35:27–36:8).
38. Joseph has dreams (Genesis 37:1-11).
39. Joseph is sold into slavery (Genesis 37:12-36).
40. Tamar gets justice from Judah (Genesis 38).
41. Joseph works for Potiphar (Genesis 39).
42. Pharaoh's cup-bearer and baker have dreams (Genesis 40).
43. Joseph is made ruler of Egypt (Genesis 41:1-45).
44. Joseph prepares for the great famine and has sons (Genesis 41:46-57).
45. Joseph's brothers come to buy grain (Genesis 42–44).
46. Joseph reveals himself to his brothers (Genesis 45:1-15).
47. Jacob's family moves to Egypt (Genesis 45:16–47:12).
48. Joseph manages Egypt's grain during the famine (Genesis 47:13-26).
49. Joseph and his sons are blessed (Genesis 47:27–48:22).
50. Jacob blesses his other sons (Genesis 49:1-28).
51. Jacob dies (Genesis 49:29–50:14).
52. Joseph treats his brothers kindly (Genesis 50:15-21).
53. Joseph dies (Genesis 50:22-26).

Significant Dates of This Time

Circa 2166 B.C., Abraham is born.
Circa 2091 B.C., Abraham enters Canaan.
Circa 2066 B.C., Isaac is born.
Circa 2006 B.C., Jacob and Esau are born.
Circa 1929 B.C., Jacob flees to Haran.
Circa 1915 B.C., Joseph is born.
Circa 1898 B.C., Joseph is sold into slavery.
Circa 1885 B.C., Joseph rules Egypt.
Circa 1805 B.C., Joseph dies.

What
Everyone
Should
Know
about
the

Bible

Heroes and Villains: The Stars in Scene 5

There are many well-known Bible heroes and villains during the time of the patriarchs. The twelve sons of Jacob are prominent characters throughout the Old Testament, for the tribes of Israel are named for them and for Joseph's two sons, Ephraim and Manasseh. Hagar, Sarah's Egyptian maid, was a prominent character, for she was the mother of Abraham's first son, Ishmael, from whom many modern Arabs have descended. There was Pharaoh, and King Abimelech, each of whom wanted Sarah as his wife. She must have been quite a beauty! Of course Potiphar and his wife were significant in unwittingly setting Joseph on course to become ruler. Pharaoh's baker and cup-bearer are well known in every roster of Bible stories. We could have quite a list, but space simply does not permit. These are some of the more prominent characters during the time of the patriarchs.

ABRAHAM

Abram, as he was named by his parents, was born and raised in Ur, a prosperous city in southern Mesopotamia. After he married his half sister Sarai, Abram migrated with his family at the age of seventy to Haran, in northern Mesopotamia. There he lived until the age of seventy-five, when the Lord directed him to migrate to the land of Canaan. Abram obeyed, and the Lord gave him the new name Abraham and his wife the new name Sarah.

In a covenant made between the Lord and Abraham, the Lord promised him that his descendants would one day inherit the land, although at that time Abraham and Sarah were too old to have children. The miracle son, Isaac, was born when Abraham was one hundred years old and Sarah was ninety. Abraham is remembered as a great man of faith, a friend of God, and a man through whom God's covenant with his people came in Old Testament times.

Bible events in Abraham's life
1. He migrates to Haran.
2. He migrates from Haran to Canaan.
3. God promises Canaan to his descendants.
4. He moves to Egypt and lies to Pharaoh about Sarah. Pharaoh expels them from Egypt.
5. He gives Lot a choice of land. Lot chooses the land near Sodom. He moves to Mamre.
6. He rescues Lot from Kedorlaomer and his allies.
7. God promises him a son.
8. Sarah gives Hagar to him as a surrogate wife so they could have a son.
9. God makes a covenant with him.
10. He bargains with God for Sodom.
11. He lies to Abimelech about Sarah.
12. Isaac is born to him and Sarah.

13. He sends Hagar and Ishmael into the wilderness.
14. He makes a covenant with Abimelech.
15. He offers Isaac on Mount Moriah.
16. He buries Sarah at Hebron.
17. He sends his servant to Haran to find a bride for Isaac.
18. He marries Keturah and has six more children.
19. He dies and is buried at Hebron.

ESAU

When Isaac's wife, Rebekah, gave birth to twin sons, the older was named Esau. He was red and hairy, even from birth. Esau was his father's favorite because he became a rugged hunter and brought home wild game that he prepared for his father. His twin brother, Jacob, was his mother's favorite. He was chosen before birth to receive the family birthright, and he did this by deceiving his father, Isaac. Esau hated his brother for this deceit, but when they met twenty years later, he forgave Jacob and returned to the land of his birth. After Isaac died, Esau moved to Edom.

Bible events in Esau's life
1. He is born to Isaac and Rebekah.
2. He sells his birthright for a bowl of lentil stew.
3. He marries ungodly wives.
4. He is deprived of his father's blessing.
5. He plans to kill Jacob.
6. He meets Jacob and is reconciled to him.
7. He says good-bye to Jacob and moves to Edom.

ISAAC

For many years, Abraham and Sarah were childless, which was a disgrace for people of that time. It was doubly difficult for them since God had promised that they would have numerous descendants, and it seemed unlikely that this would happen, since they were very old. Isaac was born when Abraham was one hundred and Sarah was ninety, so it was a miraculous birth.

When Isaac was still a lad, God commanded Abraham to sacrifice him on Mount Moriah, which was a stunning blow to the aging patriarch. On Mount Moriah, however, God provided a ram and told Abraham that he had passed a test of faith. At the age of forty, Isaac married Rebekah, a relative whom Abraham's servant brought from Mesopotamia. When Isaac was sixty, he and Rebekah had twin sons, Esau and Jacob. When Isaac was very old, Jacob tricked his father into giving the birthright to him, the younger of his twin sons.

What
Everyone
Should
Know
about
the
Bible

Bible events in Isaac's life
1. He is born to Abraham and Sarah.
2. He is willing to be offered as a sacrifice to God.
3. Abraham's servant goes to find a bride for him.
4. He marries Rebekah.
5. His twin sons, Jacob and Esau, are born.
6. He lies to Abimelech about Rebekah.
7. He refuses to fight for his wells.
8. The Lord appears to him.
9. He makes a peace covenant with Abimelech.
10. He is deceived by Jacob.
11. He blesses Jacob.
12. He refuses to bless Esau.
13. He sends Jacob to Paddan-aram to find a bride.
14. He dies at Hebron at age 180.

JACOB

For twenty years after Isaac and Rebekah married they had no children. This was a disgrace for a woman in that culture. Isaac prayed for his wife, and she had twins, whom they named Jacob and Esau. Although Esau was the older son by a few moments, God had told Rebekah before they were born that the older would serve the younger. Esau was a hunter and became his father's favorite. Jacob stayed home and became his mother's favorite.

When Isaac grew old, Jacob tricked him into giving his blessing to Jacob instead of to Esau. Esau was furious, so Jacob went to Mesopotamia to live with his uncle Laban, where he met his future wives, Leah and Rachel, Laban's daughters. In a contest to have children, Leah and Rachel gave their maids to Jacob as substitute wives.

Among the four wives, Jacob had twelve sons and one daughter. After twenty years in Mesopotamia, Jacob returned with his family to be reconciled with his brother Esau and to settle once more in his native Canaan. He later moved again when his son Joseph, whom he thought was dead, was found to be the ruler of Egypt. With several years of famine ahead, Joseph moved Jacob and his entire family to Egypt so he could take care of them.

Jacob died in Egypt, and his descendants remained there. In later years, they became slaves under a pharaoh who did not care about Joseph. Jacob's descendants became the people of Israel, bearing the name God gave Jacob on his return from the land of Mesopotamia.

Bible events in Jacob's life
1. He is born to Isaac and Rebekah.
2. He buys Esau's birthright with a bowl of stew.

3. He deceives Isaac and receives the blessing.

4. Isaac sends him to Paddan-aram.

5. He dreams of angels on a ladder to heaven, and God speaks to him.

6. God makes a covenant with him, and he makes a promise to God.

7. He meets Rachel at the well at Haran.

8. He works seven years to marry Rachel.

9. Laban deceives him by giving him Leah instead of Rachel on his wedding night.

10. He marries Rachel a week later but promises to work another seven years for Laban.

11. Reuben, Simeon, Levi, and Judah are born to him and Leah.

12. Dan and Naphtali are born to Jacob and Bilhah, Rachel's maid.

13. Gad and Asher are born to him and Zilpah, Leah's maid.

14. Issachar, Zebulun, and Dinah are born to him and Leah.

15. Joseph is born to him and Rachel.

16. He schemes to increase and strengthen his flocks and becomes wealthy.

17. He flees with his family from Laban, who pursues him.

18. Laban searches his camp for his household gods.

19. He makes a covenant with Laban and sets up a heap of stones as a memorial.

20. Angels meet him on his way back to Canaan.

21. He sends a message to Esau to come and meet him.

22. He wrestles with an angel, who dislocates his hip.

23. God changes his name to Israel.

24. He meets Esau and is reconciled with him.

25. He settles in Shechem and builds an altar there.

26. He moves to Bethel, sets up an altar, and buries idols under an oak tree there.

27. God appears to him and confirms the covenant with him at Bethel.

28. Benjamin is born to him and Rachel near Bethlehem.

29. Rachel dies, and he buries her near Bethlehem.

30. He arrives at Hebron, Isaac dies, and he and Esau bury him.

31. He gives Joseph a coat of many colors.

32. He sends Joseph to see how his brothers are doing.

33. He mourns for Joseph when his other sons show him Joseph's blood-spattered cloak.

34. He sends his sons to Egypt to buy food.

35. He reluctantly allows Benjamin to go with his brothers and sends gifts for the ruler of Egypt.

36. He receives the good news that Joseph is alive and is ruler of Egypt.

58

>

What
Everyone
Should
Know
about
the

Bible

37. He leaves Canaan with his family and goes to Egypt.
38. Joseph comes to meet him in Goshen, where he settles.
39. Joseph presents him and his sons to Pharaoh.
40. He blesses Joseph, Ephraim, and Manasseh.
41. Jacob blesses his other sons.
42. He dies and is taken back to Canaan to be buried in the cave of Machpelah at Hebron.

JOB

In the days of the patriarchs, a wealthy man named Job suddenly had his wealth removed, his health destroyed, and his family taken from him. Satan had asked God for permission to do these things to prove whether Job was faithful to the Lord only because of his prosperity. Job proved himself faithful to the Lord, not because of his prosperity, but because he loved God and trusted him.

Bible events in Job's life
1. He offers sacrifices for his children.
2. Satan afflicts him.
3. His friends visit him, and he gives honor to God.
4. He is restored and blessed by God.

JOSEPH, SON OF JACOB

Jacob and Rachel had only two sons, Benjamin and Joseph. Jacob loved Joseph more than any of the other eleven sons and showed that favoritism by giving him a beautiful, colorful cloak. The other brothers resented this, especially when Joseph told them about his dreams, which placed him above them. His older half brothers sold Joseph into slavery, and he was taken to Egypt.

Joseph remained faithful to God even when he was unjustly imprisoned in Egypt. In God's time, he interpreted a dream for Pharaoh, who promptly made him ruler of Egypt. Joseph sold grain to his brothers, who at first did not recognize him. At last, Joseph revealed himself to them and moved his entire family to Egypt so he could take care of them during the famine. This family grew during the years of silence between Genesis and Exodus. With the passing of many pharaohs, there arose one who did not remember or care about Joseph and made all of Jacob's descendants his slaves.

Bible events in Joseph's life
1. He is born to Jacob and Rachel.
2. Jacob gives him a beautiful coat of many colors.
3. He has many dreams and tells them to his brothers.

4. He goes to see his brothers at Dothan, and they sell him to traders for twenty pieces of silver.
5. He is taken to Egypt and sold to Potiphar, where he becomes a steward of Potiphar's entire household.
6. Potiphar's wife lusts for him, then falsely accuses him so that he is put into prison.
7. In prison, he interprets the dreams of the king's baker and cup-bearer.
8. The cup-bearer remembers him, and he is called to interpret Pharaoh's dreams.
9. Pharaoh makes him ruler of all Egypt and gives him Asenath for his wife.
10. Ephraim and Manasseh are born to him and Asenath.
11. He prepares for famine in Egypt.
12. His brothers come to Egypt to buy food and bow before him. He accuses them of being spies.
13. His brothers return to buy grain and find his cup in Benjamin's sack.
14. He reveals himself to his brothers.
15. He brings Jacob and his family to Egypt.
16. He receives Jacob's blessing.
17. When Jacob dies, Joseph takes Jacob's body back to Canaan and buries it in the cave of Machpelah at Hebron.
18. He forgives his brothers.
19. He dies at the age of 110.

LABAN

When Abraham sent his servant to Haran to find a bride for his son Isaac, the servant spoke with Laban. He was Abraham's nephew, the son of Abraham's brother Nahor. Laban was also the brother of Rebekah, who became Isaac's bride. Later, Isaac and Rebekah sent their son Jacob to Haran to find his bride, and Jacob served Laban for twenty years as a herdsman. Jacob married Laban's two daughters, Leah and Rachel.

Bible events in Laban's life

1. He invites Abraham's servant to his home in Haran.
2. He welcomes Jacob and hires him to work for him, agreeing to give him Rachel as his wife if he worked without pay for seven years.
3. He deceives Jacob by giving him Leah on his wedding night instead of Rachel.
4. He lets Jacob marry Rachel but makes him work another seven years for her.

60

\>

What
Everyone
Should
Know
about
the

Bible

5. He agrees with Jacob on a plan for dividing the flocks. Laban took all the solid-colored sheep, and Jacob took the speckled sheep.
6. He pursues Jacob and his family when they flee from him.
7. He accuses Jacob of stealing his household gods and searches Jacob's camp for them.
8. He makes a covenant with Jacob, says good-bye, and returns to his home.

LEAH

Jacob worked seven years for the right to marry Rachel, Laban's daughter whom he loved, but on Jacob's wedding night, Laban substituted his older daughter, Leah, without Jacob's knowing it. Jacob was angry about this but kept Leah as his wife. They had Reuben, Simeon, Levi, Judah, Issachar, and Zebulun, as well as a daughter, Dinah. Leah and her sister, Rachel, competed for Jacob's attention, and especially for the opportunity to have his children. Some time after Jacob and his family returned to Canaan but before he went to live in Egypt, Leah died and was buried in the cave of Machpelah at Hebron.

Bible events in Leah's life
1. Laban gives her to Jacob in marriage in place of Rachel.
2. Reuben, Simeon, Levi, and Judah are born to her and Jacob.
3. She gives her maid, Zilpah, to Jacob to bear children for her.
4. Reuben brings some mandrakes to her, which were superstitiously believed to stimulate fertility. We don't know today exactly what these "love apples" actually were, but in ancient times, they did have a reputation associated with sex—both as an aphrodisiac and as a fertility potion.
5. Issachar, Zebulun, and Dinah are born to her and Jacob.
6. She flees from Laban with Jacob and his family.

LOT

Before Abraham and his family left Ur for Haran, his brother Haran died, leaving his son Lot in Abraham's care. Lot accompanied Abraham into Canaan and Egypt, and when they returned to Canaan, their herdsmen argued over land for their flocks. When Abraham offered Lot his choice of the land, Lot chose the rich Jordan Valley and moved to Sodom. The combined forces of some kings from the north captured Lot, but Abraham rescued him. Later, when the Lord planned to destroy Sodom, Abraham pleaded with him to spare Lot. Lot escaped from Sodom, but when his wife looked longingly back, she turned into a pillar of salt. Lot moved to a cave, and he unwittingly fathered two sons by his two daughters. The Ammonites and Moabites descended from these two sons.

Bible events in Lot's life

1. He migrates with Abraham from Ur to Haran.
2. He moves with Abraham from Haran to Canaan.
3. He chooses the choice Jordan Valley for himself.
4. He separates from Abraham and settles near Sodom.
5. He is captured by Kedorlaomer; Abraham rescues him.
6. He entertains two angels.
7. He refuses to let the men of Sodom molest his guests.
8. Angels lead him and his family out of Sodom.
9. His wife looks back at Sodom and is turned into a pillar of salt.
10. His daughters deceive him and have sons by him.

RACHEL

After Jacob deceived his brother, Esau, and took the birthright from him, his mother, Rebekah, persuaded Isaac to send Jacob to Haran to find a wife. Jacob fell in love with his cousin Rachel, daughter of Laban, his mother's brother. For seven years, he worked without pay so that he might marry her, but on the wedding night, Laban substituted Rachel's older sister, Leah. Jacob consummated the marriage, thinking it was Rachel. Jacob had to agree to work another seven years in order to marry Rachel (though he was allowed to marry her right away), and the sisters then competed to see who could produce the most sons. Rachel, Jacob's beloved, had only two, Joseph and Benjamin, and died in childbirth with Benjamin. Rachel was buried outside Bethlehem.

Bible events in Rachel's life

1. She meets Jacob at a well in Paddan-aram, near Haran.
2. She marries Jacob after he works seven years for her and promises to work another seven years.
3. She asks Leah for some of Reuben's mandrakes to stimulate her own fertility.
4. Joseph is born to her and Jacob.
5. She steals her father's household gods.
6. She flees from Laban with Jacob and his family.
7. When Laban catches up with them and searches their camp for his gods, she hides them by sitting on them.
8. Benjamin is born to her and Jacob.
9. She dies and is buried along the way to Bethlehem.

What
Everyone
Should
Know
about
the
Bible

REBEKAH

In the days of the patriarchs, fathers often arranged their children's marriages. Even though Isaac was about forty years old, Abraham sent his servant to find a bride for him. The servant met Rebekah at a well near Haran in northern Mesopotamia and asked the Lord to verify that this was the right wife for Isaac. When he was sure that she was, the servant arranged with her family to bring Rebekah back to Isaac. After about twenty years of marriage, they had twin sons, Jacob and Esau. Many years later, Rebekah arranged for her son Jacob to take the family birthright by deceiving her husband, Isaac. She then persuaded Isaac to send Jacob to her homeland for a bride.

Bible events in Rebekah's life
1. She gives Abraham's servant and his camels a drink of water.
2. She brings Abraham's servant home to meet her family.
3. Abraham's servant asks if he can take her with him to be Isaac's wife.
4. She goes with Abraham's servant to meet Isaac and becomes his bride.
5. Jacob and Esau are born to her and Isaac.
6. Isaac lies about her, saying she is his sister.
7. She helps Jacob deceive Isaac.
8. She tells Jacob to leave home because of Esau's plan to kill him.

SARAH

Sarah was Abraham's half sister and wife. She was called Sarai at first, but God changed her name to Sarah when he changed Abram's name to Abraham. Sarah was so beautiful that two kings tried to marry her, thinking that she was Abraham's sister. She had no children until she was ninety, at which time Isaac was miraculously born. When Sarah had her own son, she became jealous of her servant Hagar, who had given birth to a son by Abraham. She coerced her husband to drive Hagar and her son, Ishmael, into the wilderness. When Sarah died at the age of 127, she was buried in the cave of Machpelah at Hebron.

Bible events in Sarah's life
1. She marries Abraham.
2. She migrates with Abraham from Haran to Canaan.
3. She moves to Egypt with Abraham because of a famine.
4. She becomes part of Pharaoh's harem because Abraham said she was his sister.
5. Pharaoh sends Abraham and her out of Egypt.
6. She gives Abraham her maid, Hagar, to bear children for her.
7. She laughs when she hears that she will have a son.
8. Abimelech sends for her because Abraham said she was his sister.

9. Isaac is born to her and Abraham.

10. She dies and is buried in the cave of Machpelah at Hebron.

Questions You May Be Asking

Where is God when you hurt?

Many believe that Job lived in northern Mesopotamia during the time of the patriarchs, probably around the time of Abraham. If the book of Job were in chronological order in the Bible, it would interrupt the early part of Genesis. What is the heartbeat of this book? The following provides some ideas.

Someone you love very much was in the car when it crashed. Where was God? A tornado rips through town and destroys your house trailer. Where is God? Your child drowns, your loved one gets terminal cancer, your mate doesn't want you anymore. Where is God? The age-old questions have been asked a million or more times, Where is God when I hurt? Doesn't he care? Is he far away beyond the most distant galaxy?

The problem of pain is mysterious. Why did God permit pain to invade the world?

Why does God let me hurt? Why does a person sometimes suffer so much before he or she dies? Why, Lord, why?

The *why* question must have plagued Job as he suffered one disaster after another. Behind the scenes we are permitted to see the overarching drama—God granting permission for Satan to test Job. It didn't seem fair, but it happened.

Job lost his possessions, then his children, then his health. His wife thoughtlessly advised him to curse God and get it over with, but Job wouldn't do it. Job suffered as much as anyone ever suffered, but he still honored God.

Why did God permit this? Why did he let a good man suffer when he could have stopped it? People have repeatedly asked this question. Behind the scenes, we see Satan inflicting the pain and God permitting it. In Job's case, it was a test of integrity. God was convinced that Job would honor him no matter what he suffered.

The *why* question may have many different answers. Perhaps we are tested to see if we will remain faithful. Perhaps there are other "behind the scenes" reasons that only God knows. Some day, in heaven, we may clearly see why. Meanwhile, it may be none of our business. Let God be God.

At the end of the story, Job's faithfulness was rewarded richly. Job had more than he ever had before. This isn't always the end of the story. Sometimes people lose their health and their loved ones and die penniless. They must wait longer for an answer.

If God is God (as he is), he does have an answer to the problem of

64

>

What
Everyone
Should
Know
about
the

Bible

pain. We may learn the answer before we die, or we may have to wait until we get to heaven. Since God is God, we, like Job, must leave the answer with God. He will always do what is right. God is sovereign and just.

What were a rich man's riches?

Abraham and Lot became very wealthy. Stocks? Bonds? Bank accounts? No, there were no such things in those days. There were no coins or currency yet. Gold and silver were in the form of art or vessels, or even in broken pieces to be weighed. For the patriarchs, wealth was mostly in animals—usually sheep, donkeys, goats, and camels. The measure of "cattle wealth" was often in the thousands of animals, such as Job's riches before he lost them—seven thousand sheep, three thousand camels, five hundred teams of oxen, and five hundred female donkeys, plus an unnamed number of male donkeys. That's a lot of feeding, watering, and cleaning!

Did You Know?

The key to the Old Testament is the covenant God demonstrated his faithfulness to Abraham by making a lasting covenant with him. It was a binding agreement, something like a marriage vow, except that it extended for generations to come. The agreement was that if Abraham would obey, love, and serve him, God would bless him and his succeeding generations. That isn't much to ask, is it? This was the old covenant that was the foundation of the Old Testament. The New Testament is a new covenant. God promises that he will be our God and will give us forgiveness for sins and a home in heaven when we die. Our part is to repent of our sins and receive his free gift. That isn't much to ask either, is it?

Sarah really was Abraham's sister Abraham told a half lie to Pharaoh and King Abimelech. He was afraid that these kings would kill him so that they could marry Sarah, so he told them that she was his sister. It was half true, for Sarah was his half sister. Terah was father of both Abraham and Sarah, but each had a different mother.

Sodom wasn't always a salty wasteland If you visit the area near ancient Sodom today, you will find a bleak, salty wasteland. It wasn't always that way. When Abraham's and Lot's herdsmen quarreled over pastureland, Abraham offered Lot his choice of location. Lot chose the land adjacent to Sodom because he regarded it as the richest pastureland. It was well watered at that time, like a garden. Perhaps the fiery destruction of Sodom destroyed the land around it.

The mountain where the Temple was built In Abraham's time, he took Isaac to Mount Moriah to sacrifice him on an altar. A thousand years later, a man named Araunah brought his grain to this mountain for winnowing. He would toss the grain into the air and the wind would blow the chaff away. David later bought Araunah's threshing floor, and Solomon built the Temple there.

The Babylonians destroyed Solomon's Temple, but after the Exile, Zerubbabel returned to begin rebuilding it. In early New Testament times, Herod rebuilt the Temple to be almost as glorious as Solomon's Temple. That Temple was destroyed in A.D. 70 by the Roman general Titus and has never been rebuilt. Today, the Dome of the Rock and the Al-Aqsa mosque stand on the former site of this Temple. This mountain is only a few feet southeast of Calvary or Golgotha, where Jesus was crucified.

Water for thirsty camels When Abraham's servant searched for a bride for Isaac, he prayed that God would show him the right girl. The one who would offer water to him and his camels would be Isaac's bride. That girl was Rebekah. Why was this so important? A thirsty camel (and the servant had ten of them) would drink twenty to thirty gallons of water, so ten would drink two hundred to three hundred gallons of water. Rebekah had to draw this water from a well, one jug at a time. She was not only beautiful, but she was ambitious and had a true servant's heart. She would make a good mother of the covenant people to come.

Israel's enemies, the Philistines Samuel, Saul, and David all fought the Philistines. They were Israel's primary enemy during the early days of the kingdom. The Philistines lived along the Mediterranean coast and were sometimes called the sea people. They may have come from Crete or another part of the Aegean Sea during the time of Israel's judges. Their chief cities were Ashkelon, Ashdod, Ekron, Gerar, and Gaza. For a long time, the Philistines were the only ones who knew how to work iron, and they made swords, spears, and plowshares. This gave them superiority over Israel in agriculture and especially in weapons of warfare. They also knew how to make iron chariots, which gave them another military advantage. Their god was Dagon, a god with a fish tail, like a mermaid.

Jacob's wives, Rachel and Leah, were his cousins Jacob's mother, Rebekah, was Laban's sister, and Laban was the father of Rachel and Leah. So Jacob married his first cousins.

The pregnancy contest Rachel and Leah were sisters, and Leah was the older one. Jacob wanted Rachel for his wife, not Leah, and he worked seven years without pay for her. Their father, Laban, switched brides when Jacob was ready to consummate his marriage. He made love to Leah, thinking that she was Rachel. Then he was stuck. He had to keep Leah and work another seven years for Rachel, his beloved. The two

66

>

What
Everyone
Should
Know
about
the

Bible

sisters were very competitive. Even in giving birth to children they had an ongoing contest.

Who won? Not Jacob's beloved wife, Rachel, but his wife Leah. She had six sons and one daughter: Reuben, Simeon, Levi, Judah, Issachar, Zebulun, and Dinah. She gave her maid Zilpah to Jacob as a surrogate mother, and Zilpah had two sons: Gad and Asher. Rachel, Jacob's beloved, had two sons, Joseph and Benjamin. She gave her maid Bilhah to Jacob as a surrogate mother, and she had two sons, Dan and Naphtali.

The complex relationships in Jacob's family Laban was Jacob's uncle. This meant that Laban was Jacob's uncle and his father-in-law. There was still another relationship between Jacob and his wives. The grandfather of Laban and Rebekah was Nahor. He and Jacob's grandfather Abraham were brothers, so Jacob and his wives were all great-grandchildren of the same man.

Jacob's sons from different mothers were half brothers, of course, but since two of those mothers were sisters, the half brothers who were their sons were also first cousins. They could literally say that their brothers were their cousins and their cousins were their brothers.

Laban was the grandfather of Rachel's and Leah's children. They were also sons of Jacob, and since Laban was Jacob's uncle, he was also their great-uncle. So their grandfather was also their great-uncle.

The sons of Bilhah and Zilpah were half brothers through Jacob to all the other brothers and the sister. Through their mothers, however, they had no blood relationship to the other brothers or sister. This was a complex family!

Slaves in Egypt When Joseph's half brothers sold him as a slave to Egypt, they probably expected that he would work under the blazing sun and die within a few years. They could not, of course, realize the various kinds of work facing a slave in Egypt. Some slaves were farm workers, bricklayers, and burden bearers, and they probably had a short life span, but some worked indoors as poultry dressers, carpenters, bakers, stone masons, metal workers, or glass blowers. Joseph was fortunate to be purchased by a slave owner, Potiphar, who soon put him in charge of his household, which was a rather plush job for a slave. The half brothers would never, in their wildest imagination, have believed that Joseph could become ruler of Egypt. They likely expected that he would soon die from his burdens.

Embalming in Egypt Both Jacob's body and Joseph's body were embalmed in the manner of the Egyptians. How was this done? The body was filled with gums and spices to preserve it, then soaked for forty to seventy days in natron or bitumen. The body was wrapped in linen strips and covered with plaster that was painted with scenes and prayers. At last, it was placed in a wooden coffin, and then sometimes in a second coffin. The two coffins, which were shaped somewhat like a human body, were also painted with scenes and prayers. This process was very time consuming and expensive, so probably the only Israelites embalmed in Egypt were Jacob and Joseph.

Discovering My Purpose from God's Plan

1. *Half lies do not produce half consequences.* Abraham's half lies about his half sister and wife Sarah brought full consequences.

2. *The road to glory is often paved with service.* Before Rebekah could become Isaac's wife and the mother of all further covenant children, she first had to water the camels of Abraham's servant. No work, no glory. The crown never precedes the cross.

3. *God does not always want what he permits.* He does not always will what he allows to happen. God did not want Job to suffer, but he permitted it so that generations of people could see his example of faithfulness. God does not want the suffering and deaths that come from hurricanes, tornadoes, fires, and other tragedies. He permits these things for reasons beyond our grasp and beyond the present moment.

4. *Everyone wants to be desired and loved for who he or she is.* Poor Leah! Her father didn't want to keep her around the house, so he secretly forced a marriage. Her husband didn't want her, for he had worked seven years for another bride. And her younger sister certainly didn't want her as her husband's other wife, with all the complications that brought. Leah was "the unwanted one" or "undesired one," but she had six of Jacob's twelve sons, including Levi, through whose tribe Moses and all other Levites, the priestly clan, would come. Also through Leah came the line of Judah, from which King David, King Solomon, and Jesus' earthly heritage came. Being undesired does not have to mean being unproductive or unblessed.

5. *If God can make you, God can fix you.* Sarah's God was too small and too limited. She knew that God had made her, but she thought that he couldn't fix her or give her a son in her old age.

6. *If God's promises aren't broken, don't try to fix them!* God promised Sarah and Abraham a baby. His promise wasn't broken, and it didn't need fixing, but Sarah tried to fix it. That fix became broken.

7. *Forced love or love on demand is not love at all.* Leah must have prayed many times for God to make Jacob love her. Sorry, Leah. Love is love only when it is a spontaneous gift of self, not just because it is desired or demanded.

68
>
What
Everyone
Should
Know
about
the

Bible

8. *Tragedy can make you or break you, build you or tear you down, make you bitter or better, bring success or failure.* Tragedy must have brought tears and even doubt to Joseph, but it led him to the ruler's mansion.

9. *Why? is often a valid question, but it is seldom answered directly.* Joseph must have asked why when his brothers sold him as a slave, when Potiphar's wife lied about him and had him thrown into prison, when Pharaoh's cup-bearer forgot him for two years, and perhaps a dozen other times. From the Pharaoh's palace, the whys were more clearly understood.

The Silent Years Between Genesis and Exodus

Characters:
No people in this scene are named in the Bible. God, of course, was still at work.

Time Period:
From the death of Joseph to the birth of Moses

Dates:
Approximately 1805 B.C.–1525 B.C.

Where Scene 6 of the Big Story Can Be Found:
This scene fits between the end of Genesis and the beginning of Exodus, so none of it is in the Bible.

In Scene 6, Find the Answers to These Questions:
How many pharaohs ruled during Joseph's time as ruler?
How many pharaohs ruled during the silent years between Genesis and Exodus?

Look for this in Scene 6
> There is not a single Bible verse about the 280 years in this time period.
> Joseph was ruler of Egypt for eighty years.

The Big Story So Far

A long time of silence

Genesis ends with the rather blunt statement that Joseph died at age 110, was embalmed, and was buried in a coffin in Egypt. That's it! This is a rather terse and ordinary ending to an extraordinary book of the Bible that begins with the creation of the universe! Exodus begins with a brief account of how the descendants of Joseph and his brothers multiplied in Egypt. That's it! This is a rather terse and ordinary beginning for a book of extraordinary events to come!

About 280 years passed from the day of Joseph's death until a "new king came to power in Egypt who knew nothing about Joseph or what he had done" (Exodus 1:8). The Bible says nothing about these 280 years except to say that the descendants of Joseph and his brothers multiplied. Apparently they multiplied more than the Egyptians did!

There is, of course, much Egyptian history recorded concerning this period, but that is not our focus here. Egyptian history of this period differs from one reference book to another. As seen below, one pharaoh may be listed under four or five slightly different names. Dates vary from source to source, so the information here is approximate.

The Middle Kingdom

Joseph came to power about 1885 B.C. It was a time of prosperity in what is known as the Middle Kingdom. Joseph's entire eighty-year rule fell within this Middle Kingdom. It was a time in Egypt for great literature, engineering projects, and exceptional prosperity.

Commerce thrived. Beautiful jewelry was common, and there was a strong emphasis on justice and rightness.

Pharaoh was considered a "shepherd" of his people, an interesting thought when you consider that Joseph came from a shepherding society and must have had a significant influence on Pharaoh. How different things would have been if God had not revealed the seven years of abundance followed by seven years of famine! Joseph saved Egypt from certain starvation and helped to move Egypt into a period of prosperity.

The pharaoh who put Joseph into power was possibly Sesostris III (sometimes called Senwosri III, Senwosret III, or Senusert III) who ruled from 1887 B.C. to 1850 B.C. He was a warrior who extended Egypt's boundaries as far as Syria. When he died, Joseph had been in power for thirty-five years. His successor, Amenemhet III, ruled from 1850 B.C. until 1800 B.C., five years after Joseph's death. Joseph was ruler of Egypt for forty-five years under this second pharaoh. Amenemhet III must have accepted Joseph's leadership as fully as his predecessor who appointed Joseph, and Joseph was ruler under these two pharaohs only, which was remarkable for an eighty-year term as ruler. This gave

72

>

What
Everyone
Should
Know
about
the

Bible

great stability to Egypt during this period of the Middle Kingdom. No wonder Egypt was at its height during Joseph's tenure!

Amenemhet III was a peaceful king who ruled Egypt during a time of great peace and prosperity, just like Joseph's entire eighty-year term as ruler of Egypt. The Genesis account ends during the reign of Amenemhet III. What happened after that?

The Second Intermediate Period and the New Empire in Egypt

In 1785 B.C., about twenty years after Joseph died, Egypt entered into the Second Intermediate Period of its history (1785 B.C.–1580 B.C.). The period of Egyptian history that followed was the New Empire, from 1580 B.C.–1085 B.C. Twenty years of the Middle Kingdom, the entire Second Intermediate Period, and 134 years of the New Empire were the years of silence between Genesis and Exodus.

What happened in Egypt during these years of biblical silence? After Joseph's death, Egypt began to decay from within. Egypt missed Joseph's great leadership!

There were five dynasties, the thirteenth through the seventeenth, during the Second Intermediate Period. During the first two of those alone, dynasties thirteen and fourteen, there were thirty-eight kings or pharaohs. The entire record of all the pharaohs is fuzzy, but it is safe to say that there may have been more than fifty pharaohs between the times of Joseph and Moses, more rulers than all the presidents of the entire United States history. No wonder the pharaoh of Moses' time knew nothing about Joseph! He probably couldn't even recite all the pharaohs since Joseph.

The Hyksos-Semite conquerors

In 1680 B.C., Asian Semite people known as Hyksos (shepherd kings who were descendants of Noah's son Shem, as were Joseph and Moses) invaded Egypt and conquered the weakened land that had rotted from within. The Hyksos adopted many of the Egyptians' cultural ways, but they were cruel to the Egyptian people. It took about 150 years before the Egyptians finally drove out the Hyksos, and they were fiercely determined never again to let a foreign power rule like this in Egypt. This helps us understand why the pharaoh who ruled when Moses was born was passionate about keeping the Hebrews in subjection.

Questions You May Be Asking

What happened during these years of silence in the Bible? Are there any Bible events during this period?

There are no Bible events during this period of silence between the close of Genesis and the opening of the book of Exodus. Nor are there any dates of significance to help us understand the Bible story.

While Joseph's family multiplied in safety and prosperity, the politics of Egypt shifted. As you look in different reference books, you will find an uncertain chronology of this period and an uncertain list of the names of the many pharaohs who ruled during this period. It was a time of great shifting of power, and with it the memory of Joseph faded.

Joseph became ruler of Egypt about 1885 B.C. and died about 1805 B.C. He was ruler of Egypt for eighty years. He apparently had full governing power until the end of his life. It is remarkable to think that this slave boy had such enormous influence over one of the great nations of the world at that time, and for such a long time.

Why is the Bible silent concerning so many years of history?

In the overall history of the people of Israel, which is the Old Testament story, there wasn't much to report during this period. It was a time of peace, prosperity, and tranquility for Jacob's descendants. The story is silent as God's covenant people lived, multiplied, and died. That's about it.

A Nation of Slaves

Israel in Egypt

Characters:
Aaron (Moses' brother); Abihu (Aaron's son); Abiram (a rebellious leader); Amram (Moses' father); Dathan (a rebellious leader); Gershom (son of Moses and Zipporah); Hur (who held up Moses' hands to ensure victory); Jethro (Moses' father-in-law); Jochebed (Moses' mother); Korah (a rebellious Levite who was Moses' cousin); Miriam (Moses' sister); Moses; Pharaoh (an evil king of Egypt); Nadab (son of Aaron); Pharaoh's daughter (who saved Moses but is not named); Zipporah (Moses' wife)

Time Period:
From Israelite slavery in Egypt through the Exodus

Dates:
From about 1526–1446 B.C.

Where Scene 7 of the Big Story Can Be Found:
The books of Exodus, Numbers, and Deuteronomy

In Scene 7, Find the Answers to These Questions:
Why was Pharaoh so paranoid about the births of the Hebrews?
The Hebrew slaves were very rich when they left on the Exodus. Where did these slaves get so much wealth?
The Tabernacle was worth about $13 million. How did a tent come to carry such a high price?

Look for this in Scene 7
> Moses was not named by his mother or father. Who named him?
> Each of the ten plagues struck at an Egyptian god or goddess. Which god did each one strike?
> The laver, or giant bronze washbowl for the Tabernacle, was made from mirrors. How did they do that?

How God's covenant people became slaves

The book of Exodus opens with Hebrews, who became known as Israel-ites, flooding the land of Egypt. The pharaoh of Egypt was terrified. The memory was fresh of the Hyksos, Asian Semitic people who conquered Egypt during the time of silence between Genesis and Exodus. Never again would Egypt allow foreign rulers to overcome them. Pharaoh's extreme solution was cruel but practical—he would make all the Hebrews slaves to keep them out of power.

These Hebrew slaves were the "children of Israel." They were covenant people, descendants of Abraham through Isaac and Jacob who carried Jacob's other name, Israel. God had made a covenant with Abraham and his descendants. God would keep his part, and he expected them to keep their part.

Exodus opens with a hopeless period for the covenant people, for they were slaves. Pharaoh had also issued a cruel edict to kill all the Hebrew baby boys. This would further reduce the population of these unwanted people.

Jochebed put her baby son into a basket and hid it among the reeds along the Nile River. There Pharaoh's daughter found him and adopted him as her own son. She named him Moses and hired Jochebed to care for him during his early years.

A slave boy becomes a prince of Egypt

When Moses was old enough, he went to the palace to live and was trained as a prince. For about the first forty years of his life, he was a prince in Egypt and was possibly in line to become the next pharaoh. As a prince of Egypt, Moses had a rigorous training program. He learned government, military skills, art, architecture, and even health care and medicine. This training would be invaluable when the Lord welded the nation of Israel together and gave the law to govern this new nation through Moses.

Moses must have known that he was a Hebrew, not an Egyptian, so when an Egyptian slave master was cruel to some Hebrews one day, Moses killed the Egyptian and buried him in the sand. Pharaoh heard about this, and Moses had to run away to Midian to escape certain death. Moses had now completed the first third of his life, the forty-year period of princely training. He had graduated abruptly from the school of Egypt.

The school of the wilderness

Moses lived in Midian for the next forty years of his life with Jethro, a priest of Midian. He married Jethro's daughter Zipporah and became

76
>
What
Everyone
Should
Know
about
the
Bible

a shepherd, taking care of Jethro's sheep. During this forty-year period, Moses was trained in "the school of the wilderness" with the Lord as his instructor. Moses served his father-in-law, Jethro, as shepherd twice as long as his ancestor Jacob had served his father-in-law, Laban, as a shepherd many years before. Jacob had no pay for fourteen of those years. Apparently Moses had no pay besides room and board for forty years. Jacob was in the business of building wealth. Moses apparently never built his own wealth, so it was not a hindrance when God called him to lead the Hebrews from Egypt.

One day, God spoke to Moses from a burning bush and commissioned him to return to Egypt and lead his people from their slavery. Moses argued with God because he didn't want to do this, but God said "go," so Moses finally decided to do it.

Warfare with the gods of Egypt

Moses returned to Egypt with his brother, Aaron, and presented God's demand to Pharaoh. This pharaoh was probably a successor to the man who was Pharaoh during Moses' childhood. Pharaoh refused to let the Israelites go, and God sent ten plagues through Moses. Each plague was open warfare against one or more gods of Egypt.

The first plague, when Moses turned the Nile River to blood, confronted the Egyptian god Hapi, the god of the river. The second plague of frogs confronted the Egyptian god Hekt, whose image was a frog.

The third and fourth plagues primarily infested cattle with flies and gnats, and the fifth plague sent a disease among the cattle. The sixth plague further inflicted both cattle and people with boils. These plagues confronted the Egyptian goddess Hathor, the cow deity; the god of the Apis bull; and the golden calves of Egypt. The sixth plague moved into the human arena, which put greater pressure on Pharaoh and his people.

The seventh plague of hail and the eighth plague of locusts struck at the very heart of the food chain for animals and people, for they struck at Egypt's agriculture. This was the very lifeline of Egypt, nurtured by the Nile and sustained by the cattle.

The ninth plague of darkness struck at the Egyptian god Re, Ra, or Amon-Ra, the sun god of Egypt. The noose was tightening in all these plagues, for Amon-Ra was one of the most important of all Egyptian gods. Without sunlight, there was no future for Egypt, not even basic survival. The Lord had started with Egypt's water supply, moved upward through the health of its animals, struck at its food supply, and lastly, had defied the god of light.

The tenth and most devastating plague was yet to come. Up to that point, the plagues had crippled Pharaoh's animals, land, and indirectly his people. Now the Lord would cripple Pharaoh himself, who thought he was a god. The tenth plague was the death of all the firstborn sons of Egypt, including the heir to Pharaoh's throne. Even the firstborn of all the Egyptian animals would die.

Pharaoh, a self-proclaimed god of Egypt, could not spare his own son from this plague from the Lord. He was defeated and so was Egypt. The people of Egypt urgently wanted the Israelites to leave—so passionately that they loaded the Israelites with vast treasures and sent them on their way. They feared that Egypt would be utterly destroyed with one more plague.

The night of the tenth plague was important for Israel, for the Lord instituted the Passover at that time. That night the Israelites ate roast lamb with bitter herbs and bread made without yeast. They sprinkled the blood of the lamb on their doorposts as a sign to the Lord to pass over those houses. When the angel of death passed through the land, he passed over (hence the word *Passover*) the houses with blood on the doorposts.

At midnight, the Lord brought the tenth plague upon Egypt. Every home in Egypt was affected. Pharaoh sent for Moses during the night and urged him to leave the country as quickly as possible. That night the Exodus began with about two million Israelites, of which six hundred thousand were men. They left their slave homes in Rameses and headed toward Succoth. Thus ended their 430 years in Egypt (Exodus 12:40).

Caught in a trap

The route of the Exodus moved toward the Red Sea. Why there? That wasn't on a direct route to the Promised Land. The answer is simple. The direct route would have put the people of Israel, freshly freed from slavery, into direct military confrontation with the Philistines. The Lord knew they were not ready for that. It would have been disastrous (Exodus 13:17-18).

You have never seen such a procession, with two million people celebrating their new freedom, singing, clapping, and shouting, with all their possessions and livestock. What a joyous people, freed at last from hundreds of years of slavery!

Succoth was their first stop. Then they camped at Etham on the edge of the wilderness. How would they find their way through the desert? The answer came quickly: A pillar of cloud appeared by day and a pillar of fire by night. It was the Lord who would personally guide his people on their journey.

The Lord ordered Moses to move the campsite to the shore of the

78

>

What
Everyone
Should
Know
about
the

Bible

Red Sea, as he knew what Pharaoh would do next. This location was a dead end—there was no way out except for the way they went in.

When word reached Pharaoh that the Israelites were camped on the shore of the Red Sea, and he realized that they were trapped in a dead end, the evil king saw his chance for revenge. He assembled his elite chariot troops. He would descend upon the former slaves and slaughter them all. They could not escape.

The Israelites saw the chariots coming in the distance. They were, of course, terrified. There was no escape from being slaughtered. They cried out to the Lord for help, then complained to Moses about the situation.

The Lord, in the pillar of cloud, moved between the chariot troops and the Israelites. Soon the Egyptians could not see where to go. Night came, and the pillar of fire gave light to the Israelites but only darkness to the Egyptians.

Pathway through the sea

Following the Lord's command, Moses stretched out his hand toward the Red Sea. Then the Lord opened a path through the sea for the Israelites to cross on dry ground. There was a wall of water on each side, but the Israelites crossed safely to the other side.

Pharaoh ordered his troops to follow, but when they got into the midst of the Red Sea, the Lord sent the walls of water crashing over them, and they were all destroyed. Pharaoh must have stood breathless on his shore of the Red Sea, watching this happen. Surely he must have admitted that Moses' God truly was God!

The Israelites had just witnessed a powerful, dramatic miracle that the Lord had performed to save them. Moses and the people burst into song, and that beautiful song is recorded in Exodus 15:1-18. Miriam, Moses' older sister, took a tambourine and led the women of Israel in rhythm and dance, singing, "I will sing to the Lord, for he has triumphed gloriously; he has hurled both horse and rider into the sea." Wouldn't you like to have heard this triumphant singing?

Slavery behind, wilderness ahead

Egypt and its slavery lay behind the Israelites, but the wilderness and its uncertainties lay ahead of them. For the next three days, they tramped through the Shur Desert with no water. Imagine going through a hot desert for three days without water!

At last the people came to a place called Marah. How thrilled they were to see water at last, and they rushed to drink their fill! They suddenly stopped, however, for the water was bitter, and they could not drink it. You can hear the people complaining to Moses, can't you?

Moses begged the Lord for help, and the Lord showed him a tree.

Moses took a branch of the tree and threw it into the water. Then the water was delicious, and everyone could drink as much as they wanted. Even the animals had plenty of water.

The caravan moved on to a place called Elim, where there were twelve springs and seventy palm trees that made a beautiful oasis in the middle of the desert. They camped there a while to enjoy this beautiful setting, but at last it was time for them to move on.

Food from the sky

Each day the Lord sent manna, a sweet waferlike substance that appeared on the ground in flakes. The Israelites had this manna for as long as they remained in the wilderness. It was the Lord's provision. They had to gather only enough for each day, except on the day before the Sabbath, when they would gather twice as much, so they would not have to gather on the Sabbath.

The Israelites moved through the Sin Desert between Elim and Mount Sinai, where they were headed. Soon they tired of eating only manna, so waves of complaints swelled up from the people. They wanted meat, and they wanted it now. Moses had led them out of Egypt to live, but as far as the people were concerned, he had led them into the wilderness to die. In Egypt they had been slaves, but at least they had had a variety of foods. Here they had freedom, but it appeared to be the freedom to starve to death.

Moses prayed, and the Lord promised meat by that evening. Where could that possibly come from? There were no animals except their own flocks and herds. That evening, the people saw dark clouds approaching, and flocks of quail descended into the camp. There was meat in abundance.

From the Sin Desert, the people moved from place to place until they came to Rephidim. Once more they were without water, and again they complained bitterly to Moses. This time, the Lord told Moses to strike a rock and water flowed from it. Moses named the place Massah (the place of testing) and Meribah (the place of arguing).

Now a new threat arose. The army of Amalek came to do battle with the Israelites. Moses commanded Joshua to call the Israelites to arms. While they fought, Moses held out his staff. As long as he held out his staff, his troops were winning, but when he grew tired and his hands lowered, his troops began losing. Quickly, Aaron and Hur found a stone for Moses to sit on, and each held up one of Moses' hands until the battle was won. The first great military adventure belonged to Israel.

News of these great miracles had by this time reached Jethro, Moses' father-in-law. Moses had sent his wife and two sons back to live with Jethro while he faced Pharaoh during the plagues. Now Jethro came to

What
Everyone
Should
Know
about
the
Bible

see Moses in the wilderness. Zipporah and Moses' two sons came with him. Imagine the conversation as Moses told his family all that had happened! There must have been much celebrating in Moses' tent that day.

Delegation of authority

The next day, Moses went to his usual place to hear the complaints of the people against one another. From morning until evening, the people lined up for Moses to judge them. Wise old Jethro saw what was happening and gave some sage advice. "Stop doing all this alone!" he advised. "Find capable honest men who can do this for you. Listen only to the most important matters."

It was excellent advice, and Moses listened to it. Soon there was a group of judges to listen to the people's complaints. Only the most difficult problems reached Moses.

The mountain of the Lord

Exactly two months after they left Egypt, the Israelites reached Mount Sinai, the mountain of the Lord. This was the destination toward which they had been moving. The Lord had much work to do here with his people.

Moses climbed the mountain to be with the Lord. At first, God's message was simple, "Now if you will obey me and keep my covenant, you will be my own special treasure from among all the peoples on earth." When Moses relayed this message to his people, they responded, "We will do everything the LORD has commanded" (Exodus 19:5, 8).

On the morning of the third day, the Lord announced his presence with powerful thunder and lightning; a dense cloud that descended from the mountain; and a loud, long blast of a ram's horn. The people trembled in fear, for they knew it was the Lord. The Lord warned the people not to climb the mountain and called Moses to the top of Mount Sinai.

There on Mount Sinai, the Lord gave Moses the Ten Commandments. He wrote them with his own finger on tablets of stone. The Lord also gave him significant parts of the law. He gave Moses detailed instructions for building the Tabernacle, a multimillion-dollar tent that would be the place of Israelite worship, and the gold furniture that would go with the Tabernacle. The Lord gave instructions for worship and for the priests who would lead that worship, even as to the garments they should wear. Aaron would be the high priest, and his sons would be his assistant priests.

A gold calf from gold earrings

All of this took many days, and the people grew restless. Some of the rebels among them came to Aaron and complained that Moses would not come back. "Make us some gods to lead us," they demanded (Exodus 32:1). Foolishly, Aaron asked for their gold earrings and molded them into a gold calf. The next day, he set up a festival to worship this idol. Then the Lord told Moses to go down from Mount Sinai and see what his people were doing.

Moses quickly descended, holding the two stones on which the Ten Commandments were written by God's own hand. When Moses saw the people dancing before the gold calf, he was so furious that he threw the two tablets of stone to the ground, where they shattered. Once in the camp, Moses ground the gold calf into powder and made the people drink it.

Moses confronted his brother, Aaron, and demanded to know what had happened. Aaron gave a lame excuse, saying, "I simply threw [their gold jewelry] into the fire—and out came this calf!" (Exodus 32:24). Moses must have been incredibly disgusted with his brother's answer.

Moses ordered the Levites to go among the people and kill with the sword those who had worshiped the gold calf. About three thousand people died that day. Moses returned to the Lord and begged him to forgive the people, but the Lord sent a terrible plague among them.

The Lord replaced the stone tablets bearing the Ten Commandments. For many years to come, these tablets were housed in the Ark of the Covenant, the gold chest that remained with the Tabernacle.

A multimillion-dollar tent

At last it was time to begin construction on the Tabernacle. The Lord chose two craftsmen who were gifted by God: Bezalel and Oholiab.

Moses invited the people to bring the gifts from which the Tabernacle would be made. Some of these were treasures the Egyptians had given them while urging them to leave Egypt. The hearts of the people were stirred to generosity, and they brought treasures beyond imagination. At last Moses had to ask them to stop giving, and then the work began.

It took a long time to make this multimillion-dollar tent. We would be dazzled to see the beauty of it, with embroidery of blue, purple, and scarlet, gold clasps, silver bases, and jewels in abundance. It was a glorious work that included about 2,200 pounds of gold, 7,545 pounds of silver, and 5,310 pounds of bronze. The gold alone would be worth much more than thirteen million dollars today.

The Tabernacle furniture was made of wood, covered with pure gold. It must have gleamed in the desert sun. At last the Tabernacle was completely set up. It must have been a breathtaking sight! Then Moses dedicated it to the Lord. The Lord's presence continued to appear as a pillar of cloud by day and a pillar of fire by night.

82

>

What
Everyone
Should
Know
about
the

Bible

Questions You May Be Asking

Why was the pharaoh so afraid of the Israelites during the time of Moses' infancy?

The frightening memories of Hyksos rulers was much fresher in the mind of the pharaoh of Moses' infancy than was the story of Joseph from centuries earlier. Never again would he let foreigners rule Egypt!

The Hyksos were Semites who were descendants of Noah's son Shem, as were Joseph and his descendants. Pharaoh feared that there would be another uprising and once again the foreign Semites would rule Egypt. It was enough to give an Egyptian king nightmares.

Too much time had passed since Joseph saved Egypt from starvation, and too many pharaohs had come and gone. It would be like Americans today getting passionate about some official almost two hundred years before George Washington.

Pharaoh's fear had everything to do with loss of power, much the same dynamic that later drove Herod to massacre the babies of Bethlehem. In a democratic society, politicians massacre each other with words. In the totalitarian society of Bible times, the sword was the weapon of choice, as words didn't work very well. Slavery was effective, too, with rigid enforcement. At first this pharaoh tried slavery but quickly drifted to the sword. He wouldn't kill grown men who could work for him, but he would kill the baby boys. Like Herod, he directed his sword at innocent children. There were too many Hebrews, or Israelites, and he had to control the population. Killing the baby boys would do it.

If Pharaoh was so anxious to enslave the Israelites and decrease their male population, why did his daughter, the princess, claim Moses and raise him in the palace?

Why did the princess, daughter of the evil Pharaoh, adopt a Hebrew slave boy? There was probably a power struggle involved. Who would inherit the throne? She was apparently not married, so she could not have a son who would inherit the throne. The son of another woman would be the next pharaoh. A son of any Egyptian woman would place that woman, not the princess, in a position of power. By adopting little Moses, she now had a son whose natural parents had no claim to Egyptian power, and he was in line with others to inherit the throne. If so, the princess would be the Queen Mother. If another person inherited the throne, the princess would possibly be executed.

What was Moses' life like as a boy?

After he went to the palace to live, Moses grew up in the royal family, receiving all the education and training given to royalty. He was in line, along with others, to become Pharaoh, the king of Egypt. He was trained for royal work, but his royal work would be for Israel, not for Egypt. No other key Bible character had such rich training. Joseph inherited power from the pharaoh, but he was not trained to exercise that power. He was never in line to become the pharaoh.

Why did Moses, prince of Egypt, escape to Midian?

Moses must have learned of his identity as a Hebrew. One day, he saw an Egyptian taskmaster beating a Hebrew slave. In a moment of passion, he murdered the Egyptian and buried him in the sand. Pharaoh learned what had happened, and Moses had to flee Egypt to save his life.

As a refugee, Moses fled alone to the land of Midian. There Moses met a band of shepherd girls, helped them to water their father's sheep, and went to live in the household of their father, Jethro. He even married one of Jethro's daughters—Zipporah.

Why would Moses risk his life to go back to Egypt?

After the pharaoh of Moses' childhood died, God commissioned Moses at a burning bush to return to Egypt with his brother, Aaron, and demand that the new pharaoh free the Hebrew slaves. This was not a request but a command and a commission. Moses was no longer a young man, being almost eighty at this time, an unlikely age for the job God was giving him.

Think of the training Moses now had—forty years of royal training as a prince of Egypt and forty years of wilderness training. Both would be needed for his future work.

What does *exodus* mean?

Exodus means "going out of." The Exodus was a great migration of about two million former slaves from their land of slavery, where they and their ancestors had lived for 430 years. It was an exodus from slavery but also an exodus into the unknown. Before them lay a strange new wilderness with not only freedom but also the fear of starvation and dehydration.

How did an unarmed band of Hebrews escape from Pharaoh's elite chariot troops?

The Hebrews were trapped on the shores of the Red Sea. Pharaoh advanced fast with his chariots. If you had been with the Hebrews that day, you would have been sure the end had come. There was simply no way for them to protect themselves against Pharaoh's armed charioteers.

Then God performed one of the greatest miracles of the Old Testament. At Moses' command, the waters of the Red Sea parted, and the Hebrews walked across the floor of the sea on dry land. When Pharaoh's troops tried to follow, the waters converged over them and they drowned.

On the Egyptian shore stood Pharaoh with all the power of Egypt at

What
Everyone
Should
Know
about
the

Bible

his disposal, but he had just been defeated by the unseen hand of God. On the opposite shore stood a victorious people with no power at all except the unseen hand of God.

Strength had become weakness, and weakness had become strength. The unseen God of Moses prevailed over all the visible symbols of Egypt's numerous gods. Surely Moses' God is God.

Why didn't the Israelites go directly to the Promised Land and enter it?

The people were free from Egyptian slavery. The Promised Land could probably be reached within two weeks or, perhaps, a month, but these freshly freed slaves were not prepared to fight major battles. They had to be trained. They also needed to learn about God's provision in a wilderness. They had to be welded together as a nation, with systems of laws and worship. All of this would take much time. They had a divine appointment at Mount Sinai, the mountain of God.

What happened at Mount Sinai? What did God do?

Moses brought his rebellious band of escaped slaves to the foot of the mountain of God, Mount Sinai. While they camped there, God welded these people into a nation with laws and a system of worship. God also gave plans for the Tabernacle, the portable multimillion-dollar tent that would be the predecessor of the Temple in Jerusalem as a center of worship.

At the foot of Mount Sinai, Moses led his people in constructing the Tabernacle, organizing the camp, and learning God's laws, especially the Ten Commandments. There he and Aaron led the people in learning to worship a holy God according to the system of worship God had established.

Great Events of This Time

1. **Moses is born** (Exodus 2:1-10).
2. **Moses kills an Egyptian and escapes to Midian** (Exodus 2:11-15).
3. **Moses meets Jethro's daughters** (Exodus 2:16-25).
4. **God speaks to Moses at a burning bush** (Exodus 3:1–4:17).
5. **Moses meets Aaron and returns to Egypt** (Exodus 4:18-31).
6. **Moses comes before Pharaoh; Pharaoh increases the slaves' workload** (Exodus 5:1–7:7).
7. **Aaron's rod becomes a serpent** (Exodus 7:8-13).
8. **The first nine plagues strike Egypt** (Exodus 7:14–10:29).
9. **Moses warns Pharaoh about the tenth plague** (Exodus 11).
10. **The Passover spares the Hebrews** (Exodus 12:1-28).
11. **The tenth plague strikes the Egyptian firstborn sons** (Exodus 12:29-36).

12. **The Exodus from Egypt begins** (Exodus 12:37–13:16).
13. **The pillar of cloud and fire leads the Hebrews** (Exodus 13:17-22).
14. **The Hebrews cross the Red Sea** (Exodus 14:1–15:21).
15. **The Hebrews encounter bitter waters at Marah** (Exodus 15:22-27).
16. **God provides food in the wilderness for the Hebrews** (Exodus 16).
17. **Moses strikes the rock at Horeb** (Exodus 17:1-7).
18. **The Hebrews defeat Amalek as Aaron and Hur hold up Moses' hands** (Exodus 17:8-16).
19. **Jethro visits and advises the appointment of judges** (Exodus 18).
20. **The people reach Mount Sinai** (Exodus 19).
21. **God gives Moses the Ten Commandments** (Exodus 20:1-21).
22. **Israel ratifies God's covenant** (Exodus 24).
23. **Instructions are given and materials are gathered for the Tabernacle** (Exodus 25–31).
24. **The Hebrews sin by worshiping a gold calf** (Exodus 32).
25. **Moses intercedes for the people and sees God's glory** (Exodus 33).
26. **Moses receives new tablets of stone** (Exodus 34).
27. **The people gladly bring gifts for the Tabernacle** (Exodus 35:1-29).
28. **The Tabernacle is constructed** (Exodus 35:30–38:31).
29. **The priests are clothed** (Exodus 39:1-31).
30. **Moses blesses the Tabernacle** (Exodus 39:32-43).
31. **The Tabernacle is assembled** (Exodus 40).

Significant Dates of This Time

Circa 1526 B.C., Moses is born.
Circa 1446 B.C., the exodus from Egypt occurs.

Heroes and Villains: The Stars in Scene 7

Space does not permit us to list all of the heroes and villains associated with the Exodus. Pharaoh, of course, was the chief villain of this period. His magicians were also villains, for they greatly deceived him and the Egyptian people. Hur was a great help to Moses when he and Aaron held up Moses' hands, assuring victory over the Amalekites. Jethro, Moses' father-in-law, was Moses' father figure for forty years while he lived with him and cared for his sheep. Moses' parents were Amram and Jochebed. The following are some of the most prominent characters during the time of the Exodus.

AARON

Like his younger brother, Moses, and his sister, Miriam, Aaron was born into a slave family. His parents, Amram and Jochebed, were descendants

What
Everyone
Should
Know
about
the

Bible

of Levi, a son of Jacob and Leah. When Moses led the Israelites from slavery, Aaron became his assistant and often spoke for him. When the Tabernacle was built in the wilderness, Aaron became the first high priest of Israel. He died before the Israelites reached the Promised Land, and was buried at Mount Hor. Many of Aaron's descendants became priests in Israel, and a number were high priests.

Bible events in Aaron's life

1. The Lord tells Moses that he will assist him and will speak for him as he leads the Israelites from Egypt.
2. He and Moses appear before Pharaoh to demand freedom for the Israelites.
3. He strikes the Nile River with his rod to turn its waters to blood.
4. He and Moses cause plagues of frogs, gnats, flies, cattle disease, boils, hail, locusts, and darkness upon Egypt.
5. He and Moses bring upon Egypt the plague of the death of the firstborn and celebrate the first Passover.
6. He and Moses lead the people of Israel from Egypt in the Exodus.
7. He and Hur hold up Moses' hands until the Amalekites are defeated.
8. He is appointed high priest, and special garments are made for him.
9. He makes a gold calf while Moses is on Mount Sinai.
10. He and his sons are consecrated for service in the Tabernacle.
11. He makes offerings to the Lord.
12. He and his sons help to move the Tabernacle.
13. His sons Nadab and Abihu are burned to death when they burn an unholy incense offering to the Lord.
14. He and Miriam criticize Moses.
15. His rod buds, signifying he is God's chosen priest.
16. He dies and is buried on Mount Hor.

MIRIAM

When the Israelites were slaves in Egypt, Amram and Jochebed suffered with their relatives. Not only were they oppressed as slaves, but they realized that their three children, Aaron, Miriam, and Moses, would also have to endure this existence. Then came the evil command from Pharaoh, king of Egypt, to kill every Israelite boy who was born. Moses, the youngest, was marked for death. Jochebed made a basket of bulrushes, put Moses in it, and hid him among the plants growing along the Nile River. Moses' older sister, Miriam, was stationed as guard, and when Pharaoh's daughter found Moses and decided to adopt him, Miriam offered her mother to nurse him. Years later, during the Exodus, Miriam was prominent as Moses' sister, leading the people in a song of victory when Pharaoh's chariot troops were drowned in the Red Sea. During the time in the wilderness, Miriam conspired against Moses' leadership and was struck with leprosy.

Bible events in Miriam's life
1. She watches over Moses in his basket boat along the Nile River.
2. She sings and dances after the Israelites cross the Red Sea safely.
3. She complains against Moses and is struck with leprosy.
4. She dies at Kadesh.

MOSES

Born as a Hebrew slave in Egypt, Moses was condemned to die along with all other Hebrew baby boys of his time. His mother, Jochebed, made a basket of bulrushes and hid Moses among the plants along the Nile River. When Pharaoh's daughter found him, she adopted him as her own son and gave Moses' mother the job of caring for him until he was old enough to live with her. Until he was forty, Moses was trained as a prince of Egypt. Moses received his name from the Egyptian princess, not from his mother.

When Moses killed an Egyptian taskmaster for abusing a slave, he fled for his life and hid in Midian. There he lived with Jethro, a priest of Midian, and married his daughter Zipporah. During the next forty years, Moses worked as a shepherd in Midian until God called to him from a burning bush to lead the people of Israel from Egypt.

During the last forty years of his life, Moses was the supreme leader of his people. He guided them through the wilderness and was an intermediary between God and the people. Moses died before he reached the Promised Land. He was forbidden to enter it because he had disobeyed God.

Bible events in Moses' life
1. He is born and hidden in a basket boat.
2. Pharaoh's daughter finds him, and he grows up in the king's palace with her.
3. He kills an Egyptian who was beating one of the Hebrew slaves and flees to the land of Midian.
4. He helps Jethro's daughters at a well in Midian, goes to live with them, and marries Zipporah.
5. The Angel of the Lord appears to him in a burning bush and commands him to lead his people out of Egypt.
6. He meets Aaron in the wilderness.
7. He appears with Aaron before Pharaoh to tell him to let the people of Israel go to the wilderness to worship God.
8. Pharaoh refuses, and God sends ten plagues.

88

>

What
Everyone
Should
Know
about
the

Bible

9. He celebrates the first Passover Feast on the night before the Exodus.
10. The tenth plague causes the death of the firstborn throughout Egypt.
11. The Israelites leave Egypt.
12. The pillars of cloud and of fire lead the Israelites through the desert.
13. He stretches out his hand, the Red Sea parts, and the Israelites cross on dry land.
14. He and his people sing their praise to the Lord after they are safely across the Red Sea.
15. He throws a branch into the bitter water of Marah to make it drinkable.
16. God sends manna and quail in the wilderness.
17. He strikes a rock at Rephidim, and water pours out for the people of Israel.
18. Aaron and Hur hold up Moses' hands until the Israelites win a battle against the Amalekites.
19. Jethro gives Moses good advice.
20. The Israelites camp at Mount Sinai while he goes up the mountain and God speaks to him.
21. God gives him the Ten Commandments.
22. God gives him more laws for the Israelites.
23. He stays on the mountain for forty days and nights. God instructs him to make the Tabernacle and the furniture for it, and gives him laws concerning the priests and the offerings.
24. The Israelites make a gold calf; Moses breaks the tablets of stone with the Ten Commandments.
25. He goes up Mount Sinai again. God gives him the Ten Commandments on tablets of stone. When Moses comes down from the mountain, his face shines.
26. He asks for gifts for the Tabernacle, and the people respond generously.
27. He oversees the building and assembly of the Tabernacle.
28. He consecrates Aaron and his sons.
29. Nadab and Abihu burn an unholy incense offering to the Lord, and they die.
30. The Lord commands Moses to take a census of the men of war.
31. Aaron and Miriam complain about him, and Miriam is struck with leprosy.
32. He sends spies into the Promised Land.
33. The Israelites are afraid to enter the Promised Land, and God punishes them by making them wander in the wilderness for forty years.
34. Korah, Dathan, and Abiram rebel; they are swallowed by the earth.

35. The Israelites rebel against Aaron. God sends a plague. Aaron's rod buds and blooms.
36. At Meribah, he disobeys and strikes the rock.
37. Aaron and Miriam die.
38. To heal the people from snakebites, he makes a bronze snake in the wilderness.
39. The daughters of Zelophehad come before him to ask for an equal inheritance with the men.
40. The Lord instructs him about offerings, feasts, and vows.
41. The Israelites fight and defeat the Midianites.
42. The Lord instructs him as to how the Promised Land should be divided.
43. In his final charge to the people of Israel, he commissions Joshua as the new leader.
44. He sings a song.
45. He blesses Israel.
46. He dies on Mount Nebo, and God buries him.

ZIPPORAH

When Moses fled from Egypt, he hid in the land of Midian and became a shepherd for the priest Jethro. In time, Moses married one of Jethro's daughters, Zipporah, and they had two sons, Gershom and Eliezer. She went to Egypt with Moses but was apparently sent home to Jethro during the time of the Exodus, possibly because of the danger involved.

Bible events in Zipporah's life
1. Moses comes to live at the home of her father; Moses marries her.
2. She and Moses have a son, Gershom.
3. She circumcises her young son.
4. She comes with her father, Jethro, to visit Moses at Mount Sinai.

What everyone should know about the book of Exodus
THE STORY OF FROM AND TO—AND WHICH IS MORE IMPORTANT
Exodus, the second book of the Bible, is a record of events that relate to the Israelites, or Hebrews, during their slavery in Egypt and their exodus from that slavery into the wilderness under Moses' leadership. Moses is the dominant figure of this book. He was a son of Hebrew slaves and was trained for forty years to become a prince of Egypt, followed by forty years of wilderness training as he cared for Jethro's sheep. He then spent forty years leading his people from slavery, welding them into a nation, and leading them toward the Promised Land.

Moses wrote the book of Exodus during the time that he led the Israelites through the wilderness, between 1450 B.C. and 1410 B.C. During this

90

>

What
Everyone
Should
Know
about
the
Bible

same time, he also wrote the books of Genesis, Leviticus, Numbers, and Deuteronomy while this information was fresh, for the author is also the main person in the books, and he was involved in its events.

Exodus is the story of an escape, springing from a trap called slavery and escaping from a land of bondage. Much of Exodus tells how the people of Israel got away from Egypt, how God led them out of their miserable conditions with stunning miracles. It is the story of Moses, God's chosen leader, and the Israelites, God's rebellious people. It's hard to lead several million rebellious people through uncharted wilderness!

More than escape *from* something, the theme of Exodus is escape *to* something. Merely leaving Egypt was not enough. What were they to do then? Exodus does not end on the safe side of the Red Sea. In a real sense, the story of Exodus begins on this "safe shore," for their new journey with God had just begun. The people of Israel had escaped from slavery to a place where God would mold them into a new nation with new laws and a new relationship with him. The first third of Exodus is about escape *from* bondage in Egypt. The last two-thirds is about escape *to* a place of being set apart as God's chosen people.

If we're truthful with ourselves, every one of us wants to escape from something. Something has become our prison. We want out, but we don't have a Moses to lead us. We may be tempted to think we don't have a God to rescue us.

Perhaps it is a health problem, a house you hate, a husband or wife who you think is unreasonable, children who don't obey, a boss who doesn't appreciate you, the mood of the country, or something that is squeezing your lifestyle. If only you could escape from that something! Many years after the Exodus, the prophet Jonah tried to escape from God's calling to go to Nineveh and found himself in a prison of sorts—in the midst of a great storm at sea, surrounded by angry sailors, and about to sink in deep waters. Knowing that the storm was the result of his disobedience, he asked the sailors to toss him into the raging sea. Jonah had gone from the frying pan into the fire or, more accurately, from a storm-battered ship into the stormy sea. At that moment, the ship looked quite good—better than it ever had. What he didn't know was that, by God's provision, a giant fish was ready to swallow him up.

If you and I learn one lesson from Exodus, it is this: The people of Israel desperately needed Moses, but Moses and his people needed God even more—to lead them from somewhere and to somewhere. Without God, the book of Exodus would be a story of disaster. The more difficult things became, the more the people needed the Lord to help them.

Are you trying to escape *from* something? Don't leave without God to guide you. Are you trying to escape *to* something? Don't go there without God to guide you. The Promised Land has no promise without the Promiser.

One of the most powerful and poignant *froms* is leaving this earth when we die. At the moment of death, *to* becomes infinitely more important than *from*. So it is throughout all of life. Once you have had an exodus from somewhere, pay special heed to where you are heading.

Moses' basket was made of papyrus When Moses' mother, Jochebed, hid him from Pharaoh's soldiers, she made a reed basket, sealed it with pitch, and set it among the reeds along the bank of the Nile River. These reeds were called bulrushes, a hollow plant that grew in abundance along the Nile. Baskets were made by weaving strips of the papyrus that came from them, sometimes in beautiful patterns.

Papyrus also was used to make scrolls on which important things could be written. Strips of the papyrus pith, or core, were laid in one direction, and other strips were laid across them. They were beaten and bonded together and made into long scrolls. Many Bible books were written on scrolls such as these. Other scrolls were made from the skins of animals.

Who was the princess who raised Moses? One of the mysteries surrounding Moses' childhood is the Egyptian princess who found him and raised him as her son. Why did she do this? Pharaoh had a death warrant on all Hebrew baby boys. It made no sense for a princess then to raise a Hebrew boy as a possible heir to the throne of Egypt. Why would the king permit it?

One theory is that the princess was Hatshepsut. Hatshepsut was the daughter of Thutmose I, whose son Thutmose II took over the throne when his father died. Hatshepsut and Thutmose II were half brother and half sister, with the same father but different mothers. They married, but had no children, so Thutmose II, the princess's half brother and husband, wanted to make the son of a woman in his harem the heir apparent.

If this happened, Hatshepsut's power would be taken from her and her descendants, so she may have considered this baby among the bulrushes as a gift from the gods, the gift of a son whom she could raise as her heir and thus assure her future power.

Later, when her half brother Thutmose II died, she seized the throne and ruled Egypt for twenty-two years. Then Moses was even more in line for the throne. He would very likely have been the next pharaoh if he had not murdered the Egyptian slave master.

There is another theory that Moses grew up under the reign of Ramses II. If that is true, Merneptah was the pharaoh of the Exodus.

The motion picture *The Ten Commandments* shows Moses growing up under Seti, father of Ramses II. Seti treated both Ramses and Moses as sons, but seemed to favor Moses. If this theory is true, Moses would very possibly have become Seti's successor, the next pharaoh instead of Ramses.

92

>

What
Everyone
Should
Know
about
the

Bible

These are all theories, of course. No one knows for sure what the true answer is.

Moses' life in three equal parts For the first forty years of his life, Moses had the finest training Egypt could offer, and this equipped him to lead the Israelites after the Exodus. The next forty years were spent near Mount Sinai as a common shepherd, tending the flocks of his father-in-law, Jethro. This was the school of the wilderness, which also gave him important training for leading the Israelites through the wilderness. The next forty years were spent leading his people from Egypt toward the Promised Land. In a very real sense, it took eighty years to train Moses for a forty-year job.

Pharaoh lost more than slaves The economy of Egypt had become dependent on the Hebrew slaves. They were farmworkers, poultry dressers, household servants, bakers, metalworkers, glassworkers, carpenters, artisans, musicians, leather makers, and most of all, bricklayers who constructed the vast cities Pharaoh demanded. Suddenly, overnight, all of this was lost. Not only that, but the ten plagues devastated Egypt. To hurry the Hebrews from the land, the Egyptians had given them vast treasures. Altogether, their loss was cataclysmic!

The Red Sea or the Reed Sea? Some scholars believe that a more likely site for the Israelites' crossing is the Reed Sea (also called the Papyrus Lake or Papyrus Marsh), rather than the body of water known today as the Red Sea. The Red Sea is 100 miles across, 1,350 miles long, and 7,200 feet deep.

The omer and ephah Some Bible versions tell us that the Israelites gathered manna into containers that held one omer per day (Exodus 16:16). How much was that? There were ten omers in an ephah (Exodus 16:36), which was about two-thirds of a bushel. So an omer was about 6.7 percent of a bushel.

These former slaves were wealthy. How did this happen? When the Tabernacle was built, the people gave millions of dollars in precious goods to help its construction. Where did former slaves get that kind of wealth? In Exodus 12:35-36, we read that after the tenth plague, the death of every Egyptian family's firstborn son, the Egyptians were frantic to get the Hebrews out of their land. To hasten them on their way, they gave the Hebrews vast riches and urged them to leave.

A washbowl made of mirrors? The enormous bowl in which the priests washed at the Tabernacle was called the laver. It was made of bronze. To make it, the women of Israel gave up the highly polished bronze mirrors that the Egyptian women had given them to hurry them out of the land of Egypt. There was no glass for mirrors in those days, but brass mirrors were highly polished reflectors. Their image was poor, but they were better than nothing.

Amalekites—the first enemies in the wilderness When the Israelites entered the wilderness, it wasn't long before they were attacked by a band of Amalekites. This was the newly freed slaves' first military adventure. Who were the Amalekites?

Amalek was the father of the Amalekites, just as Jacob, or Israel, was the father of the Israelites. Amalek was a grandson of Esau, Jacob's brother. The Amalekites were nomads who roamed the land looking for water and pasture for their flocks and herds. They added to their wealth by engaging in fierce raids, such as the one they attempted against Israel (Exodus 17:8-16).

The Amalekites' military strategy angered the Israelites. In any caravan, there are some, usually the weak or slow, who linger near the back of the line. The Amalekites knew this and attacked at the rear of their enemies' columns. Some tribes would leave these old, weak, or slow ones to their fate, but not the Israelites.

It would be six hundred more years before the Amalekites vanished from the earth.

Discovering My Purpose from God's Plan

1. *God specializes in things thought impossible.* If you need a path through a sea of difficulty or despair, God can part the waters and let you cross.
2. *A year of service may demand two years of training.* Moses trained eighty years for a forty-year work. The more significant the work, the more demanding the training may be.
3. From *may be less significant than* to. What you escape from may be less important than where you go from there. The Hebrews escaped from life-threatening slavery to a life-threatening wilderness.
4. *Your "Promised Land," the dream you have for the future, may lie on the other side of a wilderness.* Your "land of milk and honey" may be attained only by a long journey through hardship.
5. *Leadership first requires followership.* Moses could not lead the Israelites until he first served his father-in-law, Jethro, for forty years as a common shepherd.
6. *Lowly service may require royal training.* Moses' training as a prince was necessary before he could become the shepherd of a disgruntled band of former slaves.

94
>
What
Everyone
Should
Know
about
the

Bible

7. *Abundant receiving should motivate abundant giving.* We should give to God abundantly. The Israelites had received vast treasures from the Egyptians, and they gave so much for the Tabernacle that Moses had to tell them to stop.

8. *Delegate to others what they can do so that you can do what you must do.* This was Jethro's advice to Moses, and Moses listened to him.

The Long Way Home

Forty Years of Wandering

Characters:
Aaron (Moses' brother); Balaam (a false prophet); Balaam's donkey (who talked to Balaam); Balak (a Moabite king); Caleb (a good spy); Joshua (a good spy and Moses' successor); Korah (Moses' cousin who rebelled against him); Miriam (Moses' sister); Moses; Og (king of Bashan); Sihon (king of the Amorites)

Time Period:
The wilderness wanderings

Dates:
Approximately 1445 B.C. to 1406 B.C.

Where Scene 8 of the Big Story Can Be Found:
The books of Leviticus, Numbers, and Deuteronomy

In Scene 8, Find the Answers to These Questions:
Where did two million people in a barren desert find food and water?
What did a talking donkey say? Why did it talk?
What brought an advance in women's rights?
Who was the only person that the Lord buried?

Look for this in Scene 8
> After a powerful confrontation, the ground opened up and swallowed three men, their families, and their possessions.
> A bunch of grapes was so large that it took two men to carry it.
> Looking at a bronze snake cured snakebite.

The Big Story So Far

Building a nation from a bunch of slaves

Before the Israelites could leave the area of Mount Sinai, several essential tasks had to be completed. The people of Israel were only a few weeks removed from slavery. They needed to be trained to fight battles, for there would be more battles before long on the way to the Promised Land. A few military defeats would demoralize the entire camp. These people needed unity as a nation, and that had barely begun. There was much to be done in a short time.

A nation must have a constitution, or a codified system of laws. God's nation needed a codified system of God's laws. Through Moses, God gave these laws to his people at Mount Sinai.

God's nation also needed centralized worship with a place, a process, and a priesthood. Through Moses, God gave these to his people at Mount Sinai, including elaborate plans for the Tabernacle, the portable tent where God would dwell among his people. Offerings were established (Leviticus 1–7), Aaron and his sons were consecrated to the priesthood (Leviticus 8), and the Israelite feasts and festivals were appointed (Leviticus 23).

A census was needed to learn how many men of military age were available. The census showed 603,550, which was a rather formidable army. The Levites were numbered, the whole community dedicated them, and Moses and Aaron installed them into their roles as God's representatives (Numbers 8:5-26).

It was moving day, but where were they going?

With these things in place, it was time to move on toward the gateway of the Promised Land, a place called Kadesh-barnea. Two years had passed, and it was time for the Israelites to invade the land and possess it.

Along the way to Kadesh-barnea, the people began to complain again about their hardships. The Lord was angry at this and sent fire among them. When the people screamed for mercy, the fire stopped.

Before long, the foreign rabble that traveled with the Israelites began to incite a riot.

They stirred the people to think of the foods they had left behind in Egypt—the cucumbers, melons, leeks, onions, and garlic. These may not be highest on your list for your next grocery shopping, but the Israelites sorely missed these foods in the wilderness.

The Lord was angry, but he promised Moses that he would send a month's supply of meat to his people in the wilderness. Moses was shocked. A month's supply of meat for two million people? Where would God get all this meat?

The Lord sent a wind that brought quail from the sea and let them

98

>

What
Everyone
Should
Know
about
the

Bible

descend into the camp. The Israelites had meat, but the Lord also sent a plague to punish them.

As if that weren't enough, Miriam and Aaron, Moses' sister and brother, began a campaign of criticism. For that, the Lord made Miriam a leper. Moses begged God to spare Miriam, and after seven days she returned to the camp, and the Israelites moved on to Kadesh-barnea, the doorstep of the Promised Land.

First, they would send twelve spies, one from each of the twelve tribes, to scout the land.

The report was devastating. Ten of the twelve gave a bad report—the city walls were too high, the cities were too great, there were giants in the land, and there was too much to accomplish with too few resources. Two of the twelve pressed Israel to trust God for victory and possess the land.

The report of the ten prevailed. The Israelites did not trust God to give them victory. For their lack of trust, God condemned them to wandering in the wilderness for thirty-eight more years. That generation would die in the wilderness, and none of them except Joshua and Caleb, the faithful spies, would enter the Promised Land.

The day the earth swallowed some people

One day, a Levite named Korah and 250 other leaders, including Dathan and Abiram, rebelled against Moses. They demanded that Moses share the leadership role with them. They did not believe that the Lord had chosen Moses to be their sole leader.

The next day there was a great confrontation. These people had stirred up the whole camp, so everyone was there to watch. "Moses said, 'This is how you will know that the LORD has sent me to do all these things that I have done. . . . If these men die a natural death, or if nothing unusual happens, then the LORD has not sent me. But if the LORD does something entirely new and the ground opens its mouth and swallows them and all their belongings, and they go down alive into the grave, then you will know that these men have shown contempt for the LORD'" (Numbers 16:28-30). Moses had barely finished speaking when the ground opened under the tents of Korah, Dathan, and Abiram and swallowed them, their families, and all their possessions.

These people never seemed to learn their lesson. The very next morning, they began complaining that Moses and Aaron had killed their people. At that moment, a plague began to spread among the Israelites. Moses sent Aaron with an incense burner among the people, and wherever he went, he divided those who lived from those who died. That day, 14,700 people died of the plague.

Because of all the murmuring against Aaron, under the Lord's direction Moses set up a test. Each of the twelve tribes would lay a staff in the Tabernacle in front of the Ark of the Covenant. Aaron's staff would represent the tribe of Levi. Buds would form on the staff of the tribe and person of God's choosing. By the next morning, Aaron's staff had not only buds but sprouts, blossoms, and even ripe almonds!

Water problems in the wilderness

One year, in the early spring, the Israelites had another water problem. They had arrived in the wilderness of Zin and were camped at Kadesh, but there was no water to drink. Once more, the people blamed Moses.

The Lord told Moses to command water to come from a great rock, but Moses tried to get the credit for the miracle. He struck the rock twice with his staff. Water came, and so did the Lord's punishment. For his disobedience, Moses could not lead the people into the Promised Land. Another man would do it.

A healing snake

The Israelites moved on to Mount Hor. There Aaron died, and his son Eleazar became high priest in his place.

About this time, the Canaanite king of Arad attacked the Israelites and took some prisoners. Then the Israelites attacked and destroyed all of the nearby towns.

Once again, the people began to complain about their wilderness lifestyle. As punishment, the Lord sent poisonous snakes among them. The people repented and cried out to the Lord for help. The Lord told Moses what to do. "So Moses made a snake out of bronze and attached it to a pole. Then anyone who was bitten by a snake could look at the bronze snake and be healed!" (Numbers 21:9) So the bronze snake became the antidote to snakebite.

The Israelites sent word to King Sihon of the Amorites, asking for safe passage through his land. Instead, the king sent an army. The Israelites conquered the Amorites and occupied their land. Then another king, Og of Bashan, attacked the Israelites. Israel also conquered them and occupied their land.

Balak, Balaam, and the talking donkey

Balak, a Moabite king, saw what had happened to the Amorites, and he and his people were terrified. Balak sent messengers and riches far away to a man named Balaam, asking him to come and curse the Israelites. That night, God warned Balaam not to go with the messengers, so they returned home to Balak with the news.

Balak tried again. He sent a larger and more distinguished group of messengers to Balaam who told him that he could pretty well name his price. This time, the Lord permitted Balaam to go with them.

God was not pleased with Balaam, however, so he sent an angel

100

>

What
Everyone
Should
Know
about
the

Bible

to block Balaam's way with a drawn sword. Balaam did not see the angel, but his donkey did. The donkey was terrified and bolted into a field. Balaam beat the donkey and forced it back onto the path, and the donkey saw the angel again. This time, the donkey tried to squeeze through a narrow place and hurt Balaam's foot. Balaam was furious and beat the donkey again.

The third time the donkey saw the angel with a drawn sword, it lay down under Balaam. Enraged, Balaam beat the donkey again with his staff.

Then the Lord let the donkey speak to Balaam. "Why have you beat me three times?" it asked Balaam.

"You have made me look like a fool!" Balaam answered. "If I had a sword with me, I would kill you!"

"Have I ever done anything like this before?" asked the donkey.

"No," Balaam admitted.

Then the Lord let Balaam see the angel with his sword drawn, ready to kill him.

"Three times your donkey saw me and ran away," said the angel. "Otherwise, I would have killed you and spared the donkey."

"I have sinned," Balaam cried out.

"Go with these men," said the angel, "but say only what I tell you to say."

Balaam went with the messengers, and when Balak asked him to curse the Israelites, he blessed them instead. Balak was furious. This happened three times.

"Go back home!" Balak demanded.

Along the way, the Lord commanded Moses to number the people again. This time there were 601,730 men of military age. There were 23,000 Levites who were dedicated to serving the Lord.

A new day for women's rights

One day, the five daughters of Zelophehad brought a petition to Moses. Their father had died leaving five daughters but no sons. They asked for the inheritance from their father that sons would normally get. Moses took their case to the Lord. The Lord told Moses to give them their request and to establish a new law: If a man died and had no son, his inheritance should be given to his daughters. This was one of the first signs of rights for women that were equal to those for men.

Finishing a forty-year job

At last, the time came for Moses to appoint his successor. His work of leading the Israelites through the wilderness was coming to a close. The Lord told Moses to climb to the top of a high mountain and to look out over the Promised Land. Moses was also to take Joshua with him and commission him to be his successor. Then Moses presented Joshua to the people as their new leader.

Moses had one last job to do before he died. "Take revenge on the Midianites for leading [the Israelites] into idolatry," the Lord told Moses. So Moses mustered twelve thousand men, a thousand from each of the twelve tribes, and went to war against Midian. All five Midianite kings, as well as Balaam, died in that battle, and great amounts of plunder were brought to the Tabernacle as an offering to the Lord.

The Israelites were moving along the area east of the Jordan River toward the point of conquest at Jericho. As they passed through the lands to the east, the tribes of Reuben and Gad saw rich pasturelands that were ideally suited to their large flocks and herds. They approached Moses and the other leaders and asked if they could have this land as their share of the conquest.

"Are you trying to get out of your part of conquering the rest of the land?" Moses demanded. But the leaders of Reuben and Gad promised that they would help the other tribes conquer the land, then return to claim their part. So Moses granted their request, as long as they kept their word to help the other tribes in their conquest.

While the Israelites were camped east of the Jordan River preparing to enter the Promised Land, Moses gave them extensive counsel now found in the book of Deuteronomy. There are four parts: (1) Deuteronomy 1:1–4:43, a Review of God's Care for His People; (2) Deuteronomy 4:44–29:1, Principles for Godly Living; (3) Deuteronomy 29:2–30:20, a Call for Commitment to God; and (4) Deuteronomy 31:1–34:12, the Change in Leadership.

Moses said to the people, "I am now 120 years old, and I am no longer able to lead you. The LORD has told me, 'You will not cross the Jordan River.' But the LORD your God himself will cross over ahead of you. He will destroy the nations living there, and you will take possession of their land. Joshua will lead you across the river, just as the LORD promised." (Deuteronomy 31:1-3).

Moses called for Joshua and challenged him to follow the Lord as he assumed the leadership of Israel. He wrote down the law and gave it to the priests, then took Joshua with him to the Tabernacle and commissioned him to be Israel's new leader. It was then time for Moses to die.

Following the Lord's instructions, Moses climbed to the top of Mount Nebo, east of the Promised Land. The Lord showed him the length and breadth of the land. Then Moses died there on the mount, and the Lord buried him. No one knows where to find his grave.

Moses finished the work God gave him to do. For the first forty years of his life, he trained as a prince of Egypt. During the next forty years,

102

>

What
Everyone
Should
Know
about
the

Bible

SCENE 8

The
Long
Way
Home

<

103

he trained as a shepherd in the wilderness. The last forty years were spent leading the Israelites from Egypt to the threshold of the Promised Land. Moses had eighty years of training for forty years of work.

Questions You May Be Asking

How did the book of Leviticus get its name?

Leviticus was named for the Levites, the 22,000 males of the tribe of Levi from which Moses and Aaron came. These men were responsible for leading the people in worship and maintaining the Tabernacle and the systems of worship. There were 8,580 Levites ready and available to serve in the Tabernacle. That's quite a church staff, isn't it?

Why is the book of Leviticus in the Bible?

Leviticus is a guidebook for the priests and Levites of Israel. It outlines their duties in leading worship. It was also a guidebook for all Israelites concerning holy living for a holy God.

How did the book of Numbers get its name?

The band of Israelite slaves became a nation with laws, rules, a system of worship, a priesthood to help them, and a Tabernacle as the dwelling place of God among them. It was time to move on toward the Promised Land. With God's help and proper military training, they could realize their dream.

First there was a census to see how many fighting men they had. This was a numbering of the people, and from that came the name of the book of Numbers. The census showed that their nation of about two million people had 603,550 men of military age.

What were the main events of this wilderness wandering until the Israelites first reached the Promised Land?

Day by day the Israelites moved from Mount Sinai toward the doorstep of the Promised Land at Kadesh-barnea. Each time they moved, they followed a prescribed method of packing the Tabernacle for transport. Each time they stopped, they followed another procedure for setting it up.

This leg of the journey was not a happy one. It was marked by murmuring, criticism, rebellion, and lack of trust in God and Moses. The people had seen numerous awesome miracles, but still they complained and rebelled.

Four main events mark this leg of the journey: (1) leaving Mount Sinai; (2) the appointment of seventy new leaders; (3) Miriam, Moses' sister, getting leprosy when she rebels against Moses; and (4) twelve spies being appointed at Kadesh-barnea to report on the Promised Land.

When the Israelites reached the Promised Land at Kadesh-barnea, why didn't they go in?

It is not surprising to see how this complaining, rebellious band behaved at Kadesh-barnea, the doorstep of the Promised Land. The land was theirs, promised by God. All they had to do was to go in and claim it through military action.

To determine what was there, twelve spies were appointed, one from each of the twelve tribes (none from the tribe of Levi, and one each from the half tribes of Joseph—Ephraim and Manasseh). They were to scout the land and give a report.

This report was a downer. Ten of the spies reported that the residents were too big, the city walls too high, and the job too great for the Israelites. Since the people believed that the job was too big, their God became too small for them, and they refused to go in. For that, they had to wander another thirty-eight years before coming to another doorstep to the Promised Land. All the present generation had to die first; their children would go in, but they would not.

What does *Deuteronomy* mean?

Deuteronomy means "second law," suggesting a second presentation of the law found in Exodus, Numbers, and Leviticus. It wasn't a second law, of course, but a second presentation of the same law. Deuteronomy contains the presentation of the law and Moses' final instructions to his people on the eve of entering the Promised Land.

 Great Events of This Time

1. **God establishes the offerings** (Leviticus 1–7).
2. **Aaron and his sons are consecrated** (Leviticus 8).
3. **Aaron makes sacrifices** (Leviticus 9).
4. **Aaron's sons burn an unholy incense offering to the Lord, and they die** (Leviticus 10).
5. **The Israelite feasts and festivals are appointed** (Leviticus 23; Deuteronomy 16:1-17).
6. **The Israelites stone a man for blaspheming God** (Leviticus 24:10-23).
7. **The men of war are numbered** (Numbers 1).
8. **The Levites are numbered and given their duties** (Numbers 3).
9. **Israel's leaders present the dedication gifts and offerings** (Numbers 7).
10. **The Israelites install the Levites** (Numbers 8:5-26).
11. **The Israelites keep the Passover, and some men who are ceremonially unclean are allowed to participate** (Numbers 9:1-14).
12. **The people leave Mount Sinai** (Numbers 10:11-36).
13. **The Israelites complain and suffer a plague of fire** (Numbers 11:1-3).

104

>

What
Everyone
Should
Know
about
the

Bible

SCENE 8

The
Long
Way
Home

<

105

14. **God sends manna and quail in the wilderness, and Moses appoints seventy leaders** (Numbers 11:4-35).
15. **Miriam becomes leprous after she and Aaron criticize Moses** (Numbers 12).
16. **The twelve spies go into Canaan at Kadesh-barnea** (Numbers 13).
17. **The Israelites wander in the desert for forty years** (Numbers 14).
18. **Korah is rebellious** (Numbers 16:1-40).
19. **Aaron's rod buds, signifying that he is God's chosen priest** (Numbers 16:41–17:13).
20. **Moses disobeys God by striking the rock at Zin** (Numbers 20:1-13).
21. **Edom refuses passage to Israel** (Numbers 20:14-21).
22. **Aaron dies** (Numbers 20:22-29).
23. **Arad is defeated** (Numbers 21:1-3).
24. **Moses makes the bronze snake** (Numbers 21:4-9).
25. **Israel continues toward the Promised Land** (Numbers 21:10-20).
26. **Sihon and Og are defeated** (Numbers 21:21-35).
27. **Balaam's donkey talks to him** (Numbers 22–24).
28. **The Israelites have sinful relationships with the Moabites—Zimri and Cozbi are killed** (Numbers 25).
29. **Israel is numbered again—and God tells them how to divide the land** (Numbers 26).
30. **Zelophehad's five daughters receive their rightful share of land** (Numbers 27:1-11).
31. **Joshua is appointed as Moses' successor** (Numbers 27:12-23).
32. **The Midianites are defeated, and the army disobeys** (Numbers 31).
33. **The tribes of Reuben and Gad help the other tribes and settle east of the Jordan River** (Numbers 32).
34. **Moses appoints Joshua to lead the people. Moses writes the Book of the Law and places it beside the Ark of the Covenant** (Deuteronomy 31:7-29).
35. **Moses dies** (Deuteronomy 34).

Significant Dates of This Time

Circa 1445 B.C., God gives Moses the Ten Commandments.
Circa 1444 B.C., Israel camps at Mount Sinai, builds the Tabernacle, and takes the first census.
Circa 1443 B.C., Joshua sends twelve spies out from Kadesh-barnea into Canaan.
Circa 1407 B.C., Israel takes the second census, and Balaam prophesies.
Circa 1406 B.C., Joshua is appointed Moses' successor; Moses dies; the Hebrews prepare to invade Canaan.

Moses, Aaron, and Miriam are all prominent players in this scene of the Bible story. We have already shared their bios in the previous scene. The most colorful character in this scene is Balaam.

BALAAM

As the Israelites approached Canaan during their wilderness wanderings, the king of Moab grew frightened that they would attack and conquer his land as they had conquered other nearby lands. He sent a delegation to the north to persuade Balaam, a Midianite soothsayer, to come and curse Israel. At first Balaam refused, but then he went. Along the way, he was spared being killed by an angel when his donkey refused to pass a certain place in the road. When Balaam finally arrived, he refused to curse the Israelites as King Balak wanted. Balak was furious, but Balaam prophesied that Israel would conquer Moab and Edom. Later, Balaam tried to turn the Israelites from worshiping God and was killed.

Bible events in Balaam's life
1. Balak asks him to curse the Israelites.
2. On the way, an angel stops his donkey, and the donkey speaks to him.
3. He blesses Israel.
4. He tries to turn the Israelites from God and is killed.

What everyone should know about the book of Leviticus
RECONCILING IMPERFECT PEOPLE WITH A PERFECT GOD

While Moses and the people of Israel were camped at Mount Sinai, the Lord gave Moses the material we find in the book of Leviticus, which is something of a handbook for the priests and Levites. It presents their responsibilities as spiritual leaders of the Israelites and as custodians of the Tabernacle and the system of worship associated with it. Moses probably wrote this book while at Mount Sinai, around 1445 B.C., or possibly shortly thereafter as the Israelites made their way from Mount Sinai toward the Promised Land, sometime between 1445 B.C. and 1406 B.C.

WHAT IS THE CORE MESSAGE OF LEVITICUS?
HOW DOES IT RELATE TO YOU AND ME?

When Adam and Eve sinned in Eden, they were so ashamed that they hid from God. How could they talk with God now that they had the stain of sin? You and I have been trying to hide from God ever since. How could a holy God be personally involved with sinful people like us? Sin has made us spiritually unclean, so how could we ever draw close to a perfect, sinless God? How could he possibly love us and fellowship with us, or even tolerate us?

106

\>

What
Everyone
Should
Know
about
the

Bible

SCENE 8

The
Long
Way
Home

<

107

The Gospels and the story of Christ's redemption tell the complete story, but this reconciliation of sinful people with a holy God takes shape in the book of Leviticus.

Leviticus is a book about holiness, a holy God, and sinful people who strive to be holy. It is not about what we do in order to make ourselves acceptable to God, but about who God helps us to become so that we can be acceptable to him. The gospel story later reveals that we become Christlike, holy people, not by perfecting ourselves with religious activities, but by surrendering ourselves to Christ for his cleansing.

Since Leviticus was written more than fourteen hundred years before Jesus came, it could not tell the complete gospel story but could offer only a foretaste of it. The elaborate systems of sacrifice and the great feasts and festivals foreshadow forgiveness, atonement, redemption, and reconciliation. The sacrifices for sin point ahead more than fourteen hundred years to the once-and-for-all sacrifice for sin that Jesus made on the cross.

Do you long to walk and live with God, even though he is holy and you are not? Are you ever frustrated that God asks you to "be holy" (Leviticus 19:1-2), since you know it is impossible? Do you ever wonder where this holy God is when you hurt or when life seems to cave in? Do you ever think that he may be far beyond the farthest star in a place you can never reach? If you do, read Leviticus. You will begin to discover that the holy God who seems so far away is very near and very approachable.

The theme of Leviticus is holiness—the holiness of God and the holiness he wants you to achieve—not by your efforts, but by your surrender.

What everyone should know about the book of Numbers

GRATEFUL HEARTS

After the Israelites left Egypt, they made their way to Mount Sinai, a journey of only a few weeks. There, through Moses, God gave the law, including the Ten Commandments. He revealed the plans for the Tabernacle and established the priesthood and a system of worship. He gave this handbook to guide the Levites in their priestly responsibilities, and we now know it as the book of Leviticus. All of this took several months at Mount Sinai.

From Mount Sinai, God led the Israelites to Kadesh-barnea, their first doorway to the Promised Land and their first opportunity to enter it and possess it. This part of the journey, from Mount Sinai to Kadesh-barnea, was relatively short. The entire time from the beginning of the Exodus until they arrived at Kadesh-barnea was about two years.

Moses wrote the book of Numbers during the time of the wilderness wanderings, between 1443 B.C. and 1406 B.C. At Kadesh-barnea, he sent twelve spies into the Promised Land, and ten of them advised the Israelites not to go in. Their idea of God wasn't big enough for them to allow him to help them conquer the land. These Israelites were therefore condemned to wander the wilderness for thirty-eight more years.

The book of Numbers records the events from the time that the Israelites were at Mount Sinai through the entire wilderness wanderings until they camped across from Jericho, where they prepared at last to conquer the Promised Land. It takes its name from the numbering of the people near the beginning of the journey from Mount Sinai.

WHAT IS THE CORE MESSAGE OF NUMBERS?
WHAT DOES IT MEAN FOR YOU AND ME?

If you could ask for one gift today, would it be for a thankful heart? You know how repulsive an ungrateful heart can be. There is something of the giver in every gift, so an ungrateful heart depreciates not only the gift but also the giver. True giving always comes with the gift of love, and true receiving always reciprocates with loving gratitude. From a grateful heart, an even greater gift is given to the giver.

Exodus is the story of a giving God. He gave his people freedom from slavery; multiplied miracles to get them out of Egypt into a safe place; instituted the framework and charter for them to become a new nation; gave them his personal, glorious presence each day in the pillar of cloud and of fire; established a way for them to worship him; made daily provision for food in a land without food; and protected them from many dangers. He even gave them the promise of a land that they could call their own—a Promised Land. God's gifts in Exodus are stunning, and he was personally involved in every one of them. All he asked in return was for his people to follow him faithfully so he could care for them. He longed for their grateful hearts.

Numbers is the response of an ungrateful people. The more God gave, the more they grumbled and complained. The more love he showed, the more doubt and despair they exhibited. The more he poured his blessings on them, the more they heaped their curses upon him. Numbers is the record of God's giving to Israel as he led them from Mount Sinai to the doorstep of the Promised Land, a land he offered to them if they would take it. Numbers is the record of an ungrateful people who rejected God's offer and wandered another thirty-eight years in the wilderness.

You and I are tempted to stand on the sidelines of this drama and criticize these complainers. We can hardly tolerate such ungrateful people . . . until we see ourselves mirrored in them. How often each day do we show a grateful heart to a giving God? Are we thankful for each meal and his gift of food? Are we aware of his generosity each morning in his gift of the day? Are we grateful each evening for his blessings of that day? Do we worship in his house each Sunday? We can be thankful each hour as we reflect on his awesome catalog of gifts to us during the day.

If we learn anything from Numbers, let's learn to nurture a grateful heart—toward our giving God and toward others.

>

What everyone should know about the book of Deuteronomy

What
Everyone
Should
Know
about
the

Bible

LISTEN TO WORDS OF WISDOM

The forty-year journey through the wilderness was coming to an end. It was the eve of another opportunity for the people of Israel to enter the Promised Land. Thirty-eight years before, they had camped at another doorway

SCENE 8

The
Long
Way
Home

<
109

to the Promised Land. They had come through two years of miracles, with God leading, providing, and protecting them each mile of the way. God had offered them this rich land for their own if only they would go in and possess it, but they wouldn't do it.

These people had seen miracles that no other people had ever seen—miracles that only an all-powerful God could perform. They had not read about these miracles or heard stories about them, but had seen them with their own eyes, yet they rejected their miracle-working God. Now God was giving them a second opportunity. Once again, the Israelites could enter the Promised Land. Their previous rejection had cost them thirty-eight years in the wilderness. That entire generation had died in the wilderness during this time.

Now on the eve of their second opportunity, what did they need? Deuteronomy gives the answer. Their leader, Moses, gave them the wisest advice on earth at a crisis moment—obey God, trust him, choose his way, follow his directions, and possess his Promised Land. This is sage advice from a wise old man. Moses recorded this advice in the book of Deuteronomy just before his death in 1406 B.C. Joshua probably wrote the very end of the book after Moses' death.

WHAT IS THE CORE MESSAGE OF DEUTERONOMY?
WHAT DOES IT SAY FOR US?

You may be on the eve of something significant in your life. Perhaps you will soon finish school, get a new job, get married, have a baby, buy a house, buy a car, choose a new career, or search for a new church. Seek the sage advice of a wise counselor. Listen. Perhaps you will hear the same wisdom—obey God, trust him, choose his way, follow his directions, and possess his Promised Land.

Did You Know?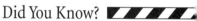

How Moses found groceries for two million people in the wilderness Stop for a moment and consider the challenge facing Moses. He had led the Israelites out of slavery in Egypt to Mount Sinai, where the Lord welded them together as a nation with laws, rules, regulations, and plans for a Tabernacle. Their overarching problem was finding food and water. This entire region was wilderness, and that meant no gardens, vineyards, grocery stores, farms, fields, wells, or much of anything else. If you were Moses, you would have to find food for two million people. The bottom line was this—without a miracle all two million, including Moses, would die of starvation and thirst. If you were Moses, would you trust the Lord enough to send groceries each day for two million people? It would take enormous faith, wouldn't it? But that's what we see in the life of Moses. He believed, and God provided.

The value of an oasis In a wilderness, an oasis is like heaven on earth. Usually, it is a place of abundant water, quite unlike the dry desert region around it. Beautiful palm trees often grow in an oasis and offer shade from the desert heat. Imagine the delight of finding an oasis after traveling for days through a hot desert land without water!

In their wilderness wanderings, the Israelites found several oases. Usually they camped at an oasis for quite a length of time. Rephidim and Kadesh-barnea were two of the most prominent oases.

Moses and Aaron were Levites—but what were the Levites? Flash back to Jacob's wedding night. He had worked seven years to marry his beloved Rachel. Unknown to him, in the privacy of his tent that night, he consummated his marriage by making love to Rachel's older sister, Leah. The sisters were switched by their father, Laban. His excuse was, "It's not our custom here to marry off a younger daughter ahead of the firstborn" (Genesis 29:26).

Jacob was furious, but the deed was done. He was duped into marrying two sisters, not just his beloved. The Scriptures suggest that he really didn't love Leah and that he favored Rachel. The two sisters became competitive over who could have the most children by Jacob. Leah won, and one of her sons was named Levi.

More than four hundred years later, Moses, Aaron, and Miriam were born into a slave home to descendants of Levi. Members of the tribe of Levi were called Levites. In the system set up at Mount Sinai, the Levites were put in charge of religious activities, including the work of the Tabernacle. Through the years, they owned no tribal portion of the Promised Land, even after the conquest by Joshua, but were supported by the other tribes. The priests came from the tribe of Levi. Their job was to preserve the law and assist the high priest.

When Korah rebelled, it was especially sad, for he was a Levite rebelling against his first cousin, Moses.

Levites served from ages twenty-five through fifty, and then they ceased work and became overseers.

Snakes in the wilderness? When the people grumbled against the Lord, he sent a plague of poisonous snakes to punish them. Only by looking at a bronze snake that Moses made could they be spared from death. Is it correct that there really were snakes in the wilderness?

Two types of snakes inhabited the wilderness—the sand viper and the carpet viper. The carpet viper was insidious. It was a snake two feet long; it hid in the sand and struck suddenly without warning. For a while the victim felt no pain even though internal bleeding had begun. By the second or third day, the victim might feel fine, but that was the beginning of death. The "poisonous snakes" of Numbers 21:4-9 may have been either carpet vipers or sand vipers. Fortunately, not all wilderness snakes were poisonous.

110
>
What
Everyone
Should
Know
about
the
Bible

SCENE 8

The
Long
Way
Home

<

111

Both the Israelites and the Egyptians had great respect for snakes. Pharaohs often put images of cobras on their headdresses. The cobra was the national symbol of Egypt.

The Ark of the Covenant–a holy gold box Since the days of Moses, the Ark of the Covenant has captured the excitement and imagination of generations of people. Even Hollywood films have glamorized it. Why was it such a special box?

First, the design for the Ark came from the Lord. No other box in all human history has been personally designed by the Creator. Second, it must have been unusually beautiful. It was carved from acacia wood, a wood also used in dyes, perfumes, and medicines. It was covered with gold both inside and outside. Gold-plated poles were used to carry the Ark, and they were held in place through gold rings at each of the four corners of the Ark. Gold molding ringed the top of the Ark.

The Ark's lid was pure gold, not gold plate. It was called the mercy seat because it was a place where God offered mercy to his people for their sins. On the lid were two gold cherubim that faced each other with wings outstretched. It was said that God was present between their wings, so this added immeasurably to the aura of the Ark.

At first the Ark contained the original stone tablets with the Ten Commandments. Later, a jar of manna, a piece of Aaron's rod that had budded, and a copy of Moses' Book of the Law were put into the Ark.

The Ark was housed in the innermost part of the Tabernacle, and later the Temple, in the place known as the Holy of Holies, where only the high priest could go only once each year.

Moving day for the Tabernacle It was no small matter to move the Tabernacle. This very large tent was made with several thousand pounds of gold, silver, and bronze.

Moving day followed an exact procedure that the Lord planned. Only Levites could disassemble the Tabernacle, move it, and set it up again. Aaron and his sons were the only Levites who could cover the Ark with the inner curtain, then again with tanned goats' skins, and lastly with a blue cloth. The bronze altar was covered with purple.

The Levite clan of the Kohathites was in charge of carrying the Ark and its accompanying bundles. They could not see or touch the items, or they would die.

Another Levite clan, the Gershonites, was in charge of transporting the curtains and the tent. The Merarites, another Levite clan, carried the Tabernacle framework, including its boards, bars, bases, pegs, and cords.

The high priest's breastpiece–an ancient jewelry store The high priest's clothing was unique and quite elaborate. His main garment was an ornate robe of blue-and-white linen with gold bells and pomegranates around its hem. Over that was an apronlike covering called the ephod, fine linen cloth embroidered with blue, purple, and scarlet thread.

A nine-inch square called a chestpiece was worn on the high priest's chest. On it were four rows of jewels, with three in each row, to represent the twelve tribes of Israel. "The first row contained a red carnelian, a pale-green peridot, and an emerald. The second row contained a turquoise, a blue lapis lazuli, and a white moonstone. The third row contained an orange jacinth, an agate, and a purple amethyst. The fourth row contained a blue-green beryl, an onyx, and a green jasper. All these stones were set in gold filigree" (Exodus 39:10-13). All of these stones had gold settings. Imagine wearing all that as your everyday dress!

The wave offering and the heave offering Many offerings at the Tabernacle involved the sacrifice of an animal. In both the wave and the heave offerings, the meat of the animal was offered to God in movements that were somewhat alike but were called by different names.

After the prayer of repentance or praise, the fat of the sacrificial animal was burned on the altar. The priest removed certain parts and waved them toward the Lord in a gesture of offering them to him. Then he gave them to the owner of the animal to cook and eat as a family.

The priest kept a portion of the meat for himself. He heaved it, lifting up those pieces toward the Lord as a way of presenting them to him. Then the priest could eat his portion. All of this meat had to be eaten within two days or else burned, for it would otherwise become "unclean" or spoiled.

Discovering My Purpose from God's Plan

1. *Faith, not fear, should guide our decisions.* At Kadesh-barnea, the Israelites were guided by fear rather than faith in the Lord, and that cost them thirty-eight more years in the wilderness.
2. *The Lord will lead us to the doorstep, but he won't make us go through the door.* We must choose to do that. The Lord led the Israelites to the doorstep of the Promised Land at Kadesh-barnea, but the Israelites had to choose to go in. They chose to remain fearful outside.
3. *Impossible promises are no longer impossible when they are God's promises.* God promised meat in the wilderness for two million people, and it happened.
4. *Greatness is no excuse for disobedience.* Moses was the great leader of the Israelites, but he was also disobedient, and that cost him dearly. He was not allowed to go into the Promised Land.

112

>

What
Everyone
Should
Know
about
the

Bible

SCENE 8

The
Long
Way
Home

<

113

5. *We shouldn't assume that we can see everything with our natural eyes.* Balaam's donkey saw an angel in the road. Balaam the prophet didn't see it, so his donkey was more spiritually perceptive than he was. When a child knows God and we don't, it's time to become more childlike.

6. *Women's equality is not new to God. Ask the daughters of Zelophehad.*

7. *Don't ask a statesman to do a general's job or a general to do a statesman's job.* Moses was the right leader to lead the new nation, but he was not the one to lead the conquest of the land. Joshua was not prepared to do Moses' work, and Moses was not prepared to do Joshua's work. God chooses his leaders wisely.

8. *There is something of the giver in every gift, so an ungrateful recipient depreciates not only the gift but also the giver.* This is one message of the book of Numbers.

Conquest Winning the Land, Losing Their Souls

Characters:
Achan (who stole the spoils of battle and caused Israel's defeat); Eleazar (Aaron's son and a high priest); Joshua; Othniel (who defeated Kiriath-sepher)

Time Period:
The conquest of Canaan

Dates:
From about 1406 B.C. until 1375 B.C.

Where Scene 9 of the Big Story Can Be Found:
The book of Joshua

In Scene 9, Find the Answers to These Questions:
How did two million people cross a great river at flood stage?
How did the walls of a great city fall outward, not inward?
How could conquered people actually conquer their conquerors?

Look for this in Scene 9
> An entire nation was defeated because of one man's petty thievery.
> The Promised Land was divided among the tribes of Israel, but one tribe received nothing.
> Joshua and Jesus had the same name. What did it mean?
> The first city to be conquered in the Promised Land was eight hundred feet below sea level.
> One of the most important helpers in the conquest of the Promised Land was a prostitute who put a red rope in her window.

Looking back to look ahead

Forty years had passed since the people of Israel had left Egypt and slavery. The Lord had lead them daily by a cloud and nightly by a pillar of fire. Each day, they ate the manna he sent, miraculous food in a barren wilderness. They saw miracle after miracle—mighty deeds that only God could perform.

Thirty-eight years before, these Israelites were at the doorstep of the Promised Land at a place called Kadesh-barnea. All they had to do was to go in and possess the land. It was theirs because God had promised it to them. He did his part, and they had to do theirs.

Ten of the twelve spies who scouted the land painted a dismal picture—the walls were too big, the people too tall, the armies too great. They believed that they couldn't do it. Two of the twelve spies said that nothing is too big for God, but the Israelites listened to the ten and ignored the two. For that they had to wander for thirty-eight more years through the wilderness. The old and faithless generation would die off so that a new generation could enter the land.

Once more, the Israelites came to the doorstep of the Promised Land, this time near Jericho. Moses, the shepherd-prince who had led the people through the wilderness, was dead. Joshua, the warrior leader, had replaced him and was ready to lead his people in military conquest.

Once again, spies visited the Promised Land, this time at Jericho. They were discovered, but a woman named Rahab hid them and begged in exchange that they would show mercy to her and her family when the Israelites defeated Jericho. The spies promised Rahab that they would be spared but she must identify her house with a scarlet rope hanging from the window.

How did two million people get across a flooded river?

There was one technical problem. The Jordan River was at flood stage and Joshua had to lead more than two million people across it. Impossible! How could he do it? God came up with yet another miracle. As he had parted the Red Sea for the Israelites to leave Egypt forty years before, so he parted the waters of the Jordan River for all the Israelites to cross over into the Promised Land.

Conquering the unconquerable

The battle for Jericho was highly unusual. It was straight from God. Jericho was one of the oldest cities in the ancient world, and it was also one of the most highly fortified, with huge walls.

God's plan was that each day for six days, Joshua and his army had to circle Jericho, with seven priests marching before the Ark of the

116

>

What
Everyone
Should
Know
about
the

Bible

Covenant. On the seventh day, Joshua and the army had to march around Jericho seven times with the priests blowing their ram's horn trumpets. When the priests gave one mighty blast, the people had to shout with a mighty shout.

Joshua followed the Lord's orders exactly. When he did so, the walls of Jericho tumbled outward, not inward. The Israelite army rushed into the city and captured it, but they remembered the promise of the spies and spared Rahab and her family.

The rest of the book of Joshua is about the incomplete capture of the Promised Land. At the next battle, at Ai, Israel was soundly defeated. Why? The Lord told Joshua that someone had sinned by stealing things that belonged to the Lord. Directed by God through a process of elimination, a man named Achan was identified. He had stolen silver, gold, and a robe. After Achan and his family were destroyed, Joshua and his army were able to defeat Ai.

Military victory—and cultural defeat

Joshua made a sad mistake when a group of Gibeonites came to him in worn garments, pretending to be friends. Without asking the Lord, Joshua entered into a covenant with them to protect them. Then, too late, Joshua discovered that he had been deceived. The Gibeonites were spared, but they had to become woodcutters and water carriers for the Israelites. Even as servants, they had a negative influence on the land.

Joshua had further conquests in both southern and northern Canaan in the Promised Land. The land was divided among the tribes of Israel except for the Levites, who did not receive land because they served Israel spiritually. The other tribes had the responsibility of caring for their families.

The land was conquered, but incompletely. Many Canaanites remained. They had a desirable lifestyle with beautiful homes, art, jewelry, and clothing. They were something like us today—materialistic and pleased about it. So while Israel conquered the Canaanites militarily, the Canaanites defeated the Israelites culturally. Before long, Israel had adopted much of Canaanite culture. This would be Israel's undoing.

Questions You May Be Asking

What is the conquest?

The forty-year wandering through the wilderness and the long, long journey to the Promised Land were over. The Israelites who refused to enter the Promised Land thirty-eight years before at Kadesh-barnea were dead, along with their leader, Moses.

Joshua had been appointed as the new leader of Israel. Moses was a shepherd-statesman, the man for the job as the Israelites were shaped into a nation and made their way from slavery in Egypt to the threshold of the Promised Land. Then the people needed a military leader, someone to lead them in a military conquest of the land. Joshua was that man.

The book of Joshua is the story of Joshua and his leadership as the Israelites invaded and conquered the land of Canaan, the Promised Land. It is a dramatic book with ten exciting and miraculous stories. The conquest was the military effort to conquer the Promised Land that God had promised to the Israelites.

How completely did the Israelites conquer the land?

They conquered the land overall, but not thoroughly. For this incomplete conquest, they would become military winners but social and spiritual losers. In a sense, they gained the world they sought but lost their souls. Those whom they vanquished militarily conquered their conquerors socially and spiritually. The winners lost, and the losers won.

The problem came from living side by side with a culture that looked more desirable on the surface than their own. The Canaanites were remarkably like us today—financially strong and morally weak, culturally desirable and spiritually undesirable.

The victors, the Israelites, wanted both worlds—to claim the religion of the Israelites, but to practice the lifestyle of the Canaanites. It sounds strangely familiar, doesn't it? God commands us to be in the world but not of the world. When what we practice is not what we preach and what we preach is not what we practice, we have a conflict within our souls.

The military conquerors became the cultural and spiritual losers. It seems that the Israelites won the smaller battle and lost the greater battle. This is a great lesson for us today, isn't it?

▰▰▰▰ Great Events of This Time

1. **The Israelites enter the land of Canaan** (Joshua 1).
2. **Spies visit Rahab and escape on a scarlet rope** (Joshua 2).
3. **The Israelites cross the Jordan River with the waters miraculously held back; they build an altar of twelve stones** (Joshua 3–4).
4. **The Hebrew men are circumcised, and the manna stops** (Joshua 5:2-12).
5. **Joshua meets the commander of the LORD's army** (Joshua 5:13-15).
6. **The people dramatically battle for Jericho, and the walls miraculously fall outward** (Joshua 6).
7. **Achan sins and brings disaster to Israel** (Joshua 7).

118

>

What
Everyone
Should
Know
about
the

Bible

8. **They battle for Ai** (Joshua 8).
9. **The Gibeonites trick Joshua** (Joshua 9).
10. **The sun and moon stand still to give Joshua time to complete the battle** (Joshua 10).
11. **The Israelites finally conquer the land as Hazor is defeated** (Joshua 11).
12. **Hebron is given to Caleb** (Joshua 14:6-15).
13. **Othniel defeats Kiriath-sepher and wins Acsah** (Joshua 15:13-19; Judges 1:11-15).
14. **The Tabernacle is set up at Shiloh** (Joshua 18).
15. **The Promised Land is divided by lots** (Joshua 18:3-10).
16. **The tribes of Reuben and Gad are sent home after a dispute over an altar** (Joshua 22).
17. **Joshua renews God's covenant with the people** (Joshua 23:1–24:28).
18. **Joshua dies** (Joshua 24:29-31; Judges 2:6-9).
19. **Joseph's bones are buried, and Eleazar dies** (Joshua 24:32-33).

Significant Dates of This Time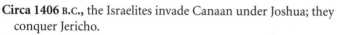

Circa 1406 B.C., the Israelites invade Canaan under Joshua; they conquer Jericho.

Circa 1406 B.C.–1375 B.C., they incompletely conquer Canaan and divide the land.

Heroes and Villains: The Stars in Scene 9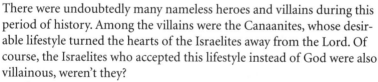

There were undoubtedly many nameless heroes and villains during this period of history. Among the villains were the Canaanites, whose desirable lifestyle turned the hearts of the Israelites away from the Lord. Of course, the Israelites who accepted this lifestyle instead of God were also villainous, weren't they?

Three individuals stand out during this period of the Bible. Their stories are given below.

ACHAN

When the Israelites first entered the Promised Land, they vowed to obey the Lord and utterly destroy the city of Jericho and all that was in it, except for Rahab and her family. Achan, a man from the tribe of Judah, secretly kept stolen goods and hid them in his tent, breaking his nation's vow. Israel's next attack, on Ai, resulted in defeat. The nation went through a long process to find the guilty person who caused this defeat. They discovered that it was Achan, who confessed and was executed by stoning.

Bible events in Achan's life
1. He secretly takes stolen goods from Jericho for himself and hides the items.
2. Israel is defeated by Ai because of his sin.
3. His sin is discovered by casting lots, and he and his family are stoned to death.

JOSHUA

Throughout the years from the Exodus until the entrance into the Promised Land, Joshua faithfully followed Moses' leadership as his assistant and military commander. Joshua is remembered as one of the two spies who recommended that the Israelites enter and conquer the Promised Land after only two years in the wilderness. He and Caleb were outnumbered, and with the decision not to invade, the Israelites were required to live in the wilderness for another thirty-eight years. When Moses died, Joshua became the leader of the Israelites and successfully entered the land with his people. The name *Joshua* is the Hebrew form of the Greek name *Jesus*. It means "Jehovah [God] is salvation," or "salvation."

Bible events in Joshua's life
1. He fights the Amalekites while Aaron and Hur hold up Moses' hands.
2. He goes with Moses part of the way up Mount Sinai.
3. He goes with eleven other spies to visit the Promised Land.
4. He gives a good report of the land and urges Israel to enter the Promised Land.
5. He is commissioned by Moses to lead the people of Israel.
6. God speaks to him after Moses' death and gives instructions about entering the Promised Land.
7. He sends spies to Jericho.
8. He leads Israel across the Jordan River.
9. Twelve stones are erected in the Jordan River as a memorial.
10. The Angel of the Lord appears to him.
11. He conquers Jericho by marching around it.
12. Ai defeats Israel because of Achan's sin.
13. He conquers Ai.
14. He reads the Book of the Law to the people of Israel.
15. The Gibeonites trick him.
16. He commands the sun to stand still.
17. He kills five Amorite kings who hid in a cave.
18. He conquers the Promised Land.
19. He gives Hebron to Caleb as an inheritance.

What
Everyone
Should
Know
about
the
Bible

20. At Shiloh, he casts lots for tribal locations.
21. He gives his final instructions to Israel.
22. He dies at the age of 110.

RAHAB

When Joshua's two spies arrived in Jericho, they were discovered. Rahab, a woman of Jericho, hid them on her roof and helped them escape. For her help, the spies pledged that she and her family would be spared in the coming conquest if she would hang a scarlet rope from her window. When Jericho fell to the Israelites, she and her family went to live among the Israelites. Rahab was a prostitute (Joshua 2:1).

Bible events in Rahab's life
1. She hides Joshua's two spies when they come to Jericho to investigate.
2. She implores the spies to save her from the destruction of Jericho and helps them to escape.
3. She and her family are saved by Joshua from the destruction of Jericho.

What everyone should know about the book of Joshua
A STORY ABOUT LOSING AND WINNING

Forty years had passed since God led the Israelites from their slavery in Egypt, through the Red Sea, and safely to the other shore. Pharaoh had been so utterly defeated that he would never bother his former slaves again. They were free! Their exodus from Egypt was complete. They were alone in the wilderness except for God. At Mount Sinai, God gave his people the charter to become a new nation with new laws. He was their new King, and he would lead them to a new land that he had promised them.

Two years passed after the Exodus from Egypt. The Israelites arrived at last at the doorstep of Canaan, the Promised Land. They could have it because God had promised it to them. They simply had to go in and take it, but they didn't believe God. Their concept of God was too small, so they rejected his promise. Because of that, they wandered in the wilderness for thirty-eight more years. All of that unbelieving, ungrateful generation had to die before a new generation could enter the Promised Land.

At the doorstep of the Promised Land once more, this new generation listened to Moses' sage advice. His counsel is written in the book of Deuteronomy. The people listened to it . . . and they obeyed.

Moses died, and Joshua led the Israelites into the Promised Land. He was not only a great military leader but also a devout follower of the Lord, so God gave him great victories. Joshua won battle after battle, and while he did not conquer the entire land, he did secure a homeland for Israel. The scoreboard said that he had won.

However, there was another side to the scoreboard. The military winner became the cultural and spiritual loser. Before long, the conquering Israelites became more and more like their Canaanite neighbors. They won the land and lost their souls. They won the lesser conquest and lost the greater battle.

If this sounds strangely modern, that's because it is. At no time in history have we been stronger economically and militarily. At no time in history have we been in more danger of losing our souls to our culture—not by conquest of culture but by default.

With God, we can gain personal victories, however, even though in the area of our finances, family, or friendships we may seem to be on the losing side. The scoreboard of daily living may say we are losing, but if we trust in the Lord, we may actually be winning. Undesirable circumstances may come at us aggressively, but our victory over them is not based on reactionary aggression. We can let God deal with those forces.

As Joshua learned, with God on your side, you will have victory regardless of what the scoreboard of life says. If you ignore God and feel secure in the land, as the Israelites did, you may gain the whole world and lose your own soul.

Except for the end of the book, which may have been written by the high priest Phinehas, Joshua wrote what we know as the book of Joshua. He wrote it sometime between the beginning of the conquest in 1406 B.C. and the beginning of the time of the judges in 1375 B.C., a period of about thirty-one years.

 ## Did You Know?

Walls too big The people of Jericho knew this and so did the Israelites. There was no way for the Israelites to conquer Jericho by climbing its walls. These walls were about twenty-five feet high and twenty feet thick. The archers of Jericho only needed to stand on top of the walls and pick the Israelites off as they tried to scale the walls. Somehow the walls must come tumbling down, but how could anyone knock down walls that high and that thick? The Israelites couldn't, but God could. All the Israelites had to do was to obey him and let him do the job. They trusted him and followed his directions exactly, and he not only caused the walls to fall down but caused them to fall outward, so that no one could ever say that the Israelites had knocked them inward. Impossible? That's where God begins, at the point of impossibility.

Jericho is eight hundred feet below sea level Jericho was, and still is, eight hundred feet below sea level. By contrast, only seventeen miles southwest, Jerusalem is three thousand feet above sea level. It is not surprising that the wealthy people of Jerusalem went to Jericho for their winter retreat, for while it was cold in the winter in Jerusalem, it was warm in Jericho. It was so warm that palms grew there in abundance, so Jericho was known as the city of palms (Deuteronomy 34:3).

The trumpets weren't like trumpets today When you think of a trumpet today, you think of a metal horn that is flared at the front end, with a

122

>

What
Everyone
Should
Know
about
the
Bible

detachable mouthpiece and valves to control the notes. The trumpets the priests blew were not like that. They were probably one of two kinds: (1) They may have been *chatsotserah*, which were long and straight and made of metal, but without valves. That kind of trumpet was like a bugle. (2) The more likely kind was the *shophar*, made from an animal horn and bent or curved in shape.

Trumpets were the most popular musical instrument at the time of Joshua, for they signaled a call to battle, proclaimed victory, informed people of important events, and announced the beginning of feasts. God chose the sound of a ram's horn to announce his presence at Mount Sinai (Exodus 19:16).

Booty, spoils, plunder In ancient warfare, victors won more than the battle. They often won vast treasures. Why would any soldier carry his wealth to the battlefield? The answer is simple. Where was there a safer place? Women and children were left at home, and a fierce fighting man would rather defend his wealth personally than trust that defense to his wife and children, so fighting men often carried much of their wealth into battle with them.

It was fair for the victor to strip all of this wealth from the dead bodies of the soldiers they had killed. It was called booty, spoils, or plunder. Much of that was in the form of gold pieces, silver, or precious stones. Weapons were also taken from the dead, and perhaps even clothing, for clothing was hard to get. If an invader conquered a city or town, booty might include the women and children, who became slaves. Some men were also taken as slaves if they were fit for hard labor.

It was considered a defilement for Israelites to touch a dead body, so Israelite soldiers who took booty had to be purified, and these rites lasted for a week. The soldiers had to stay outside the camp for a week, and they were sprinkled twice with "water of impurity."

Conquering Israelite soldiers did not keep all their booty. They shared it with other soldiers, with those who stayed home as guards, and with the priests for the Tabernacle treasury.

Sometimes the Israelite soldiers were forbidden to take booty, as at Jericho. Achan's sin was that he kept forbidden booty. For his sin, he and his family died.

The Anakim were giants When the Israelites had camped at Kadesh-barnea thirty-eight years earlier, Moses sent twelve spies into the Promised Land. The ten dissidents complained of giants, and said the Israelites were like grasshoppers next to them. That was exaggeration, of course, for the giants weren't that big.

The people of Kiriath Arba (modern Hebron) were giants known as the Anakim. Kiriath Arba was named for a man named Arba, the "father" of the Anakim. When Joshua began his conquest of the Promised Land, he gave that region to Caleb, and Caleb drove the giants into the land of the Philistines to the west. Caleb was the other spy who, with Joshua, pressed for Israel to go into the Promised Land when they were camped at Kadesh-barnea. The ten other spies were frightened by these giants and pressed equally hard for Israel not to go in. For that lack of faith in God, Israel had to wander another thirty-eight years in the wilderness.

At first, the Tabernacle was not taken to Jerusalem During the conquest of the land, the Tabernacle was set up at Shiloh. It was not erected at Jerusalem because the Israelites did not possess Jerusalem until David's reign, hundreds of years later. During the time of the conquest and the judges, Shiloh, not Jerusalem, was Israel's center of worship because that was the location of the Tabernacle.

Discovering My Purpose from God's Plan

1. *Manna was a miracle food from God, but so is your breakfast.* All food is a gift from God. The Israelites had daily manna in the wilderness, food that God miraculously gave them. You and I also have daily manna, for God miraculously gives us our daily food. Of course, we earn it, but starving people in other places would gladly work hard for food if it were available. Never take your food for granted. It is manna from heaven.

2. *The Lord is the Miracle Worker who sets aside or transcends the laws of nature.* He has that power because he established these laws. What the Creator created, he can manage or transcend.

3. *God is our Giver, but we must receive his gifts.* A gift is not truly a gift until it is received. For every giver, there must be a receiver. If we reject what he gives, his gifts are not ours to keep, no matter how much he wants us to have them. Gifts are truly gifts only when they are received. The Promised Land was God's promised gift to the Israelites, but they had to receive it. At Kadesh-barnea, they refused God's gift. At Jericho, thirty-eight years later, they accepted God's promise.

4. *"I can't" is an assault on faith. "I won't" is an assault on obedience. "I won't because I can't" is an assault on both faith and obedience.* The spies at Kadesh-barnea had failed to trust or obey God. The Israelites, at another doorstep to the Promised Land, had to reverse those decisions.

5. *God sometimes uses ungodly instruments for godly purposes.* Rahab the

What
Everyone
Should
Know
about
the

Bible

prostitute was an important link for the Israelites in helping them to conquer Jericho. Do not despise unholy instruments if God uses them for holy purposes. You and I are also unholy instruments, but we trust God to use us for holy purposes.

6. *We may lose, even when the scoreboard of life says we have won.* Or we may win, even when the scoreboard of life says that we have lost. The Israelites won militarily in Canaan, but the conquered Canaanites won culturally, infecting their conquerors with a pagan lifestyle. Military conquest was overshadowed by cultural and spiritual defeat.

Life without Rules
The Time of the Judges

Characters:
Abdon (the eleventh judge); Barak (Deborah's military leader); Boaz (Ruth's second husband); Deborah (the fourth judge); Delilah (a Philistine woman who betrayed Samson); Eglon (the king of Moab); Ehud (the second judge); Elimelech (Naomi's husband); Elon (the tenth judge); Gideon (the fifth judge); Ibzan (the ninth judge); Jabin (the king of Hazor); Jael (who killed Sisera, Jabin's general); Jair (the seventh judge); Jephthah (the eighth judge); Kilion (Chilion, Naomi's son); Mahlon (Naomi's son); Manoah (Samson's father); Naomi (Ruth's mother-in-law, the wife of Elimelech, and the mother of Mahlon and Kilion); Obed (the son of Ruth and Boaz, the father of Jesse, and the grandfather of King David); Othniel (the first judge); Ruth (a Moabite widow who married Boaz, Naomi's daughter-in-law, mother of Obed, grandmother of Jesse, and great-grandmother of King David); Samson (the twelfth judge); Shamgar (the third judge); Sisera (Jabin's military leader); Tola (the sixth judge)

Time Period:
From the time of the judges until Saul became the first king of Israel

Dates:
Circa 1375 B.C. until circa 1050 B.C., about 325 years

Where Scene 10 of the Big Story Can Be Found:
The books of Judges and Ruth

In Scene 10, Find the Answers to These Questions:
Who conquered an army of 120,000 with an army of 300?
Three women are powerful figures in this scene—Deborah, Jael, and Delilah. Who were they and what did they do?
Why did a great military leader have to sacrifice his daughter?

Look for this in Scene 10
> A battle was won by a woman with a hammer and a tent peg.
> A woman proposed to a farmer by lying at his feet.
> A man killed a lion with his bare hands.

 The Big Story So Far

The Canaanites were much like us
The Israelites had conquered the Promised Land and settled into it, but the conquest was not complete, so the Israelites had to live near their conquered neighbors. These new neighbors, the Canaanites, had a desirable lifestyle, much like the lifestyle we enjoy today. It was so attractive that the Israelites wanted it, too. It was an early version of "keeping up with the Joneses."

The Canaanites, who were conquered militarily, conquered the Israelites culturally. The Lord had commanded the Israelites to separate themselves from the Canaanites, but the Israelites, God's covenant people, did not listen. Their disobedience drove them deep into weakness and despair. They even worshiped the Canaanite gods Baal and Asherah.

The dawn of the day of judges—Othniel
The Lord raised up a new type of leader for Israel during these days, called judges. There were twelve of them, some of whom were good and some of whom were utter failures.

The first judge was Othniel. For eight years, the Israelites had been the subjects of a petty local king. When the Israelties finally cried out to the Lord, he sent Othniel to defeat the petty king. There was peace for the next forty years, and this was Israel's golden opportunity to follow the Lord.

Ehud, the left-handed warrior
The Israelites drifted into paganism again, so the Lord allowed King Eglon of Moab to defeat them and rule them for eighteen years. Once again, Israel cried out to the Lord for help and he sent a judge named Ehud, a left-handed warrior.

One day, Ehud tricked King Eglon when he delivered the tribute money. While Eglon, who was very fat, watched Ehud's right hand with the money, he failed to see the great dagger that Ehud pulled from his cloak with his left hand. Ehud drove the dagger so deeply into Eglon's belly that the king's fat swallowed the entire knife, even the handle. While his bowels were oozing out, Eglon learned a last-minute lesson that we should all learn—when our eyes are fixed on money, we may fail to see disaster lurking.

128
>

What
Everyone
Should
Know
about
the

Bible

Ehud escaped, called his people to arms, and defeated the Moabites, killing about ten thousand of their best warriors. The Israelites had peace for the next eighty years, which gave them another opportunity to follow the Lord.

When Ehud died, the Israelites drifted back easily into paganism, so the Lord allowed them to be conquered by King Jabin of Hazor and his army commander Sisera. These men had a formidable army with nine hundred iron chariots. For twenty years, they ruthlessly oppressed Israel. Then the Israelites cried out again to the Lord for help.

You're beginning to see the cyclical pattern, aren't you? Follow the Lord, become prosperous, grow spiritually weak, drift into paganism, become weakened from paganism, fall to the oppression of the enemy, suffer, cry out for the Lord's help, enjoy the Lord's rescue, follow the Lord for a while, become prosperous, and repeat the whole cycle. For the Israelites, this cycle continued throughout the time of the judges.

Victory with a hammer and a tent stake—a tale of two women

One day Deborah, a prophetess who had become judge of Israel, called for a military leader named Barak and told him, "Assemble ten thousand soldiers and go against Sisera and the Lord will give victory." Barak agreed to do this if Deborah would go with him. Deborah agreed, but told Barak, "Because you have asked this, you will not receive the honor for the victory, a woman will." Barak probably thought that Deborah was the woman who would receive that honor.

When Sisera learned that Barak had assembled ten thousand warriors, he sent his troops and his nine hundred chariots against Barak. When Barak attacked, Sisera and his troops panicked. This panic was, of course, a God thing. Sisera left his chariot and fled on foot. While he ran away, Barak killed all of his troops.

Sisera escaped to the tent of a woman named Jael, whose family was supposedly friendly to Sisera's king. Jael invited Sisera to come in and hide under some blankets. Sisera went to sleep from exhaustion and while he slept, Jael crept up to him with a hammer and a tent peg, which she drove through his head. When Barak came looking for Sisera, Jael showed him what she had done. From that time on, Israel became stronger against King Jabin until at last they destroyed him. They had another opportunity to serve the Lord.

Testing God with fleece

The old pattern followed once more. The Israelites drifted back again into paganism, so the Lord gave them over to the Midianites for seven years. The Midianites were cruel to the Israelites; they stole their crops and stripped the land bare. This reduced Israel to starvation.

Once more, the Israelites cried out to the Lord. The Lord listened and appeared as an angel to Gideon, to commission him to save the Israelites from destruction.

Gideon asked the Lord for two signs to confirm his calling. One night, Gideon placed a fleece on a threshing floor. If the fleece was wet the next morning and the ground was dry, it would be a good sign from the Lord. That is exactly what happened. The next night Gideon asked for the sign to be reversed. This time the fleece was dry and the ground around it was covered with dew. Now Gideon knew that the Lord was with him.

Gideon assembled an army and went to the spring of Harod, but the Lord told Gideon that he had too many soldiers. He had to fight with a smaller army. He had to send home all soldiers who were afraid—22,000 of them. The Lord again told Gideon that he had too many soldiers. He must ask them to drink from a spring. Those who bent down to drink, taking their eyes off their surroundings, had to go home. Those who cupped water in their hands while watching alertly around them, could stay. Now Gideon had an army of three hundred to fight the Midianite army of 120,000. Humanly speaking, this was impossible, but God specializes in things thought impossible. With God, nothing is impossible.

During the night, Gideon divided his army into three groups. Each man had a torch, covered by a pitcher, and a ram's horn. When they reached the edge of the sleeping Midianite camp, Gideon's men broke their pitchers and revealed the blazing torches. They blew their horns and shouted, "A sword for the LORD and for Gideon." Imagine what the Midianites thought as they rushed sleepily from their tents! They were surrounded, they thought, by thousands of alert warriors. The Midianites rushed around in a panic and began to fight each other (Judges 7:1-22).

Gideon's three hundred men chased the Midianites and defeated them. For the next forty years, Israel was at peace, and the Midianites never bothered them again.

Abimelech—crushed by a millstone

As soon as Gideon died, the old cycle began again. The Israelites turned once more to paganism. Gideon's son Abimelech came to power and killed seventy of his half brothers, Gideon's sons, so they could not rule in his place. It was a turbulent time for Israel, but it ended when a woman threw a millstone over a wall and crushed Abimelech.

Tola and Jair—not much to brag about

For the next twenty-three years, Tola was judge over Israel. Then Jair was judge for twenty-two years. About the only achievement of Jair was

130

>

What
Everyone
Should
Know
about
the

Bible

that his thirty sons rode around on thirty donkeys, and they owned
thirty towns. Quite an achievement!

After Jair's death, the old cycle began once more. The Israelites
turned to paganism and worshiped Baal and Asherah, wicked foreign
gods, as they abandoned the Lord. So the Lord gave them over to the
Philistines and the Ammonites, who treated them cruelly. This went
on for eighteen years. At last the Israelites cried out for the Lord to
help.

Jephthah—the man who sacrificed his own daughter

About this time, Jephthah, the son of a prostitute, became a great
warrior and led an army against the Ammonites. Then Jephthah made
a foolish vow. "If the Lord will give me victory, I will offer the first thing
that comes from my house when I return home." He probably assumed
that this would be a sheep or goat. The Lord gave him the victory, but
Jephthah's only daughter was the first to come from his house. His
vow and his victory were empty and painful because he had to offer
his daughter as a sacrifice. Beware of foolish vows, for the Lord expects
people to keep them, no matter how painful they are. Even Jephthah,
who wasn't a godly man, kept his vow despite the high cost. Jephthah
was Israel's judge for six years.

Ibzan, Elon, and Abdon—forgotten leaders

Ibzan was the next judge of Israel for seven years. Elon came next, for
ten years. Then for eight years Abdon was judge. His claim to fame
was that he had forty sons and thirty grandsons who rode on seventy
donkeys.

The strongest man alive—the weakest man alive

The cycle now began to repeat itself. Israel turned to paganism, so the
Lord handed Israel over to the Philistines for the next forty years. One
day, the angel of the Lord appeared to Manoah and his wife. They would
have a son, but he must not drink wine, eat forbidden food, or have his
hair cut. This was called a Nazirite vow. The son was Samson, probably
the most famous of the judges.

Samson was the strongest man alive and perhaps the strongest man
who ever lived. He was physically strong, but he was morally weak.
One day, he married a Philistine girl, much against his parents' wishes.
This led to a bizarre series of events until his wife's parents gave her to
another man. Samson punished the Philistines by tying the tails of foxes
together, attaching a torch between each pair, and then sending them
through Philistine grain fields.

The adventures of Samson and the Philistines would make a small
novel. One time, he killed a thousand Philistines with the jawbone of

a donkey as his only weapon. Another time, Samson carried away the large gates of Gaza.

Samson's undoing was his lust for Delilah, a Philistine temptress. Philistine leaders bribed her to find out the secret of Samson's strength. After several attempts, she finally drew the truth from Samson. It was his hair. Cut that and his strength was gone. So that is what the Philistines did. Then they gouged out Samson's eyes and took him to Gaza where they hitched him like an animal to a giant millstone and forced him to grind grain.

One day, the Philistines took blinded Samson to a great temple where they were holding a celebration. They wanted to taunt him before the three thousand Philistines gathered there, not realizing that his hair had grown again and with it his strength. Samson's last act was to pull down the temple, killing himself with the three thousand Philistines. Samson's life did not end well.

The rest of the book of Judges is a series of morbid stories that reflect the Dark Age of Israel. One man stole silver from his mother, a sorry episode in which people of the tribe of Dan willfully destroyed a town, raped a man's concubine, and fought against the tribe of Benjamin. It was truly a dark time for the nation of Israel. The measure of morality was what each person wanted to do. Personal desire overshadowed community purpose and need. Without rules, community chaos reigned.

Ruth—the brightest light of the times

Ruth is one of the bright lights of the Old Testament. Her story is thought to have taken place during the dark days of the judges, perhaps toward the end of that time and possibly during Samson's time. What a contrast there was between selfish Samson the Israelite leader and selfless Ruth the Moabite widow. Weakness with faithfulness shined brighter and left a more lasting legacy than strength with unfaithfulness.

Famine drove Naomi and her husband, Elimelech, from their home in Bethlehem to Moab. There they settled and Elimelech died. Later, Naomi's two sons married two beautiful Moabite girls. It must have been a heartbreak for her, but she accepted them as her daughters. Then Noami's two sons died. Now there were three widows. One of the most exemplary stories of the Old Testament is the tale of two of those widows.

With nothing left for her in Moab, Naomi decided to return to Bethlehem. Ruth and Orpah, the two daughters-in-law, decided to go with her. Naomi tried to persuade them to stay in Moab, where they could remarry and have an easier life. Orpah stayed, and that is the last we hear about her, but Ruth would not leave Naomi, and this is her story.

132

>

What
Everyone
Should
Know
about
the

Bible

She returned with Naomi to Bethlehem and gleaned in the grain fields of Boaz to support the two of them. Ruth became the model of a faithful, unselfish, generous person.

In time, Boaz noticed the beautiful Ruth. Naomi arranged for Ruth to show her willingness to marry this older man by lying at his feet one night in his grainfield. It was a strange way to do it, but it evidently worked, for Boaz married Ruth. Their son, Obed, became the father of Jesse, the father of the great King David. Ruth was David's great-grandmother, and she is also in the earthly genealogy of Jesus.

Questions You May Be Asking

Why is this scene called the time of the judges?

This is the approximately 350-year period from the time that the judges began to rule until Saul became Israel's first king. In principle, Israel was still a theocracy during this time, but most of the rulers or judges didn't do a very good job of letting God rule them. It was a theocracy in name only, not in practice.

What is the key message of Judges?

This simple but effective message is to obey God so that things will go well. Disobey God and things will not go well. When Israel obeyed God, he helped them, even in troubled times. When Israel disobeyed God, he left them to their own devices. It wasn't that God didn't want to help them, but their sin separated them from the God who could and would help.

Disobedience digs a deep gulf between a person or a nation and God. The greater the gulf, the greater the distance we put between God and ourselves. God is near to us, but we are not near to him. God is always on call, but we aren't talking or listening. He is ringing our doorbell, but we keep our door closed to him and pretend we're not at home.

What was life like during the time of the judges?

This is best summed up in the last verse of the book of Judges, "In those days . . . the people did whatever seemed right in their own eyes" (Judges 21:25). If that was the law of the land, you can imagine what life was like in Israel. Personal willfulness brings community chaos. Ultimately, what is best for us is best for me, and I am part of "us."

How many judges were there?

There were twelve judges: Othniel, Ehud, Shamgar, Deborah (with Barak), Gideon, Tola, Jair, Jephthah, Ibzan, Elon, Abdon, and Samson. Many Sunday school children have heard of Deborah and Barak, Gideon, Jephthah, and Samson. The others are strangers to most of us because they left small footprints.

Why is the story of Ruth included in this time of the judges?

Ruth probably fits into the history of this time, either during or slightly after this period. She is one of the brightest stars in the otherwise dark sky of Israel's history. Ruth was a faithful Moabite widow who refused to abandon her widowed mother-in-law, Naomi; instead, Ruth took care of her, gleaned in grainfields to get food for them both, and became a model of faithful conduct. "Wherever you go, I will go; wherever you live, I will live. Your people will be my people, and your God will be my God" is a keynote banner for Ruth, as for God (Ruth 1:16). With that statement and her actions she modeled godliness. Contrast the selfless faithfulness of Ruth with the selfish unfaithfulness of Samson, who possibly ruled Israel during Ruth's lifetime.

Ruth married Boaz and became the great-grandmother of King David, the greatest of all kings. Later, Jesus came in her bloodline. It was the blood of Jesus, inherited in part from Ruth, that was shed for our sins.

 Great Events of This Time

1. **Judah and Simeon fight for their territory** (Judges 1:1-21).
2. **Israel worships idols and fails to complete the conquest** (Judges 1:22–3:6).
3. **Othniel delivers Israel** (Judges 3:7-11).
4. **Ehud defeats Moab** (Judges 3:12-30).
5. **Deborah and Barak defeat Sisera, a Canaanite general** (Judges 4–5).
6. **God calls Gideon to lead Israel, and Gideon confirms the message with some fleece** (Judges 6).
7. **Gideon defeats the Midianites with an army of three hundred** (Judges 7).
8. **Gideon defeats Zebah and Zalmunna** (Judges 8:1-21).
9. **Gideon's last days** (Judges 8:28-35).
10. **Abimelech rules and Jotham gives a parable** (Judges 9).
11. **Jephthah makes a foolish vow** (Judges 11:29-40).
12. **Jephthah fights the Ephraimites** (Judges 12:1-7).
13. **Samson is born** (Judges 13).
14. **Samson gets married; he kills a lion and gives a riddle** (Judges 14).
15. **Samson sets Philistine fields on fire** (Judges 15:1-8).
16. **Samson fights the Philistines with the jawbone of a donkey** (Judges 15:9-20).
17. **Samson steals the gates of Gaza** (Judges 16:1-3).
18. **Delilah betrays Samson** (Judges 16:4-22).
19. **Samson pulls down a temple and dies with the Philistines** (Judges 16:23-31).
20. **Micah appoints his own personal priest** (Judges 17–18).
21. **The people of Benjamin are at war** (Judges 19–21).

134

>

What
Everyone
Should
Know
about
the

Bible

22. **Ruth goes home with Naomi** (Ruth 1).
23. **Ruth gleans in the fields of Boaz** (Ruth 2).
24. **Ruth and Boaz marry and have a son** (Ruth 3–4).

Significant Dates of This Time

1375 B.C., the judges begin to rule in Israel.
1367 B.C.–1327 B.C., Othniel rules as judge.
1309 B.C.–1229 B.C., Ehud rules as judge.
1209 B.C.–1169 B.C., Deborah rules as judge.
1162 B.C.–1122 B.C., Gideon rules as judge.
1075 B.C.–1055 B.C., Samson rules as judge.

Heroes and Villains: The Stars in Scene 10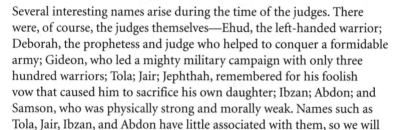

Several interesting names arise during the time of the judges. There
were, of course, the judges themselves—Ehud, the left-handed warrior;
Deborah, the prophetess and judge who helped to conquer a formidable
army; Gideon, who led a mighty military campaign with only three
hundred warriors; Tola; Jair; Jephthah, remembered for his foolish
vow that caused him to sacrifice his own daughter; Ibzan; Abdon; and
Samson, who was physically strong and morally weak. Names such as
Tola, Jair, Ibzan, and Abdon have little associated with them, so we will
focus here on the following:

DEBORAH

During the time of the judges of Israel, Deborah ruled the nation as the
fourth and greatest of the judges to that point. She was a prophetess
as well as a judge and set up court under a palm tree. The Canaanites
oppressed Israel during this period until Deborah summoned her military commander, Barak, and together they led the armies of Israel to a
great victory. This was the first such massive military campaign since
the conquest of the Promised Land 175 years earlier.

Bible events in Deborah's life
1. She sets up her court under a palm tree.
2. She and Barak defeat Sisera's army.
3. After their victory, she and Barak sing.

DELILAH

This Philistine woman was the downfall of Samson, a mighty warrior
and judge of Israel. Samson had unusual, God-given strength that was
associated with his long hair. Samson chose Delilah as his lover even

though she was one of the Philistine enemies. Delilah gradually teased Samson until he weakened and told her the secret of his strength. Delilah then called some Philistines who were hiding in her home. They cut Samson's hair, blinded him, and forced him to work as a slave. For this, Delilah received a rich reward in silver. Delilah cost Samson his sight and then his life.

Bible events in Delilah's life
1. Samson falls in love with her and visits her often.
2. She conspires with Philistine rulers to find the source of Samson's strength.
3. She deceives Samson into telling her the secret of his strength.

GIDEON

During the time of the judges, God called Gideon to lead the people of Israel. They were oppressed by the Midianites, who sent bands of warriors to steal the Israelites' food and keep them in subjection. The Israelites had forsaken their God and had turned to idols, which weakened them and kept them from organizing under God's choice of leaders.

After God called Gideon to lead them, Gideon destroyed the idols of the land, then led his army against the Midianites. To prove that Gideon's victory would be God's miracle, God instructed Gideon to send home all but three hundred men, who carried clay jars or pitchers and lanterns into a night battle. The Midianites fled, but Gideon pursued and won a great victory. Although his people wanted Gideon to rule as king, he refused, proclaiming God as the true king of Israel.

Bible events in Gideon's life
1. An angel appears to him and tells him to rescue Israel.
2. He pulls down the altar of Baal.
3. God shows him the miracle of the fleece and the dew.
4. He chooses three hundred men to fight the enemy.
5. He goes with Purah to spy on the Midianite camp.
6. He defeats the Midianites with three hundred men, armed with trumpets and clay pitchers.
7. He pursues and kills Zebah and Zalmunna, the Midianite kings.
8. He refuses to be king over Israel.
9. He makes a golden ephod.
10. He dies and is buried in the tomb of his father.

What
Everyone
Should
Know
about
the
Bible

JEPHTHAH

Jephthah was an outcast and the leader of a band of outcasts, but he proved himself a valiant warrior. When his nation needed a military commander, the people turned to Jephthah, who brought a stunning victory over the Ammonites. This wise commander made a foolish vow that if God gave him victory, he would sacrifice the first thing to walk through his doorway when he returned home. To his dismay Jephthah saw his daughter coming to meet him. We are not sure how Jephthah sacrificed his daughter, but he kept his vow. Some think that he had to kill her and offer her as a burnt offering. Others think that she was condemned to lifelong virginity, meaning that she could never marry or have children. After six years of leading his people, Jephthah died and was buried in Gilead.

Bible events in Jephthah's life
1. He runs away to live in the land of Tob.
2. The leaders of Gilead send for him to help them fight the Ammonites.
3. He is made ruler and military leader at Mizpah.
4. He makes a foolish vow.
5. He defeats the Ammonites.
6. Because of his foolish vow, he has to sacrifice his daughter.
7. He fights the men of Ephraim.
8. He judges Israel for six years.

RUTH

During a famine, Naomi moved to Moab with her husband, Elimelech. While in Moab, Naomi's husband died, and her two sons married Moabite women, Ruth and Orpah. The sons also died in Moab, leaving Naomi, Ruth, and Orpah as widows. Naomi left to travel to her former home in Bethlehem, and Ruth and Orpah went with her. Naomi encouraged both girls to go back to Moab and marry again. Orpah returned, but Ruth insisted on going with Naomi to care for her. Ruth gleaned in the fields of Naomi's wealthy relative, Boaz, gathering the stalks of grain the reapers left behind. In time, Boaz and Ruth were married and had a son whom they named Obed, who became King David's grandfather.

Bible events in Ruth's life
1. She marries Naomi's son.
2. She refuses to leave Naomi and goes with her to Bethlehem.
3. She gleans in the barley fields of Boaz.
4. Boaz is kind to her.
5. She marries Boaz, and Obed is born to them.

SAMSON

Before Samson was born, an angel told his mother that he would have great strength and would do mighty things against Israel's enemies, the Philistines. He would live under a special vow, called the Nazirite vow, which forbade him to drink strong drink, cut his hair, or do certain other things. Samson grew to be a mighty man, stronger than any other, but he was morally weak. He married a Philistine woman, an enemy of Israel.

Samson frequently abused his power, and although he did many things against the Philistines, most were personal struggles that did not lead his nation to defeat this enemy collectively. Samson lusted for women of bad reputation, such as Delilah, who ultimately persuaded him to tell the secret of his strength. Delilah turned him over to the Philistines, who weakened him, blinded him, made him a slave, and mocked him. Samson died when his strength returned and he pulled down a great Philistine temple upon thousands of his enemies.

Bible events in Samson's life

1. He is born to Manoah and his wife.
2. He kills a lion on the way to his wedding in Timnah.
3. He tells a riddle at his wedding feast.
4. He kills thirty Philistines.
5. He burns the Philistines's grain fields with torches tied to three hundred foxes.
6. With the jawbone of a donkey, he kills a thousand Philistines.
7. He carries off the city gates of Gaza.
8. He judges Israel for twenty years.
9. Delilah deceives him into telling the secret of his strength; the Philistines blind him and put him in prison.
10. He pulls down the temple of Dagon and is killed along with thousands of Philistines.

What everyone should know about the book of Judges

INTERCEPTING THE CYCLES OF LIFE

There is a sobering cycle in life. Most of us have experienced it at some time. It goes like this—work hard, succeed, be proud of our success, want more, mortgage what we have by doing something stupid, sin, lose something important, repent and confess our sin, seek God's forgiveness, get a fresh start, work hard, succeed, and the cycle begins again. Around and around it can go, up to the top and down to the bottom.

That is the story of the book of Judges. The Ferris wheel of the cycle described above repeated itself again and again, and each cycle brought greater spiritual darkness to the Israelites. Sometimes God called judges to rescue his people and give them a fresh start, but often the judges failed as miserably as their people. Samson was an example of this. The strongest man who ever lived was a poster boy for moral weakness. Physical strength

What
Everyone
Should
Know
about
the

Bible

and moral weakness are a dangerous mixture, as a long list of star athletes who have bragged about their conquests off the playing field or court will tell you.

The period of the judges could be called Israel's Dark Age. The Israelites weren't spiritually bankrupt because they were militarily weak—they were militarily weak because they were spiritually bankrupt. The book concludes with the sobering summary that "the people did whatever seemed right in their own eyes" (Judges 21:25).

A few stars shone in the dark sky during this time—bright lights such as Gideon, Deborah, and Ehud. Each was a flawed person, just like you and me, but when they let God be the driving force in their lives, light shined in the darkness. One of the most beautiful stories from the period of the judges is not even told in the book of Judges. It is in the next book of the Bible, the book of Ruth.

Times may seem dark, and may even *be* dark. You may recognize that you are a flawed person, just like all the rest of us. But when you let God be your driving force, light will shine in the darkness.

Judges was probably written by Samuel, who was born in 1105 B.C. If Samuel was the author, he was writing about events that stretched from 1375 B.C. to 1050 B.C., a 325-year period of history.

What everyone should know about the book of Ruth

A STORY OF FAITHFULNESS

The story of Ruth is a story of beauty at a time of national ugliness. It is a story of faithfulness in an unfaithful nation. One loyal, young foreign widow brought more light to this dark period than perhaps all the judges of Israel put together. Her story is so warm and wonderful that it shines like a brilliant star in the night sky of national darkness and disaster.

Ruth was, quite simply, a nobody. She was just another ordinary Moabite girl, and Israelite press for Moabites or girls wasn't too good, especially for a girl who was also a Moabite. So Ruth was already near the bottom rung of society's success ladder when Elimelech and Naomi moved into the neighborhood. Elimelech died, widowing Naomi far from home. Then Naomi's two sons married neighborhood girls named Ruth and Orpah. That must have hurt a good Israelite widow, but she determined to love these girls as her own daughters. That shows Naomi's sterling character, doesn't it?

Then life dealt another cruel blow. Naomi's two sons died, so she was a widow without sons or a husband to take care of her. Ruth and Orpah were also widows, with no one to take care of them. These three widows had only each other, and widows were very helpless in those days. There were no insurance plans, no Social Security, no widow's benefits. Naomi was a refugee who had come to Moab to escape the famine back home in Bethlehem. She was a poverty-stricken widow far from home, with some responsibility for her two poverty-stricken, widowed, Moabite daughters-in-law.

Both Orpah and Ruth went with Naomi as she set out to return to Israel, but she begged them to stay in Moab and get married again. They were young, so that would have been the sensible thing for them to do. Orpah said good-bye and went home. She probably married and had a happy life, but we never hear of her again.

Ruth, however, would not go home. "Don't ask me to leave you and turn back. Wherever you go, I will go; wherever you live, I will live. Your people will be my people, and your God will be my God. Wherever you die, I will die, and there I will be buried. May the LORD punish me severely if I allow anything but death to separate us!" (Ruth 1:16-17). Ruth was faithful and has never been forgotten.

Back at Naomi's home in Bethlehem, Ruth gleaned the grain fields, picking up grain left by the reapers. She worked so that Naomi wouldn't need to. It was hard physical work, but Ruth did it for the mother-in-law she loved. Before long, Boaz, the owner of the field, saw her and soon they were married. Ruth became the great-grandmother of King David, and an ancestor of Jesus.

Ruth is a story about what to do when life caves in. Her faithfulness made her a bright star in the dark days of the judges. Her response to life at its worst rewarded her with life at its best. Ruth is a star in the Who's Who of the Bible. If you feel that life is caving in on you, read the book of Ruth. How you respond to life at its worst may reward you, too, with life at its best.

We don't know who wrote the book of Ruth. Some think that Samuel was the author of both Ruth and Judges. If so, both books were written after his birth in 1105 B.C., in a period of history from 1375 B.C. to 1050 B.C.

◢◢◢◢ Did You Know?

The king who cut off 140 thumbs and 140 big toes After Joshua died, the Israelites asked the Lord which tribe should fight the Canaanites first. "Judah," the Lord answered. The tribe of Judah asked the tribe of Simeon to come and help them, and the tribe of Simeon agreed to do this. Together, they had a great victory over some Canaanites and Perizzites. A king named Adoni-bezek was captured. His real name was Adoni and he was from the town of Bezek. Sometimes ancients constructed their names like that—by putting their name and their city's name together.

The Israelites cut off his two thumbs and his two big toes, probably because they knew that he had made this his practice. "I have done this to seventy kings," he confessed. "Then I made them eat scraps under my table. So I deserve this." What a legacy—the person who cut off thumbs and big toes.

The Canaanites lived much the way we do We may be tempted to think that these ancient people were crude and barbaric. Actually, the Canaanites lived a lifestyle much like ours—with different toys, to be sure, but in a similar pattern of materialism. Although these people lived mostly

140

>

What
Everyone
Should
Know
about
the
Bible

by agriculture, it was a rich land with abundant crops. There were also artisans, traders, priests, musicians, and warriors among them. These were talented people in the arts, sciences, and literature. They were skilled in ceramics, music, musical instruments, and architecture. Their art treasures were made with gold, ivory, and alabaster. Their buildings were elegant. Wealthy women enjoyed cosmetics and rich jewelry, and wealthy homeowners even slept on beds of ivory. Canaanites had chariots for war and for hunting. Their lifestyle was rich and desirable.

With this rich lifestyle came pagan religion. Although the Israelites conquered the Canaanites militarily, the Canaanites conquered them socially, morally, and materialistically. It is safe to say that the Canaanite culture was similar to ours, except for our higher level of education, government, and technology. It is also safe to say that our rich culture has too often overshadowed our desire for God.

Gideon fought 120,000 Midianites with 300 soldiers. Who were the Midianites? The Midianites descended, of course, from Midian. But who was he? Flash back more than one thousand years. After Abraham's wife Sarah died, he married Keturah. One of their sons was Midian (Genesis 25:1-2), and his descendants were the Midianites.

Six hundred years later, Moses, Abraham's descendant through Jacob's son Levi, fled Egypt, hid in the land of Midian, and married a Midianite girl. Zipporah was the daughter of a Midianite priest, Jethro. Moses and Zipporah had a common ancestor—Abraham. In Midian, Moses became a shepherd, taking care of his father-in-law's sheep. Moses' descendants were all half Israelite, through him, and half Midianite, through his wife Zipporah.

Another three hundred years passed until the time of Gideon, when the Midianites forgot about their ties with the Israelites and raided their lands for seven years. They treated the Israelites with great cruelty and left them with almost nothing to eat (Judges 6:2-4).

Samson's parents took the Nazirite vow for him. What was that? In those days, a person could choose to take the Nazirite vow, either for thirty days, or for a lifetime. A child's parents could place their child under this vow even before the child was born. Samson's Nazirite vow, made by his parents, was for his entire lifetime.

The vow forbade a man from cutting his hair or shaving his beard. He could not drink wine or strong alcoholic beverages. He was not allowed to touch a dead body or even go near a dead body. The purpose of the vow was to dedicate a man to the Lord, usually for his entire lifetime.

Samson, of course, broke his vow many times. He killed many

Philistines, so he was frequently in touch with dead bodies. He made love to Philistine women, which was very much out of keeping with being dedicated to the Lord. Later, when he told the secret of his strength to Delilah, he violated his vow, and the Philistines cut his hair and robbed him of his strength (Judges 16:19).

Ruth gleaned in the fields of Boaz. What was gleaning? In the days of Ruth, harvesters accidentally or intentionally left some stalks of grain behind. Gleaners came behind the harvesters, picking up these stalks of grain and keeping them for their own food. The law of Moses required harvesters to not pick up these stalks of grain that they dropped and also to leave grain around the edge of the field. This grain was for poor people, like Ruth, to harvest. Picking it up was called gleaning.

Discovering My Purpose from God's Plan

1. *The victims became the victors and the victors became the victims.* Israel conquered the Canaanites militarily, but the Canaanites conquered the Israelites culturally. The fruit of this cultural conquest is clearly seen in the time of the judges, when everyone did what was right in his or her own eyes.

2. *Beware of the cycles of life:* Prosperity begets complacency; complacency begets spiritual weakness; spiritual weakness begets oppression from the enemy; oppression from the enemy causes people to cry out to the Lord for mercy; the Lord hears and rescues; in him, we become prosperous; and prosperity begets complacency. The cycle goes around and around, up and down, like a Ferris wheel.

3. *God specializes in things thought impossible.* Where human strength ends, God's miracles begin. When we are at the end of our rope, God is at the beginning of his. When we have exhausted our resources, God opens his treasure chest and reveals his unlimited abundance. When we are weak, he is strong.

4. *A legacy is more than an inscription on your tombstone.* A living legacy is a purpose perpetuated through children and their succeeding generations. Jair's legacy was devoid of purpose. All we remember about him is the weak fact that he had thirty sons who rode around on thirty donkeys and had thirty little villages. You would like a more purposeful legacy than that, wouldn't you? What would you like? Consider that today.

5. *Vows are promises to be kept.* Foolish vows are painful to keep. Ask Jephthah, who made a foolish vow that cost him the life of his daughter. Before you vow or promise something, consider the consequences. Don't vow something that you don't want to do. If you don't want the consequences, don't make the vow.

142
>
What
Everyone
Should
Know
about
the
Bible

6. *Obey God and things will go well.* Disobey God and life will oppress you. Look at the book of Judges. Whenever Israel disobeyed God, it became spiritually weak, then militarily weak, then oppressed by an enemy. Whenever Israel cried out to the Lord and turned to him, he helped them from the enemy's bondage and led them back into prosperity.

7. *Disobedience is the shovel that digs a great gulf between us and God.* Read about the people of Israel during the time of the judges.

8. *"I will never leave you" is the banner for faithfulness.* Faithful Ruth would never leave her mother-in-law, whom she loved deeply.

9. *Physical strength does not ensure spiritual strength.* Material abundance does not insure spiritual abundance. This is shown in the life of Samson.

10. *Never mortgage what you have to reach for something you don't have.* Samson mortgaged what he had for pleasures that he wanted.

11. *Weakness with faithfulness, as in the story of Ruth, shines brighter than strength with unfaithfulness, as in the story of Samson.* The driving force of the moment may be lost to the quiet lingering record of simple submission.

Begging for a King

Samuel and the Reign of King Saul

Characters:
Abigail (Nabal's wife, then David's wife); Abishai (David's military leader); Abner (Saul's military leader); Achish (a Philistine king); Ahimelech (a priest who helped David); David (a shepherd boy who killed Goliath the giant; the future king of Israel); Doeg the Edomite (who betrayed David and the priests); Eli (Israel's high priest); Elkanah (Hannah's husband); Goliath (a Philistine giant); Hannah (Samuel's mother); Hophni (Eli's wayward son); Jesse (David's father); Jonathan (King Saul's son and David's friend); Michal (Saul's daughter, David's first wife); Nabal (a wealthy shepherd who refused David food); Nahash (a king of the Ammonites); Peninnah (Elkanah's second wife); Phinehas (Eli's wayward son); Samuel; Saul (Israel's first king); the witch of Endor (who communicated with the dead Samuel)

Time Period:
From the birth of Samuel until the death of Saul

Dates:
Approximately 1105 B.C.–1010 B.C.

Where Scene 11 of the Big Story Can Be Found:
Parts of the books of 1 Samuel and 1 Chronicles

In Scene 11, Find the Answers to These Questions:
Who sent an offering of golden rats and golden tumors?
Who was defeated in battle by thunder?
What shepherd boy was chosen to be the next king?
Which two men attacked an army of thousands?
What warrior was more than nine feet tall?

Look for this in Scene 11
> A woman gave her only baby to a priest.
> God talked to a little boy at bedtime.

> An idol bowed down before the Ark of the Covenant.
> A hero almost died because he ate some honey.
> A man of God chopped a king into pieces.
> A widow of a fool became the wife of a future king.

 The Big Story So Far

A barren woman begs for a son

The story of Samuel begins at the Tabernacle set up at Shiloh. There the old priest Eli was in charge, with his wayward sons helping him and helping themselves. A sorrowful woman was praying, with her lips moving. Eli was angry. He thought the woman was drunk and confronted her. Then Hannah, the woman, told him her prayer. She was barren and was begging God for a son.

Hannah and Peninnah were two wives of a man named Elkanah. Peninnah had children and Hannah was barren, which was a serious disgrace for an Israelite woman at that time. Peninnah made fun of Hannah, gloating over her success and Hannah's failure in childbearing until Hannah's feelings were raw. This went on for years.

When Hannah told Eli that she had been praying for a son, Eli became sympathetic and asked the Lord to grant her request. Then a miracle happened. Hannah became pregnant and had a little baby boy that they named Samuel.

Giving a little boy to the Lord

When Samuel was weaned, Hannah took him to the Tabernacle and presented him to Eli for the Lord's service. "I am giving him to the Lord, and he will belong to the Lord his whole life," Hannah said to Eli. Imagine the mixed feelings in Hannah's heart as she left her son for the first time and headed home. Imagine little Samuel's feelings as he said good-bye to his mother, alone in a strange tent with an aging priest and his two wayward sons.

The boy Samuel learned to love the Lord at the Tabernacle, and he saw the wickedness of Eli's sons. They treated the Lord's offerings with contempt and seduced young women who assisted at the Tabernacle. Samuel knew that the Lord was not pleased with these scoundrels.

Each year, Hannah brought new clothing to Samuel, a tunic like the one a priest wore and a little boy's cloak. Each year Eli blessed Hannah and asked the Lord to give her more children. Hannah did have more—three sons and two daughters. She was barren no more, but a wonderful woman like Hannah didn't gloat to Peninnah about her childbearing successes.

One day, a prophet visited Eli and predicted the doom that would come to his family. The behavior of Eli's two sons was unacceptable

What
Everyone
Should
Know
about
the

Bible

and they would both die on the same day. God would raise up a faithful priest to lead Israel, but it would not be from Eli's family.

God speaks to a little boy

One night Eli, who was almost blind by then, had gone to bed. The boy Samuel had gone to bed, too, near the Ark of the Covenant. The seven oil lamps of the lampstand, or candlestick, as it was sometimes called, were still faintly flickering, but they were almost out.

Suddenly a voice called out in the night, "Samuel! Samuel!" Samuel thought Eli had called him and ran to ask what he wanted.

"I didn't call you," Eli told him. "Go back to bed." This happened three times. At last, Eli realized that the Lord was calling Samuel.

"Go back to bed," Eli told the boy Samuel. "If the voice calls again ask the Lord what he wants." When he did, the Lord spoke to Samuel and told him about the coming judgment of Eli's family.

The next morning, Samuel started his usual chores by opening the doors of the Tabernacle. Then Eli called to him and demanded to know what the Lord had said. Samuel was afraid, but he told Eli everything. "May the Lord do what he knows is best," Eli said.

Growing in godliness

Samuel grew to be a strong young man and the Lord frequently talked with him there at the Tabernacle. The young man Samuel shared the word of the Lord with the people and gradually shared more of God's messages with them as he grew to manhood.

Looking for help from a box instead of from God

One day, the Philistines engaged Israel in a decisive battle and the Philistines killed four thousand Israelite men. Israel retreated to decide what to do next. Then the elders had an idea. "Let's bring the Ark of the Covenant . . . into battle with us," they said. "It will save us from our enemies" (1 Samuel 4:3). So they sent to Shiloh and brought the Ark into battle. Eli's sons, the scoundrels Hophni and Phinehas, carried the Ark to the battlefield. Perhaps they thought they would get some honor from the Ark.

But the Ark was not the answer. God was the answer, and the Israelites were so far from him at that time that they did not realize this. They put their trust in "God's box" instead of in God. Apparently they didn't think of asking God for his help rather than hoping that the Ark would do the trick. The Philistines won a great victory; they killed thirty thousand Israelite men, including Hophni and Phinehas, and captured the Ark.

When ninety-eight-year-old Eli, blind and fat, heard the terrible news, he fell over backward, broke his neck, and died. It was a dark, dark day for Israel.

What to do with God's golden box

Now that the Philistines had the Ark of the Covenant, they didn't know what to do with it. It was obviously a treasure, but where should they put it? Finally, someone decided to put it in the temple of Dagon, their fish god. The next morning, they found the idol of Dagon fallen on its face before the Ark. They stood the idol up again, but the same thing happened the next night. This time Dagon's head and hands were broken off.

The Lord sent an infestation of rats and a plague of tumors on the people of that city, Ashdod. The Philistines were terrified and decided to move the Ark to another Philistine city—Gath. But as soon as it arrived in Gath, the people there suffered from a plague of tumors. They sent the Ark to another Philistine city, Ekron. The people of Ekron were terrified and begged the Philistine rulers to send the Ark back to Israel.

An offering of golden rats and golden tumors

The Philistines decided to send a guilt offering with the Ark—five gold tumors and five gold rats, since rats had spread the disease. They built a new cart, put the Ark on the cart, and hitched cows with newborn calves to it. The calves were shut up in a pen. Usually cows would go nowhere except to the pen that held their calves, but these cows went straight for Israel, lowing in protest as they went.

At Beth-shemesh, in Israel, the people were harvesting wheat. Suddenly they saw the Ark of the Covenant coming on the cart, and they were overjoyed. Then the Israelites made many offerings of thanksgiving to the Lord. Seventy men of Beth-shemesh foolishly tried to look into the Ark and died immediately. The people of Beth-shemesh were afraid to keep the Ark and asked the people of Kiriath-jearim to come to get it. For the next twenty years, the Ark remained at Kiriath-jearim in Abinadab's house.

Saved by thunder

One day there was a big meeting with Samuel in charge. He was fully grown and recognized as a leader, so apparently the people had made him a judge over Israel and were willing to listen to him. Then Samuel said to all the people of Israel, "If you are really serious about wanting to return to the Lord, get rid of your foreign gods and your images of Ashtoreth. Determine to obey only the Lord; then he will rescue you from the Philistines" (1 Samuel 7:3). The people listened to Samuel, destroyed their images, and turned to the Lord.

"Come to Mizpah," Samuel commanded. "I will pray for you." So the people gathered in a great ceremony at Mizpah. The Philistines heard about this gathering and decided that it might be a good time

148

>

What
Everyone
Should
Know
about
the

Bible

to attack. The Israelites were terrified and begged Samuel to pray, so he did.

As the Philistines arrived for battle, the Lord sent great thunder that threw the Philistines into confusion. The Israelites attacked and achieved a decisive defeat over the Philistines, and the Philistines did not bother the Israelites again for a long time.

For the rest of his life, Samuel was Israel's last judge. He is the only judge whose activities are not included in the book of Judges. When Samuel grew old, he appointed his sons as judges after him, but they were greedy. They accepted bribes and perverted justice.

The quest for a king

The Israelite leaders met with Samuel to talk about a king. They could not have Samuel's wayward sons leading them. "Give us a king!" they demanded.

Samuel was upset about this request for a king. "Do as they ask," the Lord told him. "But warn them what a king will do." The people refused to listen to Samuel's warning. They wanted a king no matter what he would do to them.

The search for Israel's first king was rather unusual. A rich and influential man named Kish lost his donkeys. They wandered away, and Kish sent his son Saul, along with a servant, to find the donkeys. Along the way, the servant remembered Samuel. "There is a man of God in this town and he may know about the donkeys," the servant suggested. So Saul and his servant went into town to find Samuel.

When Samuel saw Saul coming, the Lord spoke to him. "This is the man I told you about yesterday," the Lord said. "Anoint him to be the next king."

When they met, Samuel invited Saul to eat with him, and put him at the place of highest honor at the table. The next morning, Samuel anointed Saul as the next king. "The Lord has appointed you to be the next leader of the people of Israel," Samuel told him. Imagine Saul's surprise! He was a farmer from the lowly tribe of Benjamin who had never thought of himself as "king material." He was just looking for his donkeys. Soon after that, Samuel gathered the people at Mizpah again. It was time to reveal the new king. By using the process of choosing lots, Samuel narrowed the search tribe by tribe, then family by family within the tribe of Benjamin. Finally Saul, son of Kish, was the chosen man, but no one could find him. Then the Lord told them to look among the baggage. Saul was hiding there. At last Saul was brought out and Samuel told the people, "This is your new king."

"Long live the king!" the people shouted. Saul was thirty years old when he became king, and he ruled for forty-two years.

The price of peace–gouging out everyone's right eye

Saul's first great test as a king came a month after his anointing. King Nahash of Ammon led his army against the Israelite city Jabesh-gilead. The people begged for peace and Nahash agreed under one condition—that he gouge out the right eye of every person as a sign of disgrace.

"Give us seven days to respond," the people of Jabesh-gilead said. Before long, Saul heard about this. The Spirit of God came upon him and he cut his oxen into pieces and sent messengers with the meat throughout the land. "This will happen to your oxen if you don't join the army," was the message of the new king. It was an unusual army recruitment process, but it worked, and 330,000 men gathered to fight. Saul led them into battle and thoroughly defeated King Nahash and his army. Jabesh-gilead was spared.

Once more Samuel gathered all Israel, this time at Gilgal. There they reaffirmed Saul's kingship in a solemn ceremony, crowned him king, and offered peace offerings to the Lord.

Signs from the heavens

Samuel assembled the people again to give them a farewell address. "Make sure now that you worship the LORD with all your heart, and don't turn your back on him," Samuel told them. "But if you continue to sin, you and your king will be swept away" (1 Samuel 12:20, 25).

Samuel called for a miracle to confirm what he had said. It was not the rainy season, but Samuel called for thunder and rain. The Lord sent mighty, terrifying thunder and rain. It was a sure sign that he was there. "Fear the Lord and worship him," Samuel said again. "But if you continue to sin, you and your king will be swept away."

Two soldiers fight an entire army

One day, Saul chose three thousand special troops. Of these, two thousand stayed with Saul and one thousand went with Saul's courageous son Jonathan. Jonathan and his men attacked and defeated the Philistine garrison at Geba. Of course, the news spread to both the Philistines and the Israelites. Saul was sure that the Philistines would retaliate, so he called all his troops together to prepare for battle.

Saul was right. The Philistines gathered a vast army at Micmash with three thousand chariots, six thousand horsemen, and innumerable soldiers. It was an enormous army, far superior to Israel's army, so the Israelite men lost heart. They began to run away and hide in caves, holes, rocks, tombs, and cisterns.

Samuel had promised to come within seven days to make an offering to the Lord and beg for the Lord's presence. On the seventh day, Saul would wait no longer. He decided to take things into his own hands, and

150

>

What
Everyone
Should
Know
about
the

Bible

he made the offering to the Lord himself. He was just finishing when Samuel arrived.

"What have you done?" Samuel demanded. Saul gave a lame excuse that he just couldn't wait.

"You have disobeyed the Lord," Samuel told him. "Because of that, your dynasty will end, for God has chosen a better man to be king." Then Samuel left.

Saul must have been terrified, for now the Lord was not with him. Neither were his men, for only six hundred of them stayed there. Not only that, but except for Saul and Jonathan, these men had no swords or spears, only crude farm tools as weapons. The Philistines knew blacksmithing, but the Israelites had not yet learned, so they could not make weapons.

One day, brave Jonathan became restless while waiting for the Philistines to make the first move. Secretly, he took his armor bearer with him and went down between two rocky cliffs named Bozez and Seneh.

"Let's go across to see those pagans," Jonathan told his armor bearer. "I'm with you completely," the young armor bearer replied.

So Jonathan set up a test. "We will cross over and let the Philistines see us," he said. "If they tell us to come up and fight, we will go up. If they tell us to stay where we are, we will know the Lord doesn't want us to fight." So that was what they did.

When the Philistines saw Jonathan and his armor bearer they taunted them and told them to come up and fight. So the two climbed the cliff and killed about twenty Philistines. Suddenly the other Philistines began to panic, and as they did so, the Lord sent a great earthquake.

Saul saw from a distance what was happening. The Philistine army was melting away in every direction. A quick check showed that Jonathan was gone, so Saul guessed what had happened. Saul and his six hundred troops rushed into battle and found the Philistines killing each other, so they attacked. Soon the Israelite men who had run away came back and joined in the battle.

A foolish vow

Saul made his soldiers take a foolish oath not to eat until they had full revenge on the Philistines. Of course, the soldiers became quite weak by the end of the day even though there was plenty of honey in the forest. Jonathan had not heard Saul's demand, so he refreshed himself with some honey.

Despite their hunger, the Israelites continued to fight the Philistines, but at dusk they were faint from hunger, and began to devour the battle plunder without draining the blood, which was a strict violation of the law.

Saul wanted to chase the Philistines all night, but when the priest inquired of the Lord, the Lord was silent. "Something is wrong," Saul said. Saul went through a process and soon learned that Jonathan had eaten honey. Saul was ready to kill his own son, but the soldiers rose up against Saul and would not let him do it. Jonathan had been responsible for this great victory and they would not let Saul harm him.

Accepting the unacceptable

As time passed, Saul became a good military leader and conquered many of the local pagan kings. Whenever Saul saw a brave young man, he recruited him into the army.

One day Samuel had a powerful message from the Lord for Saul. "Destroy the entire Amalekite people, along with their animals." When the Israelites had come from slavery in Egypt, Amalek had been the first to go to battle against them.

Saul mobilized his army and went against Amalek. He warned the Kenites nearby to get out of the way so they wouldn't get hurt, and they listened. Saul destroyed all of the Amalekites except for King Agag. Saul also kept the best of the animals.

Early the next morning Samuel went to meet the triumphant Saul. "I have obeyed the Lord," Saul said, when he greeted Samuel.

"Then what is all the bleating of sheep and lowing of cattle that I hear?" Samuel demanded. Saul was caught.

"You have rejected the Lord, so the Lord will reject you," Samuel said to Saul. Then Samuel demanded that Saul bring King Agag to him, and Samuel cut Agag into pieces.

Saul pleaded with Samuel to forgive him and go to worship with him, but Samuel refused. He went home and never met with Saul again. He often grieved for Saul, however, for he knew that another person would become king in Saul's place.

The shepherd kid—the future king

"You have mourned long enough," the Lord told Samuel one day. "Take your anointing horn of oil and go to Bethlehem. Find Jesse and anoint one of his sons to be the next king."

When Samuel arrived, Jesse began to bring his sons to meet him, starting with the oldest. Eliab was tall and handsome, so Samuel thought he must surely be the chosen one, but he wasn't. Neither were any of the other sons that Jesse brought.

"Is this all your sons?" Samuel asked. "Are there any others?"

Jesse must have smiled when he remembered the boy taking care

152

>

What
Everyone
Should
Know
about
the

Bible

of the sheep out in the fields. He hadn't even tried to bring young David in. He was still a kid.

When David came, he stood before Samuel, young but dark and handsome, with pleasant eyes. "This is the one," the Lord told Samuel. "Anoint him."

With his father and brothers looking on, Samuel anointed David to be the next king of Israel. The brothers obviously didn't believe what they saw, for we see them still rejecting David as a kid later on. But the Spirit of the Lord came upon David at that time and prepared him for royal service.

Meanwhile, the Spirit of the Lord had left Saul, and in his place came a tormenting spirit. This left Saul with great depression and fear. One of Saul's servants suggested a solution. There was a talented harp player, a shepherd boy, who might soothe him. So David was brought before the king to play his harp and soothe the troubled king. David even became one of Saul's armor bearers.

Time passed. Evidently David returned to his work of taking care of the family sheep. Saul must have forgotten about David.

How do you fight a nine-foot-tall giant?

One day, the Philistines mustered a vast army for battle and camped near the Valley of Elah. This was one of Israel's strategic trade routes, so they could not afford to lose the valley. The Philistines were camped on one side of the valley, and the Israelites on the other.

The Philistines tried a new tactic. Each day they sent their giant Goliath into the valley. He was more than nine feet tall and had a powerful body and mighty weapons. "Send someone to fight me," Goliath challenged. "If he wins, all Israel wins. If I win, we Philistines take all."

The Israelite soldiers trembled in fear. Even the courageous Jonathan would not go out to fight Goliath. No one was even a close match for him.

It happened one day that Jesse sent David with some food for his soldier brothers. When David saw Goliath taunting the Israelites, he was angry. David let it be known that he would fight the giant, but his oldest brother, Eliab, was disgusted to think that "the kid" would suggest such a thing.

Word reached Saul that someone was willing to fight Goliath, but Saul's heart must have sunk when he saw that it was the harp-playing David. Still, there was no one else, and at last Saul agreed to let him do it.

With no armor, sword, or spear, David went out to meet the giant. His only weapons were a shepherd's staff, his sling, and five small stones from the dried-up brook in the valley.

Goliath was furious; it was highly insulting to see a boy come to fight him with only a sling. He cursed David and threatened to feed him to the birds.

"You come with mighty weapons, but I come in the name of the Lord," David shouted. With that, he twirled his sling and let a stone fly like a modern bullet. It pierced Goliath's forehead and he fell down. David rushed to Goliath, drew his sword, and cut off Goliath's head with the giant's own sword. Then David presented Goliath's head to King Saul.

The Israelite army went wild with joy and excitement. It was their day as they pursued the frightened Philistines and defeated them. Needless to say, David was immediately the hero of all these much older, tough career soldiers. They immediately accepted him as their own.

Jonathan was overjoyed to meet such a brave young man and instantly formed a deep friendship with David. Jonathan gave David his personal robe, tunic, sword, bow, and belt. From that time forward, they were the closest of friends.

Insane jealousy

David went to live in the palace with Saul and Jonathan, but Saul grew insanely jealous of his famous new military leader. Twice he hurled his spear at David to try to kill him, but he missed. Saul put David in charge of one thousand troops, hoping that he would be killed in battle. Instead, David brought back great military victories.

At first, Saul promised his daughter Merab to David as his wife, but he went back on his promise. At last, Saul gave his daughter Michal to David. David continued to achieve great military victories over the Philistines, and each victory made Saul even more jealous.

Once more, Saul hurled his spear at David as David played the harp for him, but David escaped. Now David knew that he must go away. He was no longer safe with Saul.

One night, David's wife, Michal, warned him to go far away. She helped him to climb from the window and escape. Then she put a large idol in David's bed and covered it to make it look like David was sleeping there. When Saul's troops came to capture David, they found only the idol.

Warrior on the run

David escaped to Ramah to see Samuel, and told Samuel all that Saul was doing to him. Samuel asked David to stay with him. Saul sent troops to get David, but as the troops came near to Samuel, they began to prophesy. Saul sent other troops, but the same thing happened. Then Saul went personally, but as he came nearby, he began to prophesy. The presence of the Lord was too great for them to come near enough to harm David.

>

What
Everyone
Should
Know
about
the

Bible

David decided to leave Samuel. He quickly found Jonathan and told him all that was happening. Jonathan could hardly believe that his father truly wanted to kill David, but he and David decided on a way to communicate with three arrows. Jonathan would learn the truth from Saul and communicate it to David.

The truth came out quickly the following night at dinner. Saul cursed Jonathan and demanded that he bring David there so that Saul could kill him. Now Jonathan knew the worst.

The next morning, Jonathan went to the field where David was hiding. He took a boy with him to chase the arrows that he shot. If he shouted to the boy, "Go farther, the arrows are ahead of you," David would know that Saul truly wanted to kill him. Jonathan shot the arrows and that is exactly what he shouted to the boy.

When the boy left, David and Jonathan tearfully said good-bye. David left, and Jonathan returned to the city.

David went alone to a place called Nob to see Ahimelech the priest, but the priest was afraid when he saw David alone. David was hungry, so the priest gave him some of the ceremonial showbread. Then David asked for a sword, and Ahimelech gave him the sword that David had taken from Goliath.

David next tried to hide with King Achish of the Philistines. When that didn't work, he moved on to the cave of Adullam. Soon his brothers and other relatives joined him there in hiding and others joined David's forces until there were about four hundred people with David.

David made a brief trip to Mizpeh in Moab, where he asked the king to protect his father and mother until things were safer. The king agreed, so David's parents moved to Moab while David was in hiding.

One day, while David was at the cave of Adullam, he longingly said, "O for a drink from the well in Bethlehem." The Philistines occupied Bethlehem at that time, so this seemed impossible, but three of David's mightiest warriors broke through the Philistine lines, drew some water from the well, and brought it back to David. David was so deeply moved that he couldn't drink it, for the three had risked their lives to get it. He poured it out before the Lord as an offering to him (2 Samuel 23:13-17).

One day, the prophet Gad told David that he should return to the land of Judah, so David went to the forest of Hereth. Saul soon heard that he was there and mobilized his forces to go after him. Saul's chief herdsman, Doeg the Edomite, happened to be at Nob when David visited Ahimelech and heard all that happened. He told Saul that Ahimelech had given David food and a sword, and had consulted the Lord for him.

Saul was furious. He sent for Ahimelech and his priests and screamed at them. Then he ordered his soldiers to kill them. When the soldiers refused to kill God's priests, Saul turned to Doeg and demanded that he do it. Without a thought, Doeg killed eighty-five priests, still dressed in their priestly garments, in bloody murder. Then he sent men to the homes of these priests and killed all their families, even the babies, and all their livestock.

David was devastated when he heard the news. "I knew Doeg would do this," he said. "I have caused the deaths of all these innocent people."

One day, news came to David that Philistines had attacked the city of Keilah and were stealing the people's grain from the threshing floors. David asked the Lord twice if he should rescue the people of Keilah and twice the Lord said he should go. So David went to Keilah and defeated the Philistines, which saved the city and its grain. You would think that those people would be grateful, but the Lord told David that they would betray him to Saul, and they did.

David and his followers, six hundred of them now, left Keilah and began roaming the countryside. The people of Ziph betrayed David by telling Saul where he was. David and his people moved on, but Saul continued to search for him. As he was about to reach David, an urgent message came to Saul that the Philistines had attacked.

Mercy for an unmerciful man

When Saul's battle with the Philistines ended, he learned that David had moved to the wilderness of En-gedi. Saul chose three thousand troops and went after him. Saul stopped in a cave to relieve himself without realizing that David and his men were in that same cave. David crept forward and cut off a piece of Saul's robe, but he would not let his men kill Saul.

As soon as Saul left the cave, David came out and called to him. "My lord, the king!" he shouted. Then he showed Saul the piece of his robe.

"I could have killed you in the cave," David said. "But I didn't. So why are you trying to harm me?" Saul was ashamed and took his troops home.

At last Samuel died. They buried him not far from his home at Ramah.

Nabal, the fool

David's next move was to the wilderness of Maon, not far from a wealthy landowner named Nabal. If ever there was a mismatch, it seemed to be the coarse, crude, selfish, mean, dishonest fool Nabal and his sweet, sensible, intelligent, and beautiful wife, Abigail.

One day David heard that Nabal was shearing his sheep near Carmel. This was usually a time of celebration when people would be in a generous mood. David had six hundred followers to feed, so he needed help.

156

>

What
Everyone
Should
Know
about
the

Bible

Why not ask Nabal? So David sent some messengers to ask the crude fellow for some food.

The men reminded Nabal that David and his followers had been protecting his shepherds and were in need of some food. Would he be kind and share some with them? But Nabal made fun of David and called him and his followers a band of outlaws who were running away from their master, King Saul.

David was furious. "Get your swords!" he commanded. So four hundred men started off with David, while two hundred remained to protect the camp.

Meanwhile, a servant told Abigail what Nabal had done. She was not only beautiful, but also a wise peacemaker who knew what David would do. Quickly Abigail gathered two hundred loaves of bread, two skins of wine, five dressed sheep, nearly a bushel of roasted grain, one hundred raisin cakes, and two hundred fig cakes. Her supplies make an interesting commentary on foods that were easily preserved in the hot Middle East.

Abigail packed this food on donkeys and hurried to intercept David and his men. She dared not tell Nabal what she was doing. When Abigail saw David, she got off her donkey and bowed at his feet. "I accept the blame for this, my lord," she said. "Please ignore Nabal, for he is a wicked and ill-tempered man, a fool. Here is a present I have brought for you."

David was deeply touched by the kindness of this beautiful woman. "Return home in peace," he told her. "We will not harm your husband."

When Abigail came home, Nabal was throwing a big drinking party. He was very drunk, so she didn't tell him what she had done until morning. When she did tell him, he was so furious that he had a stroke and was paralyzed for about ten days, and then he died.

When David heard that Nabal was dead, he asked Abigail to marry him. David also married Ahinoam from Jezreel. He was already married to Saul's daughter Michal, but Saul had given her to another man named Palti.

Slumbering warriors

Once more, the people of Ziph betrayed David by telling Saul where he was hiding. Saul took three thousand of his best troops and went to hunt for David in the wilderness. He wanted to kill him. David knew all of his movements, for he sent spies to watch Saul.

One night, David and Abishai slipped into the heart of Saul's camp past a ring of slumbering warriors. Saul was sound asleep, with his general Abner nearby. Abishai wanted to pin Saul to the ground with his own spear, but David would not let him. Saul was God's anointed, so no one must touch him.

Instead, David took Saul's spear and water jug. Then he and Abishai slipped out of Saul's camp without anyone noticing them. David climbed a hill overlooking the camp and shouted, "Wake up, Abner!" Abner did wake up and sleepily asked who was calling.

David began to mock Abner. "You haven't guarded your master very well," he said. "Look, I have crept into camp and taken Saul's spear and water jug." By now, Saul was awake and looking for those things. Then he saw David holding them.

David scolded Saul for chasing him. Saul felt guilty and asked David to forgive him. He would no longer chase David, for David had spared his life a second time. David and Saul parted and Saul went home.

At home with the enemy

David decided that he would go to live with the Philistines at Gath under the protection of the Philistine king Achish. When Saul heard where he was, he stopped hunting David. Achish, meanwhile, gave David the city of Ziklag so that he and his followers could live there. David often raided foreign cities, and the Philistines thought he had fought cities of Israel.

One day, the Philistines mustered their armies for battle with Israel. Achish wanted David and his men to go with them to fight Israel, but the other Philistine leaders would not let them.

Meanwhile, Saul was frantic with fear, for he saw the size of the Philistine army. Saul asked the Lord what to do, but the Lord no longer responded to Saul, so he decided to ask a witch who was also a medium for insight. The problem was that he had banned witches and mediums in the land, so it would be hard to find one.

Back from the dead

Some of Saul's advisers knew about a witch at Endor. Saul disguised himself and went to see her. The woman didn't want to help this stranger, for she feared for her life, but Saul swore not to hurt her. Saul then asked the woman to call Samuel back from the dead.

As soon as Samuel appeared, the woman knew that her visitor was King Saul. She was terrified, but Saul assured her that he would not hurt her.

"What do you want?" Samuel asked.

"Tell me what to do," Saul begged.

Samuel scolded Saul for his ungodliness. "The Lord will bring the whole army of Israel down to defeat," Samuel said. "The Lord has taken your kingdom from you and given it to David. Tomorrow you will be captured by the Philistines."

Saul was paralyzed with fear. The witch fed him, and then Saul and his helpers went out alone into the night to face a desperate tomorrow.

158

>

What
Everyone
Should
Know
about
the

Bible

Victory through an abandoned slave

David had gone part of the way with King Achish of the Philistines
until Achish's high-ranking officers rejected him. Then he and his men
headed home to Ziklag, but when they arrived, they found their town
sacked by Amalekites, who had burned the town and captured all the
women and children.

Through the priest Abiathar, David asked the Lord if he should chase
the Amalekites. The Lord told him to do it, so he and six hundred men
set out at once. By the time they reached the brook Besor, two hundred
men were too exhausted to go on.

Before long, David and his men found an Egyptian man abandoned
in a field. They fed him and gave him a drink, for he had not eaten or
drunk anything for three days. Then the truth came out. He was the
slave of an Amalekite. When he became sick, his master left him behind
to die.

"Will you lead us to the Amalekites?" David asked.

"I will if you will not kill me or give me back to my cruel master,"
the man replied.

The Egyptian slave led David and his men to the Amalekite camp-
ground. The Amalekites were scattered through the fields, dancing for
joy, but the party quickly stopped as David and his men rushed in and
slaughtered them during the night. Only four hundred young men
escaped on camels. David and his men found all of their wives and
children, and recovered all the plunder the Amalekites had taken plus
an enormous amount of Amalekite plunder.

When the troops arrived back at the brook Besor with the plunder,
some of David's soldiers angrily demanded that the people who stayed
behind should not share in it. David had a long-lasting rule that those
who stayed behind to guard equipment should share the plunder with
those who went to battle. David also sent some of the plunder to his
friends in Judah who had protected him as he fled from King Saul.

Death on the battlefield

The day of the great battle between the Philistines and the Israelites
came. The Philistines overwhelmed the Israelites and killed Saul's three
sons, including Jonathan. Saul was severely wounded. "Kill me!" Saul
commanded his armor bearer. Saul did not want to be captured and
tortured, but the armor bearer did not want to kill his king. So Saul took
his own sword and fell on it and his armor bearer fell on his sword, too.

The next day, the Philistines found the bodies of Saul and his sons
on Mount Gilboa. They cut off Saul's head, stripped him of his armor,
hung his body on the wall of Beth-shan, and proclaimed his death
throughout the land. So ended the life and reign of King Saul.

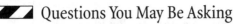 Questions You May Be Asking

How can I make sense of six complex Bible books that seem to have no consistent pattern as they present the story of the kings and kingdoms?
It's not easy. To make it more complicated, these books were written by different people at different times. For example, First and Second Chronicles were probably written as one book by Ezra, about five hundred years after the time of the kings and kingdoms. These books present much of the material from the books of Samuel and Kings for a very different audience in a very different way.

How did an unknown like Samuel come to national leadership?
The story of Samuel begins with the story of a barren woman, Hannah, who was one of Elkanah's two wives. The other wife, Peninnah, had children, and Hannah bore the shame of childlessness that barren women experienced in those days. Peninnah made life miserable for Hannah by gloating over her own fertility.

Hannah pleaded desperately with God to send a son, and miraculously, he did. Then Hannah did the unthinkable. When the boy was weaned, she gave him to God, to serve the priest Eli in the Tabernacle.

The little boy, Samuel, grew up in this great tent with an aging priest as his only day-to-day father, and with the priest's evil sons. It was not a fun-filled boyhood, but by living in God's tent, Samuel learned to love God and had a desire to serve him.

One night, God spoke audibly to the boy Samuel as he lay on his bed in the dim, flickering light of the seven-branched candlestick. God told Samuel, and Eli forced Samuel to tell him, about God's judgment on Eli's wayward family. Eli's sons could never lead Israel, so Samuel would do it.

Samuel did grow up to lead Israel while it was still a theocracy with God as king. He was a righteous ruler, but a poor father. In that way, he followed in the footsteps of old Eli, whose sons could not succeed him. Samuel didn't really have a father role model. Samuel's sons did not live as Samuel did, and God refused their succession to leadership.

How did an unknown like Saul become king?
When the people saw the inferior leadership qualities of Samuel's sons, they demanded a king. They wanted to be like the surrounding nations. God granted their wish and chose Saul, a farmer from the tribe of Benjamin, which was among the least of the Israelite tribes. At first, Saul was an effective military leader and king, but then he refused to obey God, so God made other plans. A young shepherd boy named David would be the next king.

160

>

What
Everyone
Should
Know
about
the

Bible

Great Events of This Time

1. **Hannah prays for a son, and Samuel is born** (1 Samuel 1:1-20).
2. **Samuel is consecrated to God** (1 Samuel 1:21-28).
3. **Eli's sons commit evil deeds** (1 Samuel 2:12-26).
4. **A prophet predicts Eli's doom** (1 Samuel 2:27-36).
5. **God speaks to the boy Samuel in the Tabernacle** (1 Samuel 3:1-18).
6. **Samuel becomes God's prophet** (1 Samuel 3:19–4:1).
7. **The Ark is captured and Eli dies** (1 Samuel 4:1-22).
8. **The Philistines are punished for taking the Ark** (1 Samuel 5).
9. **The Philistines return the Ark** (1 Samuel 6:1–7:2).
10. **The Philistines flee from God's thunder** (1 Samuel 7:3-14).
11. **Samuel makes his circuit** (1 Samuel 7:15-17).
12. **Israel demands a king** (1 Samuel 8).
13. **Saul searches for his donkeys** (1 Samuel 9:1–10:16).
14. **Saul becomes king** (1 Samuel 10:17-27).
15. **Saul is victorious over the Ammonites** (1 Samuel 11).
16. **Samuel reminds the people to fear God as he retires** (1 Samuel 12).
17. **Saul sacrifices wrongfully** (1 Samuel 13:8-14).
18. **Jonathan is brave at Micmash** (1 Samuel 14:1-23).
19. **Saul makes a foolish vow** (1 Samuel 14:24-46).
20. **Saul is victorious over his enemies** (1 Samuel 14:47-52).
21. **Saul destroys Amalek and keeps back the best of the spoils** (1 Samuel 15).
22. **Samuel anoints David to be the next king** (1 Samuel 16:1-13).
23. **David plays music for Saul** (1 Samuel 16:14-23).
24. **David fights the giant Goliath** (1 Samuel 17).
25. **David and Jonathan become best friends** (1 Samuel 18:1-4).
26. **Saul is jealous of David** (1 Samuel 18:5-16).
27. **David marries Saul's daughter Michal** (1 Samuel 18:17-30).
28. **Saul tries to kill David and David escapes; Saul pursues him and prophesies** (1 Samuel 19).
29. **Jonathan warns David with arrows** (1 Samuel 20).
30. **David flees to Nob and Ahimelech the priest helps him** (1 Samuel 21:1-9).
31. **David flees to Gath and pretends madness before Achish** (1 Samuel 21:10-15).
32. **David hides at the cave of Adullam and seeks protection for his parents** (1 Samuel 22:1-5).
33. **Saul kills some priests and Abiathar escapes to David** (1 Samuel 22:6-23).
34. **David rescues Keilah** (1 Samuel 23:1-14).
35. **David and Jonathan renew their friendship** (1 Samuel 23:15-18).

36. **The Ziphites betray David** (1 Samuel 23:19-29).
37. **David spares Saul at En-gedi** (1 Samuel 24).
38. **Israel mourns the death of Samuel** (1 Samuel 25:1).
39. **Abigail makes peace with David** (1 Samuel 25:2-44).
40. **David finds Saul sleeping and spares him** (1 Samuel 26).
41. **David is given Ziklag and gains Achish's trust** (1 Samuel 27:1–28:2; 1 Chronicles 12:1-18).
42. **Saul visits the witch of Endor and calls for Samuel to come back from the dead** (1 Samuel 28:3-25).
43. **David is dismissed by the Philistines and destroys the Amalekites** (1 Samuel 29–30; 1 Chronicles 12:19-22).
44. **Saul dies on the battlefield** (1 Samuel 31; 1 Chronicles 10).
45. **David learns of Saul's death** (2 Samuel 1).

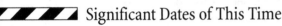

Significant Dates of This Time

1105 B.C., Samuel is born.
1080 B.C., Saul is born.
1050 B.C., Saul becomes Israel's first king.
1040 B.C., David is born.
1025 B.C., David is anointed to replace Saul; David fights Goliath.
1010 B.C., Saul dies on the battlefield.

Heroes and Villains: The Stars in Scene 11

We could list quite a few key Bible heroes and villains for this time. For example, there was Elkanah, Hannah's husband. He seemed to love Hannah and expressed his love for her, but he didn't stop Peninnah from mocking Hannah for being childless. Then there was the priest Eli, overly fat from too much rich food, and overly protective of his villainous sons. Of course, we could take a look at those sons, Hophni and Phinehas. They were villains, with few heroic virtues in them, engaging in sex with the women who came to minister at God's house, and taking offerings for the Lord as their own. They could never be Eli's successors.

The witch of Endor is an interesting character. She was a medium who dared to stick to her work despite Saul's law against this kind of thing. When Saul wanted to call Samuel from the dead, he visited this woman. There was also Michal, Saul's daughter, who fell in love with David. She and David married, but their marriage was very troubled and ended in Michal's isolation from David. Because of that, she died childless, which was a shame in ancient Israel.

We will focus on the following as key heroes or villains—Goliath and Nabal were villains for sure; Abigail, Hannah, and Jonathan were true

162

>

What
Everyone
Should
Know
about
the

Bible

heroes; Samuel was a godly man who couldn't raise his sons to succeed him; and Saul, the successful military leader, just couldn't seem to obey the Lord.

ABIGAIL

This beautiful and wise woman was married to a crude, thoughtless shepherd and landowner named Nabal. When David and his men were hiding from Saul and needed food, Nabal refused to share his food with David. Abigail wisely took food secretly to David and kept him from attacking Nabal. Shortly after that, Nabal died and David married Abigail. She lived with him in the wilderness until David became king after Saul's death.

Bible events in Abigail's life
1. She gathers food and takes it to David and his men.
2. She marries David.

ELI

When Hannah came to the Tabernacle to pray for a son, Eli was the high priest. He lived at the Tabernacle in Shiloh with his sons, who proved unworthy to take over his work. Later, when Hannah gave birth to her miracle son, Samuel, she brought the child to the Tabernacle to serve the Lord and Eli, so Samuel grew up under Eli's guidance. Eli was apparently a godly man, but he had little control or influence over his own ungodly sons.

Bible events in Eli's life
1. He prays that the Lord will grant Hannah's request.
2. Hannah brings Samuel to help him in the Tabernacle.
3. His sons are evil.
4. He blesses Hannah and Elkanah each year when they come to the Tabernacle.
5. A man of God brings him bad news about the future of his family.
6. Samuel comes to him in the night when the Lord calls Samuel.
7. Samuel tells him what the Lord said about his family.
8. When he hears about the loss of the Ark and the death of his sons, he falls and dies.

GOLIATH

David left his father's flocks to take food to his brothers who were soldiers in King Saul's army. He was surprised to find a Philistine giant challenging the Israelite army. Not one Israelite soldier would fight Goliath, who was about nine feet tall, with a massive build and state-of-the-art weapons. David offered to fight Goliath and went against him with only a slingshot and five small stones from the nearby brook. With his first shot, David sank a stone into Goliath's forehead, and after he fell, David cut off his head. The power of the Lord was greater than the power of a Philistine giant and his weapons of war.

Bible events in Goliath's life
1. He challenges the Israelites.
2. David fights him and kills him with a sling and stone.

HANNAH

A Levite from Ramah named Elkanah had two wives. Peninnah had children and taunted Hannah, who had none. Hannah prayed for a son and vowed that if she had one, she would give him to the Lord. When Hannah had the son for whom she prayed, she kept her vow and took the little boy, Samuel, to serve the Lord in the Tabernacle at Shiloh, assisting the priest Eli. Hannah's miracle son grew up to be a mighty leader over Israel.

Bible events in Hannah's life
1. She asks God for a son.
2. God answers her prayer and Samuel is born.
3. She gives Samuel back to God for as long as he lives.
4. She prays in joy and thankfulness to God.
5. She visits Samuel each year and brings him a new robe.
6. The Lord blesses her with three more sons and two daughters.

JONATHAN

When David killed Goliath, Saul's son Jonathan was among the soldiers who watched. He admired this courageous young man, David, who had dared to do what no Israelite career soldier would take on. From that day, Jonathan became David's best friend, even though he was the son of King Saul, who was insanely jealous of David and tried to kill him. As Saul's son, Jonathan was heir apparent to the throne, but he recognized that David would become the next king. Jonathan was killed in battle with his father when the Israelites and Philistines were engaged in a mighty struggle.

What
Everyone
Should
Know
about
the

Bible

Bible events in Jonathan's life
1. He defeats the Philistines single-handedly at Micmash.
2. Unaware of Saul's vow, he eats honey and is condemned to death, but the other soldiers intervene.
3. He becomes David's friend, makes a covenant with him, and gives him his robe, sword, bow, and belt.

4. He speaks to Saul on David's behalf.
5. He promises to help David, and asks David to love him and his children for as long as they live.
6. Saul throws a spear at David in anger.
7. He signals David with arrows.
8. He visits David at Horesh and encourages him.
9. He is killed in battle by the Philistines.

NABAL

Even his wife called Nabal a fool. He was very stupid and stingy when David and his men asked for food. They had protected Nabal's shepherds while hiding out from Saul, but Nabal stubbornly refused to give them any food, so David made plans to invade his ranch and destroy his people.

Nabal's wife, the beautiful Abigail, heard what her husband had done and immediately took a generous gift of food to David. When David saw her and the food, he called off his plans to punish Nabal. When Nabal heard what she had done, he had a stroke and died. Then Nabal's wife married David.

Bible events in Nabal's life
1. He refuses to give food to David and his men.
2. When he hears that Abigail gave David food, he suffers a stroke and dies.

SAMUEL

Elkanah had two wives—Hannah, who had no children, and Peninnah, who had children and taunted Hannah because she was childless. Hannah prayed for a son, and promised the Lord that she would give that son to him for his service. When Samuel was born, Hannah gave him to the Lord's work at the Tabernacle. He stayed there with the priest Eli, helping Eli care for the Tabernacle, and watching Eli's sons behave in shameful ways. When Eli died, Samuel became the priest and judge over Israel. Later, the people of Israel wanted a king instead of Samuel's sons, and the Lord had Samuel anoint Saul as king.

Bible events in Samuel's life
1. He is born to Hannah and Elkanah.
2. He is dedicated and given to the Lord.
3. He helps Eli in the Tabernacle.
4. Hannah visits him and brings him a new coat each year.
5. God calls him in the night and tells him what will happen to Eli and his family.

6. He becomes Israel's judge at Mizpah.

7. When Samuel prays, the Lord defeats the Philistines with a thunderstorm.

8. He rides a circuit to judge Israel.

9. Elders of Israel come to him and request a king.

10. He meets Saul, and the Lord tells him that Saul is the one who will rule Israel.

11. He anoints Saul with oil and proclaims him king; he reminds the people of the rights and duties of a king.

12. He calls the people together at Gilgal to renew their vows to Saul.

13. In his last address to the people of Israel, he reminds them of their responsibilities to the Lord.

14. When Saul sacrifices wrongly, he condemns his disobedience and predicts the end of his kingdom.

15. He rebukes Saul for his disobedience and kills Agag, king of the Amalekites.

16. He anoints David to be the next king of Israel.

17. He dies and is buried at Ramah.

SAUL, KING OF ISRAEL

Samuel's sons were unfit to rule Israel after him, so the people demanded a king. Saul was chosen but promptly went back to farming. However, when the Ammonites attacked Jabesh-gilead, Saul assembled an army and defeated them. From that time on, Saul was involved in numerous military campaigns, often against the Philistines.

Because of his disobedience to God, Saul was rejected as king and David was anointed. David remained loyal to Saul until Saul's death, at which time David became king over Judah, and later king of all Israel. Saul suffered from some nervous or mental trouble, perhaps severe depression; it was soothed when David played harp music for him.

Bible events in Saul's life

1. He searches for his father's donkeys and meets Samuel.

2. Samuel anoints him and proclaims him king.

3. He fights against and defeats the Ammonites.

4. He sacrifices wrongly and is condemned by Samuel.

5. He makes a foolish vow that condemns Jonathan to death.

6. He fights the Amalekites, but disobeys God, who rejects him as king.

7. David plays his harp to soothe him, and he makes David his personal armor bearer.

8. He gives David his own armor to fight Goliath.

9. He is jealous of David and throws his spear at him.

166
>
What
Everyone
Should
Know
about
the
Bible

10. He promises David his daughter Michal in marriage if he kills some Philistines.
11. He throws his spear at David again and tries to kill him.
12. He is angry at David's absence from his table.
13. He commands Doeg to kill eighty-five priests and their families.
14. He pursues David in the wilderness.
15. David spares his life but cuts off part of his robe.
16. David spares his life again and takes his spear and jug.
17. He visits the witch of Endor.
18. He is wounded in battle and dies by falling on his own sword; his body is hung on the wall at Beth-shan.

What everyone should know about the book of 1 Samuel
HOW GOD CAN USE FLAWED PEOPLE

The book of 1 Samuel was possibly written by Samuel, with writings from the prophets Nathan and Gad included. It is a record of the lives of Samuel; Saul, Israel's first king; and David, whom God chooses to succeed Saul as king.

What is the key message of 1 Samuel? God uses flawed people, such as Samuel, Saul, and David, to serve him. Here is the meaning of 1 Samuel for you:

Are you a flawed person? I must confess that I am. If you are like me, you wish you could retrieve words, misdeeds, attitudes, actions, and hurt inflicted on others. We have shot arrows into life and we wish we could pull some back almost as soon as they leave us. So what do we do about it? Do we cover our flaws and pretend that we are perfect? Or do we confess them to God and seek his forgiveness and the forgiveness of others?

If you feel that you are a flawed person, find comfort in 1 Samuel. It is a book about four of the greatest men of Israel. There was Eli, the priest. We don't have many stories about Eli, so we don't know much about him, but he must have been an impressive man to get the office. The Bible doesn't fault his work as priest, but he was a lousy father. His sons were unworthy to follow in his footsteps.

Samuel was one of the all-time great spiritual leaders of Israel. God used him in mighty ways. Samuel was a devout man of God, a prayer warrior, and a leader among leaders. Even the king trembled in his presence. But Samuel was another lousy father. He built a fine career, but his sons couldn't inherit his mantle of leadership.

Saul was a head taller than his contemporaries. He ruled Israel as its first king and he began well, even humbly. Things went from bad to worse, however, and he even began to plot murder against his son-in-law. His son Jonathan was worthy to succeed him, but Saul had so damaged his kingship that it passed out of the family to David. Saul was a flawed, weak person who committed suicide in battle.

David was Israel's greatest king. He was a supreme warrior and an unequaled psalmist who could play a harp or conquer a Philistine. He, too, was flawed as a father. For the most part, his sons were poster boys for how *not* to live. David also committed adultery, then murdered a man to cover it up.

These Bible heroes were great, but every one of them was a sinful, flawed person. The next time you feel that God can't use you because you don't measure up, remember this catalog of Bible greats. God used them all, not because of their flaws, but despite their flaws. Perhaps he will also use us with all our flaws too.

What everyone should know about the books of 1 and 2 Chronicles

A MORNING OF HOPE AFTER A NIGHT OF MISERY

Let's do a quick review of where we have come thus far in the Bible story. In Genesis, we saw the beginning of the world and its people, the story of the families of Abraham, Isaac, and Jacob. Genesis ended with Jacob's son Joseph, then ruler of Egypt, caring for his family there. Four hundred years passed before the Exodus began. Exodus is the story of Jacob's descendants, the people of Israel, who were taken into slavery in Egypt, then rescued by God through Moses. God led his people through the Red Sea to Mount Sinai, where he gave them his laws and established Israel as a nation. Leviticus is the story of a holy God and how the people of Israel could walk with him.

Numbers is the story of the Israelites from Mount Sinai to the doorway of the Promised Land. They were a grumbling, ungrateful people who refused to enter the land. The story continues with their further thirty-eight years of wandering in the wilderness until that generation had died. Deuteronomy records the wise advice of Moses when the Israelites, now a new generation, came to a new doorway to the Promised Land.

Joshua is a book of conquest—Joshua's military conquest of the land and the Canaanites' cultural conquest of their Israelite conquerors. The book of Judges describes Israel's Dark Age in the Promised Land, with judge after judge trying to lead them. Ruth is the story of a wonderful Moabite girl in the time of the judges who was faithful to her mother-in-law, Naomi. Ruth became the great-grandmother of King David and an ancestor of Jesus.

The book of 1 Samuel tells us about Samuel's life, the building of the kingdom under Saul, and the choice of David to replace Saul as the next king. Second Samuel is mostly about David's reign from 1003 B.C. to 970 B.C. First Kings tells about David's son Solomon, who at first was humble and devoted to God, but was corrupted by his thousand wives and concubines, many of whom brought pagan gods into the land. The once-devout Solomon drifted spiritually until he was preoccupied by riches and even worshiped pagan gods. For this, God took the kingdom from his descendants. The kingdom was divided, and Judah and Israel were ruled by kings descended from Ahab's son Ahaziah. Second Kings is the story of the divided kingdom from the rule of Ahaziah until Israel's people were deported to Assyria, and, much later, Judah's people were exiled to Babylon.

The captivity was a long, long night of darkness for the people of Israel and Judah. Their beloved Jerusalem and its Temple were destroyed by the Babylonians, and they were refugees far from home. Now a new day was dawning. The book of 1 Chronicles was written, according to tradition, by Ezra. It recalls how Israel got into the mess they were in and then looks

168

>

What
Everyone
Should
Know
about
the

Bible

forward to a new day of hope for the people. The book opens with extensive genealogical records, events during King David's reign, and further genealogical lists.

Second Chronicles recalls the reign of Solomon, the division of the kingdom, and the history of the divided kingdom through Judah's exile to Babylon.

Did You Know?

The menorah–seven oil lamps for the boy Samuel When he was a boy, Samuel lived at the Tabernacle, serving the old priest Eli. His bed was near the menorah, the seven-branched lampstand in the Tabernacle. Sometimes it was called a candlestick, although it had no resemblance to our candles today. The lampstand, or menorah, was an ornate golden pole on a pedestal with seven ornate branches at the top. On each branch was a small cup that held olive oil, in which there was a wick. When the wick was lit, the olive oil fueled the lamp. Each morning, a Levite priest filled the cups with the finest olive oil and lit the wicks. The menorah burned throughout the day and into the evening until the cups ran out of oil. The flames were symbolic of the Lord's presence. Picture the boy Samuel, going to sleep in the last flickering moments of the lamps on the golden stand.

The god with a fish's tail The Philistines worshiped a god called Dagon. This image had the head and torso of a man, complete with hair and beard, but from the waist down, he was a fish, like a male mermaid. Dagon was the god of rain, who was thought to bring fertility, and therefore a rich harvest, so he was also the god of grain. The Philistines built many temples to Dagon, some of which were large enough to hold thousands of people. Samson died by pulling down the supporting pillars of the Dagon temple at Gaza, killing himself and the three thousand Philistines who crowded inside the temple.

An armor bearer did more than carry armor When Jonathan went alone to fight the Philistines (1 Samuel 14), he took his armor bearer with him. When David went to fight Goliath, he not only faced the giant, but also Goliath's armor bearer (1 Samuel 17:7, 41), who carried the giant's shield. It probably weighed so much that a normal man would struggle to carry it. When Saul was mortally wounded in his battle with the Philistines, he told his armor bearer to kill him so he wouldn't be tortured if captured, but his armor bearer wouldn't do it. Saul committed suicide, and his armor bearer did also (1 Samuel 31:4-5).

Few kings would go to battle in those days without an armor bearer, who not only carried some of the warrior's weapons, but was also a personal bodyguard, defending the king or warrior with his own life. In a "clean-up operation" when victory was assured, a king or warrior often went through the battlefield inflicting mortal wounds on the enemy. His armor bearer then finished killing them.

Anointing oil had a special recipe Anointing was usually done by a prophet, a man of God. Scented oil, made according to a carefully guarded recipe, was contained in a curved animal horn. This oil was considered holy. It was consecrated to the Lord and poured over the head of the anointed one, who knelt before the man of God.

The recipe for the holy oil was a carefully guarded secret, like the recipe for a famous soft drink today. Only a few priests knew the ingredients. To steal or copy this recipe was punishable by death. No one knows the quantities used, but some of the ingredients were pure olive oil, fragrant cane, and sweet cinnamon.

Harps and lyres David played the harp and the lyre. At first, his audience was his father's flock of sheep. Then he played for the troubled King Saul. The king had a type of depression, and David's music soothed his disturbed spirit.

There were many types of harps and lyres in those days, with variations in different countries. Some were as simple and crude as David's first lyre would have been. Others were very ornate, with carvings of stags, cows, and bulls, which may have represented different parts of a choir.

Lyres had a sound box at the base. This caused the tones to resonate richly. Strings were stretched tightly between the sound box and a crossbar. Some lyres had four strings, some had six, and others had nine. The harp was different from the lyre in that it lacked a crossbar. The strings were instead stretched from a curved piece of wood.

There were many other musical instruments in those days, but David's musical instrument was either the harp or the lyre. No doubt, many of the psalms were composed as he played on his simple instrument.

Urim and Thummim—determining the will of God The day before Saul died in battle, he asked the Lord whether he would have victory or defeat in fighting the Philistines. He tried three methods: (1) dreams, (2) sacred lots (the Urim and Thummim), and (3) the prophets. God refused to answer Saul with any of these methods, so Saul turned to a medium as his last hope.

Kings would often consult a high priest to learn the Lord's will concerning an important decision. The man of God frequently used two or three stones that were kept in a pocket of the priest's breastpiece. This

170
>
What
Everyone
Should
Know
about
the

Bible

ornate rectangle was worn on his chest and was covered with twelve precious or semi-precious stones. The stones used to determine the Lord's will were called the Urim and Thummim.

We don't know how these stones were shaped, or what the man of God did with them to determine the will of God. Apparently, God would guide the way they were handled and they would inform the priest of God's will. This was sometimes called "lots," or "sacred lots," or "casting lots," which was one of the three methods Saul used.

God's command for the Urim and Thummim is found in Exodus 28:30, "Insert the Urim and Thummim into the sacred chestpiece so they will be carried over Aaron's heart when he goes into the LORD's presence."

Through the years, people have had different ideas about how these stones were used to determine God's will. Some think there were twelve stones, the same as the twelve stones on the breastpiece. For a yes from God, these stones would shine brighter than the ones on the breastpiece, or show darker for a no answer. A second theory is that within the ephod, the high priest's sacred apron, there was a golden stone or plate with the name of Jehovah engraved on it. As the high priest fixed his gaze on this, he would prophesy. A third theory is that the Urim and Thummim were two or three stones. One stone meant yes, one meant no, and if there was a third, it was blank or neutral. The one that the high priest drew out from the ephod gave God's answer.

Discovering My Purpose from God's Plan

1. *Godliness is no guarantee of good fathering.* Eli and Samuel were both godly men who were wretched fathers. Godliness is a desire to love God and walk with him. Good fathering begins with a desire to love your children and walk with them. Happy is the man who does both!

2. *People look at appearance, but God looks at the heart.* God's way works better than our way. When Samuel looked at Jesse's sons to anoint one as Israel's next king, even he assumed that the tallest, most handsome son would be God's choice, not the youngest and smallest.

3. *One person's blessing can be another person's curse.* To the Israelites, the Ark of the Covenant was a blessing. To the Philistines, it became a curse.

4. *A slingshot with God is greater than an arsenal without God.* David had a slingshot and five stones, and he had God with him. Goliath had state-of-the-art weaponry, without God. David won.

5. *What we abandon or discard may be our undoing.* The Amalekites

abandoned an Egyptian slave, thinking that he would die from his sickness. It was that slave who led David and his men to the defeat of the Amalekites. Don't think that someone who is weak or worthless is unworthy of our help. That person could be our undoing or the source of our success.

A Golden Kingdom
The Reign of King David

Characters:
Abishai (David's military leader); Abner (Saul's military leader); Absalom (David's son who tried to steal the throne); Adonijah (David's son who tried to be king when David was old); Ahithophel (Absalom's advisor); Amasa (Absalom's military leader, then David's); Amnon (David's son); Araunah (whose threshing floor David bought); Asahel (Joab's brother, murdered by Abner); Bathsheba (wife of Uriah, then David; Solomon's mother); Gad (a prophet who advised David); Hanun (an Ammonite king who insulted David); Hushai (David's advisor who pretended to advise Absalom); Ishbosheth (a relative of Saul who was king of Israel for a short time); Joab (David's general); Mephibosheth (Jonathan's son whom David took care of); Michal (Saul's daughter and David's first wife); Nathan (a prophet who advised David); Obed-edom (who housed the Ark for a while); Samuel; Saul (Israel's first king); Shemei (Saul's relative who cursed David); Solomon (son of David and Bathsheba; king over Israel after David); Tamar (David's daughter who was raped by Amnon); Uriah (Bathsheba's first husband); Ziba (Mephibosheth's servant)

Time Period:
From the time David became king until Solomon's reign

Dates:
From 1010 B.C. to 970 B.C.

Where Scene 12 of the Big Story Can Be Found:
Parts of the books of 2 Samuel, 1 Kings, 1 Chronicles, and Psalms

In Scene 12, Find the Answers to These Questions:
Why were messengers with good news executed?
Who was struck dead for touching a box?

What beautiful woman took a bath in midafternoon in an open courtyard?

Who tried to kill his father and steal his throne?

Look for this in Scene 12

> A great warrior king committed suicide on the battlefield.
> A man followed his wife, weeping.
> A king is insulted when half of his messengers' beards are shaved and their robes are cut off at the buttocks.
> Seventy thousand people die because of a census.

 The Big Story So Far

The high price of lying

The story of Samuel and Saul closed with Saul's death by suicide on the battlefield. It was the tragic end of a tragic life. The Lord had personally chosen him to be the first king of Israel. This was a fantastic honor, but Saul frequently disobeyed the Lord, and he became so insanely jealous of David that he spent many years trying to kill him.

Saul was dead, but David did not know about it for three days. David and his men had returned to their town of Ziklag to find it in ashes, with their families and goods taken by the Amalekites. With the Lord's blessing, David and his men pursued the Amalekites and regained their families, possessions, and a large amount of additional booty. Then they headed back to Ziklag, where they spent two days unaware of Israel's defeat or Saul's death.

On the third day, an Amalekite messenger came with the tragic news of the great defeat and of the deaths of Saul and Jonathan. He also told David that he had killed Saul, hoping that David would reward him.

Instead, David ordered his soldiers to kill the messenger. David believed that no one should harm the Lord's anointed, and despite all his evil, King Saul was the Lord's anointed. David wrote a funeral song for Saul and Jonathan, found in 2 Samuel 1:19-27. It ends with the powerful conclusion, "How the mighty heroes have fallen! Stripped of their weapons, they lie dead."

Who will rule after King Saul?

Then it was time to move forward. David asked the Lord if he should leave his hiding place with the Philistines and return to Judah, and the Lord said yes, to Hebron. There the leaders of Judah crowned David king over the tribe of Judah.

Abner, Saul's general, had other plans. He went to Mahanaim and proclaimed Saul's son Ishbosheth king over the rest of Israel, and he ruled for two years.

174
>
What
Everyone
Should
Know
about
the

Bible

One day, Abner led some of Ishbosheth's forces to Gibeon. David's general, Joab, also led some troops to Gibeon. The two groups sat down, facing each other. Then Abner suggested to Joab that some men from each side fight each other. Twelve warriors engaged in hand-to-hand combat, and all of them were killed. Then the two armies began to fight each other, and Joab's forces defeated Abner's forces.

Joab had two brothers, Abishai and Asahel. When Abner lost the battle, Asahel began to chase him, but Abner turned and thrust his spear through Asahel. When Joab and Abishai heard that, they began to chase Abner. At sunset, they caught up to him, but Abner begged for peace and they let him go home. They buried Asahel's body in Bethlehem.

This was the beginning of a long war between Saul's followers and David's followers. With the passing of time, David's forces grew stronger than Saul's.

One day, Ishbosheth accused Abner of having sex with one of Saul's concubines. Abner was furious, and threatened to change his allegiance to David. This terrified Ishbosheth, for he would lose the head of his army, his power base.

Abner sent word to David that he wanted to change his allegiance to him. David agreed, if he could arrange for his first wife, Michal, to come back to him. David also put pressure on Ishbosheth to return Michal to him. By this time, Ishbosheth was frightened that he would lose his power to David, so he agreed.

Saul had given his daughter Michal to David, but when David had to flee Saul's insane jealousy, Saul gave her to a man named Palti. Palti followed behind Michal, weeping as she returned to David. Abner demanded that Palti turn around and go home.

King of all Israel

Now Abner earnestly set about making David king of all Israel. He consulted with the other leaders of Israel and encouraged them to make David king. Then Abner came to Hebron with his twenty key leaders and David gave a great feast for him.

Abner had barely left when Joab came home from a military conquest with much plunder. He was furious that David had let Abner come and go in peace. Joab followed Abner, caught up with him, and plunged his dagger into him, thus avenging the death of his brother Asahel. David was angry and ordered Joab and his officers to tear their clothes and go into deep mourning for Abner. When they buried Abner, David led the procession to his grave. David fasted and mourned all that day, so the people of Israel knew that David was not responsible for Abner's death.

When the news of Abner's death reached Ishbosheth, he and his followers were paralyzed with fear. It became obvious that Ishbosheth's days as king were numbered and that David would soon become king of all Israel.

One day, two of Ishbosheth's men, Recab and Baanah, went to Ishbosheth's home at noon, slipped past the sleeping guards, and found Ishbosheth taking a nap. They stabbed him, cut off his head, and fled with it across the Jordan Valley at night. They arrived at Hebron the next day and presented Ishbosheth's head to David, thinking that he would reward them. Instead, David was furious that they would kill an innocent man while he slept. He ordered Recab and Baanah to be killed and buried Ishbosheth's head in Abner's tomb.

This event paved the way for David to become king of all Israel. The leaders of the tribes came to Hebron and asked David to be their king. David was thirty at the time, exactly the age that Saul was when he became king. David reigned forty years following Saul's reign of forty-two years.

Golden Jerusalem

David needed a better capital city than Hebron. What better city than Jerusalem? However, Jebusites, not Israelites, occupied and controlled Jerusalem. The Jebusites taunted David, saying, "You'll never get in here! Even the blind and lame could keep you out!" (2 Samuel 5:6). But David had a strategy the Jebusites had not anticipated. He sent soldiers up through the water tunnel that led into the city. Soon David had conquered Jerusalem. He made it his capital city and named it the City of David.

As time passed, David became increasingly powerful, for the Lord was with him. King Hiram of Tyre wanted to help David, so he sent carpenters and stonemasons to build a palace for David out of great cedar logs.

The sound of wind in the trees

When the Philistines realized that David's power was growing, they mobilized their forces at Rephaim. David asked the Lord if he should go to battle against them, and the Lord said yes. David had a great victory, but the Philistines gathered their forces again. David again asked the Lord if he should go to fight them. This time, the Lord told him to go behind the Philistine line and listen for wind in the trees, for that would be a signal that the Lord was moving ahead of David and his troops. David had another great victory over the Philistines. David's greatness is seen in two ways here—he consulted the Lord and he obeyed the Lord. We need to remember those two qualities.

Bringing God's golden chest to Jerusalem

It was time to bring the Ark of the Covenant to Jerusalem. David put on a great show of power but neglected to look in the law to see

176

>

What
Everyone
Should
Know
about
the

Bible

how the Ark should be handled. The Ark was placed on a new cart and David walked before it, singing and dancing. When the procession reached the threshing floor of Nacon, the oxen pulling the cart stumbled. Uzzah reached out to steady the Ark and was immediately struck dead.

David was afraid to proceed with his plans to take the Ark to Jerusalem. Instead, he sent it to the home of Obed-edom in Gath. It remained there for three months, and the Lord blessed Obed-edom's home.

David tried once more to bring the Ark to Jerusalem. This time, he must have had someone study how to handle it. They made sacrifices along the way, and David danced with joy as the Ark came into Jerusalem. The first time, David tried to do it his way. The second time, David did it God's way. God's way always works better than our way.

Final conquests

David wanted to build a beautiful temple for the Lord, so he summoned Nathan the prophet and asked him to talk to the Lord about it. When Nathan returned, he told David, "This is what the LORD has declared: You are not the one to build a house for me to live in. . . . [But] when you die and join your ancestors, I will raise up one of your descendants, one of your sons, and I will make his kingdom strong. He is the one who will build a house—a temple—for me. And I will secure his throne forever" (1 Chronicles 17:4, 11-12).

With his capital city secure and the Ark of the Covenant in Jerusalem, David turned his attention to the enemies surrounding him. First, he subdued the Philistines. Then he conquered the land of Moab, the homeland of his great-grandmother Ruth. Next came the king of Zobah, and then the Arameans when they helped the king of Zobah. King Toi of Hamath voluntarily came to David with tribute money, seeking peace. In one last conquest, David killed eighteen thousand Edomites, descendants of Esau.

Kindness to the enemy's family

One day David wondered if any of Saul's family was still alive, for he had promised his good friend Jonathan that he would be kind to Saul's family. David learned that Mephibosheth, Jonathan's crippled son, was still alive. David brought Mephibosheth to the palace to live, and he ate at the king's table.

The high cost of insulting a world leader

When King Nahash of the Ammonites died, his son Hanun became king. Nahash had conquered Jabesh-gilead in the early days of King Saul's reign, and had threatened to gouge out the people's right eyes in exchange for peace. Saul had defeated Nahash and thus spared Jabesh-gilead (1 Samuel 11). Apparently Nahash learned his lesson, for he was friendly to David throughout his reign.

Now that Nahash was dead, David wanted to renew that loyal relationship with his son, so David sent ambassadors to express his sympathy to Hanun. Hanun's advisors thought they had come to spy on the land, so Hanun seized David's ambassadors, shaved half of each man's beard, cut off their robes at their buttocks, and sent them back to David in shame.

The Ammonites realized how badly they had insulted David and feared that David would punish them, so they hired Arameans, with thirty-two thousand chariots, to fight with them. David sent Joab and the entire Israelite army to fight them. After two major Israelite victories, the Arameans surrendered and became subject to Israel.

The bath that got a king in trouble

The war with the Ammonites resumed the next spring when it was safe to fight. Joab and his troops laid siege to the Ammonite capital city, Rabbah, which today is Amman, Jordan. David was not with his troops, as he so often had been in the past. Instead, he was safely at home in his palace.

One afternoon, David got up from his nap and went for a stroll on the palace roof. As he looked down into a neighboring courtyard, he saw a very beautiful woman taking a bath. He was interested, so he sent someone to find out who she was. "Bathsheba, wife of Uriah the Hittite," was the answer.

David sent for Bathsheba and they had sex. When she became pregnant, she sent word to David. The baby's father couldn't be her husband Uriah, for he was off fighting with Joab in Rabbah. David was in trouble. He brought Uriah home and hoped that the problem would be solved by making it appear that Uriah had fathered the child.

When Uriah came home, David asked him trivial questions about the battle, then told him to go home and enjoy himself. The next morning, David learned that Uriah had slept near the palace entrance, not in bed with his wife. "The Ark and the armies of Israel and Judah are living in tents, and camping in the open fields. How could I go home to wine and dine and sleep with my wife?" Uriah said. Now David was in deeper trouble. He tried again to get Uriah to go home to be with his wife, but Uriah refused.

The next morning, David wrote a letter to Joab and sent it by Uriah. "Station Uriah on the front lines, where the battle is fiercest," the king ordered. Joab obeyed, and Uriah was killed. When Bathsheba's time of mourning ended, David brought her to the palace and they were married (2 Samuel 11).

178

>

What
Everyone
Should
Know
about
the

Bible

At that point, David may have thought that he had gotten away with something. It was all very neat, but not tidy! He had a new wife who was already pregnant. Of course, he *was* king, and kings were allowed to do anything they wanted to do, weren't they?

Their baby was born. Soon afterward, the prophet Nathan came to see David. He told the king a fictitious story, but David thought it was real. There were two men in a certain town, one very rich, the other very poor. The rich man had large flocks of sheep and herds of cattle. The poor man had only one little lamb, so precious to him that it was like a pet for him and his children. He cuddled this little lamb like his own child.

When a guest came to the home of the rich man, the rich man needed a lamb to eat. Instead of taking one of his own, he snatched the poor man's lamb from him, killed it, and ate it.

As David listened to this story unfold, his anger boiled. How could anyone be so heartless and cruel? "Anyone who would do such a thing deserves to die!" David shouted. "He must repay that poor man four lambs for his one little one."

Nathan's eyes fixed on his king. Then he pointed his finger at his face. "You are that rich man!" he shouted. "The Lord has given you everything! Why then did you despise the Lord and do such a horrible deed to Uriah? You murdered him and stole his wife. Because of this, the sword will be a constant threat to your family. The Lord will cause your own household to rebel against you. I will give your wives to another man who will have sex with them in public. You tried to get by with this secretly, but I will punish you openly!"

David must have felt the weight of the world crush down on him. He didn't get by with anything. The Lord knew and would punish him severely. "I have sinned against the Lord," he cried out.

"The Lord has forgiven you," Nathan added. "But the consequences of your sin are still there. The child will die."

Soon afterward, the baby grew very ill. David begged the Lord to spare the child; he fasted and lay all night on bare ground. On the seventh day, the baby died, so David washed, changed his clothes, and went to the Tabernacle to worship.

Bathsheba became pregnant again and gave birth to a son. She and David named him Solomon. The Lord gave him another name, Jedidiah, which means "beloved of the Lord."

A seventy-five-pound crown

Meanwhile, Joab and his troops were in the final stages of defeating Rabbah. He sent word to David to come and lead the final charge so that David, not Joab, would get the credit for the victory. It was a humble act by a not-so-humble man.

David came with reinforcements and led the charge against Rabbah, the capital city of the Ammonites. David took the crown from the head of the Ammonite king and it was put on his own head. It was a massive, glittery crown with gold and gems that weighed seventy-five pounds. Hanun must have wished a thousand times that he had not insulted David's goodwill ambassadors as he saw all his people become David's slaves. They worked for him each day with saws, picks, and axes, and they worked the brick kilns. David and his troops also took a vast amount of plunder from Rabbah that further enriched Israel.

A fractured family

The Lord's word through Nathan that the sword would come to David's family soon became a reality. The first event was a tangled web of deceit and treachery. "David's son Absalom had a beautiful sister named Tamar." Her half brother Amnon fell desperately in love and became obsessed with her. It actually wasn't love but lust, as his actions showed.

Amnon's crafty cousin Jonadab, son of David's brother Shimea, came up with a treacherous scheme. "Pretend you are ill," he said. "When your father comes to see you, ask him to let Tamar come and prepare some food for you. Tell him you'll feel better if she prepares it as you watch and feeds you with her own hands." It sounded innocent enough, so he did it, and David sent Tamar to care for him (2 Samuel 13:5-7).

While Tamar was feeding him in his bedroom, Amnon grabbed her and raped her. Then his passionate "love" suddenly turned to passionate hatred. "'Get out of here!' he snarled at her" (2 Samuel 13:15). Now he had committed a double sin against Tamar.

"No, you mustn't reject me now," she begged.

But Amnon called a servant and told him, "Throw this woman out and lock the door behind her." Tamar tore the long, beautiful robe that showed she was a virgin, put ashes on her head, and went away crying.

When Absalom heard what had happened, he pretended to pass it off, but he was plotting how to get even with Amnon. Tamar was desolate, and went to live with Absalom. David heard about it and was angry, but he did nothing.

Two years went by, and Absalom gave a great feast and invited all his brothers, including Amnon. He even invited his father, David, but David did not come. Absalom got Amnon drunk and commanded his men to murder him. The other sons of David quickly jumped on their mules and fled.

At first, the news that reached David was false. Someone said that Absalom had killed all of David's sons. Then another messenger set the record straight—he had killed only Amnon, as he had been plotting to do since Amnon had raped Tamar. David went into mourning

180

>

What
Everyone
Should
Know
about
the

Bible

for Amnon, and Absalom ran away to safety at the home of his maternal grandfather, Talmai son of Ammihud, the king of Geshur. There he stayed for three years. When David became reconciled to Amnon's death, he longed for his son Absalom. Joab knew this and set up a trick.

Joab arranged for a widow to plead to David for the life of her son, who had killed another son in a fight. When David granted the woman's request, she asked David why he didn't have the same mercy on his own son Absalom and bring him home. "Did Joab put you up to this?" David asked (2 Samuel 14:19). The woman had to tell David the truth—yes, he did.

So David sent for Joab and told him to bring Absalom back to Jerusalem, with one condition. He must live in his own house and never come to see David personally.

Stealing a father's throne

Absalom was the most handsome man in Israel. His appearance was perfect. When he cut his hair once each year, it weighed five pounds. Absalom had three sons and one beautiful daughter, whom he named for his sister Tamar.

Absalom lived in Jerusalem for two years without seeing his father. He sent for Joab to intercede for him, but Joab refused to come. He asked a second time, and Joab still refused. Then Absalom ordered his servants to set fire to Joab's barley field, which was next to his. That caused Joab to come immediately to see Absalom. Joab went to David to try to get him to see Absalom. At last David invited Absalom to come and Absalom bowed before him and kissed him.

As Nathan had warned, the sword was coming to David's family. The lust of David's son Amnon hatched a plot in David's son Absalom to murder his half brother. Absalom had to live away from his father for several years before they were reconciled. Would the family trouble end there? Unfortunately, it had just begun.

Absalom was a cunning man who wanted to be king instead of David. He bought a fancy chariot and noble horses and had fifty footmen run ahead of him. Each morning he arose early, went to the gate of the city where important matters were discussed, and sat to listen to the people.

Absalom often said, "If I were king, I could help you." Over the course of four years, Absalom stole the hearts of the people.

One day, Absalom went to Hebron, which was David's capital when he was king over Judah. Some of David's most trusted advisers, such as Ahithophel, joined Absalom in rebelling against David. Before long, a messenger arrived with the news that Absalom had been crowned king in Hebron. Instead of facing his wayward son, David fled with his loyal followers.

It was a sad procession as David and his followers descended from Jerusalem, crossed the Kidron Valley, and headed toward the wilderness. Abiathar and Zadok tried to bring the Ark of the Covenant, but David told them to return it to Jerusalem where it belonged. David also asked Abiathar and Zadok to be his spies and keep him informed.

The procession made its way up the Mount of Olives. David wept all the way, with his head covered and his feet bare. At the top, David's friend Hushai was waiting. He wanted to go with David, but David asked him to go to Jerusalem and pretend to follow Absalom as he spied for David.

Ziba met David there, too. When Saul's son Mephibosheth came to the palace to live with David, Ziba became his servant and land manager. Ziba had donkeys and food for David.

"Where is Mephibosheth?" David asked.

"In Jerusalem," Ziba answered. "He thinks this may be the time for him to become king."

How disappointed David was!

"I now give you everything that Mephibosheth owns," David said to Ziba.

The procession moved on to Bahurim. There, a member of Saul's family named Shimei came out. He ran beside the procession, throwing stones at the king and his officers and shouting horrible things at them.

"Let me go over and cut off his head," Abishai demanded.

"No," David answered. "If the Lord has told him to curse me, who am I to stop him? My own son is trying to kill me. This relative of Saul has even more reason to want me dead."

At last, when the procession reached the Jordan River, they rested.

Back in Jerusalem, Absalom asked his adviser Ahithophel what he should do next.

"Have sex publicly with David's concubines," Ahithophel advised.

That would be a point of no return, an insult to his father so grave that they could never reconcile. Tents were set up on the palace roof and Absalom had sex publicly with David's concubines. The prophet Nathan had prophesied to David that this would happen.

Ahithophel quickly advised Absalom to gather twelve thousand troops and go after David that very night, to kill David and his key people while they were weak and discouraged. Absalom wanted the advice of Hushai, whom David had sent back as a spy. Absalom thought that Hushai was loyal to him now.

"Ahithophel is very wise, but this time he has given bad advice,"

182

>

What
Everyone
Should
Know
about
the

Bible

Hushai told Absalom. "David and his men are not weak like you think. They are enraged, like a mother bear whose cubs have been taken away. If you attack, they may cause panic among your troops and you will have a major defeat. Instead, spend time mobilizing your army, and then you personally should lead the army against David."

"Hushai's advice is better than Ahithophel's," said Absalom. Ahithophel felt disgraced, so he put his affairs in order and hanged himself.

Meanwhile, Hushai quickly sent word to David to cross the Jordan River into safety, so David and his followers crossed the river that night.

Absalom mobilized Israel's entire army, except for those who followed David. Amasa was his new commander, for Joab remained loyal to David and led his troops. The troops urged David not to go to battle, since Absalom was determined to kill him.

Absalom's forces confronted David's forces in the forest of Ephraim, and David's forces beat them back. That day alone, twenty thousand men were killed. Actually, more men died because of the forest than because of the battle.

Defeat by five pounds of hair

Absalom somehow became separated from his troops and stumbled onto some of David's men. He tried to run away, but his thick hair caught in the branch of a tree. His mule kept going, leaving Absalom hanging helplessly from a tree branch. One of Joab's men ran to tell him what had happened. Joab rushed immediately to the scene and plunged three daggers into Absalom's heart. Then young armor bearers joined Joab and finished killing Absalom. They threw Absalom's body into a pit and covered it with stones, and Absalom's army fled back to Jerusalem.

Messengers were sent to tell David the news. David entered into uncontrollable grief for his wayward son, and the joy of victory quickly turned to a sense of defeat.

Soon Joab went to see David. "We saved your life today, and the lives of your family, but you make us feel ashamed. You are making it clear that we mean nothing to you. Now get out there and congratulate the troops. If you don't, not a single one of them will stay with you until morning. Then where will you be?"

It made sense, so David went out and sat at the city gate, where the people swarmed to see him.

Return of the king

Back home, the rebellious troops were having second thoughts. They remembered that David had saved them from the Philistines and Absalom had not. They decided to ask David to return and be their king.

When David headed home, hundreds came out to greet him. Shimei was there, too, fearful for his life. Remember him? He was the one who threw stones at David when he was leaving Jerusalem. True to David's character, he forgave even this vile man. Mephibosheth also came from Jerusalem.

"Why didn't you come with me?" David asked Mephibosheth.

"Ziba deceived me," he said. "You know I am crippled. I asked him to saddle my donkey, but he didn't. Then he told lies about me to you." Now David could not tell who was telling the truth, Ziba or Mephibosheth.

"You will divide the property I gave you," said David. "Half will go to each of you."

Contest of the generals

Before long, a man named Sheba revolted. He blew a trumpet and told the men of Israel to follow him. The people of Israel began to follow him, and the people of Judah stayed with David. The people were divided again.

Since Joab had killed Absalom, David appointed Amasa, who had led Absalom's troops, to be his general. He ordered Amasa to gather the troops within three days and pursue Sheba, but by the end of the three days, he had not done it. So David sent Abishai, who took Joab with him to do the job.

At a certain point, Amasa met them. Joab pretended to greet his cousin, but instead, he plunged a dagger into his belly and his bowels gushed out. Sheba, meanwhile, had moved on to his own clan at Abel-beth-maacah. Soon Joab and his forces arrived and began battering the city, but a wise woman called out for Joab to talk with her.

She asked him why he wanted to attack their city. Joab told her he didn't want to conquer the city, but he just wanted the rebel Sheba.

So the woman talked her people into killing Sheba and dumped his head over the wall to Joab, who blew the trumpet and took his forces back to Jerusalem.

Joab once again became the head of David's army.

The high price of murder

A famine came to the land and lasted three years. David asked the Lord about this famine, and the Lord said that it was punishment for Saul's murdering the Gibeonites. David summoned the Gibeonite leaders and asked what he could do to compensate them.

They said they wanted seven of Saul's sons or grandsons to execute. So that is what David did, but he spared Mephibosheth because he was Jonathan's son. David buried the seven, along with Saul's and Jonathan's bones, in the tomb of Saul's father Kish, and the famine ended.

184
>
What
Everyone
Should
Know
about
the
Bible

David's battle days ended in a skirmish with the Philistines. One of the Philistine giants cornered David and almost killed him. He would have died if Abishai had not rescued him, so David's men declared that he should not go into battle again.

A census that cost seventy thousand lives

David ordered Joab to take a census of the land. Joab didn't want to do it, but David insisted. At last the report came in that there were eight hundred thousand men in Israel and five hundred thousand men in Judah of military age. After the census, David's conscience began to bother him and he was sorry he had done it.

The Lord sent word through the prophet Gad that David must choose one of three punishments for taking this census—three years of famine, three months of fleeing from enemies, or three days of severe plague. David chose the last of these, and seventy thousand people died. When the angel of death reached Jerusalem, the Lord told him to stop.

David wondered how to make amends. At Gad's suggestion, he bought the threshing floor of Araunah the Jebusite and built an altar there. The Temple was later built there by Solomon and the Dome of the Rock stands there today.

Solomon becomes king

By now, David had grown old. Adonijah, one of David's sons, thought that this was the time to seize the throne. Like Absalom, he had never been disciplined, so he became rebellious. The sword that divided David's family was once again poised to strike.

Adonijah went to En-rogel, just outside Jerusalem, and offered sacrifices. Then he declared himself king. Nathan the prophet was not loyal to Adonijah, so he quickly went to Bathsheba and asked if she knew that Adonijah had just declared himself king. Bathsheba rushed to see David and reminded him of his promise to make Solomon king.

"Take Solomon down to Gihon Spring," David ordered Zadok the priest and Nathan the prophet. "Anoint him king and blow the trumpets." So that is what they did.

Adonijah and his guests heard the great celebration from a distance. Soon a messenger arrived with the news that David had just made Solomon king and that Solomon was already sitting on David's throne.

Adonijah's guests fled in panic. They knew that Solomon would probably kill them all. Adonijah rushed to the Tabernacle and clutched the horns of the altar in a supposedly safe place. Before long, Solomon heard this and summoned Adonijah. "Go on home!" he commanded.

Thus the reign of King David ended and the reign of King Solomon began. David was king for forty years—seven years as king of Judah only, and thirty-three as king of all Israel. Saul had been king for forty-two years, so between them, they ruled Israel for eighty-two years.

Questions You May Be Asking

Who was David? Where did he come from? Why did God choose another unknown to lead the nation?

The story of David actually begins in the rolling hillsides outside of Bethlehem, near the fields where his great-grandmother Ruth had gleaned. This youngest son of Jesse was stuck with the job of caring for the family sheep. To pass away the long hours, this talented boy learned to play the harp or lyre and to sing. David may have composed some of the psalms in his youth as he sang to his sheep, accompanied by his crude harp.

Shepherding is a lonely life, but no city person ever saw the canopy of stars, galaxies, and planets that young David saw at night. He most likely had his favorite constellations in his love affair with the stars. Under those stars, he developed a friendship with God and a heart-to-heart, mind-to-mind relationship. God and David were on good terms in a genuine friendship.

How did David's work as a shepherd prepare him for later life?

David the shepherd boy was incredibly skillful with a sling. He could hit an impossible target at a great distance. This sling was different from the forked slings we all know. It was a little leather pouch tied to the ends of two leather thongs. One was tied to a wood handle that was like a foot-long broom handle. The other thong was loose.

With one hand, the slinger would hold the loose end of the thong close to the handle with a stone inside the pouch. Round and round he would twirl it, and at last let the loose thong go. The stone would fly like a bullet to its mark.

Lions and bears often came to steal lambs, and this shepherd boy learned to fight them bare-handed. He learned to overcome his fear.

While David was just a boy, probably in his midteens, God sent Samuel to Bethlehem to meet with Jesse and anoint one of his sons to be the next king of Israel in place of the disobedient King Saul. He screened all the sons Jesse had brought, but God said no to each of them.

Puzzled, Samuel asked Jesse, "Is this all? Are there no other sons?" Jesse replied, "There's just the kid who is out in the fields taking care of the sheep." It never occurred to Jesse to bring this dark and handsome young boy to Samuel. He was the least of the least, even in this family.

He was the one God chose and the one that Samuel anointed to become the next king of Israel. Meanwhile, he was sent back to care for the family sheep. Kingship could wait.

186
>
What
Everyone
Should
Know
about
the

Bible

It's still a long way from the sheep fields to the throne. How did he get there?
Dramatic privileges often come from dynamic opportunities. David's opportunity came one day when he delivered supplies to his soldier brothers who were members of the Israelite army at war with the Philistines. They were engaged in a critical battle in the Valley of Elah, which was part of the strategic route from west to east. If Israel lost that valley, it would lose more than land. It would lose a vital trade route.

David was shocked by what he saw. A Philistine giant named Goliath came into the valley daily, challenging Israel to send someone to fight him. The winner would take all, including the enemy army. The giant was a walking military machine, almost nine feet tall with a powerful body. His armor was state of the art, and he was a highly trained fighter. No Israelite dared to face him.

Young David insisted on fighting the giant. In desperation, and with no other volunteer, Saul let him do it. David faced the giant with only a shepherd's staff and his sling. His ammunition was a pouch of five small stones gathered from the dried-up brook in the Valley of Elah.

Saul must have watched this brave boy do what his bravest soldiers would not do—face Goliath, the military machine. Saul must have thought himself crazy for putting his army's future in the hands of this kid.

The giant was scornful, but David was prayerful. The giant had weaponry, but David had God on his side. With his sling, he planted one stone in Goliath's forehead, and when he fell, David took Goliath's own sword to cut off his head and present it to King Saul.

The Israelite army went wild with triumph as they chased the Philistine soldiers and secured the victory that David had begun. When they returned, David was their hero as burly career soldiers claimed him as their military leader.

King Saul went wild with jealousy. He, the king and leader of the army, had been a coward while the teenager had done the job and won universal praise from the whole army of Israel. Saul was forced to put David in charge of parts of his army because that's what the soldiers wanted.

For months, David won great victories and escaped Saul's treachery, but Saul's jealousy became murderous. He intensely wanted to kill his military hero. At last, David had to escape from Saul into the hills.

One day, in a decisive battle with the Philistines, things turned against Saul. To avoid capture and torture, he committed suicide by his own sword. David became king over Judah, and seven years later, he became king over all Israel.

What kind of king was David?

David was a wonderful king. He was a great warrior who kept the peace with his neighbors through his military skill. He was a godly man who knew that the Lord was the real ruler of Israel. He wrote many of the psalms in our Bible that were the hymns of ancient Israel. One wonders how many of them were written when David was still a shepherd boy. David was a godly person who was loved by most of the people. Like all of us, David also had flaws and sinned.

What were David's flaws and sins?

David was an ineffective father, and his family tore at each other's throats. He lusted for Bathsheba, the wife of one of his soldiers. He got her pregnant, then had Bathsheba's husband, Uriah, murdered in battle so he could marry her.

David wanted to build a Temple for the Lord, but the Lord would not let him do it because he had killed hundreds of men in battle. David's successor had to do it.

Great Events of This Time

1. **David becomes king of Judah; there is civil war** (2 Samuel 2:1–3:1).
2. **Abner and Ishbosheth are murdered** (2 Samuel 3:2–4:12).
3. **David becomes king over all Israel** (2 Samuel 5:1-5; 1 Chronicles 11:1-3; 12:23-40).
4. **David captures Jerusalem** (2 Samuel 5:6-10; 1 Chronicles 11:4-9).
5. **David builds his palace, and God blesses David's kingdom** (2 Samuel 5:11-12; 1 Chronicles 14:1-2).
6. **David battles the Philistines, and God's presence is known by the wind in the trees** (2 Samuel 5:17-25; 1 Chronicles 14:8-17).
7. **The Ark is brought to Jerusalem from Kiriath-jearim** (2 Samuel 6; 1 Chronicles 13; 15–16).
8. **David makes plans for the Temple and prays** (2 Samuel 7; 1 Chronicles 17).
9. **David has victory over his enemies** (2 Samuel 8; 1 Chronicles 18).
10. **David is kind to Mephibosheth** (2 Samuel 9).
11. **Hanun embarrasses David's ambassadors** (2 Samuel 10; 1 Chronicles 19).
12. **David seduces Bathsheba, and Nathan rebukes him** (2 Samuel 11:1–12:25).
13. **David captures Rabbah** (2 Samuel 12:26-31; 1 Chronicles 20:1-3).
14. **Amnon rapes Tamar** (2 Samuel 13:1-37).
15. **Absalom flees and returns to Jerusalem** (2 Samuel 13:38–14:24).
16. **Absalom is reunited with David** (2 Samuel 14:25-33).
17. **Absalom rebels against his father, David** (2 Samuel 15:1–16:14).

188

>

What
Everyone
Should
Know
about
the

Bible

18. **Absalom consults his advisors** (2 Samuel 16:15–17:23).
19. **Absalom is defeated and dies** (2 Samuel 17:24–18:33).
20. **David returns to Jerusalem** (2 Samuel 19).
21. **Sheba rebels** (2 Samuel 20).
22. **There is famine and seven sons of Saul are slain** (2 Samuel 1:1-14).
23. **Goliath's brother and three other giants are killed** (2 Samuel 21:15-22; 1 Chronicles 20:4-8).
24. **Mighty men of David bring water from Bethlehem** (2 Samuel 23:8-39; 1 Chronicles 11:10-47).
25. **David buys Araunah's threshing floor** (2 Samuel 24; 1 Chronicles 21).
26. **David and Solomon plan the Temple** (1 Chronicles 22–26).
27. **Adonijah seeks the kingship, and Solomon becomes king** (1 Kings 1; 1 Chronicles 28:1–29:25).
28. **David gives his last words and dies** (1 Kings 2:1-12; 1 Chronicles 29:26-30).

Significant Dates of This Time

1010 B.C., David becomes king over Judah.
1003 B.C., David becomes king over all Israel.
1000 B.C., David captures Jerusalem and makes it his capital.
997 B.C., David sins with Bathsheba, captures Rabbah.
991 B.C., Solomon is born.
980 B.C., David's census and punishment; he buys Araunah's threshing floor, the site of the future Temple.
970 B.C., David dies.

Heroes and Villains: The Stars in Scene 12

During the reign of King David, there were several heroes and villains, some of them in unexpected places such as in David's own family. First, there was Ishbosheth, Saul's son, who claimed the throne of Israel while David was king of Judah. He was the heir apparent as son of the former king, but as David's brother-in-law (David married his sister Michal), he surely knew that Samuel had anointed David as the next king. He wasn't exactly a villain, but he wasn't a hero, either.

David's family was a mess. David's son Amnon raped his half sister Tamar, then consigned her to a life of shame and loneliness by his rejection. Another of David's sons, Absalom, murdered his half brother Amnon and later tried to kill his own father and steal the throne from him. David's son Adonijah tried to take the throne from David when he was old.

Then there is Bathsheba. What was she doing, taking a midday bath in full sight of the king on his palace rooftop? Was she inviting the king to notice her? If so, it worked. This led to David's seducing her, murdering her husband, and marrying her. David was certainly a villain in this whole affair, but Bathsheba may have been somewhat villainous, too.

David was both heroic and villainous, wasn't he? So was Joab, and so were other key leaders. Ahithophel was heroic when he served David, but villainous in betraying him. As is true of so many, heroes can also be villainous, and villains can sometimes be heroic.

Here are some key people who stand out at this time:

ABSALOM
David's third son was unusually handsome, and had long, thick hair. He had a fiery temper. He murdered his half brother Amnon in revenge for raping his sister, and later burned the grainfields of his father's general, Joab, to get his attention. Absalom rebelled against his father by trying to kill him and become king in his place. His attempt failed and he was executed by Joab and his men.

Bible events in Absalom's life
1. He is born to David and Maacah.
2. After killing Amnon for raping Tamar, he escapes and takes refuge with his grandfather, Talmai, for three years.
3. Joab tries to bring him back from exile by sending a woman of Tekoa to plead with David.
4. He returns to Jerusalem and is finally reunited with David two years later.
5. He plots to win the people's favor by talking with them at the city gate.
6. When he rebels against David, Ahithophel leaves David and joins him.
7. He has sex publicly with David's concubines.
8. He accepts Hushai's advice.
9. David's army defeats him; he is caught in an oak tree and Joab kills him.

What
Everyone
Should
Know
about
the

Bible

AHITHOPHEL
David's wise counselor was apparently a loyal officer until Absalom rebelled against his father and tried to take the kingdom from him. Ahithophel joined Absalom's rebellion and gave him counsel against David. However, when Absalom accepted the advice of Hushai, who pretended to help Absalom but was actually helping David, Ahithophel went home, put his business in order, and hanged himself.

Bible events in Ahithophel's life
1. He advises David.
2. Absalom sends for him, and he joins Absalom's conspiracy against David.
3. He advises Absalom, but God turns his advice to foolishness.
4. He is disgraced because Absalom refuses to accept his advice; he kills himself.

DAVID

During a war between Israel and the Philistines, David left the fields of Bethlehem, where he was a shepherd boy, and took food to his brothers in the Israelite army. There he saw the Philistine giant Goliath challenge the frightened soldiers of Israel. David accepted the challenge, killed Goliath, and became the hero of the army. King Saul took him to his palace to live, and David became close friends with Saul's son Jonathan. David knew that he would become the next king of Israel, for Samuel had already anointed him, but he refused to harm Saul and remained loyal to him until Saul was killed in battle. David then became king, at first over Judah, and later over all Israel. He ruled wisely and took Israel into its most prosperous period to that point. David was victorious in battle and among the nations, but he was defeated in his own household. David's son Amnon raped his half-sister Tamar, and for that he was murdered by David's son Absalom. Later, Absalom rebelled against David and tried to kill him and take over his kingdom. David is still remembered as the greatest of the Israelite kings and as the father of another great king, Solomon.

Bible events in David's life
1. He is anointed by Samuel.
2. He plays his harp to soothe the troubled King Saul.
3. He takes food to his brothers in King Saul's army.
4. He accepts Goliath's challenge to fight him and kills him with a sling, a stone, and the giant's own sword.
5. Jonathan becomes his friend and gives him his robe, sword, bow, and belt; he makes a covenant with him.
6. Saul becomes jealous of him and throws a spear at him while he plays his harp for Saul.
7. He kills many Philistines so he can marry Saul's daughter Michal.
8. Saul tries to have him killed. Michal helps him to escape.
9. He is absent from the king's table.
10. He promises to love Jonathan and his children all their lives.
11. Jonathan warns him with arrows.
12. Ahimelech lets him eat the holy bread and gives him Goliath's sword.

13. He is afraid of King Achish of Gath and pretends to be insane.
14. He flees to the cave of Adullam.
15. He defeats the Philistines at Keilah.
16. He flees to the wilderness of Ziph, where Jonathan comes to encourage him.
17. He moves to the caves of En-gedi with his men and spares Saul's life, but cuts off a piece of Saul's robe and shows it to him.
18. He asks Nabal for food. Nabal refuses, but Nabal's wife, Abigail, brings food for him and his men.
19. When Nabal dies, he marries Abigail; he later marries Ahinoam.
20. He sneaks into Saul's camp and takes his spear and jug but spares Saul's life again.
21. He goes to live at Ziklag with his men and their families.
22. Philistine commanders reject his help.
23. When he arrives back at Ziklag, he finds it burned and the women and children captured. He and his men pursue the Amalekites and defeat them.
24. He mourns for Saul and Jonathan and kills the Amalekite messenger.
25. He moves to Hebron with his family and is anointed king of Judah.
26. Abner pledges his loyalty to him.
27. He sends messengers to Ishbosheth, demanding that his wife Michal be sent back to him.
28. Joab kills Abner. He is angry and mourns for Abner.
29. He avenges the death of Ishbosheth.
30. He is anointed king over all Israel.
31. He captures Jerusalem and makes it his capital.
32. He builds a beautiful palace in Jerusalem.
33. He wars against the Philistines and Ammonites and defeats them.
34. His ambassadors are humiliated by the Ammonite king Hanun.
35. He sins against Bathsheba and her husband, Uriah.
36. After Uriah's death, he marries Bathsheba and they have a son.
37. Nathan rebukes him for his sin.
38. He is punished with the death of the baby.
39. Solomon is born to David and Bathsheba.
40. He is victorious in a series of battles.
41. Three brave men bring him water from Bethlehem.
42. He sings in thanksgiving to God for delivering him from all his enemies.
43. He attempts to bring the Ark of God to Jerusalem. Uzzah touches the Ark to steady it and is struck dead. This disturbs him and he leaves the Ark at the home of Obed-edom.
44. He brings the Ark to Jerusalem, dancing with joy; Michal sees him and despises him.

What
Everyone
Should
Know
about
the
Bible

45. He appoints musicians to sing and play in the worship services.
46. He composes psalms of thanksgiving to God.
47. He appoints Asaph and his companions to be in charge of the Ark in their daily ministry at the Tabernacle.
48. He desires to build a Temple for the Lord.
49. God speaks to him through Nathan and makes promises to him.
50. He shows kindness to Mephibosheth.
51. He is anguished when Absalom kills Amnon, and misses Absalom while he is gone for three years.
52. Joab helps bring Absalom back from exile. David refuses to see him for two years, but finally they are reunited.
53. Absalom causes people to change their allegiance from the king to him.
54. Absalom rebels against him.
55. Absalom is proclaimed king in Hebron; he flees.
56. He tells Hushai to go back to Jerusalem and confuse the advice of Ahithophel by giving him bad advice.
57. Ziba brings him gifts; Shimei curses him.
58. His forces battle Absalom's forces and Absalom is defeated; Absalom's hair gets caught in a tree, and Joab kills him.
59. He mourns for Absalom.
60. He returns to Jerusalem after Absalom's defeat.
61. Mephibosheth welcomes him back to Jerusalem.
62. Sheba rebels against him and is defeated.
63. He displeases God by taking a census of the people.
64. God tells him that he has three choices of punishment for the census; he chooses a plague.
65. The angel of death stops at Araunah's threshing floor; he buys the threshing floor.
66. He commands Solomon to build the Temple and makes preparations for it.
67. He puts Levites in charge of the Temple.
68. He reorganizes his army.
69. He assembles leaders to view the Temple plans.
70. He presents his charge to Solomon and gives him the Temple plans.
71. He gets old and has to stay in bed; Abishag is brought to keep him warm.
72. Adonijah proclaims himself as king; Bathsheba intercedes and he reaffirms Solomon as king.
73. He challenges Solomon to obey the Lord.
74. He dies at the age of seventy.

JOAB

David's half sister Zeruiah had three sons, each of whom was a hardened warrior—Joab, Abishai, and Asahel. Each of them became a commander of David's army at different times.

When David became king over Judah, Saul's son Ishbosheth took control of Israel. Joab led David's forces and Abner led Ishbosheth's forces. Abner had been King Saul's general, so it was expected that he would also command the forces of Saul's son.

When Ishbosheth insulted Abner, he transferred his loyalty to David. However, Abner had killed Joab's brother Asahel, so when the occasion was right, Joab murdered Abner.

When Jerusalem was captured, Joab was the first to enter the city, and for that, he was rewarded with the command of all David's forces. Later, David's son Absalom rebelled against David and Joab killed him. For a short time, David replaced Joab with Amasa, but Joab killed him and took back his job as commander. When Solomon became king, he ordered his bodyguard Benaiah to execute Joab as punishment for his murders.

Bible events in Joab's life

1. He is David's commander.
2. His warriors fight Abner's warriors at the pool of Gibeon.
3. He sounds the trumpet to end the battle.
4. He scolds David for being kind to Abner.
5. He kills Abner.
6. He helps David conquer Jerusalem and becomes commander of David's combined forces.
7. His army and Abishai's army help each other in fighting the Syrians and the Ammonites.
8. He obeys David's orders and puts Uriah in the most dangerous part of the battle so that he is killed.
9. He almost completes the siege of Rabbah but sends for David to finish the siege, so he can receive the honor.
10. He plans to bring Absalom back from exile by sending a woman of Tekoa to plead with David.
11. He brings Absalom back to Jerusalem.
12. Absalom sets his barley field on fire to get his attention.
13. He fights Absalom's forces; David tells him to have mercy on Absalom, but he kills Absalom as he is hanging in an oak tree.
14. He reproves David for mourning for Absalom.
15. He pursues Sheba after he rebels and kills Amasa.
16. A woman of Abel-beth-maacah throws Sheba's head over the wall to him; he blows his trumpet and his warriors return to Jerusalem.

194

>

What
Everyone
Should
Know
about
the

Bible

17. He reluctantly obeys David in taking a census.
18. He supports Adonijah as David's successor.
19. Adonijah is killed; he runs to the Tabernacle and clings to the altar, but Benaiah kills him there.

MEPHIBOSHETH

David's worst enemy was his father-in-law, King Saul, who often tried to kill him. His best friend was Saul's son, his brother-in-law Jonathan, who did all that he could to help David. Because of their strong friendship, David wanted to help Jonathan's family members after Saul and Jonathan were killed in battle. When he learned that Jonathan's son, Mephibosheth, was alive and had been crippled by a fall, David took him into his palace to eat at his table and restored Saul's family lands to him. When David's son Absalom rebelled against David, Mephibosheth remained behind in Jerusalem while David fled. His steward, Ziba, told David that Mephibosheth had stayed behind, hoping to become king, which may or may not have been true. David finally divided the land between Ziba and Mephibosheth, not knowing which one to believe.

Bible events in Mephibosheth's life
1. He becomes crippled when his nurse drops him.
2. King David shows kindness to him and lets him eat at his table.
3. He welcomes David back to Jerusalem after Absalom's defeat.

What everyone should know about the book of 2 Samuel
HOW CAN THOSE WHO FAIL EVER HOPE TO SUCCEED?
The story of David is found mostly in 2 Samuel, 1 Kings, and 1 Chronicles. It is the story of a godly man who also had failures. Can we succeed if we, too, have failed? This is the essence of 2 Samuel. The book was written around 930 B.C., shortly after the reign of King David (1010 B.C.–970 B.C.). We're not sure who wrote it. Nathan's son Zabud may have been the author (1 Kings 4:5), but the prophets Nathan and Gad contributed to it (1 Chronicles 29:29).

Here is the message of 2 Samuel: He's a failure! She's a failure!

I hope no one has ever said that about you, but I suspect that you may at some time have said that about yourself. On a dark day, when we seem to be on the bottom rung of life's ladder, we may be tempted to call ourselves failures.

If you want to know more about success and failure, read 2 Samuel. This Bible book is the story of one of history's greatest successes. If ever there was a successful warrior, king, and musician, with the heart of a spiritual giant, it was King David. He may have been the greatest king who ever lived, and is possibly one of the greatest people who ever lived. But this superstar was also a rotten failure. Despite his successes, David failed big time. David collected eight wives. Like his son Solomon,

David failed as a husband. He committed adultery with Bathsheba, then had Bathsheba's husband murdered. David was a great success, but he was also a big-time failure.

When you look at the catalog of David's failures, you may be tempted to think that God could never use him.

The portrait of David in 2 Samuel shows how an utter failure became a great success again. He truly repented and begged God to forgive him—and God did! Above all else, David wanted to honor, please, and serve God. Despite his failures, he loved God with all his heart, and God cleansed him of his sins.

If you could invite David to dinner at your house tonight, what would you like to ask him? Perhaps he could give you some tips about our forgiving God and being a forgiven sinner.

What everyone should know about the book of Psalms

MEET YOURSELF IN THE PSALMS

Imagine a church service without singing. Imagine worshiping God without music. How often have you sung a worship song or hymn and suddenly realized that the words of the song expressed just what you wanted to say to God? How did the songwriter know what you wanted to say? How did he or she know your thoughts, your emotions, your mind-set as you entered into worship?

The book of Psalms was the Israelite hymnal. It was written over a period of about 900 years, from the time of Moses, about 1440 B.C., until the time of the Babylonian captivity, about 586 B.C. Approximately seventy-three of the songs were written by King David, and some were written by Moses, Solomon, Asaph, Korah, Heman, and Ethan. Just like our hymnal, chorus book, or other collection of songs that we sing at church, Psalms is a book for worship. Each psalm is a poem that helps us express our deepest thoughts and feelings to the Lord.

Of all the books in the Bible, many people would choose the Psalms as their favorite. Most people who memorize Bible verses have memorized many verses from Psalms, probably more than from any other book of the Bible.

We meet God in the Psalms because the writers express their meetings with him. We resonate with the psalmists and we also meet ourselves in the Psalms. We meet our emotions, our longings, our hunger for God, our fear of circumstances, and our desire to walk with the Lord.

The heartbeat of the Psalms is not flippant, filled with clichés or buddy-buddy talk with the Creator. They have depth, breadth, height, and outreach. Their expressions of worship meet our deepest longings and feelings, but also rise to our highest celebration of the Creator. With the psalmists, we stand in awe before a holy God, walk through dark valleys with a God more powerful than a thousand Goliaths, and kneel before a God who has the answers to life's toughest questions.

If you're searching for God and his answers to life, you must read the Psalms. Like a thirsty person who returns again and again for refreshing water at a spring, you will return for refreshing spiritual water at the wellsprings of the Psalms.

196
>

What
Everyone
Should
Know
about
the

Bible

Bathsheba "got into hot water" by taking a bath It is ironic that her name was Bathsheba, since she caught the king's attention by taking a bath. It is less ironic when one realizes that the English word *bath* would not have been known then. Either way, Bathsheba's bathing raises some troubling questions: (1) Bathsheba's husband was away, fighting for the king. Why was she taking a bath in the open courtyard, clearly visible to the king from the flat rooftop of the king's palace? (2) Why was she bathing in midafternoon? Why not just before bedtime, or the first thing in the morning? Was this a regular time for David to take a walk on the rooftop? (3) Why didn't she protest when the king brought her to the palace to make love to her, reminding him that her husband was away fighting his battles? We don't want to fix any more blame on Bathsheba than on David, but these are troubling questions.

Even more troubling are questions about King David: (1) Why did he keep on watching this woman bathing? (2) Why did he command her presence so they could make love? (3) Why did he hatch devious plans to cover up her pregnancy and make it appear that Uriah had done it? (4) Why did he stoop to murder? Why didn't he confess to Uriah what had happened, beg his forgiveness, and give him something valuable to help make amends?

Bathsheba was not David's first wife She was David's eighth wife. The other seven were (1) Michal, Saul's daughter (1 Samuel 18:27); (2) Abigail, former wife of Nabal (1 Samuel 25:39-42); (3) Ahinoam (1 Samuel 25:43); (4) Maacah, who became Absalom's mother (2 Samuel 3:3); (5) Haggith (1 Chronicles 3:2); (6) Abital (1 Chronicles 3:3); and (7) Eglah (1 Chronicles 3:3).

Bathsheba's first husband, Uriah, was a Hittite A casual reading of the story of David and Bathsheba leads us to believe that Bathsheba's husband was an Israelite, off to war with the Israelite army. This was not true. Uriah was a Hittite (2 Samuel 11:3). As such, he was probably a mercenary, a hired soldier fighting for the money. Despite that, he showed unusual honor when he refused to enjoy the comforts of home while his fellow soldiers fought for the king (2 Samuel 11:11).

A thousand years before the time of David, the Hittites had a great empire that stretched from Lebanon to the Euphrates River. Then came the Philistines, sea peoples who conquered the Hittites. The Hittite empire did not survive, but the Hittite culture did, in parts of Syria. Uriah may have come from this Syrian line.

The city gate was the place to be Important things happened at the city gate. David's son Absalom knew this, so he went frequently to the city gates of Jerusalem to talk with people and make a case for his becoming king instead of his father, David. If you could choose the busiest and most popular meeting place in the city, it would be the city gate. It was a beehive of activity. Merchants set up their wares there each morning, just inside the gate. The city elders gathered there to talk about important things, to settle disputes, and to oversee business transactions. The city gate was the city hall and modern mall combined.

Why did King David want to buy a threshing floor? David was king, so what did he want with a threshing floor? This was a place where farmers brought their sheaves of grain, spread them out on a flat place, and trampled the sheaves to separate the grain from the stalks.

The threshing floor was in a high place where the wind was at its best. Here the farmers winnowed the grain by tossing the trampled mixture into the air. The wind blew the chaff away and the grain fell into a pile at the farmer's feet. After a farmer did this many times, the chaff was separated from the grain.

This particular threshing floor belonged to a farmer named Araunah. David had sinned by taking a census for his own pride, and the Lord gave him three choices as punishment for that sin. David chose three days of plague. On the third day, the angel of death stopped taking the lives of people at this threshing floor.

David's first motive in buying Araunah's threshing floor was to build an altar and make a sacrifice to the Lord. Later, he would have a much greater purpose, for this was the site where his son Solomon would build the Temple. Today, the Dome of the Rock, a Muslim mosque, stands on that site.

David had no royal blood, and was even part Moabite, yet he became the greatest Israelite king ever David grew up as a shepherd boy, tending his father's flocks of sheep. Shepherding was considered one of the lower occupations. David had not one drop of royal blood in him and he did not grow up as a prince, but God chose him as the king to replace the disobedient King Saul.

David descended from Jacob and his unloved wife Leah. Their son Judah had sex with his daughter-in-law Tamar, thinking she was a prostitute. From that event came Perez (Pharez or Phares). The generations that followed were: Hezron or Esron, Ram or Aram, Amminadab or Amin or Aminadab, Nashon or Naasson, Salmon, then Boaz, who married the Moabite widow Ruth. Their son was Obed and their grandson was Jesse, David's father. So through Ruth, David was part Moabite.

The psalms weren't the only Bible songs When David brought the Ark of the Covenant into Jerusalem, he composed a psalm of thanksgiving that

198

>

What
Everyone
Should
Know
about
the

Bible

is not in the book of Psalms. It is found in 1 Chronicles 16:8-36. There are other songs of the Old Testament that also are not in the book of Psalms:

Songs by the Red Sea When they had crossed the Red Sea and were finally safe from Pharaoh's elite chariot troops, the Israelites burst into a song of praise (Exodus 15:1-21).

A Song of Moses Moses composed this song and recited it as a duet with Joshua (Deuteronomy 32:1-44). Moses was about to die and Joshua was about to lead the Israelites into the Promised Land at last. The song reflects the past faithfulness of the Lord and looks forward to a wonderful future for the Israelites in the Promised Land.

The Song of Deborah and Barak After Deborah and Barak defeated King Jabin of Hazor, they recited this victory song (Judges 5). It was Israel's first great success over the chariot armies of the Canaanites. The story is in Judges 4.

Hannah's Song The barren woman Hannah prayed for a son, and Samuel was God's answer. She was so grateful that after she weaned him, she gave him to the Lord to serve the priest Eli in the Tabernacle at Shiloh. When she gave him to the Lord, Hannah sang this song, which was also a prayer (1 Samuel 2:1-10).

Discovering My Purpose from God's Plan

1. *Never harm the Lord's anointed.* Despite Saul's insane jealousy and his persistent effort to murder David, David remained loyal to Saul for as long as he lived. David's reason for not harming Saul was, "I must not harm the Lord's anointed." Be careful not to tear down someone who has been called to serve God, no matter how much you disagree with or dislike that person.

2. *We should mourn even our enemies.* When Saul, who tried for years to kill David, died in battle, David mourned his death and even wrote a funeral song for him and Jonathan (2 Samuel 1:19-27).

3. *Dramatic privileges often come from dynamic opportunities.* David's dynamic opportunity was to fight the giant Goliath. From that victory came the path to the throne, a truly dramatic privilege.

4. *Flawed people can become forgiven people.* Forgiven people can become productive people. David was flawed and sinful, but when he begged the Lord for forgiveness, the Lord used him in wonderful ways.

Rich Poverty
The Reign of King Solomon

Characters:
Adonijah (who tried to take the throne from David); Benaiah (Solomon's executioner, then his general); Jeroboam (who was advised by a prophet that he would be king of ten tribes); Nathan (a prophet who advised David); the queen of Sheba (who visited Solomon with riches); Rehoboam (Solomon's son, who succeeded him as king); Solomon (the son of David and Bathsheba who succeeded David as king); Zadok (a priest who advised David)

Time Period:
The reign of King Solomon

Dates:
Approximately 970 B.C. to 930 B.C.

Where Scene 13 of the Big Story Can Be Found:
Parts of the books of 1 Kings, 1 & 2 Chronicles, Proverbs, Ecclesiastes, Song of Songs

In Scene 13, Find the Answers to These Questions:
Why did a king almost cut a baby in two?
Who made $400 million each year tax-free?
Why was the Lord angry at the wisest man on earth for being so foolish?
Who gave a $52 billion donation to build a church? Why did he do it?
Where was there a twelve-thousand-gallon washbowl?

Look for this in Scene 13
> A feast ended in terror.
> For seven years, 183,000 workers labored to build one building.
> A woman gave $50 million to a king.

> A man had a thousand wives!
> There were fourteen hundred chariots and twelve thousand horses for one man.

The Big Story So Far

Solomon's rise to power

Solomon's rise to the throne was rather abrupt. It began with David's son Adonijah, who tried to seize the throne from his father, David. He even proclaimed himself king. Like his older brother Absalom, who tried to kill David and also tried to seize his throne, Adonijah had never been disciplined. In that way, David was a poor father.

Zadok the priest and Nathan the prophet were not on Adonijah's side. When Nathan heard what Adonijah was doing, he hurried to Bathsheba and told her. "If you want to save your life and Solomon's life, you must go at once to David and remind him that he promised that Solomon would be king. While you are still talking, I will come in and confirm what Adonijah is doing." That is the way it worked.

David promised Bathsheba again that Solomon would be king. Then he told Zadok the priest and Nathan the prophet to take Solomon to the Gihon Spring and anoint him king. "Blow the trumpets and shout 'Long live King Solomon!'" he commanded.

Before long, trumpets were sounding, and the people of Jerusalem shouted loudly to welcome their new king. It was such a noisy celebration that Adonijah heard it. His friends at the feast heard it, too, including David's trusted general, Joab. Soon a messenger brought news to Adonijah that David had just crowned Solomon king.

Needless to say, the people at that feast were terrified, including Adonijah. They could all be killed by the new king for treason, so they scattered like leaves on a windy day. Adonijah rushed to the Tabernacle and held fast to the horns of the altar, which was supposedly a safe place. Solomon sent for him and bluntly told him, "Go home!"

Counsel from King David

At last the time of David's death drew near. David spent much time with Solomon, planning the Temple. The Lord would not let David build it because he was a man of war, with much blood on his hands. Solomon was the one to do it. David actually planned the Temple and personally provided much of the wealth needed to build it.

Before he died, David had a heart-to-heart talk with Solomon about some cleanup matters. Joab had murdered two of David's generals, and he must not be allowed to die peacefully. Shimei had cursed

What
Everyone
Should
Know
about
the

Bible

David when he fled from Absalom. "You will know how to arrange a bloody death for him," David counseled.

David also advised Solomon to follow the Lord faithfully and keep his commandments. If he did, the Lord would be with him. How unfortunate that Solomon forgot this in his older years!

With things in order, David died and was buried in Jerusalem, the City of David. By this time, Solomon was firmly established as the king.

A king's cleanup campaign

Not long after David's death, Adonijah came to see Bathsheba. He wanted to ask a favor. Would Bathsheba ask Solomon to give Abishag to Adonijah as his wife? The request sounded innocent on the surface. Abishag was the young woman who had slept in David's bed to keep him warm as an old man, having no sexual relationship with him. Somehow, Adonijah thought that marrying Abishag would help him become king.

Bathsheba innocently went to Solomon with Adonijah's request. Solomon was shocked at his mother's request. "You may as well ask me to give my older brother the kingdom," he said. "He already has Joab and Abiathar the priest on his side."

Solomon decided that this was Adonijah's death warrant, so he ordered Benaiah to execute Adonijah. Then he deposed Abiathar and sent him far away. When Joab heard these things, he was frightened and ran to the Tabernacle and held onto the horns of the altar, which was supposedly a place of safety. Benaiah found him there and demanded that he come out.

"No, I will die here!" said Joab. So Solomon ordered Benaiah to execute him there and bury him. Then Solomon appointed Benaiah to lead his army, and Zadok replaced the priest Abiathar.

The king was in a cleanup mode and sent for Shimei, the man who had cursed David when he fled from Absalom. "You may build a house in Jerusalem and live here in peace," Solomon said. "But the day you set foot outside the city, you will die."

Shimei was careful to stay in Jerusalem, but three years later, two of his slaves escaped to the Philistine King Achish of Gath. Shimei went after them and brought them back to Jerusalem. Solomon sent for Shimei and reminded him of their agreement. Then Benaiah executed him.

Securing the peace

Solomon was not a warrior like his father, David, so he began a program to secure the peace. First, he made an alliance with Pharaoh, king of Egypt, and married his daughter. Thus far, Solomon showed great love for the Lord. Some think that his Song of Songs was a love song for this Egyptian princess and that he truly and passionately loved this one and only wife. It certainly isn't the love song of a man with a thousand wives, is it?

To show his love for the Lord, Solomon went to Gibeon, where he made a thousand burnt offerings. Solomon always did things in a big way! That night, the Lord appeared to Solomon in a dream and asked what he wanted. God promised to give it to him.

Solomon spoke to the Lord of his great kindness to David and to him. More than anything else, he wanted wisdom to rule his people well. The Lord was pleased with this request and promised to also give Solomon the riches, fame, and power for which he did not ask.

When Solomon woke up, he realized that it was a dream, but he returned to Jerusalem and made further offerings to the Lord before the Ark of the Covenant.

Before long, there was a test of Solomon's wisdom. Two prostitutes came to Solomon to settle an argument. Both women had babies, but one baby had died. The mother of the dead baby had switched the babies in the night so that she would have the living baby. Like little children, each of these two women said, "She did it!" How could anyone sort that one out?

"Bring me a sword," Solomon ordered. When he took the sword in his hand, he said, "Since we don't know who the real mother is, we'll cut the baby in two and give each of you half of the baby."

The woman who was not the real mother agreed, but the real mother said, "Oh, no, don't do that. Give the baby to the other woman."

"She is the real mother," said Solomon. "She loved her baby enough to give him away, rather than see him die."

Solomon's wise decision spread far and wide. As his reputation for wisdom grew, so did his wealth. Before long, Solomon had four thousand stalls for his twelve thousand chariot horses.

Building a $100 billion building—for God

The biggest and most significant event of Solomon's life was building the Temple. It was a masterpiece planned by his father David. King Hiram sent as much cedar and cypress lumber as Solomon wanted. Each year, Solomon paid him 110,000 gallons of olive oil and 100,000 bushels of wheat for this exotic lumber.

Solomon enlisted 30,000 laborers from Israel and sent them to Lebanon in shifts of 10,000. He also enlisted 70,000 laborers, 80,000 stonecutters, and 3,600 foremen to work in the quarries and at the Temple site in Jerusalem.

Never has there been a building like Solomon's Temple. King David

204

>

What
Everyone
Should
Know
about
the

Bible

had personally given more than fifty billion dollars for the Temple. Solomon started it in the fourth year of his reign and completed it in the eleventh year of his reign. You can imagine what an enormous project this was, with 183,600 workers laboring for seven years. What would that cost today? The value of the labor in today's market was probably more than the fifty billion dollars that King David gave. The Temple would easily cost more than one hundred billion dollars today. When he finished, Solomon built a magnificent palace for himself.

What a majestic celebration Solomon planned when it was time to bring the Ark of the Covenant into the Temple! The priests carried it into the Most Holy Place and placed it beneath the wings of the great cherubim. Then Solomon prayed and dedicated the Temple to the Lord. "O Lord, God of Israel, there is no God like you," he prayed. He was kneeling, with his hands raised toward heaven.

Solomon stood and shouted, "Praise the Lord! May he give us the desire to do his will and obey his commands in everything." If only Solomon could have remembered this later in his life.

The king and all his people offered sacrifices to the Lord. That day, twenty-two thousand oxen and one hundred twenty thousand sheep were sacrificed to him.

Solomon also moved his wife, the daughter of Pharaoh, to his new palace. Thus far, Solomon had one wife and a sincere desire to serve the Lord. Solomon grew richer each year. He built a fleet of ships at Ezion-geber, a port near Elath, that sailed to exotic ports and brought back wonderful things.

A queen's gift of gold and gems

News of this wise and wealthy king who lived in a golden city on a mountain reached the queen of Sheba, which some think is modern Ethiopia. She came to see Solomon and hear his wisdom. Some think that she also came to get a son who could succeed her some day. Who better to father the child than the wisest and richest man on earth?

The queen brought a gift of about fifty million dollars in gold, and of course Solomon gave her an equal amount of treasure. Tradition says that she also got her son and that he actually became one of Solomon's favorites, but this is not confirmed in the Bible. It merely says, "King Solomon gave the queen of Sheba whatever she asked for" (1 Kings 10:13). One tradition says that this son so pleased Solomon that Solomon gave him the Ark of the Covenant, and it is still in Ethiopia today.

The queen of Sheba was dazzled by all that she saw. It was a heady experience for her and her attendants to visit such splendor and talk with the wisest king in the world.

The richest man in town—the poorest man alive

In those days, gold flowed to Solomon like water. Each year, he received twenty-five tons, or about fifty thousand pounds of gold, probably as tribute. In today's gold prices, that would be an annual income of more than three hundred million dollars in gold alone. He also made a fortune from his commercial adventures, and of course from taxes and other perks. Solomon paid no taxes, so if he made, for example, $400 million each year, he kept the entire amount.

So what do you do with that much money? You become extravagant, and that's what happened to this man who had prayed so fervently at the Temple dedication. Start with two hundred shields of pure hammered gold, each weighing fifteen pounds. Add another three hundred smaller shields of pure gold. All of these hung as decorations in the Palace of the Forest of Lebanon. Next the king made a throne of pure ivory and covered it with gold. His drinking cups were pure gold, as were the other utensils in the palace. Why gold? Solomon's silver was too abundant. Solomon would have been shocked to drink from paper or plastic cups, which of course they did not yet have!

Solomon's fleet of ships returned once every three years, filled with gold, silver, ivory, apes, and peacocks. Just the thing for a man who had everything! People swarmed to talk with Solomon and when they did, they brought more rich gifts.

Solomon had fourteen hundred chariots and twelve thousand horses. What could one king do with so many?

So far, the indulgent king had focused on money, and up to this point, the Bible continues to speak of his God-given wisdom (1 Kings 10:24). Now Solomon's lust turned from money to women. "Now King Solomon loved many foreign women" (1 Kings 11:1). These were not women from the nice people next door, but from nations which had historically been enemies of Israel and worshiped pagan gods. The Lord clearly did not want Solomon or any other Israelite to marry people from these nations, for they would lead the Israelites into pagan worship (1 Kings 11:2).

Solomon turned this corner big-time. Many pagan kings had a dozen wives, and David had eight, but Solomon collected seven hundred wives and three hundred concubines. This was the turning point in Israel's history. We don't know what precipitated his wife collection, or how fast it came together, but from that point on, the history of Israel went downhill.

All that David had worked so hard to put together, Solomon was now unraveling with foreign wives who brought their pagan worship to Israel. The Israelites began to worship these evil deities, and Solomon began to worship them, also. This was the king who prayed so fervently

What
Everyone
Should
Know
about
the

Bible

and devoutly at the dedication of the Temple. The bottom line was that these wives "did turn his heart away from the LORD" (1 Kings 11:3).

The Lord was angry with Solomon. He had given this man everything—wisdom, riches, fame, and power. Now Solomon was quickly flushing it away for the sake of his lust. He was no longer the wisest man on earth, but one of the most incredibly stupid men on earth. What a turnaround!

"The LORD said to him, 'Since you have not kept my covenant and have disobeyed my decrees, I will surely tear the kingdom away from you and give it to one of your servants'" (1 Kings 11:11).

In Solomon's weakened relationship with the Lord, enemies began to arise. Among them were Hadad the Edomite, Rezon the son of Eliada, and Jeroboam the son of Nebat, one of Solomon's own officials.

Dark days on the horizon

Solomon didn't know it, but Jeroboam would become the next king, not of all Israel, but of ten tribes. This is how it happened.

Jeroboam was leaving Jerusalem one day when Ahijah the prophet approached him. Ahijah took the beautiful new cloak he was wearing and tore it into twelve pieces, one for each of the twelve tribes of Israel. "Take ten of these pieces," Ahijah told Jeroboam, "for the Lord is about to tear the kingdom from Solomon and give ten tribes to you. It won't happen now, during Solomon's lifetime, but after he dies. Follow the Lord and listen to him. He will always be with you."

Solomon must have heard the news, for he tried to kill Jeroboam. Jeroboam fled to Egypt and stayed there until Solomon died.

The time came for Solomon to die. He had ruled for forty years, just like his father, David. Solomon was buried in the city of his father, David, and his son Rehoboam came to the throne in his place.

Questions You May Be Asking

When Adonijah gave a great feast, what food did he serve?

Festive occasions were feasting occasions. We often see people giving a great feast at a festive time, such as a wedding or a royal occasion. Queen Esther gave two feasts for her husband and Haman. If you went to a Bible-time feast, what food would you expect to find?

That would depend on the wealth of the person giving the feast. A poor man's feast would be quite modest, both in menu and in presentation. A royal feast such as the one Adonijah would have given would have very exotic foods, splendid preparation and presentation, and vessels of gold and silver. Today, a highly paid chef could take the same meat that an ordinary person would prepare and present it in a much more delightful way.

First, the meats: There could have been a kid, lamb, or fattened calf, quail, pigeon, turtledove, or chicken. An exotic feast may have moved into wild game such as venison, wild kid, mountain lambs, roebucks, gazelles, hart, or antelope. Solomon might even have served peacock or just the hearts of peacock. Fish was also served. A feast would certainly include melons, dates, fresh grapes, raisins and raisin cakes, olives, fresh figs and dried figs, pomegranates, and apples. Onions, garlic, leeks, and cucumbers were also part of the meal. So were beans and lentils, pistachios and almonds. Of course there were many kinds of bread made from wheat or barley at any feast. Don't forget lots of wine, milk, and honey. Eggs were a common food and were probably prepared in many different ways. A king such as Solomon would have served exotic eggs such as peacock or quail eggs. Royalty could afford to have a chef prepare these foods in many wonderful ways.

Did Solomon grow up as a nobody, as Samuel, Saul, and David did in their childhoods?

Solomon was the first king of Israel to grow up as a prince and to receive princely training, but David was a lousy father. He raised children who tore at each other and even murdered one another. Solomon was the survivor, partly because his mother, Bathsheba, seemed to be David's favorite wife, and she persuaded him to make Solomon king.

How did Solomon become king?

When David grew old, his son Adonijah tried to seize the throne from him. Another son, Absalom, had tried that years before and succeeded for a short time, then died in battle against David's troops. Bathsheba, Solomon's mother, heard about Adonijah's rebellion and talked with David, reminding him that Solomon was supposed to be the next king. David immediately made Solomon king in his place.

What kind of king was Solomon?

At first, Solomon was a great king. In a dream, God promised him whatever he wanted. Solomon asked for wisdom to rule his people well. God was pleased and promised to also give him wealth, power, and fame. In his early years, Solomon showed great wisdom. God gave him more than any other person before Solomon's kingdom became corrupted and began to erode.

Was Solomon a good or bad husband?

By the time Solomon had collected seven hundred wives and three hundred concubines, he was an incredibly weak husband. It's hard to be a good husband to one thousand women! There couldn't have been

208

>

What
Everyone
Should
Know
about
the

Bible

much romance and loving care with so many to choose from. How could he even remember their names, let alone romance them?

There was a time early in his rule when he must have been a romantic, loving husband to the one woman in his life at that time. His passionate love is expressed in a beautiful book called Song of Songs or Song of Solomon.

That passion evidently faded through the years as he collected foreign princesses for his wives. Why? It was partly lust for sex and power. Evidently, it was mostly a political strategy. Marry a king's daughter, and the king will keep peace with you. Marry every king's daughter, and you won't have war from anyone. It seemed to work, but it was the downfall of the kingdom. Solomon traded securing the kingdom for destroying the kingdom. The very plan he used to secure peace backfired and tore the kingdom apart.

Was Solomon really the wisest man on earth?

In some ways he was, especially in his early years. The book of Proverbs was probably written in his early years, for example. These wise sayings show great wisdom, but as we see, the wisest man became the dumbest man. A good and godly king became a very ungodly ruler.

How did Solomon change from being a good king to being a bad king?

It all sneaked up on him. Like so many changes in life, it was not an abrupt new life one morning. In his growing lust for riches and women, Solomon focused on the wealth, power, and fame he had not asked God to give him. When he did, he forgot about the wisdom that he had asked for first. He began to neglect it. Solomon is a poster boy for those who would mortgage the best to gain the worst.

Solomon's many foreign wives brought their pagan gods with them. The wife and her idol were one package—love me, love my idol. Soon Solomon's people began to worship these pagan gods, and then even Solomon worshiped them. He tried to hold onto God with one hand and the pagan idols with the other. Solomon forgot the first commandment of the Ten Commandments that God gave Moses, "You must not have any other god but me" (Exodus 20:3).

God was displeased with Solomon. "The LORD was very angry with Solomon, for his heart had turned away from the LORD, the God of Israel, who had appeared to him twice. He had warned Solomon specifically about worshiping other gods, but Solomon did not listen to the LORD's command" (1 Kings 11:9-10). So the Lord promised him that he would "tear the kingdom away from [him] and give it to one of [his] servants" (1 Kings 11:11). These were harsh words, but that's what happened. As God indicated, this took place in the days of Solomon's son Rehoboam.

How did Solomon feel about all this?

He tells us this in the book of Ecclesiastes. He wrote that late in his reign, after he had tasted the bitter fruit of many things that matter little and too little of things that matter most. He uses words such as *emptiness, vanity,* and *meaningless.*

 ## Great Events of This Time

1. **Adonijah tries to become king, and David makes Solomon king instead** (1 Kings 1; 1 Chronicles 28:1–29:25).
2. **David gives his last words and dies; Solomon rules fully** (1 Kings 2:1-12; 1 Chronicles 29:26-30).
3. **Solomon destroys his enemies** (1 Kings 2:13-46).
4. **Solomon asks God for wisdom** (1 Kings 3:1-15; 2 Chronicles 1:1-12).
5. **Two women put Solomon's wisdom to the test** (1 Kings 3:16-28).
6. **Solomon appoints officials and gathers wealth** (1 Kings 4; 2 Chronicles 1:13-17).
7. **Solomon builds the Temple** (1 Kings 5–7; 2 Chronicles 2:1–5:1).
8. **The Temple is dedicated** (1 Kings 8; 2 Chronicles 5:2–7:22).
9. **Solomon gives King Hiram some cities** (1 Kings 9:10-14).
10. **The queen of Sheba visits Solomon** (1 Kings 10:13; 2 Chronicles 9:1-12).
11. **Solomon turns away from God** (1 Kings 11:1-25).
12. **Solomon dies** (1 Kings 11:26-43; 2 Chronicles 9:29-31).

 ## Significant Dates of This Time

970 B.C., David dies; Solomon becomes king.
966 B.C.–959 B.C., Solomon builds the Temple in Jerusalem.
930 B.C., Solomon dies.

 ## Heroes and Villains: The Stars in Scene 13

SOLOMON

Solomon was the son of David and Bathsheba. Through the wise and clever work of his mother and the prophet Nathan, Solomon was chosen to be king above his other brothers. At first, Solomon proved to be unusually wise and made decisions beyond human understanding. Instead of conquering his neighbors through military means, he formed political alliances with nearby kings and married their daughters to assure that they would not attack. These daughters brought their pagan gods with them, set up shrines and temples to them, and encouraged many Israelites, including King Solomon, to worship them. This was the

210

>

What
Everyone
Should
Know
about
the

Bible

beginning of the end for Israel, for pagan worship became the downfall of the nation. Later kings sometimes cleaned up the nation and led the people to worship God again, but not for long, for another king would drag the nation into idolatry again. Solomon is remembered for building the Temple that King David planned. It was a one hundred billion dollar building, a true wonder of the ancient world.

Bible events in Solomon's life
1. He is born to David and Bathsheba.
2. David charges him to build the Temple.
3. David assembles the people of Israel together and tells them that God has chosen him to be the next king; David tells them of plans to build a Temple and gives a charge to him.
4. Adonijah proclaims himself king; Bathsheba intercedes for him and David reaffirms him as his successor; Nathan anoints him at Gihon Spring.
5. He shows mercy to Adonijah.
6. He is challenged by his father, David, before he dies.
7. Adonijah again attempts to gain control of the kingdom; he has him killed.
8. He commands that Joab be killed and deposes Abiathar; Benaiah becomes his commander; he orders Shimei killed.
9. He marries one of the daughters of Pharaoh, king of Egypt.
10. He offers a thousand sacrifices at Gibeon.
11. He asks the Lord for wisdom to guide his people.
12. He makes a wise decision concerning two mothers.
13. He asks King Hiram of Tyre for building materials and craftsmen for the Temple.
14. He builds the Temple in Jerusalem.
15. He builds his royal palace.
16. Hiram makes the Temple vessels.
17. Solomon moves the Ark into the Temple.
18. He offers a prayer of dedication for the Temple.
19. He dedicates the Temple to the Lord.
20. He builds cities, walls, fortresses, and a fleet of ships.
21. He becomes wealthy and wise.
22. The queen of Sheba visits him.
23. He turns away from God.

What everyone should know about the book of 1 Kings
MORE WITHOUT GOD IS LESS, AND LESS WITH GOD IS MORE
First Kings is the story of Solomon, the richest man in town, but also the poorest man in town. It is the story of a man who had everything, but squandered what mattered

most for things that mattered least. The book continues with the consequences of the kingdom's division, and the rule of the kings of that divided kingdom through Ahab's son Ahaziah.

No one knows for sure who wrote this book. Some think that Jeremiah or some other prophet was the author. Consequently, we don't know exactly when it was written, but it was certainly after the death of Ahab in 853 B.C.

What is the message of the book for you and me? Read further.

Who is the richest person in town? Ask Solomon's neighbors. They would all tell you, "King Solomon. There has never been a richer person!" Who is the richest person in town? Ask Solomon. He will tell you, "As I looked at everything I had worked so hard to accomplish, it was all so meaningless—like chasing the wind. There was nothing really worthwhile anywhere" (Ecclesiastes 2:11). How could the neighbors think Solomon was so rich and Solomon think himself so poor? There must have been days when Solomon would have given it all to trade places with a poor man across town. The poor man was happy with nothing, while Solomon was sad with everything.

Solomon's story begins well. King David chose Solomon to be king and God said to Solomon in a dream, "What do you want? Ask, and I will give it to you!" (1 Kings 3:5). Solomon asked for an understanding mind to govern his people well. God was pleased with Solomon's request and promised him not only wisdom but also riches and honor. So far, so good. At this time, Solomon had chosen one bride, an Egyptian princess.

The story of Solomon's riches unfolds quickly in 1 Kings. He had rich food, thousands of horses, a fleet of ships, and hundreds of servants to do his bidding. The more he gained, the more he wanted. One wife wasn't enough, and he began to make peace with foreign nations by marrying their princesses. In time, Solomon had seven hundred wives and three hundred concubines, women who served as his wives without being officially married to him (1 Kings 11:3).

These foreign princesses brought with them their worship of foreign gods. Soon Solomon's people were worshiping these pagan gods, and later in life, Solomon himself worshiped them. The story of Solomon slowly erodes from the story of the wisest man on earth to the story of the most foolish man on earth who could not be content with anything. At last God spoke to Solomon and told him that his descendants would not inherit his throne. His prized kingdom would pass to strangers. Solomon's son could rule over only a small fraction of the kingdom.

Solomon learned a bitter lesson. More without God is less. Less with God is more. It is a wise lesson to learn, even from a foolish man. You and I would be wise to remember this lesson and foolish to forget it.

What
Everyone
Should
Know
about
the

What everyone should know about the book of 2 Chronicles

LEARNING FROM THE PAST

The story of 2 Chronicles is about King Solomon. It leads into the division of the kingdom under his son Rehoboam, and the rule of the kings of the divided kingdom through the exile of the people of Judah to Babylon.

Bible

According to Jewish tradition, Ezra wrote this book in about 430 B.C. It is thought that both 1 and 2 Chronicles were originally one book.

What is the message of 2 Chronicles for you and me? Read on:

Someone has quipped about 20/20 hindsight—seeing clearly what has already happened, but it is one thing to see the past and another to remember the past. It is still another to benefit from it.

Tradition tells us that Ezra wrote 1 and 2 Chronicles while the Israelites were still in exile in Babylon. In a very real sense, he is telling his captive people, "Look back before you look ahead. Learn from your past." Then he reviews the past and analyzes how they got into the mess they are in. They tasted the bitter fruit and needed to understand how the tree was planted that produced it.

The story begins with Solomon, the man who had everything—a well-known father, a great kingdom, unlimited wisdom, wealth beyond measure, and a palace filled with treasures. The Temple he built was one of the most beautiful buildings in the ancient world. He worshiped God with all his heart. What more could a person want?

That was the problem. The person who has nothing more to want always wants something more. The man who should have been content with one wife collected seven hundred wives and three hundred concubines. How could he even remember all their names? How could he relate to the children of a thousand women? Most of these women brought their pagan gods and pagan worship to Israel. Before long, even the Israelites worshiped these pagan gods, and Solomon also began to do so.

The man who had everything came to the end with his life running on empty. He was both rich and poverty stricken. When his son Rehoboam became king, the kingdom divided into the northern kingdom (Israel) and the southern kingdom (Judah). It was the beginning of the end for this nation.

In about 722 B.C., the Assyrians conquered Israel and deported the best Israelites. After another 110 years, Babylon conquered Assyria. In 586 B.C., the Babylonians conquered Judah, and exiled the best Israelites to Babylon. The once glorious kingdom was no more. Jerusalem and its beautiful Temple were completely destroyed.

A new day was dawning. In the time of Ezra and Nehemiah, there was hope of returning to the land or rebuilding Jerusalem and its Temple. The first important lesson was to learn from the past in order to avoid repeating yesterday's mistakes and sins. If God remains central, he will bring the desired success. It was a great lesson—worthy of a great time in the history of Israel and Judah.

What everyone should know about the book of Proverbs
ADVICE AT ITS BEST

If you want to read Solomon's counsel at the beginning of his reign when he walked closely with God, read Proverbs. If you want to read Solomon's counsel near the end of his reign after he had tried everything, read Ecclesiastes. Proverbs reveals a wise man not yet wealthy or wounded. Ecclesiastes reflects a wealthy and wounded man, coming to terms with the unwise choices he has made.

Solomon wrote most of the Proverbs, or at least compiled them, early in his reign, some time after 970 B.C. Agur and Lemuel contributed some of the later sections.

What is the message of Proverbs for you and me?

Life gets a little frustrating at times. There are so many options or choices facing us, and so many forks in the road. Which way should we go? We long for good advice. We need someone to help us sort out life's abundant, and often confusing, choices. We want to hear counsel from someone who has been down the road before, not from someone who has just read about our problem.

A proverb is a truth condensed into a short statement worthy of our attention. It helps us know God better, understand his truth more, and apply that truth to daily living. A proverb is life and wisdom in a nutshell, condensed down to its essence like a drop of perfume that releases its fragrance to bless all who are nearby.

When was the last time you read an advice column in your newspaper? "Dear X, I need help," someone writes. The writer may be suffering from a health problem, a bruised relationship with another person, a marriage in trouble, a bad relationship with a child or parent, or a tough time at work. If only we knew what to do! Perhaps the advice columnist can help. But has the advice columnist experienced our problem or just thought about it?

There is an advice column of sorts in our Bible. Perhaps it is more accurately called a counsel column. Proverbs was probably written early in Solomon's reign, when he was close to the Lord. Later, he had experienced the heartaches of life, and he had drifted into the arms of pagan deities.

Solomon tried it all and had it all. If you think that Solomon was supremely happy having everything, read Ecclesiastes. There, from the depths of his wounded soul, Solomon pours forth another kind of counsel.

What everyone should know about the book of Ecclesiastes

WORDS OF WISDOM FROM A WOUNDED MAN

Near the beginning of Solomon's reign, he assembled a collection of proverbs. Above all else, it is a plea for the reader to spurn ungodliness and follow godly wisdom. After identifying the author, the book begins, "[The] purpose [of these proverbs] is to teach people wisdom and discipline" (Proverbs 1:2). Again and again, the author pleads with the reader to follow God's wisdom, and not to be seduced by evil women, not to make riches more important than God, and not to be intent on satisfying human lusts. That was at the beginning of Solomon's reign, when he humbly walked with God and followed his counsel.

The scene shifts at the end of his reign. Solomon wrote another book that is unlike the first. Ecclesiastes is a brutally candid book that reflects his misguided values. The wisest man on earth became one of the most misguided men on earth, as his life was devoted to his lust for money, power, and women, the very things he had warned the reader to avoid in Proverbs. He never seemed to have enough of any of these things. He had violated the wisdom he expressed in the book of Proverbs. What happened?

The answer is found in 1 Kings 11. Here are some excerpts: "Now King Solomon loved many foreign women . . . he had 700 wives of royal birth and 300 concubines. And in fact, they did turn his heart away from the

214

>

What
Everyone
Should
Know
about
the

Bible

LORD. In Solomon's old age, they turned his heart to worship other gods instead of being completely faithful to the LORD his God, as his father, David, had been. . . . In this way Solomon did what was evil in the LORD's sight. . . . The LORD was very angry with Solomon, for his heart had turned away from the LORD, the God of Israel" (verses 1-9). Then God told Solomon that his kingdom would not pass on to his descendants. His son Rehoboam would inherit only a fraction of it.

If Solomon had followed his own counsel in Proverbs, he would never have needed to write his lament in Ecclesiastes. But he didn't follow it . . . so he did write Ecclesiastes.

For the most part, this is a book of lament. It is the cry of a man who has spent his life on a fast track to success, only to realize at the end that his "everything" was really "nothing." A palace filled with wine, women, and gold was actually nothing but a bag of empty air. "Everything is meaningless," the richest man on earth cries out. His palace filled with gold is meaningless. His thousand wives and concubines are meaningless. His powerful fleet of ships and the adoration of his people are meaningless.

Why is a lament like this in the Bible? At its conclusion, Solomon returns at last to his early wisdom, "Fear God and obey his commands, for this is everyone's duty" (Ecclesiastes 12:13). If only the king had followed his own counsel!

What everyone should know about the book of Song of Songs
WHAT IS LOVE?
Song of Songs, sometimes called Solomon's Song, is a book about love. But what is love? TV programs and Hollywood movies increasingly paint love as a casual trip to the bedroom, a quick fix for the fun of it. It's another quickie with someone new that will just as quickly be discarded. This fits in with our throw-away society, doesn't it?

According to TV and Hollywood, love is lust, occasionally elevated to passion. Is that all there is to love? According to the Bible, it isn't.

Commitment is the key to biblical love and marriage. After the honeymoon, there is a long walk together to the very end, hand in hand, heart to heart. You are mine and I am yours, even through sickness, dirty diapers, arguments, misunderstandings, and all the rest of the baggage of living together. But if love is only commitment, is the whole thing merely about "sticking through it all" no matter what? Is that all there is to it?

Song of Songs is a portrait of the passion and romance of married love, with intimate resonance. It's a rather unexpected insight on married love from a man who later collected a thousand lovers. Solomon obviously wrote it before he collected the thousand. He probably wrote this beautiful book when he was newly married to his first and only true love. We assume that he wrote it during the first ten years of his reign, probably between 970 B.C. and 960 B.C.

If you're married and your marriage has become stale, perhaps you and your mate should read this to each other, looking for the best blend of commitment and romance. Mates need to refresh their commitment, but at the same time they can refresh their romance and passion for one another.

Some believe that this is also a portrait of our loving relationship with God, beginning with utter devotion to him, then maintaining a loving daily intimacy with him. Intimacy with sin is an adulterous relationship.

Perhaps Song of Songs is both—a portrait of the wonderful love of husband and wife for each other, which in turn is a reflection, or a model, of the love between God and his people.

 Did You Know?

David was a large donor Before David died, he revealed to his son Solomon that he had gathered great treasures for his son to use in building the Temple. We won't list them all here—only the silver and gold. David gave one hundred thousand talents of gold for the Temple, which are estimated to be worth forty-five billion dollars today. The one million talents of silver were probably worth another seven billion or more dollars. Then there was an abundance of bronze, stone, craftsmen, and iron nails. David's contribution was perhaps worth more than fifty billion dollars. Never again would there be a building like Solomon's Temple.

The bronze laver was a twelve thousand gallon bowl Think of the largest tanker truck you have seen. Fill it with water and back it up to the laver, the enormous bronze washbowl in Solomon's Temple. The truck would not be able to fill this twelve-thousand-gallon bowl.

The queen of Sheba and her fifty million dollar "host gift" You have heard of hostess gifts, of course. Perhaps it is a box of candy, a book, or a silver cup. It is a thank-you gift to someone who has invited you to dinner. The queen of Sheba brought a "host gift" to Solomon. It wasn't just a box of candy or a book, but about fifty million dollars of gold. And that wasn't all. She also brought many jewels and spices. The queen used about fifty camels and drivers to bring all of these riches to Solomon. She also used many armed guards to make sure that they arrived safely.

The Temple quarries Vast amounts of stone were needed to build Solomon's Temple. Where did they get it? Actually, it came from a quarry just north of the Temple site, where the remains of the quarry can still be seen today. These enormous stone blocks were cut and chiseled to perfection at the quarry, such that the Temple was built without any need to chisel or cut the stones at the building site. Some of these enormous stone blocks can still be seen today in the Western Wall, or Wailing Wall, in Jerusalem.

216

>

What
Everyone
Should
Know
about
the

Bible

Discovering My Purpose from God's Plan

1. *The person who has nothing more to want always wants more.* Solomon is an example of this tendency.

2. *More without God is less, and less with God is more.* This is the message of 1 Kings.

3. *Materialism produces the bitter fruit of too many things that matter least and too few of the things that matter most.* As described by Solomon in Ecclesiastes, materialism is "emptiness," "vain," and "meaningless."

4. *It is good to remember the past and to profit from it.* It is best to shape the future from lessons learned in the past. Look back before you look ahead. This is the message of 2 Chronicles.

5. *Materialism is like having your car full of money so that you can buy anything you want, but having an empty gas tank so that you can't get to the store.* Solomon experienced this conflict and wrote about it in Ecclesiastes.

6. *Husbands and wives need to refresh their marital commitment, and at the same time refresh their marital romance and passion for one another.* This is the counsel of the Song of Songs.

7. *Never mortgage or leverage the best to gain the worst.* Solomon neglected the wisdom he requested from God, and focused on the things he did not request: wealth, power, and fame.

8. *It is foolish to buy security with the currency of destruction.* Solomon secured his kingdom by marrying foreign princesses and importing their pagan gods, but he did this at the high cost of destroying what he secured—his kingdom.

Tarnished Gold The Kingdom Divided

Characters:
Ahijah (a prophet who warned that the kingdom would divide); Jeroboam (who became king over the northern ten tribes); Rehoboam (who succeeded Solomon as king but eventually ruled only over the southern two tribes)

Time Period:
The division of the kingdom after Solomon died

Dates:
930 B.C.

Where Scene 14 of the Big Story Can Be Found:
Parts of 1 Kings and 2 Chronicles

In Scene 14, Find the Answers to These Questions:
Of the two kings—Rehoboam and Jeroboam—which was which?
Why did a prophet tear up a beautiful robe as an object lesson?

Look for this in Scene 14
> The cost of peace becomes higher than the cost of war.
> A kingdom split because of taxes.

Looking back to look ahead

King David was, without question, the greatest king of ancient times. He grew up as a nobody shepherd boy, but rose to the throne of all Israel and built a golden kingdom through his military brilliance. His reign is the highlight of Israel's history. Never before had Israel reached such heights of power and influence, and never would it achieve such wonderful heights again.

David's son Solomon showed greater personal wealth, political skills, and fame, but these were focused too much on Solomon, to the neglect and destruction of Israel.

Of the three kings of Israel—Saul, David, and Solomon—only Solomon was raised as a prince. Saul was a farmer, and David was a shepherd boy, and both were chosen by God to be kings. Solomon was raised to be a king—he was a prince.

When David gave the golden kingdom to Solomon, he presented him with a magnificent gift. God added to David's gift with the gift of great wisdom and the promise of riches, power, and fame. What more could a king want? He had reached the heights of glory before he began. Where now?

Solomon wanted one gift that neither his father nor the Lord had given—many foreign women. Without doubt, part of his marriage to a thousand women was his lust for sex, but these alliances were also strategic, political, and diplomatic. If Solomon married the daughter of a foreign king, that king also gave him riches and a promise of protection. Who would go to war against his daughter and her husband? Solomon must have thought he was quite brilliant. He could have lasting peace without the high cost of war, especially since he was not a military leader like his father David.

The high cost of peace

The high cost of peace was greater than the high cost of war. Each foreign wife brought in her foreign pagan idols and worship. Soon Israel was infested with pagan religions, and the Israelites began to turn from the Lord. Then even Solomon turned from the Lord and began worshiping these evil deities. That was the beginning of the end.

The Lord was angry with Solomon and talked with him about it. He told Solomon that he would take away his kingdom and give it to his servant, but that didn't stop Solomon from his pursuit of wealth, women, and wicked worship. Near the end of it all, he would write the book of Ecclesiastes, and he would label all of this excess as meaningless, empty, and foolish. By then it was too late—the damage was done and could never be undone.

220

>

What
Everyone
Should
Know
about
the

Bible

Toward the end of Solomon's life, the prophet Ahijah appeared to Jeroboam, Solomon's official, as he was leaving Jerusalem. Ahijah tore his robe in twelve pieces and gave ten of them to Jeroboam. He explained that God would tear ten tribes from Solomon's son Rehoboam, the heir to Solomon's throne, and give them to Jeroboam. Solomon must have heard about this, for he tried to kill Jeroboam. Jeroboam fled to Egypt and stayed there until Solomon died.

When Solomon died, his son Rehoboam came to the throne as the king of all Israel. Jeroboam and some other officials went to have a talk with Rehoboam. "Lighten the heavy labor and tax demands and we will serve you well," said Jeroboam.

Rehoboam asked for three days to think it over. He consulted first with his older and wiser counselors. "Tell them yes, and they will be your loyal subjects," the older counselors advised.

Rehoboam next asked his younger counselors. "If you think my father was hard on you, wait until you see what I will do," they told him to say. "I will be much harsher than my father was."

When Jeroboam returned in three days, that's what Rehoboam told him, and that stirred a revolution. "Down with David and his dynasty," many shouted. Rehoboam sent Adoniram, who was in charge of the labor force, to restore order, but the people stoned him to death. When Rehoboam heard that, he jumped into his chariot and rushed home to Jerusalem.

The kingdom divides

The people of Israel, the ten tribes to the north, immediately made Jeroboam king. Only Judah and parts of the tribe of Benjamin remained loyal to Rehoboam.

With the revolt going on, Rehoboam mustered 180,000 select troops and prepared for battle, but the Lord sent word to Rehoboam through the prophet Shemaiah not to use his army against Israel. Although Rehoboam wasn't exactly on good terms with the Lord, he listened and did not send his army to fight.

So the kingdom divided. Jeroboam ruled Israel, the northern kingdom with its ten tribes, and Rehoboam ruled Judah and Benjamin as the southern kingdom. Never again would they unite. Rehoboam's one egotistical decision had torn the kingdom apart forever. David would have wept for his grandson and for the ruined kingdom. David had risked his life again and again to build this kingdom. Even Solomon, with all his flaws, would have wept for his son and the ruined kingdom. He had mortgaged his soul to preserve the kingdom, and now it was ruined, utterly torn apart forever.

Questions You May Be Asking

How did the kingdom tear apart under Solomon's son Rehoboam?
Rehoboam inherited a vast storehouse of riches and an effective taxation system to keep his coffers filled. He inherited all that a king could desire from the richest man on earth, his father, Solomon. His subjects asked only one thing—to be treated more kindly than his father, Solomon, had treated them. "Give us some tax relief and we will serve you faithfully," they said. That seemed fair enough, and certainly a small price to pay for keeping the kingdom.

However, Rehoboam rejected the counsel of older men and accepted the counsel of younger men and answered harshly that he would be more demanding than his father. This led to rebellion. The kingdom tore apart, with ten tribes to the north of Jerusalem forming the northern kingdom of Israel. From that point south, the tribes of Judah and Benjamin were known as Judah or the southern kingdom.

What David had put together with great military skill and sacrifice, his son Solomon had mortgaged for lust and power, and Solomon's son Rehoboam carelessly caused the kingdom to tear apart. The Golden Age of Israel had come and gone with only two kings—David, who put the kingdom together, and Solomon, who squandered his father's inheritance through excessive living and foolish choices.

Solomon's riches and foreign wives had distracted him from the key means of preserving his kingdom—obeying God. As is so often the case, distractions can be more destructive than external threats. Never again would Israel know such a Golden Age as it had under King David.

Why didn't Rehoboam gather an army and defeat the rebels in the north?
He tried. But before he could go to war, God commanded him, through the prophet Shemaiah, not to do it, for he would be fighting God. This time, Rehoboam listened to godly counsel.

Are there any key prophets during this period?
No. The Lord used Shemaiah to speak to King Rehoboam, but little else is known about him.

Did the divided kingdoms ever get back together again?
Not really. This is getting a little ahead of our story, but as they existed side by side for the next two centuries, Judah often tried militarily to force Israel back into a united kingdom. By the time of King Jehoshaphat of Judah, it was obvious that this would never happen. From that time on, the two kingdoms kept a tentative peace with each other as Judah stopped trying to force them back together.

222

>

What
Everyone
Should
Know
about
the

Bible

What were these two kingdoms like after they split?
From the time that Israel split from Judah until it was conquered by
Assyria in 722 B.C., it had nineteen kings, and every one of them was
evil. Not one led a godly life, so Israel no longer enjoyed the blessings of
God. Just over two hundred years after the kingdom divided, the Assyrians, the world power at that time, destroyed Israel. Judah was wounded,
but not yet destroyed.

From the time the kingdoms divided until Judah was conquered by
the Babylonians in 597 B.C. (333 years later), Judah had twenty kings.
Eight were godly and twelve were evil, so there were times of blessing
and times of darkness.

Great Events of This Time

1. **Ahijah warns that the kingdom will divide** (1 Kings 11:29-43).
2. **Under Jeroboam's leadership the people ask Rehoboam, Solomon's
   son and successor, for a lighter tax burden. Listening to his younger
   advisors and ignoring his older and wiser counselors, Rehoboam
   threatens greater burdens. The people rebel, and the kingdom
   divides** (1 Kings 12:1-24; 2 Chronicles 10:1–11:4).
3. **Jeroboam becomes king of Israel, the northern kingdom.
   Rehoboam remains king of Judah, the southern kingdom** (1 Kings
   12:17, 20; 2 Chronicles 10:1-19).
4. **Rehoboam musters 180,000 soldiers from the tribes of Judah and
   Benjamin and prepares to go to war against Israel. God sends word
   through the prophet Shemaiah not to do it, and Rehoboam obeys**
   (1 Kings 12:21-24; 2 Chronicles 11:1-4).

Significant Dates of This Time

930 B.C., Solomon dies and the kingdom is divided under Rehoboam.

Did You Know?

Taxes split the kingdom Solomon taxed his people heavily, both in money
and in labor. When he died, a delegation came to his son, Rehoboam,
the new king. They requested that he reduce the unreasonable taxes
they had to pay, in both money and labor. A tax cut would have kept
Solomon's family in power for many years to come, but Rehoboam
would not hear of it. Instead, he promised a tax increase, and his threat
split the kingdom.

Tearing up a robe for an object lesson When you were in Sunday school or
children's church, you may have seen object lessons. Some object was

used to get a message across to you and your friends. Ahijah the prophet used his beautiful robe for an object lesson. This lesson was a very expensive one, for he tore his robe into twelve pieces. He gave ten pieces to Jeroboam and told him that they represented the ten tribes that would split from Solomon's kingdom to form the northern kingdom, Israel. The other two pieces represented the only two tribes that would stay with Rehoboam—Judah and Benjamin.

Rehoboam and Jeroboam—which was which? It's easy to get these two mixed up because their names are so similar. Rehoboam was Solomon's son who inherited the undivided nation of Israel. His stubborn refusal to ease up on taxes triggered the division of the kingdom. Jeroboam was an official in Solomon's court, and then in Rehoboam's, who led the delegation that asked Rehoboam for tax reduction. Jeroboam became the king of the northern ten tribes, which became known as the northern kingdom, or the kingdom of Israel. Rehoboam remained king, but only of the southern two tribes—Judah and Benjamin, which became known as the southern kingdom or the kingdom of Judah.

Discovering My Purpose from God's Plan

1. *Distractions are often more destructive than external threats.* We can see this in the life of Solomon. Lust for women, wealth, and power distracted him from God, and these, not external threats, became his undoing and ultimately destroyed the kingdom.
2. *Easy come, easy go. The kingdom came at great military sacrifice to David, whose life was constantly threatened.* His son Solomon squandered his inheritance spiritually, even though he built it economically. David's grandson, Solomon's son Rehoboam, squandered the entire kingdom with a momentary, selfish decision.
3. *One small decision may create centuries of change.* Rehoboam made one small decision not to decrease taxes. It split the kingdom of Israel, which would never unite fully again. The desire for gain brought loss, and greed brought division.
4. *Sometimes the cost of peace is greater than the cost of war.* Look at the price tag before you accept the easier way.

15

Wasted Opportunity
From Division to Captivity

Characters:
Abijah (who succeeded Rehoboam as king of Judah); Ahab (an evil king of Israel, Omri's son); Ahaziah (a king of Judah); Ahaziah (Ahab's son and his successor as king of Israel); Amaziah (a king of Judah); Asa (who succeeded Abijah as king of Judah); Athaliah (queen of Judah); Azariah (king of Judah); Baasha (king of Israel, succeeded Nadab); Benhadad (a king of Syria); Elah (a king of Israel, Baasha's son and successor); Elijah (a great prophet of Israel); Elisha (a great prophet of Israel, and Elijah's successor); Jehoram (one man by this name was a king of Judah, another was also known as Joram, and he was a king of Israel, Ahab's son, and Ahaziah's successor); Jehoshaphat (a king of Judah who succeeded Asa); Jehu (who killed Jezebel and became king of Israel); Jeroboam (the first king of the northern ten tribes, Israel); Jeroboam II (a later king of Israel); Jezebel (the evil wife of Ahab, king of Israel); Joash (a king of Judah); Jotham (a king of Judah); Micaiah (a prophet in Israel who advised Ahab); Naboth (whom Jezebel murdered to get his vineyard); Nadab (Jeroboam's son and successor as king of Israel); Omri (a king of Israel); Pekah (the last king of Israel); Rehoboam (Solomon's son and successor); Shemaiah (a prophet to Rehoboam, king of Judah); Shishak (a king of Egypt); Tibni (who tried to get Israel's throne, but lost it to Omri); Uzziah (a king of Judah who tried to burn incense in the Temple and became a leper); Zimri (who ruled seven days as king of Israel)

Time Period:
The period from the division of the kingdom until the captivity of Israel

Dates:
930 B.C.–722 B.C.

Where Scene 15 of the Big Story Can Be Found:
First & 2 Kings and 2 Chronicles present the historical panorama.
Joel, Jonah, Amos, Hosea, Isaiah, and Micah present the
prophetic messages of this period. The prophets Elijah and Elisha
ministered during this period, but wrote no Bible books.

In Scene 15, Find the Answers to These Questions:
Which king of Judah built a million-man army?
Who painted her face before dogs ate her?
Who went to heaven in a whirlwind, accompanied by a chariot
    and horses of fire?
Who was fed each day by some birds?

Look for this in Scene 15
> An altar split apart and ashes poured from it.
> A million-man army of Ethiopia was defeated.
> A king ruled for only seven days.
> A barrel of flour and a flask of oil were never used up.
> A certain kingdom never had a godly king.

The Big Story So Far

Requiem for a torn kingdom
David would have wept bitterly to see how his own son Solomon had
squandered his wisdom and riches, giving in to foreign women and
letting his kingdom and his own personal life deteriorate. David would
have wept bitterly upon watching his son actually worship pagan idols.

David would have shed more tears to see his grandson Rehoboam
reject wise counselors, threaten the people with harsher taxation, and
thereby cause a rebellion that would divide David's beautiful kingdom.
The kingdom did divide, with David's grandson Rehoboam as king of
the southern kingdom, Judah, and Jeroboam as king over the northern
kingdom, Israel.

Rehoboam's first act was to muster an army of 180,000 troops from
Judah and Benjamin and prepare for civil war against Israel. God sent a
message through the prophet Shemaiah warning Rehoboam not to do
this, for he would be fighting God and his plans, so Rehoboam wisely
listened to God this time and did not go to war. Perhaps he had learned
his lesson and decided to listen to the Lord.

A golden opportunity in the north
The Lord gave Jeroboam the throne of Israel, the northern kingdom.
This was Jeroboam's golden opportunity to secure his throne. All he
needed to do was to follow the Lord and keep Israel's covenant with the
Lord. That seems simple enough, doesn't it? But neither Jeroboam nor

226

>

What
Everyone
Should
Know
about
the

Bible

the next eighteen kings of Israel would follow the Lord. Throughout the history of the northern kingdom there was not one godly king.

First, Jeroboam set up pagan altars at Bethel in the north. He also made two golden calves for the people to worship. Bethel was the place where Jacob saw angels on a stairway to heaven and heard the voice of God speaking to him. Jacob would have wept to see pagan altars there.

The Temple was, of course, in Jerusalem, in the southern kingdom, so this was Jeroboam's substitute for worship at the Temple. Since Jeroboam had rejected worship of the Lord, the priests and Levites fled to the southern kingdom of Judah. Jeroboam lost the godly leaders who could have helped him to please and follow the Lord.

As Jeroboam was sacrificing at one of these pagan altars one day, a man of God approached. "This altar will split apart and ashes will pour out of it!" he cried. Jeroboam was furious. He stretched out his hand and ordered that the man of God be arrested. But as soon as he stretched out his hand, it withered before his eyes. Repentant, he begged the man of God to ask God to restore it, and God did so.

A golden opportunity in the south

Rehoboam also had a golden opportunity to lead Judah to the Lord. He should have seen what a foolish mistake he had made. He should have realized that the Lord asked him simply to obey and follow him. So what did he do?

As soon as Rehoboam had established himself, he also set up pagan altars and turned the people away from the Lord. For this, the Lord allowed Shishak, king of Egypt, to come with twelve hundred chariots and sixty thousand horsemen, capture the fortified cities of Judah, and make life miserable for Rehoboam.

The prophet Shemaiah came once more to Rehoboam. The Lord had permitted his downfall, he said, because the people of Judah had turned away from him. This time, Rehoboam and his leaders humbled themselves before the Lord. Their humility stopped further destruction from Shishak, but it did not stop the Egyptian king from stealing all the golden shields and other treasures of the Temple.

Did the two kingdoms ever try to get back together? What kind of coexistence did they have? There was continual war between the two kingdoms, and they never again united.

Abijah succeeds Rehoboam as king of Judah

When Rehoboam died, his son Abijah became king and continued to war with Israel. Jeroboam, the king of Israel, attacked the new king, hoping to conquer him. He even devised a clever military strategy to divide his troops and attack from before and from behind Abijah.

But Abijah and his people cried out to the Lord for help and depended on him, and they thoroughly defeated Jeroboam, even capturing some of his cities. God allowed Jeroboam to be defeated because he refused to follow the Lord and because Abijah had begged the Lord to help him. That made the difference.

Asa succeeds Abijah as king of Judah

When Rehoboam's son Abijah died, his son Asa (Solomon's great-grandson and Rehoboam's grandson) ruled for forty-one years. Asa loved the Lord and reformed Judah. He rebuilt the fortified cities of Judah, and mustered an army of 300,000 brave men from Judah and 280,000 from Benjamin, and provided them with spears and shields.

More important, Asa obeyed the Lord and depended on him for strength. Heeding the warnings of a man of God named Azariah, Asa made further reform in Judah by removing pagan altars and idols. He even deposed his own grandmother as queen mother because she had made a pagan Asherah pole.

One day, an Ethiopian army of one million troops and three hundred chariots attacked Asa, and he pleaded with the Lord for help. The Lord did help him and Asa thoroughly defeated the Ethiopians and took much booty home with him.

Azariah, the man of God, met Asa with a warning on his return to Jerusalem. "The Lord was with you while you were with him," he told Asa. "If you continue to seek him, he will continue to help you. If you forsake him, he will forsake you."

When Asa heard that, he continued to put away the pagan altars and idols. He would listen to the Lord and follow him.

Nadab succeeds Jeroboam as king of Israel

What was happening in the northern kingdom of Israel during this time? After Jeroboam had ruled for twenty-two years, he died and his son Nadab succeeded him. Like his father, he was evil and led Israel away from the Lord.

Baasha succeeds Nadab as king of Israel

After two years, a man named Baasha assassinated Nadab and became king. His first job was to assassinate all of the family of Jeroboam and Nadab. Not one person was left to claim the throne.

Baasha began a battle against Judah and its king, Asa, so Asa took all the Temple treasures and palace treasures and sent them to Ben-hadad, king of Syria, asking him to fight Israel for him. Ben-hadad did what Asa asked, and Baasha had to stop his aggression, but there was continued conflict between Israel and Judah throughout the days of Asa and Baasha.

Baasha ruled Israel for twenty-four years, and he was as evil as Jeroboam, Abijah, and Nadab had been. Although Jehu the prophet

228

>

What
Everyone
Should
Know
about
the

Bible

(not the Jehu who would later become king) warned Baasha to turn to the Lord, he wouldn't.

Elah becomes king of Israel

Baasha died and his son Elah became king, but he ruled for only two years. He was assassinated by a man named Zimri, who reigned as king for only seven days. Those seven days were long enough for him to kill all of Baasha's family, just as Baasha had done to Nadab's family twenty-four years earlier. Look at the pattern here of assassinations and short reigns! The people needed to cry out to the Lord for help and stability, but they would not.

Zimri rules as king of Israel for seven days

The army was not happy with Zimri. They immediately proclaimed their commander, Omri, as king. With the army against him, Zimri knew that he had lost the throne, so he committed suicide.

Tibni tries to become king, but fails; Omri succeeds Zimri as king of Israel

For a short time, there was another contestant to the throne of Israel, a man named Tibni. Omri's followers defeated Tibni's supporters, so Omri gained full control of the throne of Israel. By this time, Asa had been the king of Judah for thirty-one years.

Omri made Samaria the capital of Israel and arranged for his son Ahab to marry Jezebel, the evil pagan daughter of Ethbaal, king of the Sidonians. This marriage would bring enormous evil and sorrow to Israel, for Ahab and Jezebel became the prime villains during the next scene of Israel's history.

Ahab succeeds Omri as king of Israel

It is not surprising that when Omri died, his son Ahab became king of Israel for the next twenty-two years.

Asa had now been king of Judah for thirty-eight years. Overall, Asa was a godly king, but he, too, had his unfortunate moments. For example, several years earlier when Baasha was still king in Israel, Baasha and Asa went to war against each other. Instead of trusting God for help, as he had done when he defeated the Ethiopians, Asa sent the Temple treasures and even his palace treasures to the king of Aram to enlist his help. A man of God named Hanani rebuked Asa for that. He should have trusted the Lord, not the king of Aram. Also, in the year after Ahab became king over Israel, Asa had a disease in his feet. He should have asked the Lord for help, but he didn't. Otherwise, Asa was a godly king.

Jehoshaphat succeeds Asa as king of Judah

When Asa died, his son Jehoshaphat became king of Judah. He was only thirty-five at the time, and he ruled for another thirty-five years.

Jehoshaphat was a godly king, and under his leadership with God's blessings, Judah prospered greatly. Jehoshaphat became very wealthy and built a powerful military machine with more than a million brave men.

In Israel, Ahab made peace with Jehoshaphat. He didn't want to fight a million-man army. Ahab was the most evil king ever to reign in Israel, partly because he had an incredibly evil queen, Jezebel. It was one of the darkest days yet for the northern kingdom of Israel.

The ministry of the prophet Elijah begins

About 875 B.C., the prophet Elijah begins his ministry in the northern kingdom of Israel.

If you look at the list of Bible events for this period of history, you will see that most of them involve Elijah and his successor, Elisha. They were two of the most godly, powerful prophets of the Old Testament, and certainly have their share of well-known Bible stories. Many Old Testament miracles were performed by these two men. Neither of them wrote a prophetic book in our Bible.

Most of Elijah's work during twenty-one of his twenty-five years of ministry (from 875 B.C. to 850 B.C.) was done during Ahab's reign. He also worked during the reigns of Ahaziah and Joram, who is sometimes called Jehoram. This can be confusing, because there was also another King Jehoram in Judah. Elijah and Ahab remained bitter enemies, and Jezebel hated Elijah even more than Ahab did.

One of the greatest conflicts between Elijah and Ahab concerned a drought that came to Israel. The contest began with Elijah's prophecy. There would be no rain in Israel until he said it would rain. This, of course, did not please Ahab, so Elijah had to hide from him.

Ravens feed Elijah; the widow of Zarephath has an endless supply of flour and oil

As Elijah hid along the Brook Kerith, ravens brought food to him each day. When the brook dried up, he moved to Zarephath, where he lived with a widow and her son. When Elijah arrived at her home, she had only enough flour and oil for a bit of bread, but at his request, she fed the prophet first. You can imagine how she and her son felt. Both of them were desperately hungry as they watched the prophet eat that last bit of bread.

God rewarded her for this, for her jar of flour was never used up and her jug of oil never became empty. Later, when the widow's son died, Elijah brought him back to life.

Elijah and the prophets of Baal

One of the most famous stories about Elijah happened on Mount Carmel. Elijah gathered the people of Israel there to watch a great

230

>

What
Everyone
Should
Know
about
the

Bible

contest. The priests of the heathen god Baal placed meat on an altar and asked Baal to send fire from heaven. Of course nothing happened.

When Elijah did this, even pouring water on the meat and filling the trenches with water, fire came from heaven and burned the meat and even the altar. Elijah then commanded the people to seize the priests of Baal and execute them. After that happened, the rains came again and the long drought ended.

Queen Jezebel was furious and vowed to kill Elijah. The mighty prophet had just performed a stunning miracle, but suddenly he feared for his life and ran away to Mount Sinai, sometimes called Horeb, the mountain of God. There he fell into despair that he was the only one left who loved God.

Elijah hears a quiet voice on the mountain of God

When God told Elijah to expect his presence to pass by, Elijah thought God would be in a powerful wind, but he was not. Then Elijah thought God would be in a mighty earthquake, but he was not. When God did not appear in a great fire, Elijah was puzzled. Quietly, God appeared in a soft, gentle whisper. Sometimes God's most powerful revelations come that way (1 Kings 19:11-13).

God commanded Elijah to go home and commissioned him to anoint the next king of Aram; the next king of Israel, Jehu; and Elisha, to be Elijah's successor. From that time on, Elisha was Elijah's assistant.

Although Ahab was an evil king, God promised him victory over the Syrians and their king, Ben-hadad, in two great battles. Ahab should have executed Ben-hadad, but instead he spared him. God revealed to him that this would cost Ahab his own life.

Naboth's vineyard

One recorded event happened before this prophecy came true. Ahab wanted a rich vineyard that belonged to the man next door named Naboth. But this was Naboth's family inheritance, so Naboth refused to sell it, even to the king. Sullen and unhappy, Ahab complained to his wicked wife, Jezebel. She arranged to have Naboth killed so that Ahab could have the vineyard, but Elijah appeared as Ahab went to claim it. Elijah promised Ahab and Jezebel great punishment for this evil act.

Ahab's last battle

About this time, around 853 B.C., the godly King Jehoshaphat of Judah came to see Ahab, king of Israel, who was a very wicked man. They laid plans to go to war together against Syria to regain the city of Ramoth-gilead. "First, however, let's seek God's counsel," Jehoshaphat advised. He should have known it couldn't happen with Ahab. Of course, Ahab's false prophets predicted a great victory for them, making a dramatic show of their prediction. Jehoshaphat saw that they were false prophets and asked for a prophet of the Lord. "There is still one prophet of the Lord, but I hate him. He never says anything good," Ahab told Jehoshaphat.

Ahab called for Micaiah the prophet, who foretold Ahab's death on the battlefield. So it happened that, as Ahab and Jehoshaphat went to battle, a stray arrow hit Ahab and he died. His son Ahaziah became king of Israel in his place, and he was also an evil king.

When Jehoshaphat returned home, a prophet named Jehu scolded him. "Should a godly person help a wicked person like Ahab? Because of this God is angry at you," Jehu told him. This was not the Jehu who later became king of Israel, but a prophet by that name.

Ahaziah succeeds Ahab as king of Israel; Joram succeeds Ahaziah

Ahab's son Ahaziah had ruled Israel for about two years when he had a fatal accident and died. Then another son of King Ahab, Joram (sometimes called Jehoram), became king of Israel and ruled for twelve years. Joram was also a wicked king, as all of Israel's kings were. Remember that Judah also had a King Ahaziah and a King Jehoram.

Elijah chooses a successor

At last, about 850 B.C., it was time for Elijah to turn his work over to his successor, Elisha. But Elijah didn't die. He was taken into heaven in a whirlwind, accompanied by a chariot of fire pulled by horses of fire. What a way to go to heaven! Elisha saw this incredible sight and because he did, he inherited a double portion of Elijah's spirit, as Elijah had promised. Elisha also inherited Elijah's cloak and his prophetic ministry. Then he alone was the great prophet of the northern kingdom of Israel.

Elisha began his prophetic ministry during the reign of King Joram, a wicked son of King Ahab. He continued his work for half a century, from about 850 B.C. to 800 B.C. During this time, there were three kings of Israel—Jehu, Jehoahaz, and Joash—and five rulers of Judah—Jehoram, Ahaziah, Queen Athaliah, Joash, and Amaziah. Both the kingdom of Israel and the kingdom of Judah had kings named Jehoram, Ahaziah, and Joash. These were obviously all common names at that time.

Miracles of Elisha

232
>
What
Everyone
Should
Know
about
the

Elisha purified some bad water, helped a widow fill many jars with one little pot of oil, helped a barren woman and her husband to have a son, purified some deadly stew, fed a hundred people with twenty little loaves of bread, raised a woman's dead son to life, found a lost ax head by making it float on water, led a blinded Syrian army to the capital of Israel, told Naaman the Syrian army officer how to bathe his leprosy away, and showed his servant Gehazi a mighty angel army.

Elijah and Elisha are dramatic reminders that God provides powerful witnesses in a kingdom that desperately needs God.

Four lepers who became wealthy, but would not keep their wealth

During the days of Elisha's ministry, when Joram was still king of Israel, the Syrians laid siege to Samaria, Israel's capital city. In time, the city was reduced to utter starvation. Things were so bad that two women covenanted to eat each other's sons.

Joram was beside himself with agony. He blamed Elisha, and even sent men to capture him, but Elisha told the king that by the next day there would be abundant food in Samaria, a seemingly impossible feat.

It happened this way. That same night, four lepers decided to go into the enemy Syrian army camp and give up, hoping to either be fed or be killed. When they reached the camp, it was empty. The Syrian army had fled, leaving behind riches and food beyond belief. Suddenly these four lepers were incredibly wealthy. Feeling guilty about their discovery, the lepers told some messengers in the city. Sure enough, the next day there was abundant food in Samaria.

Jehoram, king of Judah

For our next story, we need to recall King Ahab and Queen Jezebel of Israel, two of the most wicked people of Old Testament history, and bitter enemies of Elijah.

These two villains had two sons, Ahaziah and Joram, and a daughter, Athaliah. When Ahab was killed in battle, his son Ahaziah ruled for two years, but he died in an accident. Joram, the other son of Ahab and Jezebel, became king of Israel.

About this time, Jehoram, son of Jehoshaphat, became king of Judah, but he was evil to the core even though his father Jehoshaphat had been a very godly king. As soon as Jehoram became king, he killed his own brothers to secure the throne. Then he married Athaliah, the daughter of Ahab and Jezebel.

Ahaziah succeeds Jehoram as king of Judah

Jehoram soon died from a rare disease that made his bowels fall out, and he was buried in shame. Then his twenty-two-year-old son Ahaziah (not the Ahaziah who was Ahab's and Jezebel's son) became king. He ruled only a year with great wickedness, shaped by his evil mother Athaliah. This story gets complex because two distinct men were called Ahaziah and two other men were called Joram or Jehoram.

This is how Ahaziah died. As king of Judah, he was on a visit to see his uncle, King Joram of Israel. While he was there, a rebellion took place in Israel. Jehu, who had been an officer in Ahab's army, rebelled and killed King Ahaziah of Judah along with the evil King Joram and Queen Jezebel of Israel.

Athaliah succeeds Ahaziah as queen of Judah

Now that King Ahaziah of Judah was dead, his mother, Athaliah, lusted for power and seized the throne. Remember that she was the daughter of Ahab and Jezebel of Israel.

First, she murdered all her family members, even her children and grandchildren, so none of them could claim the throne. One little grandson escaped her rampage, a baby named Joash. Ahaziah's sister, Jehosheba, hid Joash and his nurse in the Temple for six years.

Joash succeeds Athaliah as king of Judah

In the seventh year of Athaliah's reign, the priest Jehoiada called the high officials together in Judah to meet him in the Temple. There he entered into a covenant with them and showed them seven-year-old Joash.

Jehoida armed some high officials; he sent some of them to Athaliah's palace and kept some in the Temple. Then Jehoida crowned the boy Joash as king and the people loudly rejoiced. When Athaliah ran to hear what was going on, the guards seized her and executed her. The crowds cheered, for they hated their wicked queen and were glad for even a boy to rule them.

Joel's ministry in Judah

The same year that the boy Joash was crowned, the prophet Joel began his prophetic ministry in Judah by collecting and recording some of his prophesies in the book bearing his name—Joel. Under Jehoshaphat's son Jehoram, his son Ahaziah, and his widow Athaliah, Judah had become wretchedly evil, and this had continued for thirteen years. Joel warned Judah of the fruits of that evil and of the need to turn to the Lord. Joel's ministry continued for thirty-nine years until Joash was assassinated in 796 B.C. His ministry was exactly parallel to the reign of King Joash of Judah.

Jehu becomes king of Israel

With Ahab, Jezebel, and all their children dead, Jehu seized the throne of Israel. This was his golden opportunity to turn Israel toward the Lord. He started well by slaughtering all the priests of Baal and forbidding any further Baal worship, but he stopped there. He kept the worship of the golden calves alive and refused to worship the Lord as he should.

Jehoahaz succeeds Jehu as king of Israel; Jehoash succeeds Jehoahaz as king of Israel; Jonah begins his ministry in Israel

When Jehu died circa 814 B.C., his son Jehoahaz became king of Israel, but he was also a wicked king. His son Jehoash succeeded him and was

What
Everyone
Should
Know
about
the
Bible

another wicked king. This was about the time that Elisha, the great prophet of Israel, also died. Five years after Jehoash became king of Israel, Jonah began his ministry as a prophet to Israel. Eight years after that, Jonah went to Nineveh to preach, by way of a storm at sea and the great fish that swallowed him.

Joash turns from God

In Judah, Joash became an ungodly king, accepting paganism as soon as the priest Jehoida died. Joash gave orders to assassinate Jehoida's son, although Jehoida had helped to make him king. Later, some dissidents assassinated Joash. This happened in 796 B.C., the same year that Joel's thirty-nine-year ministry ended.

Amaziah succeeds Joash as king of Judah

Amaziah, Joash's son, succeeded him as king. He made some efforts to follow the Lord, but he did not do so completely. As soon as he secured the throne, he executed the people who had assassinated his father. Then he launched a successful campaign against the Edomites. But when he captured some of their pagan gods, he brought them back to worship them. Amaziah had now turned away from the Lord, and this led to his assassination.

Uzziah, also called Azariah, succeeds Amaziah as king of Judah

Now Uzziah, also called Azariah, reigned in place of his father, Amaziah. He became king of Judah at the age of sixteen. Uzziah tried to follow the Lord, but he did not completely remove the pagan places. It was the old, old story of trying to hold onto God with one hand and pagan practices with the other. Uzziah became powerful politically, economically, and militarily, but pride goes before a fall. Uzziah became proud as he became powerful, so proud that he was unfaithful to the Lord. He even entered the Temple to burn incense on the altar. Azariah the priest was frightened. He realized that Uzziah should not do this, and tried to stop him. Uzziah became angry, but he was immediately struck with leprosy and suffered with it until he died.

Jotham succeeds Uzziah as king of Judah

After Uzziah became leperous his son Jotham ruled with his father. When Uzziah died, Jotham became the king of Judah. Jotham tried to follow the Lord, but unfortunately his people did not. Jotham grew powerful; he subdued the Ammonites and forced them to pay tribute. He also engaged in several building projects.

Ahaz succeeds Jotham as the twelfth king of Judah

When Jotham died, his son Ahaz became the twelfth king of Judah. Keep this name in mind, for it will appear several times in the story to follow. During these years, both Israel and Judah went downhill spiritually. It was the old story of loving idol worship and the golden calves.

Jeroboam II rules as king of Israel

About the time of Jonah, a king named Jeroboam II had brought some military success to Israel, but he neglected to worship the Lord. The prophets Hosea and Amos cried out against the sins of Israel, but since the kings were wicked, who would lead the nation back to God?

The first exile of Israel to Assyria—734 B.C.

This first exile of Israel in 734 B.C. is interwoven with the story of Ahaz, the twelfth king of Judah. This was a critical time for Ahaz, for Israel and Syria teamed up to war against him. Although he was counseled by Isaiah, one of the all-time greatest prophets, Ahaz was petrified and refused to follow the Lord.

Pekah, king of Israel, came with violent force and killed 120,000 men of Judah in one day. Other high officials were lost in Judah, and 200,000 men, women, and children were taken back to Samaria, Israel's northern capital. Micah appeared on the scene about this time, warning the people of Israel that judgment was coming to them and pleading for their repentance.

Judah was so weakened by wickedness that it had not been able to withstand such a force. Seeing this, the Edomites came against them from the south and the Philistines came against them from the south and west. It was truly a disastrous time for Judah.

If only Ahaz had listened to Isaiah and turned to the Lord, he might have been spared. But he didn't. Instead, he turned for help to the Assyrian king Tiglath-pileser, sending palace and Temple treasures to him as payment.

During this declining period, Assyria's threat had grown in the north like a dark spreading cloud over the horizon. The prophets Amos, Hosea, Jonah, Micah, and Isaiah came on the scene, warning of disasters to come. By 743 B.C., Assyria made its first bold invasion of Israel.

In 734 B.C., toward the end of King Pekah's reign, Assyria carried many of the people of Israel into exile (2 Kings 16:7-9; 1 Chronicles 5:26). This was the first exile or captivity for Israel in 734 B.C. Tiglath-pileser also saw how weak Ahaz was in Judah, and he made life miserable for him too.

The second exile of Israel to Assyria—722 B.C.

Nine years later, in 725 B.C., another Assyrian king, Shalmaneser, came against the northern kingdom of Israel and laid siege against its capital city, Samaria, for three years (2 Kings 17:1-6). When this siege was completed in 722 B.C. by Shalmaneser's successor, the northern kingdom

What
Everyone
Should
Know
about
the

Bible

of Israel was completely conquered by Assyria. About 27,290 captives were taken back to Assyria.

Assyria left many of the lower classes of Israelites in the land, and brought in many colonists from other parts of the Assyrian empire. Before long, there was intermarriage among these colonists and the local Israelites. The hybrid offspring became the despised Samaritans. Centuries later, Jesus showed great love for these Samaritans and told the famous parable of The Good Samaritan. The woman at the well that Jesus encountered one hot day was also a Samaritan.

What happened to the people of Israel who were exiled to Assyria? Some were sent to Nineveh, Assyria's capital city. Most were sent into the less populated areas of Assyria. Some remained faithful to the Lord, and many were blended into the Assyrian population and lost their identity as part of the covenant people.

The northern kingdom was made up of the ten tribes of Israel that rebelled against Judah and parts of Benjamin. The so-called ten lost tribes of Israel weren't really lost. Their distinctiveness was lost, but their distinctiveness as a covenant people was lost long before this exile.

Thus, in 722 B.C., the northern kingdom of Israel ceased to exist.

Questions You May Be Asking

Why is it so difficult to understand this complex period of Bible history? It seems so terribly complicated.

The answer is simple—because it is so complex. First, it is the story of two kingdoms existing side by side, but each going its own way, with their paths occasionally intersecting, and at times fighting each other. It is the story of dozens of kings and queens, mostly evil, but some good. Sometimes two kings even had the same name, although they ruled in different kingdoms at somewhat different times.

To make matters more complicated, the story is woven throughout four historical Bible books—1 and 2 Kings and 1 and 2 Chronicles. The written prophecies of this period occupy six books of the Bible—Joel, Jonah, Amos, Hosea, Isaiah, and Micah.

Two of the most significant prophets of the period, Elijah and Elisha, did not leave any written works, yet they performed some of the most dramatic miracles of the Old Testament.

Great Events of this Time

Almost all Bible events of this time are stories of the northern kingdom of Israel, mostly because of the dramatic ministries of Elijah and Elisha.

Events that took place in the northern kingdom of Israel:
1. Jeroboam makes two golden calves (1 Kings 12:25–13:10).
2. Ahab marries the wicked princess Jezebel (1 Kings 16:29-34).
3. Ravens feed Elijah (1 Kings 17:1-6).
4. Elijah helps a widow of Zarephath (1 Kings 17:7-24).
5. Elijah defeats the prophets of Baal at Mount Carmel (1 Kings 18).
6. Elijah listens to a quiet voice on the mountain (1 Kings 19:1-18).
7. Elijah calls Elisha to be his successor (1 Kings 19:19-21).
8. Ahab steals Naboth's vineyard (1 Kings 21).
9. Micaiah prophesies (1 Kings 22:1-40; 2 Chronicles 18).
10. Elijah goes to heaven in a whirlwind (2 Kings 2:1-18).
11. Elisha helps a poor widow pay her debt (2 Kings 4:1-7).
12. A room is provided for Elisha (2 Kings 4:8-17).
13. Elisha raises a boy from the dead (2 Kings 4:18-37).
14. Naaman is healed of leprosy (2 Kings 5:1-14).
15. Elisha's greedy servant tries to get rich (2 Kings 5:15-27).
16. Elisha's servant sees an angel army (2 Kings 6:8-17).
17. The Syrian army tries to capture Elisha but is blinded (2 Kings 6:18-23).
18. Four lepers find a feast and riches in the enemy camp (2 Kings 6:24–7:20).
19. Jehu is anointed king and kills the kings of Israel and Judah and Queen Jezebel (2 Kings 8:25–9:37; 2 Chronicles 22:1-9).
20. Jehu kills the Baal worshipers (2 Kings 10).
21. King Jehoahaz reigns in Israel (2 Kings 13:1-9).
22. King Jehoash reigns in Israel and Elisha dies (2 Kings 13:10-25).
23. Six evil kings reign in Israel (2 Kings 14:23-29; 15:8-31).
24. Israel is taken into captivity (2 Kings 17).

Events that took place in the southern kingdom of Judah:
1. Joash becomes a boy king and Queen Athaliah is executed (2 Kings 11; 2 Chronicles 22:10–23:21).
2. Joash repairs the Temple (2 Kings 12:1-16; 2 Chronicles 24:1-16).
3. Joash turns from God and executes Zechariah the priest (2 Chronicles 24:17-22).
4. Joash pays tribute to Hazael and dies (2 Kings 12:17-21).
5. King Uzziah burns incense and gets leprosy (2 Chronicles 26).
6. Jotham becomes king of Judah (2 Kings 15:32-38; 2 Chronicles 27).
7. King Amaziah reigns in Judah (2 Kings 14:1-22; 2 Chronicles 25).
8. Jotham dies, and his son Ahaz replaces him (2 Chronicles 28).

238

>

What
Everyone
Should
Know
about
the

Bible

Significant Dates of This Time

930 B.C., Solomon dies; his kingdom divides into the northern kingdom (Israel) and the southern kingdom (Judah).

925 B.C., Shishak, king of Egypt, invades Jerusalem.

910 B.C., Abijah dies; Asa becomes king of Judah; Jeroboam, king of Israel, dies and Nadab becomes the new king of Israel.

909 B.C., Baasha kills Nadab and becomes king of Israel.

886 B.C., Baasha dies; Elah becomes king of Israel.

885 B.C., Elah is assassinated; Zimri becomes king of Israel; Omri and Tibni compete for the throne of Israel and Omri wins.

875 B.C., Elijah begins his ministry in Israel.

874 B.C., Ahab becomes king of Israel.

870 B.C., Asa, king of Judah, dies; Jehoshaphat becomes king of Judah.

857 B.C., Ben-hadad attacks Samaria for the first time; Ahab wins and spares Ben-hadad.

853 B.C., Jehoshaphat joins Ahab in battle and Ahab dies; Ahaziah becomes king of Israel, but dies from an accident; Joram son of Ahab becomes king of Israel.

848 B.C., Elijah goes to heaven in a whirlwind; Elisha begins his ministry in Israel; Jehoshaphat of Judah dies; his son becomes king and puts his brothers to death.

841 B.C., Jehu kills Joram and Jezebel and becomes king of Israel; Jehoram king of Judah dies and his son Ahaziah succeeds him, but Jehu assassinates him; Athaliah seizes the throne and kills her family; baby Joash is saved.

835 B.C., Joash becomes Judah's king; the prophet Joel begins his ministry; when the old priest Jehoida dies, Joash moves to paganism.

814 B.C., Jehu dies; his son Jehoahaz becomes king.

798 B.C., Jehoahaz, king of Israel, dies; his son Jehoash succeeds him.

797 B.C., Elisha's ministry ends.

796 B.C., Joash, king of Judah, is assassinated; his son Amaziah succeeds him; Joel's ministry ends.

793 B.C., Jonah becomes a prophet.

785 B.C., Jonah preaches in Nineveh.

783 B.C., Shalmaneser IV becomes king of Assyria.

782 B.C., Jehoash, king of Israel, dies; his son Jeroboam II succeeds him.

772 B.C., Ashur-dan III becomes king of Assyria.

767 B.C., Amaziah, king of Judah, is assassinated; his son Uzziah (Azariah) succeeds him.

760 B.C., Amos's ministry begins.

754 B.C., Ashur-ninari V becomes king of Assyria.

753 B.C., Hosea's ministry begins; Jonah's ministry ends; King Jeroboam of Israel dies and his son Zechariah succeeds him but is killed by Shallum after six months; Menahem assassinates Shallum after only one month; Menahem reigns in Israel for ten years.

753 B.C., Micah's ministry begins; King Shallum of Israel is assassinated.

750 B.C., Amos's ministry ends; Jotham becomes king of Judah.

743 B.C., Israel is invaded by Tiglath-Pileser III of Assyria.

742 B.C., Micah becomes a prophet; Pekahiah becomes king of Judah; Menahem, king of Israel, dies and his son Pekahiah succeeds him.

741 B.C., Pekah, an officer of Pekahiah, assassinates him and becomes king of Israel; he reigns twenty years; during his reign, Assyria takes the first captives from Israel.

740 B.C., Isaiah becomes a prophet to Judah.

739 B.C., Uzziah, king of Judah, dies; his son Jotham succeeds him and reigns for sixteen years.

733 B.C., Hoshea assassinates Pekah and becomes king of Israel.

730 B.C., Jotham dies; his son Ahaz becomes king of Judah and reigns sixteen years; Ahaz is wicked, and for that he suffers a great defeat at the hands of Aram (Syria) and Israel; Ahaz goes to Assyria for help and gives the Temple treasures in payment.

726 B.C.–723 B.C., the Assyrians lay a three-year siege around Samaria.

725 B.C., Ahaz of Judah dies; his son Hezekiah becomes king of Judah and rules well; the Temple is cleansed and reconsecrated.

722 B.C., the northern kingdom of Israel falls to the Assyrians.

Heroes and Villains: The Stars in Scene 15

This is one of the most complicated yet colorful scenes of Scripture. There are names worthy of attention as heroes and villains, but space does not permit us to discuss all of them. For example, Jeroboam, who became the first king of Israel, was instrumental in the division of the kingdom into Israel and Judah.

The widow of Zarephath was an incredible lady who made her last flour and oil into a cake for Elijah to eat, while she and her hungry son watched. For that faith, God rewarded her with unlimited food.

Then there was Naboth, a man who treasured his family inheritance, a vineyard, so much that he defied the most powerful person in the land—the king. Micaiah the prophet also dared to stand up against Ahab and prophesy his death. That took courage!

The poor widow whose sons were about to be sold to repay debts believed that God's prophet Elisha could somehow help her, and he did.

240

>

What
Everyone
Should
Know
about
the

Bible

Gehazi did a villainous act when he tried to get Naaman's treasure for himself, and for that he became a leper.

Athaliah, daughter of Ahab and Jezebel, was as villainous as you can get, just like her parents. She murdered all of her own family, including children and grandchildren, so that she could remain queen. We could list kings—good and bad—of Israel and Judah. But let's focus on the following.

AHAB

Omri's son Ahab (873 B.C.–851 B.C.) was one of the strongest kings of the northern kingdom of Israel. He was also a man of weak character who allowed his domineering wife, Jezebel, to lead him into wickedness and idol worship. The prophet Elijah frequently challenged Ahab and Jezebel by speaking out for God against the evil that the king and queen brought to the land. They were two of the most wicked people of that time, and their children followed in their evil footsteps. Their daughter Athaliah became queen of Judah and murdered her children and grandchildren to keep her power.

Bible events in Ahab's life

1. He marries the wicked Jezebel and becomes king of Israel after his father, Omri.
2. Elijah warns him that there will be no rain for several years.
3. He assembles the people of Israel and the false prophets of Baal at Mount Carmel for a contest.
4. He rides to Jezreel in his chariot, but Elijah outruns him.
5. He fights against Ben-hadad and the Syrians and defeats them.
6. He shows mercy and makes a covenant with Ben-hadad; a prophet of God condemns him for this.
7. He covets Naboth's vineyard; Jezebel procures it for him by murdering Naboth; Elijah prophesies against him and Jezebel.
8. He makes an alliance with Jehoshaphat of Judah.
9. Micaiah prophesies against him and he has Micaiah arrested.
10. He persuades Jehoshaphat to go to battle at Ramoth-gilead; he disguises himself but is wounded by an arrow and dies.
11. Dogs lick up his blood, just as Elijah prophesied.

ELIJAH

In the days when Ahab and Jezebel ruled over Israel, Elijah appeared as a fiery prophet. He dressed in camel's hair clothing and lived in the wilderness as John the Baptist did about eight hundred years later. Ahab had permitted Jezebel to bring her foreign gods from her native Phoenicia and to suppress the worship of the Lord. Elijah challenged four hundred of her false prophets and showed the power of God to send fire. Only when he spoke the word did a three-year drought end and rain return to the land. Elijah performed many miracles and was succeeded by Elisha, another miracle-working prophet.

Bible events in Elijah's life

1. He warns King Ahab that there will be no rain until he says so.
2. He goes to Kerith Brook where ravens feed him.
3. He performs the miracle of the widow's oil and flour.
4. He raises the widow's son from the dead.
5. He overcomes the prophets of Baal on Mount Carmel and executes them.
6. He outruns Ahab's chariot.
7. He flees from Jezebel and goes to the desert where an angel ministers to him; he goes to Mount Horeb, where God speaks to him in a soft whisper.
8. He calls Elisha to be his successor.
9. He meets King Ahab and prophesies Ahab's family's tragic end.
10. He prophesies King Ahaziah's death and calls fire down from heaven to consume Ahaziah's messengers.
11. He is taken to heaven in a whirlwind.

ELISHA

Elisha was plowing when Elijah threw his mantle over Elisha's shoulders, calling him to be his successor. For several years, Elisha followed the older prophet, then watched Elijah as he was taken up into heaven in a whirlwind. Elisha worked many miracles, including raising a boy from the dead.

Bible events in Elisha's life

1. Elijah throws his cloak on him while he is plowing, signifying that he will be Elijah's successor.
2. He slaughters his oxen, makes a feast for his neighbors, and follows Elijah.
3. He refuses to leave Elijah, asks for a double portion of Elijah's power, and sees him taken up into heaven.
4. He tears his cloak, picks up Elijah's cloak, and parts the Jordan River with it.
5. He purifies the water at Jericho.
6. Children mock him; he curses them, and bears maul them.
7. He promises King Jehoram that his men and animals will get water and that he will have victory over the Moabites.
8. He performs the miracle of the widow's oil.

242

>

What
Everyone
Should
Know
about
the

Bible

9. A couple from Shunem make a rooftop room for him; he promises them a son.
10. He restores the Shunammite woman's son to life.
11. He purifies some poisoned stew.
12. He feeds a hundred men with twenty loaves.
13. He heals Naaman of his leprosy.
14. Gehazi takes gifts from Naaman and becomes a leper.
15. He makes an ax head swim.
16. God's fiery army is revealed to him and to his servant at Dothan.
17. He prays that the Syrians may be struck with blindness.
18. He predicts relief for the besieged people of Samaria.
19. Hazael visits him at Damascus to inquire if Ben-hadad will get well; he weeps and predicts that Hazael will become an evil king of Syria.
20. He instructs a young prophet to anoint Jehu king of Israel.
21. He becomes ill; King Jehoash comes to see him; he tells Jehoash to shoot arrows out of a window, signifying his victory over Syria; he dies and is buried.

JEHU

The wicked King Ahab and Queen Jezebel had almost ruined the moral and religious fiber of the nation with the worship of Baal and other foreign gods. At last God commanded the prophet Elijah to anoint Jehu, an officer in Ahab's army, as the next king, and commanded him to destroy the household of Ahab. Jehu's fellow officers proclaimed him king, after which he rode to the capital city and executed Jezebel, her son King Jehoram, and King Ahaziah of Judah. He also executed numerous people of Ahab's family and destroyed the temple of Baal. Although Jehu began his rule well, he failed to eliminate idol worship and pagan practices from the land.

Bible events in Jehu's life
1. A prophet anoints him king of Israel.
2. He overthrows King Jehoram and fulfills Elijah's prophecy by killing him and the rest of Ahab's family.
3. He destroys the temple, worshipers, and priests of Baal.
4. He dies and is buried at Samaria.

JEZEBEL

When Jezebel, daughter of King Ethbaal of Tyre, married King Ahab of Israel, she brought her foreign gods with her. Ahab was a strong king, but a weak husband, and he let Jezebel force her pagan religions upon Israel. Her evil influence reached throughout the land, and 450 pagan priests ate at her table. She tried to kill the prophets of the Lord, including Elijah. Jezebel died when Jehu rebelled against her and her son, King Jehoram (Joram), and executed them. When Jehu came to execute Jezebel, she painted her face with cosmetics, and two men threw Jezebel to the ground from her second story window; then Jehu drove his chariot over her. Dogs ate almost all of her body before she was buried.

Bible events in Jezebel's life
1. She marries Ahab.
2. She tries to murder the Lord's prophets.
3. She sends a message to Elijah that she is going to execute him.
4. She commands that Naboth be slain and procures his vineyard for Ahab; Elijah prophesies that dogs will tear Jezebel's body to pieces.
5. She paints her face and waits for Jehu to ride up; Jehu commands eunuchs to push her out of the window; she dies and dogs eat her body, as Elijah predicted.

JONAH

God commanded the prophet Jonah to go to Nineveh to warn the people of their sin. Jonah was afraid to go with such a message, so he ran away on a ship headed for Tarshish. In the midst of a storm, the sailors discovered that Jonah was running from God and that their lives would be lost unless they threw Jonah into the sea. God had prepared a great fish to swallow Jonah and take him to land. Having learned his lesson, Jonah went to Nineveh and preached. The people repented, much to Jonah's surprise and disappointment, and God helped him to learn some important lessons through this experience.

Bible events in Jonah's life
1. God tells him to go to Nineveh.
2. He disobeys and tries to hide by sailing for Tarshish.
3. A big storm arises; the sailors throw him into the sea, and he is swallowed by a great fish.
4. He prays to God from inside the fish, and the fish spits him up onto dry land.
5. He obeys the Lord and goes to Nineveh; the people repent and God abandons his plan to destroy the city.
6. He becomes angry and God teaches him a lesson using a gourd.

NAAMAN

Syria and Israel were not especially friendly in the days of Naaman, the general of Syria's army. In fact, Naaman had captured an Israelite girl on one of his campaigns into Israel and had taken her home to serve his wife. When Naaman became a leper, this girl told him about

What
Everyone
Should
Know
about
the
Bible

a prophet in her land who could heal him. The king of Syria sent Naaman to find this prophet, named Elisha, but when Elisha told him to wash seven times in the Jordan River, Naaman was furious. He had expected that some mighty work would be performed by the prophet. At last Naaman's servants persuaded him to obey the prophet, and when he did, he was healed.

Bible events in Naaman's life
1. Elisha cures him of his leprosy when he washes in the Jordan River.
2. He brings gifts to Elisha; Elisha refuses them, but Gehazi runs after him to take the gifts for himself.

What everyone should know about the book of 2 Kings
STEWARDSHIP—WHAT WE DO WITH WHAT WE HAVE

This book is the story of the divided kingdom, from the rule of King Ahaziah of Israel until the deportation of Israel's people to Assyria, and on until the deportation of the people of Judah to Babylon. The author is not known, though some think that it was Jeremiah or some other prophet. The date when it was written is not known, either.

What is the core message of this book for you and me today?

Do you ever feel that God has shortchanged you, and that you really deserve more than he has given you? Why does your neighbor drive a better car, live in a bigger home, and take more expensive vacations to exotic, faraway places? Why is your boss the boss and not you? Why is someone else more talented, better looking, better dressed, better educated, or just plain better? If only you had more or were more!

Of course, the quest for more never stops with more, for when you get more, it is essential that you get still more, and then even more after that. In 1 Kings, we see the wisest man on earth slip into the "more" syndrome. If one wife was good, wouldn't seven hundred be better? Then toss in three hundred concubines, just in case seven hundred is not enough. His dissatisfied appetites led to his downfall. The seven hundred wives brought pagan gods that Solomon and his people began to worship. For that sin, the Lord promised to take his kingdom from his descendants, leaving only a small token for his son.

First Kings tells the story of the kingdom after Solomon's death as it divided into Israel in the north and Judah in the south. The once-glorious kingdom was on the skids, heading downward.

Second Kings is the story of thirty-nine kings—nineteen in the northern kingdom of Israel, and twenty in the southern kingdom of Judah. Of all these kings, only eight were good, and thirty-one were evil. Solomon's stewardship left very bitter fruit. The kingdom would never rise again to its former glory.

The story of these thirty-nine kings is also the story of the prophets who warned them about God and begged them to follow him. Some of these prophets wrote books of the Bible. Some, like Elijah and Elisha, did not.

God may never permit you or me to become a king or a queen, but he may give us great gifts to use wisely for his work. From 2 Kings, we should learn the lesson of good stewardship—using what we have wisely, for it is not so much about what we have as what we do with what we have.

What everyone should know about the book of Joel

SHADOWS OF THINGS TO COME

Who wrote this book and why? During the time that the prophet Joel ministered in Judah (about 835 B.C. to 796 B.C.), he wrote messages to Judah warning them about their evil and the coming judgment. Joel's ministry lasted about thirty-nine years, and corresponded with the reign of King Joash.

What is the core message of Joel for us today?

If only I knew what would happen tomorrow! Investors long to know tomorrow's stock market. If only they knew, they could make a fortune. What about tomorrow's opportunities, tomorrow's tragedies, tomorrow's crises? If only we knew!

As you read through the prophets, you will see many shadows of things to come. More than seven hundred years before Jesus, Isaiah described the suffering Savior in great detail. Zechariah portrayed Jesus riding into Jerusalem on a donkey. Daniel and Jeremiah painted pictures of things to come, as did Joel.

After predicting the coming judgment, Joel tells of the coming of the Holy Spirit (Joel 2:28–3:21). Almost eight hundred years later, Peter would preach at Pentecost, quoting this same passage (Acts 2:14-21). How could Joel possibly know this eight hundred years before it happened? God told him.

Joel was a prophet to the nation of Judah, the southern kingdom. Dates are a little uncertain, but it is thought that Joel began his ministry about 835 B.C. and ended it about 796 B.C. Like other prophets to Israel and Judah, Joel begged his people to repent and turn from their sin to God.

"Give me your hearts," God pleads through Joel (Joel 2:12). Why? "Everyone who calls on the name of the LORD will be saved" (Joel 2:32). The plea and the consequence are as timeless as yesterday and as fresh as this morning's dawn.

What everyone should know about the book of Jonah

RUNNING AWAY FROM GOD . . . BUT WHERE TO?

Jonah appeared as a prophet to Israel five years after Jehoash became king. His ministry continued through the reign of Jeroboam II, ending the same year that Jeroboam II died.

His message revealed a loving and forgiving God, even toward the wicked people of Nineveh.

What is an important message that we learn from Jonah today? Read on about running away from God, something that Jonah tried but discovered that he could not do.

When you were a child, did you ever run away? From what? Where did you go? If you are a parent, did your child ever run away? From what? Where to? How long did it take for your child to come home?

Are you running away from something or someone? What? Where are you going? What will you do? If we're honest, each of us has faced some

246

>

What
Everyone
Should
Know
about
the

Bible

time in life when we wanted to run away—from our job, from a sickness or injury, from insufficient funds, from pressure or criticism or ridicule. Perhaps you want to escape from loneliness or boredom or fear. But where to? From what to what?

We can learn from the prophet Jonah about running away. "Go to Nineveh and preach to the people," God said to Jonah. Nineveh was a great Assyrian city that was soon to become the nation's capital. Assyria was a wicked empire, and before too many years it would become Israel's mortal enemy, as it captured and took away Israel's choicest people. The Assyrians were exceptionally cruel to their captives and tortured them mercilessly.

Can you hear Jonah arguing with God? "Those people are wicked. They deserve to die. You should send them all to hell." Have you ever talked like that about some person or nation? Jonah just couldn't do what God wanted, so he ran away.

You probably know the story of Jonah. Jonah boarded a ship and went below to sleep. God sent a violent storm and the sailors feared for their lives. Though they were pagan, they realized that someone had done something wrong. Even pagans are instinctively sensitive to right and wrong. "Get up and pray to your God!" the sailors demanded.

Jonah had a problem. He was running away from God. How could he talk with the God he was running away from? You know the rest of the story. At Jonah's suggestion, they threw him into the violent sea. It looked like the end for Jonah, but God had created a very special fish to swallow Jonah and spit him out on the shore near Nineveh.

At last Jonah went to Nineveh and preached, and a revival broke out. The king of this pagan city repented, so God forgave them and spared them the judgment he had planned. Jonah wasn't happy about this. He had hoped that God would send all 120,000 of these wicked people into eternal punishment, and he grumbled about God's mercy. Then through the lesson of a gourd vine, God taught Jonah something about forgiveness (Jonah 4).

When God tells you to go, then go. Don't run away. If you do, you'll run right into the arms of a waiting God.

What everyone should know about the book of Amos

TARNISHED GOLD, RIGGED SCALES

Your friend has a big smile on his face as he brags about his new job, new car, new house, and new toys. You're almost jealous as you think of your same old job, same old car, same old house, same old toys. You're almost jealous until you recall what your friend's wife told your wife this morning. The man's new toys have come at the high price of neglect—almost abandoning his wife and children, ignoring God, and selling his soul to climb the ladder of success. The dark shadow of divorce lurks in the wings, ready to tear the family apart. The man would have his toys but no loving family to help him enjoy them, and his family would have everyone and everything except the one person they loved so very much.

Like alcohol, the quest for things is intoxicating. Like drugs, it is addictive. It is like cancer. Before we know we have it, it's already eating the heart out of life, and we are totally oblivious to it.

So it was in the days of Amos, a prophet during the golden years of Israel in the northern kingdom. New trade routes had just opened, crops were abundant, people prospered, beautiful homes were built, and elegant public buildings spoke of wealth. What a wonderful time to be alive in the northern kingdom!

But an insidious disease was invading the land. It was raw, rampant materialism, the love of and lust for things. While some slept on beds of pure ivory, others sold themselves and their children into slavery just to survive. Sound familiar? Some things never change.

The old-fashioned way of earning wealth was just too old fashioned for Amos's neighbors. Merchants cheated their customers with rigged scales, diluted good grain by adding husks, and gouged the poor with exorbitant interest rates that made them even poorer. This was the golden age in Israel, but it was tarnished gold weighed on rigged scales. Prosperity was tainted by ugly dishonesty and bribery. It was the "me, my, and mine" generation, when people lived for self at the expense of others. Amos, a simple herdsman, got what he had the hard way—by working for it—but God called him to leave his home in Judah and go north to preach against Israel's sins.

Amos's message is clear for materialistic people—then and now. There is nothing wrong with having money, even lots of money. It's not what we have, but how we got what we have and how we use what we have that makes a difference. We are called to godly ways of gaining what we have and godly stewardship of what we have gained. It is not mine, but ours: mine and God's. I must keep him in the midst of how I get my wealth and how I use my wealth.

What everyone should know about the book of Hosea

LOVE BEYOND REASON

Is love always reasonable, or is there love that reaches beyond rational behavior? To love the truly lovely person makes sense. We would call that reasonable or logical. To love the truly unlovely person defies logic. How can it be? Ask the Lord, who loves us with unreasonable love.

The story of Hosea, the first of the Minor Prophets in the Bible, is also a story of unreasonable love. Hosea was a prophet to Israel, the northern kingdom, during its last days and its last six kings. Amos, another minor prophet, was in Israel at the same time. Amos and Hosea probably knew each other.

At this same time, in the southern kingdom of Judah, Isaiah and Micah were prophets. Hosea became a prophet only thirty-one years before the northern kingdom, Israel, was defeated by the Assyrians. It was a time of national disgrace when kings and peoples were unfaithful to God.

When Hosea was young, he must have dreamed of the lovely, godly young woman he would marry. They would love each other and together would raise their children for the Lord. These are the dreams of many godly young people.

But God commanded Hosea to marry an ungodly, adulterous woman.

248
>

What
Everyone
Should
Know
about
the
Bible

Hosea's children would not come from him, but from the affairs of his wife, Gomer, with her lovers. It was unreasonable. How could God ask Hosea to love a woman like Gomer? But God did, and Hosea obeyed. When Gomer hit bottom and became a slave, Hosea bought her back. This is still an object lesson today that helps us understand the unreasonable and unfathomable love God has for us.

Why would God command Hosea to love this fallen woman? Hosea's unreasonable love for an adulterous woman would be an object lesson to an adulterous nation about God's unreasonable love for that nation. Despite their wickedness, God still loved them, as Hosea loved Gomer.

Thankfully, God doesn't ask you to marry an unfaithful person to provide an object lesson, but through the story of Hosea and the book he wrote, God reveals his unreasonable love for you and me despite our sinfulness. He also offers a model for us, that we might love the unlovely with an unreasonable love and seek to win them to a loving God through his Son, Jesus.

What everyone should know about the book of Isaiah

WINDOW ON TOMORROW

Under King David, Israel had been militarily, socially, economically, and spiritually in its golden age. His son Solomon started out humbly following the Lord, but the lust for women and wealth caught up with him. The more he got, the more he wanted, and the cycle of wanting and getting was a never-ending story. His greatest sin was in permitting his thousand women—wives and concubines—to bring pagan gods into Israel. Before long, the Israelites were joining in worship of these evil deities, and King Solomon also began to worship them. God was displeased, and this was the beginning of the end for the kingdom. The kingdom divided under Solomon's son Rehoboam, who kept only two tribes, called Judah, or the southern kingdom. Israel, or the northern kingdom, split off with ten tribes.

With Rehoboam and Jeroboam began a period of declining kingdoms in Judah and Israel. Altogether, there were thirty-nine kings in the two kingdoms, but only eight honored God. During this period of the divided kingdoms and the exile that followed, prophets arose. There were twelve minor prophets, not because their ministry was small, but because the Bible books they wrote were smaller. Two prophets, Elijah and Elisha, did not write Bible books. Four other prophetic books—Isaiah, Jeremiah, Daniel, and Ezekiel—are "major" prophets because of the size of their books. Jeremiah also wrote the book of Lamentations.

Isaiah became a prophet in 740 B.C., when Jotham was king of Judah. He ministered primarily to Judah but also to other nations—warning them to repent and turn to God. His ministry stretched across the reigns of five kings of Judah—Uzziah, Jotham, Ahaz, Hezekiah, and Manasseh, and four kings of Israel—Menahem, Pekahiah, Pekah, and Hoshea.

Isaiah is the first book of prophecy in the Bible, and Isaiah is considered the greatest of all the prophets. He was the son of nobility and was possibly of royal blood. One ancient tradition says that Isaiah was King Amaziah's nephew, King Uzziah's first cousin, and King Joash's grandson. According to another tradition, he was executed by Manasseh after sixty years of ministry by being sawed into pieces between two planks.

In the first half of the book, chapters 1–39, Isaiah fiercely condemns the wickedness of the people and their need to repent and turn to God. The last twenty-seven chapters are a message of hope that looks forward to the coming Messiah, Jesus. Some of the greatest passages of the Bible are in these chapters, especially the suffering Servant prophecy from Isaiah 52:13–53:12. It is stunning to see how accurately Isaiah foretold the suffering Jesus more than seven hundred years before he came. Isaiah 55 is another well-known passage.

Isaiah not only foretold the future seven hundred years in advance, but many of his prophecies speak to a much more distant future. Only God could speak so clearly through an ordinary man. Isaiah is quoted in the New Testament more than any other prophet.

What everyone should know about the book of Micah
BLIND TO THE WEEDS GROWING IN THE GARDEN OF PROSPERITY
What famous person would you like to meet? Is it a basketball star, a movie star, a great musician, a famous author? You are getting nervous and excited as this famous person is about to enter the room. People all around you are whispering. Then the door opens and that famous person walks through. It's always been this way, hasn't it? Everyone pays special attention to the rich and famous, the stars, the great athletes. If he is tall and handsome, it doesn't hurt either. If she is drop-dead beautiful and rich as Solomon, the excitement is unbearable.

People have always favored the rich, the attractive, the famous, the stars of their generation. These people are set up on pedestals too high for any person to endure. Some can hang on, but many fall.

It was this way in Micah's time. The rich and famous weren't sports heroes or movie stars, but they were often the merchants or high officials. They commanded great admiration in a prosperous society.

Micah's time, from 742 B.C. to 687 B.C., was prosperous in both the northern and the southern kingdoms. There were rich and famous people everywhere, and other people adored them. In the garden of prosperity, there were noxious weeds, many of the same pesky weeds as in our society.

Affluence brought materialism, which lulled the prosperous to sleep. To the north, a giant called Assyria was awakening and would one day devour the northern kingdom. Insensitivity to the rising threat was accompanied by insensitivity to their need for God. If I'm rich enough, why do I need God? I have everything I need. Micah's neighbors were insensitive to the military power that would destroy them and equally insensitive to the God who could prevent that destructrion, the greater power who could save them. They ignored Assyria and God. They were simply too busy with their comforts and with the distraction those comforts brought. Does that sound contemporary?

Micah preached about the coming judgment of God against his people,

250

>

What
Everyone
Should
Know
about
the

Bible

who were ignoring him. Samaria would be destroyed. Judgment would come upon the rulers of Israel who should rule justly for God, but did not.

Micah spoke also of hope. A great king would come with origins from the distant, eternal past. He would be born in an insignificant Judean village called Bethlehem. Of course, this great king was Jesus, and the prophecy was made seven hundred years before he came.

In the prophets, judgment and hope often go together. God judges his people for their sins, but he never leaves them there. He always offers hope for the future. Perhaps that lesson of hope is one of Micah's greatest lessons for us.

Did You Know?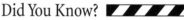

Two seasons, not four The seasons in ancient Israel were not the same four that we have. Their seasons were divided into two—the rainy season and the dry season. The rainy season began in October and ended in May. The dry season ran from June through September. When the early rains came in October, there was great celebration, for this assured that crops could grow. Without the rainy season, the soil became hard and produced no crops for the May harvest. When the prophet Elijah told King Ahab that there would be no rains until he said so, he was indirectly saying that there would be famine. No rains, no water, no crops, no food. This was incredibly serious. People would die of thirst and starvation.

No godly kings in the northern kingdom During the 208 years that the northern kingdom survived, there were nineteen kings. Not one of them was a godly king. That was one major reason that the northern kingdom did not survive as long as the southern kingdom, which lasted another 141 years after the northern kingdom fell. Of the twenty kings of Judah, eight were godly and twelve were ungodly. Those eight made the difference for Judah.

Let's get some perspective on the time periods:

1. The time of the patriarchs, from Abraham through Joseph, was about two hundred years.
2. The time during which the patriarchs' descendants lived in Egypt was about four hundred years.
3. The time that the Israelites were in the wilderness was about forty years.
4. The time of the judges was about three hundred years.
5. The reign of King Saul lasted for forty-two years.
6. King David reigned for forty years.
7. The reign of King Solomon lasted for forty years.

8. The duration of the northern kingdom of Israel was 208 years.
9. The duration of the southern kingdom of Judah was 340 years.
10. The duration of the southern kingdom beyond the end of the northern kingdom was 141 years.
11. The time from Abraham to Jesus lasted more than two thousand years.
12. The exile lasted for approximately seventy years.
13. From exile and foreign rule until the time of Jesus was more than five hundred years.
14. The life of Jesus on earth was about thirty-three years.
15. The time of the apostles was about eighty-five years.
16. The Christian era, from the time of Jesus until now, has been about two thousand years.

To get perspective, let's compare some periods of United States history with the periods above:

1. From the earliest colonial times until now has been about four hundred years.
2. From the Declaration of Independence until now has been about 230 years.
3. From Christopher Columbus until now has been about five hundred years.

The descendants of the patriarchs were in Egypt for as long as the entire United States history from the earliest colonial days. Either the time of the judges or the history of the southern kingdom of Judah would take United States history back beyond the Declaration of Independence. The time of exile and foreign rule before Jesus, about five hundred years, would take United States history all the way back to Christopher Columbus.

The time from Abraham to the time of Jesus on earth was approximately the same as from the time of Jesus until now—more than two thousand years.

The kings who ruled the longest Of all the kings of Judah and Israel, did any rule longer than King David, who ruled forty years? In the northern kingdom, only one ruled longer, as Jeroboam II ruled forty-one years. In the southern kingdom, three ruled longer: Asa, forty-one years; Uzziah, fifty-two years; and Manasseh, fifty-five years. Joash ruled for forty years.

Of these kings, Asa was truly godly and Jeroboam II was ungodly; Uzziah, Manasseh, and Joash had partly godly and partly ungodly reigns.

252
>
What
Everyone
Should
Know
about
the
Bible

The kings who ruled the least time In the northern kingdom, seven kings ruled for two years or less: Nadab, two years; Elah, two years; Zimri, seven days; Ahaziah, two years; Zechariah, six months; Shallum, one month; and Pekahiah, two years. All were ungodly kings.

In the southern kingdom, four kings ruled for two years or less: Ahaziah, one year; Amon, two years; Jehoahaz, three months; and Jehoiachin, three months. All were ungodly kings.

Zarephath When Kerith Brook dried up, God commanded Elijah to go to Zarephath, where a poor widow would take care of him. Zarephath was a village along the coast of the Mediterranean Sea, between Tyre and Sidon, and thus was in Phoenicia, which is modern Lebanon.

Baal There were many heathen gods named Baal, since the word was often used as a generic term for a local heathen god. Generally, the worship was similar, with Baal credited with controlling rain, crops, fertility, fruit, and cattle. In ancient Israel and Judah, agriculture was the primary source of income and food, so superstitious farmers who did not know the Lord gravitated to their local Baal, their pagan deity of fertility and prosperity.

There were high places and altars for the worship of Baal, and sometimes Baal was represented by an idol. Incense and burnt sacrifices were sometimes offered to Baal, sometimes even the sacrifice of children by their parents.

The contest between Elijah and the prophets of Baal on Mount Carmel was the most dramatic encounter in the Scriptures between the worship of Baal and worship of the Lord.

Cloaks were a luxury Elisha inherited Elijah's cloak, and with it performed miracles. Most people had a cloak in Bible times, but usually only one. It was their luxury item. Today we go to the store and buy clothing, often at very cheap prices. Not so during Bible times. The woman of the house had to make cloaks for her family, which was tedious handwork. First, she had to spin the fibers, thread, or yarn. Some were from animal hair, some from flax. With a loom, she then wove the threads into cloth, and from that cloth, she carefully cut and sewed the pieces together. Imagine doing that for all your clothing!

Grapes were more than grapes, so a vineyard was more than a vineyard Today we buy bunches of grapes at the grocery store and often think little about their origin, which is probably far from the store. In Bible times, grapes, olives, figs, wheat, and barley were the most important crops. These foods were not merely crops but life itself. Without these five crops, the ancient food supply would be almost exhausted. Wheat and barley were vital for bread, the one essential staple in ancient society.

Grapes were essential, too. From grapes came wine, and in ancient lands, which often had unsafe water, wine was an important drink. Grapes were dried and were sometimes made into little cakes. With no refrigeration available, dried grapes, figs, and other fruits were essential foods for travel, military operations, and even day-to-day survival.

Naboth could not easily give up his vineyard to King Ahab, for it was an important source of his family's food supply. What good would Ahab's gold be without food to eat?

Olives were more than olives; they were oil While we're talking about foods, let's remind ourselves of the importance of olives in ancient cultures. First, people ate them, as we do today. More importantly, olive oil was extracted from olives, and this oil was used as fuel for lamps, so olives were important for light. Olive oil was also an important ingredient in cooking and in anointing oil.

A room on a roof? Who would want that? The kind couple of Shunem built a room on their roof for Elisha and his helper. Who would want a room on a roof? If you live in snow country, it sounds even less appealing. Imagine sleeping in a rooftop room with snow blowing.

However, this was not snow country. It was a warm, often hot climate so the rooftop room was not only acceptable, but desirable, for the gentle breezes blowing through on a hot night would be most welcome.

Houses in Bible times were built from stone or mud bricks, depending on which was available. In our times, even children have private rooms, but then, almost no one had a private room. Entire families often slept in the same room, so a room especially for the prophet and his helper was a luxury.

Windows were merely openings in the walls, for glass windows were not yet in common use and would have been too expensive for the average person even if they had been available. Glass was available, but it was uncommon for windows. Large sheets of clear glass, as we have today, were not available in those days.

Wealthy people often had a courtyard around their houses, protected by a wall.

Jezebel painted her face—with what? When Jehu came to execute Jezebel, she painted her face with cosmetics. Was she hoping to change his mind with makeup, or possibly seduce him? Was she so vain that she wanted to die with her makeup on? But what cosmetics did she have?

Today, when you visit a mall, you encounter perfume stores, cosmetics stores, beauty salons, nail salons, and much more. You have a choice of hundreds of brands of perfumes, blush, lipstick, eye shadow, and many other types of cosmetics. Jezebel, of course, did not have any of this. She would have given half her kingdom, and perhaps even her king, for what you own. But what did she have?

In those days, women could paint their faces with colors (2 Kings 9:30). They could also draw heavy black lines around their eyes. They had lipstick, blush, and facial paints that came from iron or copper ore mixed with water. They also had nail polish, made with henna plant dye, which colored the fingernail. The skin was colored with reddish-brown pigments that were supposed to make the woman more beautiful. Olive oil mixed with spices made perfume. Some cultures used the essence of flowers, such as the essence of lotus in Egypt.

Discovering My Purpose from God's Plan

1. *Golden opportunities can become lost opportunities.* Gold offered is not gold received. Gold at arm's length is worthless. Golden opportunities are golden only if accepted and redeemed. Both Jeroboam and Rehoboam had golden opportunities to obey the Lord and prosper. Both squandered those golden opportunites and the "gold" melted away and turned to ashes.
2. *What we have is not as important as what we do with what we have.* This is the message of 2 Kings. Making good use of the little bit we have is more important than having an abundance that we cannot use, or that we squander. Possessing little but having a relationship with God is much better than having an abundance but not knowing God.
3. *It's hard to pray to God when you're running away from him.* How can you be running away if he is close enough to hear you pray? This is a lesson Jonah learned as he tried to run away from God, but discovered that God was always there, as close as his whispered prayer. You can't hide from an omnipresent God, for he is everywhere.
4. *Even a fish's belly can be a great classroom if the teacher is the Lord.* In the belly of the fish, Jonah took a crash course in Obedience 101.
5. *If you try to run away from God, you may actually run into his open arms.* You may think you are escaping from God, but actually you are escaping to God.
6. *It's not what we have that counts, but how we got what we have and how we use what we have.* We are called to godly ways of gaining what we have and to godly stewardship of what we have gained. It is not mine, but ours: mine and God's. I must keep him in the midst of how I get my wealth, and how I use my wealth, and be mindful of the needs of other people.

7. *Like alcohol, the quest for things is intoxicating.* Like drugs, it is addictive. Materialism is like cancer before we discover that we have it—it's eating the heart out of life, and we are totally oblivious to it. So Israel was in the days of Amos, and so it is in our culture today.

8. *To love the truly lovely person makes sense.* We would call that reasonable and logical. To love the truly unlovely person defies logic. How can it be? From a human perspective, we can love only the lovely. From God's perspective, we must love even the unlovely, for he loves both the lovely and unlovely.

9. *Godliness is loving God and others as God loves us and others.*

10. *Affluence brings materialism, and materialism lulls the prosperous to sleep, oblivious to the noxious weeds growing in the garden of prosperity.* This is a vital lesson from the prophet Micah.

11. *In the prophets, judgment and hope often go hand in hand.* God judges his people for their sins, but he never abandons them. He always offers hope for the future. Perhaps that is one of Micah's greatest lessons for us.

12. *God's most powerful revelations come as a gentle whisper.* Elijah expected God in a mighty wind, a great earthquake, and a roaring fire, but he came with a gentle whisper. Look for God in the silences of life as much as in visible or audible signs.

Everything Falls Apart
Israel Taken Captive

Characters:
Amon (son and successor to King Manasseh of Judah); Daniel (deported to Babylon during this time); Eliakim (Josiah's son and successor, renamed Jehoiakim); Gedaliah (governor of Judea appointed by Nebuchadnezzar); Habakkuk (a prophet during this time); Hezekiah (a king of Judah); Hilkiah (the priest who found the Book of the Law in the Temple); Isaiah (a prophet during this time); Jehoiachin (son and successor to Jehoiakim, king of Judah); Jehoiakim (Josiah's son and successor, named Eliakim at first); Jeremiah (a prophet during this time); Josiah (a king of Judah); Manasseh (Hezekiah's son and successor as king of Judah); Mattaniah (renamed Zedekiah; Jehoachin's brother and successor as the last king of Judah); Merodach-baladan (king of Babylon during Hezekiah's reign); Nabopolasser (a king of Babylon, father of Nebuchadnezzar); Nahum (a prophet during this time); Nebuchadnezzar (a king of Babylon, son of Nabopolassar); Pharaoh Neco (the Egyptian king who killed Josiah); Sennacherib (king of Assyria during Hezekiah's reign); Shaphan (the secretary who read the Book of the Law to Hilkiah and Josiah); Zedekiah (first named Mattaniah; Jehoiachin's brother and successor as the last king of Judah); Zephaniah (a prophet during this time)

Time Period:
Between the captivity of the northern kingdom of Israel and the captivity of the southern kingdom of Judah

Dates:
722 B.C.–581 B.C.

Where Scene 16 of the Big Story Can Be Found:
Second Kings and 2 Chronicles present the historical panorama. Isaiah, Nahum, Obadiah, Jeremiah, Zephaniah, and Habakkuk present the prophetic messages of this period

in Judah. Daniel and Ezekiel present prophetic messages of this period in Babylon.

In Scene 16, Find the Answers to These Questions:
Assyria captured one kingdom and Babylon captured the other. Which was which?
Which king tore his robes when the Bible was read to him?
Which king cut the Bible into pieces and burned it as it was read to him?

Look for this in Scene 16
> An angel killed 185,000 enemy soldiers in one night.
> Four lepers inherited a fortune, but refused to keep it.
> The only copy of the Bible of that time was lost, then found.
> A king watched his sons be murdered, then had his eyes gouged out.
> An eight-year-old boy became king.

 The Big Story So Far

Looking back to look ahead
During its 208-year history, the northern kingdom of Israel had nineteen kings. Every one of them was a pagan, ungodly leader who turned people away from the Lord. During its 344-year history, the southern kingdom of Judah had twenty kings, a much longer average tenure for its kings than for those of Israel. Although twelve of them were evil, eight of them were godly. It was the godly eight who gave Judah its much longer life.

A basic principle pervades the Old Testament and our lives today. When rulers pleased the Lord and followed him, he brought safety and prosperity to the nation. When they did not, he did not help them. Israel had no godly leaders and Judah had eight. That made a difference.

Looking back, the people of Israel had many golden opportunities. Although they were bound in slavery in Egypt for hundreds of years, God personally involved himself in leading them from that slavery toward their own new Promised Land.

When the Israelites escaped from Egypt, God personally led them to Mount Sinai where he gave them his law and magnificent instructions for his Tabernacle and worship. There, under Moses' leadership, he welded the former slaves into a nation and a covenant people. All they had to do to prosper was to follow and obey the Lord. That isn't much to ask of them, or of us, is it?

The next part of Israel's history is a troubled time, beginning with a wasted opportunity to enter the Promised Land after only two

258
>
What
Everyone
Should
Know
about
the
Bible

years. Their lack of faith in God sent them back into the wilderness to wander for another thirty-eight years. It was a grueling time, with their food mostly limited to the daily manna. At last, after forty years in the wilderness, the Israelites entered the Promised Land and conquered Jericho in a miraculous battle. This was a high point in their history.

The Promised Land was theirs by promise, but their conquest was incomplete. As time passed, and they failed to fully conquer the Promised Land, the winsome lifestyle of the inhabitants, the Canaanites, became more appealing to many of the Israelites than their own worship of the Lord. The Israelites won militarily, but lost to their enemies morally, spiritually, and culturally. They tried to hold onto God with one hand while they worshiped pagan deities with the other hand.

This continued through the time of the judges, selected leaders who were supposed to head a theocracy, but who seldom honored God. There were judges such as Samson who seemed more intent on having sex with Philistine women than with leading his nation righteously. There were a few such as Deborah and Gideon, who served the Lord and had military successes. Samuel was the last of the judges, and he was also a prophet. He led during the transition between the judges and the kings. His story is not in the book of Judges, but opens the first book bearing his name. Unfortunately, Samuel was an incompetent father with unrighteous sons, so they could not succeed him in leading Israel, and the people demanded a king.

God gave Israel a king named Saul. He began well and finished poorly by refusing to obey the Lord. God chose a humble shepherd boy to be the next king and gave him a mighty victory over a Philistine giant named Goliath. When Saul died in battle, David became king.

Israel entered its golden era under King David. He was mostly a godly person, although like us, he had his moments of sin and repentance. Under David, the kingdom grew and prospered to an amazing degree. David's son Solomon inherited vast riches and power and had every opportunity to secure his throne and his father's throne for generations to come.

Although Solomon began well by seeking God's wisdom in ruling his people well and by writing the beautiful books of Proverbs and Song of Songs, he became infected with lust for money, women, and power. At one point, he had a thousand wives and concubines. Imagine trying to remember their names, never mind their birthdays!

Solomon became a wretched husband, father, and king. His foreign wives brought in their pagan deities, and before long, the Israelites were worshiping these other gods in direct violation of the first commandment. In time, Solomon joined this foreign worship and departed from the one true God. His wretchedness is expressed in the book of Ecclesiastes, which he wrote later in life.

When Solomon died, his son Rehoboam had one golden opportunity to keep the kingdom within the family. If he would only treat his people well, they would serve him, but he ridiculed the idea and the kingdom split into the northern kingdom of Israel and the southern kingdom of Judah, where Jerusalem was located. Rehoboam and his successors were a mixed bag—there were twenty kings, but only eight were godly. This was still better than the northern kingdom, which had nineteen ungodly kings.

The ungodly condition of the northern kingdom rotted it from within, and it lasted only 208 years. The partially godly condition of the southern kingdom kept it going for 136 years longer.

At last, in 722 B.C., Assyria captured Israel, bringing to an end the political history of the northern kingdom. Hosea's prophetic ministry ended with the demise of the kingdom of Israel. About seven years later, Hosea would finish writing the book with his name. Micah's prophetic ministry to the kingdom ended with the defeat of Israel in 722 B.C. but continued for thirty-five more years in Judah.

It would be another 136 years before the Babylonians captured Jerusalem and the southern kingdom, so they had another golden opportunity to follow the Lord during that time.

Judah has 136 years of opportunity

What happened in Judah during those 136 years? Let's backtrack a little into the time before Israel was taken into exile to understand this. We will go back to the reign of Ahaz, the twelfth king of Judah. At the age of twenty he ruled four years with his father. While Ahaz was still in his midtwenties, Israel and Syria teamed up to come against Judah.

Pekah, king of Israel, came against Judah with such violent force that he killed 120,000 of their men in one day. Israel took 200,000 men, women, and children back to their capital city of Samaria. Judah was desperately weak from its wickedness and this weakened it even more severely. Realizing that, the Edomites attacked from the south, and the Philistines come from the south and west. It was a low point for Judah.

If only Ahaz had listened to the great prophet Isaiah and turned to the Lord, he would have saved Judah. But he didn't. Instead, he sent his Temple and palace treasures to the Assyrian king, Tiglath-pileser, asking him to go against Israel and Syria. Assyria fought Israel and

260

>

What
Everyone
Should
Know
about
the

Bible

Syria in 734 B.C., resulting in the first captivity of the people of Israel. Tiglath-pileser also saw how weak Judah had become, so he made life miserable for Ahaz until he died. Ahaz's son Hezekiah became king of Judah about 725 B.C. at age twenty-five.

Ahaz had been an ungodly king, but Hezekiah was a godly king of Judah. He removed the pagan high places, smashed the pagan sacred stones, and cut down the pagan Asherah poles. He even destroyed the bronze snake that Moses had made in the wilderness, for the people of Judah had begun to burn incense to it. He was the most righteous of all the kings of Judah (2 Kings 18:5).

Assyria began its siege of Samaria, the capital of the northern kingdom, in the fourth year of Hezekiah's reign. During the sixth year, Assyria completely defeated Israel and took many captives. In the fourteenth year of Hezekiah's reign, Assyria came against Judah and conquered several cities. Hezekiah paid tribute to Assyria's king Sennacherib. He gave him Temple and palace treasures and even stripped gold from the Temple doors to give him. During this period, Judean kings often gave Temple and palace treasures to buy the help of a foreign king.

Assyria threatens Judah

This was not enough for Sennacherib, who sent his commander in chief, a personal representative, and a huge army to taunt Hezekiah. "If you do not surrender, we will put Jerusalem under siege," they said.

Hezekiah tore his clothes and put on sackcloth when he heard what the Assyrians said. It looked grim, for they had conquered Israel only eight years earlier, completely destroying the northern kingdom. Hezekiah sent his officials to talk with the prophet Isaiah about this.

The Lord's message came back to Hezekiah. "Do not be disturbed by this blasphemous speech," he said. . . . "I myself will move against him, and the king will receive a message that he is needed at home. So he will return to his land, where I will have him killed with a sword" (2 Kings 19:6-7).

Sennacherib sent another grim, threatening letter to Hezekiah. When Hezekiah received the letter, he went to the Temple and spread it out before the Lord. Then he prayed fervently.

Isaiah sent a message to Hezekiah. "The Lord has heard your prayer. The armies of Sennacherib will not enter Jerusalem."

One angel kills 185,000 soldiers

That night, the angel of the Lord went through the Assyrian camp and killed 185,000 of Sennacherib's troops. When Sennacherib saw that, he broke camp and went home, greatly humbled. One day, two of his sons murdered him with the sword. They escaped to a foreign country, and another son, Esarhaddon, became king of Assyria.

Extended life

About this time, Hezekiah became deathly ill. Isaiah the prophet went to visit him. He told the king to set his affairs in order, for he would die. Then Hezekiah turned his face to the wall, praying and weeping.

Isaiah had not yet left the middle courtyard when the Lord sent him back. "I have heard your prayers and seen your tears," the Lord said to Hezekiah. "I will add fifteen years to your life."

"What sign do I have that this will happen?" Hezekiah asked Isaiah.

"Would you like the shadow of the sundial to go forward ten steps or backward ten steps?" Isaiah asked.

"It always goes forward," said Hezekiah. "Make it go backward." So it did.

Soon after this, Merodach-baladan, the son of Babylon's king, sent well-wishers and a gift to Hezekiah. Hezekiah foolishly let his pride get the best of him, and he showed them all his treasures. At this point, Babylon had not yet conquered Assyria, so Hezekiah apparently did not see them as the threat they would become.

Isaiah came back to see Hezekiah and told him how foolish he had been. "A time is coming when everything you have will be carried to Babylon. Even some of your descendants will be taken away." Concluding that these events would not happen during his lifetime, Hezekiah breathed a sigh of relief. How sad that he did not grieve for his descendants!

Manasseh succeeds Hezekiah as king of Judah

When Hezekiah died, his son Manasseh became king of Judah, and he ruled in Jerusalem for fifty-five years. Manasseh began his reign as an evil king. He rebuilt the pagan shrines and constructed altars to the pagan god Baal. He built pagan altars and set up an Asherah pole in the Temple of the Lord. Manasseh even sacrificed his own son in a pagan fire ritual and murdered many innocent people. Hezekiah would have wept to see his son do all these things. The Lord spoke to Manasseh and his people, but they paid no attention, so the Lord allowed the army commanders of Assyria to capture Manasseh. They put a hook in his nose, bound him with bronze shackles, and led him away to Babylon. This same year, Isaiah's prophetic ministry ended. Some say that Manasseh had him sawn asunder between planks before Manasseh was transported to Assyria.

In his distress, Manasseh humbled himself before the Lord and prayed for help. The Lord heard him and helped him return to Jerusalem, possibly as a puppet king of the king of Babylon. Then Manasseh realized that the Lord is truly God. He removed the pagan gods, images,

What
Everyone
Should
Know
about
the

Bible

and altars from the Temple, and threw them out of the city. He restored
the altar of the Lord and sacrificed offerings to him. He begged the
people of Judah to serve the Lord.

Nahum's prophetic ministry in Judah

During this time in Judah, Nahum began his prophetic ministry. His
plea was to God. Why didn't God punish wicked Assyria? God's message
was clear and simple—he does punish evil and would in time punish
Assyria. It was only forty-two years after Nahum's ministry ended that
Babylon defeated Assyria.

Amon succeeds Manasseh as king of Judah

When Manasseh died, his son Amon became king of Judah. He was
twenty-two and reigned for only two years as an evil king. Amon's
officials conspired against him and assassinated him. Soon there was
an uprising, and the people killed the officials who assassinated Amon.
They made Josiah king of Judah.

Josiah succeeds Amon as king of Judah

Josiah was only eight years old when he became king. He reigned as a
godly king for thirty-one years. This same year, 640 B.C., Zephaniah the
prophet, who like Josiah was a fourth-generation descendant of King
Hezekiah, began to prophesy. He preached judgment for Judah's sin and
the coming Day of the Lord.

When he was sixteen, Josiah began to bring sweeping reforms to
Judah. He sought the Lord and began to purge the pagan high places,
Asherah poles, carved idols, and cast images.

About this time (627 B.C.), Jeremiah began to prophesy. His ministry
would extend beyond the end of Judah. He spoke of God's coming judgment against Judah for the sins of the past. This caused some to plot
against Jeremiah, but he faithfully kept on preaching and calling Judah
to repent.

In the eighteenth year of Josiah's reign (about 622 B.C.), the king
began a building program to restore the Temple. In the process, Hilkiah
the priest found a copy of the Book of the Law, probably a scroll, tucked
away in a forgotten place. Shaphan the secretary read it to Hilkiah and
then he read it to King Josiah.

Josiah tore his robes when he heard the Scriptures. "The Lord must
be very angry because our fathers have not kept his word," Josiah said.
Then Josiah sent for some word from Huldah the prophet.

"The Lord says he will bring disaster on this place and its people,"
she said. "But because you, the king, have humbled yourself before the
Lord, this will not happen during your lifetime."

That same year, Zephaniah's prophetic ministry ended.

Babylon becomes the world power instead of Assyria

About this time, there was a vast change in world power. For many centuries, Babylon and Assyria had contended for power, but for the most part, Assyria had prevailed. When Israel was taken into exile, Assyria was the world power.

In 626 B.C., a powerful figure named Nabopolassar founded an independent dynasty known as the neo-Babylonian or Chaldean regime. Under Nabopolassar and his son Nebuchadnezzar, Babylon rebelled against Assyria and established the Babylonian empire. By 612 B.C., Babylon was the world power. Both father and son were skilled in military warfare, and they rebuilt old Babylon to be a splendid cultural center. Both men also sent military expeditions to gather wealth and capture artisans who could help develop their magnificent city.

Habakkuk's prophetic ministry

In this same year (612 B.C.), Nahum's prophetic ministry ended and Habakkuk's began. The book he wrote was a book of "whys." Why was God permitting Judah to get by with so much evil? God's answer was that they would be punished and that he was already preparing the Babylonians to do so. Why use a greater evil to punish a lesser evil? God answered that the Babylonians were temporary. They, too, would be punished. Habakkuk's book also addressed the declining kingdom of Judah.

Jehoahaz succeeds Josiah as king of Judah

For some mysterious reason, Josiah went into battle against Pharaoh Neco of Egypt in 609 B.C. Egyptian archers shot Josiah; he returned to Jerusalem badly wounded and died. Josiah's twenty-three-year-old son Jehoahaz became king. He reigned for only three months, and that short reign was evil. Pharaoh Neco captured Jehoahaz, put him in chains, and levied a heavy tribute from Judah.

Eliakim (Jehoiakim) succeeds Jehoahaz as king of Judah

Pharaoh Neco made Josiah's other son Eliakim his puppet king and changed his name to Jehoiakim. He was only twenty-five at the time, and he reigned as an evil king for eleven years. How did the godly Josiah raise two ungodly sons? One wonders. Jehoiakim had to levy heavy taxes to pay Pharaoh Neco the tribute that he demanded.

What
Everyone
Should
Know
about
the

Bible

Daniel, Shadrach, Meshach, and Abednego are exiled to Babylon

Judah was now weak and vulnerable. Egypt ruled over Judah, and the rising power of Babylon was an even greater threat. Before long, in 605 B.C., Nebuchadnezzar sent his forces to Judah, drove the Egyptians out, took control of Judah, and made Jehoiakim a puppet king for three years. He also took the first captives from Judah to Babylon, including the four young men Daniel, Shadrach, Meshach, and Abednego (Daniel 1:1-7).

Nebuchadnezzar valued the wealth he could gather from a place like Judah, and he valued even more the wealth in artisans and future government leaders such as these four young men.

Jehoiakim burns the Scriptures

Jehoiakim was a rebellious and ungodly puppet king. When Jeremiah wrote a scroll and it was read to Jehoiakim, the king cut it into pieces and threw it into a firepot that warmed his palace. This scroll was replaced with another, which has become our book of Jeremiah. At last, Jehoiakim rebelled against Nebuchadnezzar. He provoked the king of Babylon and other neighbors such as the Moabites, Ammonites, and Arameans, who sent expeditions against him.

Jehoiachin succeeds Jehoiakim as king of Judah

Jehoiakim died, and his son Jehoiachin ruled in his place. He was eighteen, and he reigned for only three months before Nebuchadnezzar laid siege to Jerusalem and took Jehoiachin prisoner to Babylon. Nebuchadnezzar also took Judah's treasures and many other key people, including Ezekiel, who became a prophet to the common man in Babylon.

Zedekiah succeeds Jehoiachin as the last king of Judah

Nebuchadnezzar appointed Jehoiakim's brother Mattaniah as a puppet king and renamed him Zedekiah. He was twenty-one and he reigned for eleven years. Zedekiah was not a very loyal puppet king for Nebuchadnezzar. Before long, it became apparent to Nebuchadnezzar that Zedekiah wasn't responding as expected, so Nebuchadnezzar came again with an army and laid a siege against Jerusalem from January 587 B.C. to July 586 B.C.

When the Babylonians broke through Jerusalem's wall, Zedekiah and his close followers fled. Nebuchadnezzar's soldiers soon captured him and brought him before the Babylonian king. Nebuchadnezzar forced Zedekiah to watch him execute his sons, then he gouged out his eyes so that it was the last thing he ever saw. Then he took Zedekiah in chains to Babylon. Eighty other high officials of Judah were executed.

A month later, Nebuzaradan, captain of Nebuchadnezzar's bodyguard, ordered the confiscation of the final Temple treasures, the destruction of the Temple, and the burning of Jerusalem. It was all over. The rest of Judah was carried away into captivity, and only the poorest people were left to care for the land. It was a time for weeping, and that is what Jeremiah's book of Lamentations is all about.

King Nebuchadnezzar of Babylon appointed Gedaliah as governor of Judah. There would be no more kings of Judah. A dissident named Ishmael thought that Gedaliah cooperated too much with the Babylonians and assassinated him. This led to the sixth deportation of Judeans to Babylon in 581 B.C.

A few remaining Judeans forced Jeremiah to flee with them to Egypt (2 Kings 25:22-26; Jeremiah 40–44). Israel was no more, and with this conquest and deportation Judah was no more.

Questions You May Be Asking

What was Hezekiah's tunnel?

When Sennacherib prepared to attack Jerusalem, Hezekiah got ready for his attack. One of his precautions was to secure water that would be available during a possible siege. Hezekiah had a tunnel dug through almost eighteen hundred feet of solid rock. This connected a spring with the pool of Siloam, and brought plenty of water into the city. An inscription can still be seen today at the south end of this tunnel that describes its construction. Visitors can still wade through the waters of this tunnel.

How did the Assyrians treat their captives?

The Assyrians were especially skilled in warfare and exceptionally cruel to their captives. When Assyrians came against a city, they first built great walls of earth around their camp, complete with ramps, towers, and roads. They assaulted the city with mighty battering rams and pounded the city walls and gates incessantly.

One method of torture was to impale a captive by jamming him down alive onto a sharp pole. Death took two or three days and loved ones often had to watch helplessly from a nearby city wall. Assyrians also cut their victims in pieces, crushed them with hammers, or blinded them by gouging out their eyes. One of the worst tortures was flaying—pulling small strips of skin from the captive a little at a time until the pain was so intense that the person died.

Where was the Book of the Law found?

When Josiah had the Temple repaired, his workmen found a copy of the Book of the Law, the first five books of our Bible. How could a large scroll like that be lost? Where did they find it? It is possible that it was tucked away in a dusty old chest, but wouldn't someone have found it in the decades of ungodliness that preceded Josiah? Josiah's evil father, Amon, and grandfather Manasseh probably tried to destroy every copy of the Scriptures during their fifty-six-year reigns. Some think that this copy of the Scriptures was in the cornerstone of the Temple and was

What
Everyone
Should
Know
about
the

Bible

thus hidden from Manasseh's and Amon's destructiveness. The stone may have been opened for repairs during the reconstruction of the Temple.

How did Josiah pay for the restoration of the Temple?
Repairing the Temple and restoring its services were costly, so Josiah asked for contributions from his people. The Levites collected the money and gave it to Hilkiah the high priest so he could pay the workmen. What was this money? Coinage had just begun in other places, but not yet in Judah. Paper currency would not exist for many years, and there were no credit cards. Money was usually gold or silver that could be weighed. It could be whole pieces of art or broken pieces of metal. Don't picture the people dropping coins or currency into an offering plate just yet.

Great Events of This Time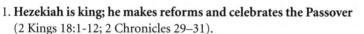

1. **Hezekiah is king; he makes reforms and celebrates the Passover** (2 Kings 18:1-12; 2 Chronicles 29–31).
2. **Sennacherib attacks Hezekiah** (2 Kings 18:13-37; 2 Chronicles 32:1-19; Isaiah 36).
3. **An angel destroys the Assyrian army** (2 Kings 19; 2 Chronicles 32:20-23; Isaiah 37).
4. **Hezekiah becomes ill** (2 Kings 20:1-11; 2 Chronicles 32:24-26; Isaiah 38).
5. **Hezekiah foolishly shows some Babylonians his treasure** (2 Kings 20:12-21; 2 Chronicles 32:27-33; Isaiah 39).
6. **Manasseh and Amon are wicked kings of Judah** (2 Kings 21; 2 Chronicles 33).
7. **Josiah repairs the Temple and the Book of the Law is found** (2 Kings 22; 2 Chronicles 34:1-28).
8. **Josiah reads the Book of the Law to his people** (2 Kings 23:1-3; 2 Chronicles 34:29-32).
9. **Josiah makes reforms and celebrates the Passover** (2 Kings 23:4-27; 2 Chronicles 34:33–35:19).
10. **Josiah dies in battle** (2 Kings 23:28-30; 2 Chronicles 35:20–36:1).
11. **Judah declines under kings Jehoahaz, Jehoiakim, and Jehoiachin** (2 Kings 23:31–24:17; 2 Chronicles 36:2-10).
12. **Judah falls and Jerusalem is destroyed; their return is prophesied** (2 Kings 24:18–25:21; 2 Chronicles 36:11-21; Jeremiah 39:1-10).
13. **Jehoiachin is released and Gedaliah is murdered** (2 Kings 25:22-30; Jeremiah 40–43).

 Significant Dates of This Time

722 B.C., the northern kingdom of Israel falls and Judah remains.

715 B.C., Hezekiah becomes Judah's king; Hosea's ministry ends.

701 B.C., Sennacherib of Assyria besieges Jerusalem, and Hezekiah gives his treasure to Sennacherib as tribute.

696 B.C., Hezekiah, king of Judah, dies. His son Manasseh becomes king of Judah and rules fifty-five years; he takes Judah back into paganism.

687 B.C., Micah's prophetic ministry ends.

681 B.C., Isaiah's prophetic ministry ends; the Assyrian king Sennacherib is assassinated by his sons and his son Esarhaddon succeeds him; Manasseh is captured and taken with a hook in his nose to Babylon; Manasseh repents, turns to God, and reforms Judah.

669 B.C., Ashurbanipal becomes king of Assyria.

663 B.C.–612 B.C., Nahum's prophetic ministry.

641 B.C., Manasseh dies; his son Amon becomes king of Judah; he reigns two years and is assassinated by his officials.

640 B.C., Judeans kill Amon's assassins; they make Amon's son Josiah king of Judah at age eight; Zephaniah becomes a prophet of Judah.

627 B.C.–586 B.C., Jeremiah becomes a prophet; Josiah attacks paganism in Judah and repairs the Temple.

622 B.C., the Book of the Law is found in the Temple; Josiah reads it to his people.

621 B.C., Zephaniah's ministry ends.

612 B.C.–589 B.C., Habakkuk becomes a prophet; Assyria's capital of Nineveh is destroyed by the Babylonians.

609 B.C., King Josiah is killed in battle; Babylon completely conquers Assyria.

608 B.C., Nebuchadnezzar's first captivity of Judah; Daniel is taken captive to Babylon.

603 B.C., Jehoiakim burns Jeremiah's scroll.

602 B.C., Jehoiakim rebels against Nebuchadnezzar.

601 B.C., Daniel and his friends are appointed as Babylonian officials; Nebuchadnezzar has a dream.

597 B.C., The second captivity of Judah; Ezekiel is taken to Babylon; Jehoiakim, king of Judah, dies and his son Jehoiachin succeeds him at age eighteen; Jehoiachin is taken to Babylon; Nebuchadnezzar installs Jehoiachin's uncle Mattaniah as a Judean king and renames him Zedekiah; Jeremiah prophesies under Zedekiah.

593 B.C.–571 B.C., Ezekiel prophesies in Babylon.

268
>
What
Everyone
Should
Know
about
the

Bible

589 B.C., Ezekiel's ministry ends.

586 B.C., Judah falls to Babylon; Zedekiah must watch his sons be murdered; he is blinded and taken captive to Babylon; Jerusalem and the Temple are destroyed; Jeremiah is forced to stay with the new governor Gedaliah; the book of Lamentations is written; Gedaliah is assassinated.

Heroes and Villains: The Stars in Scene 16

This period of Bible history has a long list of heroes and villains. The Assyrian kings Sennacherib, Esarhaddon, and Ashurbanipal might top the list of villains. These were brutal people who often treated prisoners with great cruelty. Micah, Isaiah, Jeremiah, Nahum, Zephaniah, Daniel, Ezekiel, and Habakkuk were prophetic heroes.

Nebuchadnezzar, king of Babylon, was a mixed bag. He could be both ruthless and kind, as is seen in his treatment of Daniel and his three friends. Manasseh, king of Judah, was also a mixed bag. He started out being incredibly evil, and then had a turning point when he was captured, had a hook put in his nose, and was taken to Babylon. He became a somewhat godly king after that. Jehoiakim, king of Judah, was so evil that he burned Jeremiah's scroll as it was read to him. We will focus now on three heroic figures of this period.

HEZEKIAH

Ahaz, Hezekiah's father, had submitted himself to Assyria. When Hezekiah became king, he joined some other kingdoms, against Isaiah's advice, to break the yoke of Assyria. Sennacherib, king of Assyria, swept down and forced Hezekiah and his allies into submission. Hezekiah did much to bring his people back to the worship of the Lord. He cleansed the Temple, restored the services, and set up a great Passover celebration. When Sennacherib came against the land again, Hezekiah took the threats of the Assyrians and spread them out before the Lord, pleading for his help. The angel of the Lord struck 185,000 Assyrians dead and forced the survivors to retreat. Hezekiah is remembered for the tunnel that he cut through rock from a spring outside Jerusalem that brought water into the city.

Bible events in Hezekiah's life

1. He rules Judah in a way that pleases the Lord.
2. He cleanses the Temple.
3. He restores the service in the Lord's Temple.
4. He makes a great Passover celebration.
5. He asks the people to contribute tithes to the priests and Levites.

6. He pays tribute to Sennacherib.
7. The Assyrians insult him.
8. He receives a threatening letter from Sennacherib, takes it to the Temple, and spreads it out before the Lord, praying for deliverance.
9. Isaiah sends a message to him from the Lord predicting the Assyrians' defeat.
10. The angel of the Lord kills 185,000 Assyrians.
11. He becomes sick, prays for healing, and his life is prolonged.
12. He shows ambassadors of Babylon the treasury, and Isaiah rebukes him.
13. He builds storehouses, cities, and a water tunnel.
14. He dies and is buried in the royal tombs.

JEREMIAH

In the declining days of the kingdom of Judah, Jeremiah was called as a prophet to warn the nation that it would pay dearly for turning from the worship of God. Jeremiah's message angered many of his fellow Judeans, who thought he was a traitor. The prophet began his ministry under Josiah, who tried to bring his nation back to God, although his efforts were not sufficient.

When Josiah died, his son Jehoahaz ruled for only three months before he was taken to Egypt. Jehoiakim, brother of Jehoahaz, ruled during the next eleven years and tried to silence or kill Jeremiah. When Jeremiah dictated his prophecies to Baruch and they were read to Jehoiakim, the king burned them.

Jehoiakim's son Jehoiachin ruled next, but he ruled for only three months before he was carried off to Babylon. Nebuchadnezzar appointed Zedekiah, who ruled for eleven years, protected Jeremiah, and sought his advice from time to time. When Zedekiah finally rebelled against Babylon, the Babylonians laid siege to Jerusalem. After a year and a half, Jerusalem fell, and with it, the kingdom of Judah. Jeremiah died in Egypt of old age, having been forced to go there with some of his countrymen. They had murdered the governor that Babylon had appointed over Judah.

Bible events in Jeremiah's life
1. God calls him.
2. He learns the lesson of the potter's clay.
3. He is beaten and put in stocks.
4. He cries to the Lord because of his troubles.
5. He prophesies against Judah and is saved from execution.
6. He warns Judah to submit to Babylon.
7. He denounces Hananiah and predicts his death.

What
Everyone
Should
Know
about
the
Bible

8. Jehoiakim throws him into prison.
9. He buys a field at Anathoth.
10. Jehoiakim burns his scroll.
11. He tells Zedekiah that he will be captured by the king of Babylon; Zedekiah puts him in the palace prison.
12. He is thrown into a cistern, and Ebed-melech rescues him.
13. After Jerusalem is conquered, Nebuzaradan sets him free; he goes to live with Gedaliah.
14. He warns Johanan not to go to Egypt, but Johanan doesn't listen.
15. He is taken to Egypt with a remnant of Judah and dies there.

JOSIAH

Josiah was an eight-year-old boy when he became king of Judah. As Josiah grew older, he began to destroy many pagan practices and places of worship. He was the last king to make a sincere effort to return Judah to the worship of the Lord. While remodeling the Temple, the Book of the Law was found and read to Josiah, who then tried to lead his nation to observe its teachings. Josiah died when he foolishly entered a battle against Pharaoh Neco of Egypt. The nation mourned the passing of its thirty-nine-year-old monarch who had brought new hope to the land.

Bible events in Josiah's life
1. He destroys the high places, idols, and altars of Baal.
2. He repairs and cleanses the Temple.
3. Hilkiah finds the Book of the Law in the Temple. Shaphan reads it to Josiah, and he tears his clothes in repentance.
4. He reads the Book of the Law to all of the people.
5. He makes a covenant with the Lord to follow him.
6. He makes many reforms and destroys idolatry in the land.
7. He makes a great Passover feast.
8. He disguises himself in the war against the Egyptians; archers kill him and he is buried in the royal tombs.

What everyone should know about the book of Nahum
EVIL WILL BE PUNISHED

In Nahum's days, Assyria in the north was the world power, with the splendid city of Nineveh as its capital. Nineveh was magnificent, with enormous walls that reached for eight miles around the city. The library of Nineveh had about twenty thousand books in the form of clay tablets. About sixty-six years before Nahum began his ministry, Assyria had already destroyed the northern kingdom and had taken the best of its people into captivity. Those left behind and the people of Judah felt the cruel pressure of this great world power.

Why didn't God punish such an evil empire? Assyria seemed to be getting by with its wickedness. Had God gone to sleep? Was he too far away? Didn't he care?

You may have heard these same questions. Where was God when my child died? Didn't he care? Was he too far away when we lost our home? Was he asleep when I had that terrible accident? Look at the newspaper articles and TV programs about evil despots around the world. Wickedness seems to thrive, and God just lets it happen. Where is he, anyway?

These questions are timeless, for evil is ever present. The same people who question God forget about their own bent toward evil, however. The northern kingdom fell because its people turned against God and practiced evil. The southern kingdom was in danger for the same reason. Where is God? He's there with you. But are you there with him? Remember that if you expect God to judge your neighbor's evil, you must also expect him to judge your evil.

Nahum's message was simple. God does see and punish evil according to his timetable, not ours. He would punish evil Assyria. It was only forty-two years after Nahum's ministry ended that God did what he had promised. The Babylonians so completely destroyed Nineveh, Assyria's capital city, that when Alexander the Great visited the area, he could not even see where it had been.

God is still God, and he still punishes evil, but he does it according to his own timetable.

What everyone should know about the book of Obadiah

WHEN GOD'S PEOPLE STUMBLE, DON'T CHEER

He was a well-known pastor in town, but he got into trouble and had to leave. Some wept, while others cheered, making fun of "that preacher." They actually seemed happy to see a preacher fall in life's mud. If Obadiah were there, he would have roundly scolded those people, just as he scolded the Edomites.

Judah, the southern kingdom, was getting deeper and deeper into sin and trouble. They had abandoned God, and now the armies of Babylon were coming against them. It was a dark day for God's people. The Babylonian armies came three times, pillaging, robbing, and taking choice people away to Babylon. Neighbors should have wept, but the Edomites to the south cheered and even helped the Babylonians rather than their distant relatives, the people of Judah. Sometimes the Edomites captured Judeans and turned them over to Babylon. Why? The Israelites were descendants of Jacob and the Edomites were descendants of his twin brother, Esau. Family feuds never seem to die!

Flash back to a Bedouin tent of long ago. There is Jacob, feeding his blind father the savory meat of young goats and deceiving him into giving him, not his older brother, Esau, the blessings. When Esau discovered the deceit, he was furious and pledged to kill Jacob when their father died. Jacob fled to Haran, married two daughters of his uncle Laban, and grew prosperous. When Jacob returned to the land, he made peace with Esau, but the two parted, with Esau moving south. The Edomites were Esau's descendants, and they never mixed well with the descendants of Jacob. Now, more than a thousand years later, the blood of the twin brothers was still like oil and

272

>

What
Everyone
Should
Know
about
the

Bible

water. Isaac and Rebekah might have wept if they could have looked ahead and seen the descendants of their twin boys such bitter enemies.

Why? Obadiah had this vision about the Edomites: "Because of the violence you did to your close relatives in Israel. . . . When they were invaded, you stood aloof, refusing to help them" (Obadiah 1:10-11). During the Israelites' journey to the Promised Land, when they wanted safe passage through Edomite lands, the Edomites instead met them with an army (Numbers 20:14-21). Now, when Babylon was plundering Judah, the Edomites "stood aloof, refusing to help them."

The Edomites must have felt quite secure in their home, the beautiful carved city we know today as Petra. Obadiah broke that bubble. "You have been deceived by your own pride because you live in a rock fortress and make your home high in the mountains. . . . I will bring you crashing down" (Obadiah 1:3-4).

Today, there is nothing left of the Edomites and their rock fortress, and their carved city, Petra, is nothing but a tourist attraction. Never laugh, cheer, or mock when God's people fall. When God is grieving, who are we to cheer?

Some think that Obadiah lived and ministered from about 855 B.C. to 840 B.C. during the reign of Jehoram, king of Judah. This is possible. It seems more likely that his ministry fits here during the declining days of Judah, when the Edomites helped the Babylonians against their distant relatives. Obadiah wrote a book, but we know almost nothing about the man.

What everyone should know about the book of Jeremiah
LAST CHANCE!
About a hundred years after Isaiah, God called Jeremiah to be a prophet. Isaiah prophesied during the years that Assyria was the world power. Assyria captured the northern kingdom of Israel only eighteen years after Isaiah began his ministry. Since Isaiah's time, Babylon had defeated Assyria and had become the world power. Then Babylon threatened the southern kingdom of Judah, and Jeremiah was an unwanted counselor to Judah's last five kings.

Babylon came against Jerusalem three times, the last time to destroy it and carry away Judah's best people to Babylon. During this time, Jeremiah warned the kings and the other people of Judah to surrender to Babylon and be spared, but many thought he was a traitor.

Jeremiah was Judah's last chance. If Judah repented and begged God's forgiveness, they would be spared. If not, they would be captured by Babylon. No matter what Jeremiah said, it seemed that no one listened, so in 586 B.C., Babylon captured Judah and destroyed Jerusalem and its beautiful Temple.

Is it possible that God is giving you a last chance to turn to him? If so, read Jeremiah. The last chance may be just that—the last one.

What everyone should know about the book of Lamentations
TEARS, TOO LATE
When was the last time you cried? For what? Was it a wedding or a funeral? Was it a celebration of a person added to your family, or the mourning of a life taken from

you? Lamentations is Jeremiah's lament for the wounded, broken city that was once Jerusalem, the jewel of the world. It was once the golden city, with its great stone walls and magnificent Temple reflecting the rays of the sun. Therein was the problem. The people of Judah and Jerusalem thought that their city was so golden that it could not be destroyed, much as the builders of the Titanic sincerely believed that it could not sink.

Day after day and year after year for forty years, Jeremiah preached, begged, warned, and pleaded for Judah and Jerusalem to repent and turn to God. "Beg God for forgiveness. Perhaps he will spare you from Babylon." All Jeremiah's preaching fell on deaf ears, for the last five kings of Judah and their people simply would not listen.

Jeremiah suffered much for his faithful preaching. Jeremiah was imprisoned in a dark, damp well. He went hungry and he was impoverished. That lifestyle would wear down the best preacher.

Three times Babylon came against Jerusalem. Each time it inflicted pain and suffering, and each time it exiled key people. In 608 b.c., Babylon carried Daniel and his friends back with them. Eleven years later, in 597 b.c., the Babylonians took Ezekiel. In 586 b.c., Babylon made one final attack in which they destroyed Jerusalem and the Temple.

The golden city was no longer golden, but only a pile of rubble, a place for weeds to grow. Jeremiah wept for a wounded city in utter ruin. He wept for something that had happened but did not need to happen. He had begged and pleaded, but no one would listen.

When it's too late, there is nothing left but tears, and so it was for Jeremiah. The city was in ruins and its people were captives. No wonder Jeremiah wept and wrote a book of lament.

What is the message of Jeremiah for us today? When God speaks through his Word or his messengers, listen! Understand what he is saying and do something about it. If sin is the problem, repent and beg him for forgiveness. If the people of Judah had only done that, things would have been much different.

What everyone should know about the book of Zephaniah

A DAWN OF HOPE AFTER A NIGHT OF HOPELESSNESS

More than eighty years had passed since the northern kingdom had come to an end. Assyria, the world power at that time, had conquered Israel but not Judah. Both kingdoms had their share of wickedness, but Judah was blessed with more godly kings than the northern kingdom had.

When Zephaniah began his prophetic ministry in 640 b.c., a new king named Josiah came to Judah's throne. He had a lot of work to do, for his two predecessors, Amon and Manasseh, had inflicted much evil on Judah. Josiah was a godly king who was passionate about turning the kingdom around for God. Perhaps Zephaniah was a godly influence on him. Josiah was the one bright light in Judah's dark night of hopelessness. Not only

274

>

What
Everyone
Should
Know
about
the

Bible

the kings before him, but also the other kings to follow would promote evil in the land.

Zephaniah had two messages for his people in Judah. The first was a thundering condemnation of Judah's sin and a warning about God's coming judgment for that sin. If Zephaniah wrote this book in the last year of his ministry (621 B.C.), his prophecy of judgment was fulfilled in only thirty-five years, when Babylon would destroy Judah and Jerusalem and deport its key people.

Zephaniah focused at first on Judah's night of hopelessness. Sin brings judgment, and judgment was coming soon for Judah. Then he focused on the dawn of hope after judgment. The glory of it all was that "the LORD himself, the King of Israel, will live among you!" (Zephaniah 3:15). Like so many other prophets, Zephaniah promised that after God's judgment would come glorious hope, especially when Jesus, the King of Israel, would come.

What everyone should know about the book of Habakkuk

WHY, WHY, WHY?

Habakkuk was like a little child, asking incessant why questions. If you're a parent, you have heard it a thousand times. "Why? Why? Why?" Too often, we hurriedly say, "Because," and expect that to be the final answer.

Habakkuk had at least two why questions for God. Why was God permitting the people of Judah to get away with so much sin? God's answer was simple—they would be punished. He was already preparing the Babylonians for that task.

Habakkuk had another question. Why would God use people even more evil than the people of Judah to punish them? Was it right for God to punish a lesser evil with a greater evil? Why would God do such a thing?

Again, God's answer was simple. The Babylonians were a temporary instrument to punish God's people. They, too, would be punished for their evil.

Habakkuk's questions are our questions. We ask them all the time, don't we? Why is God permitting so much evil all around us? God's answer is probably the same as the one he gave to Habakkuk. God will punish evil, even our own. We may not like the instrument he chooses, but the choice and the timing are his.

Habakkuk was a prophet in Judah during the dark days when Babylon was rising up against it. He probably saw Babylon's three campaigns against Judah—the first when Daniel and his friends were taken to Babylon, the second when Ezekiel was taken, and the third, when Judah was totally defeated and Jerusalem was destroyed. Habakkuk's ministry began in the closing days of the good King Josiah, and continued through the next four evil kings of Judah.

The third and last scene in Habakkuk is Habakkuk's prayerful hymn to God. A footnote at the end says, "For the choir director: This prayer is to be accompanied by stringed instruments."

Habakkuk probably wrote this book, addressed to the declining kingdom of Judah, between 612 B.C. and 589 B.C. Habakkuk began his ministry the year the Assyrians conquered Babylon, three years before King Josiah was killed in battle and four years before Daniel and his friends were deported to Babylon.

CONSEQUENCES

"I can do what I please when I please. So what?" Have you ever heard that? The "so what" is called "consequences," the fruit of seeds planted, the results of work done, or the bitter results of sin committed. "It won't happen to me," is another familiar saying. That was the problem with Judah and Jerusalem in the time of Ezekiel.

Let's back up a little and do a refresher course with some dates to help us see where Ezekiel fits: 722 B.C. was the end of the northern kingdom as Assyria conquered Israel and took captives back to Assyria. In 609 B.C., about 113 years later, Babylon conquered Assyria, and only one year later, in 608 B.C., Babylon, as the new world power, took some captives from Judea, including Daniel and his friends. In 597 B.C., only eleven years later, Babylon took more captives from Judea, including Ezekiel; four years later, in 593 B.C., Ezekiel became a prophet to the Judean captives in Babylon. In 586 B.C., seven years later, the Babylonians conquered Judea completely and destroyed Jerusalem.

From this, it is obvious that Jeremiah and Ezekiel preached to the people of Judea—Jeremiah to those remaining in Judah, and Ezekiel, a captive in Babylon, to the other Judeans taken captive there. Jeremiah and Ezekiel probably knew each other, and perhaps communicated with each other. Ezekiel also undoubtedly knew Daniel, who had already been in Babylon for nine years and had already won favor with the king. Daniel moved in the circle of royalty with other high officials. Ezekiel moved among the common people of Judah who had been carried away to Babylon.

In chapters 1–24 of Ezekiel, we see Ezekiel warning the Judeans that Judah and Jerusalem were about to fall. It was already too late for the Judeans in Babylon to do much about this except to repent and ask God to help.

In chapters 25–32, Ezekiel warned of the overthrow of the heathen nations around Judah. In chapters 34–48, he spoke of Israel's glorious future.

Ezekiel was a priest, but he also was a street preacher for twenty-two years. He, like Jeremiah, paid a heavy price in suffering for his preaching, mostly through what God commanded him to do to illustrate his preaching. This included lying on his side for more than a year, eating only an ounce of food each day, cooking over manure, shaving his beard and hair, and not being permitted to show grief when his wife died.

The people of Judah thought that "it would never happen to them." Judah could not fall, and Jerusalem, the golden city, could never be destroyed. In their minds, there were no consequences for their sins, but the consequences came only seven years after Ezekiel began to preach. Judah was defeated and Jerusalem was destroyed.

Did You Know?

The Book of the Law To us today, finding a lost copy of the Scriptures seems strange and raises many questions. How many Bibles do you have in your house? your church? the local Christian bookstore?

What was this Book of the Law that King Josiah's workmen found in the Temple? How much of our Scriptures did it contain? What did it look like? Why was it lost?

The Book of the Law was a scroll on which was written the first five books of our Bible, sometimes called the Book of Moses, or the law of Moses, because it is generally thought that Moses wrote them. These would include Genesis, Exodus, Leviticus, Numbers, and Deuteronomy. The shining core of these books was the Ten Commandments. All of this was written in Hebrew.

A scroll was made of either animal skin or parchment that was rolled on two rollers. As it was read, it was rolled from one roller to the other. Parchment was made from papyrus. The pith was removed from the stem and laid in parallel strips. Then other rows of pith were laid across these strips and they were pounded together. When it dried, it was a form of ancient paper.

Why would a copy of the Scriptures be lost in the Temple? Was it the only copy known at that time? It had been seventy-four years since the evil King Manasseh had begun his reign. During most of his reign he was very ungodly, and the Scriptures were probably hidden in the Temple. The reign of his son was also evil. Some copies may have been found and destroyed, but one remained hidden until Josiah's workmen found it. Some think that it was in the cornerstone and was found when the cornerstone was opened for repairs. This must have been the only copy known, for what it said came as a great surprise to everyone. Imagine having the very last copy of the Bible on earth hidden for many years, and then suddenly having it brought to light!

Assyria and Babylon—two great empires that dominated Israel and Judah Both Assyria and Babylon were very old. Assyria dated back to about 3,000 B.C., but did not become a world power until much later. Around 1,000 B.C., Assyria began to grow in power. During the years when Assyria had its greatest contacts with Israel and Judah, several famous Assyrian kings appeared—Shalmaneser, Tiglath-pileser, Sargon, Sennacherib, Esarhaddon, and Ashurbanipal. Israel was taken into captivity toward the end of Shalmaneser V's reign.

Sennacherib, king of Assyria, tried to conquer Judah during Hezekiah's reign. In his weakness, Hezekiah begged the Lord to help him, and the Lord sent an angel to destroy 185,000 of Sennacherib's troops in one night.

Sennacherib conquered Babylon and destroyed the city in 689 B.C. He immediately made a law that Babylon could not be rebuilt for seventy years, but his own son Esarhaddon rebuilt the city. The Babylonians grew to great power and overthrew Assyria in 612 B.C.

Israel was taken into captivity by the Assyrians. Judah was taken into exile by the Babylonians.

Nebuchadnezzar Nebuchadnezzar was the only truly great king of Babylon. He ruled from 605 B.C. to 562 B.C. He invaded Judah three times and took captives back to Babylon. Nebuchadnezzar is remembered for his magnificent building programs, the brilliance of his military exploits, and for taking the best Judeans to Babylon for leadership training. Daniel and his three friends were four such Judeans. After Nebuchadnezzar died, his empire began to crumble, making it easy for Cyrus the Mede to conquer it during a drunken orgy by Babylon's king, Belshazzar.

Hooks in your lips Assyrians and Babylonians could be quite cruel to prisoners. The Assyrians were especially cruel. One practice in those days was to put large hooks in the nose or lips of prisoners, even a king. Needless to say, the prisoners kept pace with those ahead, lest the hooks tear their noses or mouths apart. King Manasseh of Judah was taken to Babylon with a hook in his nose. This experience humbled him and he sought the Lord.

The Babylonians punished King Zedekiah of Judah by murdering his sons while he watched, then gouging out his eyes with a spear so that the last sight he ever saw was the murder of his sons.

Discovering My Purpose from God's Plan

1. *God is God and he still punishes evil.* Judgment may not come as quickly as we wish, but it will come.
2. *Never laugh at, mock, or cheer God's people when they fall.* When God is grieving, who are we to cheer? This is Obadiah's message.
3. *Your last chance may be just that—your last one.* Don't miss it! This is a message from Jeremiah.
4. *Remain faithful to the Lord, no matter where, no matter what.* This is what Daniel and his friends did in Babylon.

Life in a Strange Land

The Exile and Return to the Land

Characters:
Abednego (the Babylonian name for Azariah, one of Daniel's three friends deported to Babylon); Ahasuerus (another name for Xerxes, Esther's husband and a Persian king); Artaxerxes (son and successor of Xerxes, Esther's husband; also called Longimanus); Belshazzar (the last Babylonian king); Cyrus the Persian (also called Cyrus the Great, head of the Persian Empire); Daniel (a member of the Judean royal family who was deported to Babylon and became a top leader there; he wrote the book of Daniel); Darius the Mede (who conquered Babylon and made Cyrus king; several Medo-Persian rulers were named Darius); Esther (also called Hadassah, queen of the Persian Empire, wife of Xerxes or Ahasuerus); Ezra (who wrote the books of Ezra and Esther and led a group back to Israel to re-establish worship there); Haggai (a prophet during this time); Haman (an evil prime minister who tried to destroy the Jews during Esther's time); Malachi (the last prophet of this time, author of the last book of the Old Testament); Meshach (the Babylonian name of Daniel's friend Mishael); Mordecai (Esther's older cousin, who became prime minister of the Persian Empire); Nebuchadnezzar (the Babylonian king during Daniel's earlier years); Nehemiah (who wrote the book of Nehemiah and led a group back to Israel to rebuild Jerusalem's walls); Shadrach (the Babylonian name of Daniel's friend Hananiah); Vashti (Xerxes' queen whom he deposed before he married Esther); Xerxes (the Greek name for Ahasuerus, Esther's husband); Zechariah (a prophet during this time); Zedekiah (the last king of Judah)

Time Period:
From the destruction of the Temple until the Temple was rebuilt

Dates:
586 B.C.–515 B.C.

Where Scene 17 of the Big Story Can Be Found:
Second Chronicles, Daniel, Ezra, Esther, and Nehemiah carry the
historical thread; Daniel, Ezekiel, Haggai, Zechariah, and Malachi
give the prophetic messages

In Scene 17, Find the Answers to These Questions:
How did a Jewish orphan become queen of the Persian Empire?
How was a cup-bearer commissioned to rebuild the walls of
    Jerusalem?
Did Jesus walk in the fiery furnace?
How did a young foreign captive become a prince of the
    Babylonian Empire?
Who wrote the last book of the Old Testament? What kind of
    work did he do?

Look for this in Scene 17
> A man is hanged on a gallows that he built to hang another
  man.
> Someone walked in a fiery furnace without getting burned.
> God wrote twice with his own hand—the Ten Commandments
  and handwriting on a wall.
> Hungry lions couldn't eat.
> Esther's stepson sent Nehemiah to rebuild Jerusalem's walls.
> Daniel is known for his Judean name rather than his
  Babylonian name, Belteshazzar. Daniel's friends were
  known by their Babylonian names, Shadrach, Meshach, and
  Abednego. Their Judean names were Hananiah, Mishael, and
  Azariah.

The Big Story So Far

Looking back to look ahead

Let's go back to Abraham, the father of the Israelite people. He was a
shepherd who spent endless hours studying the stars and talking with
their Maker. Abraham had no church to attend, no Bible to read, no
conferences, no Bible studies, no hymns, and no books to read to help
him know God. He had only the stars and the other fingerprints of the
Creator, which were all around him. His close family members may have
been the only other believers that he knew, unless he met Job, another
shepherd in northern Mesopotamia. The Bible gives no hint that he did,
but it is possible.

    Abraham knew the Lord and loved him fervently. Because of that, the
Lord talked with Abraham personally and entered into a covenant with

280

>

What
Everyone
Should
Know
about
the

Bible

him. It was a simple covenant with far-reaching consequences. "Obey me, love me, and follow me," the Lord said. "If you do, I will be your God and you will be my people." The covenant is the foundation on which the Old Testament rests and upon which all believers build their faith in God.

The Lord renewed this covenant with Isaac, with Jacob, whom he renamed Israel, and with Jacob's sons. In a moment of insane jealousy, ten of these sons sold their young half brother Joseph as a slave bound for Egypt. If they had not done this, the story of the Bible would have been little more than the story of a Bedouin tribe that took care of sheep and goats. God does not create evil, but he uses evil to create good.

In Egypt, Joseph interpreted two important dreams for Pharaoh, and the king saw immediately that God was with this bright young man. Pharaoh made him ruler of all Egypt, primarily to manage the grain program during seven years of plenty to prepare for seven years of famine. Joseph continued as ruler for eighty years, during the long reigns of two pharaohs.

Between Genesis and Exodus, there is a period of silence in the Bible of approximately 280 years. In United States history, that would take us back to about fifty years before the Revolutionary War.

The silence is broken by a pharaoh too far removed from Joseph to care about his people. He was paranoid that the Hebrews, now numbering almost as many as all the Egyptians, would conquer Egypt the way that some other Semites, the Hyksos, had done years before. To prevent that, he made them slaves, and they served Pharaoh for many, many years.

God miraculously let the son of a Hebrew slave be adopted by Pharaoh's daughter and raised as a prince of Egypt for forty years. When Moses murdered a cruel Egyptian, he fled to Midian; there he became a shepherd, like his ancestors, for the next forty years, learning in the school of the wilderness.

God sent Moses back to Egypt to demand freedom for his people. Pharaoh refused, and God sent ten terrible plagues. After the tenth, the death of all the Egyptian firstborn sons, Pharaoh set the Israelites free.

God personally led his people through the wilderness with a pillar of cloud and of fire. He led them to Mount Sinai, where he gave them the law, elaborate instructions for building the Tabernacle, and a system of worship and priesthood. He welded them together as a nation and prepared them for their Promised Land.

After two years, the Israelites had a golden opportunity at Kadesh-barnea to enter the Promised Land and conquer it, but their lack of trust in the Lord stopped them. They thought that their God was simply not big enough for the job at hand. For that lack of faith, they had to wander in the wilderness for another thirty-eight years until that entire unbelieving generation died—except for Caleb and Joshua, the spies with faith that God would give the Israelites the Promised Land.

At last, a new generation entered the Promised Land and conquered Jericho. The conquest continued, but it was not completed thoroughly. Soon the Israelites were living in the company of the pagan Canaanites who had occupied the land. The pagan culture was attractive to them, and although they had won militarily, they lost morally and spiritually by becoming more and more like their pagan neighbors.

Judges ruled Israel for almost four hundred years. In this theocracy, God was king, but the people did not treat him as king. They did what was right in their own eyes. The people desired a human king, and Saul was chosen.

Saul ruled for forty-two years. God had personally chosen him, so he had a golden opportunity to lead Israel righteously. Saul did not follow the Lord, however. Instead, he spent many years as king venting his jealousy at David, and even trying to kill him.

When Saul died on the battlefield, David became king of Judah and king of all Israel seven years later. He loved the Lord and led his people to fulfill the covenant. At last, they were covenant people in practice as well as in name. David had big-time faults, but overall he was a good king.

When David died, his son Solomon became king. He began well, and at first was a devout follower of the Lord. Then he drifted into a love of wealth and women until he had collected a thousand wives and concubines. These were mostly foreign women who brought in their pagan idols and worship. Before long, Israel and King Solomon were worshiping these pagan deities. It was the beginning of the end. Solomon had grown up as a prince, but he lived most of his later life as a royal spendthrift and a spiritual pauper—incredibly wealthy, but spiritually bankrupt.

When Solomon died, his son Rehoboam had a golden opportunity to build on Solomon's successes and wealth, but his pride turned his heart away from his people and his God. The kingdom divided into the northern kingdom of Israel with ten tribes and the southern kingdom of Judah with the tribes of Judah and Benjamin.

The story of the divided kingdom is a story of missed opportunities, misappropriated gifts from God, and mismanagement of resources. The northern kingdom never had one godly king among its nineteen ungodly kings! The southern kingdom had eight godly kings

282
>
What
Everyone
Should
Know
about
the
Bible

and twelve ungodly rulers. Israel rotted from within faster than Judah did, and by 722 B.C., it fell to the Assyrians and its best people were carried away.

Judah lasted 136 years longer before it fell to the Babylonians and its best people were carried off to Babylon. David's golden kingdom was completely destroyed. He would have wept to see its beauty squandered.

What happened to the people of Israel when they were taken to Assyria? Many simply melted into the new society and lost their identity as covenant people. Some kept their covenant identity in this faraway land, but blended into the culture. A few kept their distinctive spirituality and culture.

How the Judeans were treated in Babylon

What about the people of Judah? King Nebuchadnezzar had a policy that the Assyrians did not have of bringing the best young people from captured lands and training them to be Babylonian artisans and leaders. This policy brought Daniel, Shadrach, Meshach, and Abednego to Babylon. It also brought Ezekiel to Babylon, although he became a street preacher, while Daniel became a king's associate.

The Judeans in Babylon were permitted to gather together, even for worship. They could continue with such practices as circumcision, observing the Sabbath, and praying with their face toward Jerusalem. However, they were not allowed to observe their high festivals.

Daniel's rise to power in Babylon

The story of Daniel and his friends is, of course, the most dramatic story of this time.

Daniel and his friends were members of the royal family, or at least were nobility (Daniel 1:3). Josephus, a Jewish historian from Jesus' time, says that they were related to King Zedekiah. How they were related is not known.

Daniel and his friends were very unlike the wicked Zedekiah, for they were devoted to the Lord, just as Zedekiah's godly father, King Josiah, had been. Josiah's godly influence is seen in these young relatives. Josiah would have been pleased to see his influence reach all the way to the palace of Babylon.

Daniel and his teen friends were among the royal captives of the first Babylonian exile of 605 B.C. Nebuchadnezzar and his father were in a building mode, seeking to make old Babylon into a stunning place. To accomplish this, Nebuchadnezzar engaged in several military adventures, first to get wealth, and then to get the brightest young men of these societies to help him build and govern. It was a very wise move, for it brought a freshness and diversity from these other cultures.

The Babylonian Empire ends; the Persian Empire begins

The night of Belshazzar's feast, Belshazzar was killed and the Babylonian Kingdom ended. Darius the Mede conquered Babylon at age sixty-two. Darius saw immediately what an important person Daniel was, so he appointed Daniel and two others to rule the leaders of the 120 provinces of the kingdom. The other two men were jealous and tricked the king into making a law that condemned Daniel for praying. For that, the king was forced to put Daniel into a den of lions, but God protected him through the night and the next morning Darius threw the other two men and their families into the lions' den, but they did not survive. Daniel continued to prosper throughout the reigns of Darius and his successor, Cyrus the Persian. The rest of the book of Daniel records his visions of the future.

Cyrus was a very kind emperor. In 538 B.C., he decreed that the Israelites might return to their homeland (Ezra 1–2). When they returned, the Temple rebuilding began in 536 B.C. (Ezra 3), but was stopped again in 530 B.C. (Ezra 4).

Eight years later, Darius I (not Darius the Mede who conquered Babylon) became the king, or emperor. Two years after that, in 520 B.C., Haggai and Zechariah began to preach that the work on the Temple should resume. Darius ordered that this should happen and the work was completed in 515 B.C.

Xerxes becomes ruler of the Persian Empire, and Esther becomes his queen

In 486 B.C., twenty-nine years after the Temple was completed, Xerxes became the ruler of the Persian Empire. It was a vast empire with worldwide power. Seven years later, he became dissatisfied with his queen, Vashti, and deposed her. After testing many beauties, he chose Esther to be his new queen.

Esther had been raised by her older cousin Mordecai, a minor palace official indirectly associated with the king. Unfortunately, Xerxes chose the very evil Haman to be his prime minister. It was expected that everyone would bow to him as he went by, but Mordecai refused. This filled Haman with rage and he plotted how to kill not only Mordecai, but all Jews in the empire. He even persuaded Xerxes to go along with that law.

Mordecai sent a message to Esther to do something about this. Esther was not only beautiful, but very bright, which was probably the reason that Xerxes wanted her as his queen. Esther invited the king and Haman to two banquets. At the second, she told the king that Haman was trying to kill her and all her people. This infuriated the king, and he hanged Haman on the gallows he had prepared for Mordecai. Then he made Mordecai his new prime minister.

284

>

What
Everyone
Should
Know
about
the

Bible

Artaxerxes succeeds his father, Xerxes, as ruler of the Persian Empire

Xerxes was succeeded in 465 B.C. by Artaxerxes, Xerxes' son and Queen Esther's stepson. As queen, Esther probably had considerable influence over him, for he continued the strong favor toward the Jewish people that Xerxes had already shown. He granted permission for Ezra the priest to return to the land in 457 B.C., where he taught Judah the law of God and helped to beautify the Temple, which had been completed for about sixty years. Ezra also helped to restore the Temple service (Ezra 7–8).

The first six chapters of the book of Ezra record events that happened prior to Esther's time as queen. The last four chapters of Ezra record events that happened after Esther's time as queen. Esther was apparently queen for fourteen years, from 479 B.C. until Artaxerxes became the ruler in 465 B.C.

Nehemiah the wall builder; Malachi the last Old Testament prophet

Thirteen years after Ezra went to Jerusalem, Nehemiah had a great desire to return and rebuild the walls of the city. He was a cup-bearer for Artaxerxes and apparently was on very good terms with him. The king granted him permission to return and rebuild the walls. We find the story of the wall building in the book of Nehemiah. Nehemiah went to Jerusalem in 445 B.C., returned to Babylon in 433 B.C., and went back to Jerusalem the next year, in 432 B.C.

The Old Testament story ends with Nehemiah's work of rebuilding the walls of Jerusalem and his return to Jerusalem in 432 B.C. Two years later, in 430 B.C., Malachi became a prophet. He wrote the last book of the Old Testament, and thus, the story of the Old Testament ends.

Questions You May Be Asking

What happened to the exiles taken to Babylon?

The exiles were captives and could not return home under the Babylonians. They apparently made a decent living. Some even succeeded in business and became so wealthy that they did not want to return to their land when they later had the opportunity to do so.

Like the Israelites deported to Assyria, the Judeans deported to Babylon had different reactions to the pagan gods. Some remained faithful to the Lord, but many assimilated into the culture and lost their distinctives as covenant people.

What about Ezra, Nehemiah, and Esther? Weren't they exiles also?

Ezra, Nehemiah, and Esther were descendants of the exiles from Israel and Judah. They lived after the Temple was completed in 515 B.C. By the time they came on the scene, the Babylonian empire had been captured, and the new empire of the Medes and Persians, the Persian Empire, had come to power.

The book of Ezra is a little confusing. Did all of this happen at one time?

Ezra 1–6 records the first return to the land of Israel, especially to Jerusalem, in 538 B.C. The rebuilding of the Temple was finally completed in 515 B.C.

The story of Esther interrupts the book of Ezra. It comes after the events of Ezra 6 and before the events of Ezra 7–10. Esther was queen from 479 B.C. until 465 B.C., when her stepson Artaxerxes became king. Ezra 7–10 picks up the story seven years after Esther ceased to be queen. The story of Nehemiah begins thirteen years after Ezra returned to Jerusalem, or twenty years after Esther ceased to be queen.

How long did Artaxerxes rule over Persia?

Esther's stepson Artaxerxes ruled Persia for forty years. He had another name: Longimanus. All three—Ezra, Nehemiah, and Esther—would have known him.

Great Events of This Time

1. **Ezekiel has a vision** (Ezekiel 1:1–2:8).
2. **Daniel doesn't eat the king's food** (Daniel 1).
3. **Daniel interprets a dream for King Nebuchadnezzar and is promoted** (Daniel 2).
4. **Shadrach, Meshach, and Abednego are cast into the fiery furnace** (Daniel 3).
5. **Nebuchadnezzar has a dream and Daniel's interpretation comes to pass** (Daniel 4).
6. **There is handwriting on the wall at Belshazzar's feast** (Daniel 5).
7. **Daniel is thrown into the lions' den** (Daniel 6).
8. **The first exiles return** (Ezra 1–2).
9. **The rebuilding of the Temple begins** (Ezra 3).
10. **The Temple rebuilding is stopped** (Ezra 4).
11. **King Darius orders the Temple rebuilding to resume** (Ezra 5–6).
12. **Queen Vashti displeases the king** (Esther 1).
13. **Esther becomes queen** (Esther 2:1-20).
14. **Mordecai discovers treason** (Esther 2:21-23).
15. **Haman tricks the king** (Esther 3–4).
16. **Queen Esther gives some banquets** (Esther 5–6).
17. **Haman is defeated** (Esther 7–8).
18. **The Feast of Purim is observed** (Esther 9).
19. **Ezra returns to Jerusalem** (Ezra 7–8).

>

What
Everyone
Should
Know
about
the

Bible

20. **There is revival in Jerusalem** (Ezra 9–10).
21. **Nehemiah prays for his homeland and begs to go home** (Nehemiah 1:1–2:10).
22. **Nehemiah inspects the Jerusalem walls by night** (Nehemiah 2:11-16).
23. **Nehemiah builds the Jerusalem walls despite the opposition** (Nehemiah 2:17–7:3).
24. **Ezra reads the law and God's covenant is renewed** (Nehemiah 8–10).
25. **Cities around Jerusalem are repopulated and the Jerusalem walls are dedicated** (Nehemiah 11–12).
26. **Nehemiah initiates reforms and expels foreigners** (Nehemiah 13).
27. **Malachi prophesies** (the book of Malachi).

Significant Dates of This Time

Circa 605 B.C., Daniel and his friends are taken in captivity to Babylon.
Circa 604 B.C., Daniel and his friends enter the king's service.
Circa 603 B.C., Jehoiakim burns Jeremiah's scroll.
Circa 602 B.C., Jehoiakim rebels against Nebuchadnezzar.
Circa 601 B.C., Daniel and his friends are appointed as officials in Babylon; Nebuchadnezzar has a dream.
Circa 597 B.C., the second captivity of Judah; Ezekiel is taken to Babylon; Jehoiakim king of Judah dies and his son Jehoiachin succeeds him; Jehoiachin is taken to Babylon; Jehoiachin's uncle Mattaniah is installed by Nebuchadnezzar as a puppet king and his name is changed to Zedekiah; Jeremiah prophesies under Zedekiah.
Circa 593 B.C., Ezekiel begins to prophesy in Babylon.
Circa 586 B.C., Judah falls to Babylon; Zedekiah must watch his sons be executed before he is blinded; Jeremiah stays with Gedaliah, the new governor; Jeremiah writes Lamentations; Gedaliah is assassinated.
Circa 584 B.C., Daniel's friends are thrown into the fiery furnace.
Circa 562 B.C., Nebuchadnezzar, king of Babylon, dies.
Circa 553 B.C., Daniel has his first vision.
Circa 542 B.C., Belshazzar gives a feast; there is handwriting on the wall; Belshazzar is killed; Darius the Mede conquers Babylon.
Circa 540–539 B.C., Daniel is thrown into the lions' den; Darius deserts to Cyrus of Persia and helps Cyrus to overthrow his enemies.
Circa 538 B.C., Cyrus decrees the first return to Jerusalem and the first Jewish exiles leave Babylon.
Circa 536 B.C., Temple reconstruction begins; Daniel's ministry ends with his last vision.
Circa 530 B.C., the Temple work is halted.

Circa 522 B.C., Darius I becomes king of Persia.

Circa 520 B.C., Haggai and Zechariah preach about the Temple; the Temple work resumes.

Circa 515 B.C., the new Temple is completed in Jerusalem.

Circa 486 B.C., Xerxes becomes king of Persia.

Circa 479 B.C., Esther becomes queen of Persia.

Circa 474 B.C., Haman gets a decree to destroy the Jews.

Circa 473 B.C., the first Festival of Purim is celebrated.

Circa 465 B.C., Artaxerxes I becomes king of Persia.

Circa 458 B.C., Ezra returns to Jerusalem.

Circa 445 B.C., Nehemiah goes to Jerusalem; he builds the Jerusalem walls.

Circa 433 B.C., Nehemiah returns to Babylon.

Circa 432 B.C., Nehemiah goes back to Jerusalem.

Circa 430 B.C., Malachi becomes a prophet; the Old Testament ends.

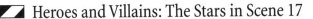

Heroes and Villains: The Stars in Scene 17

Nebuchadnezzar was both a hero and a villain. He was both kind and harsh with Daniel and his friends. For the most part, he was kind, but when Shadrach, Meshach, and Abednego refused to bow to the king's golden image, he was furious and had them thrown into a fiery furnace.

Belshazzar was a villain, doing his best to mock God and the Temple. He paid for this with his life the night of his evil feast.

Mordecai was heroic. He raised Esther, trained her, guided her, and became prime minister of the Persian Empire.

Haman, prime minister of the Persian Empire, was a villain. He wanted to murder all the Jews. He didn't realize that the queen was a Jew, and he was executed for his evil plots.

Darius the Mede, who conquered the Babylonians, was kind to the Jews and let some return to the land. So did Cyrus, an even kinder king.

The following are all heroes:

DANIEL

Daniel was born as a Jewish nobleman. He was captured by Nebuchadnezzar and taken to Babylon in 605 B.C. He and some other young Jewish noblemen were trained for the king's service for three years. Daniel also had the gift of prophecy and the courage to tell the king what he did not want to hear. Daniel faithfully worshiped God, regardless of the cost. He was eventually promoted to be one of three presidents over Babylon. As far as we know, Daniel never returned to his homeland, Judah, but remained in power in Babylon.

288
>
What
Everyone
Should
Know
about
the

Bible

Bible events in Daniel's life
1. He is taken to Babylon in exile and is chosen for the Babylonian king's service; he refuses to eat the king's food.
2. He becomes the king's personal counselor.
3. He interprets Nebuchadnezzar's dreams.
4. The king makes him a ruler over all Babylon.
5. He interprets the handwriting on the wall and Belshazzar promotes him.
6. He prays to God and is thrown into a lions' den; God delivers him.

ESTHER (Also called Hadassah)

During the years when Judah was exiled into Babylon, which was later part of the Persian Empire, a young Jewish orphan named Hadassah grew up in the home of her older cousin Mordecai. They lived in the city of Shushan, where Mordecai served as a minor palace official. When King Xerxes, or Ahasuerus, divorced his wife, he searched for a new queen. Esther's beauty, intelligence, and charm captivated him and he married her. Later, the king's prime minister, Haman, arranged for the Jews to be executed in revenge for Mordecai's refusal to bow to him. Esther persuaded the king to execute Haman instead and to grant unusual privileges to the Jewish people.

Bible events in Esther's life
1. Mordecai brings her to the king's palace.
2. King Xerxes (Ahasuerus) makes her his queen.
3. Mordecai urges her to go to the king and plead for the Jews.
4. The king holds out his scepter to her.
5. She invites the king to a banquet, and then to a second banquet.
6. She asks the king to spare her life and the lives of her people.
7. She saves her people.
8. She helps to establish the annual Feast of Purim for the Jews.

EZRA

Despite the opposition of the Samaritan people already living in the vicinity of Jerusalem, the Temple was rebuilt in 515 B.C. Fifty-eight years later, Ezra, a direct descendant of the high priest Aaron, received permission from the Persian king to go to Jerusalem to institute religious reforms. He took eighteen hundred Jewish people with him on the nine hundred-mile trip from Babylon to Jerusalem. When he arrived there, Ezra worked eagerly to reestablish the authority of the law of Moses and the worship associated with it. Later, when Nehemiah rebuilt the walls of Jerusalem, Ezra read the law of Moses to the people and encouraged them to follow it.

Bible events in Ezra's life

1. He moves from Babylon to Jerusalem; Artaxerxes gives him all he needs, plus permission for anyone else to go with him.
2. He takes treasures to the Temple in Jerusalem and offers burnt offerings to the Lord.
3. He proclaims a public fast and commands Jewish leaders to put away their foreign wives.
4. He reads the Book of the Law to the people.
5. He instructs the people concerning the Feast of Tabernacles.
6. He makes a prayer of commitment.

NEHEMIAH

While the Jewish people were captive in the Persian Empire, Nehemiah was the cup-bearer to King Artaxerxes, Queen Esther's stepson. Nehemiah was thus a high official who was trusted by the king. Nehemiah persuaded the king to send him to Jerusalem to rebuild the walls of the city. When he returned to the king of Persia, the people of Jerusalem lapsed back into their careless ways, forsaking the worship of the Lord. Nehemiah returned again, this time with Ezra, and stirred the people to numerous reforms in their worship and lifestyle.

Bible events in Nehemiah's life

1. He weeps and mourns for Jerusalem and prays that the Lord will grant his request.
2. He asks King Artaxerxes to send him back to Jerusalem.
3. He goes to Jerusalem, surveys the walls at night, and asks the officials of Jerusalem to rebuild the walls.
4. Sanballat and Geshem mock him.
5. He starts to rebuild the walls; Sanballat and Tobiah hinder the work.
6. He rebukes the nobles and rulers of Israel for their unfair dealings with the people.
7. He finishes building the walls.
8. Sanballat, Tobiah, and Geshem plot to kill him; he refuses to meet them.
9. He numbers the people of Jerusalem and Judah; the people give him money for the work.
10. When Ezra reads the Book of the Law, the people weep and he comforts them.
11. He signs the sealed document of commitment to the Lord and agrees with the people to care for God's house.
12. The walls are dedicated; he leads half of the leaders of Judah on a walk on top of the walls and then into the Temple to praise the Lord.

290

>

What
Everyone
Should
Know
about
the

Bible

13. He removes Tobiah from the Temple, restores the Levites to their
work, and condemns commerce on the Sabbath.

What everyone should know about the book of Ezra

IT'S TIME TO CLEAN UP YOUR LIFE

In 586 B.C., Babylon's mighty army swept into Judah, conquered its people,
destroyed Jerusalem and its Temple, and deported its best people back to
Babylon. Nineteen years earlier, Babylon had already captured and deported Daniel
and his friends.

Forty-seven years after Babylon conquered Judah, at a low point in Babylon's life,
King Cyrus of Persia, with the help of Darius, conquered Babylon. With Cyrus came a
new attitude toward the conquered people of Judah. The following year, he permitted the Jews to begin their return to the land—once under Zerubbabel, when the
Temple was rebuilt; once under Ezra, when the people were called to clean up their
lives spiritually; and once under Nehemiah, when the walls of Jerusalem were rebuilt.

The story of Esther took place between the time of Zerubbabel's visit and the time
of Ezra's visit. Zerubbabel finished rebuilding the Temple in 515 B.C. Esther became
the queen wife of Xerxes, king of Persia, only thirty-seven years later. Ezra visited Jerusalem twenty-one years after Esther became queen. Nehemiah went to Jerusalem
thirteen years after that.

Ezra was a priest, teacher, and writer. Most of all, he was a powerful influence for
God. His mission was to call people to repent of their sins, confess their sins, and
seek forgiveness from God. He then called people to clean up their lives for God.

Somehow, Ezra won favor with the Persian king and thus received a royal edict
to go to Jerusalem to bring about a spiritual revival. He took eighteen hundred Jews
from Babylon with him and halted nine days later at a place called Ahava. There, they
discovered that no Levites were among them, so several were persuaded to join the
caravan. After fasting and praying for three days, they left for Jerusalem and arrived
four months later after a journey of nine hundred miles. Think about that the next
time you take a two-hour, nine-hundred-mile flight!

The events of this part of the book of Ezra, chapters 1–6, take place before the
story of Esther. The rest of the events described in Ezra, in chapters 7–10, take place
after the story of Esther.

These final four chapters of Ezra are the story of one man who made a difference.
He called his people with revival-like passion to turn back to God and clean up their
lives. This is the message of the book—before moving ahead, weep for your sins, beg
God for forgiveness, and then ask him to be with you.

What everyone should know about the book of Esther

FOR SUCH A TIME AS THIS

Esther (or Hadassah) had four strikes against her. First, she was a refugee in a
faraway land, and refugees don't usually command much political clout. Second,
she was Jewish in a Persian society. As the story unfolds, it becomes obvious
that some people in high places at that time despised the Jewish people. Third,

she was an orphan. With both parents dead, she was raised by her older cousin Mordecai. Fourth, she was a woman, and women in those days were rather low on the ladder of power and success. Women had to keep their place in a man's society.

With all that against her, Esther should have headed toward the bottom of society's junk pile. Surprise! Flash forward and you see Queen Esther. She was the queen of the entire Persian Empire and she had enormous influence on the king. How Esther went from A to Z is the story of the book.

What was a Jewish orphan girl doing in Babylon, anyway? When Babylon conquered Judah and its capital city, Jerusalem, in 586 B.C., they brought many choice Judean people to Babylon. Esther's grandparents or even great-grandparents were probably among those captives.

Esther was a young nobody, an orphan raised by her cousin Mordecai, who was a minor official. Then the king became angry with his queen, Vashti, and divorced her. At the suggestion of some officials, he had a beauty contest to see which young lady pleased him the most. Of all the young ladies in the land, Esther won. She must have been incredibly beautiful, but so were hundreds of others. More importantly, a queen must have remarkable poise, wit, conversational ability, social grace, and a royal demeanor. Clearly, Esther was the most queenlike of all. Her godliness must have been a shining light.

Artaxerxes' wicked prime minister despised Jews because the Jew Mordecai refused to bow down to him, so he plotted to hang Mordecai and murder all the Jews in the empire. His plot backfired and he was hanged on the gallows he built for Mordecai. Esther persuaded the king to spare the Jewish people and helped her cousin Mordecai get the prime minister's job.

Although the name of God is never mentioned in the book, the presence of God is clearly seen throughout. Some call this "God-consciousness," an awareness that God is there controlling history even though he is not identified.

The key phrase of the entire episode is "who knows if perhaps you were made queen for just such a time as this?" (Esther 4:14). God gave Esther an opportunity after preparing her to respond in God's way.

Who knows but that you have been brought to a God-given opportunity "for such a time as this"? The timing is God's, the opportunity is God's, and you are God's. Like Esther, seize the moment on God's behalf and make it happen. Then you will have profited from the story of this nobody who became a dynamic somebody 2,500 years ago.

292 | *What everyone should know about the book of Nehemiah*

> | **KEEP ON KEEPING ON**

What Everyone Should Know about the

Thirteen years after Ezra returned to Jerusalem to call his people to repentance, Nehemiah persuaded his king to send him to Jerusalem to rebuild its walls. This was the third return to the land—the first was under Zerubbabel to rebuild the Temple, the second was under Ezra to rebuild the soul of the people, and the third was under Nehemiah to rebuild the walls of Jerusalem.

Bible

The story of Nehemiah tells of personal sacrifice to get a job done for God. Nehemiah was the cup-bearer for the Persian monarch, and thus a high official with a personal relationship with the king. He was comfortable and wealthy. Why would a man who has everything want to do grungy work for God in a faraway place? God sent him, that's why.

Visitors from Jerusalem told Nehemiah of the city's disgrace, with its walls still torn down from Babylon's conquest years before. Nehemiah was so troubled by the news that he wept, fasted, and prayed for days.

The next spring, Nehemiah was serving the king, but he appeared sad as he did it. This was a serious matter, for it was not right to appear sad before the king, but the king cared for Nehemiah and asked him about his sadness. Nehemiah told him the sad news about Jerusalem, and the king was sympathetic. He gave Nehemiah money, supplies, and an armed guard to return to Jerusalem and rebuild its walls.

The book of Nehemiah is the story of that wall building. Nehemiah faced strong resistance from Israel's nearby enemies, for they felt threatened, but he persisted. He kept on going until the walls were rebuilt.

The great lesson of the book is to persist in God's work until it is accomplished, for it is God's work.

What everyone should know about the book of Daniel
REMAINING FAITHFUL, NO MATTER WHERE, NO MATTER WHAT

Daniel, Jeremiah, Ezekiel, Obadiah, and Habakkuk were contemporaries. They lived and worked during the dark days leading up to Judah's defeat and Jerusalem's destruction. Ezekiel preached to the Judean refugees in Babylon, and Jeremiah, Obadiah, and Habakkuk preached to the Judeans back home. Daniel was headed toward high places in Babylon, where he became a statesman and a prophet.

Six important stories give us insight into Daniel's life in Babylon: (1) Daniel and his friends refuse the king's rich food (Daniel 1); (2) Daniel interprets a dream for Nebuchadnezzar and is promoted (Daniel 2); (3) Daniel's three friends are thrown into a fiery furnace for refusing to bow to a golden statue (Daniel 3); (4) Nebuchadnezzar has another dream and Daniel gives the interpretation (Daniel 4); (5) Daniel reads the handwriting on the wall at Belshazzar's pagan feast (Daniel 5); and (6) Daniel is thrown into a den of lions, and God protects him (Daniel 6). These stories span many years, from Daniel's youth to his old age.

Daniel and his friends were members of the royal family, or at least the nobility (Daniel 1:3). Josephus, a Jewish historian during Jesus' time, says that they were related to King Zedekiah. They were not like this wicked king, for they were devoted to the Lord, just as Zedekiah's godly father, King Josiah, had been. Josiah's influence is probably seen in these young relatives. Josiah would have been pleased to see his godly influence reach all the way to the palace of Babylon.

The story of Daniel and his friends tells of God's faithfulness, no matter where, no matter what. When Daniel and his teenage friends arrived as captives in Babylon, they were offered a remarkable opportunity. As Judean royalty or nobility, they were invited to eat the king's food and train to be leaders in Babylon. All they had to do was to obey the king no matter what. Daniel and his friends would obey the king as long as they did not have to disobey their Lord. The first test was about the king's food, which probably had been offered to idols. Who wouldn't want to eat royal delicacies? Daniel and his friends didn't if it meant favoring the pagan gods, so they risked their lives and futures to be faithful to their God. God honored them and they became high officials.

So it was with Daniel's friends when they refused to bow down to the golden statue. For that, they would be sentenced to burn to death in a fiery furnace, but God again honored and protected them. In Daniel's old age, he risked his life by telling King Belshazzar that God would punish him and remove his kingdom, and God honored Daniel for that. Later, Daniel refused to stop praying, and for that he was put into a den of hungry lions. God protected him and rewarded him for his faithfulness.

What does Daniel have to do with us? His life is a model of faithfulness—no matter where, no matter what. God honors that kind of faithfulness, in Daniel and in us.

What everyone should know about the book of Haggai

PRIORITIES—WHAT'S FIRST?

"I don't have time to go to church." Have you ever heard that? "I don't have time to read my Bible." "I don't have time to pray."

When a person says that, he or she really means, "Something else seems more attractive to me, so that's where I will spend my time." Perhaps it is the golf course, a picnic, a favorite TV program, or any one of a dozen other things. Every person on earth has the same amount of time as every other person, so no one can honestly say, "I don't have time to do something." God gave each of us twenty-four hours in each day—no more and no less, but each of us has a different set of priorities. What we value most, we put first in our life. We all have the same time, but not the same priorities.

In 586 B.C., the Babylonians captured Judah and destroyed Jerusalem and its Temple. Forty-eight years later, the Babylonians were conquered by the Persians, and the new king let some people of Judah return to rebuild the Temple. Some returned with enthusiasm and began to rebuild, but time passed and priorities changed. It increasingly seemed more important for them to build their own homes and take care of their own desires. Before long, work on the Temple slowed to a halt. Rebuilding the Temple was no longer a high priority.

When Haggai and Zechariah became prophets in 520 B.C., Haggai focused his ministry on rebuilding the Temple, and he challenged the people to make that a top priority. God sent this message through Haggai, "Why are you living in luxurious houses while my house lies in ruins?" (Haggai 1:4).

Haggai's challenge sparked the enthusiasm of Zerubbabel and the others who had returned, so they began to work again on God's house, the Temple. Haggai is a great example of a man who made a difference. Without his passionate plea, the Temple might never have been rebuilt. With it, work began again.

God may also use you as that one person who makes a difference for him.

294

>

What
Everyone
Should
Know
about
the

Bible

What everyone should know about the book of Zechariah

ENCOURAGING THE DISCOURAGED

When things aren't going the way you hoped, you sink into discourage-ment. You're not alone. Every one of us gets discouraged, probably more often than we want to admit. So it was with the people of Judah. Think how discouraged you would be if your nation was conquered, your capital destroyed, your church burned to the ground, and your family taken away to a foreign country, perhaps never to return. It's discouraging just to think about it.

That's what happened to the people of Judah. In 586 B.C., the Babylonians made their third campaign against Judah and its capital city, Jerusalem. This time, they thor-oughly conquered the people, destroyed the city and its Temple, and took the best of the people back to Babylon. You can imagine how discouraged these people became.

In 538 B.C., by a God-ordained miracle, some were sent back to rebuild the Temple. At first their enthusiasm was high, but then reality and discouragement set in as they saw the enormity of the task. They were working with rubble that was strewn among weeds. They needed houses to live in and had careers to build. Before long, work on the Temple slowed, then came to a halt.

In 520 B.C., God called two prophets, Haggai and Zechariah, to preach to the Temple builders. Their primary mission was to stir the people into making the Temple building their number one priority. Their prophetic ministry was to encourage the discouraged to get up and get going. The people listened to Haggai and Zechariah. They were encouraged, and even excited, to get up and get going, so the Temple was finished.

Zechariah's work as a prophet was not finished, however. Much of his prophecy is encouragement and hope for the future. The promised Messiah was coming and would bring hope far beyond the building of a city and its Temple. At the end of the age, the Messiah will come back again and set up his eternal kingdom.

What everyone should know about the book of Malachi

FAILURE IS NOT FINAL

Would you or I say, "I want to be a failure"? Of course not. We all want to succeed, although each of us has a different measuring stick for success. The people of Judah wouldn't say, "I want to be a failure" either, but they were failures. Malachi was writ-ing to a group of people who had failed again and again.

For many generations, the people of Judah had practiced idolatry, wallowed in sin, and shown great unfaithfulness to God. Occasionally, a godly king arose, only to be followed by other ungodly kings. Judah failed to please God, and this was the great-est failure of all.

Failure to please God was followed by a failure to keep their nation together. A world power called Babylon came against them three times, taking choice people away each time. Daniel and his friends were deported with the first group. Ezekiel was deported with the second group. The third campaign was the worst, for the Babylonian army defeated Judah, destroyed Jerusalem and its Temple, and deported many of its people. That was a big-time failure.

Some people returned, but they failed for a time to rebuild the Temple. Then, when the Temple was finally rebuilt, they failed to keep their love for the Lord alive. Malachi makes a catalog of their failures to live for God: They have contempt for God's name, they engage in false worship, they break God's laws, they keep the tithes and offerings for themselves, and they are arrogant.

The most obvious failure was the loss of distinction between God's people and all other people. Does that sound familiar? It is a failure today, isn't it?

Like many other prophets, Malachi concludes his book with a promise for the future. Someone like Elijah would come to announce the Messiah. That, of course, would be John the Baptist. The Messiah would come with hope for the hopeless and forgiveness for the sinner. That would be Jesus.

As the Old Testament draws to a close, a light shines toward the New Testament to come almost five hundred years later. The Messiah would come to turn failures into significance.

Did You Know?

Daniel had another name Daniel was his real name, given to him at birth. The Babylonians gave him a new name, Belteshazzar. This name was probably used by the Babylonians throughout his years there. They would not have known him as Daniel.

Shadrach, Meshach, and Abednego also had other names We know Daniel by his Judean name, not his Babylonian name, Belteshazzar. We know Shadrach, Meshach, and Abednego by their Babylonian names, not their Judean names, Hananiah, Mishael, and Azariah.

No pork chops for Daniel The king's food had three types of problems for Daniel and his friends: (1) foods that had been offered to pagan idols; (2) the king's rich wines; and (3) foods considered unclean by the Judeans, such as camels (Leviticus 11:4), rabbits (Leviticus 11:6), pigs (Leviticus 11:7), ravens (Leviticus 11:15), and owls (Leviticus 11:16-18). Some think that Daniel and his friends were vegetarians by choice, but they may have been vegetarians by default. Vegetables would not be offered to idols and would therefore not be "unclean" by Judean standards, so they were safe to eat. Any meat was suspect unless it could be positively identified and it was known for sure that it had not been offered to idols.

What God wrote with his fingers God wrote two important messages with his own hands: (1) the Ten Commandments, which he wrote twice on tablets of stone (Exodus 24:12; 34:28); and (2) the handwriting on the wall at Belshazzar's drunken party (Daniel 5).

The fourth person in the fiery furnace When Shadrach, Meshach, and Abednego refused to bow before the king's golden image, the king had

296
>
What
Everyone
Should
Know
about
the
Bible

them thrown into a smelting furnace or a kiln for baking mud bricks. When the king's men threw these three into the furnace, a fourth person appeared with them. Nebuchadnezzar said that the fourth person looked like a divine being, or like a god (Daniel 3:25). He would not have known about Jesus, so he could not have called him that, but some believe that Jesus was walking with these three faithful men in the intense flames. Later, Nebuchadnezzar said that the Most High God had sent his angel to rescue the three (Daniel 3:28), but of course, this was a pagan king speaking. He would not have known if the being was an angel or the Son of God.

A purple robe for Daniel When Daniel read the handwriting on the wall to King Belshazzar, the king gave him a purple robe, as he promised. Why purple? Purple dye, from a tiny part of the murex shellfish, was almost more valuable than gold, and certainly more rare. Purple dyes were in great demand by the wealthy and by royalty, so a purple robe was a status symbol.

Esther's royal husband–Xerxes or Ahasuerus? We sometimes find the name of Esther's husband as *Xerxes*, and sometimes we see it as *Ahasuerus*. Both are correct. *Xerxes* is the Greek form of his name and *Ahasuerus* is the Hebrew form.

Nehemiah was sent back to Jerusalem by Esther's stepson The successor to Esther's husband, Xerxes, was his son Artaxerxes I, who ruled from 464 B.C. to 424 B.C. Esther was not his mother, but Esther's husband was his father. As far as we know, Esther never had children. As his father's queen, Esther may have had considerable influence on young Artaxerxes as he grew up. If so, her influence would have been significant in helping Nehemiah return to rebuild the walls of Jerusalem.

Discovering My Purpose from God's Plan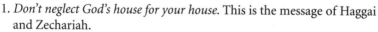

1. *Don't neglect God's house for your house.* This is the message of Haggai and Zechariah.
2. *Would I give up the luxury of the king's court for the pain of wall building? Nehemiah did.* Would I give up any luxury to do God's work, no matter how menial?
3. *God is with his faithful people—in a fiery furnace or a den of hungry lions.* Daniel and his friends discovered that.
4. *Divine appointments do not come from human ingenuity.* See Daniel, Esther, Ezra, and Nehemiah. God specializes in arranging the impossible. We need help, even with the possible.

5. *Be careful to read what God has written.* Belshazzar offered a fortune just to know what God's handwriting said. We can read God's writing, the Bible, without it costing us one cent. If a pagan king valued God's handwriting that much, we who love God should value it infinitely more.

A Time of Silence
Between the Old and New Testaments

Characters:
Alexander the Great (a leader of the Greek or Macedonian Empire); Antiochus III (a leader of the Seleucids); Antiochus IV (Antiochus Epiphanes, a leader of the Seleucids); Antipater (an Edomite ruler of Judea for the Romans); Herod the Great (a ruler of Judea for the Romans); Judas Maccabaeus (a Jewish leader who continued rebellion against the Seleucids); Mattathias (a Jewish leader who rebelled against the Seleucids); Philip (the father of Alexander the Great); Seleucus IV (a leader of the Seleucids); Simon (a Maccabean governor)

Time Period:
From Malachi until the birth of Jesus

Dates:
Approximately 430 B.C.–6 or 5 B.C.

Where Scene 18 of the Big Story Can Be Found:
This is a period of silence in the Bible. There is no Bible source for it.

In Scene 18, Find the Answers to These Questions:
Who conquered the world by the time he was thirty?
Who sacrificed to Zeus on the altar of the Jewish Temple?
What is the Septuagint?

Look for this in Scene 18
> An Edomite is a Roman ruler.
> Seven books that sound as if they could be books of the Bible, but which are not accepted by anyone as Scripture.
> Fourteen books accepted by some as Scripture but not included in the Old Testament as we know it.
> A commentary on the law of Moses, compiled by Jewish religious leaders.

From the time of Malachi, who closed the curtain on the Old Testament story, until the birth of Jesus in 6 B.C. or 5 B.C. was a period of about 425 years. If we move back through United States history, that would take us to the earliest colonial days, about 150 years before the Revolutionary War. This is another long period of biblical silence, like the time between Genesis and Exodus.

Not one Bible event is mentioned during this 425-year period. No books written during this time are accepted by all Christians as part of the Bible. There are fourteen books that are often referred to as the Apocrypha, eleven of which are accepted by some Christians as authentic Bible books, mostly within the Catholic Church. For the most part, Protestant Christians do not accept any of these books as true Bible books.

During this period of biblical silence, world power shifted enormously, from the Persians to the Greeks to the Romans. There was relative freedom for the Jewish people in Palestine, or Judea, during this time. It was also a period when significant influences arose that would shape events in the life of Jesus, such as the rise of the synagogue, the rise of Pharisees, Sadducees, and Essenes, and the translation of the Old Testament into Greek. During this time, Greek influence dominated the world scene, even in the Roman Empire. Here are some of the influences during this period of biblical silence.

The Persian Empire

The Persian Empire had been the world power for about a hundred years before the time of Malachi and the close of the Old Testament. It would remain in power for another hundred years.

From 486 B.C.–465 B.C., Xerxes I, or Ahasuerus, Esther's husband, was the ruler. He was succeeded by his son and Esther's stepson, Artaxerxes I, who ruled from 464 B.C.–424 B.C. Esther must have had great influence on him while he was growing up, for he was quite favorable toward the Jews. He permitted Ezra to go to Jerusalem to restore proper worship, and he let Nehemiah go to Jerusalem to rebuild the walls. The Persian Empire survived until 331 B.C.

The Greek or Macedonian Empire

Almost thirty years earlier, Philip, father of Alexander the Great, was gaining power over the Greek states. When he died in 336 B.C., Alexander came to power and within five years had conquered the Persian Empire in three decisive battles. Alexander went on to establish the Greek or Macedonian Empire, conquering much of the known world by the time he was thirty. Alexander was still young when he died in Babylon in 323 B.C., and his kingdom was divided among four of his

300
>

What
Everyone
Should
Know
about
the

Bible

generals. One wonders what would have happened if he had lived another ten years.

The Greek conquest was more than a military victory. It was a cultural victory that left Greek influence on language, literature, and art for many years to come. About 280 B.C.–150 B.C., the Old Testament was translated into Greek and became known as the Septuagint. This released the great truths of the Old Testament Scriptures from the Jews to the entire Gentile world. Many years later, the Romans still clung to Greek culture and language, and even the Hebrew writers of the New Testament penned their message in Greek.

The Ptolemies and Seleucids

When Alexander the Great died, his empire was divided among four of his generals. Egypt was then under rulers known as the Ptolemies. Syria was under the rule of the Seleucids. For 122 years, Israel, or Palestine, was ruled by the Ptolemies, who were quite favorable to the Jews. In 198 B.C., Antiochus III drove the Ptolemies from Palestine and annexed it to the Seleucid Empire. He was succeeded by Seleucus IV, and then by Antiochus IV, known also as Antiochus Epiphanes. During this time of the Seleucid rule, the Greek influence in dress, names, language, and morality was impressed upon the Jews. Antiochus Epiphanes profaned the Temple by offering sacrifices to Zeus on the altar of burnt offering. The Seleucids attempted to stamp out the Jewish religion, but angered the Jews to the point that they rebelled.

The Maccabean Revolt and the Hasmonean Period

The Jewish revolt began under a man named Mattathias, who used guerrilla warfare against the Seleucids. He died after a short time, and his son Judas Maccabaeus took over as the leader of the rebellion. He continued to use his father's method of guerrilla warfare, and at last he defeated three Syrian generals at Emmaus. The family of Judas Maccabaeus was sometimes known as the Maccabees or the Hasmonaean family.

Judas Maccabaeus continued the struggle against the Seleucids until he died in 161 B.C. The leadership passed to his brother Jonathan, who continued to lead the struggle for Jewish independence. In 143 B.C., Simon became governor. There would be five more rulers of the Maccabean or Hasmonean Period when the Jewish people had a somewhat autonomous rule. At last, in 63 B.C., the Romans conquered the land under their general Pompey.

Roman Rule

From 63 B.C., the Romans ruled the known world for centuries beyond the time of Jesus on earth. They appointed Antipater as ruler of Judea. He was an Idumaean or Edomite, a descendant of Esau. His son Herod the Great became the king of Judea. To build favor with the Jews, Herod rebuilt the Temple with great splendor, and this was the Temple that Jesus often visited. This was the same Herod that murdered the babies of Bethlehem in an attempt to kill the newborn king, Jesus.

The Apocrypha

During the time between the Old and New Testaments, fourteen books were written that were accepted as Scripture in the Septuagint and later in the Latin Vulgate, though they were never included in the Old Testament as we know it. The Roman Catholic Church accepts eleven of the fourteen as part of Scripture. We will list the fourteen here, but it is beyond the boundaries of this book to do more than that: 1 and 2 Esdras, Tobit, Judith, The Remainder of Esther, The Wisdom of Solomon, Ecclesiasticus, 1 and 2 Maccabees, Baruch, The Song of the Three Children, The Story of Susanna, Bel and the Dragon, and The Prayer of Manasses.

Pseudepigrapha

Seven other books written during the period from 200 B.C. to A.D. 200 are not accepted by anyone as Scripture. They are the Assumption of Moses, the Ascension of Isaiah, the Book of Enoch, the Book of Jubilees, the Sibylline Oracles, the Psalms of Solomon, and the Testaments of the Twelve Prophets.

The Talmud

Jewish religious leaders compiled their commentary on the law of Moses from 300 B.C. to A.D. 500. This work was known as the Talmud.

The Sanhedrin

During the time between the Testaments, the Sanhedrin became the Jewish high court. It was comprised of seventy leaders, and was significant in the life of Jesus, as it condemned him to death.

The Pharisees, Sadducees, Essenes, and Scribes

The Pharisees were a strict, rigid, legalistic, separatist group that formed around 168 B.C. The Sadducees, by contrast, were worldly priests who denied the resurrection and eternal punishment. Because of their worldly ways, these aristocratic leaders were oriented toward Greek culture. The Essenes were like monks. The scribes copied the Scriptures, and because of that, became quite knowledgeable about the Scriptures, and became prominent religious leaders.

Synagogues

With the Temple destroyed and the people deported to Assyria and Babylonia, the Jews needed a local place for worship and learning. These places were the synagogues. Jesus taught in the synagogues in Nazareth and Capernaum.

God the Son

Jesus Before Bethlehem

Characters:
Jesus Christ, God the Son

Time Period:
From eons before creation until Jesus was born in Bethlehem

Dates:
From eternity past until 6 B.C.–5 B.C.

Where Scene 19 of the Big Story Can Be Found:
John 1:1-18

In Scene 19, Find the Answers to These Questions:
How could a baby create the world?
Why did Jesus come as a baby? Why wasn't he a great, powerful person?

Look for this in Scene 19
> Some people knew Jesus was coming, even hundreds of years before he was born.
> Without the cradle, there could not have been the Cross.

The Big Story So Far

The Christmas story is more than a Christmas story

The Christmas story, which has stirred the imaginations of people of all ages for hundreds of years, focuses on the birth of a baby in Bethlehem. He was born in a stable, cradled in a manger, and wrapped in swaddling clothes. Add to that the angels appearing to the shepherds and the visit of the wise men. What would Christmas be without this glorious story? Despite the efforts of our secular society to cover it up, it remains the focal point of Christmas. The birth of the baby Jesus is much more than just a Christmas story, of course. It is the Incarnation that offers redemption for you, me, and all who believe.

God the Son is without beginning or ending

To understand the birth of Jesus at Bethlehem, the life he lived on earth, and the sacrifice he offered on the cross, we must first go back thousands of years to the creation of the universe. God the Father, God the Son, and God the Holy Spirit were already in existence, creating all things. The triune God—Father, Son, and Holy Spirit—had been there for eons before Creation, planning every snowflake, every flower, every animal, and every human being who would ever live. God the Son, whom we know as Jesus because of his visit to earth, was always there. He was and is God—God the Son, the second person of the Trinity. The life of Jesus on earth was but a small chapter in the everlasting life of God the Son, from eons past through eons yet to come.

God the Son—the Creator

The apostle John, who probably knew Jesus better than any other human being knew him, wrote a Gospel about Jesus affirming that he truly was and is the Son of God, the Messiah. John opens his Gospel with the remarkable words, "In the beginning the Word [Jesus] already existed. The Word was with God, and the Word was God. He existed in the beginning with God. God created everything through him, and nothing was created except through him. The Word gave life to everything that was created, and his life brought light to everyone. The light shines in the darkness, and the darkness can never extinguish it" (John 1:1-5).

Heaven is the home of the triune God, the Father, Son, and Holy Spirit. It has always been his home and always will be. Except for the few years Jesus lived on earth, he lived in his heavenly home for all the time before that and will live there for all time in the future.

Jesus' life on earth was planned before Creation

Hebrews 13:8 says, "Jesus Christ is the same yesterday, today, and forever." He is eternal. In John 8:58 Jesus says, "I tell you the truth,

304

>

What
Everyone
Should
Know
about
the

Bible

before Abraham was even born, I Aᴍ!" Later Jesus prays, "Now, Father, bring me into the glory we shared before the world began" (John 17:5). Jesus—God the Son—has always lived, just as God the Father and God the Holy Spirit have always lived. Jesus also says to the Father, "They can see all the glory you gave me because you loved me even before the world began!" (John 17:24). Peter speaks of Jesus' life before Creation when he says, "God chose him [Jesus] as your ransom long before the world began" (1 Peter 1:20). God's plans for the incarnation of Jesus, the life of Jesus on earth, the death of Jesus on the cross, and the resurrection and ascension of Jesus were all in place long before the dawn of Creation.

The force that holds the universe together

Not only were the plans for all of this in place before Creation, but God the Son was personally there at Creation, bringing all things into existence. He remains with Creation and holds it together. Colossians 1:15-17 affirms this: "Christ is the visible image of the invisible God. He existed before anything was Created and is supreme over all Creation, for through him God created everything in the heavenly realms and on earth. He made the things we can see and the things we can't see—such as thrones, kingdoms, rulers, and authorities in the unseen world. Everything was created through him and for him. He existed before anything else, and he holds all creation together."

The phrase "he holds all creation together" is staggering. Think of the binding forces, such as atoms and molecules, that hold our bodies and all Creation together. All that is in us and in the universe is bonded together with forces beyond our comprehension. Scripture tells us here that Jesus is the one to whom those forces are given. It is his job to hold together the universe he helped create.

The Christ of the Old Testament

In a very real sense, the entire Old Testament is the prelude to Jesus' birth at Bethlehem. Every person and every event fit into the remarkable story of all stories and lead to his coming as a baby at just the right time. A long line of prophecies in the Old Testament point to Jesus' coming. The priestly system anticipates the great High Priest to come. The sacrificial system foreshadows the Lamb of God, whose sacrifice for our sins is the pinnacle of history. Jesus came to Bethlehem for two purposes: (1) to be sacrificed on the cross for our sins (the preeminent purpose); and (2) to gather and train a select few to lead and build his church after he returned to heaven. Revelation 13:8 speaks of "the Lamb [Jesus] slain from the foundation of the world" (ɴᴋᴊᴠ). Jesus' crucifixion, and all that led to it, was in God's eternal plans long before Creation.

In the fullness of time

There was an appointed time for the Son to come to earth and an appointed time for him to die on the cross. The Scriptures describe these divine appointments this way: "When the right time came, God sent his Son" (Galatians 4:4). Some versions say, "When the fullness of time came," meaning that Jesus came when time was fully ripe or prepared for it. He was not a moment too early and not a moment too late.

Questions You May Be Asking

Why did Jesus come as a little baby? Why didn't he, the Son of God, come with great power and glory?

In God's remarkable plan of redemption, a blood sacrifice was needed to pay the price for our sins. Life is in the blood. We can't fully understand this mystery, but its prelude is found in the Old Testament sacrifices for sin. No animal is great enough to redeem all believers of all time from sin. The sacrifice must be preeminent—beyond all other sacrifices. God the Son was willing to make that sacrifice for us, and that required a body. He took on a human body at Bethlehem, and his body, fully grown, was sacrificed on the Cross.

How can God be one person, but three persons?

This is one of the mysteries we must accept as Bible truth without fully understanding it. God's ways are not our ways. Who can fully understand the person and the mind of the Creator of the universe? A poor comparison might be how one person can *seem* to be three or more persons to others. For example, Joe is the president of a corporation, a husband, and a father. To his employees he is one person, to his wife he is a radically different person, and to his children he is still another person. This is a poor comparison because these are only perceived differences in the same person, while God is actually three persons in one.

How could the prophets know ahead of time about Jesus' coming and predict details of his person and work?

All Scripture is given, or inspired, by God (2 Timothy 3:16). God spoke through godly people. The prophets did not know about events hundreds of years in the future, but God did, and he revealed it to them and through them.

What
Everyone
Should
Know
about
the
Bible

Great Events of This Time

Before Creation, the triune God—Father, Son, and Holy Spirit—planned all that would be created and all that would happen. The Creation of the universe set the stage for this great drama, and the Old Testament prepares us for Jesus' incarnation, life, crucifixion, resurrection, and ascension.

Discovering My Purpose from God's Plan

1. *Without the cradle, there could not have been the Cross.* Without the birth of Jesus, there could not have been the sacrifice of Jesus for our sins. Jesus first had to be born in order to die.
2. *The Christmas story and the Easter story are essential to one another and are intimately related in the plans and purposes of God.*
3. *The Cross always precedes the crown. Jesus will someday return as King of kings and Lord of lords, but he first had to die for our sins.* Our cross must always precede our crown—we will reap a reward after we pay the price for it, not before.

Bloodline for the Blood

The Genealogies of Jesus

Characters:
Jesus; Joseph (the adoptive father of Jesus); Luke (the author of the book of Luke); Mary (the mother of Jesus); Matthew (the author of the book of Matthew)

Time Period:
The entire Old Testament period from Adam to Jesus

Dates:
From an unknown time until 6 B.C.–5 B.C.

Where Scene 20 of the Big Story Can Be Found:
Matthew 1:1-17; Luke 3:23-38

In Scene 20, Find the Answers to These Questions:
Why is so much space in the Bible devoted to Joseph's genealogy, since he wasn't Jesus' father?
Why didn't Jesus descend from royalty instead of common, ordinary people?

Look for this in Scene 20
> The bloodline of Jesus, whose blood was the sacrifice for our sin, came from flawed people.
> Jesus was part Moabite.

The entire New Testament is the story of God the Son coming to earth to become a sacrifice for our sins. The Cross towers over all of history: All world events before the Cross point to it, and all world history after the Cross points back to it. The four Gospels compose the scriptural record of Jesus' life on earth leading to the Cross. The theme of these books isn't so much the life of Jesus as it is the person and work of Jesus.

Credentials for Jesus' legal father

Some people might be startled to see that the story of Jesus in Matthew's Gospel begins with a long genealogy rather than an account of his birth (Matthew 1:1-16). The record in Matthew gives a long list of Joseph's ancestors—the line of Jesus' legal father—rather than the bloodline through Mary that Luke records. Because Matthew is writing to a Jewish audience, he gives credibility to Jesus' ancestry through his legal father, even though that father was adoptive. This genealogy connects Jesus' ancestry to Abraham. Matthew's Jewish audience would have recognized and accepted such a lineage. It was not necessary for them to go back beyond Abraham for that fatherly set of credentials.

Jesus' bloodline

The genealogy in Luke is probably Mary's ancestry (Luke 3:23-38). The record in Matthew says that Joseph's father was Jacob. Here it says Heli, who was probably Joseph's father-in-law, Mary's father. Why doesn't Luke just say that? Perhaps giving a long genealogy of a woman wasn't a culturally acceptable thing to do at that time.

If this is Mary's genealogy (Bible scholars accept it as such), these ancestors are in the bloodline of Jesus' human body, which he sacrificed on the cross. The blood he shed for our sins came through these ancestors.

Flawed family

If you were expecting a list of perfect people, forget it. Though Jesus himself was without sin (and therefore qualified to offer himself as a sacrifice for our sins), through Mary he came from a long line of sinful people. The Bible is clear that they were people just like you and me—flawed and sinful.

Abraham heads the list of flawed people. He was a godly man, to be sure. But he also deceived Pharaoh into thinking that Sarah was his sister, not his wife. He later repeated this same deception with the Philistine king Abimelech. Abraham and Sarah also lacked the faith to believe that God would give them a son through Sarah, for they both contrived to have that son through Sarah's Egyptian maid, Hagar. This lack of faith in God's promises brought untold grief to the family.

310

>

What
Everyone
Should
Know
about
the

Bible

Isaac was obedient to God in many ways, but in his old age he almost gave the birthright and the covenant lineage to Esau instead of Jacob. Surely in his heart of hearts he knew better, for Esau had married two Hittite wives. How could a pagan be the mother of a covenant son or of future covenant generations? The human explanation is that old Isaac enjoyed the savory wild game Esau hunted for him. With his appetite for meat, Isaac almost broke the chain of covenant relationships. Isaac was a flawed, sinful man.

Jacob was a godly man, but he deceived his brother, Esau, and blatantly lied to his blind father, Isaac, when he disguised himself as Esau.

The story of the birth of Perez is shocking even by today's standards. Judah had sex with a prostitute, who turned out to be Tamar, his widowed daughter-in-law, in disguise. Later when Judah learned that his daughter-in-law was pregnant, he threatened to kill her. But she showed him his own seal, cord, and walking stick, which he had left as payment to the woman he thought was a prostitute. This established Judah as the father of Tamar's child, so he left her alone.

Obed, King David's grandfather, was the son of the Moabite widow Ruth. Though there was nothing overtly sinful about Ruth's life, she was Moabite, a descendant of Lot and his older daughter. Lot's daughter got her father drunk one night so that she could have sex with him and have a baby (Genesis 19:30-38). That baby was Moab, Ruth's ancestor and therefore King David's ancestor. Historically the Moabites were enemies of the Israelites. But through Ruth, David and all of his descendants were part Moabite.

King David was a godly man who built a golden kingdom. Overall, he led a godly life, and he wrote many of the psalms. But the story of David and Bathsheba is infamous—how he seduced her, then had her husband murdered so he could marry her. The great king Solomon was born of David and Bathsheba. David, Bathsheba, and Solomon are all in Jesus' bloodline.

All of this is to show that the blood of Jesus Christ, given for our sins, came from the flawed, sinful people in Mary's bloodline. When we know this, we realize how wise God's plan was.

Questions You May Be Asking

Why does Matthew's genealogy start with Abraham instead of Noah or Adam?
Why not go back further, to Noah or even to Adam, the way Luke's genealogy does? For the Jewish audience to whom Matthew was writing, it was important to establish that the father's lineage was from Abraham. Although Joseph was not the bodily ancestor of Jesus, he was the legal father, and that was sufficient. Luke was a Gentile physician,

writing to Gentiles and to people everywhere, so the link to Abraham was not as significant as it was for Matthew's audience. Thus, Luke gives Mary's genealogy all the way back to Adam.

Why are we talking about the sins of Mary's ancestors?

It was Jesus' blood from Mary's bloodline that was offered on the cross for our sins. It is comforting to know that this bloodline was composed of sinners, for we who are redeemed by Jesus' blood are also sinners. If every one of Jesus' ancestors was spotlessly sinless, we might feel we could never measure up.

Discovering My Purpose from God's Plan

1. *Life is in the blood. For us to have forgiveness of sins and everlasting life, a blood sacrifice had to be made.* Jesus' sacrifice was the ultimate sacrifice, the only one sufficient to cover the sins of the world.

2. *The bloodline that led to the cross, where Jesus shed his blood for us, came through the lineage of a woman, not a man.* Joseph's bloodline was of no consequence at the cross. But for the Jewish people of that time, the lineage of Joseph, Jesus' legal father, was significant.

3. *Heritage is significant in God's plan of salvation.* Think of it! Almost two chapters of the Bible are dedicated to Jesus' earthly heritage—one to his bloodline, the other to his legal line. Heritage is also significant in God's plans for you and me. Give full attention to it.

Announcing the Birth of the King
Preparing for Jesus' Birth

Characters:
The angel Gabriel (who announced John's birth); Elizabeth (the mother of John the Baptist); the Holy Spirit (Jesus' "father"); Jesus; John the Baptist (who announced the Messiah's coming); Joseph (Mary's fiancé and Jesus' legal father); Mary (the mother of Jesus); Zechariah (the father of John the Baptist)

Time Period:
The year leading up to Jesus' birth

Dates:
6 or 5 B.C.

Where Scene 21 of the Big Story Can Be Found:
Matthew 1:18-25; Luke 1:5-80

In Scene 21, Find the Answers to These Questions:
Why couldn't Zechariah speak until his son was born?
Which angel spoke to Zechariah and to Mary?

Look for this in Scene 21
> There are two miracle babies, but the miracles are very different. How so?
> Mary could have been stoned to death.
> Jesus is a Greek name, not a Hebrew one.
> The same angel who spoke to Mary also spoke to Daniel five hundred years earlier.

The Old Testament prophecy of John the Baptist

The story of John the Baptist begins about 425 years before he was born. The prophet Malachi, who wrote the last book of the Old Testament, closed his book with these words: "Look, I am sending you the prophet Elijah before the great and dreadful day of the LORD arrives" (Malachi 4:5). Malachi was predicting the coming of John the Baptist, a man who was like the prophet Elijah even in the way that he dressed. John was the forerunner of the Messiah, the one to announce Christ's appearing.

Gabriel announces the birth of John the Baptist

The Gospel of Luke opens with the story of John's coming birth. The setting is the Temple, where each morning a priest was scheduled to enter the Holy Place to burn incense. There were thousands of priests, so the task rotated among the twenty-four orders of priests, and within an order one priest was chosen by lot. The lot fell to the aged priest Zechariah, in the order of Abijah, a descendant of Moses' brother Aaron. Zechariah and his wife, Elizabeth, had longed for a son, but like Abraham and Sarah thousands of years before, they were too old. Their hopes were gone.

On this particular morning, the angel Gabriel appeared to Zechariah as he offered the incense in the Holy Place. He announced that Zechariah and Elizabeth would have a son who would turn many to the Lord.

And, like Abraham and Sarah, Zechariah doubted that God could do this because he and his wife were too old. Because of his doubt, the angel said that Zechariah would not be able to speak until his son was born. This son would be John the Baptist.

Gabriel announces Jesus' birth

Six months later Gabriel appeared to a young virgin named Mary, who was engaged to a carpenter named Joseph. "You have found favor with God," the angel told Mary. "You will have a son and will name him Jesus. He will be called the Son of the Most High, and his kingdom will never end."

Mary was puzzled. She and Joseph were not married yet, and she was still a virgin. How could she have a baby?

"The Holy Spirit will come upon you, so your son will be the Son of God," the angel told her. Mary realized she would face public shame for becoming pregnant before she was married, but she quickly agreed to obey the Lord.

Mary visits Elizabeth

The angel told Mary that her cousin Elizabeth was also pregnant, so Mary hurried to see her where she lived near Jerusalem. As soon

314

>

What
Everyone
Should
Know
about
the

Bible

SCENE 21

Announcing
the Birth
of the
King

<

315

as Mary spoke to her, Elizabeth's baby leaped in her womb and Elizabeth was filled with the Holy Spirit. Elizabeth blessed Mary with a beautiful song.

Mary responded with a beautiful song of her own, a poem of praise to the Lord. Mary stayed with Elizabeth for three months, then returned home to Nazareth.

Birth of John the Baptist

At the appointed time, Elizabeth's baby was born. Friends, family, and neighbors came together to express their joy at the baby's circumcision, when he was eight days old. The friends and neighbors wanted to name him Zechariah, for his father, but Elizabeth insisted that his name was John. Zechariah still could not speak, so he wrote on a tablet that the baby's name was John. Immediately Zechariah was able to speak again.

Zechariah was filled with the Holy Spirit and prophesied. His prophecy was also a song of praise to the Lord that foretold the ministry of his son, John.

An angel speaks to Joseph

Meanwhile, Joseph learned that his fiancée, Mary, was pregnant. In those days this was a serious problem punishable by being stoned to death. Joseph loved Mary and did not want to hurt her, so he decided that he would break the engagement quietly. One night, an angel of the Lord appeared to Joseph in a dream and told him that Mary's child was conceived by the Holy Spirit, not by another man, and that the child should be named Jesus. So Joseph proceeded with the wedding, but he had no sexual relationship with Mary until after the birth of Jesus.

Questions You May Be Asking

The name *Jesus* doesn't sound like a Hebrew name. Was it?

The name *Jesus* is a Greek form of the Hebrew name *Joshua*. This reflects three things: (1) the strong Greek influence at that time; (2) that God himself named his Son; and (3) that Jesus had come to bring salvation to all people, including the Gentiles.

How were Jesus and John the Baptist related?

Elizabeth was Mary's older cousin or aunt, so Jesus was either the first or second cousin of John the Baptist.

Gabriel was an archangel. But what is an archangel?

An archangel is one of the highest orders of angels. The extrabiblical Book of Enoch, which was written in the first or second century B.C., names four archangels: Michael, Raphael, Gabriel, and Uriel. Muslims believe that the Koran was given to Muhammad through Gabriel.

▰▰▰ Great Events of This Time

1. **John's birth is announced to Zechariah in the Temple** (Luke 1:5-25).
2. **Jesus' birth is announced to Mary** (Luke 1:26-38).
3. **Mary visits Elizabeth** (Luke 1:39-56).
4. **John the Baptist is born** (Luke 1:57-80).
5. **Jesus' conception is explained to Joseph** (Matthew 1:18-25).

▰▰▰ Significant Dates of This Time

Circa 6 B.C.–5 B.C., the birth of Jesus and John the Baptist.

▰▰▰ Heroes and Villains: The Stars of Scene 21

ZECHARIAH

Elizabeth's husband, Zechariah, was a priest who served part of the time in the Jerusalem Temple. During one such period of service, the angel Gabriel appeared to Zechariah and told him that he and Elizabeth would have a son. It was difficult for Zechariah to believe this, for he and his wife were very old, but they did have a son and named him John. Later their son was called John the Baptist. His work was to prepare people for the coming of the Messiah. Zechariah was a godly man, and Elizabeth was a godly woman; they raised John to earnestly seek God's will for his life.

Bible events in Zechariah's life

1. He burns incense in the Temple; the angel Gabriel appears to him and promises him a son.
2. Because of his doubt, he becomes speechless.
3. A son is born to him and Elizabeth; he writes on a tablet that the child's name is John.
4. His speech comes back, and he praises God.

ELIZABETH

When Mary of Nazareth learned that she would become the mother of the Messiah, she visited her cousin (or aunt) Elizabeth, who lived with her husband, Zechariah, near Jerusalem. Both Elizabeth and her husband were Aaron's descendants. Elizabeth was also expecting a miracle son when Mary visited, for according to human standards, she was too old to bear a child. Later Elizabeth gave birth to John the Baptist, and Mary gave birth to Jesus.

Bible events in Elizabeth's life

1. An angel promises Zechariah that Elizabeth will have a son.
2. Mary comes to visit her, and her baby leaps within her.

316

>

What
Everyone
Should
Know
about
the

Bible

SCENE 21

Announcing
the Birth
of the
King

<

317

3. A son is born to her and Zechariah.

4. They name their son John. He becomes known as John the Baptist.

MARY, JESUS' MOTHER

Mary willingly accepted God's offer through the angel Gabriel for her to become the mother of the Messiah. This brought shame from those who would not believe that God was the child's father. Mary's husband-to-be, Joseph, almost divorced her but was told in a vision from God that this child was truly God's Son. With Joseph, Mary went to Bethlehem, where Jesus was born.

Bible events in Mary's life

1. The angel Gabriel appears to her and announces Jesus' birth.
2. She visits her cousin Elizabeth.
3. She sings in praise to God.
4. She goes to Bethlehem with Joseph; Jesus is born.
5. She receives the shepherds who come to see the baby Jesus.
6. She receives the wise men when they come to see Jesus.

JOSEPH, MARY'S HUSBAND

Joseph could trace his ancestry back to Abraham and King David, which was quite an honor. His home was in Nazareth, where he worked as a carpenter. When Joseph was betrothed to Mary and learned that his bride-to-be was expecting a baby, he decided to break their engagement privately. He could have made a public issue out of it and had Mary stoned to death. An angel appeared to Joseph and assured him that Mary's child was truly God's Son and not the son of a stranger, so Joseph took Mary as his wife and accepted God's Son as his own.

Bible events in Joseph's life

1. An angel appears to him in a dream.
2. Mary becomes his wife.
3. He journeys with Mary to Bethlehem.
4. Jesus is born in a manger.
5. Shepherds visit the manger.
6. The wise men visit the boy Jesus.

What everyone should know about the book of Matthew

THE STORY OF A KING WHOSE KINGDOM NEVER ENDS

Matthew was also known as Levi and was a Jewish tax collector. The Jewish people in Matthew's time despised tax collectors because they were fellow Jews who collected unfair taxes for their Roman captors. They usually collected more than the Romans demanded and grew rich off the excess. When Jesus called Matthew to follow him, he left his tax booth and became one of the Twelve. His name was later changed to Matthew. Little did Matthew realize that he would write the first book of our New Testament.

Matthew's Gospel connects well with the Old Testament, for it is filled with Old Testament prophecies concerning Jesus. There are fifty-three quotes from the Old Testament and seventy-three additional references to the Old Testament in this Gospel. This close connection with the Old Testament was essential for Matthew's Jewish audience.

The key purpose of Matthew's Gospel was to give clear evidence to the Jewish people that Jesus was the Messiah, the Son of God, the One the Jewish people expected.

What does Matthew's Gospel have to say to us today?

Every king who has ever lived has wanted his kingdom to be inherited by his son and to be passed down to his grandson, great-grandson, and succeeding grandsons until the end of time. But no earthly king has ever seen this dream come true.

David was perhaps the greatest king who ever lived. He built a kingdom that is often called the Golden Kingdom of Israel. Sadly, within two generations it had been torn apart by the foolishness of his son and grandson.

Matthew writes about a king who came in a very unkingly way and ruled on earth in a way that no other king would have thought wise. Royalty means power and the ability to bring subjects into servitude, but the king Matthew describes was the "servant of all." How could any king endure by being a servant to all his subjects? How could such a kingdom survive?

Enter King Jesus, who was born in a manger and never owned his own home. He had no money to call his own, and no possessions. King Jesus lived below the poverty level and served everyone. His kingdom will indeed last forever.

And as for power? Someday every knee will bow and every person will admit that this Jesus is truly the King of all kings and Lord of all lords. No other king who ever lived has earned those titles.

Who wrote the story of this king whose kingdom never ends? It was a scoundrel named Matthew, a hated Jewish tax collector who stole money from his people to give to the Romans. Who would choose a man like that to tell a kingly story? Jesus did.

First, Jesus changed Matthew into a new person, a believer and follower of King Jesus. No longer would he steal from his people and give money to the Romans. No longer would he get rich at the expense of the poor. This new person would no longer be called Levi, but Matthew. Now his job was to follow Jesus, then tell us the story of the King of kings. His story is so important that it opens the entire New Testament.

A king whose kingdom never ends? Yes, that's King Jesus. Matthew's story was written first for the Jewish people, but now it is your story too.

> *What everyone should know about the book of Mark*

THE FAST-MOVING VIDEO OF JESUS' LIFE

Matthew wrote his account of Jesus' life for Jewish believers, but Jesus' story was also intended for Roman believers. Many Romans accepted Jesus as Savior, and they needed a "story of Jesus" written for them.

The Roman believers couldn't get too excited about ancient Jewish gene-

Bible

SCENE 21

Announcing
the Birth
of the
King

<

319

alogies. Matthew wrote about such things for the Jews, but the Romans wanted a fast-paced account of the life of Jesus. What was he like? What did he do? What will he do for me?

So Mark wrote a story of miracles and action-filled events. It moves like a video rather than a slide show. Mark's Gospel is the shortest of the four, and it spends much more time on Jesus' actions than on his teachings.

Mark's Gospel is also appealing to today's fast-moving, practical, action-oriented, media-centered world. If you want to ponder Jesus' life and teachings, linger with Luke or meander with Matthew. If you want to be up and doing, march with Mark.

Not many people would volunteer to be a servant, but Jesus, God the Son, did just that. If we follow Jesus, we must also be servants—for him and for our neighbors. Do you want to be Jesus' servant? Read Mark.

Who wrote this Gospel? Mark's name was derived from his Roman name, Marcus. His Jewish name was John. To get to know the very human Mark, take a look in the garden of Gethsemane the night a mob came to arrest Jesus. You will see a naked young man running for his life. He didn't do much better years later, when he volunteered for missionary duty with Paul and Barnabas. Life got tough, and Mark quit almost before he got started. Paul wasn't happy with this young quitter and refused to take him on his second missionary journey, so Barnabas took Mark with him on a short-term missions trip to Cyprus. Much later Mark became Paul's staunch helper (2 Timothy 4:11; Philemon 1:24).

Mark was not one of the Twelve. Since Mark didn't walk with Jesus daily, as the apostles did, where did he get his information? Some believe that the content was Peter's, as filtered through Mark's consciousness. Peter grew to love Mark so much that he called him his son (1 Peter 5:13).

If you want to understand Mark better, watch him as he may have helped his mother, Mary, host Jesus and the apostles for the Last Supper in his mother's home. This was a gathering place for Jesus and the disciples, and it continued to be the gathering place for the believers after Jesus ascended into heaven. There the Holy Spirit appeared. There the believers held a prayer meeting for Peter when he was in prison. There Peter, freed by an angel, knocked on the door and was finally let in.

What everyone should know about the book of Luke

THE CHRIST OF COMPASSION

Have you ever wondered why God chose four different people to write the story of Jesus on earth? Wouldn't one account be enough? Not really.

The story of Jesus by Matthew was written for the Jewish people by a former Jewish tax collector. The story of Jesus by Mark was written for Romans by a young man whose mother's home in Jerusalem was the meeting place of the followers of Jesus. Now the story of the compassionate Jesus needed to be told through different eyes.

Enter a medical doctor, Luke. He was probably Greek, and if so, he was the only Greek to write a section of the Bible. He was certainly a Gentile, not a Jew. He was not one of the Twelve, so he did not walk with Jesus personally.

Luke sees his world through eyes of compassion. He focuses on the births of John the Baptist and Jesus as no other Gospel writer does. He pays special attention to illness, disease, suffering, and miracles.

Luke was a man of culture; he loved poetry, beauty, grace, and prayer. He speaks of women and children with a more loving voice than others would do. He reveals a Savior who had great compassion for the needy.

Since Luke did not walk with Jesus for three years as the twelve apostles did, where did he get his information? Some think that this highly educated doctor had learned to be an investigative reporter, and that he gathered wonderful accounts from people who were with Jesus. If this is true, he may have probed deeper and lingered longer than other writers. Imagine such a heart-to-heart conversation with Mary about the birth of Jesus. No other Gospel writer could have brought forth the wonderful story we read in Luke as well as a medical doctor could.

What everyone should know about the book of John

THE LIVING PORTRAIT OF THE SAVIOR

Matthew, the former Jewish tax collector, tells the story of Jesus for the Jewish people. Mark wrote the story of Jesus for Roman believers. Dr. Luke tells the story of the compassionate Jesus, who healed the sick and showed love to the unlovely.

But another story of Jesus was still needed, something quite unlike the other three Gospels. If Mark's Gospel is a fast-paced action video, John's Gospel is an art gallery, filled with elegant classical portraits of Jesus.

Here in John's gallery, do you see the painting of Jesus the Lamb of God? It's beautiful and tender, isn't it? What about the portrait of Jesus the Bread of Life or Jesus the Light of the World or Jesus the Good Shepherd? See also the True Vine, the Resurrection and the Life, and the Way, the Truth, and the Life. What a gallery of masterpieces!

For these portraits the Lord needed a special, tenderhearted person who was personally close to the heart of Jesus. That was John, the man who leaned on Jesus at the Last Supper and the man who walked closely with him for three years. John was the loving disciple who could paint beautiful portraits with his words.

John was so close to his subject that when Jesus was dying on the cross, Jesus chose him to take care of his mother, Mary. That tells us what Jesus thought of John.

John wrote his Gospel so that we might know Jesus as our Lord and Savior. He also wrote three Epistles, 1, 2, and 3 John, and the magnificent book of Revelation.

Did You Know?

Daniel and Mary have something in common The angel Gabriel spoke to Daniel more than five hundred years before he spoke to Zechariah and Mary (Daniel 8:16 and 9:21).

The name *Jesus* is the Greek form of the Hebrew name *Joshua* This means "Jehovah [God] is salvation."

SCENE 21

Announcing
the Birth
of the
King

<

321

Mary's pregnancy brought her the highest glory and the lowest shame Because Mary was the mother of Jesus, her pregnancy gave her greater honor than any other woman. No other woman in human history has become pregnant by the Holy Spirit. Mary's pregnancy also brought great shame, for to her friends, family, and neighbors, it appeared that she became pregnant as the result of an adulterous relationship, and they viewed Jesus as an illegitimate child.

Discovering My Purpose from God's Plan

1. *Cultural shame and heavenly glory may come in the same package.* Mary's pregnancy brought her cultural shame as well as heavenly glory. The same may be true for you when you act in obedience to the Lord.

2. *Cultural glory and heavenly shame may also come in the same package.* If Mary had refused to become the mother of Jesus, she would have had cultural approval but would have lost heavenly glory.

3. *Yesterday's scoundrel may be tomorrow's saint.* Take Matthew, who was once a hated tax collector but became the author of the first book of the New Testament. Jesus changed him, and he can also change others.

4. *Glorious endings may come from humble beginnings.* Who would have thought that the baby in the manger would redeem the world?

A Majestic, Ordinary Childhood
Jesus' Early Years

Characters:
Angels (who appeared to shepherds to announce Jesus' birth); Anna (an old woman in the Temple who waited for the Messiah); Caesar Augustus (who decreed the census that took Mary and Joseph to Bethlehem); Herod the Great (who slaughtered the babies of Bethlehem); an innkeeper of Bethlehem; Jesus; Joseph (Jesus' legal father); Mary (Jesus' mother); Simeon (an old man in the Temple who waited for the Messiah); teachers in the Temple (whom Jesus taught when he was twelve); wise men (who brought gifts to Jesus)

Time Period:
From the birth of Jesus until he was twelve

Dates:
Circa 6 or 5 B.C.– A.D. 7

Where Scene 22 of the Big Story Can Be Found:
Matthew 2:1-23; Luke 2:1-52

In Scene 22, Find the Answers to These Questions:
Why was Jesus born in a stable instead of a house?
How many angels sang to the shepherds?

Look for this in Scene 22
> There were two Bethlehems. Which was which?
> The shepherds saw a dazzling light that was far greater than the angels' appearance. What was it?
> A twelve-year-old boy taught the teachers.

 The Big Story So Far

A specific prophecy seven hundred years previous

About seven hundred years before Jesus was born, the prophet Micah wrote, "But you, O Bethlehem Ephrathah, are only a small village among all the people of Judah. Yet a ruler of Israel will come from you, one whose origins are from the distant past" (Micah 5:2). The prophecy is very specific. The Messiah would be born in Bethlehem of Judah.

There was one problem. Mary was expecting Jesus, and she and Joseph lived in Nazareth, about seventy miles north of Bethlehem of Judah (also called Judea). There was absolutely no reason for them to leave Nazareth and go that far during the latter part of Mary's pregnancy. Was there?

What took Mary and Joseph from Nazareth to Bethlehem?

It just so happened that the emperor, Caesar Augustus, decreed that a census be taken of the entire Roman world. Bethlehem of Judea was the ancestral home of both Mary and Joseph, who were descendants of King David, so they had to leave Nazareth and go to Bethlehem. God's plans transcend all other plans, even those of the Roman emperor.

The divine appointment for the Messiah to be born in Bethlehem of Judea had been made seven hundred years before, but Mary and Joseph arrived in Bethlehem on the eve of her delivery to find the inn completely booked. "No room in the inn," the innkeeper said, "but you may sleep in the stable."

The Incarnation—majestic humility

Mary gave birth to her firstborn son. She wrapped him in cloths and placed him in a manger, a feeding trough from which the animals ate. The Christmas story wouldn't have been quite the same if he had been born in a room in the inn or in a palace. Words such as *stable, manger, swaddling clothes,* and *firstborn son* have resonated in our hearts and minds every Christmas for centuries. These are words that speak of humility—the Son of God coming to earth in the lowliest way.

The greatest choir on earth

324

\>

What
Everyone
Should
Know
about
the

Bible

The story shifts to the lonely hillsides east of Bethlehem, where shepherds were taking care of their sheep. They too had a divine appointment, for an angel appeared with the message that the Messiah had been born in Bethlehem. His message was confirmed by the grandest angel choir ever heard since the dawn of Creation—about two hundred million angels from "the armies of heaven" (Luke 2:13). No wonder the shepherds were terrified!

The *shekinah* glory of the Lord
And if that weren't enough to overwhelm your imagination, "the radiance of the Lord's glory surrounded them" (Luke 2:9). The full brilliance of the Lord's glorious presence lit up the hills east of Bethlehem. This *shekinah* glory (a sign of the Lord's presence) was far more dazzling than the two hundred million angels.

The first visitors
As quickly as all of this appeared, it departed. Suddenly the shepherds were alone with their sheep. "Let's go to Bethlehem! Let's see this thing that has happened, which the Lord has told us about," they said (Luke 2:15). So they left their sheep and made their way to the stable. That night, these humble shepherds became evangelists, telling everyone about the child they had seen. Those who heard about it were amazed.

As Mary looked with wonder at the infant in the manger, she treasured all these things in her heart.

The day Jesus was named
When Jesus was eight days old, Joseph and Mary circumcised him and gave him the name Jesus, as the Lord had instructed through Gabriel. Later they went to the Temple for Mary's purification rites. Imagine their surprise when two older people, Simeon and Anna, rushed to see Jesus. These two godly people praised God that they had seen the Messiah for whom they had waited so long.

Wise men and rich treasures
Perhaps two years passed before wise men came from the east, following an amazing star that led them to Bethlehem. We know it was about two years because Herod slaughtered the infants of Bethlehem who were that age or younger. The wise men brought great gifts to Jesus, including gold, frankincense, and myrrh. These treasures may have provided the finances for Jesus and his parents when they fled to Egypt.

The coming of the wise men alerted King Herod to the "newborn king," whom he viewed as a grave threat to his throne. He ruthlessly ordered all infants in Bethlehem under the age of two to be slaughtered. Before this could happen, an angel warned Joseph in a dream, and Joseph quickly fled to Egypt with Mary and Jesus. They lived there for about two years until Herod died and the angel told them it was safe to return home.

Back to Nazareth, the childhood home of Jesus
At last Joseph and Mary safely returned to Nazareth, and Joseph resumed his work as a carpenter. Since every Jewish boy at that time had to learn a trade, Jesus became an apprentice to Joseph.

Each year Joseph, Mary, and Jesus went to Jerusalem to celebrate the Passover feast, as was expected of every Jewish man. Each family built a rough booth from sticks and lived in it during the week of the feast. The Passover was like a great family reunion with many celebrations.

When Jesus was twelve, he and his parents went again to Jerusalem for the Passover. At the end of the week, Mary and Joseph headed home with their friends and neighbors, who traveled together in a caravan for protection. Mary and Joseph assumed that Jesus was with relatives, so for a while they were not troubled by his absence. As time passed, they grew more concerned and looked everywhere for him. At last they returned to Jerusalem and searched for three days before they found him in the Temple, teaching the learned teachers of the law. How surprised they must have been to see their twelve-year-old son doing this!

Jesus returned to Nazareth with Mary and Joseph and grew up there. Joseph likely died before Jesus began his ministry, for he is never mentioned again in the Scriptures.

Questions You May Be Asking

How do we know that there were two hundred million angels with the shepherds?

We don't know for sure, but in Luke 2:13 we are told that the angel was "joined by a vast host of others" from "the armies of heaven." We encounter the armies of heaven again in Revelation 9:16, which tells us that there were two hundred million angels. Isn't it likely that these were the same angels who celebrated Creation with the morning stars?

Why did Micah and Luke refer to Bethlehem as Bethlehem of Judea (or Judah)? Why not just call it Bethlehem?

There were two villages named Bethlehem—the one in Judea where Jesus was born, and one in Galilee, seven miles northwest of Nazareth. Mary and Joseph would have passed by the Bethlehem that was seven miles away to go to the Bethlehem that was seventy miles away. The one Micah described is Bethlehem of Judah (or Judea). God knew which Bethlehem was which seven hundred years before Jesus was born.

What was "the radiance of the Lord's glory" that surrounded them?

The glory of the Lord that lit up the hills of Bethlehem is sometimes called the *shekinah glory*. It is the brilliance of the personal presence of the Lord. The word *shekinah* does not appear in the Bible.

Great Events of This Time

1. **Jesus is born** (Luke 2:1-7).
2. **Angels appear to some shepherds** (Luke 2:8-14).

326
>
What
Everyone
Should
Know
about
the
Bible

3. **Shepherds visit the baby Jesus** (Luke 2:15-20).
4. **Simeon and Anna see Jesus** (Luke 2:21-38).
5. **Wise men visit Jesus with gifts** (Matthew 2:1-12).
6. **The family flees to Egypt** (Matthew 2:13-15).
7. **Herod slaughters the babies of Bethlehem** (Matthew 2:16-18).
8. **Jesus grows up in Nazareth** (Luke 2:39-40).
9. **Jesus instructs the teachers in the Temple** (Luke 2:41-52).

Significant Dates of This Time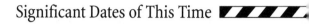

6 B.C.–5 B.C., Jesus is born, and angels and shepherds appear.
5 B.C.–4 B.C., the wise men visit, the holy family escapes to Egypt, and Herod slaughters the Bethlehem babies.
4 B.C.–3 B.C., Jesus and his family return to Nazareth.
Circa A.D. 6–A.D. 7, Jesus teaches the teachers in the Temple.

Heroes and Villains: The Stars of Scene 22

HEROD THE GREAT

Many years before Jesus was born, Herod the Great took possession of Palestine and ruled with an iron hand for thirty-four years. He was a cruel and heartless ruler who murdered innocent babies in an attempt to kill the Christ child. He even murdered his own wife Marianne and their children. Herod was loyal to the Roman emperors and named many of his far-flung building projects after them. The ruins of many of these projects remain today.

Bible events in Herod the Great's life
1. He brings the wise men to him and asks them to search for the Messiah and let him know where he is.
2. He becomes very angry when the wise men do not return and orders all the baby boys in Bethlehem to be killed.

JOSEPH, MARY'S HUSBAND

Joseph faithfully cared for Jesus and hid him in Egypt for a time to protect him from Herod. The last time Joseph is mentioned in the Bible is when he and Mary are with twelve-year-old Jesus at the Temple. Joseph probably died before Jesus entered his public ministry, leaving Mary as a widow.

Bible events in Joseph's life
1. He presents an offering at the Temple and brings Jesus to be dedicated.

2. An angel of God visits him in a dream.
3. He flees to Egypt with Mary and Jesus.
4. He returns to Nazareth with Mary and Jesus.
5. He takes Jesus to the Passover in Jerusalem and finds him in the Temple with the teachers.

MARY, JESUS' MOTHER

With Joseph, Mary went to Bethlehem, where Jesus was born, then moved on to Egypt to protect him from Herod. She returned to Nazareth and lived with Joseph until he died, apparently before Jesus' ministry began. Mary faithfully followed Jesus, even to the foot of the cross where he was crucified. She was among the women who came to his tomb the morning after the Sabbath ended. Mary lived with the apostle John after Jesus' death and ascension.

Bible events in Mary's life
1. With Joseph, she takes Jesus to the Temple.
2. She goes to Egypt with Joseph and Jesus.
3. She returns to Nazareth with Joseph and Jesus.
4. She goes to Jerusalem for the Passover with Jesus and Joseph; she and Joseph find Jesus in the Temple with the religious teachers.
5. She goes to a wedding in Cana with Jesus.
6. She and her other sons go to visit Jesus.
7. She stands beneath Jesus' cross, and Jesus tells John to take care of her.
8. She is present at a prayer meeting in the upper room after Jesus' ascension.

Did You Know?

The manger was not a wooden box Paintings often mistakenly show the manger as a wooden box, like those traditionally used on Midwestern grain farms. The manger was actually a stone trough made by hollowing out the center of a large stone block.

The inn was not a modern motel When you visit a motel today, you expect a certain level of hospitality—a private room; a bath with a toilet and tub; a clean, comfortable bed with a mattress, sheets, and pillows; clean towels; a restaurant with good food; and possibly a swimming pool and some game rooms. The inns of Bible times, such as the one at Bethlehem, were not like that. If you were fortunate, you might have a private room, but even that wasn't guaranteed. Forget about the bathroom with toilet and tub, skip the restaurant with food and table service, and don't even dream of game rooms and swimming pools. You might have a large courtyard for your animal to share with other animals. If all rooms

What
Everyone
Should
Know
about
the

Bible

were filled, you might also sleep and eat your own food there in the courtyard with the animals. You would be grateful to have a safe place to get off the street at night.

The cold winter night may not have been as cold as you think We often picture the Bethlehem hills on the night of Jesus' birth as wintry and bitterly cold. Winter nights were cold, but probably not as cold as what many Americans experience. The coldest temperature ever recorded in Israel is nineteen degrees Fahrenheit, but that was unusual. And it does snow occasionally in Jerusalem. But the night of Jesus' birth was probably not much colder than forty degrees Fahrenheit.

Jesus was probably not born on December 25, in the year 0 Jesus was probably born between 6 B.C.–5 B.C. No one knows for sure which day of the year he was born. During the fourth century A.D., the Western church settled on December 25 and the Eastern church settled on January 6 as the day to celebrate Christmas.

Discovering My Purpose from God's Plan

1. *There could have been no redemption without Incarnation, no death without birth, and no sacrifice without a body.* The birth of Jesus was pivotal to all that came after it. Remember to thank Jesus for his incarnation through his birth at Bethlehem.
2. *A person of great value deserves gifts of great value.* Read about the wise men, who brought expensive gifts to honor Jesus. Remember this when you give gifts.
3. *Wisdom and age are not always traveling companions.* Jesus was only twelve, but he taught the Jewish religious teachers. The teachers, who were much older, knew less about heaven than Jesus did.

Locusts and Wild Honey
John Prepares the Way

Characters:
Jesus; John the Baptist (who announced the coming of the Messiah); Satan (who tempted Jesus)

Time Period:
About thirty years after Jesus was born

Dates:
Circa A.D. 25–A.D. 26

Where Scene 23 of the Big Story Can Be Found:
Matthew 3:1-17; 4:1-11; Mark 1:1-13; Luke 3:1-22; 4:13; John 1:19-34

In Scene 23, Find the Answers to These Questions:
Why did the perfect Son of God want to be baptized?
Why did John call Jesus "the Lamb of God"?

Look for this in Scene 23
> A king's herald ate locusts.
> Jesus had a cousin.
> Satan memorized Scripture.
> Jesus defeated Satan with quotes from Deuteronomy.

The Big Story So Far

The King's herald

In days of old a herald often announced the coming of a king, perhaps with great fanfare. The King of kings was coming, but who would announce him? God sent as his herald a rugged wilderness preacher who dressed in rough garments, as Elijah had done, and even ate locusts and wild honey. His name was John the Baptist, and he was Jesus' cousin. This was the baby, now grown, who was promised to Zechariah and Elizabeth.

Throngs of people came to hear this rough hewn preacher, who was so different from the professional Pharisees, Sadducees, and scribes. John preached the people's need to repent, confess their sins, and get right with God. When they did, he baptized them in the Jordan River.

John defined his mission by quoting from Isaiah 40:3-5: "It's the voice of someone shouting, 'Clear the way through the wilderness for the LORD!'" John was called to prepare a pathway for the Messiah.

"I baptize with water those who repent of their sins and turn to God," John preached. "But someone is coming soon who is greater than I am—so much greater that I'm not worthy even to be his slave and carry his sandals. He will baptize you with the Holy Spirit and with fire."

That special someone was the long-awaited Messiah. The people didn't know it then, but his name was Jesus.

Baptizing the Son of God

When he was about thirty years old, Jesus came to the place where John was preaching and asked John to baptize him. John was shocked. Jesus was not a sinner who needed to turn from his sins. Why did he need to be baptized?

"I need to be baptized by you," John replied.

But Jesus insisted, mostly to set an example for others, so John baptized him in the Jordan River. When Jesus came up from the water, heaven opened and the Holy Spirit descended like a dove and landed on him. A voice from heaven called, "This is my dearly loved Son, who brings me great joy."

The greatest battle of all is between Satan and Jesus

332
>
What
Everyone
Should
Know
about
the
Bible

After his baptism, Jesus was led by the Spirit into a lonely place, probably in the nearby mountains. There Jesus fasted for forty days and forty nights, and he was often in prayer to his heavenly Father. When Jesus was desperately weak and hungry, Satan came to tempt him. If Jesus were to yield to Satan's temptation, all his future ministry would be destroyed. If he resisted, he could move ahead with his ministry.

Satan tempted Jesus three times to sin. First he tried to get Jesus to turn the nearby stones into bread. Jesus was famished from forty days of fasting, but he reminded Satan that the Scriptures tell us to feed on the Word of God (Deuteronomy 8:3).

Satan tried a second time. He took Jesus to the pinnacle of the Temple and tempted him to throw himself down to prove that he was God's Son. Satan even quoted Scripture, but Jesus used Scripture correctly to resist Satan, quoting Deuteronomy 6:16: "You must not test the LORD your God."

Once again Satan put Jesus to the test. This time he offered a power alliance. Satan would give Jesus power over the whole world if only he would bow down and worship him. Jesus again responded with Scripture: "You must fear the Lord your God and serve him" (Deuteronomy 6:13).

Satan was defeated. He knew then that he could not make Jesus sin, so he went away. Then angels came to Jesus and ministered to him. His great battle with the devil was over.

Who is this rugged preacher?

Meanwhile the Jewish leaders in Jerusalem sent priests and Levites to ask John the Baptist who he was. Was he the Messiah? John said no. Was he Elijah come back to life? Again, John said no. He wasn't even a prophet.

"I am a voice shouting in the wilderness, 'Prepare a straight pathway for the Lord's coming.'"

"Then what right do you have to baptize?" they asked.

"I baptize only with water," John replied. "But there is one among you who will soon begin his ministry. I am not worthy even to be his slave." John was announcing the Messiah's coming to them, but they were blind and deaf to his message.

The Lamb of God

The next day, John saw Jesus coming. "Look!" he shouted to the people. "There is the Lamb of God who takes away the sin of the world. I testify that he is the Son of God."

John had now fulfilled his life's mission—to announce the coming of the Messiah, the Son of God. Isaiah had prophesied John's mission seven hundred years earlier (Isaiah 40:3). The last prophet of the Old Testament had also prophesied John's mission more than four hundred years earlier (Malachi 4:5). At last John had arrived.

Questions You May Be Asking

Why did John baptize people?

Baptism is symbolic of the washing away of our sins, and of identification with Christ's death, burial, and resurrection. Today three modes of baptism are practiced among different groups of Christians: (1) In immersion, the person being baptized is fully submerged under water. Baptists and other evangelical groups use this mode. In the past some groups practiced trimersion, submerging the baptized person three times, once each for the Father, Son, and Holy Spirit. (2) Water may be poured over the head of the person who is baptized. (3) Water may be sprinkled over the person who is baptized. Some groups baptize infants, and some reject infant baptism.

Why was Jesus tempted? Satan didn't really think he could tempt God, did he?
Satan could not tempt God, of course. But Jesus had taken a human body upon himself, and with it our humanity, so Satan could tempt Jesus the man. In Hebrews we read, "This High Priest of ours [Jesus] understands our weaknesses, for he faced all of the same testings we do, yet he did not sin" (Hebrews 4:15). From this we gather that Jesus faced human temptations throughout his lifetime on earth, not this one time only.

Why did Jesus insist that John baptize him?
Jesus certainly had no sin, and it was he who would die, be buried, and rise again, so he did not need baptism. Just as Jesus submitted to all the temptations we face so that he would understand our weaknesses and help us resist them (Hebrews 4:15), so he also submitted to baptism to set an example for us and to relate to us more fully.

What was John's primary purpose in life?
John's main purpose was to announce the Messiah's coming. He did not live very long after he fulfilled his purpose, but his work was done.

 Great Events of This Time

1. **John the Baptist preaches; some priests and Levites ask who John is** (Matthew 3:1-12; Mark 1:1-8; Luke 3:1-18; John 1:19-34).
2. **Jesus is baptized** (Matthew 3:13-17; Mark 1:9-11; Luke 3:21-22).
3. **Jesus is tempted** (Matthew 4:1-11; Mark 1:12-13; Luke 4:1-13).

 Significant Dates of This Time

Circa A.D. 25–A.D. 26

What
Everyone
Should
Know
about
the
Bible

Heroes and Villains: The Stars of Scene 23

JOHN THE BAPTIST
In their old age, the priest Zechariah and his wife, Elizabeth, had a miracle son and named him John. He later became known as John the Baptist because he preached to people in the wilderness and baptized those who

repented of their sins. John wore coarse garments made of camels' hair, ate locusts and wild honey, and proclaimed the Messiah's coming to those who came to hear him. John baptized his cousin Jesus and identified him as God's Son, the Messiah. John met his death when Herodias tricked her husband, Herod Antipas, and demanded John's head on a platter.

Bible events in John the Baptist's life
1. He is born to Elizabeth and Zechariah.
2. He lives in the wilderness, and God speaks to him.
3. He proclaims news of the Messiah and baptizes believers.
4. He baptizes Jesus.
5. He points to Jesus as the Lamb of God.
6. He baptizes at Aenon and discusses Jesus' baptism with the disciples.
7. He condemns Herod Antipas and is thrown into prison.
8. He sends his disciples to ask Jesus a question.
9. He is beheaded by King Herod.

Did You Know?

Satan has done his Bible memory work Many are surprised to hear Satan quoting Psalm 91:11-12. Does the devil know the Bible? Of course he does. He can probably quote more memory verses than you can. He quotes Scripture for his own evil purposes, to deceive us. When we quote Scripture, it should be to please and honor God.

Jesus answered the devil from Deuteronomy All three Scripture verses that Jesus quoted to resist Satan's temptations come from Deuteronomy. Should we memorize Old Testament verses? Jesus did. Deuteronomy has many great passages that are vital to us today.

Dress code in the wilderness John the Baptist dressed much like Elijah, in hairy clothing (2 Kings 1:8). His "girdle" was a wide leather belt. Locusts were a poor man's food (Leviticus 11:21-22), and wild honey was plentiful in the hollows of logs and trees. Would you like to have Sunday dinner at John's house?

Father, Son, and Holy Spirit in one place Throughout Scripture, we encounter the Father, Son, and Holy Spirit individually, but it's not too often that all three are mentioned at the same time. At Jesus' baptism, the Holy Spirit descends on him like a dove, and we hear the voice of the Father from heaven. The Trinity—God the Father, God the Son, and God the Holy Spirit—was evident in one place at one time.

The Mount of Temptation is the traditional site of Jesus' temptation The Mount of Temptation is only a short distance west of Jericho. This traditional site of Jesus' temptation is very barren, a true wilderness.

 Discovering My Purpose from God's Plan

1. *Food without labor; fame without effort; power without service—we are all tempted with the same three temptations that Satan threw at Jesus.*

2. *Temptation is most vicious when we are most vulnerable.* Satan exploits our weakness to further weaken us. God works through our weakness to further strengthen us.

3. *Angels minister to us when we successfully resist temptation.* Angels ministered to Jesus when he had won his fight against Satan in the wilderness.

4. *The "Kingdom of Heaven" and the "Kingdom of God" mean the same thing.* The two terms are often used interchangeably.

Lamb of God

Jesus' Early Ministry

Characters:
Andrew (Jesus' first follower); John the Baptist; Nathanael (an early follower of Jesus); Nicodemus (a Pharisee who came to see Jesus one night); Philip (an early follower of Jesus); the Samaritan woman at the well; Simon Peter (Jesus' second follower)

Time Period:
Jesus' early ministry

Dates:
Circa A.D. 26–A.D. 27

Where Scene 24 of the Big Story Can Be Found:
Matthew 4:12; Mark 1:14-15; Luke 3:19-20; John 1:35–4:42

In Scene 24, Find the Answers to These Questions:
Why did Jesus whip some merchants?
Who was Jesus' first follower?
Why would someone hate the woman at the well?

Look for this in Scene 24
> Jesus made wine for a wedding.
> John 3:16 was first quoted to a Pharisee.
> The woman at the well was a Samaritan.
> Jacob dug the well where Jesus met the Samaritan woman.

The preparation for Jesus' ministry had ended. John the Baptist, the Messiah's herald, had announced to the world that Jesus, the Lamb of God, was indeed the Messiah, the Son of God for whom they had waited for centuries. He had come! He was here!

Jesus had been baptized. He had wrestled with Satan and won. Then he was ready to begin his ministry.

Jesus' first followers

The day after John the Baptist declared that Jesus was the Lamb of God, John was standing with two of his disciples, Andrew and another man, when Jesus came by. "Look! There is the Lamb of God!" John said again. The two disciples immediately followed Jesus to the place where he was staying and spent the rest of the day with him. Then Andrew hurried to find his brother and tell him the news.

"We have found the Messiah," Andrew told his brother. He brought his brother, whose name was Simon, to Jesus.

"You are Simon, son of John," Jesus said. "From now on you will be known as Cephas (or Peter)."

The next day Jesus left for Galilee. Along the way he asked Philip to follow him. Philip, like Andrew and Peter, was from Bethsaida, a town in Galilee. Before long Philip was convinced that Jesus was truly the Messiah, so he hurried to find his brother.

"We have found the Messiah," Philip told Nathanael. "He is from Nazareth."

Nathanael must have laughed when he heard that. Nazareth was an unimportant, virtually unknown little village without much of a reputation. "Can anything good come from Nazareth?" he asked.

But Nathanael went with Philip to see this man. As he approached, Jesus said, "Here is a good Israelite."

"How do you know me?" Nathanael asked.

"I saw you while you were under the fig tree before Philip found you," Jesus answered.

Nathanael must have caught his breath. Only God could see like that. "You really are the Messiah, God's Son," Nathanael whispered.

"You will see much greater things than that," Jesus said. "You will one day see heaven open and the angels of God ascending and descending on the Son of Man."

If Nathanael remembered his Scripture, he would have thought of the ladder that Jacob saw in a dream at Bethel, with angels of God ascending and descending on it. Could Jesus have been that ladder?

338

>

What
Everyone
Should
Know
about
the

Bible

The wedding in Cana

When Jesus and his friends arrived in Galilee, they went to a wedding in the village of Cana. Perhaps the bride or groom was a relative or a close friend of the family. Jesus' mother, Mary, was there and so were Jesus' new disciples.

Something went wrong with the wedding plans. Long before the end of the festivities, the host had no more wine. Mary told Jesus about the problem. She also told the servants, "Do whatever Jesus tells you."

There were six jars nearby, each large enough to hold twenty to thirty gallons. "Fill those to the brim with water," Jesus told the servants, so they did.

About that time the master of the wedding reception came by and tasted the water in the jars. He was so excited that he called the bridegroom over. "Usually people serve the best wine first," he said. "But you have reserved the best wine until the last."

This was Jesus' first public miracle, and it confirmed for his disciples that he was the Messiah. Then Jesus and his disciples visited Capernaum for a few days.

Jesus and the money changers

When the Passover came, Jesus and his disciples went to Jerusalem. It was expected that every Jewish male would take part in the Passover each year. When Jesus went into the Temple, he saw merchants selling cattle, sheep, and doves. There were money changers sitting at their tables, cheating those who needed the proper currency or denominations. Jesus had seen this many times before, but at last he could do something about it. He made a whip from cords and drove the merchants and money changers from the Temple, scattering their coins everywhere. This angered the religious leaders because they received some of the profit from these sales.

Nicodemus visits Jesus

One night, while Jesus was still in Jerusalem, staying at a friend's house, a Pharisee named Nicodemus came to see him. Nicodemus was a member of the Sanhedrin, the Jewish council of seventy.

"Rabbi, we know that you have come from God," he said. "No one could do the miracles you do unless God has sent him."

But Jesus knew why Nicodemus had come, so he went directly to the topic of everlasting life.

"You must be born again," Jesus told him.

Nicodemus was startled. How did Jesus know what he really wanted to discuss?

"How can I be born a second time?" he asked.

"Your first birth is earthly, from a human mother," Jesus said. "Your second birth is spiritual, from God."

Then Jesus told Nicodemus the truth that has been memorized by more people than any other verse in the Bible: "For God loved the world so much that he gave his one and only Son, so that everyone who believes in him will not perish but have eternal life. God sent his Son into the world not to judge the world, but to save the world through him" (John 3:16-17). There is the essence of salvation in just a few simple words. God loves us, gave his Son for us, and wants to save us and give us eternal life. The one condition is that we believe in Jesus as the Savior, the Messiah.

We don't know when Nicodemus became a believer—it was probably that very night. But after Jesus was crucified, Nicodemus cared for Jesus' body and helped to bury it.

We next find Jesus in the Judean countryside with his disciples, who were baptizing people. John the Baptist was at a place called Aenon near Salim, also baptizing, but a dispute had come up between John's disciples and Jesus' disciples. John's disciples weren't happy that Jesus' disciples were baptizing more people than John was. When John heard this, he quickly ended the dispute. "He is greater than I," John told his disciples. "He is the Son of God."

The Samaritan woman at a well

When Jesus heard about the disciples' dispute, he left Judea and the region near Jerusalem and headed home to Galilee. His route took him through Samaria. At the town of Sychar, Jesus and his disciples stopped at Jacob's well to rest. While the disciples went into town to buy food for lunch, Jesus stayed by the well.

Before long a Samaritan woman came to the well for some water.

"Will you give me a drink?" Jesus asked her.

The woman was startled. Usually Jewish people didn't talk with the hated Samaritans, and it was even more unusual for a Jewish man to speak to a Samaritan woman.

Jesus and the woman entered into a lively conversation. At last Jesus said to her, "Bring your husband here."

"I have no husband," she answered.

Jesus must have smiled at that. "That's right," he said. "You have had five husbands, but the man you are living with now is not your husband."

The woman was amazed. How did this stranger know so much about her? "You are a prophet," she said. "Some day the Messiah will come. He will know all things."

"I am the Messiah," Jesus told her.

340

>

What
Everyone
Should
Know
about
the

Bible

With that the woman ran back into town and told all her friends and neighbors about Jesus. Soon great crowds of people came out from Sychar, and many believed in Jesus as the Messiah.

Then Jesus headed home toward Galilee.

Questions You May Be Asking

Why were money changers in the Temple?

People came from all over the world to observe the Passover in Jerusalem, for it was expected that every Jewish male would go there each year. This meant that people who came to Jerusalem had different kinds of coins from their homelands. They couldn't spend foreign money in the Temple, so they had to exchange it for Jewish money. Money changers charged them excessive rates for the exchange and cheated people who had nowhere else to turn. Jesus was angry about this cheating. He was also angry that merchants had turned God's house into a mall.

Why were merchants selling oxen, sheep, and doves in the Temple?

These animals were sacrificed as burnt offerings to the Lord. It was more convenient to buy them at the Temple than to roam the city looking for animals to buy. Merchants who sold these animals undoubtedly charged much more than their value, so people were cheated twice—once when they changed their money and again when they bought their animals.

What kind of whip did Jesus use?

The whip Jesus used to drive the money changers and merchants from the Temple was a simple one made of cords. It was a gentle type of whip compared to the one the Romans (with the permission of the Jewish religious leaders) later used against Jesus. That one had pieces of metal embedded in it to tear the flesh apart.

Great Events of This Time

1. **Jesus calls his first disciples** (John 1:35-51).
2. **At Cana Jesus turns water into wine** (John 2:1-12).
3. **Jesus cleanses the Temple at Passover** (John 2:13-25).
4. **Jesus talks with Nicodemus** (John 3:1-21).
5. **John's disciples fear that Jesus is becoming greater than John** (John 3:22-36).
6. **John is imprisoned; Jesus travels through Samaria toward Galilee** (Matthew 4:12; Mark 1:14-15; Luke 3:19-20; John 4:1-3).
7. **Jesus meets a Samaritan woman at a well** (John 4:4-42).

Circa A.D. 26–A.D. 27

 Heroes and Villains: The Stars of Scene 24

NICODEMUS

The Pharisees, who were Jewish religious leaders, hated Jesus because he taught people that their rules were too harsh. They also feared that too many people would follow Jesus, which would cause the Romans to punish the nation and take away the Pharisees' important positions. Most Pharisees openly opposed Jesus and his disciples.

Early in his ministry Jesus was visited by the Pharisee Nicodemus, who asked him about the Kingdom of God. Nicodemus may have become a secret believer at that time. Toward the end of Jesus' ministry when the council of religious leaders made plans to crucify him, Nicodemus, who was also a member of the council, gathered enough courage to mildly protest the murderous plot. After Jesus was crucified, Nicodemus came forth openly with another prominent council member, Joseph of Arimathea, to claim Jesus' body and anoint it for burial with expensive spices.

Bible events in Nicodemus's life
1. He comes to see Jesus at night.
2. He speaks up for Jesus at the Feast of Tabernacles.
3. He provides spices to embalm Jesus' body and helps with his burial.

PETER

Simon, also called Peter, was a fisherman from Bethsaida who was in partnership with his brother Andrew as well as James, John, and their father, Zebedee. Andrew brought Peter to Jesus early in his ministry and followed Jesus faithfully from that time on. Peter was unusually loyal to Jesus, except for the infamous incident the night before the Crucifixion, when he denied his Lord. This uneducated fisherman became one of the great leaders of the early church, and he preached with mighty power and eloquence after the Holy Spirit came upon him. Tradition says that he was crucified in Rome during the time of Nero. By his own request he was executed with his head down so that his death would be different from that of his Lord. Peter is recognized as the author of the epistles bearing his name in the New Testament.

Bible events in Peter's life
1. Andrew brings him to Jesus.
2. Jesus asks Peter to follow him.

342

>

What
Everyone
Should
Know
about
the

Bible

3. Jesus visits his house and heals his mother-in-law.

4. Jesus chooses him as one of his twelve apostles.

5. He goes with Jesus, James, and John to Jairus's house, where Jesus raises Jairus's daughter from the dead.

6. He walks on the water toward Jesus, begins to sink, and calls for help.

7. He confesses that Jesus is the Christ, the Son of God.

8. Jesus rebukes him.

9. He goes with Jesus, James, and John to a mountain where Jesus is transfigured.

10. Tax collectors ask him about Jesus' taxes; he catches a fish with a silver coin in its mouth.

11. He protests when Jesus washes his feet at the Last Supper.

12. Jesus predicts that Peter will deny him.

13. Jesus takes him, James, and John apart from the other disciples in Gethsemane; Peter falls asleep.

14. He cuts off Malchus's ear with a sword, and Jesus rebukes him.

15. He denies Jesus, then goes out and weeps.

16. He and John run to the tomb on the morning of the Resurrection.

17. Jesus appears to him and several other disciples on the shore of the Sea of Galilee; Jesus tells him three times to feed his sheep.

18. He gathers with other disciples for a prayer meeting in an upper room after Jesus' ascension; he speaks to the disciples about choosing a replacement for Judas.

19. He is present at Pentecost when the Holy Spirit comes upon the apostles; he preaches a sermon to the Jews assembled there.

20. He and John heal a lame man at the Temple.

21. He preaches from Solomon's colonnade at the Temple.

22. He and John are arrested, put in prison, and appear before the Jewish council; he speaks to the council, and they are set free.

23. He exposes the sin of Ananias and Sapphira.

24. Crowds seek his healing shadow; he heals many people.

25. He and John are thrown into prison; an angel sets them free.

26. He and John are brought before the Sanhedrin, forbidden to preach about Jesus, beaten, and released.

27. He is sent with John to Samaria where the Holy Spirit comes upon the Samaritan believers by the laying on of hands; he rebukes Simon the magician for trying to buy the Holy Spirit.

28. He heals Aeneas and raises Dorcas from the dead.

29. He stays at the home of Simon the tanner, where he has a vision of a sheet filled with unclean animals; Cornelius sends for him.

30. He visits Cornelius and baptizes him and his family.

31. He is criticized for associating with the Gentiles; he explains his actions.
32. King Herod Agrippa I arrests Peter and puts him in prison; an angel frees him, and he visits a prayer meeting at John Mark's house.
33. He attends the Jerusalem conference and upholds the liberty of the Gentiles.

PHILIP, THE APOSTLE

Like Peter and Andrew, Philip was a resident of Bethsaida, a little fishing village by the Sea of Galilee. Jesus called him to be his disciple in the early years of his ministry. Philip then brought Nathanael to Jesus. Philip also brought others, especially Gentiles, to Jesus.

Bible events in Philip's life
1. Jesus calls him; he finds Nathanael and brings him to Jesus.
2. Jesus chooses him to be one of the twelve apostles.
3. Jesus tests him with a question.
4. Greeks come to him and ask to see Jesus.
5. At the Last Supper, he asks Jesus to show the disciples the Father.

Did You Know?

Where was Cana of Galilee? The traditional site of Cana is known as Kefr Kenna, about five miles northeast of Nazareth. There are three other possible sites, one of which is Kana-el-Jelil, a little north of Kefr Kenna.

What kind of celebration was the wedding at Cana? Weddings in Jesus' time did not take place in a church, as ours do today. The arrangements for marriage began with betrothal, a period similar to an engagement but more binding. The wedding itself began when the bridegroom dressed in his finest clothes, went to the bride's house, and escorted her back to his house, which was filled with the people who had been invited. The wedding celebration lasted between seven and fourteen days. It began with singing, shouting, and playing musical instruments. There was a great feast with plenty of wine. When the festivities ended, the bridegroom took his bride to the wedding chamber to consummate their marriage.

The house where Nicodemus came to see Jesus We don't know for sure which house this was, but it may have been the home of John Mark's mother. The disciples also may have waited for the risen Jesus there, and still later they may have waited there for the coming of the Holy Spirit. Nothing is said about Mark's father, so his mother may have been a wealthy widow. This is the same Mark who wrote the Gospel of Mark.

344
>
What
Everyone
Should
Know
about
the
Bible

Why did the Jewish people hate the Samaritans? Flash back to 722 B.C., when
the Assyrians conquered the northern kingdom of Israel and its capital
city, Samaria. Assyria took many of the choicest people into captivity
and left behind many of the poorer people who were considered inferior. The people who were left behind intermarried with the foreigners
the Assyrians brought into the land. The Jewish people of Jesus' time
hated this mixed race, called Samaritans, because of racial prejudice.

What was Jacob's well? The well where Jesus talked with the Samaritan
woman was the well that Jacob had dug hundreds of years before.
When Jacob came home from Haran with his wives and his livestock,
he settled briefly near this place and dug the well, which at one time
was 240 feet deep. Joseph is buried nearby.

Discovering My Purpose from God's Plan ▰▰▰▰

1. *Jesus is not racially prejudiced.* In his time, racial prejudice was focused
   mostly against the Samaritans, the mixed race that settled in ancient
   northern Israel. Jesus showed that he loves all people, no matter what
   race they are.
2. *Jesus knew how to have fun.* We see him enjoying the festivities at the
   wedding at Cana, even making wine for the bridegroom.
3. *A house is sometimes more than a home.* The house of Mark's mother
   may have been a meeting place for Jesus and his disciples. Perhaps
   Nicodemus heard the gospel there also. It may have been the place
   where they celebrated the Last Supper and where the disciples waited
   for the risen Christ, chose the disciple to replace Judas, and waited
   for the Holy Spirit. Think of the ministry this wonderful woman
   may have had in her house, and think of the ministry you can have
   in yours!

The First Miracles

Jesus in Galilee and Jerusalem

Characters:
Herod Antipas (who imprisoned John the Baptist); Herodias (who married Herod Antipas); Jesus and his disciples; John the Baptist (who was imprisoned for criticizing Herod Antipas); Matthew (or Levi, the tax collector who followed Jesus); some Nazarene neighbors (who almost killed Jesus); an official in Capernaum (whose son Jesus healed); Peter; several sick people whom Jesus healed

Time Period:
Jesus' early ministry

Dates:
Circa A.D. 27

Where Scene 25 of the Big Story Can Be Found:
The Gospels: Matthew, Mark, Luke, and John. See "Great Events of This Time," page 353, for specific references.

In Scene 25, Find the Answers to These Questions:
Since the demons knew that Jesus was God's Son, why didn't the religious leaders know?
Why did Jesus' neighbors in his hometown try to kill him?
How do we know that Peter was married?

Look for this in Scene 25
> Jesus healed a boy without seeing him or touching him.
> A man was brought to Jesus through the roof.
> A tax collector wrote the first book of the New Testament.

The Big Story So Far

Near Sychar the arms of the gospel reached wide to embrace the hated Samaritans, a mixed race of Jews and Gentiles. With Jesus' marvelous reception at Jacob's well by the people who swarmed out from Sychar, who could doubt that the gospel is for anyone and everyone?

From Jacob's well, Jesus went northward to Galilee, where his hometown of Nazareth was located. His Galilean neighbors had been in Jerusalem and had seen him do wonders there, so they welcomed him. These wonders should have been sufficient evidence that Jesus was the Messiah, but as we'll see, it wasn't enough. Even his hometown would reject him.

Long-distance healing

Jesus' first stop in Galilee was Cana, where he turned water into wine. About this time a royal official from Capernaum was concerned for his sick son. When this official heard that Jesus had returned to Galilee, he hurried to Cana to meet him and begged him to come to Capernaum to heal his son.

"Go home," Jesus told him. "Your son is well."

The man believed Jesus and hurried home. Along the way his servants met him with the incredible news that his son was well—and the fever had left him at the exact time Jesus had said he would be well. The man and his entire household became believers and accepted Jesus as the Messiah.

John the Baptist is imprisoned

John the Baptist rebuked Herod Antipas because he had married Herodias, the wife of his brother, Herod Philip I. Herod angrily put John into prison. Later, this same Herod would judge Jesus before his crucifixion. Herod stealing his brother's wife was but one of many vile sins that infected the Herodian clan.

The not-so-friendly Nazarene neighbors

On the Sabbath Jesus went to the synagogue at Nazareth and stood up to read. The scroll of the prophet Isaiah was given to him. Jesus unrolled it and began to read from Isaiah 61:1-2, which is a prophecy concerning the coming Messiah.

After reading the Scripture, Jesus rolled up the scroll, handed it to the attendant, and sat down to speak. Everyone stared at him, listening intently.

"This Scripture has come true today before your very eyes."

The people whispered good things to one another about this preacher, but they wondered aloud, "How can this be? This is just Joseph's son."

348

>

What
Everyone
Should
Know
about
the

Bible

Jesus continued, "You probably wonder why I don't do miracles here as I do elsewhere, but a prophet is not honored in his own hometown."

Then Jesus began to speak of the foreigners God had favored over the course of Israel's history. The mood quickly changed from sweet talk to fury. Jesus' neighbors were so angry that they mobbed him and took him to a high cliff, intending to push him to his death. But Jesus slipped through the crowd and left.

A new home for Jesus

Jesus' hometown of Nazareth had rejected him, so he moved to Capernaum and taught in the synagogue there every Sabbath. The people were amazed at the authority of his preaching, which was not like that of the religious leaders.

One day a man possessed by a demon came to the synagogue. He began shouting at Jesus, "Go away! I know who you are—the Holy One sent from God."

The demon recognized Jesus as the Messiah, even when the people did not.

"Be silent," Jesus commanded. "Come out of the man!"

The demon threw the man on the floor and left him. The people were amazed, marveling at the power Jesus had, even over evil spirits. Of course, the news spread like wildfire throughout the region.

Peter's mother-in-law

When Jesus left the synagogue that day, he went to Peter's home. According to tradition, Peter lived in Capernaum a short distance from the synagogue. When they arrived at his home, they found Peter's mother-in-law sick with a high fever.

"Please heal her," everyone begged.

Jesus stood by her bedside and commanded the fever to leave her. Immediately the woman was well, and she got up and prepared a meal for them.

After sunset that evening people brought the sick and demon-possessed to Jesus, and he healed many of them. He drove out demons, but he commanded the demons to keep quiet, for they knew that he was the Messiah.

A healing ministry

Early the next morning while it was still dark, Jesus left the house and went to a lonely place to pray. When the disciples found him, they urged him to come back, for everyone was looking for him.

"We must go somewhere else," Jesus said, "so I can preach there also. That is why I have come."

Jesus and his disciples went throughout Galilee, teaching in the synagogues, preaching the Good News of God's kingdom, and healing sick people. News of Jesus' miracles spread far and wide, and many brought sick friends and relatives to him for healing. Before long large crowds swarmed around Jesus wherever he went.

One day a man with leprosy knelt before Jesus and begged Jesus to heal him. No one would touch a leper in those days, because they might also get the disease, but Jesus reached out and touched the man.

"Show yourself to the priest and do the rituals for cleansing," Jesus told him. The man was healed instantly and went all over the region telling people of the miracle. This brought even greater crowds to Jesus.

Through the roof to Jesus

When Jesus returned home to Capernaum, four men brought a paralyzed friend on a cot, hoping that Jesus would heal him. But they couldn't get through the crowd to the house where Jesus was healing others. One of them had an idea—they climbed up on the roof, pulled aside some of the loose roofing material, and let the man down through the opening. When Jesus saw their faith, he said, "Take heart, son! Your sins are forgiven."

Some nearby teachers of the law were angry when they heard this.

"Blasphemy!" they shouted. "Only God can forgive sins."

Of course, they didn't realize that Jesus was God the Son.

"Is it easier for me to say that his sins are forgiven or to tell him to get up and walk?" Jesus asked. "But I will prove that I have authority to forgive sins."

Then Jesus spoke again to the paralyzed man: "Stand up, take your mat, and go on home, because you are healed."

The man jumped up and went home. Great awe and fear swept through the crowd when they saw this. Jesus unquestionably had the power to heal and to forgive sins.

This was just one of many times that the religious leaders challenged Jesus and his authority. He was a threat to them. They were the official religious leaders in Israel—how could they let this carpenter from Galilee overshadow them?

Levi follows Jesus

350

>

What
Everyone
Should
Know
about
the

As Jesus walked along the Sea of Galilee, he passed by the tax collection booth of a man named Levi. Like all tax collectors, Levi was despised by other Jewish people. Tax collectors gathered taxes for Rome, but they collected more than Rome required and kept the extra for themselves. They got rich by cheating their fellow Jews.

Jesus may have talked with Levi many times, urging him to follow him, but if so, today *was* different. Levi had reached a decision. He would leave his tax booth and follow Jesus. We remember Levi by a different name—he was Matthew, who later wrote the first book of the New Testament.

Levi had a big feast for Jesus at his house, and he invited many tax collectors and friends.

The Pharisees, of course, thought that all of these people were the worst of sinners. "Why do you eat and drink with tax collectors and sinners?" they demanded of Jesus.

"Healthy people don't need a doctor; sick people do," Jesus answered. "I have come to call sinners, not those who think they are already good enough."

A time to feast and a time to fast

One day the disciples of John the Baptist asked Jesus, "Why do we and the Pharisees fast, but your disciples don't?" Jesus answered that while he was still with them, it was time to celebrate. The time to fast would come later.

At the pool called Bethesda

It was time once again to go to Jerusalem for a Jewish feast. Near the Sheep Gate there was a pool called Bethesda, which was surrounded by five covered colonnades. Many sick people gathered there, for tradition held that the first person to go into the waters after they were stirred up would be healed. One man had been there for thirty-eight years, waiting hopelessly to get into the water and be healed.

"Do you want to get well?" Jesus asked him.

It seemed a strange question, but the man answered, "When the waters stir, I have no one to help me in. Someone else is always ahead of me."

"Pick up your mat and walk," Jesus told the man. Immediately the man was healed, so he picked up his mat and carried it away. This happened on the Sabbath, when people were not to do any work, even carrying a mat, so it wasn't long before some religious leaders accused the man of breaking the law. They were angry at the man who was healed but even more angry at Jesus. It was more important to them that the Sabbath laws were kept than that someone should be healed.

Harvesting on the Sabbath

On the way back to Galilee, Jesus and his disciples passed by a grain field. The disciples were hungry, so they plucked some grain and ate it. This stirred the religious leaders up again, for again this happened on the Sabbath. Even plucking a few grains to eat was considered work.

Jesus told them, "The Sabbath was made for man, not man for the Sabbath. So the Son of Man, Jesus, is Lord even of the Sabbath."

A man with a withered hand

On another Sabbath Jesus saw a man in the synagogue who had a withered hand. The religious leaders were watching Jesus to see what he would do. They didn't care about the poor man and his hand—they were only concerned about whether or not Jesus would heal on the Sabbath, for that was considered work and was not to be done.

"Is it legal to work by healing on the Sabbath?" they asked him.

"If any of you had a sheep that fell into a well on the Sabbath, wouldn't you work to get it out? Of course you would! How much more valuable is a person than a sheep! Yes, it is right to do good on the Sabbath."

Then Jesus told the man to stretch out his hand, and he healed him. The Pharisees and other religious leaders began making plans to kill Jesus. Jesus left that area and went along the Sea of Galilee, where large crowds swarmed around him, hoping to be helped or healed. To avoid the crush of the crowd, Jesus asked his disciples to prepare a small boat in which he could sit and teach them.

Questions You May Be Asking

Did Jesus heal many kinds of sickness?

The four Gospels record thirty-five miracles of Jesus, of which twenty-three are miracles of healing. He gave hearing to the deaf, sight to the blind, and speech to the mute. He helped the lame to walk, restored a withered or deformed hand, healed paralytics, drove out demons, and cured leprosy.

Do we know where Capernaum is today?

The ruins of Capernaum are now called Tell Hum. They are located along the northwest shore of the Sea of Galilee, about twenty miles east of Nazareth. There are ruins of an ancient synagogue and of what some think is the foundation of Peter's house.

How do we know that Peter was married?

The story in Matthew 8:14-17; Mark 1:29-34; and Luke 4:38-41 is about Jesus healing Peter's mother-in-law. To have a mother-in-law, a man must first have a wife!

If evil spirits knew that Jesus was the Messiah, why didn't they accept him?

The answer is simple. They belonged to the devil, and he controlled them, so they could not accept Jesus. How sad for them to know that Jesus was the Messiah and yet not be able to accept him. The Pharisees did not even recognize that Jesus was the Messiah.

352

>

What
Everyone
Should
Know
about
the

Bible

Great Events of This Time

1. **Jesus heals a nobleman's son** (John 4:43-54).
2. **Jesus teaches at the synagogue in Nazareth, and people try to throw him off a cliff** (Luke 4:16-30).
3. **Jesus moves to Capernaum** (Matthew 4:13-17).
4. **Jesus performs the miracle of the great catch of fish** (Luke 5:1-11).
5. **Jesus calls four disciples** (Matthew 4:18-22; Mark 1:16-20).
6. **Jesus teaches in the synagogue at Capernaum and heals a man with an unclean spirit** (Mark 1:21-28; Luke 4:31-37).
7. **Jesus heals Peter's mother-in-law** (Matthew 8:14-17; Mark 1:29-34; Luke 4:38-41).
8. **Jesus tours Galilee, teaching and healing** (Matthew 4:23-25; Mark 1:35-39; Luke 4:42-44).
9. **Jesus heals a leper who tells everyone about it** (Matthew 8:1-4; Mark 1:40-45; Luke 5:12-16).
10. **A paralyzed man is lowered through a roof to Jesus** (Matthew 9:1-8; Mark 2:1-12; Luke 5:17-26).
11. **Jesus calls Matthew** (Matthew 9:9; Mark 2:13-14; Luke 5:27-28).
12. **Matthew gives a dinner party** (Matthew 9:10-13; Mark 2:15-17; Luke 5:29-32).
13. **Jesus speaks of wineskins and patched garments** (Matthew 9:14-17; Mark 2:18-22; Luke 5:33-39).
14. **Jesus heals a sick man on the Sabbath at the pool of Bethesda** (John 5:1-18).
15. **Jesus' disciples pick grain on the Sabbath in the wheat fields** (Matthew 12:1-8; Mark 2:23-28; Luke 6:1-5).
16. **Jesus heals a man with a withered hand** (Matthew 12:9-14; Mark 3:1-6; Luke 6:6-11).
17. **Jesus teaches and heals great multitudes by the Sea of Galilee** (Matthew 12:15-21; Mark 3:7-12).

Significant Dates of This Time ▰▰▰▰

Circa A.D. 27

Heroes and Villains: The Stars of Scene 25 ▰▰▰▰

MATTHEW

Levi, son of Alphaeus, collected taxes at a customs booth at Capernaum, along the road from Damascus to Jerusalem. This was the same road where Jesus would appear to Saul, who would become his follower. Like all publicans, Levi was a wealthy man because tax collectors took more from the people than Rome required and kept the extra. When Jesus called him to become his disciple, Levi left his prosperous business and apparently changed his name to Matthew. Jewish tax collectors, who were employed by the Roman government, were usually hated by their fellow Jews, and Matthew was probably no exception. However, his name has been precious to centuries of Christians because his Gospel is one of the most widely read and best loved accounts of the life of Jesus Christ on earth.

Bible events in Matthew's life
1. Jesus meets him at his tax office and calls Matthew to follow him.
2. He invites Jesus to dinner.
3. He is chosen as one of the twelve apostles.
4. He takes part in all of the activities of the Twelve.

Did You Know?

The hole in the roof Because of how houses are made today, you might be horrified at the thought of making a hole in the roof to let a friend through it. But in Bible times roofs were different, often made of mud mixed with straw. It was a simple matter to pull aside a small part of this roof and then replace it.

A prophet is not honored in his hometown To the people of Nazareth, Jesus was the boy next door. How could he be the Messiah? He was Joseph the carpenter's son. Perhaps he'd once made a cart wheel for them. The Messiah? They couldn't believe it—they saw him grow up. He was too close for them to see who he really was.

Leprosy was the scourge of Jesus' time Today we speak of AIDS as the scourge of society—partly because it is so deadly and partly because we have yet to find a satisfactory cure. In Jesus' time, leprosy was the scourge. Leprosy was a skin disease that caused patches of skin to turn white and often disfigured the fingers or toes. It was a dreaded disease, and victims were forced to call out "Unclean!" in the presence of others so that everyone could keep their distance. The victim had to live away from his family. It was up to the priests to determine whether or not a person was infected or if an infected person had healed. When Jesus healed lepers, he instructed them to visit a priest to confirm their healing, go through the purification rites, and be restored to society and Temple life.

354
>
What
Everyone
Should
Know
about
the

Bible

Discovering My Purpose from God's Plan

1. *Honor the prophet next door.* The people of Nazareth had the awesome privilege of living with the Messiah, but their privilege became their downfall. They couldn't accept the boy next door as the Messiah.

2. *Privilege may be our downfall.* Economic wealth may breed spiritual poverty. Educational wealth may deprive us of wisdom. Military wealth may create a spirit of self-dependence that deprives us of God's greatest resources. The privilege of proximity may make us too close to someone to give that person the honor he or she may deserve.

3. *Wisdom requires that we recognize the distinction between good and evil.* If we confuse the two in either direction, we are in trouble. Evil forces can see good but cannot accept it, just as good forces can see evil and not accept it. The demons recognized Jesus as the Messiah. The Pharisees did not. Instead they rejected the Messiah and made plans to murder him. Beware when you see evil and consider it good or see good and consider it evil.

Jesus and the Twelve
Choosing the Disciples

Characters:
Jesus and the Twelve: Andrew (Peter's brother); Bartholomew; James; James the son of Alphaeus; John; Judas son of James; Judas Iscariot; Matthew (formerly called Levi); Philip; Simon Peter; Simon the Zealot; Thomas (who would later doubt Jesus' resurrection)

Time Period:
Near the midpoint of Jesus' ministry

Dates:
Circa A.D. 28

Where Scene 26 of the Big Story Can Be Found:
Matthew 5–7; Mark 3:13-19; Luke 6:12-49

In Scene 26, Find the Answers to These Questions:
Why did Jesus pray all night?
Why did Jesus choose twelve apostles? Why not eleven or thirteen?
What are the Beatitudes?

Look for this in Scene 26
> Apostle or disciple—what is the difference?
> Which of the apostles had two names?

Jesus' all-night prayer session

Have you ever prayed all night in a secluded place? Perhaps you have done something similar prior to a significant event in your life. Before choosing his twelve apostles, Jesus went to a secluded mountainside and prayed all night, talking over his choices with his heavenly Father.

Choosing the Twelve

When morning came, Jesus called his disciples together and identified the Twelve he had chosen as his apostles. They were Simon, also called Peter; Andrew, Peter's brother; James; John; Philip; Bartholomew; Matthew, formerly called Levi; Thomas, who would later doubt Jesus' resurrection; James, son of Alphaeus; Simon the Zealot; Judas, son of James; and Judas Iscariot, who would later betray Jesus.

After this Jesus went with his apostles to a level place. A great crowd of disciples swarmed around Jesus and the Twelve, including people from Judea and Jerusalem and even from the coast of Tyre and Sidon. All of these people wanted to hear Jesus teach, to be healed, or to bring family or friends to be healed. They knew that if they just touched Jesus they would be healed, for healing power flowed from him.

The Sermon on the Mount

As the crowds grew, Jesus went with his disciples to a mountainside to teach. His teaching there has become known as the Sermon on the Mount. The sermon begins with the Beatitudes—a series of "Blesseds" that on the surface seem to be rules for happiness. In a larger sense, the Beatitudes and the rest of the sermon that follows establish Jesus' view of his kingdom, which looks nothing like a worldly kingdom. Here in this world, who can be happy when persecuted? Who can be a chief by first becoming a servant, a leader by first becoming a follower, a rich person despite economic poverty?

Jesus made it clear in his sermon that he did not come to abolish the law of Moses but to fulfill it. The law remains, not as a burden but as a blessing. It is not to be used as a whip but as a guide; it is not to be a presentation of human will but of the will of God. The law shows us how to live for God and obey him. Jesus' gospel transcended the law, for it set holier standards than the law's rigid requirements.

At that time the law had been compromised by the Jewish religious leaders. They saw the law as a whip, as a rigid set of rules to be followed, even if it meant rejecting God's Son and disobeying God. These leaders had added to the law and created extra guidelines that kept them in positions of authority. Jesus cut through all of this with the simple message, "Love God with all your heart, soul, mind,

358

>

What
Everyone
Should
Know
about
the

Bible

and strength, and your neighbor as yourself; obey God because you love him." This is the essence of the covenant God originally made with Abraham and continued to affirm with Abraham's descendants through Isaac and Jacob.

The people were amazed at Jesus' teachings, for they were so unlike the teachings of their religious leaders. The religious leaders, who wanted to hold on to their power, had made the whole law into a burdensome and superficial ritual. Jesus came to make it a significant blessing. The purpose behind the religious leaders' teachings was for people to obey them. The purpose behind Jesus' teachings was the same as that of the law—for people to obey God.

Questions You May Be Asking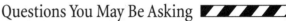

Why did Jesus choose twelve apostles? Why not fourteen or ten?
The number twelve had symbolic meaning to the Jewish people. There were twelve sons of Jacob, and thus twelve tribes of Israel. Because of this, the number twelve took on special significance and appeared a number of times in the history and worship of Israel: Moses set up twelve pillars around an altar he built at the foot of Mount Sinai (Exodus 24:4); there were twelve jewels in the high priest's breastpiece (Exodus 28:21); there were twelve loaves or cakes of bread in the Holy Place (Leviticus 24:5); Moses used twelve rods to test the authenticity of Aaron and the Levites (Numbers 17:1-9); Joshua placed twelve stones in the Jordan River when he crossed to begin the conquest (Joshua 4:9); Solomon appointed twelve officers (1 Kings 4:7); Elijah made an altar of twelve stones to challenge the priests of Baal (1 Kings 18:31).

What is the difference between an apostle and a disciple?
A disciple was a follower. Jesus had many disciples, including the Twelve whom he chose to be his apostles. *Apostle* means "messenger," someone chosen and sent with a special commission for a certain task. The Twelve were the select group that Jesus would train during his time on earth. They would build his church after he ascended into heaven. All other followers were disciples. Until the Twelve were chosen as apostles, they were also disciples.

Great Events of This Time

1. **Jesus chooses twelve apostles** (Mark 3:13-19; Luke 6:12-16).
2. **Jesus preaches the Sermon on the Mount** (Matthew 5–7; Luke 6:17-49).

Significant Dates of This Time

Circa A.D. 28

Heroes and Villains: The Stars of Scene 26

JOHN THE APOSTLE

John was one of the two sons of Zebedee, a prominent fisherman on the Sea of Galilee (the other son was James). When Jesus called James and John to follow him, they responded and became two of his twelve disciples. Their mother, Salome, was possibly the sister of Mary, Jesus' mother. If this is true, then they were Jesus' cousins. Jesus called James and John the "sons of thunder," probably because they were filled with energy and zeal. John is the author of the four books of the New Testament that bear his name, as well as Revelation.

Bible events in John's life
1. Jesus calls him to be his follower.
2. He goes with Jesus and James to Peter's home, where Jesus heals Peter's mother-in-law.
3. Jesus chooses him as one of the twelve apostles.
4. He goes with Jesus, Peter, and James to Jairus's house, where Jesus raises Jairus's daughter from the dead.
5. He witnesses Jesus' transfiguration.
6. He and James want to call fire down from heaven to destroy the Samaritans; Jesus rebukes them.
7. He and James ask Jesus for a special place in his kingdom; the other disciples become angry.
8. He asks Jesus who will betray him.
9. Jesus takes him, Peter, and James apart from the other disciples in Gethsemane; John falls asleep.
10. From the cross, Jesus tells him to take care of Jesus' mother, Mary.
11. He and Peter run to the tomb on the morning of the Resurrection; he realizes that Jesus has risen from the dead.
12. The resurrected Jesus appears to him and several other disciples on the shore of the Sea of Galilee; he is the first to recognize Jesus.
13. He gathers with other disciples in an upper room for a prayer meeting after Jesus' ascension.
14. He and Peter heal a lame beggar at the Temple.
15. He and Peter are arrested and put in prison; they appear before the Jewish council and are set free.
16. He and Peter are thrown into prison; an angel sets them free.
17. He and Peter are called before the Sanhedrin and are forbidden to preach about Jesus; they are beaten and released.

360

>

What
Everyone
Should
Know
about
the

Bible

18. He is sent with Peter to Samaria, where the Holy Spirit comes upon the Samaritan believers through the laying on of hands.

Did You Know?

Two apostles with the same name Among the twelve apostles, there were two Simons—Simon Peter and Simon the Zealot. There were two named James—James the brother of John and son of Zebedee, and James the son of Alphaeus. There were also two named Judas—Judas the son of James and Judas Iscariot.

Two men named John John the Baptist was the forerunner of Jesus, and later became one of his followers. He was arrested by Herod and subsequently beheaded. John the apostle and his brother, James, were sons of Zebedee. They were also disciples, or followers, of Jesus.

Apostles with two names Bartholomew was also known as Nathanael, the man Philip brought to Jesus. Thomas was sometimes called Didymus, which means "the twin," and James the son of Alphaeus was also known as James the Less, possibly because he was younger or shorter than James the brother of John.

Discovering My Purpose from God's Plan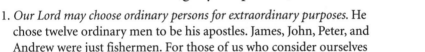

1. *Our Lord may choose ordinary persons for extraordinary purposes.* He chose twelve ordinary men to be his apostles. James, John, Peter, and Andrew were just fishermen. For those of us who consider ourselves ordinary, this is a great comfort.
2. *Our Lord permits evil and good to work together until he separates them.* When Jesus chose the Twelve, he chose Judas Iscariot even though he knew that Judas would betray him. If you wonder why evil sometimes works side by side with good, remember Judas. There will come a time of accounting.
3. *The gospel is a blessing, not a burden.* It frees us from sin rather than oppressing us.

A Prophet in His Own Country

Jesus in Galilee Again

Characters:
Jesus and his disciples; Joanna, wife of Chuza; Mary Magdalene (from whom Jesus cast out seven demons); a Roman centurion (whose servant Jesus healed); Simon the Pharisee (who served dinner to Jesus); Susanna; a widow of Nain (whose son Jesus raised from the dead); a woman who washed and anointed Jesus' feet (at Simon the Pharisee's house)

Time Period:
About midpoint in Jesus' ministry

Dates:
Circa A.D. 28–A.D. 29

Where Scene 27 of the Big Story Can Be Found:
Matthew 8:5-13; 11:2-24; 12:38-45; Mark 3:20-30; Luke 7:1–8:2; 11:14-32

In Scene 27, Find the Answers to These Questions:
Who washed Jesus' feet with her tears?
Why was a Roman centurion humble?

Look for this in Scene 27
> Where did guests lie down to eat dinner?
> A woman had seven demons, but Jesus drove them out.

The Big Story So Far

The Sermon on the Mount was over. The vast crowd of people was awed by Jesus' teachings, which were filled with power and purpose and were unlike the rituals and teachings of the self-serving Pharisees and Sadducees. Jesus left the mountain and went home to Capernaum.

A humble centurion

Before Jesus reached Capernaum, some Jewish elders approached him with a bold request. A Roman centurion had asked them to beg Jesus for help because his highly valued servant was near death. Would Jesus come and heal him?

"This man deserves your help," the elders said. "He loves our nation and has even built our synagogue." So Jesus started with them toward the centurion's house.

Along the way some of the centurion's friends met Jesus with a message from him. "Please don't trouble yourself to come to my house," the centurion said. "I'm not worthy to have you visit. Please just say the word, and my servant will be healed. I know this is true because I have men under me and they obey my authority."

"I haven't seen such faith among the people of Israel," Jesus said. He sent a message to the centurion that his servant was healed, and the servant was healed at that very moment.

The widow of Nain's son comes back from the dead

Not long after that, Jesus and his disciples passed through the little town of Nain. A great crowd was with them, as usual. As they approached the town gate, a funeral procession was coming out. The dead person was the only son of a poor widow, who now faced a life of poverty without her son to take care of her.

Jesus had great sympathy for the woman. "Don't cry," he said.

These were comforting words, and she appreciated the concern, but that didn't bring her son back.

Jesus walked up to the coffin. Everyone was quiet, waiting to see what he would do.

"Young man," he said, "Get up!"

The dead man sat up and began to talk, and Jesus gave him back to his mother. The crowd was amazed and filled with awe when they saw this.

"A great prophet has come to us," they said.

News of this miracle spread far and wide.

Was Jesus really the Messiah?

About that time, some disciples of John the Baptist came to see Jesus. John had heard about Jesus' miracles and wanted Jesus to confirm that he was the Messiah.

What
Everyone
Should
Know
about
the

Bible

"Go back to John and tell him about the miracles you have seen," Jesus told them. This would confirm that he was the Messiah, for only God's Son could do such miracles.

When John's disciples left, Jesus told the people nearby, "John is more than a prophet, for he was the one sent to announce my coming."

Then Jesus quoted Malachi 3:1, which had prophesied John's coming hundreds of years earlier: "Look! I am sending my messenger, and he will prepare the way before me."

Dinner at Simon's house

One day a Pharisee named Simon invited Jesus to dinner. While Jesus reclined at the table to eat, which was the custom, a woman with a bad reputation in that town came to Jesus with an alabaster jar of perfumed ointment. She stood behind him, washing his feet with her tears and wiping them with her hair. She kissed his feet and poured ointment on them.

When the Pharisee saw this, he was indignant. He said to himself, "If Jesus were a prophet, he would know what kind of woman she is."

Jesus not only knew that, he also knew Simon's thoughts. He told Simon a story about two debtors—one who owed much, another who owed little. "Neither had the money to pay the man back, so he forgave them both," Jesus said. "Which do you think loved him more?" Simon had to admit that the man who had the greater debt forgiven would have the greater love.

Jesus scolded Simon for his lack of love and courtesy. "When I came into your house, you gave me no water to wash my feet, but she has washed my feet with her tears," Jesus said. "You gave me no kiss of greeting, but she has not stopped kissing my feet. You put no olive oil on my head, as you should have done, but she has anointed my feet with perfumed ointment. Her many sins are forgiven, so she loves me much."

Then Jesus turned to the woman and said, "Your sins are forgiven."

Healing the needy

After that, Jesus traveled from one town to another, announcing the Good News concerning the Kingdom of God. The Twelve went with him, as well as some women he had healed. These included Mary Magdalene, who was delivered from seven demons; Joanna, the wife of Chuza, who was Herod's business manager; Susanna; and many others who were supporting Jesus and his disciples with their personal resources.

Jesus entered a house with a great crowd surrounding him. It was so crowded that they couldn't eat. Some people brought in a demon-possessed man who was also blind and mute. Jesus healed him by driving out the demon and restoring his sight and speech. The people there were astonished and began to ask if this could be the Messiah.

This kind of talk infuriated the Pharisees. "He gets his power from Satan, the prince of demons," they said.

"Any kingdom that fights against itself cannot stand," Jesus told these hard-hearted people. Satan would not cast out demons from people—he would be hurting his own cause.

"If I am casting out demons by the Spirit of God," Jesus said, "then the Kingdom of God has arrived among you. Remember that if you speak blasphemy against the Holy Spirit, you cannot be forgiven. Be careful, for on the judgment day you will give an account for every thoughtless word you speak."

On another day some Pharisees and other religious leaders came to see Jesus. "Teacher, we want to see a miracle to prove that you are from God," they said.

How could they ask such a thing? It had only been a few days since Jesus had driven out a demon and restored the sight and speech of the same man. They surely knew that he raised the widow of Nain's son from the dead. What greater miracle did they want?

"The only sign I will give you is from the prophet Jonah," Jesus said. "When the evil people of Nineveh heard Jonah preach, they repented. But you have someone greater than Jonah here, and you won't believe."

A visit from Jesus' mother and brothers

While Jesus was talking, his mother and brothers came to speak with him. Someone told Jesus that they were outside, waiting to see him. Then Jesus told the crowd around him that all of his disciples were his mother and brothers, just like anyone who does the will of the Father in heaven. Jesus established a new relationship: When we accept him, we enter the family of God.

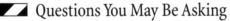 Questions You May Be Asking

How could Jesus heal the sick, give sight to the blind, and raise the dead to life?
Jesus is God the Son, the One who participated in the creation of the universe. He who made all life certainly has authority to fix any part of it that is broken.

Why did Jesus recline at the dinner table at Simon the Pharisee's house?
In that culture, that was the posture for eating. We sit in chairs around a table, but there people reclined on their sides, resting on something like a bench.

366
>

What
Everyone
Should
Know
about
the
Bible

What did a centurion do?

A centurion was a Roman army officer who was in charge of one hundred men. It was the job of a centurion to supervise crucifixions, including Jesus' crucifixion. A centurion named Cornelius accepted Jesus under Peter's ministry (Acts 10). Julius was a centurion who escorted Paul to Rome (Acts 27:1-3).

Great Events of This Time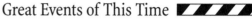

1. **Jesus heals a centurion's servant** (Matthew 8:5-13; Luke 7:1-10).
2. **Jesus raises the son of the widow at Nain** (Luke 7:11-17).
3. **John asks Jesus if he is the Messiah** (Matthew 11:2-19; Luke 7:18-35).
4. **Jesus puts a curse on three towns** (Matthew 11:20-24).
5. **A woman anoints Jesus' feet** (Luke 7:36-50).
6. **Jesus tours Galilee with his disciples. Mary Magdalene is healed, and women help Jesus with his work** (Luke 8:1-3).
7. **Jesus heals a blind and mute demoniac** (Matthew 12:22-37; Mark 3:20-30; Luke 11:14-28).
8. **Some Pharisees ask Jesus for a sign from heaven** (Matthew 12:38-45; Luke 11:29-32).

Significant Dates of This Time

Circa A.D. 28–A.D. 29

Heroes and Villains: The Stars of Scene 27

MARY MAGDALENE

After Jesus cast seven demons from her, Mary Magdalene followed him faithfully. She was there when he was crucified and when he was buried. She prepared spices to anoint his body. On the first day of the week Mary visited his tomb with some other women and found the tomb empty. She went to tell the other disciples what she had seen. She saw Jesus in the garden and spoke with him. Mary is honored as one of Jesus' most devoted followers.

Bible events in Mary Magdalene's life
1. She travels with Jesus and the apostles through Galilee.
2. She is present at Jesus' crucifixion.
3. She watches as Jesus is buried.
4. She buys spices and brings them to Jesus' tomb on the morning of the Resurrection.
5. An angel tells her that Jesus is risen; she hurries to tell Peter and John the news.
6. Jesus appears to her after his resurrection.

▟▟▟▟ Did You Know?

Funerals were often held the same day the person died In a hot climate, and in the absence of modern preparations for burial, bodies began to decay quickly, so it was necessary to hold the funeral right away. Often there were mourners who were paid to wail and cry, adding to the grim reality of death. The body was wrapped in cloth and carried on a bier (like a cot). Graves were more shallow then than they are today.

Why was the widow of Nain in such great trouble? In those days a widow depended on her oldest son or another close relative to take care of her. If she had no close relatives who were living, the son became her lifeline. The widow of Nain apparently had lost her only means of support—there was no life insurance, Social Security, savings accounts, or anything else she could depend on. Widows in this situation often had to beg.

Common courtesies Simon the Pharisee was rude to Jesus. He neglected three common courtesies that any thoughtful host would give a guest: (1) water for the guest to wash his feet, or better, to wash the guest's feet himself; (2) a kiss of greeting; and (3) anointment with oil or perfume to honor the guest.

▟▟▟▟ Discovering My Purpose from God's Plan

1. *The devil doesn't do godly things, and he doesn't undo ungodly things.* Jesus reminded the Pharisees that Satan would never destroy his own work—by casting out his own demons, for example—just as God would never destroy his own work.
2. *Authoritative teaching comes from authorized teachers.* God authorized Jesus to teach.
3. *As we receive much from Jesus, we should give much to Jesus.* Some women who traveled with Jesus and the Twelve had been healed or had demons driven from them, so they helped support Jesus and his ministry. "When someone has been given much, much will be required in return; and when someone has been entrusted with much, even more will be required" (Luke 12:48).

The Greatest Stories Ever Told

The Parables of Jesus

Characters:
A baker; a farmer; Jesus and his disciples; and a pearl merchant

Time Period:
About midpoint in Jesus' ministry

Dates:
Circa A.D. 28–A.D. 29

Where Scene 28 of the Big Story Can Be Found:
The Gospels: Matthew, Mark, Luke, and John. For specific references, see "Great Events of This Time," page 372.

In Scene 28, Find the Answers to These Questions:
What is the difference between a story and a parable?
Why was Jesus hiding religious truth from religious leaders?

Look for this in Scene 28
> A certain pearl was worth everything a man owned.
> What is the smallest seed of all?

Stories that are more than stories

Jesus was the greatest storyteller of all time. His stories were parables—stories with two parallel meanings. One is the obvious narrative, a story the majority of people will accept at face value. The other meaning is a deeper spiritual truth for the true seeker.

Jesus taught in parables because certain people hated him, especially the Pharisees and the Sadducees. They controlled the Jewish religious system, and they controlled it for their own purposes. They wanted to remain in power, and Jesus' popularity threatened their power. When Jesus taught great spiritual truths through parables, the spiritually blind could not see the meaning while the spiritually alert could.

Jesus often used parables when he taught in public, but when he was alone with his disciples, he explained their meaning.

Jesus' use of parables was prophesied in a psalm: "O my people, listen to my instructions. Open your ears to what I am saying, for I will speak to you in a parable. I will teach you hidden lessons from our past—stories we have heard and known, stories our ancestors handed down to us" (Psalm 78:1-3). There are parables in the Old Testament as well, but Jesus told more of them.

Storyteller in a boat

Jesus began his ministry of parables along the Sea of Galilee. Jesus was on the shore of this large lake when an immense crowd began to gather around him, pressing him closer and closer to the water. Jesus got into a boat, sat down, and taught the people with parables.

The parable of the sower

A farmer planted some seed by scattering it in his field. Some fell on a footpath with hard soil, and the birds flew down and ate it. Other seed fell on shallow soil with underlying rock. The plants grew quickly but soon wilted and died. Other seed fell among thorns. The plants started to grow but were choked out. Some seeds fell on fertile soil and produced a wonderful crop.

Later the disciples asked Jesus the meaning of this parable, so he explained it to them. The seed is the Good News of the Kingdom of God. The hard soil represents minds that do not understand it, so Satan comes and snatches it away. Some people receive the Good News with gladness, but when troubles come, their soil is too shallow to support the crop. The thorns represent the cares of the world that choke out the Good News in a person's heart. The fertile soil represents the hearts of those who fully accept God's message and produce a good harvest for him.

370

>

What
Everyone
Should
Know
about
the

Bible

The parable of the wheat and the weeds

Jesus told another parable about weeds. The Kingdom of Heaven is like a farmer who plants good seed. While everyone is asleep, his enemy plants weeds among the wheat, so that they grow in the same field together. The farmer's servants want to pull up the weeds, but the farmer does not want to hurt the wheat. He orders the servants to let the two grow together until harvest time. Then the weeds can be separated and burned, and the wheat can be gathered into the barn.

The parable of the mustard seed

The Kingdom of Heaven is like a mustard seed that is planted in a field. Although it is the smallest of all seeds, it grows to become the largest of garden plants, growing into a tree where birds can find shelter.

The parable of the yeast

The Kingdom of Heaven is like yeast that a woman uses to bake bread. She uses a large amount of flour, and the yeast permeates all of the dough.

The parable of the treasure in a field

The Kingdom of Heaven is like a treasure that a man discovers in a field. He carefully hides the treasure again, then in his excitement sells all that he has to buy the field.

The parable of the pearl of great price

The Kingdom of Heaven is like a pearl merchant who discovers a pearl of great value. He sells everything he has to buy that pearl.

The parable of the fishing net

The Kingdom of Heaven is like a fishing net that a fisherman throws into the water to gather all kinds of fish. When the net is full, the fisherman drags it to shore and sorts out what he has caught. He keeps the good fish and discards the worthless fish. At the end of the world, the angels will sort out the godly from the ungodly. The ungodly will be discarded into the fire, where there will be great weeping and sorrow.

The parable of a lamp under a basket

Would anyone light a lamp and put it under a basket or under the bed? Of course not! A lamp is placed on a stand, where its light will shine throughout the room. Things now hidden will one day come to light.

The parable of the growing plant

The Kingdom of Heaven is like a farmer who plants seeds in a field. The seeds sprout and grow without the farmer's help. First the blade grows, then the heads of wheat, and then the grain ripens. At last when the grain is ripe, the farmer brings his sickle and harvests it.

Great Events of This Time

1. **Jesus teaches parables from a boat** (Matthew 13:1-3; Mark 4:1-2; Luke 8:4).
2. **Jesus tells the parable of the sower** (Matthew 13:3-23; Mark 4:3-20; Luke 8:5-15).
3. **Jesus tells the parable of the wheat and the weeds** (Matthew 13:24-30).
4. **Jesus tells the parable of the mustard seed** (Matthew 13:31-32; Mark 4:30-32; Luke 13:18-19).
5. **Jesus tells the parable of the yeast** (Matthew 13:33; Luke 13:20-21).
6. **Jesus tells the parable of the hidden treasure in a field** (Matthew 13:44).
7. **Jesus tells the parable of the pearl of great price** (Matthew 13:45-46).
8. **Jesus tells the parable of the fishing net** (Matthew 13:47-50).
9. **Jesus tells the parable of the lamp under a basket** (Mark 4:21-22; Luke 8:16-18; 11:33-36).
10. **Jesus tells the parable of the growing plant** (Mark 4:26-29).

Significant Dates of This Time

Circa A.D. 28–A.D. 29

Did You Know?

Parables The word *parable* comes from the Greek word *paraballo,* which means "to put beside." It puts two truths side by side—one the simple story line, the other a hidden spiritual truth.

Parables use imagery from everyday life Look at the images in the parables Jesus told: farmers, seed, planting, harvesting, a lamp, a basket, weeds, mustard seed, yeast, treasure, a field, a pearl, a fishing net. There is nothing complicated about them.

Discovering My Purpose from God's Plan

1. *Great truths can come in simple packages, as in Jesus' parables.* He taught the profoundest truths with the simplest stories.
2. *All truth is God's truth.* All falsehoods are from the devil.
3. *People can be spiritually blind as well as physically blind.* Spiritual blindness hides truth from the soul just as physical blindness hides sights from the mind.

The Creator Transcends His Creation

The Miracles of Jesus

Characters:
Herod Antipas; Herodias (Herod's evil wife); Jairus, his wife, and his daughter; Jesus and his disciples; John the Baptist (who was beheaded after Salome's dance); Salome (Herodias's evil daughter)

Time Period:
About the midpoint of Jesus' ministry

Dates:
Circa A.D. 29

Where Scene 29 of the Big Story Can Be Found:
The Gospels: Matthew, Mark, Luke, and John. For specific references, see "Great Events of This Time," page 380.

In Scene 29, Find the Answers to These Questions:
What is a miracle?
Whose head on a platter was served to a girl after a dance?

Look for this in Scene 29
> There was a group of demons named Legion.
> The demons ran into some pigs.
> Mourners were paid to cry.

The Big Story So Far

How do we know that Jesus is the Messiah, the Son of God? He taught well and spoke words of wisdom from heaven, but the most powerful evidence to those around him (and to us) was his miracles. By performing miracles, Jesus proved that he had authority over demons, the wind and the waves, sickness, and even death. Only God's Son could command the forces of the universe he created.

The "almost" disciples

The crowd was growing around Jesus, so he told his disciples they must go to the other side of the Sea of Galilee. As they were preparing to board their boats, a religious teacher came to Jesus. "Teacher, I will follow you no matter where you go," he said.

"Foxes have dens and birds have nests, but I am homeless," Jesus told him. Would he still want to follow a homeless man?

Another would-be disciple said, "Let me first go home and stay with my father until he dies."

"Follow me now," Jesus said.

Tomorrow may be too late.

The wind and the waves obey

Jesus got into the boat with his disciples and started across the lake. Suddenly a terrible storm arose, with waves crashing into the boat. But Jesus was sleeping through it all. At last the disciples woke him, shouting, "Lord, save us! We're going to drown!"

"Where is your faith?" Jesus asked.

Then he stood up and commanded the wind and the waves to be still. The disciples must have gasped with amazement that anyone would dare do such a thing! But suddenly all was calm.

"Who is this?" the disciples wondered. "Even the wind and the waves obey him." It should have been obvious—only the Son of God could command his creation like that.

A legion of many demons

When Jesus and his disciples arrived on the other side of the Sea of Galilee, they were in the land of the Gerasenes. A demon-possessed man ran toward them from a cemetery, where he lived among the tombs. This wild man could not be restrained. When people had tried to bind him, he broke the chains. No one was strong enough to control him. Day and night this poor man roamed the tombs and hillsides, screaming and hitting himself with stones. He was completely under the control of the demons within him.

The man saw Jesus coming from a distance. He ran to Jesus and fell

374

>

What
Everyone
Should
Know
about
the

Bible

down before him with a piercing scream, for Jesus had already told the demons to leave the man.

Then the demons spoke to Jesus. "Why are you bothering us, Jesus, Son of the Most High God? Don't torture us!" Even they recognized that Jesus was the Son of God.

"What is your name?" Jesus asked.

"Legion, because there are many of us in this man," the demons answered. Then the demons begged Jesus not to send them to a distant place but into a herd of pigs nearby.

Jesus commanded the demons to leave the man and gave them permission to enter the pigs. When they did, all two thousand pigs rushed down the hillside into a lake and drowned.

The herdsmen who took care of the pigs ran throughout the countryside and into the nearby city, spreading the news. Crowds hurried out to see for themselves. They gathered around Jesus and the formerly possessed man, who was now fully clothed and perfectly sane. The people were so frightened that they asked Jesus to go away and leave them alone. As Jesus prepared to leave, the man begged to go with him.

Jesus told him, "Go home and tell your friends what wonderful things the Lord has done for you."

There is a time to walk with Jesus and a time to take the Good News to others.

Jairus's daughter is raised from the dead

Once more Jesus crossed the Sea of Galilee. As soon as he landed on the shore, a vast crowd gathered around him. A synagogue ruler named Jairus urgently pushed through the crowd to Jesus. He knelt at Jesus' feet and begged him to heal his dying twelve-year-old daughter. This was a bold thing for Jairus to do. The highest-ranking Jewish leaders hated Jesus; they thought he was a fraud and had even convinced themselves that he was working miracles by the power of Satan, so they were making plans to kill him.

Jesus began walking with Jairus toward his home, with the crowd jostling around them. Everyone wanted to be near Jesus to receive help or healing.

Suddenly Jesus stopped and looked around. He realized that power had gone out from him. "Who touched me?" he asked.

The disciples were amused. Who touched him? Dozens—no, hundreds—were pushing and shoving to be near him. But Jesus kept looking around. He knew who had touched him and why, but he wanted the woman to make her healing public.

Slowly a woman knelt at Jesus' feet. Trembling with fear, she told her story. She had been bleeding for twelve years and spent all she had on doctors, but no one could heal her. Instead she kept getting worse. She thought, *If I just touch Jesus' clothes, I will be healed.* And when she did, the bleeding stopped. She was healed completely.

"Your faith has healed you," Jesus said. "Go in peace and enjoy your good health."

This incident delayed the trip to Jairus's house. Jairus was getting more nervous by the minute, for his daughter was very sick, even at the point of death. At that very moment some people arrived from Jairus's house with the sad news that his daughter had died. Why trouble Jesus further? What could he do now?

"Don't be afraid," Jesus told Jairus. "Only believe."

When they arrived at the house, the paid mourners were already there, wailing and moaning.

"Why all this commotion?" Jesus said. "The child is not dead but asleep."

The mourners laughed at him. Of course she was dead. There was no question about that.

Jesus put the mourners out of the house, then took Jairus and his wife and the disciples who were with him to the little girl's bedside. Everyone could see that she really was dead. What now? It was hopeless!

Jesus tenderly took the little girl's hand in his and looked into her lifeless face. "Little girl, get up!" Jesus whispered.

Suddenly the little girl opened her eyes. Then she got up and walked around. Everyone was amazed, and Jairus and his wife were filled with great joy, but Jesus told them to keep this a secret.

The miracle of sight

When Jesus left Jairus's house, two blind men followed him, shouting, "Have mercy on us, Son of David!" They followed him all the way into the house where he was staying.

"Do you believe I can help you see?" Jesus asked.

"Yes," they answered.

Then Jesus touched their eyes. "Your faith will make you see!" he said, and they were healed instantly.

This news was too good to keep, so the men told everyone about their miraculous healing.

376

>

What
Everyone
Should
Know
about
the

The miracle of restored speech

After these men left, some people brought Jesus a man who couldn't speak because he had a demon in him. Jesus cast out the demon, and immediately the man could speak. The crowds who saw this were amazed.

"Nothing like this has ever happened before in Israel," they said.

Once again the Pharisees claimed, "He casts out demons by the power of Satan."

Bible

Visiting the synagogues

Jesus went back to his hometown of Nazareth and taught in the synagogue again. Everyone was amazed at his teaching.

"Where does he get the authority for his teaching and miracles?" they asked. "He's just a carpenter's son. We know his mother, Mary, and his brothers—James, Joseph, Simon, and Judas. His sisters live here among us. What makes him so great?"

Once again Jesus said, "A prophet is not honored in his own hometown." Because of this he did not do many miracles around Nazareth.

Jesus traveled extensively in the cities and villages of the area, teaching in the synagogues and proclaiming the Good News about the Kingdom. Wherever he went, he healed many people with all types of sickness and disease. Jesus felt pity for the people, who were like sheep without a shepherd.

"The harvest is great, but the workers are few," Jesus told his disciples. "Pray to the Lord of the harvest to send more workers." Then Jesus called the Twelve together and gave them authority to cast out evil spirits and heal every kind of sickness.

John's head on a platter

Meanwhile Herod Antipas arrested John the Baptist and put him in prison at the behest of his evil wife Herodias. John had told Herod many times that it was illegal for him to marry Herodias because she was the wife of Herod's brother Philip. Herod would have executed John, but he was afraid it would start a riot.

At a birthday party for Herod, Herodias's daughter Salome performed an exotic dance that greatly pleased him, so he promised to give her anything she wanted. At her mother's urging, Salome demanded the head of John the Baptist on a platter. Herod regretted his promise, but he couldn't get out of it, so he ordered John's beheading. John's head was brought to the girl on a platter, and she gave it to her mother, Herodias.

Later when Herod heard about Jesus, he was afraid, for he thought that John had risen from the dead. Who could do such miracles but John?

Feeding the five thousand . . . and more

When Jesus heard about John's death, he went to a lonely area, but crowds soon gathered around him. Before long there were five thousand men, plus all the women and children. That evening Jesus' disciples came to him with a problem. "This is a desolate place," they said, "and it is getting late. There is no food here. You should send the crowds home."

"Feed them!" Jesus said.

The disciples were surprised. How could they feed thousands of people when they had no food? They looked around but found only one boy who had been thoughtful enough to bring food, and he had only five little loaves and two small fish.

"Bring them here," Jesus said.

Jesus must have smiled as he asked the boy if he could have his lunch. Of course, the boy was happy to give it to Jesus. He would gladly go hungry so Jesus could have something to eat.

Jesus gave thanks for the food and began to divide it up. The disciples took baskets filled with bread and fish and distributed it to all of the people. Everyone in the crowd had plenty to eat, and there were twelve baskets of leftovers.

Walking on water

It was getting late, so Jesus sent his disciples across the Sea of Galilee. Then he went up into the hills to pray, alone at last.

Out on the lake the disciples were having a terrible time, for a strong wind had risen, and they were fighting the great waves. Making it ashore seemed almost hopeless.

About 3:00 in the morning, Jesus came across the lake to the disciples, walking on the surface of the stormy water. The disciples screamed, thinking he was a ghost. But Jesus called out to them, assuring them it was he.

The impetuous Peter had to do something. "Let me walk on the water to you," Peter called to Jesus. So Jesus invited him out of the boat.

Peter climbed over the side and began to walk toward Jesus. But then he looked at the great waves. He was terrified and began to sink.

"Save me, Lord!" he cried out.

Jesus reached out his hand and grabbed Peter. "Why did you doubt?" Jesus asked. "You don't have much faith, do you?"

As soon as Jesus climbed into the boat, the wind stopped.

"You really are the Son of God," the disciples said, and they worshiped him.

Jesus, the Bread of Life

Jesus and his disciples finally landed at Gennesaret after a long, long night on the sea. The news spread quickly that Jesus was there, and the crowds gathered again, bringing their sick friends and relatives to be healed. They begged Jesus to let them just touch the hem of his robe so they could be healed.

News of the feeding of the five thousand men, plus women and children, had spread over the whole area. Jesus was staying at Capernaum, and people came there looking for him.

"You are looking for me because I fed you," Jesus told the people, "not because you're interested in what I have to say."

>

What
Everyone
Should
Know
about
the

Bible

"What does God want us to do?" they asked.

"Believe in me, the one whom God has sent," Jesus said.

But the people wanted bread to eat. That was more important to them than the Messiah. They lost sight of the Son of God because of a basket of bread.

"I am the bread of life," Jesus told them. "Those who come to me will never get hungry again."

The people grumbled at this. They knew Jesus was the son of Joseph. They knew his family. How could he be bread from heaven? How could he be the Messiah? Many disciples left Jesus at this time and stopped following him.

Festival in Jerusalem

Jesus and his disciples went to Jerusalem for a festival, and the religious leaders confronted Jesus there. "Why do your disciples ignore the ceremonial hand washing?" they demanded.

"And why do you ignore some direct commandments of God?" Jesus replied. "For example, God commands you to love your father and mother, but you think you don't need to care for your parents if you give money to God. You hypocrites! Isaiah prophesied about you when he said that some would honor God with their lips while their hearts were far from him."

Then Jesus told the crowds, "You are not defiled by what you eat, but by who you are, which determines what you say and do."

When Peter asked Jesus to explain, Jesus said, "Evil thoughts and actions come from within, out of the heart of people, not from without." Guard your heart more than your food!

Questions You May Be Asking

Why did the people of Nazareth refuse to believe that Jesus was God's Son?
They saw him grow up. They knew his mother and his half brothers and half sisters. If they knew him so well, how could he be the Son of God? Familiarity breeds contempt.

How could the people who saw the multiplication of the loaves and fish not see how miraculous that was? Why were they so preoccupied with food?
They did see the miracle, but their taste for bread was stronger than their taste for godliness. When they saw that Jesus could make bread and fish from almost nothing, they wanted more. Hunger for food overcame their hunger for God.

Why did people pay mourners to wail when someone died?
It was customary to lament for the dead at the graveside. The professional mourners lamented with eulogies and dirges, and were sometimes

accompanied by flutes. They provided a grim atmosphere for a grim event. These mourners, usually women, made a career of it. The job was passed from mother to daughter.

Great Events of This Time

1. **Jesus stills a storm** (Matthew 8:23-27; Mark 4:35-41; Luke 8:22-25).
2. **Jesus heals a demon-possessed man in the land of the Gerasenes and sends the demons into a herd of pigs** (Matthew 8:28-34; Mark 5:1-20; Luke 8:26-39).
3. **Jesus heals Jairus's daughter** (Matthew 9:18-19, 23-26; Mark 5:21-24, 35-43; Luke 8:40-42, 49-56).
4. **A woman is healed by touching the hem of Jesus' cloak** (Matthew 9:20-22; Mark 5:25-34; Luke 8:43-48).
5. **Jesus heals two blind men** (Matthew 9:27-31).
6. **Jesus cures a mute demoniac** (Matthew 9:32-34).
7. **Jesus returns to Nazareth** (Matthew 13:53-58; Mark 6:1-6).
8. **Jesus sends out the disciples two by two** (Matthew 9:35–11:1; Mark 6:7-13; Luke 9:1-6).
9. **John the Baptist is beheaded following Salome's dance** (Matthew 14:1-12; Mark 6:14-29; Luke 9:7-9).
10. **Jesus feeds five thousand men, plus women and children** (Matthew 14:13-21; Mark 6:30-44; Luke 9:10-17; John 6:1-15).
11. **Jesus walks on water** (Matthew 14:22-33; Mark 6:45-52; John 6:16-21).
12. **Jesus heals the sick at Gennesaret** (Matthew 14:34-36; Mark 6:53-56; John 6:22-24).
13. **Jesus is the Bread of Life; some of Jesus' followers desert him** (John 6:25-71).
14. **Jesus' disciples are accused of being unclean** (Matthew 15:1-20; Mark 7:1-23).

Significant Dates of This Time

Circa A.D. 29

What
Everyone
Should
Know
about
the

Heroes and Villains: The Stars of Scene 29

HEROD ANTIPAS

Jesus called Herod Antipas a fox, for he was a cunning man. He was tetrarch of Galilee and ruled over part of the territory that his father, Herod the Great, once ruled. The Jewish people were offended when Herod Antipas married Herodias, his brother's evil wife. Herodias hated John the Baptist for criticizing their marriage, and she tricked Herod into ordering John's death. This same Herod later judged Jesus before he was crucified.

Bible events in Herod Antipas's life

1. He becomes angry when John the Baptist condemns him, so he has John thrown into prison.
2. He gives a party; Salome dances for him and asks him for the head of John the Baptist.
3. He orders John the Baptist to be killed.
4. Pilate sends Jesus to him; he mocks and ridicules Jesus and sends him back to Pilate; he and Pilate become good friends.

Did You Know?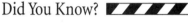

The demons knew that Jesus was God's Son, but the religious leaders didn't
How could demons know that Jesus was God's Son? Jesus had authority over them and could drive them out of the person they inhabited. Why didn't the religious leaders know that Jesus was God's Son? They were hard-hearted and would not believe in Jesus or allow him to have authority over them.

There is a time to linger with Jesus and a time to go out with the Good News
When Jesus sent the Twelve out to share the Good News, it was time for them to leave his presence and go to others with the gospel. For us too there is a time to linger and a time to go out into the world with the Good News.

The harvest was great but the laborers were few Jesus saw what no one else could see—the vast expanse of human need. People saw the sick and diseased nearby, but Jesus could see them worldwide. The people saw one small segment of evil, but Jesus could see its entire extent.

Discovering My Purpose from God's Plan

1. *Our hunger for God should be greater than our hunger for food.* The people who saw the miracle of the loaves and fish should have learned that.
2. *If even the demons recognized Jesus as the Son of God, how much more should we?*
3. *Only God's Son could work the miracles that Jesus did, for only the Creator can supersede creation.* Jesus' miracles make it evident that he is truly God's Son.
4. *The identity of God's Son can be lost in a basket of bread.* For many

who enjoyed the feeding of the five thousand, Jesus was no more than a source of food. While looking to him for more food, they missed the greater message that the Son of God, the long-awaited Messiah, was in their midst.

Reaching the Gentiles

Jesus beyond Galilee

Characters:
The blind man of Bethsaida; the crowd that Jesus fed; Elijah (who appeared at Jesus' transfiguration); a Gentile woman near Tyre and Sidon; Jesus and his disciples; Moses (who appeared at Jesus' transfiguration)

Time Period:
About midpoint in Jesus' ministry

Dates:
Circa A.D. 29

Where Scene 30 of the Big Story Can Be Found:
The Gospels: Matthew, Mark, Luke, and John. For specific references, see "Great Events of This Time," page 388.

In Scene 30, Find the Answers to These Questions:
Whose daughter had a demon?
How did Peter get his tax money from a fish?
Who will be the greatest in the Kingdom of Heaven?
How often, according to Jesus, should we forgive someone?

Look for this in Scene 30
> Feeding the four thousand was actually feeding about eight thousand.
> Moses and Elijah appeared with Jesus.

The Big Story So Far

Daughter with a demon

Jesus left his home region of Galilee and went to the region of Tyre and Sidon. Thus far his ministry had been mostly among the Jewish people, but now he was extending it into the region inhabited by Gentiles.

A Gentile woman came to see Jesus. "My daughter has a demon tormenting her," the woman said. "Have mercy on me, O Lord, Son of David."

Jesus tested this woman to see how strong her faith was. "I was sent to the Jewish people, not the Gentiles," he said. "Should I take food from the children and throw it to the dogs?" Jesus didn't mean that, of course, for he loved all people, even the Gentiles. He had already opened his arms to the Samaritans when he talked with the woman at the well. How would the woman respond to such an answer?

"Even dogs are permitted to eat crumbs that fall from their master's table," she said. Jesus must have smiled when he heard that. The woman had passed the test. She truly did believe.

"Your faith is great," Jesus said to her. "Your prayer is answered." At that moment, the woman's daughter was healed.

Healing a deaf and mute man

When Jesus returned to Galilee, some people brought a poor man to him who was both deaf and mute. They begged Jesus to lay his hands on the man and heal him. Jesus took the man to a quiet place and put his fingers into the man's ears. Then he moistened his own fingers and touched the man's tongue. Immediately the man could hear and speak perfectly.

Feeding the four thousand . . . and more

Not far from the Sea of Galilee, Jesus walked to the top of a hill and sat down. A large crowd brought their sick and diseased friends and neighbors for healing, and Jesus healed them all. This went on for three days. Jesus felt sorry for the people, for they were getting hungry. As at the feeding of the five thousand, the disciples scouted for food and found only seven small pieces of bread and a few small fish. How far would that go among four thousand men? With the women and children, there were probably eight thousand people altogether.

As he did before, Jesus took this small amount of food, thanked God for it, and began to break it into pieces. Then he gave it to his disciples, who distributed it throughout the crowd. When they were finished, there were seven baskets of leftovers.

Request for a bonus miracle

One day the Pharisees and Sadducees came to test Jesus. They asked him to do a miracle that would prove he was God's Son, the Messiah. Where

384
>
What
Everyone
Should
Know
about
the

Bible

had they been? Jesus had healed hundreds of people. He had given sight to the blind and hearing to the deaf. He had raised people from the dead and had commanded the wind and the waves to obey him. He had driven demons from people. What more could they possibly need? Jesus scolded them for their unbelief. Only hard-hearted people would still be asking for a miracle after seeing so many.

Healing a blind man at Bethsaida

When Jesus arrived at Bethsaida, some people brought a blind man to him for healing. They begged Jesus to touch and heal the man. Jesus took the man from the village and put spit on his eyes. Then he put his hands on the man and asked if he could see.

"I see people, but they look like trees walking around," the man said. "I can see, but not clearly." Jesus placed his hands over the man's eyes again, and suddenly the man could see completely.

Peter's great confession

From Bethsaida Jesus and his disciples left Galilee again and went north to Caesarea Philippi. Along the way Jesus asked his disciples, "Who do people say I am?"

"Some say that you are John the Baptist, some say Elijah, and others say that you are another prophet," they answered.

"Who do you say I am?" Jesus asked.

Peter was the first to reply. "You are the Messiah," he said. "You are the Son of the living God." Jesus must have smiled at Peter's words, but he warned him not to tell others who he was because they would not understand.

The Transfiguration

Jesus took Peter, James, and John onto a high mountain. As the disciples watched, Jesus' appearance changed so that his face shone like the sun and his clothing became dazzling white. Then Moses and Elijah appeared and began to talk with Jesus. They knew Jesus well, for they had already spent hundreds of years with him in heaven.

Impetuous Peter was always ready to do something at a moment's notice, even if he hadn't thought it through. He said, "Lord, I will make booths to shade the three of you, if you wish." Peter wasn't thinking— Jesus, Moses, and Elijah didn't need shade.

Suddenly a bright cloud came over Jesus, and a voice spoke from the cloud. "This is my beloved Son, and I am fully pleased with him. Listen to him." It was the voice of God, speaking from heaven. The disciples were afraid, but Jesus touched them and comforted them.

As the voice faded, Jesus' appearance went back to normal. "You must not tell others what you have seen," he said to them.

Healing a boy with seizures

When Jesus and the disciples reached the foot of the mountain, a large crowd was waiting for them. A man knelt before Jesus. "Have mercy on me, Lord," he said. "My son has seizures and suffers terribly. He even falls into fire or water. I brought him to your disciples, but they couldn't heal him."

Jesus rebuked his disciples for their lack of faith. Then he rebuked the demon in the boy, forcing it to leave him. The boy was completely well.

Later the disciples asked Jesus what had gone wrong when they had tried to drive out the demon. "You didn't have enough faith," Jesus said. "If you have faith as small as a mustard seed, you could tell this mountain to move, and it would."

Getting taxes from a fish

When Jesus and the disciples returned to Capernaum, some Temple tax collectors asked Peter, "Doesn't Jesus pay the Temple tax?" Peter was sure that Jesus did, but he went to ask him. Before Peter could say anything, Jesus spoke. He knew what Peter was about to ask.

"Do kings tax their own people or the foreigners they have conquered?" Jesus asked Peter. Peter must have smiled. Kings taxed the foreigners they conquered, of course.

"So the citizens are free," Jesus said. "However, we don't want to offend the Temple tax collectors, so go down to the lake and throw in a line with a hook. When you catch a fish, open its mouth and you will find a coin. It will be enough to pay my Temple tax and yours."

The greatest in the Kingdom of Heaven

The disciples came to Jesus asking, "Which of us will be the greatest in the Kingdom of Heaven?" Jesus was sorry to hear their question, for it was about power, not service.

Jesus asked a little child to join them. "Unless you become like little children, you will never get into the Kingdom of Heaven," he told them. "Anyone who becomes as humble as this little child will be greatest in the Kingdom of Heaven. Anyone who welcomes such a child welcomes me. If anyone causes one of these little ones to lose faith, it would be better for that person to be thrown into the sea with a large millstone around his neck."

Casting out demons in Jesus' name

Another time, the disciples saw a man casting out demons in Jesus' name. They told him to stop, then they asked Jesus if they had done the right thing. "No, you should not have stopped him," Jesus said. "A person is either for me or against me."

What
Everyone
Should
Know
about
the

Bible

How often should we forgive someone?

Peter had a serious question for Jesus. "How often should I forgive someone?" he asked. We don't know what prompted this question. Perhaps someone had wronged him two or three times, and Peter had forgiven him each time so far. Wasn't that enough? Should he stop? What if it got up to seven times? Wouldn't seven be the limit?

"No, you should forgive someone seventy times seven," Jesus said.

Then Jesus told a parable about a king who wanted to check up on the debts people owed him. He found one man who owed him millions of dollars. The king called for the man and demanded full payment, but the man couldn't pay it. So the king ordered the man and his family to be thrown into prison until he paid everything. The man pleaded for mercy, and the king felt sorry for him and forgave his debts.

This same man soon ran into a fellow servant who owed him a small amount of money. He demanded instant payment, but the man could not pay. He knelt down and asked for forgiveness, but the creditor would not forgive him and had the man jailed until he could pay his debt.

When other servants saw what happened, they were angry and told the king. So the king called the unforgiving creditor back to him and rebuked him. "You evil man! I forgave your debt of millions of dollars, and you wouldn't forgive another's debt of just a few dollars." Then the king had this evil man thrown into prison until he could pay all of the debt.

Jesus said, "Likewise, you must forgive your brothers and sisters if you expect your heavenly Father to forgive you." Since God has forgiven us, we should forgive others.

Questions You May Be Asking

Why is this woman of Tyre called a Syrophoenician in some Bible versions?

She was Phoenician by race, and she lived in a region of Syria, thus *Syrophoenician*. She also was a Canaanite, which is a more general term for people who lived in the larger area known as Canaan. The important distinction was that she was a Gentile, not a Jew.

Where was Caesarea Philippi?

Caesarea Philippi was about thirty miles northwest of Capernaum, where Jesus lived. It was one of the ten towns known as the Decapolis. It was in the high foothills of Mount Hermon, about 1,200 feet above sea level, whereas Capernaum was about 680 feet below sea level. Caesarea Philippi was a summer retreat from the heat of Capernaum, and Capernaum was probably a winter retreat from the cold of Caesarea Philippi.

Where was Jesus transfigured?
Some think this event took place at Mount Hermon, just above Caesarea Philippi. Others think it was at Mount Tabor, though this is less likely.

 Great Events of This Time

1. **Jesus speaks with the Syrophoenician woman** (Matthew 15:21-28; Mark 7:24-30).
2. **Jesus heals a man who is deaf and mute** (Mark 7:31-37).
3. **Jesus feeds four thousand men, plus women and children** (Matthew 15:32-39; Mark 8:1-10).
4. **Some Pharisees and Sadducees ask Jesus for a sign; Jesus gives the lesson of the leaven** (Matthew 16:1-12; Mark 8:11-21; Luke 12:1-12).
5. **Jesus heals a blind man at Bethsaida** (Mark 8:22-26).
6. **Peter makes his confession** (Matthew 16:13-20; Mark 8:27-30; Luke 9:18-27).
7. **Jesus is transfigured** (Matthew 17:1-13; Mark 9:2-13; Luke 9:28-36).
8. **The disciples cannot heal a boy possessed with demons** (Matthew 17:14-21; Mark 9:14-29; Luke 9:37-45).
9. **Jesus provides tax money out of a fish's mouth** (Matthew 17:24-27).
10. **The disciples argue about who will be the greatest** (Matthew 18:1-10; Mark 9:33-37; Luke 9:46-48).
11. **A man is found casting out demons in Jesus' name** (Mark 9:38-50; Luke 9:49-50).
12. **Jesus tells the parable of the two debtors** (Matthew 18:21-35).

 Significant Dates of This Time

Circa A.D. 29

 Did You Know?

There were two towns named Bethsaida One Bethsaida was west of Capernaum. The other, Bethsaida Julias, was on the eastern side of the Jordan River as it enters the Sea of Galilee. The Bethsaida in this scene was probably the second one.

The Temple tax Every Jewish male was supposed to pay the Temple tax each year to help with the upkeep of the Temple. The tax was a half shekel per person per year. Since the amount was small, payment was probably not always enforced.

388

\>

What
Everyone
Should
Know
about
the

Bible

Discovering My Purpose from God's Plan

1. *We are either for Jesus or against him.* That's what Jesus said. We cannot be neutral.
2. *If we seek unlimited forgiveness, we must give unlimited forgiveness.* As we forgive others, God will forgive us.
3. *God spoke twice from heaven to affirm that Jesus was his Son—once at Jesus' baptism, and the second time at his transfiguration.*

A Not-So-
Festive
Feast
Jesus in
Jerusalem

Characters:
Jesus and his disciples; the man blind since birth; the
Pharisees and other religious leaders; a woman caught in
adultery

Time Period:
About midpoint in Jesus' ministry

Dates:
Circa A.D. 29–A.D. 30

Where Scene 31 of the Big Story Can Be Found:
Luke 9:51-56; John 7:1–10:21

In Scene 31, Find the Answers to These Questions:
Why does the world hate Jesus?
Why did the religious leaders hate the Son of God?
Why did the Samaritans turn against Jesus?

Look for this in Scene 31
> The Light of the World
> The Good Shepherd

The Big Story So Far

Onward to Jerusalem

Jesus went from village to village throughout Galilee, avoiding the region of Judea, where the Jewish leaders were plotting to kill him. When the time came for him to attend the Feast of Tabernacles in Jerusalem, which is in Judea, Jesus' brothers urged him to go. At the time they did not believe Jesus was the Messiah, so they scoffed, "Go to Jerusalem, where more people will see your miracles. You can't be famous if you stay here in Galilee."

"You go ahead," Jesus said. "I will come at the right time. The world doesn't hate you, but it does hate me, because I confront the world about its sin and evil."

Jesus left for Jerusalem after his brothers, but he went secretly through Samaria. Jesus wanted to go through a certain Samaritan village, but the people there turned Jesus and his disciples away. They did not want to associate with Jesus because he was headed for Jerusalem and they believed people should worship nearby, at Mount Gerizim. James and John were insulted. "Shall we call fire down from heaven to burn them up?" they asked. But Jesus rebuked them, and they went on to another village.

The Feast of Tabernacles

When Jesus reached Jerusalem, some Jewish leaders who wanted to kill him searched for him and asked others if they had seen him. Some people said good things about Jesus, but most of them were too afraid of the religious leaders to do it publicly.

Midway through the festival, Jesus went to the Temple to teach. When the religious leaders heard his teaching, they were amazed at his wisdom, for Jesus had not been trained in their schools. Jesus explained that he was not teaching his own ideas, but God's wisdom.

"You're demon-possessed," some people shouted at Jesus.

"I heal a person on the Sabbath, and you are offended; but you work when you circumcise your baby boy on the Sabbath, if that's when the day falls," Jesus told them.

Some people nearby wondered why the religious leaders didn't kill Jesus if they wanted to. Did they secretly know he was the Messiah? The leaders tried to arrest Jesus, but they couldn't do it, for the time for his sacrifice had not yet come.

Many in Jerusalem believed that Jesus was the Messiah. "Can we expect greater miracles from the Messiah than the ones Jesus is doing?" they argued.

On the last day of the festival, Jesus shouted to the crowd, "If you are

392

>

What
Everyone
Should
Know
about
the

Bible

thirsty, come to me! Come, for the Scriptures say that rivers of water will flow from me."

Some who heard him believed he was the Messiah. Others said it was not possible. How could the Messiah come from Galilee? The Messiah would be a descendant of King David, born in Bethlehem. Of course, they did not realize that Jesus was descended from David, through both his mother and his legal father, and that he had indeed been born in Bethlehem.

Temple guards came to arrest Jesus, but they returned to the religious leaders without him in custody. "Why didn't you arrest him?" the religious leaders demanded.

"We have never heard anyone speak as he does," they answered. Then the leaders mocked the guards, but Nicodemus, the Pharisee who had come to see Jesus one night, spoke in Jesus' defense.

"Is it right to convict a man before he is given a hearing?" he asked. Then the other Pharisees mocked Nicodemus.

The woman caught in adultery

After spending the night on the Mount of Olives, Jesus returned to Jerusalem the next morning. He sat down and began to teach the people, but as he was speaking, some religious leaders brought a woman they had caught in the act of adultery and put her in front of the crowd. Of course, they didn't bring the man, only the woman. They wanted to find a reason to condemn Jesus, and this woman might be their way to do it.

"Teacher, this woman was caught in the act of adultery," they said to Jesus. "The law of Moses says we must stone her to death, but what do you say we should do?"

If Jesus were to say they should stone her, he would not be the compassionate Jesus the crowd thought he was. If Jesus were to say they should not stone her, he would not be upholding the law of Moses. The religious leaders thought they had him trapped.

Jesus stooped down and began to write in the dust with his finger while the leaders shouted at him. Perhaps he was writing the sins of each of those leaders. When he stood up, he spoke to them. "Let those who have never sinned throw the first stone," he said. The leaders looked down at the dust. One by one, they dropped their stones and walked away. At last there was no one there but Jesus and the woman.

"Go and sin no more," Jesus told her.

The Light of the World

As the woman quietly slipped away, Jesus began to teach again. "I am the Light of the World," he said. "If you follow me, you won't stumble through the darkness; I will give you the light that leads to life. I have been sent here by my Father."

"Who is your father?" the religious leaders asked angrily. If Jesus were to say that God was his Father, he would be admitting publicly that he was the Messiah, the Son of God.

Jesus said, "If you knew me, you would know my Father also."

Jesus also said to the religious leaders, "I am going away. You will search for me and die in your sin. You cannot come where I am going." The religious leaders didn't understand what he was saying.

Jesus talks about his crucifixion

Then Jesus spoke more clearly about the future: "When you lift me up on the cross, you will realize who I am." At this, many believed in him.

Jesus continued his dialogue with the religious leaders. They said he was possessed by demons, and when he said that he existed even before Abraham, it was too much for them. They picked up stones to kill him, but he suddenly disappeared.

Healing a man blind since birth

Later Jesus saw a man who had been blind since birth. The disciples asked Jesus why the man was blind. Had his parents sinned? Had he sinned?

"He is blind so the power of God may be seen in him," Jesus said. Then Jesus spit on the ground, made mud with his saliva, and put the mud over the blind man's eyes.

"Go, wash in the pool of Siloam," Jesus told the man. He obeyed, and immediately he could see.

The people who saw this were amazed. They knew this was the blind beggar, but he was no longer blind. Some people took him to the Pharisees, who asked the man what had happened. He had been healed on the Sabbath day, and no work, not even healing, should be done on the Sabbath.

Some religious leaders didn't believe that the man had been blind, so they sent for his parents. The parents confirmed that he was truly their son, and that he had been blind since birth, but they didn't know how he had been healed.

The religious leaders didn't care that the blind man was healed. They just wanted to trap Jesus by proving he had broken the Sabbath by working. They banned the man from the synagogue, so he could not worship there again. Then the man returned to Jesus.

"Do you believe in the Messiah?" Jesus asked.

"Yes, but who is he?" the man answered.

"You are looking at him," Jesus said.

So the man worshiped him.

Some Pharisees who stood nearby heard everything. Jesus said to them, "I have come into the world to give sight to the blind and to show those who think they can see that they are blind."

394

>

What
Everyone
Should
Know
about
the

Bible

The Pharisees knew Jesus was talking about them. "Are you telling us that we are blind?" they asked.

"Yes, you are guilty because you think you can see, even though you are blind," Jesus answered.

The Good Shepherd

Jesus began to teach again. "I am the Good Shepherd," he said. "The Good Shepherd lays down his life for his sheep. No one can take my life from me. I lay down my life voluntarily."

When Jesus taught these things, the people were divided again. Some thought he was the Messiah, and others thought he was crazy or demon possessed.

Questions You May Be Asking

Why did the Pharisees and other religious leaders hate Jesus so much that they wanted to kill him?

These people saw Jesus work miracles that no human being could perform. They heard teaching so profound that it had to have come from God. All the evidence indicated that Jesus was the Messiah. But if the religious leaders accepted Jesus as the Messiah, they would have to give up their positions of power and serve the people. They couldn't do it; power meant more to them than truth. The only way they could preserve their power was to kill Jesus.

Why did the Samaritans turn against Jesus?

Jesus was going to Jerusalem to worship. Samaritans thought God should be worshiped at Mount Gerizim, not in Jerusalem. So they turned against Jesus because he was going to Jerusalem to worship.

Great Events of This Time

1. **Jesus' brothers give bad advice because they don't believe in him as the Messiah** (John 7:1-9).
2. **A Samaritan city rejects Jesus, and the disciples want to destroy it** (Luke 9:51-56).
3. **Jesus teaches at the Feast of Tabernacles; the guards are afraid to arrest him** (John 7:10-53).
4. **Jesus forgives a woman caught in adultery** (John 8:1-11).
5. **Jesus says he is the Light of the World; Jewish leaders try to stone him** (John 8:12-59).
6. **At the pool of Siloam, Jesus heals a man born blind** (John 9).
7. **Jesus is the Good Shepherd** (John 10:1-21).

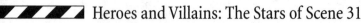

Significant Dates of This Time

Circa A.D. 29–30

Heroes and Villains: The Stars of Scene 31

JAMES THE APOSTLE

James and his brother John were sons of a fisherman named Zebedee. Together they conducted a prosperous business on the Sea of Galilee. Their mother, Salome, was possibly the sister of Mary, Jesus' mother, and she was a devout follower of Jesus throughout his ministry on earth. Jesus called James and John "the sons of thunder," probably because of their abundant energy and zeal. James was executed by Herod Agrippa I, who was trying to please the Jewish leaders.

Bible events in James's life

1. He leaves his fishing business to follow Jesus.
2. He goes with Jesus and John to Peter's home, where Jesus heals Peter's mother-in-law.
3. Jesus chooses him to be one of the twelve apostles.
4. He goes with Jesus, Peter, and John to Jairus's house, where Jesus raises Jairus's daughter from the dead.
5. Jesus calls James and the other apostles together, instructs them, and sends them out to minister.
6. He goes with Jesus, Peter, and John onto a mountain, where Jesus is transfigured before them.
7. He and John want to call down fire from heaven to destroy the Samaritans; Jesus rebukes them.
8. When he and John ask Jesus for a special place in his kingdom, the other disciples become angry.
9. He goes with Jesus, Peter, and John apart from the other disciples at Gethsemane; James falls asleep.
10. Jesus appears to him and several other disciples on the shore of Galilee after he rises from the dead.
11. He is murdered by Herod Agrippa I.

Did You Know?

The pool of Siloam The pool of Siloam, where the blind man was healed, was seven hundred years old, dating back to the time of King Hezekiah. When the Assyrians threatened Hezekiah in Jerusalem, he ordered his people to dig an underground tunnel to the Gihon Spring. This provided water to Jerusalem when the Assyrians laid siege to the city.

396
>
What
Everyone
Should
Know
about
the
Bible

The Feast of Tabernacles The Feast of Tabernacles had other names—the Feast of Booths, the Feast of Shelters, and the Feast of Ingathering. It was held during the Jewish month of Tishri. It began five days after the Day of Atonement and lasted for eight days. This feast celebrated the completion of the harvest. During this festival, people lived in little booths made of branches and sticks (or sometimes in tents) to remind them of the way their ancestors lived in the wilderness. It was supposed to be a joyous time, but the Pharisees were trying to make it a miserable time for Jesus.

Mount Gerizim This mountain in Samaria is almost three thousand feet high and sits next to Mount Ebal. When the Israelites entered the Promised Land, they were to shout blessings from Mount Gerizim and curses from Mount Ebal. Later when the Israelites returned from Babylon, they refused to let the Samaritans worship with them in Jerusalem. The Samaritans built a temple on Mount Gerizim, and it became the Samaritans' place of worship.

Discovering My Purpose from God's Plan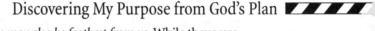

1. *Those closest to us may also be farthest from us.* While they were growing up, Jesus and his brothers lived in the same household and shared the same dinner table. But until he rose from the dead, they could not believe their half brother was the Messiah. It was only after the Resurrection, when Jesus was distanced from them, that they believed.
2. *A time of great joy can turn into a time of great sorrow.* The Feast of Tabernacles was supposed to be a time of celebration and joy, but the Pharisees made it a time of sorrow and suffering for Jesus. They deliberately tried to kill him during this joyful celebration.
3. *A practical moment may produce eternal blessing.* Hezekiah dug the pool of Siloam to give his people water to drink. Seven hundred years later, this pool would help to show the world that Jesus was the miracle-working Messiah.

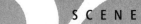

32

Sending the Seventy
Jesus in Judea

Characters:
The Good Samaritan; Jesus and his disciples; Martha (Jesus' busy friend at Bethany); Mary (Jesus' listening friend at Bethany); the rich fool; some Pharisees and other religious leaders; the seventy (whom Jesus sent out)

Time Period:
About midpoint in Jesus' ministry

Dates:
Circa A.D. 29–A.D. 30

Where Scene 32 of the Big Story Can Be Found:
Luke 10:1–11:13, 37-54; 12:13-48; 13:6-9

In Scene 32, Find the Answers to These Questions:
Why did Jesus send seventy people into nearby villages?
Why was the Good Samaritan called good?

Look for this in Scene 32
> A man worked hard so that thieves could inherit his estate.
> What does it mean to shake the dust from your shoes?

Sending seventy

After the Feast of Tabernacles Jesus and his disciples traveled throughout Judea. Although the religious leaders had tried to kill him, it was not yet time for Jesus to die, so they were not able to do it.

Jesus chose seventy of the disciples and sent them by pairs into the Judean villages that he planned to visit. "I am sending you like lambs among wolves," he told them. "Don't take money or a traveler's bag or an extra pair of sandals. Accept hospitality. Heal the sick, and tell people that the Kingdom of God is near. If a town does not welcome you, wipe the dust of that town from your feet and move on. Whoever accepts you accepts me, and whoever rejects you rejects me."

The seventy went out as Jesus instructed. When they returned, they reported joyfully, "Lord, even the demons obey when we use your name."

Jesus thanked the Father for giving wisdom to ordinary people and for keeping the simple message from those who thought they were so wise.

What must I do to inherit eternal life?

One day an expert in religious law tested Jesus with a question: "Teacher, what must I do to inherit eternal life?"

"What does the law of Moses say?" Jesus asked him.

"Love God with all your heart, soul, strength, and mind," the man answered. "And love your neighbor as yourself."

"You have answered your own question," Jesus told him. "Do this and you will have eternal life."

"But who is my neighbor?" the man asked, still trying to test Jesus.

The parable of the Good Samaritan

To answer this religious leader's question, Jesus told a parable. We usually call this the parable of the Good Samaritan.

A Jewish man was traveling from Jerusalem to Jericho when he was attacked by bandits. They stripped him of his clothing and money, beat him, and left him half dead by the side of the road. A Jewish priest came by, but he didn't want to get involved, so he crossed to the other side of the road and left the poor man lying there. Then a Temple assistant came along, but he also passed by, leaving the injured man lying by the road.

Finally a Samaritan man came by. Although Jewish people despised Samaritans, he took pity on the injured man. He knelt down and put medicine and bandages on his wounds. Then he put the man on his donkey and took him to an inn, where he took care of him. The next day he gave the innkeeper two pieces of silver and told him to take care of the man. He even offered to cover any extra expenses that might come up.

400

>

What
Everyone
Should
Know
about
the

Bible

Then Jesus asked the religious teacher, "Which of these three was a neighbor to the injured man?"

What could the man say? "The one who showed mercy to him," he answered.

Jesus must have smiled. The man had answered both of his own questions. "Go and do the same," Jesus said.

The best dinner in Bethany

On his way back to Jerusalem, Jesus stopped in Bethany, where his friends Mary, Martha, and Lazarus lived. Martha immediately became preoccupied with making a big dinner, while Mary sat near Jesus' feet, listening to his teachings. Before long Martha complained to Jesus. "It's not fair for Mary to sit here while I'm working so hard," she said. "Tell her to come and help me."

"My dear Martha, you are burdened with many details," Jesus said. "Mary has chosen what is more important, and I won't take it from her."

Hopefully Martha forgot about the dinner preparations and sat down with Mary to listen to Jesus.

The Lord's Prayer

The disciples asked Jesus to teach them how to pray. Jesus gave them the wonderful prayer that we know as the Lord's Prayer. This is what he prayed:

"Father in heaven, may your name be honored. May your Kingdom come soon. Give us our food each day, and forgive us our sins, just as we forgive others who sin against us. And don't let us yield to temptation."

Cleaning the outside of the cup

A Pharisee invited Jesus to his home for a meal. He was surprised when Jesus sat at the table without performing the ceremonial washing. Jesus knew what he was thinking and responded before he could say anything.

"You Pharisees are very careful about cleaning the outside of a cup or dish, but inside you are filthy—filled with greed and wickedness. You need to clean up the inside as well as the outside. You tithe your income but forget about justice and the love of God. Keep on tithing, but don't forget to honor God. You love the honored seats in the synagogues and greetings in the marketplace, but you are corrupt. You crush people with impossible religious demands, but you won't lift a finger to help with their burdens. You even build beautiful tombs for the prophets your ancestors murdered. You hide the truth from your followers. You don't want to go into God's kingdom, and you keep others from going in."

The Pharisees and the religious leaders were furious. From that time on, they tried to trap Jesus with hostile questions.

The parable of the rich fool

While Jesus was teaching, someone asked him to help divide his father's estate fairly. Jesus refused to be a judge over such things. Then he cautioned the people about greed for money. He emphasized his point with the parable of the rich fool.

There was once a rich man with a productive farm. He had wonderful crops, and his barns were overflowing with grain. So the man thought, *I will tear down these barns and build bigger ones. I will be able to sit back and enjoy life without a care in the world. I can eat, drink, and be merry.*

But God said to the rich man, "You fool. Tonight you will die, and who will get your riches then?" Of course, the man couldn't take his wealth with him. After his death, perhaps all he had hoarded for himself would simply be stolen by thieves.

Jesus' lesson was simple. "A person is a fool if he stores riches on earth but neglects to store riches in heaven," he said.

The parable of the unexpected return

Jesus told another parable about a master and his servants. Suppose that a man put his servant in charge of his household and went on a trip. When the master returns from the trip unexpectedly and finds that the servant has been faithful, he rewards the servant. But suppose the servant did not think his master would return so soon, and he misman-aged the estate. Suddenly the master returns and finds the servant doing a terrible job. This servant is severely punished. This is how it will be when Jesus returns to earth.

The parable of the fig tree

Jesus also told a parable about a fig tree. A man planted a fig tree in his garden but was disappointed when it did not bear fruit. For three years the plant produced nothing. At last the man said to his servant, "Cut that worthless tree down and get it out of here. It is taking up space I could be using for a fruitful tree."

The gardener begged to let the tree live. "Please, let's give it one more year," he said. "I will give it extra care. If it still does not bear fruit, then we can cut it down."

Fruitfulness is a symbol of godly living. God will tolerate ungodly, unproductive living for a while, but not forever.

>

What
Everyone
Should
Know
about
the

Bible

Questions You May Be Asking

Why did Jesus tell his disciples to wipe the dust from their feet if a village rejected them?
This was an act of rejection. If a village rejected Jesus' message and his messengers, the disciples were to ritually reject the village.

Why was the rich man a fool?

He spent all his time and effort building his riches on earth, which he could not take with him when he died. He neglected to store riches in heaven, where he would always have them.

Great Events of This Time

1. **The seventy (or seventy-two) are sent out** (Luke 10:1-24).
2. **Jesus tells the parable of the Good Samaritan** (Luke 10:25-37).
3. **Jesus visits Mary and Martha** (Luke 10:38-42).
4. **Jesus teaches his disciples how to pray** (Luke 11:1-13).
5. **A Pharisee invites Jesus to dinner** (Luke 11:37-54).
6. **Jesus tells the parable of the rich fool** (Luke 12:13-21).
7. **Jesus tells the parable of the unexpected return** (Luke 12:35-48).
8. **Jesus tells the parable of the fig tree** (Luke 13:6-9).

Significant Dates of This Time

Circa A.D. 29–A.D. 30

Heroes and Villains: The Stars of Scene 32

MARTHA

Martha lived with her sister, Mary, and her brother, Lazarus, in the village of Bethany, about two miles east of Jerusalem. Jesus often visited their home and became a close friend. Martha busied herself with household chores while her sister Mary listened to Jesus. When Lazarus became sick and died, Martha sent for Jesus. When Jesus arrived, she expressed her trust that he would help.

Bible events in Martha's life

1. She prepares dinner for Jesus; she complains to him about Mary, and Jesus rebukes her.
2. She runs to meet Jesus and complains about his delay in coming to heal Lazarus.

MARY OF BETHANY

The sister of Martha and Lazarus lived with them at Bethany. Martha was apparently the housekeeper and cook, and Mary's role wasn't as carefully spelled out. Mary sat and listened to Jesus one day while Martha busied herself with meal preparations. When Martha complained, Jesus said that Mary had chosen the better part. Mary was present when Jesus raised her brother Lazarus from the dead. On one occasion Mary poured ointment on Jesus' feet and wiped them with her hair. Jesus said that she was anointing him for his burial.

Bible events in Mary of Bethany's life
1. Jesus commends her for her interest in hearing him teach.
2. She runs to meet Jesus after Lazarus dies; she weeps.
3. She shows devotion to Jesus by anointing him with costly ointment.

Did You Know?

Judea was a district The territory surrounding Jerusalem was called Judea. It was about fifty-five miles from east to west and about the same length from north to south. Galilee, Perea, and Samaria were other districts.

Bethany was a suburb of Jerusalem The little village where Mary, Martha, and Lazarus lived was about two miles east of Jerusalem, on the eastern slope of the Mount of Olives. The small village of El-Azariyeh is there today, including the traditional ruins of Lazarus's tomb.

Discovering My Purpose from God's Plan

1. *The currency of heaven lasts longer than the currency of earth.* The rich fool spent all his time and effort to gain riches he couldn't take with him, and he neglected to gain riches he could send on ahead to heaven.
2. *The best work may be to sit and listen.* Jesus commended Mary for skipping the meal preparations to listen to him.
3. *Return love for hatred.* The Good Samaritan was hated by the Jewish people, but he responded with love to the wounded Jewish man.
4. *Prayer is a multifaceted jewel.* In the Lord's Prayer, Jesus taught us to pray for food and clothing, to praise God, to ask forgiveness for sins, to desire to know the will of God in our lives, and other diverse requests. Prayer is not just getting, but giving; not just asking, but praising; not seeking just our own will, but God's will.

Are You the Messiah— or Not?

Jesus in Bethany

Characters:
Jesus and his disciples; Lazarus the beggar; Lazarus of Bethany (whom Jesus raised from the dead); Martha of Bethany; Mary of Bethany; some Pharisees and other religious leaders; the Prodigal Son; the rich man who treated Lazarus the beggar poorly; a shepherd who looked for his lost sheep

Time Period:
About the midpoint of Jesus' ministry

Dates:
Circa A.D. 29–A.D. 30

Where Scene 33 of the Big Story Can Be Found:
The Gospels: Matthew, Luke, and John. For specific references, see "Great Events of This Time," page 410.

In Scene 33, Find the Answers to These Questions:
Which leader did Jesus call "that fox"?
Why did Jesus feel like a hen with her chicks?

Look for this in Scene 33
> A young man almost ate the pigs' food.
> Angels celebrate in heaven.

The Big Story So Far

Teaching at the Feast of Dedication

After the Feast of Tabernacles in Jerusalem, Jesus had been ministering in Judea, the region surrounding Jerusalem. Then he returned to Jerusalem to attend the Feast of Dedication, or Hanukkah. It was December, and Jesus was teaching in the part of the Temple known as Solomon's porch or Solomon's colonnade.

Jewish leaders surrounded him. "Tell us plainly—are you the Messiah or are you not?" they demanded. If Jesus said he was, they would accuse him of blasphemy for claiming to be God's Son. If he said he was not, they would tell the people not to listen to him or follow him. It was another of their trick questions.

"I have already told you the answer," Jesus said, "but you won't believe me. You should believe because of the miracles you see me do. But yes, the Father and I are one." This infuriated the religious leaders, so they picked up stones to kill him.

Then they tried to arrest Jesus, but he left before they could do it. He crossed the Jordan River, and many followed him and believed in him.

That fox, Herod Antipas

In Jerusalem some religious leaders warned Jesus, "Herod Antipas wants to kill you, so you had better go away from here."

"Go tell that fox that I will keep on casting out demons and doing miracles of healing," Jesus answered.

Like a hen protects her chicks

Jesus began to mourn for Jerusalem. "O Jerusalem, Jerusalem," he cried out. "I have often longed to protect you like a hen protects her chicks, but you wouldn't let me."

Jesus was able to look ahead and see that the Romans would destroy the city and its Temple several years later, around A.D. 70.

Healing a man with swollen arms and legs

One Sabbath day Jesus was invited to the home of a Pharisee. The religious leaders watched him closely, for a man was there with swollen arms and legs, and they wondered if Jesus would heal him.

Jesus knew their thoughts. "Does the law permit a person to be healed on the Sabbath day or not?" he asked.

They refused to answer, so Jesus touched the sick man, healed him, and sent him away.

Then he scolded the religious leaders. "You all work on the Sabbath day," he said. "If your cow falls into a pit, you do your best to get it out!"

Jesus noticed that all the religious leaders who came to dinner were trying to get the best seats at the table, so he gave this advice: "Don't try

406

>

What
Everyone
Should
Know
about
the

Bible

to get the best seat. If a more respected person comes along, the host must demote you, perhaps even to the foot of the table. That will shame you, not honor you. Instead start at the foot of the table, and your host may promote you to the head of the table. Then you will be honored."

The parable of the great feast

One man at the table said to Jesus, "What a great honor to be in the Kingdom of God!" In response Jesus told this parable.

A man prepared a great feast and sent out many invitations. When the feast was ready, he sent a servant to bring in the guests, but each one made excuses. One had just bought a field and had to inspect it. Another had just bought some oxen and wanted to try them out. Another had just married, so he couldn't come.

When the servant told the master what the invited guests had said, the master was angry. "Go out into the streets and alleys and invite the poor, crippled, lame, and blind," he said.

But there was still room at the banquet table. So the host told the servant to go out again and find other strangers to come so the table would be filled.

"None of those I invited at first will ever taste the food I prepared for them," the host said.

Jesus told this story to remind his listeners that God invites many to his banquet table in heaven, but those who make excuses will never taste its bounty.

The parables of the lost sheep, the lost coin, and the Prodigal Son

Jesus told three parables about the lost and found.

A shepherd had a hundred sheep, and one was missing. He left the ninety-nine and searched for the one lost sheep until he found it. When he did, he rejoiced over that lost sheep more than over the ninety-nine that didn't wander away. In the same way, our Father in heaven does not want one of his sheep to wander, and he rejoices whenever a lost sheep is found.

A woman had ten silver coins. When she lost one, she lit a lamp, looked in every corner, and swept her whole house until she found her lost coin. When she did, she invited her friends and neighbors to rejoice with her because she found her lost coin. Likewise, the angels rejoice when one lost sinner repents and comes to God.

A man had two sons. One day the younger asked his father for his share of the inheritance. Then he went far away and wasted all of his money on wild living. About that time a famine swept over the land. The young man became so desperate that he got a job feeding pigs. He even wished he could eat the pig food to satisfy his hunger. At last he realized how good he had it before he left home.

"I will go home to my father and confess my sin to him," he said. "I will tell my father that I am not worthy to be his son, so I will work as a hired servant." So the young man headed home.

When he was still far away, his father saw him coming. The father was so overjoyed to see his lost son that he ran out to him, hugging and kissing him. Then the father had a great feast for his son, who had been lost but was found again.

The older brother grumbled about all the fuss, but his father explained that his lost son had been found, and that was reason enough to celebrate.

The parable of the unjust steward

Jesus told another parable. A rich man hired a manager but soon learned that he was a dishonest man who stole from his master. The rich man called for the manager and fired him, so the man became worried about his future. What could he do now? He might not be able to get another good job.

Then the manager came up with a plan. He quickly called for all the people who owed his master money and cut each person's debt. The rich man wasn't happy about this, but he admired the man's cleverness. All of these people would now owe the manager.

Jesus wasn't approving of this man's dishonest ways, but he used the parable to make this point: Use your worldly resources to benefit others and thereby win friends. True generosity also brings a reward in heaven.

The parable of the rich man and Lazarus

In another parable Jesus told, a rich man lived in great luxury, while a diseased beggar named Lazarus pleaded for scraps from the rich man's table. One day the beggar died. Because he loved the Lord, he went to heaven, where he was in Abraham's presence. The rich man also died and went to a place of torment. The rich man was able to see the beggar in heaven.

"Father Abraham," the rich man cried out, "send Lazarus here to dip the tip of his finger in water and cool my tongue, for I am suffering greatly in these flames."

"Do you remember that during your lifetime you had everything and Lazarus had nothing?" Abraham answered. "Now he is comforted, but you are in anguish. There is also a great gulf separating us, and no one can cross it in either direction."

The rich man tried one more request. "Please, Father Abraham, send Lazarus to my home to warn my five brothers, so they will not come to this place of torment," he begged.

"Moses and the prophets have already warned your brothers," he said. "All they need to do is read and heed those warnings."

408

>

What
Everyone
Should
Know
about
the

Bible

"No, Father Abraham," the rich man said. "If someone came from the dead, they would turn from their sins."

"If they will not listen to Moses and the prophets, they will not listen to someone returning from the dead," Abraham said.

The rich man learned a bitter lesson—sometimes it really is too late.

The parable of the unprofitable servant

In another one of Jesus' parables, a servant comes in from a hard day of work plowing or shepherding, but he can't sit down to eat before he does his chores. First he prepares and serves dinner to his master. The master doesn't even thank the servant, for he is just doing his job.

"Likewise," Jesus told his disciples, "when you obey me, do not expect praise, for you are servants doing your duty."

Raising Lazarus from the dead

One day some messengers came to Jesus with an urgent message from Mary and Martha in Bethany. Their brother Lazarus was so sick they feared he would die. Could Jesus come quickly and heal him?

Jesus did not leave for Bethany for two days. His disciples could not understand the delay, but Jesus knew what he was doing.

When Jesus finally arrived in Bethany, the news came to him that Lazarus had already died and been buried. Many from nearby Jerusalem had come to pay their respects and comfort Mary and Martha.

Martha went to meet Jesus. "Lord, if you had been here, my brother would not have died," she said.

"Your brother will rise again," Jesus told her.

Martha said she knew that he would rise again on the resurrection day.

"I am the resurrection and the life," Jesus said. "Those who believe in me, even though they die, will live again. Because they believe in me, they will have eternal life and will never truly die. Do you believe me, Martha?"

"I have always believed that you are the Messiah, the Son of God," Martha answered.

When Mary saw Jesus, she repeated Martha's sentiments: "Lord, if you had been here, my brother would not have died."

The two sisters took Jesus to Lazarus's tomb, and Jesus wept. The tomb was a cave with a stone rolled across the opening. Jesus called to some men nearby, "Roll the stone away!"

Martha was taken aback. "Lord, he has been dead for four days," she said. "By now the smell will be terrible."

"If you believe, you will see the glory of God," Jesus said. He prayed, thanking the Father for hearing his prayer.

Then Jesus shouted, "Lazarus, come out!"

At the opening of the tomb the figure of a man wrapped in grave clothes slowly appeared.

"Unwrap him and let him go!" Jesus commanded.

News of this great miracle soon spread to the Pharisees, Sadducees, and other religious leaders in Jerusalem. They were alarmed to hear it. If Jesus continued to do miracles like this, the whole nation would follow him, and they would lose their jobs! So they stepped up their efforts to kill Jesus. When news of their plots reached Jesus, he left Jerusalem and stayed in the wilderness with his disciples.

 Questions You May Be Asking

How could religious leaders want to kill a man who raised someone from the dead?

The Pharisees, Sadducees, and scribes were religious leaders who had a great amount of political power. Jesus was attracting a large following because of his miracles and wise teachings. These leaders were insanely jealous of the attention people were giving to Jesus and of the number of people who followed him. Jesus was a threat to them. Their religious system forced the people to obey every detail of their rules, especially the ones about doing no work on the Sabbath. But Jesus knew that his work, like healing people and giving them new life, was more important than the Sabbath.

Why didn't Jesus just zap the people who wanted to kill him? Couldn't he have?

Yes, of course he could have. He could have called down thousands of angels to destroy them. However, Jesus came to earth to die on the cross for our sins. Zapping his enemies would have cut those plans short.

What was winter like in Israel, such as at the Feast of Dedication?

The month of Chisleu was a thirty-day month equivalent to late November and early December on our calendars. Winter began in this month. It is somewhat stormy, with snowfall on the mountains and sometimes in Jerusalem. The rainy period is mostly during our months of December, January, and February.

Great Events of This Time

410
>
What
Everyone
Should
Know
about
the

1. **Jesus heals a woman on the Sabbath** (Luke 13:10-17).
2. **At the Feast of Dedication, some Jews again try to stone Jesus** (John 10:22-39).
3. **Jesus teaches near the Jordan River** (John 10:40-42).
4. **Jesus warns against Herod and sheds tears for Jerusalem** (Luke 13:31-35).

Bible

5. **Jesus heals a man with swollen arms and legs** (Luke 14:1-6).
6. **Jesus tells the parable of the seat at a wedding feast** (Luke 14:7-14).
7. **Jesus tells the parable of a great feast that is shunned by the invited guests** (Luke 14:15-24).
8. **Jesus tells the parable of the lost sheep** (Matthew 18:10-14; Luke 15:1-7).
9. **Jesus tells the parable of the lost coin** (Luke 15:8-10).
10. **Jesus tells the parable of the Prodigal Son** (Luke 15:11-32).
11. **Jesus tells the parable of the unjust steward** (Luke 16:1-18).
12. **Jesus tells the parable of the rich man and Lazarus** (Luke 16:19-31).
13. **Jesus tells the parable of the unprofitable servant** (Luke 17:5-10).
14. **Jesus raises Lazarus from the dead** (John 11:1-44).
15. **The chief priests plot to kill Jesus** (John 11:45-54).

Significant Dates of This Time

Circa A.D. 29–A.D. 30

Heroes and Villains: The Stars of Scene 33

LAZARUS OF BETHANY

With his sisters Mary and Martha, Lazarus lived in the village of Bethany, about two miles east of Jerusalem. Today we would call it a suburb of Jerusalem. Jesus often visited these three and became their close friend. While he was ministering in another place, the news reached Jesus that Lazarus was sick. Jesus delayed going to him so that Lazarus would die and Jesus could raise him up again to show God's glory. After a while Jesus went to Bethany and raised Lazarus from the dead, even though he had been buried for four days. The news of this stunning miracle made the chief priests even more determined to kill Jesus, for they were afraid that the whole nation would follow him.

Bible events in Lazarus's life
1. He becomes sick and dies.
2. Jesus raises him from the dead.
3. He helps prepare a supper for Jesus.

Did You Know?

The Feast of Dedication This was a joyous feast, held on the twenty-fifth day of the Hebrew month Chisleu, which is the latter part of our November and the early part of our December. The feast lasted for eight days. The people lit many lights in the Temple and in their homes, and they carried palm fronds and other branches to celebrate.

Perea Jesus' ministry during this time was focused in Perea, but sometimes he went to Jerusalem. The word *Perea*, or *Peraea*, does not appear in the Bible. Josephus and others define Perea as a small territory on the east side of the Jordan River, across from Samaria and Judea. Jerusalem and Bethlehem were located in Judea, which was sometimes called Judah. The region of Perea is sometimes called "the land beyond the Jordan." John the Baptist probably baptized in Perea. Today this territory is part of the kingdom of Jordan, with Amman as its capital.

 ## Discovering My Purpose from God's Plan

1. *There is greater joy in finding something that was lost than in keeping something and never losing it.* Even the angels celebrate when a lost soul comes to God.
2. *Pride can bring great shame, and humility can bring great honor.* A proud person who seeks first place is shamed when put into last place. A humble person who seeks last place is honored when put into first place.

Moving toward the Cross

Jesus Returns to Jerusalem

Characters:
Blind Bartimaeus; the children Jesus loved; laborers in the vineyard; the mother of James and John; a Pharisee and a tax collector who pray in the Temple; a rich young ruler; ten lepers whom Jesus healed; a vineyard owner; the widow who kept asking; Zacchaeus

Time Period:
Toward the end of Jesus' ministry

Dates:
Circa A.D. 30

Where Scene 34 of the Big Story Can Be Found:
The Gospels: Matthew, Mark, Luke, and John. For specific references, see "Great Events of This Time," page 421.

In Scene 34, Find the Answers to These Questions:
Why did lepers show themselves to a priest?
Why did a mother ask for her sons to sit at Jesus' right and his left?
Why did people throw their cloaks on the ground for a donkey to walk on?

Look for this in Scene 34
> A camel goes through the eye of a needle.
> A short tax collector climbs a big tree.

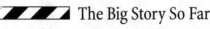

The Big Story So Far

During his ministry in Perea, Jesus visited Jerusalem to attend the Feast of Dedication, which was in late November and early December. When Jesus returns to Jerusalem, it is April, but the Gospels don't record anything about what he did during the intervening months. Jesus evidently went back to Galilee because the story picks up with Jesus leaving Galilee to make his way to Jerusalem for the annual Feast of the Passover.

Nine ungrateful lepers

As Jesus reached a village on the border between Galilee and Samaria, ten lepers approached him but kept their distance. Lepers were not permitted to come near "clean" people, lest they infect them. The lepers cried out, "Jesus, Master, have mercy on us!"

"Show yourselves to the priests," Jesus said. This was a way of telling them that they were healed, for it was a priest who determined if a person had leprosy or if he or she was healed of leprosy.

The lepers could see immediately that they were healed. All ten rushed off to find a priest to declare them clean, but one went back to thank Jesus.

"Didn't I heal ten?" Jesus asked. "Where are the other nine? Does only this Samaritan come back to give glory to God?"

The parable of the widow who kept asking

Along the way toward Jerusalem, Jesus told his disciples two parables about prayer. The first was the parable of the widow who kept asking.

There was once a poor widow who had been treated unjustly. She came to a godless judge to get justice. He had contempt for everyone, and each time this widow came, he turned her away. She persisted, coming back to the judge again and again and again. Eventually he grew tired of seeing her and decided to grant her request just to keep her away.

"Learn a lesson from this evil judge," Jesus told his disciples. "Even he was willing to give justice to a persistent petitioner. How much more will God give justice to his people if they persist in praying?"

The parable of the Pharisee and tax collector

Jesus told a second parable about prayer.

Two men went into the Temple to pray. The Pharisee prayed this prayer: "I thank you, God, that I am not a sinner like everyone else, especially like that tax collector over there. I tithe, fast, and behave myself."

The tax collector, sometimes called a publican, stood at a distance. He dared not even look up to heaven as he prayed in sorrow, "O God, be merciful to me, for I am a sinner."

414

>

What
Everyone
Should
Know
about
the

Bible

Jesus told his disciples, "I tell you, the sinner, not the Pharisee, went home justified before God." Prayer is not a time for pride but for humility.

Jesus loves children

One day some parents brought their children to Jesus so he could touch them and bless them. But the disciples told the parents not to bother Jesus. He was too important to spend time with children.

When Jesus saw that, he was displeased with the disciples. "Let the children come to me. Don't stop them!" Jesus told the disciples. "The Kingdom of God belongs to such as these. Anyone who doesn't have the faith of a little child cannot get into the Kingdom of God."

Then Jesus took the children into his arms, put his hands on their heads, and blessed them.

What must I do to have eternal life?

A rich young man came to Jesus asking, "What must I do to have eternal life?"

"Do you keep the Ten Commandments?" Jesus asked him.

"Yes, I try to keep all of them," the young man answered.

"Then sell everything you have and follow me," Jesus said.

Disappointed, the young man turned away from Jesus. He could try to keep the Ten Commandments, but to give up his riches to follow Jesus was too much. He would not do it.

Jesus sadly watched the young man leave. "It is very hard for a rich person to get into heaven," he said. "It is easier for a camel to go through the eye of a needle."

"Then who can be saved?" the disciples asked.

"No one can be saved by themselves," Jesus answered. "But with God, anything is possible."

The rewards of following Jesus

Peter said, "We have given up everything to follow you. What will we get out of it?"

"When I sit upon my throne in heaven, you will also sit on twelve thrones," Jesus said. "Everyone who gives up homes, family, or property for my sake will receive a hundred times as much. Many who seem important now will be unimportant in heaven, and many who seem unimportant now will be important in heaven."

The parable of the laborers in the vineyard

Jesus continued to teach about values with this parable:

The Kingdom of Heaven is like a vineyard owner who went into the marketplace of the town one morning to hire workers. He agreed to pay some workers the usual daily wage and sent them to work in his vineyard. About nine o'clock, he was passing through the marketplace and saw some more workers waiting to be hired, so he hired them and told them he would pay a fair wage. He did the same thing the rest of the day—at noon, at three in the afternoon, and even at five in the afternoon.

That evening at about six o'clock, the owner told the foreman to pay the workers, beginning with the last ones hired. Those hired at five o'clock were amazed to receive a full day's wages. When those hired earlier came for their wages, they received the same amount. They began to grumble. How could the owner pay them the same amount as the people who worked only one hour?

The owner said, "I paid you a full day's wage, just as we agreed and as you deserve. Why are you unhappy if I pay others more than they deserve? I have been fair to you and kind to them."

Foretelling his destiny

Along the way to Jerusalem, Jesus talked privately with the Twelve. He told them what would happen to him in Jerusalem—that he would be betrayed and sentenced to die and that the religious leaders would hand him over to the Romans, who would mock him, whip him, and crucify him. On the third day he would rise from the dead. This should have been clear to the disciples, but when all these events happened, it was as if they completely forgot Jesus' words.

Sitting at the right and the left

The mother of James and John, the sons of Zebedee, brought her two sons to Jesus and knelt before him to ask a favor. "In your kingdom, will you put one of my sons at your right hand and the other at your left?" she asked.

"You don't know what you're asking," Jesus said. "My Father has prepared the thrones next to me; even I will not decide who sits on them."

The other ten apostles were indignant when they heard what James and John wanted, but Jesus taught them all an important lesson. "Kings and rulers of this world lord it over their subjects," Jesus said. "Among you, whoever wants to be a leader must first become a servant. Whoever wants to be first must be a slave to the others. Even I came not to be served, but to serve, and to give my life as a ransom for many."

Blind Bartimaeus

Jesus and his disciples passed through Jericho. Along the way they saw a blind beggar named Bartimaeus and a second blind man sitting by the road. When the two blind men heard that Jesus was coming, they began to cry out for him to heal them. Some people nearby told them to be quiet, but they cried out even more.

416

>

What
Everyone
Should
Know
about
the

Bible

"What do you want me to do?" Jesus asked the men.

"Open our eyes so that we may see," they begged.

Jesus touched their eyes, and immediately they could see. Then they joyfully followed Jesus.

A short tax collector named Zacchaeus

A rich and influential tax collector named Zacchaeus lived in Jericho. Zacchaeus wanted to see Jesus, but he was too short to get a good look at him over the crowds. So he ran ahead of the crowd, climbed a sycamore tree, and looked down at Jesus as he came by.

Jesus must have smiled to see this short little rich man up in a tree. "Zacchaeus, come down," he said. "I'm coming home with you for lunch." Zacchaeus hurried down from the tree. Not only did he see Jesus, but he would serve Jesus lunch in his home.

Some of the religious leaders didn't like this. They didn't think Jesus should eat with sinners such as tax collectors, but with "nice people" like themselves.

During lunch Zacchaeus had a heart-to-heart talk with Jesus. He made a decision to follow him. "I will give half of my wealth to the poor," he told Jesus. "If I have overcharged anyone on their taxes, I will give them back four times what I took."

"Salvation has come to this house today," Jesus said. "I have come to seek and to save people like this, people who are lost."

Salvation came to Zacchaeus's house because Zacchaeus gave his life to Jesus, not because he gave his money to the poor.

The parable of the wise investments

As Jesus neared Jerusalem, he told another parable. A nobleman was called away to a distant empire to be crowned king. Before he left, he called some servants and gave them money to invest for him.

When the man returned from his long trip, he brought in his servants to find out what they had done with the money. The first servant had earned ten times what his master had given him. The master was pleased and made him ruler over ten cities. The second servant had earned five times what the master had given him. The master was pleased and made him ruler over five cities. The third servant had earned nothing and had only the original amount of money. The king was displeased. "Take the money from him and give it to the one who earned the most," he commanded.

Some people objected. "That servant already has much," they argued. "Why give him more?"

"To those who use their resources wisely, more will be given," the king answered. "What little the unfaithful have will be taken from them."

On the Friday afternoon six days before the Passover, Jesus and his disciples arrived in Bethany. Word had spread that he was coming, so people came from Jerusalem to see Jesus and also to see Lazarus, whom Jesus had raised from the dead. The Pharisees and other religious leaders were making plans to kill both Jesus and Lazarus.

The Triumphal Entry

On Sunday Jesus sent two disciples into a nearby village. He told them that they would find a young colt that had never been ridden, and they should untie it and bring it to Jesus. If the owner asked what they were doing, they should tell him that the Master needed it.

It happened just as Jesus said. They found the colt and untied it, and the owner asked what they were doing. They told him the Master needed it, and they brought the colt to Jesus. They threw their garments over it for Jesus to sit on as he rode on the colt to Jerusalem.

A crowd gathered quickly and spread their cloaks on the road ahead of Jesus. As he descended the Mount of Olives, the crowd of disciples began to shout and sing, praising God for Jesus and his miracles. Some of the Pharisees in the crowd were angry. "Tell them to stop!" they shouted at Jesus.

"If they keep quiet, the stones along the road will burst into cheers," he said.

This had been prophesied more than five hundred years earlier by the prophet Zechariah: "Rejoice, O people of Zion! Shout in triumph, O people of Jerusalem! Look, your king is coming to you. He is righteous and victorious, yet he is humble, riding on a donkey—riding on a donkey's colt" (Zechariah 9:9).

As Jesus rode into Jerusalem, he wept for it. This city would turn on him, and in less than forty years, it would be totally destroyed by the Romans.

Teaching in the Temple

On Tuesday, Jesus went into the Temple, in Jerusalem, to teach. The religious leaders challenged his authority to teach and to drive out merchants from the Temple. Who gave him this authority?

"I will tell you if you first answer this question," Jesus said. "Was John's baptism from heaven or merely from men?"

The religious leaders were trapped. If they said it was from heaven, Jesus would ask why they didn't accept it. If they said it was from men, they would be mobbed, for the people believed John was a prophet.

"We don't know," they answered.

"If you won't answer my question, I won't answer your question," said Jesus.

What
Everyone
Should
Know
about
the

Bible

The parable of the two sons

Jesus told another parable. A man asked each of his two sons to work in his vineyard. One son said no, but later he changed his mind and went to work. The other son said yes, but he also changed his mind and never went to work. Which of the two obeyed his father? The answer is obvious, isn't it? Obedience is not merely saying we will do something, but actually doing it.

The parable of the wicked caretakers

Jesus told a parable to the Pharisees and other religious leaders.

A vineyard owner worked hard to plant his vineyard. He built a wall around it, and he built a winepress and a lookout tower. Then he leased the vineyard to some caretakers and moved to another country.

At harvest time, the owner sent some servants to collect his share, but the wicked caretakers grabbed the servants and beat them, killing one and stoning another.

Then the owner sent a larger group to collect his money, but the wicked caretakers treated them in the same way.

At last the owner sent his son, thinking that the caretakers would surely honor him. But the wicked caretakers grabbed him, took him to the vineyard, and murdered him.

Jesus looked at the religious leaders. "What do you think the owner will do now?" he asked.

The religious leaders were indignant. They knew what they would do in the same situation. "The owner will put those men to a horrible death and lease the vineyard to others who are faithful," they said.

How could they be so blind? Jesus pointed at them. "Likewise, God will take the kingdom from you and give it to a nation that will produce the right fruit," he said.

Now they understood! They were the wicked caretakers who even wanted to kill God's Son. They were furious. They wanted to arrest and kill Jesus, but they couldn't do it with the crowds nearby. They would have to wait for a better time.

The parable of the wedding feast

Jesus told other parables about his kingdom. This one is similar to one he told earlier about another banquet.

A king prepared a great wedding feast for his son and invited many guests. When the banquet was ready, he sent his servants to notify the guests, but the guests refused to come. He sent other servants, but the guests ignored them too. Some seized the messengers and treated them shamefully, even killing some of them.

The king sent his army to destroy the murderers and burn their city. Then he commanded his servants to go out and find other guests who would come and appreciate the banquet. But one man came in improper clothing, so the king had him thrown out of the banquet hall.

Giving to Caesar and to God

The Pharisees and other religious leaders were working hard to find a way to trap Jesus. At last they thought they had it.

"Tell us, is it right to pay taxes to the Roman government?" they asked.

Jesus saw through their trap and recognized the evil in their hearts. If he said yes, the people would turn against him. If he said no, the leaders would report him to the Romans. "Show me the Roman coin you use for the tax," Jesus said.

So they handed him the coin.

"Whose picture is on the coin?" Jesus asked.

"Caesar's," they said.

"Well then, give to Caesar what belongs to Caesar, and give to God what belongs to God," Jesus answered.

Jesus' reply amazed the religious leaders. They had no good response, so they went away.

The poor widow's rich gift

While Jesus was in the Temple with his disciples, he watched rich people putting their money into the horn-shaped collection boxes. A poor widow came by and dropped in two small coins that were almost worthless.

"This poor widow gave more than all the rest of them together," Jesus said. "They have given only a small part of their surplus, but she has given everything she has."

▨▨▨▨ Questions You May Be Asking

What was a publican?

This was another name for the Jewish people who were tax collectors for the Romans. They were hated by their fellow Jews, for they often collected more than the Romans required and kept the difference. Matthew was Levi the tax collector before Jesus called him to be a disciple. Zacchaeus was a chief tax collector, a higher rank than the one Matthew held. The Jewish people classed the publicans with prostitutes and other vile sinners.

Why did the vineyard owner go to the marketplace to hire workers?

It was the custom in Jesus' time for workers to gather in the market-place of a town, hoping that someone would hire them for the day.

420

>

What
Everyone
Should
Know
about
the

Bible

This is still the custom in some parts of the world today, such as in certain villages in China.

Why did Jesus weep for Jerusalem when he rode into the city?
There were two reasons. First, Jesus longed for Jerusalem to accept him for who he was, God's Son, but the people of Jerusalem were about to crucify him. Second, Jesus could look ahead to A.D. 70, when the Roman general Titus would destroy Jerusalem completely, leveling the Temple.

Great Events of This Time

1. **Jesus heals ten lepers** (Luke 17:11-19).
2. **Jesus tells the parable of the widow who kept asking** (Luke 18:1-8).
3. **Jesus tells the parable of the Pharisee and the publican** (Luke 18:9-14).
4. **Jesus blesses the children** (Matthew 19:13-15; Mark 10:13-16; Luke 18:15-17).
5. **Jesus challenges the rich young man** (Matthew 19:16-30).
6. **Jesus tells the parable of the laborers in the vineyard** (Matthew 20:1-16).
7. **James and John want to sit at Jesus' right and left** (Matthew 20:20-28; Mark 10:35-45).
8. **Jesus heals blind Bartimaeus** (Matthew 20:29-34; Mark 10:46-52; Luke 18:35-43).
9. **Jesus meets Zacchaeus** (Luke 19:1-10).
10. **Jesus tells the parable of the wise investments** (Luke 19:11-27).
11. **The Passover crowds in Jerusalem await Jesus' coming** (John 11:55-57).
12. **Jesus makes his triumphal entry** (Matthew 21:1-11; Mark 11:1-11; Luke 19:28-44; John 12:12-19).
13. **Jesus teaches in the Temple** (Matthew 21:23-27; Mark 11:27-33; Luke 19:45–20:8; John 12:20-50).
14. **Jesus tells the parable of the two sons** (Matthew 21:28-32).
15. **Jesus tells the parable of the wicked caretakers** (Matthew 21:33-46; Mark 12:1-12; Luke 20:9-19).
16. **Jesus tells the parable of the wedding feast** (Matthew 22:1-14).
17. **Jesus provides a coin for Caesar** (Matthew 22:15-22; Mark 12:13-17; Luke 20:20-26).
18. **Jesus comments on the poor widow's two coins** (Mark 12:41-44; Luke 21:1-4).

Significant Dates of This Time

Circa A.D. 30

Heroes and Villains: The Stars of Scene 34

ZACCHAEUS

While the honored religious leaders of Jesus' time rejected him, some of the hated tax collectors sought him out. Zacchaeus was one of them. When Jesus passed through Jericho, where Zacchaeus lived, Zacchaeus wanted to see him. But he was a short man and could not see over his taller neighbors as they lined the roads to watch Jesus pass by. Zacchaeus climbed into a sycamore tree. When Jesus arrived at the tree, he called for Zacchaeus to come down and take him to his house. Zacchaeus gladly invited Jesus home with him. As a result of this encounter, Zacchaeus gave himself to Jesus and pledged to restore the money he had wrongfully received.

Bible events in Zacchaeus's life
1. He climbs a tree to see Jesus.
2. Jesus visits him at his home.
3. He repents of his sins.

Did You Know?

The eye of the needle Jesus said it is harder for a rich person to get into heaven than it is for a camel to go through the eye of a needle. If he was referring to a sewing needle, no rich person could ever get into heaven because a camel could never fit through such a tiny space. But we know that there are many wealthy people who are devout Christians, so Jesus must not have meant that kind of needle.

At that time cities usually had walls around them, and the gate in the wall often had a smaller gate within it. When the larger gate was closed at sunset, the smaller gate was kept open for a while. It was easy for a person to walk through this smaller gate, but a camel would have to kneel down and crawl through. It would be hard, but not impossible. This gate was called the eye of the needle or the needle's eye. Some think Jesus was referring to this, not to the eye of a sewing needle.

The daily wage In Jesus' time a day's wages was approximately one denarius. The denarius was a Roman coin that would be worth about sixteen cents today. The workers in the vineyard were probably paid that one little coin for a long day of work under the hot sun.

What
Everyone
Should
Know
about
the
Bible

Discovering My Purpose from God's Plan

1. *Persistent prayer pays off, and God encourages it, as Jesus indicated in his parable about the persistent widow who sought justice. If something is worth praying for, pray persistently.*

2. *Things or people that seem important here on earth may be unimportant in heaven. Things or people that are unimportant here may be important in heaven.* God's values are not the world's values, and vice versa.

3. *Obedience requires action, not just talk.* Saying yes to God is not enough; we must do what we say. That's the message of the parable of the two sons.

4. *Prayer and pride do not mix.* Prayer is a time for humility, as we understand from the parable of the publican and the Pharisee.

5. *To be a leader, you must first be a servant.* That's Jesus' way.

6. *Salvation does not come because of the amount of money we give to others, but by how much of our life we give to God.*

7. *More is given to those who are faithful, and what little the unfaithful have is taken away from them.* That is the lesson of the parable of the wise investments.

8. *Fairness is giving people what they deserve.* Mercy is not giving them the punishment they deserve. Kindness or generosity is giving people *more* than they deserve.

Lengthening Shadows
The Road to the Cross

Characters:
Jesus and his disciples; Judas Iscariot; Mary of Bethany; Satan; Simon the leper

Time Period:
Toward the end of Jesus' ministry

Dates:
Circa A.D. 30

Where Scene 35 of the Big Story Can Be Found:
The Gospels: Matthew, Mark, Luke, and John. For specific references, see "Great Events of This Time," page 429.

In Scene 35, Find the Answers to These Questions:
What happened when five foolish bridesmaids forgot their lamp oil?
Why would Jesus send goats away from him?

Look for this in Scene 35
> Tuesday was actually Wednesday.
> Spikenard is poured from an alabaster jar onto Jesus' head.

Jesus predicts the destruction of Jerusalem in A.D. 70

On Tuesday afternoon Jesus left the Temple with his disciples to go to the Mount of Olives. The disciples proudly pointed out the enormous, beautiful stones with which Jerusalem and the Temple were built. Then Jesus sadly told them what would happen in just a few years.

"Not one stone will be left upon another," Jesus said.

Later when they were all on the Mount of Olives, the disciples asked Jesus, "When will these things happen? Will we have a sign before you return and the end of the world comes?"

"Don't look for a sign in every troubled time," Jesus told them. "There will be wars, famines, earthquakes, and many other horrors, but these are only the beginning of the troubles. My followers will be persecuted and hated because of me, but the Good News must be preached throughout the world so that all nations will hear it. Be careful of rumors about my coming, for many false messiahs will appear. I will come on the clouds of heaven with great power and glory. I will send angels forth with a mighty trumpet blast to gather my chosen ones from the ends of the earth. No one except my Father knows the day or hour when I will return. When I come unexpectedly, people will be doing business as usual, just as they were when the Great Flood came in Noah's time."

The parable of the fig tree

Jesus told six parables to illustrate his teachings. The first was about a fig tree.

Jesus said, "You know that summer is near when the fig tree's buds appear and its leaves begin to sprout. Likewise, when you see the events I described, you know the time of my return is drawing near. Stay alert and watch!"

The parable of the master and his servants

Jesus' second parable compared his coming to a man who left for a trip, giving each of his servants instructions about the work they were to do while he was gone. He also told the gatekeeper to watch for his return.

"Beware," said the master, "for I could come back without notice at any time of the day or night. Don't let me find you sleeping if I return without warning. Watch carefully for my return."

The parable of the faithful or unfaithful servant

A similar parable was about a master who put a servant in charge of his household. Part of his job was to feed his family. If the master returned

426

>

What
Everyone
Should
Know
about
the

Bible

and found the servant doing a good job, he would reward him. If the servant was evil and thought that he could get by with something, and then the master made a surprise return, the master would punish the servant and banish him from his home.

The parable of the ten bridesmaids

The Kingdom of Heaven is like ten bridesmaids who took their lamps and went to meet the bridegroom. Five of these girls were foolish, for they took no oil for their lamps. The other five were wise and brought oil with them.

The bridegroom was delayed, so they all lay down and slept until midnight. Suddenly someone shouted that the bridegroom was coming. The five foolish girls had run out of oil, and they asked the other five to share theirs. But there wasn't enough oil for everyone, so the five foolish girls ran off to buy some. While they were gone, the bridegroom came and everyone went in to the wedding feast and locked the door. When the five foolish girls finally came back with oil, it was too late to get in.

Those who think they can wait and are too late may find that they are locked out of heaven.

The parable of the talents

Another of Jesus' parables, sometimes called the parable of the talents, is similar to another one he told. A talent was a measure of gold that would be the equivalent of half a million dollars today.

The Kingdom of Heaven is like a wealthy man who went on a long trip. He gave one servant five bags, or talents, of gold. He gave another two bags, and he gave the third one bag. He asked each of these servants to invest his money wisely while he was gone.

When he returned, the wealthy man called for his three servants to give him an account of their investments. The servant with five talents had ten after investing. The master was pleased and gave this servant more responsibilities and a reward. The servant with two talents had four after investing, and the master also rewarded him. The servant with one talent had dug a hole and buried the money, so he had only the one talent to give back. The master was not pleased with this servant. He ordered other servants to take the talent from him and give it to the one who had ten talents.

The parable of the sheep and the goats

"When I return in my glory and all the angels with me, I will sit upon my glorious throne," Jesus said. "The nations will be gathered before me, and I will separate them as a shepherd separates sheep and goats, with the sheep on my right hand and the goats on my left hand. To the sheep I will offer my kingdom, but I will send the goats away from me."

How does Jesus know his sheep? These are the people who trust him as Savior and Lord and believe that he is God's Son. He also expects them to serve him well.

"When I was hungry, you fed me," Jesus said about his sheep. "When I was thirsty, you gave me a drink. When I was a stranger, you took me in. When I had no clothing, you clothed me. When I was sick, you took care of me. When I was in prison, you visited me."

The disciples were puzzled. "When did we do all these things for you?" they asked.

"When you did it for the least of my people," Jesus answered.

We do not get to heaven by doing nice things for people, but we do nice things for people because we love and follow Jesus.

Jesus predicts his crucifixion

On Tuesday evening, which for Jewish people was the beginning of Wednesday, Jesus told his disciples that the Passover would come in two days, and after that he would be crucified. The disciples still did not seem to understand this, for Jesus' crucifixion came as a surprise to them.

Meanwhile, the chief religious leaders got together and plotted how to kill Jesus. They didn't want to do it during Passover, for that might turn the people against them.

Mary anoints Jesus with ointment

That same evening Jesus had dinner in Bethany at the home of Simon the leper, whom he had evidently healed. While he was there, Mary the sister of Martha and Lazarus brought an alabaster jar of expensive ointment and poured it on Jesus' head as an act of love and worship.

The disciples were indignant because the ointment was worth a lot of money. Judas Iscariot, the disciple who would later betray Jesus, was the most vocal. "Why wasn't this ointment sold and the money given to the poor?" he demanded. Judas didn't really care about the poor—he just wanted more money so he could steal it.

"Leave her alone," Jesus said. "You will always have the poor with you, but you will not always have me with you. Wherever the gospel is preached throughout the world, this woman's wonderful deed will be remembered."

Satan enters Judas Iscariot

At that time Satan entered into Judas Iscariot. Judas went to the religious leaders and talked with them about how he could betray Jesus. For his betrayal they gave him thirty pieces of silver.

What
Everyone
Should
Know
about
the
Bible

Questions You May Be Asking

Why was Tuesday evening considered the beginning of Wednesday?
For the Jewish people of Jesus' time, sunset marked the end of the current day and the beginning of the new day. What we know as Tuesday evening, therefore, the Jewish people would call the beginning of Wednesday.

What kind of oil did the bridesmaids use in their lamps, and what were the lamps like?
Lamps in Jesus' time were like little covered saucers with a hole in the top. The lamp was filled with olive oil and had a wick inserted into it.

Great Events of This Time

1. **On the Mount of Olives Jesus tells his disciples about the destruction of Jerusalem** (Matthew 24–25; Mark 13:1-37; Luke 21:5-28).
2. **Jesus tells the parable of the fig tree** (Matthew 24:32-41; Mark 13:28-32; Luke 21:29-33).
3. **Jesus tells the parable of the gatekeeper** (Mark 13:34-37).
4. **Jesus tells the parable of the master and his servants** (Matthew 24:45-51).
5. **Jesus tells the parable of the ten bridesmaids** (Matthew 25:1-13).
6. **Jesus tells the parable of the talents** (Matthew 25:14-30).
7. **Jesus tells the parable of the sheep and the goats** (Matthew 25:31-46).
8. **Jewish leaders secretly plot against Jesus** (Matthew 26:1-5; Mark 14:1-2; Luke 22:1-2).
9. **Mary anoints Jesus' feet** (Matthew 26:6-13; Mark 14:3-9; John 12:1-11).
10. **Judas bargains to betray Jesus** (Matthew 26:14-16; Mark 14:10-11; Luke 22:3-6).

Significant Dates of This Time

Circa A.D. 30

Did You Know?

An alabaster jar of spikenard Different Bible versions translate the words for Mary's jar and its contents in different ways. You may see the word *spikenard*, or *nard*, for the ointment. Some call her jar an alabaster box. The ointment was a very expensive fragrant oil from the Himalayan mountains and other mountains of India that was sometimes used to anoint royalty. Alabaster is a soft marble stone from Egypt. Mary had a jar that was probably imported from Egypt filled with ointment imported from India. This suggests that Mary and her family were quite wealthy.

Would you rather be a sheep or a goat? In Jesus' story goats got some bad press. The sheep represented Jesus' followers, while the goats represented those who rejected him. Sheep follow a shepherd obediently, but goats do not. In the Middle East it is common to see a long line of sheep following after their shepherd. Goats will stay in the crowd, so to speak, but you won't see a line of them following their shepherd because they are too rebellious.

Discovering My Purpose from God's Plan

1. *"Too late" sometimes really is too late.* The five foolish bridesmaids learned that they were too late for the wedding feast, and they could not get in. If we are too late in making a decision to accept Jesus, it will be too late to get into heaven, his home.
2. *Invest personal talents wisely.* Don't dig a hole and bury them—use them or lose them.
3. *We don't get to heaven by doing godly things for needy people, but by becoming godly people.* We become godly people when we accept Jesus as our Savior. Then we are expected to do godly things for needy people.

36

Last Hours

The Upper Room and Gethsemane

Characters:
Jesus and his disciples, especially James, John, Judas Iscariot, and Peter

Time Period:
Toward the end of Jesus' ministry

Dates:
Circa A.D. 30

Where Scene 36 of the Big Story Can Be Found:
Matthew 26:17-30, 36-46; Mark 14:12-26; Luke 22:7-30, 39-46; John 18:1-30

In Scene 36, Find the Answers to These Questions:
Why did the Son of God wash dirty feet?
What was the menu for the Last Supper?

Look for this in Scene 36
> They reclined to eat at the Last Supper.
> Jesus sang a hymn.

Preparing for the Passover and the Last Supper

On Wednesday Jesus evidently spent the day resting with his disciples in Bethany, just two miles east of Jerusalem. Our story resumes on Thursday afternoon. The Festival of Unleavened Bread, which began with the Passover, had arrived. It was time to prepare the Passover supper for Jesus and his disciples, the one that has become known as the Last Supper.

Jesus sent Peter and John into Jerusalem to prepare the Passover meal so that they could all eat it together. Jesus gave them very specific instructions: "When you enter Jerusalem, a man with a pitcher of water will meet you. Follow him to the house he enters and ask the owner if we may use the upstairs guest room so that I may eat the Passover meal with my disciples. He will take you upstairs to a large room already set up. Prepare our Passover meal there."

The Last Supper

Peter and John went into Jerusalem, and everything happened exactly the way Jesus said it would. When the time came for supper, Jesus went with the Twelve to the upper room, and they reclined at the table together.

"I have longed to eat this meal with you before my suffering begins," Jesus told them. "I will not eat this meal with you again until it is fulfilled in the Kingdom of God." Jesus was announcing that this was their last supper together, but the disciples apparently still didn't grasp what he meant about suffering. Jesus told them several times that he would be crucified, but it still seemed to be a surprise for them when it happened.

The disciples began to argue among themselves about who would be the greatest among them. How this must have grieved Jesus! He had the answer to their argument: "Whoever wants to be chief must be a servant, just as I am serving you," he said. The arguing stopped—no one wanted the job of being a servant to the others.

But Jesus set the example of servant leadership for them. He got up from the table, removed his outer robe, wrapped a towel around his waist, and poured water into a basin. He began to wash the disciples' dirty feet, wiping them with the towel. Certainly this was servant leadership, for no one else would want that job!

When Jesus came to Peter, Peter protested, "You will never wash my feet!"

"If I don't, you will not belong to me," Jesus responded.

Impetuous Peter hastily replied, "Then wash my hands and head as well, not just my feet."

Jesus put on his robe and reclined again at the table. "Do you know what I have done?" he asked. "If I have served you this way, you should serve one another."

432

\>

What
Everyone
Should
Know
about
the

Bible

Then great anguish came over Jesus. "One of you will betray me," he said. He must have looked deep into the eyes of Judas Iscariot, down to his soul.

Peter motioned for John, who was sitting next to Jesus, to ask who he was talking about. Jesus answered, "The one to whom I give the bread when I dip it into the sauce."

Then Jesus dipped the bread and gave it to Judas Iscariot. As soon as Judas ate the bread, Satan entered into him. "Do it now!" Jesus whispered to him. "Do it quickly!"

The others didn't understand what Jesus meant. Judas was their treasurer, so some thought that Jesus was sending him to pay for the food or to give some money to the poor. After Jesus spoke to him, Judas slipped away from the table and into the night.

After Judas left, Jesus said to the others, "The time has come for me to enter into my glory. God will be glorified because of all that happens to me, and he will soon bring me into my glory. It won't be long now before I leave you, and you cannot go where I am going. I leave you the commandment that you should love one another just as I have loved you."

"Where are you going?" Peter asked.

"You can't go with me now, but you will come later," Jesus answered.

"Why can't I go with you?" Peter asked. "I am ready to die for you."

"Die for me?" Jesus asked. "No, Peter, not really. Before the rooster crows twice tomorrow morning, you will deny three times that you even know me."

Peter and all the other disciples argued that they would never desert Jesus or deny him, but Jesus could see what they could not.

The cup of wine

Jesus took a cup of wine and gave thanks for it. "Share this among yourselves," he said, "for I will not drink wine again until the Kingdom of God has come." The disciples sipped from the cup and passed it from person to person.

"This cup is my blood of the new covenant, which I will shed for many to take away their sins," Jesus told them.

The loaf of bread

Jesus lifted a loaf of bread and gave thanks for it. "This is my body, given for you," he said. "Eat this in remembrance of me."

A long farewell

After the supper Jesus gave a long farewell discourse to the disciples. This is found in the Gospel of John, chapters 14, 15, and 16. Among the many other things Jesus shared with his disciples, he told them that he was going away to prepare a home for them (and for us) in heaven, and that he would come back someday to take us there. He called himself "the Way, the Truth, and the Life." He is the only way to heaven, the only way to the beautiful home he is preparing for us. He also spoke of the coming of the Holy Spirit.

A prayer of intercession

The entire seventeenth chapter of the Gospel of John is a prayer of intercession that Jesus prayed for his disciples. After this prayer Jesus and his disciples sang a hymn and left the upper room to go to the garden of Gethsemane on the Mount of Olives, overlooking the eastern wall of Jerusalem.

Praying in the garden

In the garden Jesus took Peter, James, and John apart from the others. Then he told them to wait while he went alone to pray. "My soul is crushed with grief, to the point of death," he told them. "Stay here and watch with me." Then Jesus went on a few paces to pray.

Jesus knelt down with his face to the ground and prayed, *My Father, if it is possible, take this cup of suffering from me. But I want your will, not mine, to be done.*

When Jesus returned to Peter, James, and John, they were asleep. "Couldn't you stay awake with me this one hour?" he asked. "Stay alert and pray, or temptation will overpower you. You want to do this, but your body is weak."

Jesus left the three again and prayed, *My Father, if this cup of suffering cannot be taken from me, then let your will be done.* He returned to the three and found them still sleeping, so he went back a third time to pray, repeating his plea to the Father. Then he returned again to the three.

"Still sleeping?" Jesus asked. "Look, the time has come for me to be betrayed into the hands of sinners. Get up! My betrayer is coming."

Questions You May Be Asking

Do we know the hymn that Jesus and the disciples sang at the close of the Last Supper?

Yes, it was most likely the Hallel, but you won't find it in your church hymnal. Instead it's in your Bible, in Psalms 113–118. Can you picture Jesus singing this beautiful hymn with his disciples before he entered his passion?

What was the menu for the Last Supper?

The traditional Passover menu included unleavened bread, red wine mixed with water, bitter herbs, vinegar or salt water in which the bitter herbs were dipped, charoseth (a mixture of almonds, apples, raisins,

What
Everyone
Should
Know
about
the

Bible

and other foods), and the sop, or morsel (a wafer or cake of unleavened bread, something like a potato chip), which was used to dip into food.

Where was Judas Iscariot seated?
Judas must have grabbed the best seat at the table, for he sat next to Jesus in the seat of greatest honor. John sat on the other side of Jesus, and Peter sat across the table in the seat of least honor.

Why did people recline at the table instead of sitting in chairs?
This was the Roman custom of that time. The people were in a semi-reclining position. They rested with their left side and arm propped up on pillows, and they ate with their right hands.

Great Events of This Time

1. **The disciples make Passover preparations** (Matthew 26:17-19; Mark 14:12-16; Luke 22:7-13).
2. **The disciples and Jesus celebrate the Last Supper** (Matthew 26:20-30; Mark 14:17-26; Luke 22:14-30; John 13:1-30).
3. **Jesus prays in the garden of Gethsemane** (Matthew 26:36-46; Mark 14:32-42; Luke 22:39-46; John 18:1).

Significant Dates of This Time

Circa A.D. 30

Heroes and Villains: The Stars of Scene 36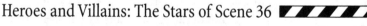

JUDAS ISCARIOT
Judas and his father, Simon, both had the surname Iscariot, which probably meant that they were from Kerioth, a town in southern Judah. The other eleven disciples apparently never suspected Judas as a traitor. He appeared to be a loyal follower from the first, only turning against Jesus when it became clear that he would not lead an earthly kingdom against the Romans. Judas was apparently a good businessman and was thus appointed to handle money for the Twelve.

On the night of the Last Supper, Jesus revealed that one of the Twelve would betray him. He then told Judas privately to go and do his evil work. Judas sold Jesus for thirty pieces of silver, led the mob to the garden of Gethsemane, betrayed Jesus with a kiss, suffered remorse for his evil, told the chief priests he had betrayed innocent blood, threw the silver on the floor of the Temple, and committed suicide.

Bible events in Judas Iscariot's life
1. He is chosen as one of Jesus' disciples.
2. Jesus predicts that Judas will betray him.

3. He objects to Mary's extravagance when she anoints Jesus with ointment.
4. He discusses with the chief priests how he might betray Jesus to them; they give him thirty pieces of silver.
5. Jesus gives him dipped bread at the Last Supper, signifying that he would betray him.
6. Satan enters into him, and he leaves the Last Supper.
7. He betrays Jesus with a kiss.
8. Filled with remorse, he brings the thirty pieces of silver back to the chief priests and throws the money on the Temple floor.
9. He runs away and hangs himself.

 Did You Know?

Thirty pieces of silver The religious leaders paid Judas Iscariot thirty pieces of silver to betray Jesus. These were probably silver shekels, used to pay the Temple tax for two people. The actual coin could have been the tetradrachma of Tyre. This was a silver coin about the size of a United States half dollar. The head of the coin had a picture of a god of Tyre, Baal Melcarth, with a wreath or laurel. On the reverse side of the coin was an eagle with a victory palm.

The upper room No one knows for certain where the upper room for the Last Supper was, but some identify it as the upstairs room in the home of Mary the mother of John Mark. The traditional tourist site is on the second floor of the same building where David's tomb occupies the first floor. Of course, it would have been a bit of a problem for Mary's home to have David's tomb on the first floor.

The route to Gethsemane From the upper room, Jesus and his disciples probably went out of Jerusalem through the gate in the south wall that is called the Dung Gate today. They would have descended Roman-built stone steps into the Kidron Valley, then climbed back up the other side of the valley into the garden of Gethsemane. From Gethsemane there is a clear view of the eastern walls of the city, the Golden Gate through which Jesus rode in his Triumphal Entry, and the Temple structure rising above the walls.

>

What
Everyone
Should
Know
about
the

Bible

Discovering My Purpose from God's Plan

1. *Godly events are no time for ungodly conduct.* What an inappropriate time and place for the disciples to argue—at the Last Supper! This should remind us to avoid arguments in church settings.
2. *A servant is not greater than his master, as Jesus told the disciples.* Think

of every humble act Jesus did. How can we be so proud when we remember Jesus' example?

3. *Never betray Jesus with a kiss of affection*—that is, avoid misguided affection for ungodly things.

The Greatest Sacrifice
Jesus' Trial, Crucifixion, and Burial

Characters:
Barabbas (a criminal released instead of Jesus); Caiaphas (the high priest); Herod Antipas (a ruler of Galilee who judged Jesus); Jesus and his disciples (especially John, Judas Iscariot, and Peter); Joseph of Arimathea (a rich man who helped to bury Jesus in his tomb); Malchus (a servant of the high priest); Mary (the mother of Jesus); Mary (the wife of Cleopas); Mary Magdalene; the mob; Nicodemus (a Pharisee who helped to bury Jesus); Pontius Pilate (a Roman governor); a Roman centurion and Roman soldiers (who crucified Jesus); the Sanhedrin, or Jewish council

Time Period:
Toward the end of Jesus' ministry

Dates:
Circa A.D. 30

Where Scene 37 of the Big Story Can Be Found:
The Gospels: Matthew, Mark, Luke, and John. For specific references, see "Great Events of This Time," page 446.

In Scene 37, Find the Answers to These Questions:
Who gave up his own tomb so that Jesus could be buried there?
How many angels stood by to rescue Jesus?
Why didn't Jesus ask the angels to help him?

Look for this in Scene 37
> How did some men blaspheme by claiming that someone else had done so?
> Where did the money come from to buy the potter's field where Judas Iscariot was buried?

The Big Story So Far

The mob and the kiss of betrayal

With flickering torches, a mob of thugs armed with swords and clubs wound their way up the side of the Mount of Olives into the garden of Gethsemane. The mob was led by Judas Iscariot, and they came from the high priest and the other religious leaders. Judas had told them he would identify Jesus with a kiss, so he brazenly came up to Jesus and kissed his cheek. "Greetings, Teacher," he said.

Jesus looked deep into Judas's soul. "How can you betray the Son of God with a kiss?" he asked. Those words must have penetrated the very marrow of the betrayer.

When the thugs in the mob saw this prearranged signal, they grabbed Jesus. The guards who came along arrested and bound him. Peter had a sword with him, so he pulled it out and slashed wildly at a servant of the high priest, whose name was Malchus, and cut off his ear.

"Put your sword away, Peter," Jesus said. "Those who use the sword may also die by the sword. Don't you know that I could call twelve legions of angels down to protect me?" Then Jesus restored the servant's ear.

Jesus turned to the mob. "Have you come here with swords and clubs as though I were a robber?" he asked. "I was with you every day in the Temple, but you wouldn't touch me. Nevertheless, this is all happening so the Scriptures will be fulfilled."

All of this happened very late Thursday night or very early Friday morning, according to our calendar, since Jews start their day at sundown, or about six in the evening. Thus the Last Supper, the time in the garden of Gethsemane, Jesus' arrest, and his early trials all occurred on the Jewish Friday.

Jesus is taken before Caiaphas

The mob took Jesus to Caiaphas, the high priest, and he assembled the Sanhedrin, which was the Jewish high council. These scoundrels found false witnesses to lie about Jesus, probably paying them to do so. Someone is always willing to do such things for a price. The witnesses' testimony didn't seem very good, so the high priest went after Jesus himself, but Jesus would not answer him.

The high priest demanded, "Are you the Messiah or not?"

"I am," Jesus answered. "You will see me sitting at the right hand of God, and coming with the clouds of heaven."

When he heard that, the high priest tore his clothes as a sign of anguish.

"Why do we need any more witnesses?" he shouted to the council. "You have heard this man's blasphemy. What is your verdict?" The

What
Everyone
Should
Know
about
the

Bible

majority of the council members condemned Jesus to die. Some even began to spit on him. They blindfolded him and hit him.

"Who hit you that time, prophet?" they mocked.

Even the guards who led Jesus away began to hit him.

Peter denies Jesus

Meanwhile Peter sneaked into the courtyard of the high priest's home, where Jesus was being judged, and warmed himself by a fire. A servant girl saw Peter and accused him of being with Jesus. Peter denied it, and as he did, a rooster crowed. Another servant girl accused him of being with Jesus, and Peter denied it again. Later some other people accused him of being with Jesus.

This time Peter began to curse. "I swear to God, I don't even know that man," he shouted. Immediately the rooster crowed again.

At that moment Jesus was being led past the place where Peter was standing, and he heard what Peter said. When Peter looked into the face of Jesus, he remembered Jesus' prediction: that Peter would deny him three times before the rooster crowed twice. In his great remorse Peter ran from the courtyard, crying bitterly.

Jesus before the Sanhedrin

After daybreak the Sanhedrin assembled formally, and Jesus was brought before it. "Tell us if you are the Messiah," they demanded.

"If I tell you, you won't believe me," Jesus said. "And if I ask you a question, you will not answer. But the time is coming when I will be at God's right hand in a place of power."

"Then you claim to be God's Son!" they shouted.

"Yes, you are right when you say that," Jesus answered.

"We do not need witnesses," they all said. "We have heard his blasphemy." They believed that it was blasphemy for anyone to claim to be God or God's Son. Oddly enough, they thought the Son of God spoke blasphemy when he was telling the truth, and they thought they themselves were pure though they spoke lies.

Judas repents, too late

When Judas Iscariot learned that Jesus had been condemned to die, he was filled with remorse. He took the thirty pieces of silver back to the religious leaders. "I have sinned, for I have betrayed an innocent man," he moaned.

"What do we care about that?" the religious leaders snorted. "That is your problem."

So Judas threw the money on the Temple floor, then went out and hanged himself. The religious leaders picked up the money and tried to find a good use for it.

"We can't put it into the Temple treasury, since it's against the law to accept money paid for murder," they said.

What strange morals these men had! It was all right for them to pay for the betrayal of Jesus, but it wasn't all right to put the "murder money" into the Temple offering.

They decided to use the money to buy a potter's field, where they could bury strangers. The field became known as Akeldama, or Aceldama, the field of blood.

Jesus is judged by Pilate

Jesus' trial before Caiaphas, the high priest, ended early in the morning. The Jewish council, or Sanhedrin, could condemn a man to death, but they couldn't actually kill him. Only the Romans could carry out an execution. So they sent Jesus to the Roman governor, Pilate, hoping he would officially pronounce the Roman death sentence.

The religious leaders would not go into the Roman headquarters because they thought this would defile them, which would prevent them from celebrating the Passover. It was another case of backward morals—it was all right to murder a miracle-working prophet, but they wouldn't defile themselves by entering a Roman building. Because they wouldn't go in, Pilate went out to meet them.

"What is your charge against this man?" he asked.

"He's a criminal," they said.

"Then judge him by your own laws," Pilate responded.

"Only the Romans can execute a man," they said. So Pilate went inside and ordered Jesus to be brought before him.

"Are you the king of the Jews?" Pilate asked.

"I am not an earthly king," Jesus responded. "My kingdom is not of this world."

"So you are a king," said Pilate.

"Yes, you are right," Jesus said. "I was born for that purpose. I came to bring truth into the world."

"What is truth?" Pilate asked.

Then Pilate went out to the religious leaders again. "I find nothing wrong with this man," he said, but the religious leaders became even more urgent. Then they mentioned Galilee. Pilate didn't want to deal with Jesus' case, so he decided to send Jesus to Herod Antipas, who happened to be in Jerusalem at that time.

Jesus is judged by Herod Antipas

Herod was glad to see Jesus. He had heard about Jesus' miracles and hoped Jesus would do a magic trick or two for him. Jesus would not even talk with Herod; he remained silent before him. Meanwhile the

What
Everyone
Should
Know
about
the
Bible

religious leaders stood there, shouting and yelling terrible things about Jesus. Soon Herod grew tired of this. He placed a royal robe on Jesus, made fun of him, and sent him back to Pilate. These two, who had been enemies, became friends that day because of Jesus' trial.

Jesus is judged by Pilate again
Jesus was brought back before Pilate. The religious leaders had gathered a crowd to support them, and they pressed Pilate to condemn Jesus to death.

By this time Pilate realized that the Jewish leaders had arrested Jesus because they were jealous of him. He wanted to let Jesus go, but he knew he had to do it in the right way. Each year the Roman governor released one Jewish prisoner at Passover, and the people could choose which one would be set free. "Should I release the king of the Jews or Barabbas?" Pilate asked. He was sure the religious leaders would release Jesus, for Barabbas was a notorious criminal.

"Barabbas! Barabbas!" the leaders shouted. They also stirred up the crowd to cry out for Barabbas's release.

Jesus is sentenced to be crucified
"What should I do with Jesus?" Pilate asked.

"Crucify him! Crucify him!" they shouted.

Pilate was too much of a coward to go against them, so he ordered the Roman soldiers to flog Jesus with lead-tipped whips and take him away to be crucified.

Roman soldiers were notoriously brutal. They called out the entire battalion to flog Jesus. They dressed him in a purple robe, jammed a crown made of thorns down on his head, and mocked him. They beat him, spit on him, and made fun of him. When they finally became bored of this, they took him away to be crucified.

On the way to the cross
When Jesus was too exhausted to carry his own cross, the soldiers forced an onlooker, Simon from Cyrene in North Africa, who had just arrived in Jerusalem, to carry Jesus' cross. His sons were Alexander and Rufus.

Jesus is crucified
The procession made its way to a hill called Golgotha, which means "Place of the Skull." Some people offered Jesus wine drugged with myrrh to ease his pain, but he refused it. The Roman soldiers nailed Jesus to the cross, then gambled for his clothing. This fulfilled the prophecy in Psalm 22:18: "They divide my garments among themselves and throw dice for my clothing." Two robbers were crucified with Jesus that day, one on each side of him.

The crucifixion took place at nine o'clock on Friday morning. Jesus prayed, "Father, forgive them for they don't know what they are doing."

Pilate ordered a sign that read "Jesus of Nazareth, King of the Jews" to be written in Hebrew, Latin, and Greek and nailed to Jesus' cross. The religious leaders didn't like the sign and asked Pilate to change it to "He said he was king of the Jews."

"What I have written, I have written!" Pilate angrily responded, and he refused to change the sign.

Many mocked Jesus as he hung on the cross. "If you are the Son of God, prove it by coming down from the cross," they said.

"He saved others, but he can't save himself," some religious leaders shouted.

One of the robbers joined the crowd in mocking Jesus, but the other did not. He pleaded, "Jesus, remember me when you come into your kingdom."

"Today you will be with me in paradise," Jesus promised the dying man.

Jesus' mother, Mary, as well as Mary the wife of Cleopas and Mary Magdalene were there at the foot of the cross. When Jesus saw his mother standing with John, he called down to them, asking John to take care of her.

At noon darkness came across the whole land and lasted until three o'clock. Then Jesus called out in a loud voice, *"Eloi, Eloi, lema Sabachthani,"* which means, "My God, my God, why have you abandoned me?" Some thought that he was calling for Elijah. One person filled a sponge with vinegar and put it to his mouth to drink.

Then Jesus cried out in a loud voice, "Father, into your hands I entrust my spirit." With those last words, he died.

At that moment strange and wonderful things began to happen. The curtain of the Temple was torn in two from top to bottom. The earth shook, rocks split apart, and tombs opened. Many godly people who had died rose from the dead and appeared to others in Jerusalem after Jesus' resurrection.

The Roman centurion and other soldiers at the crucifixion were terrified by the earthquake and all that had happened. "Truly this was the Son of God," they said.

From a distance Mary Magdalene, Jesus' mother, and the mother of James and John were watching. For them it was a time of intense sorrow.

The Jewish leaders did not want the bodies to remain on the crosses through the Sabbath day, which would begin that evening at six o'clock, so they asked Pilate to break the men's legs to hasten their

444

>

What
Everyone
Should
Know
about
the

Bible

death. The soldiers broke the legs of the two robbers, but when they came to Jesus, they saw that he was dead already. So they did not break his legs, but one soldier pierced his side with a spear, and blood and water poured out. These things fulfilled the Old Testament prophecies in Exodus 12:46; Numbers 9:12; Deuteronomy 21:22-23; and Psalm 34:20. The Old Testament prophecies in Psalm 22:16 and Isaiah 53:5 prophesied that Jesus would be pierced.

Joseph of Arimathea claims the body of Jesus

As evening approached, a wealthy man from Arimathea named Joseph, who was one of Jesus' followers, went to Pilate and asked for Jesus' body. Pilate called for the centurion and asked if Jesus was already dead. When the centurion said that he was, Pilate gave Jesus' body to Joseph.

Joseph of Arimathea carefully took Jesus' body from the cross and wrapped it in a linen cloth. Nicodemus, the man who came to Jesus by night, joined Joseph and brought seventy-five pounds of embalming ointment made from myrrh and aloes to put on Jesus' body. Together they wrapped Jesus' body and placed it in Joseph's new tomb in a garden near Golgotha.

Questions You May Be Asking

Why was Peter carrying a sword?

This is one of those strange, unexplained things in the Bible. Why would any disciple of Jesus carry a sword? And was it a short sword or a full-size one? Did Jesus know that Peter carried a sword? We don't know if Peter carried it regularly or just for this occasion, but it seems that none of the other disciples had a weapon of any kind.

What was the Sanhedrin?

The Sanhedrin was the Jewish high council during the Greek and Roman periods. It was composed of seventy men, plus the high priest, who acted as president. We don't know much about succession, but some think it was a job for life, and successors were appointed by the other council members. The members were chief priests (the high priest or anyone who had been a high priest, and members of privileged families from which high priests were taken), scribes or Pharisees, and elders, who were mostly secular nobility or tribal heads. Josephus said that the high priests in Jesus' time were Sadducees, but the Pharisees dominated the council.

Why couldn't the religious leaders put Judas's money into the Temple treasury?

Deuteronomy 23:18 forbade the use of tainted money for the Temple treasury, especially money gained from prostitution. Apparently the religious leaders extended this ban to include money paid for murder.

1. **Judas betrays Jesus** (Matthew 26:47-56; Mark 14:43-52; Luke 22:47-53; John 18:2-11).
2. **Jesus stands before Annas, Caiaphas, and the council** (Matthew 26:57-68; Mark 14:53-65; Luke 22:63-71; John 18:12-14, 19-24).
3. **Peter denies Jesus** (Matthew 26:69-75; Mark 14:66-72; Luke 22:54-62; John 18:15-18, 25-27).
4. **Judas hangs himself** (Matthew 27:1-10; Acts 1:18-19).
5. **Jesus stands before Pilate** (Matthew 27:11-14; Mark 15:1-5; Luke 23:1-5; John 18:28-37).
6. **Jesus stands before Herod Antipas** (Luke 23:6-12).
7. **Jesus returns to Pilate and is condemned to die** (Matthew 27:15-26; Mark 15:6-15; Luke 23:13-25; John 18:38–19:16).
8. **Roman soldiers scourge Jesus** (Matthew 27:27-30; Mark 15:16-19).
9. **Jesus proceeds to the cross** (Matthew 27:31-34; Mark 15:20-23; Luke 23:26-31; John 19:17).
10. **At Jesus' crucifixion, soldiers gamble for Jesus' clothing** (Matthew 27:35-36; Mark 15:24; Luke 23:32-38; John 19:18-24).
11. **Jesus hangs on the cross and dies** (Matthew 27:38-56; Mark 15:27-41; Luke 23:39-49; John 19:25-30).
12. **Joseph and Nicodemus bury Jesus** (Matthew 27:57-66; Mark 15:42-47; Luke 23:50-56; John 19:31-42).

Significant Dates of This Time

Circa A.D. 30

Heroes and Villains: The Stars of Scene 37

CAIAPHAS

By Jesus' time, the high priest of Israel was no longer appointed because of his godliness but because of political reasons. The high priest who presided over Jesus' trial was not as concerned about whether Jesus was truly the Son of God as he was about preventing an uprising against Rome. Caiaphas's father-in-law, Annas, was also called a high priest, for he had once served in that office, but he was more of an emeritus high priest.

Bible events in Caiaphas's life

1. He meets with a council of Pharisees and tells them that one man must die for the people.
2. Jesus is sent to his house; he questions him and accuses him of blasphemy.

446

>

What
Everyone
Should
Know
about
the

Bible

3. He meets with a council to judge Peter and John for preaching in the Temple.

JOSEPH OF ARIMATHEA

This wealthy member of the Sanhedrin became a secret disciple of Jesus. Although he was afraid to speak out against Jesus' crucifixion, he gathered the courage to ask for Jesus' body so that he might bury him in his own new tomb. Along with Nicodemus, Joseph anointed Jesus' body, wrapped it in burial cloth, and laid it in the tomb.

Bible events in Joseph of Arimathea's life
1. He asks Pilate for Jesus' body.
2. He helps to embalm Jesus and buries him in his own new tomb.

PONTIUS PILATE

During Jesus' ministry, Pontius Pilate served Rome as the fifth procurator of Judea. He represented the emperor and reported directly to him. Pilate's job was to keep peace in the land, and that required keeping peace with the Jewish leaders. He had offended them several times prior to Jesus' trial to the point that they complained directly to Caesar. Now Pilate was on trial, so when Jesus came before him, he was caught between seeking justice for an innocent man and seeking political expediency. Pilate tried numerous ways to free Jesus, but when the Jewish leaders taunted him, saying he was not a friend of Caesar's, Pilate yielded and gave orders for Jesus to be crucified. Tradition says that Pilate was later recalled to Rome for another political mistake; he was banished and committed suicide.

Bible events in Pontius Pilate's life
1. The council of religious leaders brings Jesus to him for trial.
2. He questions Jesus and finds no fault in him.
3. He sends Jesus to Herod, and Herod sends Jesus back to Pilate.
4. His wife tells him to leave Jesus alone.
5. He orders Jesus to be beaten and brings him out to the people.
6. He washes his hands of guilt and delivers Barabbas to the people.
7. He delivers Jesus to be crucified.

Did You Know?

Twelve legions of angels A legion was the largest unit in the Roman army, made up of about six thousand soldiers. Twelve legions of angels would be seventy-two thousand angels. That would be quite an angel army!

Live by the sword, die by the sword Soldiers in Bible times lived and died by the sword. They used it for protection and were often killed by it in combat. Jesus was telling Peter that the sword can bring death as well as protection. This was not the time to protect themselves with weapons, for Jesus came to die for our sins on the cross.

Blasphemy The religious leaders considered blasphemy to be anything spoken against God. When Jesus claimed to be God's Son, they were sure that he wasn't, so they thought he was blaspheming. But Jesus said that speaking against the Holy Spirit is blasphemy, so the religious leaders were blaspheming when they accused the Son of God of speaking blasphemy.

The potter's field This fulfilled the Old Testament prophecies in Zechariah 11:13; Jeremiah 18:2; 19:2; 32:6-15. Akeldama may still be seen today, just south of the old city of Jerusalem.

Discovering My Purpose from God's Plan

1. *Life and death are intertwined.* In the forest old trees must die to give new trees nourishment and life. Jesus had to die to give us everlasting life, and we must live for him to bring death to sin.
2. *There are times for angels to protect, and times for them to stand by.* Jesus had at least seventy-two thousand guardian angels at his disposal, but he would not let one of them help him.
3. *The religious leaders killed the Son of God because he claimed to be the Son of God.* If Jesus had claimed to be God's Son but really wasn't, it would have been blasphemy. Since Jesus claimed to be God's Son and he really was, it was the religious leaders who committed blasphemy against God when they rejected and crucified God the Son. They sinned by condemning Jesus to death for the supposed sin of telling the truth.

38

The Dawn of Hope
Jesus'
Resurrection
and
Ascension

Characters:
Angels; Cleopas and a friend (who walked with Jesus on the road to Emmaus); Jesus and his disciples (especially James, John, Nathanael, Peter, and Thomas); Joseph of Arimathea (who helped to bury Jesus in his own tomb); Mary (the mother of Jesus); Mary Magdalene; Nicodemus (who helped to bury Jesus); the Roman soldiers who guarded Jesus' tomb

Time Period:
Toward the end of Jesus' ministry

Dates:
Circa A.D. 30

Where Scene 38 of the Big Story Can Be Found:
The Gospels: Matthew, Mark, Luke, and John; and Acts. For specific references, see "Great Events of This Time," page 455.

In Scene 38, Find the Answers to These Questions:
Why did Pilate station a guard at Jesus' tomb?
When did James finally believe in Jesus as the Messiah?

Look for this in Scene 38
> Angel clothing—what was it like?
> Jesus shared Old Testament prophecies about himself twice.

The Big Story So Far

It was approaching sundown, about six o'clock, and the beginning of a new day on the Jewish calendar. This had been the most momentous day in all of history because Jesus, the Son of God, was crucified for our sins. Joseph of Arimathea asked Pilate for Jesus' body, and he and Nicodemus prepared it for burial in Joseph's new tomb, near Golgotha. Mary Magdalene, Mary the mother of Jesus, and some other women from Galilee watched from a respectful distance. At last the women went home and prepared spices and ointments to place on Jesus' body after the Sabbath ended early Sunday morning.

A guard at Jesus' tomb

Meanwhile the religious leaders were still paranoid about Jesus. They went to Pilate and asked him to station a guard at the tomb, for they remembered that Jesus had said he would rise from the dead in three days. They wanted to be sure that the disciples would not steal Jesus' body and claim he had risen, so Pilate granted their wish and stationed a guard at the tomb. He even sealed the stone, probably with his own seal.

Jesus rises from the dead, and women visit Jesus' tomb

The Sabbath ended at sundown on Saturday, but it was too late in the evening for the women to go to the tomb. They waited until early Sunday morning, which was considered the first day of the week. Before they arrived, there was a great earthquake as an angel descended from heaven, rolled the stone away from Jesus' tomb, and sat upon it. His appearance was like lightning, and his garments were as white as snow. Pilate's guards were so frightened that they lay there like dead men.

As dawn broke on Sunday morning, the third day after Jesus was crucified, the women came to the tomb with spices and ointments to put on Jesus' body. They wondered who would roll the heavy stone away for them.

As the women approached the tomb, they found the stone already rolled away. They rushed into the tomb and saw two angels in white sitting there. "Why are you seeking the living among the dead?" they asked. "He is not here. He is risen! Do you remember how he said that he would be crucified, and on the third day he would rise again? Now go and tell his disciples and Peter that you will see him."

The women rushed from the tomb and hurried back to tell the disciples. For a while the disciples would not believe them. They called it idle talk.

Mary Magdalene meets Jesus

Mary Magdalene returned to the tomb alone and stood there crying. The two angels appeared again and asked her why she was crying.

450

>

What
Everyone
Should
Know
about
the

Bible

"Because someone has taken my Lord's body, and I don't know where they have laid him," she answered. As she spoke, she turned her head and saw a man in the garden. She supposed he was the gardener.

"Sir," she called to the man. "If you have taken him away, tell me where you have laid him."

"Mary!" the stranger said.

Immediately Mary recognized the voice of Jesus. She rushed to Jesus and started to hug him. "Rabboni, Master!" she said.

"You must not cling to me," Jesus told her. "I have not yet ascended to my Father. But go back and tell the disciples what you have seen."

Peter and John visit Jesus' tomb

Mary rushed back to the upper room where the disciples were still waiting. She told them that she had seen Jesus and what he had said to her.

Peter and John ran from the room to see for themselves. John ran faster than Peter. When he arrived at the tomb, he stooped and looked in, but impetuous Peter rushed past him into the tomb. The two men saw the grave clothes, neatly folded up. When they saw these things, they went back to the upper room to tell the others.

Meanwhile the guards told the religious leaders what had happened at the tomb. Surely they would believe in Jesus as the Messiah when they heard he had risen from the dead, but their hearts were so hard that they could not believe. They paid the soldiers to lie, to say they had fallen asleep and the disciples had stolen Jesus' body while they slept. That became the official party line.

On the road to Emmaus

That afternoon two disciples decided to leave the upper room and go home to Emmaus, about seven miles west of Jerusalem. As they walked along, they talked about all the things that had happened. Suddenly Jesus joined them, but they didn't recognize him.

"What is your deep discussion?" Jesus asked. "What are you so concerned about?"

Cleopas answered, "You must be the only person in Jerusalem who hasn't heard of all the things that have happened the last few days."

"What things?" Jesus asked. The two men told about Jesus and how they had thought he was the Messiah, but that he had been crucified. They told how the women had found the empty tomb and how Peter and John had also failed to find the body of Jesus.

"You find it so hard to believe all that the prophets wrote in the Scripture," Jesus scolded. "Didn't the Scriptures clearly predict that the Messiah must suffer all these things before he could enter his glory?"

As they walked along, Jesus quoted one prophecy after another that told of his coming.

At last they reached Emmaus. Jesus started to go on, but the two men urged him to stay with them, since it was getting late. As they sat down to eat, Jesus took a small loaf of bread and thanked God for it. Then he broke it and gave it to them. Suddenly they recognized him, but the moment they did so, he disappeared.

"Didn't our hearts feel strangely warm as he talked with us?" they both asked. Although it was getting dark and was therefore unsafe to travel, the two hurried back to Jerusalem to tell the news to the other disciples. They rushed into the room, but before they could say a word, some other disciples greeted them with their own good news.

"The Lord is truly risen!" they said. "He appeared to Peter."

Then the two men told their story about Jesus. As they were telling the story, Jesus appeared there among them.

Jesus visits the disciples in the upper room

"Peace be with you," Jesus said. The whole group was very frightened, for they thought they were seeing a ghost.

"Why are you so frightened?" Jesus asked. "Why do you doubt who I am? Look at my hands and feet. Touch me and see that I am not a ghost." They were still filled with doubt, mingled with joy and wonder. Then Jesus ate some fish to prove that his body was human and very much alive.

Jesus taught the disciples all the prophecies of the Old Testament that predicted his coming. He breathed on them and told them to receive the Holy Spirit.

Thomas was absent on this Sunday evening, so he still doubted that Jesus was alive. "Unless I see the scars in his hands and put my finger into the wound in his side, I will not believe," he said.

Doubting Thomas believes

Eight days later the disciples were together again in the upper room. This time Thomas was with them. Although the doors were closed and locked, Jesus suddenly stood among them. Then Jesus had a little talk with Thomas.

"Put your finger here on my hands," he said to Thomas. "Put your hand into the wound in my side. Stop your unbelief! Believe in me!"

"My Lord and my God," Thomas said.

"You believe because you have seen me," Jesus said. "Blessed are those who believe even though they have not seen me."

Jesus meets the disciples in Galilee

As the days passed, many of the disciples went back to Galilee. Peter decided to go fishing, so several of the others joined him—Thomas the

452

>

What
Everyone
Should
Know
about
the

Bible

Twin, Nathanael, James and John, and two other disciples. They fished all night and caught nothing.

At dawn they saw a man standing on the beach, but they couldn't see who he was. "Throw your net on the right-hand side of the boat!" the man shouted. When they did so, it became so filled with fish that they couldn't pull the net into the boat.

"It is the Lord!" John said to Peter. Impetuous Peter put on his outer robe, for he had stripped it off for work. He jumped into the water and swam to shore because he just couldn't wait for the boat. The others brought in the boat and the fish. They saw a charcoal fire that Jesus had made, and fish frying on it. Jesus even had bread for them.

When the disciples dragged their net to shore, they counted the fish in the net. There were 153 large fish, but the net had not torn.

"Come and have some breakfast," Jesus said. So Jesus served them the bread and fish.

After breakfast Jesus had a talk with Peter. "Do you love me more than these?" Jesus asked. Perhaps Jesus pointed to the boat, the nets, and the fish.

"You know that I do," Peter answered.

"Feed my lambs," Jesus said. Then Jesus repeated the question.

"Do you love me?" he asked this time.

"Yes, Lord, you know that I love you," Peter answered. Then Jesus asked Peter his question a third time, and Peter was grieved.

"Feed my sheep!" Jesus said to Peter. "When you were young, you could go wherever you liked, but when you are old, you will stretch out your hands and others will take you where you don't want to go." Jesus was gently telling Peter that he too would be crucified, just as Jesus was. Then Jesus gave one last instruction to Peter. "Follow me," he said.

Then Peter saw John standing nearby. "What about him?" he asked Jesus.

"If I want him to remain alive until I return, what is that to you?" Jesus asked Peter. "You follow me." This started a rumor that Jesus had said John would not die.

Jesus meets the disciples on a mountain in Galilee

Later the eleven disciples went to a mountain in Galilee where Jesus had said he would meet them. Jesus also appeared to five hundred disciples at one time and to his half brother James (1 Corinthians 15:6). James had apparently not believed in Jesus as the Messiah until this time. Perhaps this appearance caused James to fully accept Jesus as the Messiah, for James became a leader in the Jerusalem church. Jesus appeared to his disciples from time to time for forty days after his resurrection.

The great commission

Jesus gave his disciples a special commission. He said, "I have been given all authority in heaven and on earth. Therefore, go and make disciples of all the nations, baptizing them in the name of the Father and the Son and the Holy Spirit. Teach these new disciples to obey all the commands I have given you. And be sure of this: I am with you always, even to the end of the age" (Matthew 28:18-20).

Jesus ascends into heaven

When they all returned to Jerusalem, Jesus taught his disciples again, showing them the prophecies of the Old Testament that spoke of his coming. He also told them about the coming of the Holy Spirit, whom they must wait for.

Then the time for Jesus' ascension had come. Jesus led his disciples to the Mount of Olives, near Bethany. He blessed them, then ascended into heaven as they watched. In heaven Jesus sat down at the right hand of God.

Questions You May Be Asking

Do angels wear clothing? What kind?

The Bible tells us several times that angels have dazzling white robes. The face of the angel who rolled the stone away from Jesus' tomb shone like lightning, and his clothing was as white as snow (Matthew 28:3). In Luke 24:4, the two angels who were at the tomb when the woman came to put spices on Jesus' body had dazzling robes. The angels who appeared to the disciples at Jesus' ascension were like white-robed men (Acts 1:10).

Why didn't Peter have his outer robe on when he fished?

The Bible tells us that he had stripped for work. It would have been impractical for a fisherman to be throwing out and pulling in nets in his long outer robes. Workers would remove their outer robes and "gird their loins," as some Bible versions put it. This means they would tie together their inner robes so that they fit them snugly and would not get in their way.

Where was Jesus when he ascended into heaven?

The Bible says that Jesus was near Bethany on the Mount of Olives when he ascended into heaven. A small domed structure on the Mount of Olives, called the Chapel of the Ascension, marks one traditional site. Russian Christians have built a Russian Orthodox church and bell tower over a second traditional site of the ascension. The original church was built by Queen Helena, mother of the Roman emperor Constantine,

454

>

What
Everyone
Should
Know
about
the

Bible

who lived from A.D. 248–A.D. 327. The present structure is about nine hundred years old.

Great Events of This Time

1. **Some women visit Jesus' tomb** (Matthew 28:1-10; Mark 16:1-8; Luke 24:1-12).
2. **Peter and John visit Jesus' tomb** (John 20:1-9).
3. **Mary Magdalene goes to Jesus' tomb** (Mark 16:9-11; John 20:11-18).
4. **The Jewish leaders concoct a story** (Matthew 28:11-15).
5. **Jesus speaks with two disciples on the road to Emmaus** (Mark 16:12-13; Luke 24:13-35).
6. **Jesus appears to his disciples when Thomas is absent** (Mark 16:14; Luke 24:36-43; John 20:19-23).
7. **Thomas doubts the Lord** (John 20:24-31).
8. **Jesus performs a fishing miracle** (John 21).
9. **Jesus appears to five hundred disciples and gives the great commission** (Matthew 28:16-20; Mark 16:15-18; Luke 24:44-49; Acts 1:1-8; 1 Corinthians 15:6).
10. **Jesus ascends into heaven** (Mark 16:19-20; Luke 24:50-53; Acts 1:9-11).

Significant Dates of This Time

Circa A.D. 30

Heroes and Villains: The Stars of Scene 38

JAMES THE BROTHER OF JESUS

James and the other sons of Joseph and Mary were Jesus' half brothers. These half brothers did not recognize Jesus as the Messiah during the early years of his ministry. Apparently when Jesus appeared to James after the Resurrection, James became a believer, and he later became the head of the church in Jerusalem. He was involved in numerous events in the early church, including the election of Matthias to replace Judas Iscariot as an apostle, counseling Paul to take the gospel to the Gentiles, and heading the Jerusalem council in which he supported Paul's position concerning the Gentiles and their freedom from the law. He was the author of the epistle of James. He was executed by the high priest around A.D. 62.

Bible events in James's life
1. He speaks at the council in Jerusalem.
2. He meets with Paul in Jerusalem when Paul returns from his third missionary journey.

THOMAS

Thomas is remembered as the doubting disciple. He was one of the Twelve who followed Jesus, but after Jesus rose from the dead, he refused to believe it until he saw the nail prints in Jesus' hands and put his hand into the wound in Jesus' side. When Jesus appeared to Thomas and invited him to touch his wounds, Thomas believed. Jesus told him that others who have not seen Jesus alive or touched his wounds but still believe are blessed.

Bible events in Thomas's life
1. Jesus chooses him to be one of the twelve apostles.
2. When Jesus tells the disciples that Lazarus is dead, he says they should go and die with Lazarus.
3. At the Last Supper he protests to Jesus that he does not know where Jesus is going or how to get there.
4. He doubts that Jesus rose from the dead; when Jesus appears eight days later, he exclaims "My Lord and my God."
5. Jesus appears to him and several other disciples on the shore of Galilee after rising from the dead.

Did You Know?

Emmaus We do not know exactly where the Emmaus of Jesus' time was located. There have been at least four suggestions through the years, but two rise to the top as most likely. One is present-day Imwas, or Amwas. Early pilgrims as far back as the fourth century thought that this was the right place. However, it is about twenty miles from Jerusalem, and the Bible says that Emmaus was seven miles. The other traditional site is El Kubeibeh, or Qubeibeh. It is about seven miles northwest of Jerusalem, so it fits the Bible's account of the distance.

Resurrection appearance of Jesus The time between Jesus' resurrection and his ascension was a period of forty days. How many times did Jesus appear to his disciples during these forty days? The Bible records the following appearances: (1) Sunday morning to Mary Magdalene in the garden; (2) Sunday morning to Peter; (3) Sunday afternoon to two men on the road to Emmaus; (4) Sunday evening to the disciples in the upper room, with Thomas absent; (5) the following Sunday to the disciples in the upper room, with Thomas present; (6) later, to seven disciples at the Sea of Galilee; (7) to five hundred disciples; (8) to James, his half brother; (9) to his disciples again in Jerusalem; and (10) to his disciples when he ascended into heaven.

What was Jesus doing during those forty days when he was not with

456

>

What
Everyone
Should
Know
about
the

Bible

his disciples? He must have had very important work to complete, but we do not know what it was.

Discovering My Purpose from God's Plan

1. *The Resurrection distinguishes Christianity from all other religions.* We have hope for life beyond the grave because Jesus rose from the dead, thereby conquering death forever.
2. *The Ascension, which was witnessed by the disciples, proves that Jesus is in heaven, where he is preparing an eternal home for us.* How could we expect to go to heaven if he were not already there? Heaven without Jesus would not be heaven at all. He is its focal point.
3. *Jesus' scars are marks of honor.* They turned Thomas's doubt into faith and hope. We will probably see them on Jesus in heaven, as evidence of his great sacrifice for us. Revelation 5:5-6 speaks of the Lamb who was killed as the heir to the throne. Jesus is that wounded Lamb of God.

Ordinary People for Extraordinary Work
The Life of the Early Church

Characters:
Ananias (who lied about the sale of his land); Annas (a former high priest who was still considered a high priest); Barnabas (who sold land and gave money to other believers); Caiaphas (a high priest); the seven deacons (Nicanor, Nicolas of Antioch, Parmenas, Philip, Procurus, Stephen, Timon); Gamaliel (who counseled his fellow council members); the Holy Spirit; Jesus' disciples (especially John and Peter); Joseph Barsabbas (also known as Justus, one possible replacement for Judas Iscariot); Matthias (who was chosen to replace Judas Iscariot as the twelfth apostle); Philip (one of seven deacons who became an evangelist); Sapphira (wife of Ananias who lied about the sale of their land); Stephen (one of seven deacons who became the first martyr)

Time Period:
The beginning of the early church

Dates:
Circa A.D. 30–A.D. 35

Where Scene 39 of the Big Story Can Be Found:
Acts 1–8

In Scene 39, Find the Answers to These Questions:
Was the sin of Ananias and Sapphira the sin of not giving enough or the sin of lying about the amount they gave? What kind of work did the seven deacons do?

Look for this in Scene 39
> How much do we hear later about Judas Iscariot's replacement?
> Who was the "Son of Encouragement"?
> Who was the first martyr?

Jesus completed his majestic work on earth. The Son of God, whom the Scriptures foretold many times, became human. He chose the Twelve to carry on his work, he taught them, revealed his divine nature to them through his miracles, died on the cross for our sins, rose from the dead to conquer death and give us hope for eternity, and ascended to the right hand of God in heaven. He gave his disciples the commission to go into all the world to preach and teach the gospel, and he promised to be with them in their work. Jesus also promised that the Holy Spirit, the third person of the Trinity, would come to be with his people. The Holy Spirit will not leave us; his presence is always with us.

Waiting in the upper room and choosing Judas's replacement

After Jesus' ascension into heaven, the disciples walked the half mile back to the upper room in Jerusalem. While the 120 disciples waited for the Holy Spirit to come, they prayed and took care of some important business. The Twelve were no longer the Twelve, for Judas Iscariot had betrayed Jesus and committed suicide. They needed a replacement. Peter seemed to be the spokesman for this event.

The disciples nominated two men to be the twelfth apostle to replace Judas. One was Joseph Barsabbas, also known as Justus, and the other was Matthias. The disciples prayed for the Lord's choice, and when they cast lots, Matthias was the choice. This is the first and last time that he appears in the Bible record.

The coming of the Holy Spirit

Seven weeks had now passed since Jesus' resurrection, and it was a little more than a week after Jesus' ascension. It was Pentecost, and the believers were still meeting together in the upper room. Suddenly a sound came from heaven like a mighty roaring wind, and it filled the entire house. What looked like little tongues of fire came upon each of them. Everyone present was filled with the Holy Spirit and began to speak in other languages.

Godly Jews from many nations had come to Jerusalem for Pentecost, and they ran to see what was happening. They were astonished to hear local people speaking the languages of the nations from which they came.

"How can this be?" they wondered, for there were Parthians, Medes, Elamites, people from Mesopotamia, Judea, Cappadocia, Pontus, the province of Asia, Phrygia, Pamphylia, Egypt, the area of Libya toward Cyrene, Rome, Crete, and Arabia. These local people were speaking to them in their many languages, telling them what great things God had done.

What
Everyone
Should
Know
about
the

Bible

SCENE 39

Ordinary
People for
Extraordinary
Work

<

461

There are always cynics in the crowd. "They're drunk!" they said. That was a foolish explanation, for how could getting drunk cause people to speak in a dozen or more languages?

Peter's great sermon

When Peter heard what some were saying, he stepped before the people and gave a great speech. "Of course we're not drunk," he said. "This is the outpouring of the Holy Spirit that was prophesied by the prophet Joel." Peter went on to tell these people that they had crucified the Son of God, and that Jesus had risen from the dead. They must repent of their sins and turn to God for salvation.

The power of the Holy Spirit was upon Peter and that crowd, so about three thousand people turned from their sin and accepted Jesus that day. The new church was growing fast! The believers joined together in devoting themselves to godly teaching, fellowship, prayer, and the Lord's Supper.

The fellowship of the early church

With the power of the Holy Spirit, the apostles performed many miracles. The believers formed such a strong fellowship that they began to sell their possessions and share what they had with others who had less. There was great joy among the believers, and the Lord added many more to them each day.

Healing a lame man at the Temple

About three o'clock one afternoon, Peter and John went into the Temple to pray. At the entrance called the Beautiful Gate sat a man who was lame from birth. Friends carried him there each day so he could beg to earn a living. When he saw Peter and John, he asked them for money.

"Look at us!" Peter commanded. The man looked, expecting a coin or two. "We have no money," Peter said. "But we will give you something far more valuable. In the name of Jesus Christ of Nazareth, get up and walk."

Peter took the lame man by the right hand and helped him up. Suddenly, the man's feet and anklebones were healed. He jumped up and began to walk, leap, and praise God. Then he went into the Temple with them.

When people realized that this was the lame beggar who sat by the Temple gate, they were amazed. People swarmed around the man, who was clinging to Peter and John as they stood on Solomon's colonnade.

Peter had a crowd now, and he couldn't waste an opportunity to preach to them. He preached a sermon about Jesus, the Son of God, whom they had rejected and crucified. This same Jesus had risen from the dead. It was Jesus, not the disciples themselves, who had healed this man.

Peter and John are arrested and tried

While Peter was preaching, some religious leaders arrived. Peter's sermon greatly disturbed them, especially when he said that Jesus had risen from the dead. They arrested Peter and John and jailed them until morning, but it was too late to stop the flow of people into Jesus' church. Now almost five thousand men, plus women and children, had accepted Jesus as Savior.

The next day the religious leaders took Peter and John before the Sanhedrin, the Jewish high council. Annas, the former high priest, and Caiaphas, the current high priest, were there along with other relatives of the high priest. These men were bullies, and they expected these poor, uneducated fishermen to cower before them. The council demanded, "By what power have you done this miracle?"

"By the power of Jesus Christ of Nazareth, the one whom you crucified," Peter asserted. He was filled with the Holy Spirit, so he was not afraid of these men. "This is the same Jesus who was prophesied in the Scriptures as the coming Messiah. There is salvation in no other person but him."

Peter utterly amazed the council. A rugged fisherman was preaching to them with great power, eloquence, and wisdom. How could this be? He had no training.

The man who was healed was standing there also, so they could not dispute the miracle. They sent Peter and John from the room while they deliberated. "What shall we do with these men?" they wondered. "They have performed a miracle, and everyone in Jerusalem knows about it." They decided to punish Peter and John and set them free.

When they called Peter and John back into the room, they warned them never to teach about Jesus again. But Peter and John responded, "Does God want us to obey him or you? We can't stop telling people about the wonderful things we have seen and heard."

The council members were frustrated now, so they threatened Peter and John some more and let them go. They didn't know how to punish them without starting a riot. Peter and John went back to the other believers and told them what had happened. The believers prayed together, praising God and asking him to give them boldness in teaching and preaching.

Sharing possessions

In those days the believers had a powerful sense of unity. They often sold what they owned and gave the money to the apostles to distribute among all the believers. Hence there was no poverty among them. Joseph was nicknamed Barnabas, which means "son of encourage-

462

>

What
Everyone
Should
Know
about
the

Bible

SCENE **39**

Ordinary
People for
Extraordinary
Work

<

463

ment." He was a member of the tribe of Levi and came from Cyprus. He sold a field he owned and gave it to the apostles to be distributed to those in need.

The deception of Ananias and Sapphira

It seems that someone always tries to beat the system, especially if the system seems to be working. Ananias and his wife, Sapphira, sold some property. With his wife's agreement, Ananias brought part of the money to the apostles, claiming that he was bringing all of it to them.

Peter knew what had happened. "Ananias, why has Satan filled your heart with lies and deceit?" he asked. "The money was yours to keep, or to give part of it, or to give all of it. But you have lied to God about the amount you gave."

As soon as Ananias heard this, he dropped dead. Everyone there was terrified. Some young men quickly wrapped his body in a sheet and buried him. About three hours later, Sapphira came to see Peter. She had not yet heard what had happened to Ananias.

"Tell me," said Peter. "Was this the price you received for your land?"

"Yes, that was it," she said.

"You two have conspired in lying to the Lord," Peter told her. "The young men who buried your husband are outside, waiting to bury you too." Sapphira also dropped dead, and the young men buried her beside her husband. This incident stirred great fear in the church.

Released from prison by an angel

The apostles were performing many miracles in those days, and the believers met regularly on Solomon's colonnade, sometimes called Solomon's porch, at the Temple. Many new people joined them, so there were crowds of new believers. People brought the sick to the apostles for healing, and some were healed if even Peter's shadow fell on them. Many brought sick friends and relatives from villages surrounding Jerusalem.

All of this activity stirred violent jealousy among the high priest and his friends, the Sadducees, so they arrested the apostles and put them in jail. That night an angel of the Lord opened the prison doors and let them out, so the apostles went to the Temple at daybreak to preach.

The next morning the high priest called the Sanhedrin together and sent Temple guards to get the apostles from jail, but the guards came back with a disturbing report. "The jail was locked, and the guards were all in place outside, but when we opened the prison gates, no one was there," the Temple guards said. At that moment someone came with the news that the apostles were in the Temple teaching.

Peter and John before the council again

The captain of the Temple guards took his men to the Temple and arrested the apostles again. The guards treated the apostles gently because they were afraid of the vast crowds of people.

"Didn't we tell you to stop preaching about this man Jesus?" the high priest demanded. "You are filling Jerusalem with your teaching and blaming us for his death."

"We must obey God rather than men," Peter answered. "You did crucify Jesus, but God raised him from the dead. Then God put him into a place of high honor at his right hand. We and the Holy Spirit are witnesses of these things."

The council was furious to hear this and wanted to kill the apostles. Gamaliel, a highly respected teacher of the law, ordered the apostles from the chamber. Then he addressed the other council members. "Be careful what you do to these men," he advised. "Leave them alone. If they are doing these things on their own, it will come to nothing. If these things are of God, you cannot stop them, and you may even be fighting God."

The council accepted Gamaliel's advice. They brought the apostles back, had them flogged, and again ordered them to stop teaching about Jesus. The apostles left the council rejoicing in their sufferings for Jesus. They continued to teach and preach about Jesus every day.

Grumbling in the new church and the appointment of seven deacons

There was soon grumbling and discontent among the believers. The Greek-speaking believers said that the Hebrew-speaking believers were discriminating against them, shortchanging their widows in the daily distribution of food.

The Twelve called a meeting of the believers. "We apostles should be preaching and teaching, not distributing food," they said. "Let's appoint seven men who are full of the Holy Spirit and wisdom to administer the food program."

This was a good idea, so they chose the following men to be the first deacons: Stephen, Philip, Procurus, Nicanor, Timon, Parmenas, and Nicolas of Antioch, a Gentile convert. The Twelve prayed for them.

Stephen, the first martyr

Stephen, one of the seven deacons, was a godly man who performed many amazing miracles among the people. Such gifts tend to arouse jealousy. Some men from the Synagogue of Freed Slaves, as it was called, came to debate Stephen, but none could match his wisdom and his debating skill. They persuaded other men to lie about Stephen, and he was brought before the Sanhedrin. The false witnesses made their case. When the council members looked at Stephen, his face was radiant.

464

>

What
Everyone
Should
Know
about
the

Bible

SCENE 39

Ordinary
People for
Extraordinary
Work

<

465

"Are these things true?" the high priest asked.

Stephen gave a long speech, much of it recalling the history of Israel. The council listened patiently until Stephen reached his conclusion. "You stubborn people," Stephen said. "You murdered the Messiah." Then Stephen looked up into heaven. "Look, the heavens have opened and Jesus is standing in the place of honor at God's right hand," he cried out.

It was too much for the council members. They held their hands over their ears, drowned out Stephen's voice with their shouts, and dragged him from the council chambers. The lying witnesses took off their cloaks and laid them at the feet of a young man named Saul, and the people stoned Stephen. As he died, Stephen prayed, "Lord Jesus, receive my spirit. Lord, don't punish them for this sin." After he died, some godly men buried him.

A wave of persecution and the spread of the gospel

This event triggered a wave of great persecution for the church in Jerusalem, so the believers, except for the apostles, fled into Judea and even Samaria. Saul was one of the leaders in this persecution, and he went all over the area to devastate the church. He dragged men and women from their houses and threw them into jail.

Meanwhile the believers who fled Jerusalem were now taking the gospel to other places. This was a valuable lesson for the church—sometimes persecution moves us out to share the gospel in new places.

Philip went to Samaria to escape the persecution in Jerusalem, and he took the gospel with him. Crowds listened intently, for they saw Philip perform miracles. He healed paralyzed and lame people and cast out evil spirits, and there was great joy in that city.

Simon the sorcerer had often been called the Great One by his fellow Samaritans. He was influential because of the magic he performed. Along with many others, Simon came to believe in Jesus and was baptized. As he followed Philip around, he was amazed at the miracles Philip performed. These were no mere magic tricks!

News of what was happening in Samaria reached Jerusalem, so the apostles sent Peter and John to join Philip. They prayed for the new believers to receive the Holy Spirit. When Simon the former sorcerer saw this, he offered to buy the gift of bestowing the Holy Spirit.

"Turn from your wickedness and pray to the Lord for forgiveness," Peter scolded. Then Simon begged Peter to pray for him. As Peter and John returned to Jerusalem, they preached the gospel in other Samaritan villages along the way.

The Gaza Road miracle

Meanwhile an angel of the Lord gave Philip some new orders: "Leave Samaria and go south, to a desert road that runs from Jerusalem to

Gaza." Philip must have wondered why the Lord would make him leave the marvelous work in Samaria to go to a lonely desert road. But when the Lord said go, Philip went.

Before long a chariot came along the road. Inside sat the treasurer of Ethiopia, a very important man from this African nation. The Lord told Philip to join the Ethiopian, and the man invited Philip into his chariot. He was reading a scroll that was part of the book of Isaiah.

"Do you know what you are reading?" Philip asked.

"How can I?" the man answered. "I need someone to help me." So Philip explained the passage, which was from Isaiah 53:7-8, foretelling Jesus' crucifixion. Philip then gave him a clear presentation of the gospel message. The Ethiopian became a new believer and asked Philip to baptize him.

As soon as they came to a place with water, Philip baptized the Ethiopian treasurer. When they came up out of the water, the Holy Spirit suddenly took Philip away, so the treasurer went home to Ethiopia, rejoicing in his new faith.

 ## Questions You May Be Asking

Why were women and children not counted?
At the feeding of the five thousand and the feeding of the four thousand, the number given was the number of men, "in addition to all the women and children" (Matthew 14:21; 15:38). In Acts 4:4, we read that there were five thousand new believers, "not counting women and children." Why not count the women and children? The answer is simple. In in those days, women and children were not considered to be as important as men. Occasionally a woman is so significant to a Bible story that she simply must be given top billing. Such cases include Esther, Ruth, Lydia, Dorcas, and Deborah.

What was the sin of Ananias and Sapphira?
They lied to God and his people. The property was theirs to keep or sell. No one had asked for it. When they sold the property, the money was theirs to keep or to give. No one had asked for it. Their sin was in giving part of the money and claiming it was all of the money. Don't lie to God—he knows what is in your heart.

Who were the Sadducees?
The Sadducees, like the Pharisees, were more of a party than a priestly group. They were mostly wealthy aristocratic landlords, both priests and laymen. The Sadducees were more accepting of the Greek culture and the Roman political system than the Pharisees. The Sadducees accepted only the Torah, and they rejected many of the traditions of the Phari-

466

>

What
Everyone
Should
Know
about
the

Bible

sees. The Sadducees did not believe in the final resurrection of the dead, as the Pharisees did.

Great Events of This Time

1. **The disciples pray in the upper room, and Matthias is chosen to succeed Judas Iscariot** (Acts 1:12-26).
2. **The Holy Spirit comes at Pentecost** (Acts 2:1-41).
3. **The early church grows** (Acts 2:42-47).
4. **Peter and John heal a lame man at the Temple** (Acts 3:1-26).
5. **Peter and John stand before the religious leaders** (Acts 4:1-31).
6. **Early Christians live and work in unity** (Acts 4:32-37).
7. **Ananias and Sapphira lie to God** (Acts 5:1-11).
8. **The apostles heal the sick** (Acts 5:12-16).
9. **The apostles are thrown into prison; they are released on the advice of Gamaliel** (Acts 5:17-42).
10. **Seven deacons are chosen** (Acts 6:1-7).
11. **Stephen stands before the council; he is stoned to death** (Acts 6:8–8:1).
12. **Saul persecutes the Christians** (Acts 8:1-3).
13. **Philip goes to Samaria** (Acts 8:4-13).
14. **Peter and John go to Samaria, where Simon tries to buy the Holy Spirit** (Acts 8:14-25).
15. **Philip encounters the Ethiopian treasurer** (Acts 8:26-40).

Significant Dates of This Time

Circa A.D. 30–A.D. 35

Heroes and Villains: The Stars of Scene 39

ANANIAS

With his wife Sapphira, Ananias came up with a clever plan. They sold their property and pretended to give all of the money to the community of believers. Instead they kept back part of it. For their sin of deceit, both Ananias and Sapphira died. Their sin was not in keeping the money but in lying to the others and to God by pretending to give it all.

Bible events in Ananias's life
He conspires with his wife, Sapphira, to sell their land and pretend to give all the proceeds to the believers.

BARNABAS

Barnabas was the nickname of Joseph, a Levite from Cyprus. He became a Christian in the early days after Jesus ascended to heaven, and he was an unusually devout man. Barnabas sold his property and gave the money to help support the poorer Christians. When Paul became a Christian, most believers were afraid to accept him, but Barnabas assured them that Paul was truly a believer. Barnabas led the work at Antioch and brought Paul there to help them. Then the church sent the two of them on the first missionary journey. When Barnabas wanted to take his cousin, John Mark, on the second missionary journey, Paul refused because Mark had deserted them on the first journey. Paul took Silas on his second journey, and Barnabas took Mark on a missions trip to Cyprus. From this point on, Paul's work is recorded through his epistles, and little is said about Barnabas and his work.

Bible events in Barnabas's life
1. He sells his land and distributes the money to needy believers.
2. He helps Saul (Paul) to be accepted by the believers after his conversion.
3. He works with the church at Antioch and brings Saul (Paul) from Tarsus to work with him.
4. With Paul, he takes a collection to the believers in Jerusalem.
5. He goes with Paul on the first missionary journey.
6. He is with Paul at Antioch of Pisidia.
7. He is almost killed at Iconium.
8. He is mistaken for the Greek god Zeus (or Roman, Jupiter) at Lystra.
9. He returns with Paul from the first missionary journey.
10. He ministers at Antioch and takes part in the council at Jerusalem.
11. He argues with Paul about taking John Mark on the second missionary journey; he takes John Mark with him to Cyprus.

PHILIP THE EVANGELIST

When the apostles became overburdened with the affairs of the early church, seven men were appointed as deacons to carry on daily services to the believers. Philip (not the apostle who followed Jesus) was appointed as one of those deacons. When persecution came to Jerusalem, Philip fled to Samaria and preached there with great power. He next went along the Gaza Road, where he helped an Ethiopian official to understand the Scriptures concerning the Messiah and how Jesus fulfilled them. Philip moved to Caesarea, where Paul visited him and his four daughters on his travels toward Jerusalem.

What
Everyone
Should
Know
about
the

Bible events in Philip's life
1. He is chosen to be a deacon and serve others.
2. He preaches and works miracles in Samaria.
3. He talks with an Ethiopian official and wins him to Jesus.
4. Paul visits his home in Caesarea.

Bible

SCENE 39

Ordinary
People for
Extraordinary
Work

<

469

SAPPHIRA

Sapphira's name means "beautiful," but she and her husband, Ananias, conspired to do something very ugly. During the time of the early church, many Christians sold their property and gave the money to the entire fellowship, to be distributed among those who had less. Ananias and Sapphira sold their property and gave part of it to the fellowship but claimed that they gave it all. Their conspiracy was evil, not because they kept part of their money but because they pretended to give all of it. For their sin, both of them died and were buried.

Bible events in Sapphira's life
1. She conspires with her husband, Ananias, to sell their land and pretend to give all the proceeds to the believers.
2. She dies and is buried next to her husband.

STEPHEN

Serving the other believers became too burdensome for the apostles of the early church, so seven men were appointed for this work and were called deacons. Stephen, one of these seven, was a godly man, but the religious leaders of the day hated him because he was a prominent believer. Some liars brought false charges against him and had him stoned to death. Among those present at Stephen's death was Saul of Tarsus, who would later become Paul, a great leader of the Christian church.

Bible events in Stephen's life
1. He is chosen to be a deacon and serve others.
2. He is taken before the council and wrongly accused; he is stoned to death.

What everyone should know about the book of Acts
THE STORY OF THE EARLY CHURCH AT WORK

There is no other book in the entire Bible that is quite like Acts. At no previous time in human history was the Holy Spirit working so dynamically among God's people. Acts is often called the Acts of the Apostles. It is more accurately the Acts of the Holy Spirit through the Apostles.

Jesus' ministry on earth lasted for approximately three years. He chose his disciples, walked with them daily, trained them, and empowered them. However, they did not have full power to serve God until Jesus left and the Holy Spirit came. At Pentecost the Holy Spirit brought to believers a dynamic power that people had never before known.

When the Holy Spirit came, the believers had a new boldness. They were no longer afraid of powerful people, for the Holy Spirit within them was a greater power. They preached, taught, and shared the gospel. Thousands believed, accepted Jesus, and became witnesses for him.

The gospel witness began in Jerusalem, but persecution drove people away to other places. As they went, they took the Good News with them. Persecution fueled the spread of the gospel.

The first half of Acts is mostly the story of Peter, and the second half is mostly about Paul. The lives of both men reveal God's remarkable choices. When Jesus chose Peter the fisherman, he was rough, sinful, impetuous, and untrained. What did he have to offer? Paul was a highly trained Jewish leader who brutally persecuted Christians. What an unlikely candidate for taking the gospel to the ends of the earth, especially to the Gentiles. But God chose these two unlikely men to do remarkable work for him.

What happened after Jesus ascended into heaven? What happened in the early church? If you've ever wondered, Acts is the book for you.

Did You Know?

Solomon's porch or colonnade The Temple of Jesus' time, built by Herod the Great, had a roofed colonnade, or porch, surrounding it on all four sides. The eastern colonnade was called Solomon's porch because of the tradition that Solomon had a similar one. This porch was about fifty feet wide, and it was lined by three rows of white marble columns, each about forty feet high. The roof of the porch was cedar. The floor was mosaic stone.

Prayer times at the Temple The traditional prayer times in the Temple were morning, noon, and at three in the afternoon.

Annas and his family Annas was a powerful figure even when he was no longer high priest (A.D. 6–A.D. 15). He had enough political clout to get five sons, one son-in-law, and one grandson into the high priest's position after him. The sons were Eleazar (A.D. 16–A.D. 17), Jonathan (A.D. 36–A.D. 37), Theophilus (A.D. 37–A.D. 41), Matthias (A.D. 42), and Annas, who was evidently named for his father (A.D. 61). His son-in-law was Caiaphas (A.D. 18–A.D. 36), who served the longest term. He also had a grandson named Matthias (A.D. 65–A.D. 66).

Discovering My Purpose from God's Plan

What
Everyone
Should
Know
about
the

1. *Don't lie to God, for he knows your heart.* Lies can be told by what you say or what you don't say. Sometimes what you don't say is a greater lie than what you do say.

2. *Persecution or tragedy may force us to take the gospel to places we might not have gone otherwise.* The persecution in Jerusalem forced the believers to take the gospel into Judea and Samaria.

3. *God may sometimes ask us to leave a thriving work for him to go to*

Bible

an uncertain work. But the small beginnings of the new work may be even greater than the thriving work we left. Philip left a thriving work in Samaria to go to a lonely desert road. There he met the treasurer of Ethiopia and won him to Christ, opening a whole nation (Ethiopia) and continent (Africa) to the gospel.

A Murderer Becomes a Missionary

Saul's Conversion

Characters:
Ananias (a Christian in Damascus who helped Saul); Barnabas (who befriended Saul); Saul the Pharisee (who became Paul the apostle)

Time Period:
The conversion of Saul

Dates:
Circa A.D. 35

Where Scene 40 of the Big Story Can Be Found:
Acts 9

In Scene 40, Find the Answers to These Questions:
What passionate persecutor became a passionate missionary?
Why did a great and powerful man escape from a city in a basket?

Look for this in Scene 40
> Old friends become new enemies; old enemies become new friends.
> The Son of Encouragement comes to the rescue.

We now come to one of the most dramatic events in the history of the Christian church. The story begins with a mass murderer named Saul, who spewed hatred and venom against the Christians. He was certain that Jesus was a fake and a blasphemer, and he was bent on destroying the young church. But one moment of heavenly drama changed everything. Saul became Paul, a mighty missionary and ultimately a martyr for Jesus. He authored many of the Epistles in our Bible and forever changed the church that he once tried to destroy. This is how it happened.

Saul, passionate persecutor

Saul was passionately destroying the Lord's followers by sending some to prison and murdering others. He was perhaps the greatest threat to the young church, as he forced many to flee Jerusalem into Judea and even Samaria. Saul didn't realize it then, but his vicious persecution was effectively helping to spread the gospel beyond Jerusalem, as the fleeing believers took the gospel with them to far places.

One day Saul went to the high priest with a request for letters addressed to all the synagogues of Damascus. Not content with persecuting Jesus' followers in Jerusalem, Saul now wanted to take his vicious ways to Damascus. He would bring these hated believers back to Jerusalem in chains so that they could not continue spreading lies about this fake Messiah, Jesus. How dare they promote this blasphemer!

A voice from heaven changes a life forever

Saul got the letters he wanted and headed toward Damascus. He was almost there when a brilliant light from heaven suddenly beamed down on him, a divine spotlight focusing on this one murderous man. It was brighter than the sun and seemed to penetrate his soul.

"Saul, Saul, why are you persecuting me?" a voice called down from heaven. Saul was terrified. He had never heard a voice from heaven before. Was this truly the voice of God?

"Who are you, sir?" Saul asked. He must have been trembling with fear at having God speak to him.

"I am Jesus, the one you are persecuting!" the voice said. "Now get up and go into Damascus, and you will be told what to do."

Saul was stunned. Jesus was truly God's Son, and he was in heaven. The truth must have struck him with monumental force. He had been persecuting the Son of God, the Messiah!

Saul's men stood speechless, for they too had heard the voice from heaven, but they saw no one. When Saul stumbled to his feet, he realized he had been struck blind. The mighty Saul, coming in power to Damas-

474

>

What
Everyone
Should
Know
about
the

Bible

cus to put believers in chains, instead was led into the city like a helpless child who had been brought low before God. The great Saul was greatly humbled so that the Spirit of God could fill him and use him in mighty ways.

Saul remained in Damascus for three days without food and water, waiting for instructions from the Lord. What must his thoughts have been during those three days? *I heard the voice of Jesus from heaven! He truly is the Messiah, and he is at the right hand of God. We were all wrong. And we crucified him. We murdered God's Son. I have murdered his followers. Can he ever forgive me? Will he?*

Saul's sight is restored, and his soul is renewed

Meanwhile the Lord spoke to a man of Damascus named Ananias and told him to go over to Straight Street to meet Saul of Tarsus. "I have shown him in a vision that you are coming," the Lord said.

Ananias was terrified. "But Lord, I have heard frightening things about this man. He has come to Damascus to arrest every believer."

"Go and do what I say," the Lord told him. "I have chosen Saul to take the gospel to the Gentiles and to kings as well as to the people of Israel. I will show him how much he must suffer for me."

Ananias obeyed the Lord and went to Straight Street, where he found Saul. He laid hands on him and said, "Brother Saul, the Lord Jesus, who appeared to you on the road, has sent me to restore your sight. Be filled with the Holy Spirit." As soon as Ananias said this, Saul could see again, and something like scales fell from his eyes. He got up, was baptized, and ate some food.

Saul had gone from being a passionate persecutor to a man of powerful convictions. He had come to destroy believers, but he became one of them. That's what Jesus can do! Saul stayed with the believers and went into the synagogues to preach that Jesus is the Son of God.

Old friends become new enemies; old enemies become new friends

Saul's preaching created quite a stir. "Didn't he come here to persecute Jesus' followers?" people asked. "How then can he be preaching that Jesus is the Son of God?"

Saul's preaching became more powerful until the Jewish leaders could stand it no longer. They simply had to kill this man, or he would upset everything.

Saul somehow learned of their plot to murder him, and that they were waiting for him at the city gate day and night. So during the night, some believers put him into a large basket and let him down over the wall away from the gates.

Saul went back to Jerusalem to meet with the believers there, but they were all understandably afraid of him. How did they know that his conversion wasn't just a trick to learn who the believers were so he could murder them? How could they trust this man who had brought so much misery upon them?

Barnabas, Son of Encouragement

Enter Barnabas, the man who sold some property and gave the money to the apostles to distribute to other believers. Barnabas must have had some heart-to-heart talks with Saul and became convinced that he truly was a new believer. Barnabas lived up to his name, Son of Encouragement, by assuring the believers that Jesus had changed Saul. So the believers accepted Saul because of Barnabas.

Saul began to preach the gospel boldly. He debated with some Greek-speaking Jews, but they plotted to murder him. When the Jerusalem believers heard about this, they took Saul to Caesarea and sent him home to Tarsus for a while.

The persecution died down, and the church had peace throughout Judea, Galilee, and Samaria as it grew in numbers and strength. Believers walked daily in awe of the Lord and in the comfort and power of the Holy Spirit.

 ## Questions You May Be Asking

How could Paul debate with Greek-speaking Jews?

Paul was a learned man who fluently spoke both Greek and Aramaic. Greek was the main language of the civilized world in Jesus' time, much as English has become the language of today's world.

Why did the persecution of the church suddenly die down?

Saul was the most dynamic force behind the persecution of the church. When he accepted Jesus, that dynamic force was reversed. Many who saw the fruits of his conversion must have realized that the gospel was true after all and that Jesus was surely the Messiah.

 ## Great Events of This Time

1. **Saul is converted** (Acts 9:1-9).
2. **Saul recovers and preaches in Damascus** (Acts 9:10-22).
3. **Some Jews plot Saul's death, and he escapes in a basket** (Acts 9:23-25).
4. **Barnabas helps Saul at Jerusalem** (Acts 9:26-31).

Significant Dates of This Time

Circa A.D. 35

476

>

What
Everyone
Should
Know
about
the

Bible

Heroes and Villains: The Stars of Scene 40

PAUL

Saul, who was later known as Paul, grew up in the city of Tarsus in Cilicia. He was a well-educated man who was familiar with the languages and culture of his time, and he was a Roman citizen, which was a great honor in those days. He was trained to be a religious leader of the Jews and was a prominent member of their inner circle. When the Christians multiplied, Saul persecuted some and imprisoned others.

One day Jesus spoke personally to Saul on the road to Damascus, and Saul suddenly realized that Jesus was God's Son. He turned around completely and became as zealous for Jesus as he had been against him. He became a leader among the Christians and made three extensive missionary journeys, including visits to Asia and Europe. Paul (as he was called after his conversion) wrote many of the Epistles in our New Testament. He is considered by many to be the greatest person in the New Testament, after Jesus.

Bible events in Paul's (Saul's) life

1. Stephen is stoned; those who stone him lay their cloaks at Saul's feet, showing Saul's consent for Stephen's death.
2. Saul goes toward Damascus to persecute the believers, but Jesus speaks to him along the way, and he is converted.
3. Saul is led blind into Damascus, where he regains his sight and preaches; the religious leaders try to kill him, but he escapes in a basket.
4. He returns to Jerusalem, where the believers are afraid of him; Barnabas intercedes for him.
5. When Barnabas works at the church in Antioch, he goes to Tarsus and brings Saul back to work with him.
6. He goes to Jerusalem with Barnabas to take a collection to the believers there, and he returns to Antioch with John Mark.
7. First missionary journey: The church at Antioch consecrates him and Barnabas and sends them forth on their journey, along with John Mark.
8. First missionary journey: He visits Salamis and Paphos on Cyprus, where Saul is now called Paul; he strikes Bar-jesus blind.
9. First missionary journey: He goes from Cyprus through Attalia and Perga to Antioch of Pisidia, where he preaches but is rejected. John Mark deserts Paul and Barnabas at Attalia.
10. First missionary journey: He visits Iconium, then Lystra, where he and Barnabas are mistaken for gods.
11. First missionary journey: He returns to home base at Antioch, going through Derbe, Lystra, Iconium, Antioch of Pisidia, Perga, and Attalia.

12. He remains at Antioch for some time with Barnabas

13. He is sent to the Jerusalem council with Barnabas to discuss Gentile believers and circumcision with other delegates.

14. Second missionary journey: After he and Barnabas separate over the issue of taking John Mark, he takes Silas and goes through Syria, Cilicia, Derbe, and Lystra, where he meets Timothy.

15. Second missionary journey: He and Silas take Timothy with them and travel through Phrygia and Galatia, then go to Mysia and Troas, where Paul has a vision of a man from Macedonia pleading with him to go there. Some think this Macedonian man in the vision was Luke, who lived at Philippi in Macedonia, and who then joined Paul on his journey.

16. Second missionary journey: He goes from Troas to Macedonia, passing through Samothrace and Neapolis; at Philippi he meets with Lydia, who becomes a Christian.

17. Second missionary journey: He heals a slave girl at Philippi and is thrown into prison where an earthquake frees him and Silas; the jailer and his family are converted.

18. Second missionary journey: He passes through Amphipolis and Appollonia to Thessalonica, where people attack Jason's house looking for Paul and Silas.

19. Second missionary journey: He visits Berea, where believers search the Scriptures to see if Paul's message is true.

20. Second missionary journey: He visits Athens, where he preaches on Mars Hill.

21. Second missionary journey: He visits Corinth, where he stays and works with Aquila and Priscilla, and later with Titius Justus.

22. Second missionary journey: He makes a vow at Cenchrea before sailing to Jerusalem by way of Ephesus and Caesarea.

23. Second missionary journey: He reports to the church at Jerusalem, then returns home to Antioch, where he remains for some time.

24. Third missionary journey: He visits the believers in Galatia and Phrygia on the way to Ephesus, where the sons of Sceva try to cast out demons, and people burn their incantation books.

25. Third missionary journey: Demetrius, an Ephesian silversmith, starts a riot against Paul and Silas.

26. Third missionary journey: He passes through Macedonia to Greece, then back through Macedonia to Troas, where Eutychus falls from a window.

27. Third missionary journey: He goes to Jerusalem by way of Assos, Mitylene, Chios, Samos, Miletus, Cos, Rhodes, Patara, Tyre, and Caesarea, where Agabus predicts Paul's imprisonment.

What
Everyone
Should
Know
about
the
Bible

28. At Jerusalem, he meets with James and elders of the church; he visits the Temple, where he is taken prisoner.
29. At Jerusalem, he is imprisoned at Antonia Fortress and then is taken before the council.
30. When Paul's nephew discovers a plot against Paul's life and reports it to the Roman commander, Paul is transferred to Caesarea.
31. Felix judges him at Caesarea.
32. Festus judges him at Caesarea.
33. King Agrippa II judges him at Caesarea.
34. Voyage to Rome: He sails on a ship from Adramyttium, stopping at Sidon, then sailing past Cyprus, Cilicia, and Pamphylia; he stops next at Myra in Lycia, then sails on to Fair Havens, Crete, where Paul suggests that they winter.
35. Voyage to Rome: He sails toward Phoenix, but a storm drives them to sea, and the ship is wrecked on Malta (or Melita).
36. Voyage to Rome: On Malta, a poisonous snake bites Paul, but he lives.
37. Voyage to Rome: On Malta, Paul heals the governor's father, and after wintering there, he proceeds toward Rome.
38. Voyage to Rome: After stopping at Syracuse, Rhegium, and Puteoli, Paul meets with some believers at the Market of Appius and the Three Inns, or Three Taverns.
39. Voyage to Rome: For two years Paul lives in a rented home, meeting with those in Rome who come to talk with him.
40. Paul is evidently released from his house arrest in Rome, probably because the statute of limitations has run out. He ministers for a while but is arrested again. He is imprisoned in Rome and executed.

Did You Know?

Damascus Today Damascus is the capital of Syria. In Jesus' time it was a great city about 175 miles northeast of Jerusalem, in the Roman province called Syria. It was part of the Decapolis, ten cities that had formed an alliance. There were evidently many Jews and many new Christian converts in Damascus.

Straight Street Two main streets ran parallel through Damascus. One was named Straight Street for obvious reasons—it was very straight. This street still exists in modern Damascus, running from the eastern gate to the middle of the city.

Tarsus Paul grew up in Tarsus, a city that still exists ten miles inland from the southern coast of modern Turkey. In Paul's time this region was the Roman province of Cilicia. The gateway to Tarsus is through the

Taurus Mountains. It was a cultural center on a major Roman highway, so Greek culture and Roman military and political power converged there. Paul probably grew up under the best of circumstances, for his father was a devout Jew and a Roman citizen, which gave Paul Roman citizenship by birth. Paul's father was probably affluent, which gave Paul the resources for the best training and education.

Discovering My Purpose from God's Plan

1. *Some people come to Jesus like Saul did—in a blinding moment.* Some are nurtured through childhood to love Jesus. When Saul became Paul, he must have wished he had known Jesus throughout his childhood. Even though he had diligently studied the Scriptures and looked forward to the coming of the Messiah, he missed a lot during those growing-up years.

2. *The school of suffering in which we are the teachers may become the school of suffering in which we are the students.* Saul inflicted suffering on believers, but the Lord said that he would suffer for him as a believer.

3. *The worst may become the best, with Jesus' help.* Saul, the mass murderer, was one of the worst persecutors of the early church, but he became Paul, one of the best apostles and missionaries. Pray for those that you think are hopeless, so they may have hope and bring hope to others.

4. *If you claim the name, live up to the name.* Christians should be Christlike. Barnabas, the Son of Encouragement, lived up to his name by encouraging the Jerusalem believers to trust Saul and by encouraging Saul as a new believer.

A Fisherman's Greatest Catch
Peter's Ministry

Characters:
Aeneas (whom Peter healed); Agabus (a prophet); Cornelius (a Roman centurion that Peter led to Christ); Dorcas (also known as Tabitha, whom Peter raised from the dead); Herod Agrippa I (who killed James); James (who was murdered by Herod); Nicolas of Antioch (one of seven deacons; he helped establish the church at Antioch); Peter; Saul (Paul); Simon (a leathermaker, or tanner, of Joppa, where Peter stayed)

Time Period:
The early church

Dates:
Circa A.D. 35–A.D. 40

Where Scene 41 of the Big Story Can Be Found:
Acts 9–12

In Scene 41, Find the Answer to This Question:
Who was criticized for leading an important man to Jesus?

Look for this in Scene 41
> A king died of worms.
> A sheet filled with unclean animals was lowered from the sky.

Gentiles

More than two thousand years before Jesus came, God made a covenant with a shepherd named Abraham. It was a simple covenant—God said love, obey, and follow me, and I will be with you and take care of you. This covenant, at the heart of the Old Testament, was inherited by Abraham's descendants through the centuries. Throughout those centuries, Gentiles rejected God and his covenant. They were pagans.

A new day dawned when the Son of God came to earth. He died for the sins of all people, including Gentiles. The time was ripe for all nations to come to the Savior. The new covenant, presented through the New Testament, is as simple as the old covenant—God says love, obey, and follow me, and I will be with you and take care of you.

But who would open the way for the gospel to go to the Gentiles? One of the seven deacons, Nicolas of Antioch, was a Gentile who had come to Christ, and there were probably others. The Lord would soon open the way for vast numbers of Gentiles to come to him.

At times we are sure that the Lord has a sense of humor. Who would you choose to take the gospel to the Gentiles? You and I would probably choose a Gentile convert, but God chose the most die-hard Jew of all Jews—Saul, persecutor and murderer of Christians—to be his apostle to the Gentiles. Unthinkable! Unbelievable!

Jesus spoke to Saul on the road from Jerusalem to Damascus as Saul was on his way to capture Christians and bring them back to Jerusalem in chains.

When Saul fully comprehended that Jesus was the Messiah, who was now in heaven with God the Father, he became a passionate evangelist, missionary, and writer of Scripture. God also chose him to be the great missionary to the Gentiles. "Saul is my chosen instrument to take my message to the Gentiles," the Lord told Ananias (Acts 9:15).

Meanwhile, the apostle Peter, one of the Twelve, would also get into the business of taking the Good News to Gentiles. Peter didn't know it, but the Lord would lead him away from Jerusalem and pave the way for his own ministry to non-Jewish believers.

Peter heals Aeneas

482

>

What
Everyone
Should
Know
about
the

Bible

Peter was traveling from place to place. One day he stopped at Lydda, which was a little more than halfway from Jerusalem to Joppa. Peter had a divine appointment to visit the home of Aeneas, a believer who had been paralyzed and bedridden for eight years. Aeneas had probably given up hope of ever walking again.

"Aeneas, get up and walk!" Peter said to him. And that's what Aeneas did. The news of this miracle spread all over the region around Lydda and nearby Sharon, and many people became believers in Jesus because of it.

Peter raises Dorcas from the dead

Not far away, in Joppa, a woman named Tabitha (whose Greek name was Dorcas) was always doing something for others—sewing, cooking, serving. Everyone loved Dorcas, so it was a great blow to the believers when she became sick and died. They sadly prepared her body for burial. Then someone heard that Peter was nearby in Lydda, so the believers of Joppa sent for him. Perhaps he could comfort them.

When Peter reached Dorcas's home, her friends took him to the upstairs room where her body lay. The room was filled with widows, who wept and showed him all the clothing that Dorcas had made for them. Peter asked all of them to leave the room, then he knelt beside Dorcas's bed and prayed. Then he said, "Get up, Tabitha!"

Dorcas sat up and looked at Peter. When she stood up, Peter called for her friends to come back into the room. There was Dorcas, alive and well! The news of this miracle raced through the town and beyond, and many believed in Jesus. Peter stayed on for a while in Joppa, living at the home of Simon, a leatherworker, or tanner.

Peter leads Cornelius, a Roman centurion, to Jesus

A Roman army officer named Cornelius lived in Caesarea, just a few miles north of Joppa on the seacoast. He was a captain in the Italian Regiment. Cornelius was a devout man who believed in the God of Israel, as did his entire household.

About three o'clock one afternoon, he saw a vision of an angel of God coming toward him. The angel spoke his name: "Cornelius!"

Cornelius stared at the angel in terror. "What do you want?" he asked.

"God has noticed your prayers and your gifts to the poor," the angel said. "Send some men to Joppa to a man named Simon Peter. He is staying with Simon the leatherworker, by the seashore. Ask him to come to your home."

When the angel left, Cornelius called for two servants and a godly soldier, told them what had happened, and sent them to Joppa to find Peter. Peter knew nothing about this.

The next day around noon, as Cornelius's messengers were approaching Joppa, Peter went up to Simon's rooftop to pray. He was hungry, but lunch was still being prepared.

As he prayed, Peter had a vision. He saw the sky open, and something like a large sheet was let down by its four corners. In the sheet were all sorts of animals, reptiles, and birds. A voice spoke to Peter in the vision.

"Get up and eat, Peter," the voice said. Peter looked at all the animals and other creatures. Every one of them was considered unclean according to Jewish standards, which meant they were not acceptable for a good Jew to eat.

"Never, Lord," Peter answered. "I have never eaten anything forbidden by our Jewish laws."

"If God says that something is acceptable, you must not say it is unacceptable," the voice said. This same vision was repeated three times. Peter was perplexed. What did this mean?

As Peter wrestled with the meaning of his vision, the Holy Spirit spoke to him. "Three men have come for you," he said. "Go with them without hesitation. I have sent for them."

Peter went down to see the men. "I'm the one you are looking for," Peter said. "Why have you come?"

The men told Peter about Cornelius's vision, and they stayed at Simon's house for the night. The next day Peter left for Caesarea with some other Joppa believers and Cornelius's servants. When they arrived in Caesarea, Cornelius was waiting anxiously for Peter. He had called together his entire household and other close friends to meet him.

As Peter entered his home, Cornelius bowed down before him.

"Stand up!" Peter said. "I'm just a human being like you." So they talked and then joined the others Cornelius had gathered. Peter reminded them that it was against Jewish laws for him to be in a Gentile home like this, but that God had shown him in a vision that no one must be considered unclean. Cornelius told Peter and the others about his vision, and Peter shared the message about Jesus the Messiah and Savior with Cornelius's household and friends.

As Peter talked, the Holy Spirit came upon all those present. The Jewish people from Joppa were amazed to see that the Holy Spirit had come upon Gentiles also and to hear these people speaking in other languages and praising God.

Peter baptized Cornelius and all the others who had received the Holy Spirit, and Cornelius invited Peter to stay with him for several days.

This incredible news spread quickly to the apostles and other believers in Judea. When Peter arrived back in Jerusalem, some Jewish believers criticized him, but Peter told them about his vision. He told them how the Holy Spirit had come upon Cornelius and his household and friends as he shared the gospel with them. This answered the critics' objections, and they praised God for what had happened.

A new church at Antioch

The believers who fled Jerusalem during the persecution after Stephen's death went as far as Phoenicia, Cyprus, and Antioch of Syria. They

484
>
What
Everyone
Should
Know
about
the

Bible

preached the Good News, but only to Jewish people. However, some believers from Cyprus and Cyrene began to preach to the Gentiles in Antioch. Large numbers of these Gentiles accepted Jesus as Savior. When the church at Jerusalem heard about this, they sent Barnabas to Antioch. He was filled with joy to see what had happened there.

Barnabas went on to Tarsus to find Saul. He brought Saul back to Antioch, and the two of them stayed with the believers there for a full year, teaching many of them. It was at Antioch that believers were first called Christians.

During this time some prophets traveled from Jerusalem to Antioch. One of them, a man named Agabus, stood up in a meeting and predicted that a great famine was coming upon the whole Roman world. This did happen later during the reign of Claudius. When the believers in Antioch heard this, they took a collection for their fellow believers in Judea. They gave these gifts to Barnabas to be distributed as needed to believers in Jerusalem.

Herod persecutes the Christians; an angel releases Peter from prison

About this time King Herod Agrippa I began to persecute some believers. He even had the apostle James, John's brother, killed with a sword. When Herod saw how much this pleased the Jewish leaders, he arrested Peter during the Passover and put him in prison. He stationed four squads of four soldiers each to guard Peter. Herod planned to bring Peter to a public trial after Passover, but while Peter was in prison, the believers held a powerful prayer meeting for him.

The night before Peter's trial, Peter was asleep and chained between two soldiers, with other guards stationed at the prison gate. Suddenly an angel appeared to Peter in a bright light and tapped him gently.

"Get up!" the angel said. "Get dressed and put on your sandals. Put on your cloak and follow me." The chains fell from Peter as the angel spoke, so Peter followed the angel from the prison cell.

Peter thought this must be a vision. How could this actually be happening? They passed the first and second guard posts and came to the main iron gate, which opened by itself. As they passed through the gate and walked down the street, the angel disappeared.

By now Peter realized that this was really happening. *The Lord sent his angel and saved me from Herod and from the Jewish leaders who wanted to kill me,* he thought. Peter hurried to the home of Mary, the mother of John Mark, where the believers were holding a prayer meeting for him. He knocked at the gate, and a servant girl named Rhoda came to open it. When she heard Peter's voice, she ran back inside and told everyone that Peter was at the door.

"You are out of your mind!" the people said. "It must be his angel."

They had prayed much for Peter, but they couldn't believe their prayers would be so tangibly answered.

Peter kept knocking until at last someone opened the door. The people were all amazed that it really was Peter. He motioned for them to be quiet and came into the house. Peter told them all that had happened, then he quietly went away to another place.

At dawn there was a great commotion in the prison. Herod Agrippa ordered a thorough search for Peter, but they couldn't find him. After Herod questioned the guards, he ordered all of them to be executed, then left Judea to stay for a while in Caesarea.

Herod dies from worms

Herod was angry with the people of Tyre and Sidon, so their leaders sent a delegation to make peace with Herod because they depended on Herod's country for their food. First they made friends with Blastus, Herod's personal assistant, and through him they got an appointment with Herod.

Herod put on his royal robes, sat on his throne, and made a speech to them. The visitors gave him a great ovation, shouting, "It is the voice of a god, not of a man."

At that moment an angel of God struck Herod with a sickness because he accepted the people's worship. He was consumed by worms and died.

The gospel of Jesus was spreading rapidly, and there were many new Christians. When Barnabas and Saul finished their mission in Jerusalem, they returned to Antioch and took John Mark with them.

Questions You May Be Asking

Why did Jewish believers in Jerusalem criticize Peter for his work with Cornelius?

The Jewish people thought that all Gentiles were pagans. Through the centuries, Gentiles had for the most part been pagans who refused to believe in the Lord. There were a few Gentiles over the years who had believed in the Lord. For example, Job was probably a Gentile because he seemed to have no relationship to Abraham.

The Jewish religion in Jesus' time was prejudiced against Gentiles. Jews thought that Gentiles were unclean and incapable of loving the Lord. Even the Jewish Christians held this belief until it became obvious that the Gospel was intended for Gentiles as well.

Who was Herod Agrippa?

Two men were named Herod Agrippa. The man who died of worms was Herod Agrippa I, the grandson of Herod the Great, who slaughtered the babies of Bethlehem. Herod Aristobulus, one son of Herod

486
>

What
Everyone
Should
Know
about
the

Bible

the Great, had three children—Herod Agrippa I, Herod Chalcis, and Herodias, who prompted her evil daughter Salome to request the head of John the Baptist. The entire Herod clan was evil.

Great Events of This Time

1. **Peter heals Aeneas** (Acts 9:32-35).
2. **Peter raises Dorcas** (Acts 9:36-43).
3. **Peter has a vision of unclean animals; Cornelius and his household are converted** (Acts 10).
4. **Peter is criticized for his work with Gentiles** (Acts 11:1-18).
5. **Christians go to Antioch and start a church** (Acts 11:19-26).
6. **Agabus prophesies a famine** (Acts 11:27-30).
7. **James is killed, and Peter is put into prison** (Acts 12:1-5).
8. **Peter is released from prison** (Acts 12:6-19).
9. **Herod Agrippa I dies** (Acts 12:20-25).

Significant Dates of This Time

Circa A.D. 35–A.D. 40

Heroes and Villains: The Stars of Scene 41

CORNELIUS

Until Cornelius was converted, the gospel had been given mostly to Jewish people. Peter was surprised when the Lord gave him specific orders to take the gospel to this Roman centurion who was stationed at Caesarea. A Roman centurion had supervised Jesus' crucifixion, but it was probably not Cornelius, for Cornelius was a godly man who searched for the right way. When Peter came, he and his household accepted Jesus as Savior and Lord. They became the first prominent Gentile converts.

Bible events in Cornelius's life
1. He has a vision of an angel.
2. He sends for Peter.
3. He becomes a believer when Peter visits him.

DORCAS

Tabitha, who is better known to us as Dorcas, lived in Joppa during the time of the early church. Dorcas helped her townspeople generously, so when she died, they mourned her death and sent for Peter, the great apostle. The weeping widows told of Dorcas's gifts and good deeds. Peter then raised Dorcas from the dead.

Bible events in Dorcas's life
1. Dorcas does many good deeds for her fellow townspeople in Joppa.
2. Peter raises her from the dead.

KING HEROD AGRIPPA I

This King Agrippa, the first of two mentioned in the New Testament, is referred to merely as Herod. The emperor in Rome had appointed him ruler of the Jews, so he tried to please the Jewish leaders, first by executing James. Then he imprisoned Peter, with the intent of executing him as well. But an angel took Peter from prison. In a stroke of vanity, Agrippa put on dazzling robes and appeared before a crowd of people, who cried out that he was a god. Agrippa accepted their claim, but he died five days later of a horrible disease with worms.

Bible events in Agrippa I's life
1. He murders James, the brother of John.
2. He arrests Peter and puts him in prison.
3. He dies a horrible death when people worship him as a god.

 Did You Know?

Joppa Today, Joppa is Jaffa, a suburb south of Tel Aviv, Israel. There is a Russian monastery in Joppa that some consider to be the burial place of Dorcas (also called Tabitha).

Caesarea Two villages were named Caesarea. One was on the seacoast, and the other was Caesarea Philippi, where Peter declared Jesus to be the Messiah. Caesarea, where Cornelius lived, was about thirty-two miles north of Joppa and about twenty-five miles south of Mount Carmel. Today, Caesarea has beautiful ruins from Roman times and later. In Roman times, it was the capital of Judea, where the Roman procurators governed the land.

Sharon Peter's fame spread throughout the region of Sharon, which is a Hebrew name meaning "plain." It refers to the great plain known as the Plain of Sharon, which stretches for about fifty miles from Joppa to Haifa and Mount Carmel.

Herod Agrippa I died of worms. What worms? Some believe that these were roundworms, which are pinkish yellow, about ten to sixteen inches long, and about one-fifth of an inch in diameter. These worms multiply in a person's intestine and often form a compact ball with their interlocking bodies, which obstructs the intestine and produces severe pain. Today, surgery can remove the ball of worms, but there was no

488
>
What
Everyone
Should
Know
about
the

Bible

such procedure in Herod's time. This was a very painful and shameful way to die, especially for a high official such as Herod.

Discovering My Purpose from God's Plan

1. *Never call unacceptable what God has called acceptable.* That was God's message to Peter through his vision and Cornelius's. Likewise, never call acceptable what God has called unacceptable.
2. *Evil and righteousness are both contagious.* The entire Herod family was infected with evil, and they infected each other and those they associated with. Cornelius, a Roman centurion, might have been expected to be evil, but he encouraged the spread of the gospel and righteousness through his entire household, family, and friends.
3. *If you pray, expect answers.* Otherwise, why pray? Peter's friends prayed fervently for him, but they did not believe it when their prayers were answered.

To All the World

Paul's First Missionary Journey

Characters:
Bar-Jesus (also called Elymas, the sorcerer who challenged Paul); Barnabas (Paul's partner on this journey); Barsabbas (also called Judas, who returned from Jerusalem to Antioch with Paul); the governor of Cyprus; Hermes (also called Mercury, a god of Greece and Rome; Paul was mistaken for this god at Lystra); John Mark (also called Mark, who started on this journey with Paul and Barnabas, then deserted them); Silas (who returned from Jerusalem to Antioch with Paul); Zeus (also called Jupiter, a Greek and Roman god; Barnabas was mistaken for Zeus at Lystra)

Time Period:
Paul's first missionary journey and the council in Jerusalem

Dates:
A.D. 46–A.D. 50

Where Scene 42 of the Big Story Can Be Found:
Acts 13–15

In Scene 42, Find the Answers to These Questions:
Who were Judaizers, and what did they want?
Why was Saul's name changed to Paul?

Look for this in Scene 42
> Two men are mistaken for two gods.
> What did the Jerusalem council do?

Looking back before looking ahead

Before he ascended into heaven, Jesus gave one last instruction to his disciples: "You will receive power when the Holy Spirit comes upon you. And you will be my witnesses, telling people about me everywhere—in Jerusalem, throughout Judea, in Samaria, and to the ends of the earth" (Acts 1:8). At the time, the disciples could not comprehend the coming of the Holy Spirit. Nor could they comprehend taking the gospel, whatever that would come to mean, beyond Jerusalem—certainly not to the pagan Gentiles all over the world.

When the Holy Spirit came, the disciples were changed from fearful, cowering fishermen and tax collectors to bold, powerful preachers and teachers. In Jerusalem thousands responded to their message and accepted Jesus as Savior, so the church grew at a breathtaking rate. This of course stirred the hatred and jealousy of the Jewish religious leaders, who had already crucified Jesus. A young Pharisee named Saul became especially passionate against these believers. He began a brutal campaign of persecution by jailing, hurting, and even killing Christians.

Saul's persecution forced many Christians to flee Jerusalem and go elsewhere throughout Judea and Samaria. Wherever they went, they took the gospel story with them and shared it with those they encountered. What they were not yet ready to initiate willingly, they did to flee Saul's persecution. Saul unwittingly began the spread of the gospel he was trying to stop but would later give his life to continue.

Jesus spoke to Saul when he was on his way to Damascus to persecute Christians in that city. Saul was changed in an instant, for he now had divine proof that Jesus was the Messiah and was with God in heaven. Saul, the murderous Pharisee, would become Paul, the passionate missionary for Jesus.

This new Saul became a lightning rod for the wrath of the Jewish religious leaders. He was a marked man. Barnabas counseled Saul to go home to Tarsus and wait for the Lord's instructions, and he helped to send him on his way. Saul remained there until a church began to form in Antioch of Syria. Then Barnabas brought Saul back to work with him in Antioch.

The church at Antioch

The church at Antioch had several prophets among its members. It was there that believers were first called Christians, and it was this church that would start the great missionary movement. One day as the people of this church were worshiping, the Holy Spirit spoke to them: "Separate Barnabas and Saul for special work I have for them." After the believers

492

>

What
Everyone
Should
Know
about
the

Bible

continued to fast and pray, they laid hands on Barnabas and Saul to commission them for missionary service.

Paul's first missionary journey: Cyprus

Led by the Holy Spirit, Saul and Barnabas went first to the seaport of Seleucia, where they sailed with John Mark for the island of Cyprus, Barnabas's homeland. In Salamis, they went first to the synagogue to preach. Then they preached from town to town across the entire island until they reached Paphos, the capital city of Cyprus on the far western side.

The governor of Cyprus invited Saul and Barnabas to visit and share the word of God with him, but a Jewish sorcerer named Bar-Jesus, or Elymas, urged the governor not to listen to these men. He was trying to keep the governor away from the Christian message.

Paul (Saul's new name from this time on) was filled with the Holy Spirit. He looked intently at the sorcerer and condemned him. "You son of the devil—you are perverting the way of the Lord, so he will strike you blind." As soon as Paul said that, Elymas became blind, groping here and there and begging for someone to help him. The governor was astonished at this and quickly became a believer in Jesus.

Paul's first missionary journey: Paphos, Perga, Pamphylia

From Paphos the three men sailed for Pamphylia and landed at the port town of Perga. For some reason John Mark decided not to continue on this missionary journey, and he went home to Jerusalem. This later created a serious rift between Paul and Barnabas because Barnabas defended his young nephew, but Paul refused to take him on his second missionary journey. Why did John Mark leave the group? Possibly he was homesick. Possibly he wanted to avoid the threats of the hard journey ahead. Possibly it had become obvious by now that Paul, not Barnabas, would be the leader of the group. Paul may not have been the encourager that Barnabas was.

Paul's first missionary journey: Antioch of Pisidia

Paul and Barnabas traveled inland to Antioch of Pisidia. This city should not be confused with Antioch of Syria, where their home church was located. On the Sabbath day they went to the synagogue and were invited to speak. Paul gave a rather lengthy sermon (which is recorded in Acts 13), telling about Jesus the Messiah and how he and Barnabas had come to share that Good News with everyone. As they left the synagogue, they were invited to come back the next Sabbath to preach some more.

The next week, the whole city turned out to hear Paul and Barnabas. The Jewish leaders became jealous when they saw the crowds, so they slandered Paul and argued with his teachings.

"We were required to give this Good News first to you Jewish people," Paul said. "But you have rejected it, so now we will offer it to the Gentiles." The Gentiles were glad to hear this and thanked the Lord for his message. Many became believers, and the gospel spread throughout that region. The believers were filled with joy and with the Holy Spirit.

This further agitated the Jewish religious leaders, so they stirred up the town against Paul and Barnabas. A mob gathered to run them out of town, so they went on to Iconium.

Paul's first missionary journey: Iconium, Lystra, Derbe

When Paul and Barnabas reached Iconium, they first went to the synagogue as usual and preached so powerfully that many Jews and Gentiles believed. Like the Jewish leaders in Antioch of Pisidia, the Jewish leaders here were jealous and stirred up distrust among the people.

Paul and Barnabas stayed at Iconium for some time, and many accepted Jesus because of them, but the town became divided between those who were for Paul and his message and those who were violently against it. At last those against it formed a mob to attack and stone Paul and Barnabas to death. Paul and Barnabas quickly left Iconium and moved on to the cities of Lystra and Derbe, in the region of Lycaonia, where they again preached the gospel.

In Lystra Paul and Barnabas saw a man who had been crippled since birth. As the man listened intently to Paul's preaching, Paul spoke to him. "Stand up!" he commanded. The man immediately jumped up and started walking.

The crowd was amazed to see this miracle and immediately thought that Paul and Barnabas were gods. They thought Barnabas was the Greek god Zeus, and that Paul was the god Hermes. The crowd sprang into action, and the priest of the temple of Zeus and others brought oxen and wreaths of flowers, preparing to sacrifice to the apostles at the city gate.

Paul and Barnabas were dismayed when they saw this. "No, no, no, we are merely human beings like you," they said. "We have come to bring you the Good News about Jesus. You should turn from all these things to the living God." But it was hard for Paul and Barnabas to keep the crowd from going ahead with the sacrifices.

About that time some jealous Jewish leaders arrived from Antioch of Pisidia and Iconium and quickly turned the worshiping crowd into a murderous mob. They stoned Paul and dragged him from the city, thinking that they had killed him. The believers surrounded Paul, who got up and went back into the city. The next day he and Barnabas left for Derbe.

494

\>

What
Everyone
Should
Know
about
the

Bible

Paul's first missionary journey: Back to Lystra, Iconium, Antioch of Pisidia, Pamphylia, Perga, Attalia, and home to Antioch of Syria

After preaching in Derbe, where many believed in Jesus, Paul and Barnabas made their way back through Lystra, Iconium, and Antioch of Pisidia, strengthening the believers to continue in their faith and reminding them that they would be persecuted. In each church Paul and Barnabas appointed elders and prayed for them with fasting.

From these towns Paul and Barnabas went back toward Jerusalem through Pisidia to Pamphylia. They preached again in Perga, then went on to Attalia. At last they took a ship to Antioch of Syria and their home church. They called the church together and gave a full report about this first missionary journey, telling all the wonderful things that God had done and how he had opened the gospel to the Gentiles. They remained in Antioch of Syria with their fellow believers for some time.

Letter to the Galatians

Circa A.D. 49, while he was in Antioch, Paul wrote a letter to the believers in Galatia that we know as the book of Galatians in our Bible. There is a bit of uncertainty as to whether this Galatia was the Roman province of Galatia where Paul and Barnabas had just been on their first missionary journey or whether it was another territory by that name. It would seem logical that Paul was writing to churches he had just visited.

News had reached Paul in Antioch of Syria that certain Jewish teachers who professed to be Christians insisted that people must follow the ancient Jewish customs in order to be saved. This undermined the gospel teaching that Christ would save anyone directly, and not by means of another system. Paul wrote the wonderful letter we call Galatians to assure the believers that the gospel was a gift to any believer, not merely to those who followed Jewish regulations. It was a charter of Christian freedom in Christ.

The Jerusalem council

The next year, circa A.D. 50, some men arrived from Judea and began to teach the Christians in the Antioch church that they must first keep the ancient Jewish custom of circumcision in order to be saved. Paul had just dealt with this issue in his letter to the Galatians; he and Barnabas disagreed with these teachings. Many Gentiles were becoming Christians, and they were not first becoming Jews before becoming Christians.

Paul and Barnabas were sent to Jerusalem to resolve this matter, accompanied by some local believers in Antioch of Syria. The church in Jerusalem welcomed Paul and Barnabas, and the two told of the wonderful things the Lord had done on their first missionary journey. However, some Christians who had been Pharisees before their conversion insisted that all Gentile converts must be circumcised according to the law of Moses.

The apostles and elders of the Jerusalem church assembled what we know as the Jerusalem council. After a long discussion, Peter stood up and talked about his work among the Gentiles, and Paul and Barnabas added some more about their work. James, the half brother of Jesus and a leader of the Jerusalem church, stood up and urged them not to trouble the Gentile converts with Jewish regulations.

"We should, however, urge the Gentile converts to abstain from eating meat sacrificed to idols, from sexual immorality, and from consuming blood or eating the meat of strangled animals," he counseled.

The apostles and elders of the Jerusalem church agreed with James, and they chose delegates to send with Paul and Barnabas to Antioch of Syria to report on this meeting. One delegate was Judas, also known as Barsabbas, and the other was Silas. The whole group carried a letter to the church at Antioch of Syria from the Jerusalem leaders. The decision in Jerusalem had been unanimous, and the Jerusalem church leaders wanted the leaders of Antioch to know about it. They believed that Gentiles should not be burdened with Jewish laws and regulations, but should accept Jesus directly and personally. They also followed James's advice and counseled the Gentiles to abstain from the things he had mentioned.

There was great joy in the church at Antioch of Syria when the four delegates read the letter from the Jerusalem church. Judas and Silas spoke at length with the Christians in Antioch, encouraging them and strengthening them, and then the two went back to Jerusalem. Paul and Barnabas remained in Antioch of Syria, assisting those who were teaching and preaching the word of the Lord.

Questions You May Be Asking

Why did Saul's name change to Paul while he was in Cyprus?
Saul was his Jewish name, and Paul was his Greek and Roman name. Paulos was Greek, and Paulis was Latin. Saul was moving abruptly from a ministry to the Jews to a ministry to the Gentiles, so his name change reflected that change in his ministry.

Why were the Jewish religious leaders so violently against Paul, a learned Pharisee?
The Scripture clearly says that they were jealous because crowds came to listen to his powerful message about Jesus. The people did not come to hear them (Acts 13:45). Jealousy was also behind Jesus' arrest, trials, and crucifixion—the Jewish religious leaders were jealous because the crowds followed Jesus and not them.

496

>

What
Everyone
Should
Know
about
the

Bible

Why did Paul and Barnabas go first to the synagogues? Why didn't they just go directly to the Gentiles?
As ardent Jewish believers, they felt that they should offer the Good News about Jesus to their own people first. If the Jewish people accepted it, Paul and Barnabas would be delighted. If they rejected it, they would take the message to the Gentiles instead.

Great Events of This Time

1. **Paul begins his first missionary journey** (Acts 13:1-5).
2. **Bar-Jesus tries to keep the governor from believing and is struck blind** (Acts 13:6-12).
3. **Paul preaches at Antioch of Pisidia** (Acts 13:13-52).
4. **Paul and Barnabas are rejected by the Jews at Iconium** (Acts 14:1-7).
5. **Paul and Barnabas are mistaken for gods, and Paul is stoned** (Acts 14:8-20).
6. **Paul strengthens the Christians as he returns to Antioch** (Acts 14:21-28).
7. **Paul attends the council at Jerusalem around** A.D. 50 (Acts 15:1-35).

Significant Dates of This Time

Circa A.D. **49,** Paul wrote to the Galatians.
Circa A.D. **50,** the Jerusalem Council convened.

Heroes and Villains: The Stars of Scene 42

MARK

John Mark is the author of the second Gospel and as a young man accompanied Paul and Barnabas on their first missionary journey. For some reason, Mark deserted them along the way and returned home. Barnabas, who was Mark's cousin, wanted to take Mark along on the second missionary journey, but Paul refused. They disagreed so sharply that they separated; Paul took Silas with him, and Barnabas took Mark. Paul and Mark did not let their relationship remain strained, however, for Paul later spoke highly of Mark. John Mark's mother, Mary, lived in Jerusalem. Believers met at her home a number of times, and it may have been the home with the upper room where Jesus ate the Last Supper with his disciples. Mark was probably the young man who ran naked from the garden of Gethsemane when the mob arrested Jesus.

Bible events in Mark's life
1. He runs away naked when Jesus is arrested in Gethsemane.
2. He goes with Saul (Paul) and Barnabas to Jerusalem with a collection for needy believers.

3. He goes with Saul (Paul) and Barnabas on their first missionary journey.
4. He leaves Paul and Barnabas at Attalia and returns home.
5. He goes with Barnabas on another missionary journey after Paul refuses to let him go on his second missionary journey.

SILAS

Barnabas accompanied Paul on his first missionary journey, but when they made plans for their second journey, Barnabas and Paul parted company. Barnabas wanted to take John Mark, but Paul refused because Mark had deserted them on their first journey. Barnabas and John Mark traveled together to Cyprus, and Paul chose Silas to travel with him on the second missionary journey. Silas is probably also called Silvanus in the New Testament. He was a Roman citizen, which helped him on certain occasions when he traveled with Paul. Silas was the scribe to whom Peter dictated his first epistle.

Bible events in Silas's life
1. He accompanies Paul and Barnabas to the church at Antioch of Syria with news from the Jerusalem council.
2. He goes with Paul on his second missionary journey.
3. He is imprisoned with Paul at Philippi.
4. People search Jason's house for him and Paul at Thessalonica.
5. He ministers with Paul at Berea.
6. He remains at Berea with Timothy while Paul goes on to Athens.

What everyone should know about the book of Galatians
SHOULDN'T I DO SOMETHING DIFFICULT TO ACCEPT JESUS?
What if you had to push a marble a hundred miles with your nose to become a Christian, or walk to the top of Mount Everest? What if you had to carry a two-hundred-pound weight for a mile or do ten thousand push-ups? Accepting Jesus seems too easy. We should have to earn it, shouldn't we?

That's what some Judaizers, or Jewish zealots, were teaching the believers in Galatia. You can't just accept Jesus as Savior. That is too easy. You must first become Jewish—go through the rituals, be circumcised, and follow certain laws and regulations. No, you can't make it too easy. You have to qualify for the Christian life. This was the same old problem of false teachers teaching their own doctrine rather than the doctrine of Christ.

Paul was back home in Antioch of Syria when this problem came up, so he had to write the Galatians a letter. We call that letter the book of Galatians.

Salvation is a gift, Paul wrote. God gives it to you. You can't earn it or qualify for it—you simply must have the faith to accept it. When you do, you

What
Everyone
Should
Know
about
the
Bible

are truly free. For that reason, Galatians is often called the charter of Christian freedom. Christ's death has freed us from sin, from condemnation, from the penalty of sin, and even from the demands of the law.

This new freedom is not the freedom to live an ungodly lifestyle, but the freedom to follow Christ. We are free to live under the direction of the Holy Spirit, who brings great changes in our lives. When we long to be free indeed, we must find our freedom in Jesus.

Paul's letter to the Galatians was written a year before the council in Jerusalem, where the leaders of the Jerusalem church, along with Paul and Barnabas, had to deal with this same issue. Some believers in Jerusalem, especially Pharisees who had become Christians, also believed that people first had to become Jewish before they could become Christians. After prayer and discussion, the Jerusalem church leaders unanimously agreed with Paul, Barnabas, and their leader, James, the half brother of Jesus: Gentiles could come directly to Christ for salvation and did not need to become Jewish first.

Did You Know?

Galatia Galatia was a region, not a city, but there is a bit of uncertainty as to which region or territory it was. The Roman province of Galatia included the cities that Paul and Barnabas visited on their first missionary journey. There was also an old ethnographic territory of Galatia that was somewhat different, but it seems logical that Paul would write to churches he had recently visited.

Antioch of Syria Antioch of Syria, the capital of the Roman province of Syria in Paul's time, was on a major trade route. This was one of sixteen cities that Seleucis Nicator founded to honor his father Antiochus. The city had about five hundred thousand people in Paul's time, and its cosmopolitan population included Jews and Gentiles. The first Gentile church, which became the mother church for many other Gentile churches, was here at Antioch. The church at Antioch was the sending church for Paul on all three missionary journeys.

Discovering My Purpose from God's Plan

1. *A gift rejected by some may become a gift accepted with joy by others.* When the Jewish leaders rejected the gospel, the Gentiles joyfully accepted it.
2. *The best gifts are free—starting with salvation from sin, the greatest gift of all.* Add to that the gifts of sunshine and rain, the beautiful work of creation all around us, the stars, animals, and life itself. We do not earn any of these gifts for they are indeed gifts—they are free.

3. *Jealousy is a fire that consumes reason.* The Jewish religious leaders in the towns Paul and Barnabas visited were offered the greatest gift of all—salvation through Jesus. The Bible tells us it was jealousy, not logic or reason, that prompted them to reject this great gift and even try to destroy the messengers.

4. *Evil seeks to destroy the messenger along with the message.* It was not enough for the leaders to destroy the message that Paul and Barnabas brought; they also wanted to destroy the messengers who brought the unwanted message.

5. *What people most need to hear may be what they least want to hear.* So it was with the gospel as Paul and Barnabas brought it to the synagogues.

Revisiting the Flock
Paul's Second Missionary Journey

Characters:
Aquila (a tentmaker and Paul's host at Corinth); Barnabas (Paul's companion on his first journey, but not the second); Crispus (a Corinthian synagogue leader who believed in Jesus); Damaris (a convert at Athens); Dionysius (a convert at Athens); Gallio (the governor of Achaia when Paul was at Corinth); Jason (Paul's host at Thessalonica); Luke (the author of Acts who joined Paul on this journey); Lydia (a seller of purple, and Paul's hostess in Philippi); Mark (John Mark); Paul; a Philippian jailer who came to Christ; Priscilla (a tentmaker, wife of Aquila, and Paul's hostess at Corinth); Silas (Paul's companion on this journey); Sosthenes (a synagogue leader at Corinth who was beaten for challenging Paul); Timothy (who went with Paul on part of this journey); Titius Justus (one of Paul's hosts at Corinth)

Time Period:
Paul's second missionary journey

Dates:
A.D. 50–A.D. 52

Where Scene 43 of the Big Story Can Be Found:
Acts 15:36–18:23

In Scene 43, Find the Answers to These Questions:
What caused Paul and Barnabas to separate?
How did the demon-possessed girl at Philippi know that Paul and Silas were sent from God?
Who were the three tentmakers who lived and worked together?

Look for this in Scene 43
> The gospel was taken to Europe for the first time.
> A woman sold purple cloth.
> Where was the altar to an unknown god?

Paul and Barnabas separate

After some time had passed, Paul said to Barnabas, "Let's go back to each city we visited before and see how the believers are doing." Barnabas thought this was a great idea and wanted to take John Mark with them. Paul was still unhappy with John Mark because he had deserted them at the beginning of the first missionary journey. Paul stubbornly refused to let him go, and the disagreement became so sharp that the two men separated. Barnabas took John Mark with him and went to Cyprus. Paul chose Silas, one of the two delegates from the Jerusalem council, to go with him.

Paul's second missionary journey: Cilicia, Galatia, Antioch of Pisidia, Iconium, Derbe, Lystra

Paul and Silas went north through Syria, then westward through Cilicia, where Paul's hometown of Tarsus was located, encouraging believers as they went. Next they went into the Roman province of Galatia, in which the towns of Antioch of Pisidia, Iconium, Lystra, and Derbe were located. These locations can be confusing for us because parts of the districts of Phrygia, Pisidia, Lycaonia, and Isauria were part of the Roman province of Galatia.

Paul's second missionary journey: Timothy joins Paul and Silas

Paul and Silas stopped briefly at Derbe before going on to Lystra, where the people had thought that Paul and Barnabas were gods. There they met Timothy, a young believer whose father was Greek and whose mother was a Jewish believer. Timothy had a good reputation in Lystra and Iconium, so Paul asked him to join their missionary team. Because of the Jews in the area, he arranged for Timothy to be circumcised. Then the three of them went through several towns of that area, working with the believers.

Paul's second missionary journey: Phrygia, Galatia, Mysia, Troas

Paul and Silas traveled to other regions. Perhaps Timothy left them, for he is not mentioned again on this trip. They went through Phrygia and Galatia, for the Lord told them not to go to Asia. When they came to the borders of Mysia, they headed northward toward Bithynia, but the Lord would not let them go there either. As they went through Mysia to the town of Troas, Paul and Silas must have wondered about these closed doors—first Asia, then Bithynia. Why?

Paul's second missionary journey: vision of a man from Macedonia

One night Paul had a vision in which he saw a man from Macedonia, which is in northern Greece. The man in the vision pleaded with him

502

>

What
Everyone
Should
Know
about
the

Bible

to come over and help them, so Paul and Silas decided to go into Macedonia. Some think that the man in the vision was Luke, for Luke joined Paul and Silas at this point. Luke may have been from Philippi, which was in Macedonia.

The Lord had closed doors to Asia and Bithynia, so Paul and Silas could go to Philippi. This was the first missionary work in Europe.

Paul's second missionary journey: Troas, Samothrace, Neapolis, Philippi
Responding to the plea to go to Macedonia, Paul, Silas, and Luke boarded a boat at Troas and sailed to the island of Samothrace, then on to Neapolis, the seaport for Philippi. They crossed inland to Philippi and stayed there for several days.

On the Sabbath they went to a riverbank at Philippi where they had heard some people met for prayer. Some women came along, and they talked with them. One was Lydia from Thyatira, who was a merchant of expensive purple cloth. She believed in God, so when Paul preached, it was easy for her to accept Jesus as Savior. She and the members of her household were baptized. She urged Paul and Silas to be guests at her home, so they stayed there for a while.

One day as the believers were going to the place of prayer, a demon-possessed slave girl followed them. She was a fortune-teller, so she earned much money for her owners. The girl followed behind Paul and his group shouting, "These men are servants of the Most High God. They have come to tell you how to be saved." Once again the demons recognized the presence of God when religious people seemed to miss it. This went on day after day until Paul turned to the girl and commanded the demon to leave her. It obeyed immediately.

The girl's owners were furious. She had been making so much money for them, and now their income was gone. They grabbed Paul and Silas and dragged them before the authorities in the marketplace. They even formed a mob against them, so the city officials ordered Paul and Silas to be stripped and severely beaten with wooden rods, then thrown into prison. The jailer was given strict orders not to let them escape, so he put them into the inner dungeon and clamped their feet in stocks.

About midnight Paul and Silas were singing and praying while the other prisoners listened. Suddenly there was a great earthquake that shook the prison. The doors flew open, and the chains fell off of every prisoner. The jailer woke up and saw the doors open. Assuming that the prisoners had escaped, he drew his sword and was about to kill himself. He would rather die by his own sword than be tortured to death by officials.

"Stop! Don't do that!" Paul shouted. "We are all here."

The jailer was trembling as he called for lights, ran into the dungeon, and fell down before Paul and Silas. Perhaps he too had heard their singing and praying.

"Sirs, what must I do to be saved?" the trembling jailer asked.

"Believe on the Lord Jesus Christ, and you will be saved, along with your entire household," they answered.

They shared the gospel with the jailer and the others in his household. After the jailer had washed their wounds, he and every member of his household were baptized. He took Paul and Silas into his home and fed them, and the jailer and all his household rejoiced in the Lord.

The next morning, the city officials decided to let Paul and Silas go, so the jailer told them the good news. Paul told the jailer, "These men have beaten us publicly without a trial and jailed us, which is not legal for them to do to Roman citizens. We will not leave secretly. They must come personally to free us."

The city officials were alarmed to hear that Paul and Silas were Roman citizens, so they came to the jail and apologized to them, begging them to leave the city. The two went to Lydia's home, where they met with the believers, and then they left Philippi.

Paul's second missionary journey: Amphipolis, Apollonia, Thessalonica, Berea
Paul and Silas next traveled through the towns of Amphipolis and Apollonia, apparently without stopping to preach. When they came to Thessalonica, they went to the synagogue for three Sabbaths to share the gospel with the people. Some believed, including some Greek men and many important women of the city.

As usual, the Jewish religious leaders were jealous, so they formed a mob to start a riot. The mob gathered at Jason's house, where Paul and Silas were staying. Paul and Silas were not at home, so the mob dragged Jason and some believers from his home and took them before the city council. This created quite a stir, but the city council let Jason and his friends go.

That night the believers sent Paul and Silas on to Berea. They went first to the synagogue as they usually did. The people of Berea were more open minded than others they had met. They listened carefully to Paul's message and searched the Scriptures each day to verify what he said. Many believed in Jesus because of this, including some prominent Greek men and women.

But there were always troublemakers. Some of the Jewish leaders in Thessalonica heard that Paul and Silas were in Berea, so they sent delegates to stir up trouble. The believers responded quickly by sending Paul on to the coast. Apparently it was safe to keep Silas and Timothy at Berea, but not Paul. The believers who went with Paul escorted him

504

>

What
Everyone
Should
Know
about
the

Bible

all the way to Athens, then they returned to Berea to ask Silas and Timothy to join Paul soon.

Paul's second missionary journey: Athens

While Paul waited for Silas and Timothy in Athens, he debated with the Jews in the synagogues and spoke daily in the public square to all who would listen. He also debated with some Greek philosophers. They even took Paul to the council of philosophers, or the Areopagus, which met on Mars Hill, so they could listen to Paul for new ideas, as many people of Athens did.

Paul spoke to this group, reminding them of their altar to an unknown God. Paul told them that his God was that unknown God, so they should get to know him. They listened carefully until he spoke of the Resurrection. Some laughed at that idea, but others wanted to hear more. Although the discussion ended, some of these people became believers. One was Dionysius, a member of the council, and another was a woman named Damaris.

Paul's second missionary journey: Corinth

From Athens Paul went to Corinth, where he met Aquila and his wife, Priscilla, who were tentmakers by trade, as Paul was. These Jewish people had been expelled from Italy because of Claudius Caesar's order to deport all Jews from Rome. Since they shared a common trade, Paul stayed with them and probably helped them make tents.

As usual, Paul went to the synagogue each Sabbath, trying to convince both Jews and Gentiles to accept Jesus as Savior. At last Silas and Timothy arrived from Macedonia, so Paul stopped making tents and began preaching the gospel full-time. When the Jewish people there rejected Paul and his message, he turned his full attention to the Gentiles.

After that, Paul stayed in the home of a Gentile named Titius Justus, who lived next door to the synagogue. Crispus, the leader of the synagogue, and his entire household believed in the Lord, and so did many others.

One night the Lord spoke to Paul in a vision and told him not to be afraid but to keep on sharing the gospel, for he would be with Paul. So Paul stayed on at Corinth for another year and a half.

From Corinth, Paul writes two epistles to the Thessalonians

During this time, Paul wrote two epistles to the young church at Thessalonica. Earlier we read that Paul and Silas were thrown into prison and then released at Philippi. From there they made their way to Thessalonica, around A.D. 51, and preached in their synagogue for three Sabbaths. A large number of people believed, but the Jewish leaders were jealous, so they started a riot. They attacked Jason's house and dragged him and some believers before the city officials. Out of this event a church grew in Thessalonica.

When Timothy and Silas rejoined Paul in Corinth, they brought word that the Thessalonian Christians were holding up well under persecution but that they had some grave concerns about Christians who died before Jesus' return. Paul wrote 1 Thessalonians to this church to help them understand more about Christ's second coming. The Thessalonians were confused; they had expected Christ to return immediately, but some of their Christian brothers and sisters had died, and Jesus had not yet come. What did that mean?

Paul wrote that those who died before Christ returned had no disadvantage over those who were alive. Those who are alive and waiting for Christ's return should always be alert, for he could come back at any time.

While Paul was still in Corinth, he wrote a second letter to the Thessalonians to clarify their understanding of Jesus' second coming. The Thessalonian believers had suffered mounting persecution, so they thought that Jesus would come at any time. They even interpreted Paul's first letter to mean that Jesus would come immediately. This took away their incentive to plan for the future, and some became idle and even disorderly.

In this second epistle, Paul wrote that Christ's second coming could be at any time, but that it would not happen until after "a great rebellion against God" (2 Thessalonians 2:3), so it would not be immediately. Second Thessalonians was written a few weeks or months after 1 Thessalonians, probably around A.D. 52. The Thessalonians (and all believers) should be alert to Christ's coming, but it should not keep them (or us) from planning for the future and working hard for tomorrow.

Paul's second missionary journey: Corinth, Caesarea, Jerusalem, Antioch of Syria

When Gallio became governor of Achaia, some Jewish leaders under Sosthenes, the leader of the local synagogue, thought it was a good time to pressure him about Paul. They even brought Paul before him with their accusations.

Paul was ready to make his defense, but Gallio interrupted. He spoke sharply to the Jewish leaders and told them that he didn't want to get involved in their arguments about Jewish law. When Gallio ordered the mob out of the courtroom, they grabbed Sosthenes and beat him there, but Gallio refused to stop them.

Paul stayed in Corinth for some time after that, then sailed for the coast of Syria, taking Priscilla and Aquila with him. When they arrived at Ephesus, Paul left the others behind and went into the synagogue to

506

>

What
Everyone
Should
Know
about
the

Bible

debate with the Jews. They asked him to stay a while, but he felt that he should move on. He went next to the port of Caesarea. From there he went to the church in Jerusalem and then back up to his home church in Antioch of Syria.

Questions You May Be Asking

How could the demon-possessed girl know that Paul and Silas were servants of God and would tell people how to be saved?
The same thing happened with Jesus. Demons recognized that he was God's Son, even though the religious leaders couldn't see it. That was because the demons were obedient to Jesus, while the religious leaders weren't. When Jesus commanded demons to leave a person, they obeyed. They knew he had power over them. The demon in this girl recognized Jesus' power in Paul and Silas.

Why were the officials at Philippi alarmed after they had beaten Paul and Silas?
Roman citizens had significant rights in those days, so citizenship was greatly prized. Some wealthy people bought their citizenship, and others were born as children of Roman citizens, so they became citizens by birth. Still others earned citizenship through some special service. Paul was born a Roman citizen. It was illegal for anyone to beat a Roman citizen without a trial. The officials would be in trouble with Rome for what they had done, and they knew it.

Great Events of This Time

1. **Paul and Barnabas separate for Paul's second missionary journey** (Acts 15:36-41).
2. **Timothy joins Paul and Silas** (Acts 16:1-3; 2 Timothy 1:5).
3. **Paul has a vision about Macedonia** (Acts 16:6-10).
4. **Paul meets Lydia** (Acts 16:11-15).
5. **Paul and Silas are kept in the Philippian jail** (Acts 16:16-40).
6. **Paul visits Thessalonica** (Acts 17:1-9).
7. **The Bereans receive Paul's message** (Acts 17:10-15).
8. **Paul preaches on Mars Hill** (Acts 17:16-34).
9. **Paul spends time at Corinth with Priscilla and Aquila** (Acts 18:1-11).
10. **Paul writes 1 and 2 Thessalonians from Corinth.**
11. **Gallio frees Paul, and Sosthenes is beaten** (Acts 18:12-17).
12. **Paul returns to Antioch through Ephesus** (Acts 18:18-22).

Significant Dates of This Time

Circa A.D. 50–A.D. 52

PRISCILLA

Priscilla fled from Rome with her husband, Aquila, when the emperor Claudius expelled the Jews. They moved to Corinth and set up a tent-making business, which employed them at the time that Paul arrived. Since Paul was also a tentmaker, he worked in their business and lived in their home. Later Priscilla and Aquila moved to Ephesus and used their home as a place of worship. Priscilla is always mentioned with Aquila, and her name is often mentioned first. Both of them were very effective workers in the early church.

Bible events in Priscilla's life

1. She and Aquila are tentmakers in Corinth; they take Paul into their home.
2. She sails with Aquila and Paul to Ephesus, where she remains.
3. She helps Apollos learn the gospel.

AQUILA

When the Roman emperor Claudius forced the Jewish people to leave Rome, Aquila and his wife, Priscilla, moved to Corinth and set up a tentmaking business. Paul, also a tentmaker, lived with them for a year and a half. Aquila and Priscilla had Christian worship services in their home and were active in promoting the gospel of Christ in Corinth.

Bible events in Aquila's life

1. He and Priscilla are tentmakers in Corinth; they take Paul into their home.
2. He sails with Priscilla and Paul to Ephesus, where he remains.
3. He helps Apollos learn the gospel.

LYDIA

When Paul arrived in Philippi, he met a widow named Lydia, who sold purple cloth to earn her living. Lydia and her household accepted Jesus, and she opened her home to Paul and his companions. Lydia came from Thyatira, the center from which she obtained her purple cloth.

Bible events in Lydia's life

1. She accepts the message of the gospel and is baptized; she opens her home to Paul and his companions.
2. She opens her home for believers to meet with Paul.

TIMOTHY

Timothy's mother, Eunice, was a Jewish woman who had become a Christian. His father was Greek, and perhaps not a Christian, for only

508

>

What
Everyone
Should
Know
about
the

Bible

Eunice and her mother, Lois, are mentioned as godly influences on Timothy. Timothy was probably converted to Christ on one of Paul's visits to his hometown, Lystra. He joined Paul on part of his second missionary journey. He and Paul traveled through Macedonia, but he stayed at Berea while Paul continued on.

Timothy joined Paul again at Athens and went on a special mission to Thessalonica, returning to report to Paul at Corinth. Timothy went with Erastus to prepare the way for Paul's third missionary journey and was later joined by Paul. Timothy was with Paul during his later captivity, traveled with him when he was released, and worked with the Ephesian church while Paul was absent. When Paul was imprisoned in Rome the second time, Timothy went to be with him. Two New Testament books bear his name; they are the letters Paul wrote to him.

Bible events in Timothy's life
1. Paul and Silas meet Timothy at his home at Lystra; he goes with them on the second missionary journey.
2. He remains at Berea with Silas while Paul goes on to Athens.
3. Paul sends him into Macedonia.

What everyone should know about the book of 1 Thessalonians
BE READY FOR YOUR APPOINTMENT
Life is filled with appointments. We choose a specific hour of a specific day—one o'clock on the afternoon of January 1. It may be a wedding, a funeral, a ball game, a concert, or a business meeting, but it is an appointment, and everyone involved is expected to be there.

When Jesus came as a baby to the manger of Bethlehem, it was a divine appointment, or as some Bible versions call it, "the fullness of the time" (Galatians 4:4, NKJV). It was a specific time on God's calendar, and it happened not a moment too early or too late. The appointed time had come, and the king arrived on schedule.

Much of 1 Thessalonians is about King Jesus' second appointment here on earth, sometimes called the Second Coming. We don't know the appointed hour, but God knows. It will happen at a specific point in time, and the King will keep his appointment, arriving not a moment too late or too early.

Since we don't know God's appointed time, we must be prepared for that appointment at any time. He could come ten minutes after you read this, or ten years, or much longer.

This next appointment will not be in a manger of an insignificant little village. It will be accompanied by "the voice of the archangel, and with the trumpet call of God" (1 Thessalonians 4:16). It will not be with humble quietness, but "with power and great glory" (Matthew 24:30). Every eye will see him, and nations will cry with great sorrow if they have rejected him. He will not come this time as the baby of Bethlehem, but as the King of kings and Lord of lords.

When he comes, it will be too late to prepare for his coming—that would be like trying to train for a race after the starting whistle blows. The time to prepare is now.

Paul wrote 1 Thessalonians circa A.D. 51, while he was ministering in Corinth on his second missionary journey.

What everyone should know about the book of 2 Thessalonians

GET UP AND GET GOING UNTIL THE FINAL WHISTLE BLOWS

At some time we all dream of getting away from something—bills we can't pay, a demanding boss, bad parent-child relationships, a diagnosis that will send us on a downward spiral, the sudden death of a loved one, unreasonable expectations, or a dozen other nightmares. So it was in Thessalonica, a Greek city in Macedonia.

Thessalonica was a major seaport. It was also at the crossroads of four major Roman roads. Like Corinth and Ephesus, Thessalonica was prosperous and enjoyed its location as a port and a crossroads of major trade routes. Thessalonica also had the usual problems that went with prosperity—paganism, materialism, and self-centeredness. Who would want to escape from such a rich lifestyle?

The Christians in Thessalonica weren't trying to escape their lifestyle, but persecution. When Paul established the church there on his second missionary journey, the religious leaders of Thessalonica persecuted him. It was to be expected that other Christians would be persecuted.

The Christians of Thessalonica dreamed of escaping this persecution. When Paul wrote about Jesus' second coming in his first letter to them, the people seized on this wonderful thought. Christ would return any day now, and in him they would find their escape. Many quit their jobs and sat around waiting . . . waiting . . . waiting. That's what they thought Paul meant they should do.

Paul returned to Corinth and had his hands full. He couldn't drop everything and rush back to Thessalonica, so he wrote a second letter, which we know as 2 Thessalonians. This is what Paul told them:

God will certainly punish those who persecute his people, but that may not happen for a while. Don't sit around waiting for Christ to return. It could be soon, but it may not be, so get up and get busy until he comes. When he comes, Christ does not want to find you loafing, but working for him. Get up and get going! Keep going until the appointed time for the King's coming has arrived.

Did You Know?

Timothy's family We learn more about Timothy's family in 2 Timothy 1:5. In Acts we learn that his father was a Greek Gentile. In 2 Timothy we learn that his mother, Eunice, a Jewish believer, was a godly woman, as was her mother, Lois.

Lydia was a merchant of purple cloth In Paul's time, purple cloth was unusually expensive because the purple dye came from a tiny part of the murex shellfish. It took many of those shellfish to dye a small amount of

>

What
Everyone
Should
Know
about
the

Bible

cloth. The purple cloth was usually bought only by the very wealthy, especially those of royal or noble blood. A dyer's guild was located in Lydia's hometown of Thyatira. Why was a woman a merchant of this expensive cloth? We don't know, but she may have inherited the business when her husband died. Lydia was probably quite wealthy because of this business.

Stocks When Paul and Silas were put into the Philippian jail, the jailer put their legs into stocks. These were wooden posts with large iron bolts that clamped them together. A prisoner in stocks had no hope of escaping, but stocks didn't stop the Lord!

Discovering My Purpose from God's Plan

1. *Doors may close to one opportunity so they can open to another opportunity.* When you find doors closing to something you want, perhaps you should ask what doors are opening. Likewise, some doors may open so that others may close.
2. *Heritage does not save a person, but it can provide a link of godliness that will lead a person to Christ.* Timothy's mother and grandmother were godly women who evidently left their mark on him.
3. *God specializes in the impossible.* There was no possible way for someone to escape from a dungeon with their hands or feet in stocks. God can do anything, and he freed Paul and Silas from the stocks and the dungeon.

The Last Great Journey
Paul's Third Missionary Journey

Characters:
Agabus (a prophet in Caesarea); Apollos (an eloquent speaker); Aristarchus from Thessalonica (who traveled with Paul); Demetrius (a silversmith of Ephesus who started a riot against Paul); Diana (also called Artemis, a goddess of the temple at Ephesus); Eutychus (a young man who fell asleep when Paul preached at Troas); Gaius from Derbe (who traveled with Paul); James (a half brother of Jesus and leader of the Jerusalem church); Mnason (Paul's host in Jerusalem, an early disciple from Cyprus); Philip (an evangelist at Caesarea); Sceva (whose seven sons tried to cast out demons at Ephesus); Secundus from Thessalonica; Sopater from Berea; Timothy; Trophimus from Asia; and Tychichus from Asia (all of whom traveled with Paul)

Time Period:
Paul's third missionary journey

Dates:
A.D. 53–A.D. 57

Where Scene 44 of the Big Story Can Be Found:
Acts 18–21

In Scene 44, Find the Answers to These Questions:
Why were seven silly sons beaten by a demon-possessed man?
Why were the silversmiths of Ephesus so passionately against Paul?
Who fell asleep and fell to his death while listening to a sermon?

Look for this in Scene 44
> An eloquent preacher didn't yet know the gospel.
> Someone was healed with handkerchiefs.

Paul's third missionary journey: Galatia, Phrygia, Derbe, Lystra, Iconium.

After some time at his home church in Antioch of Syria, Paul left for his third missionary journey. He went first through Galatia and Phrygia, encouraging the believers to walk with the Lord. Since he went by land, he would have traveled first through his hometown of Tarsus, then on to places such as Derbe, Lystra, and Iconium, where many had come to Christ on earlier visits. Finally he made his way toward Ephesus.

Eloquent Apollos

Meanwhile a Jewish believer named Apollos, who was an eloquent speaker and knew the Scriptures well, had arrived in Ephesus from Alexandria in Egypt. He spoke enthusiastically about the Lord, but he only knew about John's baptism. When Aquila and Priscilla heard him, they explained more to him about Jesus and his work on the Cross.

Apollos had been considering a trip to Corinth in Achaia, so the believers in Ephesus encouraged him to go and sent a letter asking the believers there to welcome him. When he arrived, he preached powerfully about Jesus the Messiah and engaged some of the Jewish leaders in public debate.

During the time that Apollos was in Corinth, Paul arrived in Ephesus and met with a dozen believers there. "Did you receive the Holy Spirit when you believed?" he asked them. They had not, for they apparently had become believers through Apollos before he accepted Jesus, so they also only knew about John's baptism. Paul explained the gospel and baptized them, and the Holy Spirit came upon them.

Paul's third missionary journey: three years in Ephesus

Paul went to the synagogue in Ephesus and preached for the next three months. Some rejected his message, so Paul left the synagogue and took some believers with him. They now met at the lecture hall of Tyrannus. This continued for the next two years, so people throughout Achaia heard the gospel. The Lord also gave Paul great power to work miracles. People were healed even if their friends placed handkerchiefs on Paul and touched the sick or demon-possessed.

The seven silly sons of Sceva at Ephesus

A strange and almost comical incident took place about this time. The seven sons of Sceva, a Jewish high priest, must have seen Paul drive out demons in Jesus' name. They thought they would try it, perhaps like trying a new magic trick, but when they commanded an evil spirit to come out of a man, the spirit said to them, "I know Jesus, and I know about Paul, but who are you?"

The man with the evil spirit jumped on these seven men and gave

514

>

What
Everyone
Should
Know
about
the

Bible

them such a severe beating that they ran naked and bleeding from the house. That probably ended their "healing" ministry rather abruptly.

The story of the seven silly sons spread throughout the region, bringing new respect for the Lord. A revival stirred some believers to confess their sinful practices and seek forgiveness. Many of them had been practicing evil magic, so they now brought their expensive books of incantations, or dark magic, and burned them in a great public bonfire. This also encouraged the spread of the gospel.

From Ephesus, Paul writes 1 Corinthians

While Paul was living in Ephesus, he wrote a letter to the believers in Corinth, probably about A.D. 55. We call this letter 1 Corinthians, although it was his second letter to them; the first letter has been lost. That letter was sent with Timothy to the believers in Corinth, and it prompted the Corinthians to write to Paul in Ephesus.

First Corinthians is Paul's response to their letter, which raised questions about marriage, food sacrificed to idols, and spiritual gifts. Paul's letter answered these questions. He also wrote about divisions among them, and the problems of living in an immoral, pagan city. Paul told them not to dress like pagans, eat like pagans, or live like pagans, lest people think they were pagans.

After about three years in Ephesus, Paul made plans to leave for Macedonia and Achaia. He wanted to return to Jerusalem and hopefully go from there to Rome, so he sent Timothy and Erastus ahead to prepare the way.

Ephesus: the silversmith riot

Before Paul could leave Ephesus, some serious trouble erupted. Demetrius had a large silversmith business in Ephesus, with several employees that made silver idols of the Greek goddess Artemis, or Diana. The gospel was turning people away from the worship of Diana, and this was hurting the silversmith business, so Demetrius called his employees and other craftsmen together and stirred them into a mob. He talked about their loss of income and the insult to their great goddess Artemis. The more Demetrius talked, the more their anger boiled over.

"Great is Artemis of the Ephesians!" they began to chant. Before long others joined the mob. The crowd surged to the amphitheater, dragging Gaius and Aristarchus, Paul's traveling companions from Macedonia, with them. Paul wanted to go too, but the Christians in Ephesus restrained him.

Inside the amphitheater, the crowd was getting nasty. They were shouting one thing and another, and it was all very confusing, especially because most of the people didn't know why they were there to begin with. Someone pushed a man named Alexander to the front to speak, but when the crowd saw that he was a Jew, they kept shouting, "Great is Artemis of the Ephesians!" for two more hours.

At last the mayor came to speak. He quieted the crowd and began to talk reasonably with them. "Of course everyone knows how great Artemis is, so why keep shouting about it?" the mayor reasoned. "You have brought these men here, but they have not stolen anything or even said anything bad about Artemis. If Demetrius and his men have a case against them, let them bring it to the courts, and the judges will decide what is right. If you keep rioting like this, the Roman governor may make trouble for us, especially since there is no good reason for this riot. Please go home before we all get into trouble with the Roman governor."

The people listened to the mayor and went home. The silversmith riot was over.

Paul's third missionary journey: Macedonia

Paul could see that it was time for him to move on, so he said good-bye to the Christians and left for Macedonia, encouraging believers along the way. While in Macedonia, Paul wrote 2 Corinthians, circa A.D. 56–A.D. 57. This letter was about the false teachers who had infected the church at Corinth. To gain more power, the false teachers had to do something to decrease the power of the gospel. They tried by falsely criticizing Paul and Jesus. If they could make Paul and Jesus look bad, perhaps they could make their own pagan ways look good. Paul wasn't in Corinth to defend himself, so he wrote to them from Macedonia.

Paul's third missionary journey: three months in Corinth

From Macedonia, Paul went to Greece, where he stayed for three months, spending most of this time in Corinth. While there, he wrote an epistle to the Roman Christians, which is the book of Romans in our Bible. This was circa A.D. 57.

Paul longed to visit the believers in Rome, but first he had to return to Jerusalem with contributions from the believers in Macedonia and Achaia, where Philippi and Achaia were located.

Paul paints a grim picture of paganism in his letter to the Romans. He warns believers that we, too, must beware of pagan influences in our lives. Like the pagans, we are trapped in the prison called sin, waiting for someone to free us. That someone is Jesus, who alone can truly free us from our sin.

Paul's third missionary journey: back to Macedonia and Philippi

When Paul learned that some Jews were plotting against his life, he went back to Macedonia, probably to Philippi. Several men were traveling with Paul, including Sopater from Berea, Aristarchus and Secun-

516
>
What
Everyone
Should
Know
about
the
Bible

dus from Thessalonica, Gaius from Derbe, Timothy, and Tychichus
and Trophimus from the province of Asia. These companions went
ahead to Troas and waited for Paul to arrive from Philippi.

Paul's third missionary journey: Troas, where Eutychus fell to his death

The believers in Troas met for a long service. Since Paul was leaving the
next day, he preached through the evening until midnight. The room
where they were meeting was upstairs, and it was lit by many flickering
lamps.

A young man named Eutychus was sitting on an open window ledge,
listening to Paul. When he became drowsy and fell asleep, he dropped
from the window to his death three stories below.

Paul rushed down, took Eutychus into his arms, and restored him to
life. Then the believers all went back upstairs and finished the service by
celebrating the Lord's Supper. After that, Paul preached until dawn—
but Eutychus probably didn't sit on the window ledge anymore.

Paul's third missionary journey: Assos, Mitylene, Kios, Samos, Miletus, Cos, Rhodes, Patara, Tyre, Ptolemais, Caesarea, Jerusalem

While Paul's companions went ahead by ship, Paul traveled by land
to Assos, where they met up again and traveled together to Mitylene.
The next day they passed by the island of Kios, and the following day
they crossed to the island of Samos. The day after that, they landed at
Miletus.

Paul sent a message to the believers in Ephesus that he could not
take the time to visit them, but that he would welcome it if some of
them wanted to visit him. He had to hurry to get to Jerusalem in time
for Pentecost.

When elders from Ephesus came to see Paul, he gave them the grim
news that the Holy Spirit had repeatedly told him that jail and suffering awaited him in Jerusalem. He felt that he must go anyway, so these
believers would never see him again. Then Paul warned them about
false teachers. When he finished speaking to them, he knelt and prayed
with them. They wept, embraced, and said good-bye.

Paul sailed to the island of Cos, then on to Rhodes the next day,
and then to Patara, where they changed ships for Phoenicia and passed
Cyprus. At last they landed at Tyre, in Syria, and stayed for a week with
local believers who warned Paul against going to Jerusalem. After a week
the entire congregation at Tyre went to the ship with Paul, knelt, prayed,
and said good-bye.

Ptolemais was the next stop, where Paul met with believers for a day.
After that he went to Caesarea and stayed for several days in the home
of Philip the evangelist, one of the seven deacons who had been chosen to distribute food. Philip had the gift of prophecy, and he had four

unmarried daughters. While Paul was there, another prophet named Agabus came to visit. He took Paul's belt and bound his feet and hands with it.

"The Holy Spirit tells me that the Jewish leaders in Jerusalem will bind the owner of this belt and turn him over to the Romans," he said. When they heard Agabus, Paul's traveling companions and the local believers urged Paul not to go to Jerusalem, but Paul told them he was willing to die for the sake of the Lord Jesus.

Paul left for Jerusalem, accompanied by some believers in Caesarea. They went to the home of Mnason, one of the early disciples from Cyprus, and the believers in Jerusalem welcomed Paul.

The next day Paul met with James, Jesus' half brother, and other leaders of the Jerusalem church. Paul gave them an account of what the Lord had done among the Gentiles, and they praised God for this.

The leaders also told Paul how many Jewish people had come to believe in Jesus but still took the law of Moses very seriously. These people had been told that Paul was teaching Gentile believers to turn their backs on the law of Moses by not circumcising their children or following other Jewish customs.

The leaders of the Jerusalem church had a suggestion. Paul should accompany four men to the Temple and join them in a purification ceremony. This would help the Jewish believers know that Paul still treasured Jewish customs. Paul agreed with this suggestion, and he went through the purification ritual the next day. He accompanied the four men to the Temple, where they publicly announced their vows, the time they would end, and the sacrifices that each of them would offer.

Questions You May Be Asking

Why did Paul go back to some of the same places on his three missionary journeys? Why didn't he go to new places each time?

Becoming a believer in the world of Paul's time was an invitation to persecution and difficult living. The Jewish religious leaders who still hated Jesus and Paul wanted to persecute the Christians. In addition, the pagan lifestyle, while not hostile, was alluring. The attraction of paganism may have been an even greater threat than the persecution of the Jewish leaders. These new Christians needed sound teaching, frequent encouragement, and counsel. Paul returned several times to encourage and strengthen the believers.

How could Apollos teach about the Lord if he didn't even know Jesus?

At first the vibrant speaker Apollos taught what he knew as a faithful student of the Old Testament Scriptures. He also had the testimony of John the Baptist. Until he met Aquila and Priscilla, who shared the gospel with him, he apparently did not realize that Jesus had died for his sins.

518
>

What
Everyone
Should
Know
about
the

Bible

Why would Paul insist on going to Jerusalem when he had been warned several times that he would face jail and persecution there?

Paul said that he was constrained to go. This suggests that the Holy Spirit was leading him to go to Jerusalem. Going there meant imprisonment and time in Caesarea to witness to two Roman governors and King Agrippa. It also led Paul to go to Rome, where he undoubtedly had many opportunities to witness.

How far did Paul travel on his missionary journeys?

Let's use the third missionary journey as an example. From Antioch of Syria, where Paul's home church was located, it was about one hundred miles over land to Tarsus, Paul's hometown. From there it was another one hundred fifty miles to Iconium, almost another one hundred miles to Antioch of Pisidia, and about two hundred miles more to Ephesus. Corinth was almost two hundred miles west by sea, and Philippi, in Macedonia, was about three hundred miles north of there by sea or land. Altogether Paul probably traveled about one thousand miles for this journey and two thousand miles on his second missionary journey. Remember, overland travel was largely done on foot. That's a lot of walking!

Great Events of This Time

1. **Paul's third missionary journey begins** (Acts 18:23).
2. **Priscilla and Aquila help Apollos, and Paul helps believers in Ephesus** (Acts 18:24–19:12).
3. **Paul meets the seven sons of Sceva** (Acts 19:13-16).
4. **The books of evil are burned** (Acts 19:17-20).
5. **Paul meets Demetrius, and the silversmiths riot** (Acts 19:21-41).
6. **Paul writes 1 Corinthians while in Ephesus.**
7. **While Paul is in Greece, he learns of a plot against him** (Acts 20:1-6).
8. **Paul writes 2 Corinthians from Macedonia.**
9. **Paul writes Romans at Corinth.**
10. **Eutychus is at Troas** (Acts 20:7-12).
11. **Paul meets the Ephesians on his return trip to Jerusalem** (Acts 20:13-38).
12. **Paul stays with Philip the evangelist and hears Agabus's prophecy** (Acts 21:8-14).
13. **Paul returns to Jerusalem and meets with the elders** (Acts 21:15-26).

Significant Dates of This Time

Circa A.D. 53–A.D. 57, Paul makes his third missionary journey.
Circa A.D. 55, Paul writes 1 Corinthians from Ephesus.
Circa A.D. 55–A.D. 57, Paul writes 2 Corinthians from Macedonia.
Circa A.D. 57, Paul writes Romans from Corinth.

Heroes and Villains: The Stars of Scene 44

APOLLOS

When he visited Corinth, arriving from his native Alexandria in Egypt, Apollos spoke eloquently to the Jewish people. At first he preached the message of John the Baptist, but when he learned the full story of the gospel of Christ, he preached that. Because he was such a good speaker, some began to say that they were followers of Apollos. Paul encouraged the people not to follow Paul or Apollos, but to follow Christ. Apollos moved to Crete, and he and Paul remained good friends.

Bible events in Apollos's life

1. When Apollos preaches at Ephesus, Aquila and Priscilla share the gospel with him.
2. When he goes to Achaia, the Ephesian believers write a letter urging the people there to receive him warmly.

What everyone should know about the book of Romans

HOW CAN WE GET OUT OF OUR OWN PRIVATE PRISON?

The first part of Romans paints a dark picture of pagans wallowing in their wickedness. We nod our heads as we read of their dark deeds and the judgment and punishment that await them. We will be ever so happy when they are punished. Have you ever heard a news report of a wicked person who committed an evil crime? What is your first thought? You are probably anxious to see this evil person captured and punished. That would make you happy, wouldn't it?

Would it make you equally happy if this person accepted Jesus and became a passionate believer? We like to nod our heads as we speak of the punishment of the wicked. We stop nodding if the wicked repent and escape the punishment we want them to have.

In Romans, Paul suddenly turns the tables. "You believers have just condemned yourselves," he says. That's because your sins are punishable too. Perhaps we haven't committed murder or persecuted anyone, but we may have gossiped and hurt someone. We may have cheated a little and brought heavy consequences on someone else. Our "dark deeds" may not be as consequential as the dark deeds of the pagans, but they are still unacceptable to God.

We, like the pagans, imprison ourselves in sin, and we can't get out. We are trapped, and there we will remain until someone mercifully frees us. Who can do that? In Romans, Paul gives the answer: Jesus. He alone can set us free, and he wants to do so, but we must ask.

Paul was in Corinth toward the end of his third missionary journey when he wrote Romans. It was circa A.D. 57, and he would soon head toward Jerusalem to take a collection to the poor there.

520

>

What Everyone Should Know about the

Bible

What everyone should know about the book of 1 Corinthians

MUST WE BE DIFFERENT FROM THE CROWD?

Until you understand the city of ancient Corinth, you cannot fully understand the books of 1 and 2 Corinthians.

Corinth was a Greek city of about half a million people. Some lived below the poverty line, but most lived above it. Many were affluent, sophisticated, educated people who lived an enviable lifestyle. They had lots of *things*—money, fine houses, and servants or slaves.

Corinth was a port city and thus a center of commerce. Sailors, businessmen, educators, and tradesmen came from all parts of the world. With them, they brought various lifestyles, and goods worthy of many modern malls. Corinth also had its own version of the Super Bowl or the all-star games. It was a sports center and a host city for the Isthmian Games, which were something like the Olympics.

It's hard to criticize ancient Corinth—it had education, sophistication, business, affluence, an enviable lifestyle, and wealth—what is there to condemn? These things themselves were not the issue, but rather what the people did with all these things. Corinth's problems were similar to ours. God doesn't condemn what we have, but he does judge what we do with what we have and so it was in Corinth.

The enviable Corinthian lifestyle encouraged immorality, pagan practices, and misplaced love. Money, for example, is not a problem, but the love of money leads to many difficulties. Education, sophistication, and possessions are not problems in themselves, but when we take our eyes from God and fix them on things, we have a big problem.

First Corinthians was a letter to the Corinthian Christians about their lifestyle, not their doctrine. Paul's advice: Don't live like your neighbors. Be careful not to adopt their pagan practices, lest you also adopt their pagan gods. If you dress, live, and eat like the pagans, it may be difficult to distinguish you from the pagans. If you're different, your difference can be a way of witnessing.

Paul wrote 1 Corinthians near the end of his three-year ministry in Ephesus on his third missionary journey, circa A.D. 55. He wrote 2 Corinthians from Macedonia sometime between A.D. 55 and A.D. 57, when he was still on his third missionary journey.

What everyone should know about the book of 2 Corinthians

HOW SHOULD WE HANDLE FALSE TEACHING?

When Paul wrote his last letter to the church at Corinth, he warned them about the pagan lifestyle. He encouraged them to be different and to avoid living like the pagans did lest they become pagan or look like pagans. If the pagans saw Christians adopting their ways, how would Christians attract them to Christ's ways?

Now a different problem affected the church at Corinth. False teachers had come on the scene. People couldn't accept both these new teachings and Christ's teachings, which Paul had shared with them.

The false teachers wanted power. To gain more power, they had to see Christ and Paul decrease in power, so they falsely criticized Paul and Christ and affirmed the pagan practices. If they could make Paul look bad and pagan practices look good, they could win.

You would think true believers would see through this kind of scam, but some didn't. Paul was far away in Macedonia on his third missionary journey, so he wasn't there to defend himself. He had to write a letter, which we know as 2 Corinthians.

 ## Did You Know?

The books of magic were not like our books When you read this story, don't picture a book like ours. These books were scrolls, written by hand on a long roll of parchment. A scroll may have been thirty feet long, which is a lot of handwriting. The scroll was wound up on two rollers, and it had to be rolled from one to the other to be read. Making a scroll like this took a scribe many days, and few people could write, so books were expensive. These books were incantations used in dark magic. When a person became a true believer, it was not possible to continue practicing evil magic and still practice the presence of God.

Artemis, or Diana Artemis of the Ephesians was a somewhat different goddess than the Artemis worshiped in other places. In Ephesus she was a lusty goddess of female fertility. Like many ancient fertility gods and goddesses, crop fertility was associated with worshiping her. Female slaves would dress in short skirts with one breast bared to serve in the temple of Artemis at Ephesus. This temple apparently did not practice prostitution, however, as the temples of many other fertility gods or goddesses did.

Discovering My Purpose from God's Plan

1. *The road to the mountaintop may lead through the valley.* For Paul to reach Rome, where he longed to witness, he first had to be imprisoned for two years in Caesarea.
2. *Our greatest threats are often from within, not from without.* The threat of temptations to sin and lead ungodly lives may be more ominous for us than the threat of persecution.
3. *Beware when you long for the ungodly to be judged for sin, lest you condemn yourself for your sin.*

Paying the Price

Paul's Arrest and Trials

Characters:
Agrippa (King Herod Agrippa II, who judged Paul at Caesarea); Felix (the governor who judged Paul at Caesarea); Festus (Porcius Festus, the second governor who judged Paul at Caesarea); Paul; Paul's nephew; a Roman commander (who imprisoned Paul in Jerusalem); Tertullus (a lawyer who represented Jewish leaders at Caesarea); Trophimus (a Gentile companion to Paul in Jerusalem)

Time Period:
Paul's arrest in Jerusalem and his trials in Jerusalem and Caesarea

Dates:
A.D. 57–A.D. 59

Where Scene 45 of the Big Story Can Be Found:
Acts 21–26

In Scene 45, Find the Answers to These Questions:
Which two languages could Paul speak fluently?
What Greek slave became a governor?

Look for this in Scene 45
> A nephew saved his uncle's life.
> Two governors and a king judged Paul at Caesarea.

Trouble in the Temple

One day some of the Jewish leaders from Asia saw Paul in the Temple. They had stirred up trouble for him back home, and now they would make trouble for him in Jerusalem. They quickly incited a mob against Paul by grabbing him and yelling for others to help them.

"Help!" they cried out. "This man teaches against our people and tells everyone to disobey our laws. He speaks against the Temple, and he even brings Gentiles into it!" Earlier that day they had seen Paul in the city with the Gentile Trophimus, and they lied about Paul bringing him to the Temple. This stirred up quite a mob, and a riot soon began. They dragged Paul from the Temple and closed the gates behind them. As the mob was trying to kill Paul, the Roman commander called out his soldiers and officers and went into the midst of the mob, and the people stopped beating Paul.

The Roman commander arrested Paul and bound him with two chains. When he couldn't find out who Paul was or what he had done, he took Paul to the Antonia Fortress. The mob became so violent that the soldiers had to lift Paul above their heads to carry him. The mob kept shouting, "Kill him! Kill him!" even though many of them didn't even know who he was.

Paul spoke to the commander in Greek. "May I have a word with you?" he asked. The commander was surprised to hear Paul speaking Greek. This was the language used by the more sophisticated, or cultured people, not the language of a common criminal.

"Are you the Egyptian who led a rebellion and took four thousand men out into the desert?" the commander asked.

"No, I am a Jew from Tarsus in Cilicia," Paul answered. "Please let me talk with these people."

The commander gave him permission, so Paul stood on the steps and addressed the people in their language, Aramaic. Suddenly the crowd became quiet.

Paul gave a long speech, telling about his training, his work as a Pharisee, and his persecution of the Christians. He also told about his conversion. The crowd kept quiet until Paul mentioned the word *Gentiles*. Then they went crazy again, throwing off their cloaks, throwing dust into the air, and demanding that Paul be killed.

Since the commander did not know Aramaic, he did not know what Paul had said to stir the people up again. He brought Paul back into the fortress and had him tied down in order to flog him. "Is it legal for you to whip a Roman citizen without a trial?" Paul asked.

"Are you a Roman citizen?" the commander asked.

524

>

What
Everyone
Should
Know
about
the

Bible

"Yes!" Paul said.

"I am too," said the commander. "But I had to buy mine, and it cost me much."

"I am a Roman citizen by birth," Paul said.

The commander was frightened because he had almost flogged a Roman citizen without a trial. The soldiers were also afraid.

Paul before the Jewish council

The next day the commander removed Paul's chains and took him into a meeting with the Jewish high council. Paul began to speak to the council, and when he mentioned that he was a Pharisee and was on trial because of the resurrection of the dead, it started a big argument. The Pharisees argued that Paul was right. The Sadducees, who did not believe in the resurrection, argued that he was wrong. The shouting grew louder and louder, with the council members tugging at Paul from both sides. At last the commander took Paul back to the fortress.

That night the Lord spoke to Paul. "Be encouraged," the Lord said. "As you have told the people about me here in Jerusalem, so you will preach the gospel in Rome." This is what Paul had dreamed of doing for a long time.

The next morning a group of more than forty Jews took an oath not to eat or drink until they had killed Paul, and they told the leading priests and other religious leaders what they had done. "Tell the commander to bring Paul back here," they said. "We will kill him on the way."

Somehow Paul's nephew heard about this plot and told Paul about it. Paul told an officer to take the young man to the commander, and Paul's nephew told the commander what he had heard. The commander listened carefully and told the young man to keep this a secret.

Then the commander sprang into action. Bringing together two hundred soldiers, two hundred spearmen, and seventy horsemen, he left that night at nine o'clock for Caesarea. The commander was kind to Paul, and provided a horse for him to ride.

The commander sent Paul to Governor Felix with a letter. He told the governor that the Jewish leaders wanted to kill him for some technicality about their law; therefore, as a Roman citizen, he did not deserve imprisonment or death.

That night they rode as far as Antipatris. The soldiers returned to the fort the next morning, and the horsemen delivered Paul to Felix, the governor in Caesarea. The governor asked Paul what province he was from, and Paul told him he was from Cilicia. Felix decided to hear Paul's case himself when his accusers arrived.

Paul judged by Felix

Five days later Ananias the high priest, some other Jewish leaders, and the lawyer Tertullus came to press charges against Paul. Tertullus was the first to address the governor. He accused Paul of stirring up trouble, speaking against Rome, and defiling the Temple.

Paul was next. He told the governor that he had not stirred up trouble, had not spoken against the Temple, and had not spoken against Rome. These men were lying. "However, I admit that I follow the Way, which they call a sect," he said. "I firmly believe the Jewish law and the law of Moses."

Felix was already familiar with the gospel and with the Christians. He adjourned the meeting and said he would make a decision when the garrison commander arrived.

A few days later Felix and his wife, Drusilla, a Jewish woman, listened to Paul as he clearly set forth the gospel. He spoke to them about righteousness, self-control, and the judgment to come. Felix was terrified and told Paul, "Go away for now. I will call for you at a more convenient time." He also hoped that Paul might bribe him, so he talked with him often.

Paul judged by Porcius Festus

Paul remained in this situation for two years. At last Porcius Festus became governor instead of Felix, but Felix left Paul in prison.

Festus had a visit from the Jewish leaders while he was on a trip to Jerusalem. Again they made their accusations against Paul and asked Festus to bring him back to Jerusalem for trial, hoping to kill him along the way. Festus told them to come to Caesarea to make their case.

More than a week later Festus returned to Caesarea and started Paul's trial the very next day. Paul's accusers were there too. Paul told Festus that these accusations were certainly not true, and that he had done nothing against the Jewish laws, the Temple, or the Roman government.

"Are you willing to go to Jerusalem and stand trial before me there?" Festus asked.

"No. This is the official Roman court, so I should be tried here," Paul answered. "You know that I am not guilty. Since I am innocent, no one has the right to turn me over to these men. I appeal to Caesar."

Festus talked this over with his advisers. "Very well, then," he said. "You have appealed to Caesar, so you shall go to Caesar."

Paul judged by King Agrippa

A few days later King Agrippa arrived with his sister Bernice to congratulate Festus on his new job. Festus talked with them about Paul. "The Jewish leaders have accused him of things that pertain to their religious law," he said. "He appealed to Caesar, so he is in jail until I can send him there."

>

What
Everyone
Should
Know
about
the

Bible

"I would like to hear him personally," said King Agrippa. So the next day Agrippa and Bernice arrived with great pomp and with military and civic dignitaries. Paul was brought in to present his case.

"I need help to know what to write to Caesar about this man," Governor Festus said. "So King Agrippa, help me to articulate the charges against him."

When Agrippa asked Paul to speak, Paul gave a lengthy talk. He recalled his training, his work as a Pharisee, his persecution of the Christians, his conversion, and his ministry. Paul recounted how the Jewish leaders had arrested him in the Temple because of his work with the Gentiles.

Then Paul spoke directly to Agrippa. "King Agrippa, do you believe the prophets?" he asked. "I know that you do."

Agrippa interrupted, "Do you think you can make me a Christian so quickly?"

When Agrippa, Bernice, and Festus conferred privately, they all agreed that Paul had done nothing worthy of death or imprisonment. "He could be set free if he hadn't appealed to Caesar," Agrippa told Festus.

Questions You May Be Asking

Why was the commander surprised that Paul spoke Greek?

Greek was the language of more sophisticated people, and Aramaic was the inclusive language of the Jews. The commander expected a commoner to speak his native language, not the Greek language. The commander was even more impressed with Paul's Roman citizenship. Only a select few had that, for citizens were either born a citizen, bought their citizenship for an enormous price, or earned it through some very special service to Rome. Paul was a Roman citizen by birth, and this gave him many privileges.

Why were the Roman governors in Caesarea instead of Jerusalem?

Jerusalem was the center of Jewish worship and political life because the Temple and the Jewish Sanhedrin were there. Caesarea was the capital of the Roman province of Judea, the place from which the Roman procurators governed the nation. Peter shared the gospel with the Roman centurion Cornelius at Caesarea.

What did it mean to appeal to Caesar?

A Roman citizen could appeal for a trial before Caesar, the emperor of Rome, if he felt that he did not receive a fair trial at the local level. It was unfair for Festus to suggest that Paul be tried in Jerusalem, for as a Roman citizen, Paul should have been tried in Roman courts, not in Jewish courts.

Great Events of This Time

1. **Paul is arrested at the Temple** (Acts 21:27–22:21).
2. **Paul is scourged by the Romans and brought before the Jewish council** (Acts 22:22–23:11).
3. **Paul's nephew warns him of a plot to kill him, and Paul is taken to Caesarea** (Acts 23:12-35).
4. **Paul stands before Felix** (Acts 24).
5. **Paul stands before Festus and appeals to Caesar** (Acts 25:1-12).
6. **Paul stands before Herod Agrippa II** (Acts 25:13–26:32).

Significant Dates of This Time

Circa A.D. 57–59

Heroes and Villains: The Stars of Scene 45

KING AGRIPPA II

When Paul was held prisoner at Caesarea, King Agrippa came for a visit, heard Paul, and judged that he had done nothing worthy of death. The son of Agrippa I, he had gradually taken over the rule of his father's territories after Agrippa I died of worms. When the Jews revolted against Rome in A.D. 70, Agrippa sided with Rome. He and his sister Bernice then retired to Rome, where he lived until his death in A.D. 100.

Bible events in Agrippa II's life
Agrippa II judges Paul.

FELIX

The Roman emperor Claudius freed the Greek slave Antonius Claudius, who was then given the name of Felix. Supported by the emperor, Felix went about his business of procuring funds for Rome by cruel and oppressive methods. He persuaded Drusilla, the wife of a minor king, to marry him instead, and since she was Jewish, he learned a lot about Jewish beliefs from her. When Felix was the governor of Judea and listened to Paul's message, he appeared to be convicted of sin, but he also seemed to want Paul to buy his freedom. He kept Paul imprisoned at Caesarea for two years until he was replaced by Festus.

Bible events in Felix's life
1. Paul is delivered to Felix at Caesarea.
2. He judges Paul.

528

>

What
Everyone
Should
Know
about
the

Bible

FESTUS

The Roman governor who succeeded Felix was Porcius Festus. He was a more just ruler than Felix, and he refused to let the religious rulers in Jerusalem dictate their will to him. When King Agrippa II visited Caesarea, Festus brought Paul before him, and he confirmed what Festus thought—that Paul had done nothing worthy of death. Although Festus seemed fair, Paul realized that he might turn him over to the religious leaders for political reasons, so Paul appealed to Caesar for trial.

Bible events in Festus's life
1. He judges Paul at Caesarea.
2. He brings Paul before Agrippa II.

Did You Know?

Antonia Fortress When Herod the Great built the Temple that stood during New Testament times, he built a fortress at the northeastern corner and named it Antonia Fortress in honor of Mark Antony, Herod's friend and patron. This is one of two possible sites for the trial of Jesus before Pilate. The fortress had four towers, one at each corner.

King Agrippa Two men in the New Testament were named King Agrippa, and both were in the Herod family. King Herod Agrippa I had five children—Herod Agrippa II, Bernice, Drusilla, Drusus, and Mariamne. Bernice was married at the age of thirteen to Marcus, the son of Tiberias Julius Alexander. When he died, she married her uncle, Herod Chalcis. When he died, she went to live with her brother King Agrippa II, who judged Paul. There were rumors of incest because of their intellectual affinity. King Agrippa I, father of Herod Agrippa II, was the son of Herod Aristobulus, who was the son of Herod the Great, the one who slaughtered the babies of Bethlehem to try to kill the baby Jesus.

Discovering My Purpose from God's Plan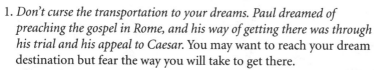

1. *Don't curse the transportation to your dreams. Paul dreamed of preaching the gospel in Rome, and his way of getting there was through his trial and his appeal to Caesar.* You may want to reach your dream destination but fear the way you will take to get there.
2. *The Lord may use pagan instruments for Christian purposes.* He used the Roman governors to get Paul to Rome, where he could preach the gospel.
3. *The Roman procurators showed greater fairness to Paul than the Jewish leaders did.*

Shipwreck and Beyond
Paul's Journey to Rome

Characters:
Agrippa II (King Herod Agrippa II, who judged Paul at Caesarea); Aristarchus (a Macedonian who went with Paul on this journey to comfort him); Bernice (Agrippa's sister); Caesar (Nero; Paul appealed to him for judgment); Epaphras (a Colossian messenger); Epaphroditus (who brought Paul offerings from Philippi); Julius (a Roman centurion who guarded Paul on this journey); Onesimus (a slave owned by Philemon; both accepted Christ under Paul); Philemon (owner of the slave Onesimus, who was won to Christ under Paul); Publius (a host to Paul and other shipwrecked men at Malta)

Time Period:
Paul's journey to Rome

Dates:
A.D. 59–A.D. 62

Where Scene 46 of the Big Story Can Be Found:
Acts 27–28

In Scene 46, Find the Answers to These Questions:
Who was bitten by a poisonous snake and didn't die?
What four "prison epistles" did Paul write from Rome?

Look for this in Scene 46
> Who was shipwrecked on an island?
> What was the figurehead of Castor and Pollux?

The Big Story So Far

Looking back before looking ahead

For two years Paul had been kept in prison at Caesarea. The jealous
Jewish leaders had charged him unfairly in Jerusalem for disturbing the
peace, speaking against Rome, and desecrating the Temple by bringing
a Gentile into it. It wasn't enough for them to murder Jesus. Now they
wanted to murder Paul, and they hoped to get the Romans to do the job
for them.

Caesarea was the Roman provincial capital of Judea, so Paul was sent
there to stand trial before the governor. Felix was the first to hear Paul.
He wanted a bribe, so he kept Paul in prison for two years and spoke
with him occasionally. Festus was next. He brought Paul to trial immediately but was under pressure from the Jewish leaders to take Paul back
to Jerusalem for trial. They planned to murder him on the way.

Paul knew that he could never get a fair trial in Jerusalem, so he
appealed to Caesar, which he had the right to do as a Roman citizen.
After Paul's appeal, King Agrippa II and his sister Bernice listened to
Paul. They and Festus thought that Paul could have been freed if he
had not appealed to Caesar.

Paul had dreamed of preaching the gospel in Rome. He had not
dreamed of getting there in this way, but God works in mysterious ways.
Paul would go to Rome under the auspices of the Roman government.

Setting sail for Rome

At last the time came to send Paul to Rome. He and some other prisoners were guarded by a Roman centurion named Julius, captain of the
Imperial Regiment. Aristarchus, a Macedonian from Thessalonica,
came along on the journey to encourage Paul.

The first ship for the journey was based in Adramyttium and was
scheduled to make several stops along the coast of Asia. The first of
those stops was Sidon, where Julius kindly let Paul go ashore to meet
with some friends, who gave him supplies for the journey.

Leaving Sidon, the ship faced strong headwinds, so it changed direction and sailed north of Cyprus and the mainland. The journey took the
ship along the coast of Cilicia and Pamphylia, with another stop at Myra
in the province of Lycia. There Julius and his prisoners changed ships,
boarding an Egyptian ship from Alexandria that was bound for Italy.

The new ship had rough sailing for the next few days, but at last
they came to Cnidus. There was still a strong headwind, so they went
past the leeward side of Crete and passed the cape of Salmone. After a
great struggle, they finally reached Fair Havens, past the city of Lasea.
The ship was now behind schedule, and because it was late autumn, the

What
Everyone
Should
Know
about
the

Bible

weather was becoming dangerous for long voyages. Paul talked with the ship's officers about this.

"If we go ahead now, we will have great trouble and even risk a shipwreck," he said. The ship's captain and owner of the ship didn't agree with Paul. What did this prisoner know about sailing? Besides, Fair Havens would be a poor winter harbor because it was too exposed. Most of the crew wanted to go on to Phoenix, farther up the coast of Crete, and spend the winter there.

Storm at sea

With a light wind blowing from the south, the sailors thought this was their opportunity to move on. They lifted the anchor and kept close to shore, but there was a sudden change in the weather, and a northeaster caught the ship and blew it out to sea. The wind was too strong, so they had to give up steering and let the ship drift.

The wind blew them past a small island named Cauda, where they decided to bring on board the lifeboat they were towing. The sailors put rope bands around the ship to strengthen it. They were now afraid that the ship would be driven onto the sandbars of Syrtis near the coast of Africa, so they lowered the anchor to see if they could slow the ship's drift.

Powerful winds continued to batter the ship the next day, so the crew began to throw the cargo overboard. With no change for the better by the next day, they began to throw the ship's equipment and everything else they could find overboard. The storm raged on for days, so at night they were in utter darkness, with no stars to guide them.

At last Paul called the crew together and spoke to them. "You should have listened to me back at Fair Havens," he scolded. "You would have prevented all this tragedy. But be encouraged. Last night an angel of the Lord told me we will be shipwrecked on an island, but everyone will be spared."

The storm roared on for fourteen days as the ship was driven across the Sea of Adria in the central Mediterranean Sea. About midnight of the fourteenth day, the sailors sensed that the ship was near land. When they took soundings, they found that the water was only 120 feet deep, later only ninety feet. The sailors were now afraid of crashing on the rocks of a shore, so they threw out four anchors and prayed for daylight.

The sailors started to lower the lifeboats. They pretended to be taking care of the anchors, but their plan was to abandon the ship. Paul warned the commanding officer and the soldiers with him, "Unless those sailors stay on board, we will all die." This time they listened to Paul. They cut the ropes to the lifeboats and let them fall into the sea.

As night gave way to early dawn, Paul urged everyone to eat. Then he took bread, gave thanks for it, and ate some. Everyone was encouraged, so all 276 of them ate. After that, the crew threw the rest of the cargo overboard to lighten the ship.

Shipwreck

When morning came, they saw land, but they did not recognize where they were. They hoped to guide the ship through a bay with treacherous rocks so they could ground the ship safely on the beach. The sailors cut the anchors, lowered the rudders, raised the foresail, and headed toward shore, but the ship hit a shoal and ran aground. The bow was stuck, and the stern was smashed repeatedly by giant waves. Before long the ship began to break apart.

The soldiers wanted to kill the prisoners to make sure they didn't escape, but the commanding officer wanted to keep Paul safe, so he wouldn't let them do it. He ordered everyone who could swim to jump overboard and head for land. Those who couldn't swim got to shore on planks or other broken timbers from the ship. Thus everyone arrived safely.

On the island of Malta, or Melita

On shore, the survivors learned that they were on Malta, or Melita. The people were kind to the shipwrecked men, and since it was cold and rainy, they built a fire to warm them.

As Paul gathered an armload of sticks for the fire, a poisonous snake crawled from the sticks and sank its fangs into Paul's hand. The island people saw what happened and assumed he would die quickly. *Perhaps he's a murderer,* they thought. *He escaped the sea, but he will have justice here.*

Paul shook the snake from his hand into the fire, but he didn't die! The people watched him closely, expecting him to drop dead at any minute. When time passed and nothing happened, they decided that he was a god, not a murderer.

At home with Publius

Near the shore of Malta, the chief official, Publius, had an estate. He took the survivors into his home for three days to feed and care for them. At that time, Publius' father was sick with fever and dysentery, so Paul laid his hands on the man and prayed for him, and he was instantly healed.

Soon the other sick people of the island came, and Paul healed them too. When it was time for the survivors to board another ship leaving Malta, the people showered Paul and the others with many supplies for their trip.

534

>

What
Everyone
Should
Know
about
the

Bible

Onward to Rome

Three months after the shipwreck, Paul and the others set sail for Rome
on another ship. This one was also from Alexandria in Egypt, and it
had the twin gods Castor and Pollux as a figurehead. The ship stopped
at Syracuse for three days, then sailed to Rhegium. The next day, with
a south wind blowing, it sailed up the coast to Puteoli, where it landed.
Paul and the soldiers stayed with some believers there for seven days
before heading on to Rome.

Believers in Rome had heard that Paul was coming, so they went to
greet him at the Forum on the Appian Way. More believers joined the
crowd when the group arrived at the Three Taverns. Julius the centurion and his soldiers who were guarding Paul must have been greatly
impressed that so many people risked their lives to greet Paul. It was
dangerous to be a Christian in Rome at this time, but these people
publicly risked their lives to be with Paul. Paul was greatly encouraged
by all of these believers, and he thanked God for them.

House arrest in Rome: witnessing for Jesus

In Rome the guards permitted Paul to rent his own private home,
although he was guarded by a soldier at all times. This gave Paul the
freedom to witness to many people in Rome, which was something he
had long dreamed of doing.

Three days after they arrived, Paul asked the local Jewish leaders to
visit him. He told them how he had been arrested and shared the gospel
with them, telling them that Jesus was the Messiah for whom they had
waited.

"We have heard nothing bad about you from Judea," they said. "We
want to hear what you have to say, for we know nothing about Christians except that they are denounced everywhere."

A time was set and a large number of people came to Paul's house
to hear him. He taught them about Jesus from the Old Testament
Scriptures—from the books of Moses, which are the first five books of
our Bible, and from the prophets. He sometimes lectured all day, from
morning until evening.

As in other places, some people believed in Jesus as Savior and some
did not. When Paul felt that he had done all he could among his fellow
Jews, he began sharing the gospel with the Gentiles.

For the next two years, Paul lived in his rented house in Rome. He
welcomed his many visitors and shared the gospel with them, and no
one tried to stop him.

Paul writes four epistles: Ephesians, Colossians, Philemon, and Philippians

During the two years Paul was imprisoned in this rented house, he
wrote four epistles that are included in our Bible: Ephesians, Colossians,

Philemon, and Philippians. Paul went to Rome in A.D. 59; he wrote the first three of these epistles circa A.D. 60, and Philippians circa A.D. 62. When Paul wrote the first three letters, he sent them out with the same messengers at the same time.

There was a large number of Gentiles in the church at Ephesus, but the Gentile Christians and Jewish Christians had problems accepting each other, which led to disunity in the church. Actually this problem was more widespread than Ephesus, so Paul wrote the book of Ephesians as an encyclical letter to be shared with other churches.

The Jewish believers still had a strong attachment to the law of Moses and the Jewish customs, so they were displeased that uncircumcised Gentiles called themselves disciples of a Jewish Messiah. They felt that these believers should first become Jewish by following the Jewish rituals and customs, and then become Christian believers. Wasn't Christianity a Jewish offshoot?

The Gentiles in turn became prejudiced against these prejudiced Jewish people. Prejudice breeds prejudice and racism breeds racism. Paul wrote the letter to the Ephesians to urge Jewish and Gentile believers to accept one another, for we are all one in Christ.

The second epistle that Paul wrote while imprisoned in Rome was Colossians, a letter to the church at Colossae. Paul was in the vicinity of Colossae during his second and third missionary journeys; although it is likely that he visited the Colossians, there is no record that he actually did so.

Epaphras, one of the Colossians, brought word to Paul in Rome that a dangerous heresy was infecting the church in Colossae. This heresy, like many today, was a mixture of strange philosophies, religions, and rituals mixed in with a bit of Christianity. Philosophers were groping for an understanding of mysteries beyond their comprehension, legalists were focusing on what they must do to become Christians, ascetics were devising austere and humiliating requirements for becoming a Christian, and some were teaching that Christians must reach God through angels as intermediaries. Mix all of these together, and you have quite a religious brew!

Paul's letter to the Colossians focused on one truth that supersedes the rest—that Jesus Christ is Lord over all, and that accepting him as Savior means accepting him as a personal Savior and Lord. God the Son created and sustains the world. God the Son forgives our sins and helps us walk with him. Yes, doctrines and teachings are important, but the person of Christ is the most important, for everything else points to him. Jesus, not the angels, is the way to God. He provides the free gift of salvation; it is not the fruit of austere and humiliating requirements.

536

>

What
Everyone
Should
Know
about
the

Bible

At the church in Colossae, Paul had a dear friend named Philemon whom he had led to the Lord. This man had a slave named Onesimus, who had stolen some money from his master and had run away to Rome. If caught, Onesimus could be put to death, for the Roman world had no sympathy for runaway slaves. They were their masters' property and had no rights.

It happened that Onesimus met Paul in Rome, accepted Jesus as Savior, and now faced a dilemma. Onesimus had to return to his master, Philemon, and beg forgiveness because he could not be a Christian and remain a runaway slave.

Philemon owed Paul for his salvation, and Paul reminded him of that as he asked that Philemon accept Onesimus back, forgive him, and hopefully, as a brother in Christ, free him. We don't know what Philemon did, but tradition says that he did accept Onesimus back and offered him forgiveness and freedom.

The book of Philippians was written primarily as a thank-you letter to the church at Philippi. While Paul was under house arrest in Rome, he must have wondered if the church at Philippi had forgotten him. It had been ten years since the Macedonian call on his second missionary journey, when he crossed into Europe with the gospel, beginning at Philippi.

Dr. Luke joined Paul's team at Philippi. This was probably Luke's hometown, so he may have been practicing medicine there. Lydia, the wealthy merchant of purple cloth worked in Philippi, and it was the home of the jailer who uttered the famous words "What must I do to be saved?" as he and his household accepted Christ as Savior. The church at Philippi was a great church, and Luke became its pastor for six years.

While Paul was wondering if they had forgotten him, Epaphroditus arrived from the church at Philippi with an offering for Paul. He apparently had almost lost his life in delivering this to Paul. To avoid criticism, Paul usually did not accept offerings for his ministry, but instead earned his living by making tents. But he did accept money from the church at Philippi. Surely Luke and Lydia were two of the big donors.

Bubbling with thanksgiving for this generous gift, Paul wrote his letter to the church at Philippi and sent it back with Epaphroditus. He thanked them for their offering, told them how the gospel was spreading in Rome, and mentioned some new believers in Nero's court.

More than anything, the letter to the Philippians is a declaration of great joy. Paul was a prisoner, possibly facing death, but he was glowing with the joy that he had in Jesus. He wanted the Philippians to share in that joy, and he wants us to share in it too.

Questions You May Be Asking

Where was the Sea of Adria?

This was in the central Mediterranean Sea and should not be confused with the Adriatic Sea.

Who were the gods Castor and Pollux?

In Greek mythology, Castor and Pollux were sons of the Greek god Zeus. Castor was a horseman and Pollux a boxer. They were considered part of the constellation Gemini, or "the Twins," and were regarded as deities who helped sailors. That's why the ship carried their emblems.

Great Events of This Time

1. **Paul sails for Rome** (Acts 27:1-8).
2. **Paul is shipwrecked** (Acts 27:9-44).
3. **Paul spends time on Malta** (Acts 28:1-10).
4. **Paul arrives at Rome and is under house arrest for two years** (Acts 28:11-31).

Significant Dates of This Time

Circa A.D. 59, Paul's journey to Rome.

Circa A.D. 60, Paul writes Ephesians, Colossians, and Philemon while under house arrest in Rome.

Circa A.D. 61, Paul writes Philippians.

Circa A.D. 62, Paul is released from house arrest, probably because the statute of limitations ran out.

What everyone should know about the book of Ephesians

THE CHURCH IS A TEAM

You've probably watched a great team play basketball, football, soccer, or hockey. At times one person may be the star, but he or she can't do it alone. The star needs the rest of the team to play—and win—the game.

You've probably listened to a great orchestra or choir. One person may sing or play a solo, but the soloist can't do it all. He or she needs the others.

You've probably seen the same thing in the church. When God's people work together as a team, things go much better. When an individual tries to be the star or soloist and forgets the rest of the team, it doesn't work well.

This was Paul's message to the church at Ephesus. Be a team! Unite! You need each other. Work together in unity. This is true in a local congregation and in the church worldwide.

Like Corinth, Ephesus was a proud, rich port city where prosperous people lived side by side with the poor. One of the largest temples in the world—the temple of Diana, or Artemis—was at Ephesus, so pagan worship

538

>

What
Everyone
Should
Know
about
the

Bible

abounded. Like Corinth, Ephesus was a center of the pagan lifestyle. Both were like our large cities today.

It is not surprising that a pagan lifestyle infected the church, but prejudice also affected it. The Jewish Christians thought the Gentiles should first become Jewish in order to become Christian. The Gentiles resented the Jewish Christians' rejection. With prejudiced, disunified living came self-centered living. The church needed to be a team, but everyone wanted to be the star, or even the whole team.

Ephesians is a call for unity and teamwork in the church. It must have grieved Paul, chained to a guard in Rome, to have to write about such things. In this letter Paul gives practical pointers about teamwork, and he soars into the heavenlies with sublime language and images.

What everyone should know about the book of Colossians
DON'T LOSE YOUR HEAD!
Without your head, you couldn't live. You could lose a hand, a foot, a tooth, an arm, a leg, or your hair, and you could still have a quality life. But if you lose your head, it's all over. Your head houses your brain, which controls all that you do. Your head also has your eyes, ears, mouth, tongue, and nose. Without a head, a person is dead.

In the same way the church without its true head is also dead. The letter to the Colossians is a reminder to keep Jesus Christ as the head of the church. Without Christ as head, the church is dead.

The people of Colossae knew this already, but they still debated it. They sampled other ideas, like some Christians do today. A few new rituals, some angels, other religions, spirituality without God—sound familiar? Soon Christianity is watered down. It has lost its head.

The greatest threat to the church today is the same as the threat to the church at Colossae. It is a threat from within more than a threat from without. Materialism, hedonism, and self-centeredness are often mixed in with our Christian devotion. Not only do they dilute it, they often nullify it.

We can't lose our head, for without our head we are dead. Our head is Jesus Christ.

What everyone should know about the book of Philemon
HOW MUCH SHOULD WE FORGIVE?
Onesimus was a runaway slave. He was not just a servant to his master Philemon, he was a slave—his master owned him, as you own a car or a pair of shoes. If Onesimus's master, Philemon, caught him, he could have Onesimus put to death. The law was on the owner's side. The slave had no rights; there was no court where he could plead his case, no lawyer to defend him, and no judge who would grant him justice.

Life became a bit more complicated for Onesimus. He ran away to Rome and tried to get lost there, but you can't hide from God, even in Rome. Onesimus had a divine appointment with a missionary named Paul, and he accepted Jesus as Savior.

Now Onesimus had God's forgiveness, but to be safe he needed the forgiveness of his master, Philemon. It just so happened that Paul knew Onesimus's master. In fact, Paul had led Philemon to accept Jesus, just as he led Onesimus to accept Jesus. Philemon owed Paul his salvation. Paul wanted no reward, but he did want Philemon to forgive his runaway slave and accept him back as a brother in Christ.

Paul wrote a letter to Philemon, begging him to forgive Onesimus. Then he sent Onesimus back to Colossae, where Philemon was a prominent member in the Colossian church.

"Give him the same welcome you would give me," Paul wrote. That would be quite a welcome! "If he has stolen anything from you, I will repay it," Paul said. "I won't mention that you owe me your very soul!"

We don't know what happened when Onesimus delivered the letter. We can only imagine that Philemon welcomed him and perhaps even freed him from his slavery.

How much should we forgive? Ask Onesimus. "Much," he would say. "Everything." And Philemon would surely agree with him.

What everyone should know about the book of Philippians
WHERE CAN WE FIND JOY IN DEFEAT?

Paul sat in a rented house in Rome, probably chained to a guard while awaiting trial for his life. His crime was preaching the wonderful Good News about Jesus. For that, he might die.

Almost no one wanted to visit Paul while he was a prisoner. If they were caught and identified as Christians, they could also become prisoners. Epaphroditus came, however, bringing a gift from the church at Philippi.

Paul wrote the letter we know as Philippians as a thank-you note, but it was not written as an obligation. Though living as a prisoner, and possibly near death, Paul did not wallow in pity but punctuated his letter with notes of joy.

This little letter is a model for how we can handle defeat when it comes—and it will come. The scoreboard of life may say that we have lost, but the heavenly scoreboard says that we have won, big time. Like Paul, we can sing with joy.

Did You Know?

Malta, or Melita Melita is the ancient name for the island we know today as Malta. The Phoenicians established colonies there circa 1000 B.C. The island is about sixty miles south of Sicily, and the Romans acquired it in 218 B.C., long before they conquered Palestine. Even though the Roman world moved steadily toward Greek as the accepted language, the people of Melita kept their own native tongue. In some Bible versions, Luke refers to these people as barbarians, mostly because they had not adopted the culturally accepted Greek language. Their behavior was certainly not barbaric to Paul and his companions, was it?

The Forum on the Appian Way Different Bible versions treat this name in different ways. Some call it the Forum on the Appian Way. Others call it

540
>
What Everyone Should Know about the

Bible

Appii Forum, and still others call it the Market of Appius. This place was forty-three miles southeast of Rome. It was a station on the famous Appian Road, which led from Rome to Naples.

The Three Taverns This wasn't a tavern but a town about thirty miles southeast of Rome on the Appian Road, which leads from Rome to Naples. The name has also been translated as the Three Shops.

Discovering My Purpose from God's Plan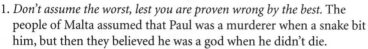

1. *Don't assume the worst, lest you are proven wrong by the best.* The people of Malta assumed that Paul was a murderer when a snake bit him, but then they believed he was a god when he didn't die.
2. *Godly sensitivity may prevail over technical excellence.* The sailors knew sailing, but Paul knew God. If the sailors had listened to Paul, it would have spared them the loss of a ship and all its cargo.
3. *The gift of love may prompt a gift of goods.* Paul lovingly healed the people of Malta and expected nothing in return, but when they sailed for Rome, the people loaded him and the others with supplies.
4. *The power of presence is the greatest gift of love at a time of need.* Paul needed encouragement when he entered Rome as a prisoner. Fellow believers publicly risked their lives to be with him in person during this time.
5. *Prejudice breeds prejudice, and racism breeds racism.* The Jewish and Gentile believers of Paul's time allowed their prejudice against each other to breed counteracting prejudice.
6. *A team is a team only if it is unified.* The church at Ephesus learned that they should set aside their prejudices against each other and become unified so they could work together as a team.
7. *The gospel brings many kinds of freedom.* It freed Philemon and Onesimus from their sins, and it freed Philemon to respond to his slave in a Christian way, perhaps by granting him forgiveness and freedom.
8. *Joy is too good to keep to ourselves.* If we have it, we must share it. Paul had the joy of Jesus even though he was imprisoned in Rome, and he had to share it with his friends at Philippi.

Characters:
Nero (the Roman emperor who executed Peter and Paul);
Paul; Peter

Time Period:
From Paul's first house imprisonment in Rome until his
execution

Dates:
A.D. 62–A.D. 67

Where Scene 47 of the Big Story Can Be Found:
1 and 2 Timothy, Titus

In Scene 47, Find the Answers to These Questions:
Where did Paul go between his two imprisonments?
Did he write any books of the New Testament during this
    interim?

Look for this in Scene 47
> Nero's wife may have been worse than the incredibly
    wicked Nero himself.
> The city of Rome burned.

A Quiet Time

Paul's Writings from Rome

The Big Story So Far

Paul's release and second imprisonment

The Bible narrative in the book of Acts ends with Paul in Rome under house arrest, waiting for trial before the emperor. Paul's story doesn't end there, however. We know that Paul was released from that imprisonment, possibly because the emperor Nero was too busy with other things to bother with him.

We also know that Paul had a ministry after he was released from house arrest, because he wrote 1 Timothy and Titus before he was imprisoned a second time in Rome.

Paul probably went to Macedonia, perhaps to the wonderful church at Philippi, and some think he wrote 1 Timothy and Titus from there. Both letters were written circa A.D. 64. Paul expected to meet Titus in Nicopolis soon and spend the winter there.

Then Paul was arrested again, possibly in Nicopolis or at Troas, and was taken back to Rome for trial. Tradition says that he was in the Mamertine Prison this time. Conditions there were much more severe than house arrest, and from that prison he was taken for execution, probably in A.D. 67. Peter also spent time in the Mamertine Prison, and tradition says that he was crucified upside down, possibly not long after Paul's execution.

Questions You May Be Asking

Why did the emperor Nero release Paul from his first imprisonment but execute him during his second imprisonment?

At first, Nero wasn't bothered much by the Christians. He was consumed with evil, but it seemed to find expression more through his wild lifestyle than through persecuting others. Paul's first imprisonment was during this period of relative peace in Nero's reign.

In A.D. 64, the year after Paul was freed from his first imprisonment, Nero married Poppaea. Her influence apparently changed him for the worst. That same year, much of Rome burned in a fire that was probably instigated by Nero so he could build a grand new Rome. He blamed the Christians for the fire to divert blame from himself. This began a reign of terror against the Christians. Paul was a victim of this movement. As one of the most prominent Christians of that time, he was a marked man when he was imprisoned the second time.

Why was Peter crucified upside down?

Like Paul, Peter was a victim of Nero's reign of terror against Christians. Tradition says that Paul was beheaded on the Ostian Way and that Peter was crucified. It is said that when Peter was about to be crucified, he

544

>

What
Everyone
Should
Know
about
the

Bible

asked to die upside down because he considered himself unworthy to die in the same way as his Lord.

Great Events of This Time

1. Paul apparently goes to Macedonia by way of Miletus and Troas.
2. Paul writes 1 Timothy from Macedonia (1 Timothy 1:3).
3. Paul writes a letter to Titus from Macedonia; he is about to leave for Nicopolis in Greece to spend the winter and wants Titus to join him there (Titus 3:12).
4. Paul is arrested, possibly at Nicopolis or Troas, and is returned to Rome.
5. Paul writes 2 Timothy from prison in Rome (2 Timothy 1:8).
6. Paul is martyred in Rome.

Significant Dates of This Time

Circa A.D. 54–68, Nero, perhaps the most evil of all Roman emperors, rules.
Circa A.D. 64, Paul writes 1 Timothy and Titus, probably from Macedonia. Paul is likely arrested and sent to Rome.
Circa A.D. 64, fire burns much of Rome, and the evil Roman emperor Nero blames the Christians for it.
Circa A.D. 64, Nero marries Poppaea, who seems to intensify his evil ways.
Circa A.D. 66–67, Paul writes 2 Timothy while imprisoned in Rome.
Circa A.D. 67, Paul is martyred.

What everyone should know about the book of 1 Timothy
HOW CAN I BECOME A GOOD LEADER?
A young pastor has begun his ministry. He wants to be a good leader for his people. How can he do this? A young mother wants to be a good leader for her children. A young army officer has just graduated from the academy and now wants to become a good military leader. A scientist, educator, political leader, and researcher all dream of becoming good leaders in their chosen field. How does this happen?

The book of 1 Timothy is a manual of Christian leadership. Paul, an elder statesman, writes to young Timothy to help him understand how to become a good leader. We too can find out how by reading 1 Timothy.

Paul wrote this letter circa A.D. 64 from Rome or Macedonia (most likely from Philippi in Macedonia) just before his final imprisonment. Death was near now, for Paul would become a martyr within perhaps three years from that time.

This same year, Nero married Poppaea, who seemed to intensify his evil ways against Christians. Rome also burned that year. Nero blamed the Christians for this and began a reign of terror against them. He murdered them in the most brutal ways he could devise.

Leadership in parenting, pastoring, education, scientific endeavors, military achievement, or any other discipline is based on one fundamental truth—good leadership depends first upon good living and good character.

First build your life. Then leadership will flow naturally from that exemplary life.

For a Christian, life-building that produces leadership is nurtured by prayer, holiness, unity, morality, discipline, reason, modesty, honor, faithfulness, and all other traits of exemplary character and living.

What everyone should know about the book of 2 Timothy

WHAT WOULD YOU SAY TODAY IF YOU WERE TO DIE TOMORROW?

Life has crushed you about as much as it can. You are chained in a dark, damp prison. Your crime is that you are a Christian who has faithfully witnessed for Jesus. Few will visit you because they fear for their lives.

That was Paul's condition. Before, he had been imprisoned in Rome in a rented house, but that was before Emperor Nero made an all-out effort to persecute Christians. Paul was probably imprisoned in the Mamertine Prison this time. He was a prominent, passionate Christian, and Nero wanted him dead—fast!

Before Paul died, he wanted to give one last word to his good friend Timothy—and to us. This letter, the book of 2 Timothy in the Bible, is probably the last thing Paul wrote, perhaps in A.D. 66 or 67.

What would you expect a person to say on the eve of his execution? Would he grumble? complain? curse? pity himself? Not Paul. His last letter is a note of encouragement and counsel to the young man who would continue part of Paul's ministry.

Paul called Timothy "my dear son," saying, "May God the Father and Christ Jesus our Lord give you grace, mercy, and peace" (2 Timothy 1:2). Paul goes on to say, "I thank God for you" (v. 3) and "I long to see you again" (v. 4). Paul's encouragement and counsel continues throughout the book.

By the time Timothy received this letter, it was probably too late for him to visit Paul, who may already have been executed. Timothy may even have received the news of his death with the letter. Imagine reading this letter from a mentor and friend and knowing that he wrote it to you on the eve of his death.

What everyone should know about the book of Titus

WHAT KIND OF PERSON WILL MAKE A GOOD LEADER?

Timothy and Titus had much in common. Both were young pastors groomed by Paul, and both looked to Paul for counsel. Both wanted to know how to be effective Christian leaders and pastors.

Paul wrote to Titus about A.D. 64, between his two Roman imprisonments, about the same time that he wrote his first letter to Timothy. He probably wrote from Macedonia. His advice to Titus and Timothy is similar.

What kind of person makes a good leader? Paul's answer is that a good leader must be a good person. A godly person makes a godly leader.

What are some qualities of a good or godly person? Paul tells Titus that a godly leader should be discreet, disciplined, exemplary, holy, loving, rever-

546
>
What
Everyone
Should
Know
about
the
Bible

ent, serious, temperate, and trustworthy. A person gets these qualities from God's Word. Trust in the Scriptures and live their teachings. Walk the talk, and talk the walk.

How can anyone hope to develop these awesome qualities? It is a daunting task. But with the help of the Holy Spirit, discipline, and especially devotion and surrender, we can accomplish it.

Discovering My Purpose from God's Plan

1. *Walk the talk, and talk the walk.* To serve as a godly person and a godly leader, both are essential.
2. *A good leader must first be a good follower.* To expect others to follow is first to expect yourself to follow.

Letters That Last Forever

The Other Epistles

Characters:
Domitian (son of Vespasian; Roman emperor from A.D. 81–A.D. 96 who sent his son Titus to destroy Jerusalem); Galba (one of three Roman emperors in A.D. 68–A.D. 69); James (the author of the book of James); John (the author of the Gospel of John; 1, 2, and 3 John; and Revelation); Jude (the author of the book of Jude); Nero (Roman emperor from A.D. 54–A.D. 68 who executed Peter and Paul); Otho (one of three Roman emperors from A.D. 68–A.D. 69); Paul (the possible author of the book of Hebrews); Peter (the author of 1 and 2 Peter); Titus (who destroyed Jerusalem in A.D. 70; he was Roman emperor from A.D. 79–A.D. 81); Vespasian (Roman emperor from A.D. 70–A.D. 79); Vitellius (one of three Roman emperors from A.D. 68–A.D. 69)

Time Period:
When the New Testament letters other than Paul's were written

Dates:
A.D. 49–A.D. 96

Where Scene 48 of the Big Story Can Be Found:
Hebrews; James; 1, 2, and 3 John; Jude; 1 and 2 Peter; Revelation

In Scene 48, Find the Answers to These Questions:
What threat arose that was worse than the Roman persecution?
Which three of the twelve apostles wrote books of the Bible?

Look for this in Scene 48
> Which two books of the Bible were written by Jesus' half brothers?

The Big Story So Far

The Bible story in the book of Acts ends with Paul's first imprisonment in Rome, but history and tradition have provided some insights into his release and his ministry until he was arrested again, sent to prison in Rome (probably at the Mamertine Prison), and executed.

Paul wrote many of our New Testament books as letters to churches or to individuals. The other books of the New Testament were all written before the time of Paul's execution, except for John's three epistles and Revelation.

Significant Dates of This Time

Circa A.D. 49–A.D. 50, James wrote his epistle.
Circa A.D. 62–A.D. 64, Peter wrote 1 Peter.
Circa A.D. 65, Jude wrote his epistle.
Circa A.D. 67, Peter wrote 2 Peter.
Circa A.D. 67–A.D. 70, Hebrews was written, possibly by Paul.
Circa A.D. 70, Jerusalem was completely destroyed by Titus.
Circa A.D. 85–A.D. 90, John wrote 1 John.
Circa A.D. 90, John wrote 2 John and 3 John.
Circa A.D. 95, John wrote Revelation.
A.D. 54–A.D. 68, Nero was the Roman emperor.
A.D. 68–A.D. 69, Galba, Otho, and Vitellius were Roman emperors.
A.D. 70–A.D. 79, Vespasian was the Roman emperor.
A.D. 79–A.D. 81, Titus was the Roman emperor.
A.D. 81–A.D. 96, Domitian, another son of Vespasian, was the Roman emperor.

What everyone should know about the book of Hebrews

THE BETTER WAY

You come to a fork in the road and read the signs. One points to the right and says "The Better Way." Another points to the left and says "The Worse Way." Which way would you want to take? Why would anyone in his right mind want to follow "The Worse Way"? Yet millions of people make that choice every day.

Each day brings us to a new crossroads with unwritten signs that point to a better way and a worse way. Millions choose the worse way or even the worst way. Perhaps that path looks easier or more attractive, or it is filled with goodies that entice us. Whatever the attraction, we too often turn left and follow the worse way even against our better judgment.

The book of Hebrews is a book about the better way, and that way is Jesus. And what or who is Jesus better than? Jesus is better than the

550
>
What
Everyone
Should
Know
about
the
Bible

prophets (1:1-3); the angels (1:4–2:18); Moses the lawgiver (3:1-19); or Joshua, the leader of the conquest of the Promised Land (4:1-16). He is better than Aaron the high priest, for Christ is the great High Priest forever (4:14–5:10).

Hebrews reveals Christ as the source of hope in a hopeless situation. Rather than wallow in hopelessness, we can turn to him for lasting hope.

Next time you come to a crossroads in life, remember the unseen signs and choose the better way, who is Jesus.

Some think that Paul wrote the book of Hebrews, but this is not certain.

What everyone should know about the book of James

FAITH OR WORKS—WHICH SAVES US?

James was Jesus' half brother (Matthew 13:55). At first James didn't realize that his half brother was the Messiah (John 7:5). It must have been a dramatic day after Jesus' resurrection when James finally believed (Acts 1:14). James led the Jerusalem church and penned this letter to believers everywhere circa A.D. 49. The famous Jewish historian Josephus says that James was martyred by the high priest thirteen years later, in A.D. 62. That was the year that Paul was released from his first imprisonment, his house arrest in Rome.

Apparently there was controversy in the church about faith and works. Which saves us? James wrote to Christians who had scattered when they were persecuted in Jerusalem. We are saved by faith, James wrote, but we show evidence of our salvation by our works. How can we show that we are godly if we live ungodly lives?

Faith without works is a dead faith. Works without faith are dead works. They might be nice, but they are not the fruit of godliness.

What everyone should know about the book of 1 Peter

HOW SHOULD WE LIVE IN THE FACE OF PERSECUTION?

Times were tough for Christians in the early church. Most of the Roman emperors were blatantly evil men. Nero was the worst of the worst. In A.D. 64, Rome burned, and history points to Nero as the perpetrator. He had dreams of rebuilding Rome as a city of wonder, but first the old city had to be destroyed. Of course, Nero couldn't take the blame for burning his own city, so he blamed the Christians.

At this time, Paul would soon be imprisoned a second and final time, and he would soon become a martyr for Christ. Peter was living in Rome, and he suffered persecution like many other Christians. Peter would die shortly after Paul was executed. It was the eve of Nero's worst persecutions. The purpose of Peter's letter was to encourage other Christians to live triumphantly through persecution, even when there was no way out of it.

Christ suffered intense persecution and died on the cross because of it. Can his followers expect to escape all persecution and suffering?

In the midst of suffering and persecution, we Christians can strive for holiness, Christlikeness, godliness. That is the heart of Peter's first letter. Because of his writings, Peter was considered the apostle of comfort.

What everyone should know about the book of 2 Peter

STANDING FIRM AGAINST FALSE TEACHERS

Peter was living in Rome. Like other Christians, he suffered persecution. The emperor Nero had burned Rome, hoping to rebuild a golden city based on heavy taxation. He certainly couldn't let the people blame him for Rome's destruction, so he blamed the Christians and set out to persecute them mercilessly.

The year that Peter wrote his second letter may have been the very year that Paul was martyred. Peter's own life was also in danger, for he was a Christian leader living in Rome. He was probably martyred shortly after Paul's death. An early church father, Origen, said that Peter was crucified upside down because he did not feel worthy to be crucified in the same way that Jesus was.

Christians looked to Peter for words of wisdom. In his first letter, he encouraged them to endure persecution and come through as godly, holy people.

As if persecution from the Romans weren't enough, a new threat had arisen from false teachers. Rome was a threat from without, and false teaching was an even more insidious threat from within.

Peter's second book warns Christians to stand against false teaching by studying, knowing, and understanding the Word of God. Heresy withers when the light of God's Word shines upon it.

Heresy still invades the church today. Watch out for false teachers who are out of sync with the Scriptures. A godly teacher will be in sync with God's Word.

What everyone should know about the book of 1 John

KEEPING CLOSE TO THE FAMILY OF GOD

Long before he wrote this epistle, John was a fisherman on the Sea of Galilee. He spent his life catching fish, selling fish, catching more fish, and selling those fish. There is nothing wrong with a fishing career. Fishermen feed hungry people, and that is worthwhile; but there was a higher calling waiting for John.

One day Jesus came along the shore of the sea and watched John fish. "Follow me," Jesus said. John left his fishing business and followed Jesus. His life changed dramatically. He didn't know it then, but he discovered later that he was enrolled for three years in the greatest school in history, the training of the Twelve, with the Son of God as the teacher.

John was at the Last Supper and in Gethsemane with Jesus. He was present at the two greatest events in history—the crucifixion and resurrection of Jesus. Of all the twelve apostles, Jesus chose John to take care of his mother when he was gone. What an honor!

John lived longer than any of the other eleven (or twelve, with Matthias). He outlived Paul too. When he wrote this beautiful letter, he was probably at least ninety. He would live to be one hundred, which is old by today's standards but was unheard of in his day. He would spend his last days exiled on Patmos. When he wrote 1, 2, and 3 John, he was still ministering in Ephesus.

Bible

At the heart of civilized society is a yearning for strong family life. Good families have a glue that holds them together.

John's letter is about another kind of family—the family of God. It is held together with the same kind of glue as an earthly family—love. When we love the Lord and love each other, we have discovered the glue that binds families together, both our human family and the family of God.

Somehow our family glue is intimately related to the glue that binds together the family of God. Love God first. Love others, including your family, second. Love yourself last. When we have our love relationship with God intact, we can build a proper love relationship with our family members.

What everyone should know about the book of 2 John
WHERE DOES LOVE COME FROM?

In his first epistle John wrote about the love of God's family and the love of our earthly family. The formula is quite simple. Build a strong love relationship with God, and it is much easier to build a strong love relationship with family, as well as those outside our family.

John was an old and wise man when he wrote this second epistle—perhaps ninety-five years old. He would soon be exiled to the lonely island of Patmos, where he would write Revelation, one of the most stunning books in the Bible. Before he left Ephesus, he wanted to help his followers know more about the greatest topic in the Bible—love.

Where is love found? "God is love" (1 John 4:8), so we cannot possibly understand love until we understand more about God. Know God and you will know love.

Don't try to practice love on your own because you will fail. Get in sync with the love of God, and you will get in sync with the love of others. It just works better that way.

That's the message of 2 John, and the apostle John should know. He loved Jesus with all his heart.

What everyone should know about the book of 3 John
THE HOSPITALITY OF LOVE AND THE LOVE OF HOSPITALITY

This very small book of the Bible, only one short chapter, is a profile of two men—Gaius and Diotrephes—who are contrasting figures in the same church. Gaius is the model of hospitable love as he cares for the traveling teachers, even those who are strangers. No traveling teacher ever went away from Gaius's presence hungry or homeless.

Diotrephes is the model of an unloving person with no hospitality. No traveling teacher ever had dinner or stayed overnight with him. To make matters worse, this rascal even threatened to put anyone out of the church who showed loving hospitality to traveling teachers. If John ever came back to that town, he would tell Diotrephes a thing or two about love and hospitality.

Which of these men are you like?

This third epistle of John was written when John was about ninety-five. He was about to be banished from Ephesus to the island of Patmos, where God would draw aside the curtain of the future and John would write Revelation.

What everyone should know about the book of Jude

THREATS FROM WITHOUT, THREATS FROM WITHIN

If you are a Christian, you will be persecuted at some time, in some way. That's just the way it is. Since the world hates Jesus, it will instinctively hate his followers. Since the ungodly persecuted Jesus, they will also persecute his followers.

Persecution is not our greatest threat, however, and that's what the book of Jude is all about. We must guard even more against threats from within.

In his letter to the church, Jude warns his brothers and sisters in Christ to be on guard against false teachers who had infected the church. It's only natural to recognize and guard against persecution, but we can easily be caught off guard by false teaching—soft, sweet words that sound so good but sow the seeds of inward destruction.

False teaching is usually not an all-out assault with lies. We wouldn't fall for that. Instead false teaching is often half truth, half lies. The half truth makes it sound okay, so we are more willing to accept the half lies.

Jude's message to the church is simple. Be on guard against persecution that threatens from without, and be equally on guard against false teaching that threatens from within. Don't let the half truths sugarcoat the half lies. False teachers will be judged, and with them the followers who accept their teachings.

Jude was one of Jesus' half brothers, born of Mary and Joseph. James, who wrote the epistle of James, was Jude's full brother. Like Jesus' other half brothers, Jude apparently did not believe in Jesus as the Messiah until after the Resurrection (Acts 1:14).

Jude's closing statement is often used as a doxology in church services today.

◤◢◤◢◤◢ Discovering My Purpose from God's Plan

1. *Half truth makes half lies palatable.*
2. *Threats from within are more dangerous than threats from without.*
3. *Watch out for false teachers.* How can you tell who is false? They will be out of sync with the Word of God. How can you tell if a teacher is godly? He will be in sync with God's Word.
4. *Each day brings us to a new crossroads with unwritten signs that point to a better way and a worse way.* Millions choose the worse way. Beware of that way, for sometimes it may even be marked as the better way.
5. *Christ is the source of hope in a hopeless situation.* When we feel hopeless, we can turn to him for lasting hope.
6. *At the heart of civilized society is a yearning for strong family life.*

554

>

What
Everyone
Should
Know
about
the

Bible

Good families have a glue—love—that holds them together, and dysfunctional families would give a fortune for that glue.

7. *Our family glue is intimately related to the glue that binds the family of God together.* Love God first. Love others, including your family, second. Love yourself last. When we have our love relationship with God intact, we can build a proper love relationship with one another as family members.

8. *Get in sync with the love of God and you can get in sync with the love of your spouse, your children, or your family.*

Characters:
Jesus (the author of Revelation); John (the writer and recorder of Revelation)

Time Period:
Eternity yet to come

Dates:
Endless time before us

Where Scene 49 of the Big Story Can Be Found:
The book of Revelation

A Glimpse of Tomorrow
Revelation and Beyond

The Big Story So Far

Why is the Bible so important?

What purpose for life can you discover in the Bible? Why bother reading it? Why so much fuss about one book out of millions?

Why has the Bible remained the best seller of all ages? Why do people spend vast amounts of money to share the Bible with people around the world? Why do thousands of missionaries give up home and family to share the Bible with people in remote places? Why not just skip the whole thing and go on with life as it is? Why waste time on all this? Why not just eat, drink, and be merry?

One reason is that the Bible has endured. Two thousand years have passed since Jesus came to earth, about the same number of years that elapsed between the time of Abraham and the time of Jesus. So the Old Testament has endured for about four thousand years. Still, the world-wide reception of both the Old and New Testaments keeps growing every year.

Empires and emperors rise and fall, and they are soon forgotten, but God's Word endures. The once-mighty Assyrian empire is no more. Who but historians could name their emperors? The great Babylonian empire is completely gone. Who ruled that empire? You may know the name of Nebuchadnezzar, but how much do you know about him? Alexander the Great's Greek empire has disappeared. His name is well known, but who knows much about him? And the mightiest of all ancient empires, the Roman Empire, is all but forgotten except in history books. We remember Caesar Augustus, not because of his great-ness but because the Bible has kept his name alive through the centuries.

The Bible has endured through all of this. As Isaiah said, 2,700 years ago, "The grass withers and the flowers fade, but the word of our God stands forever" (Isaiah 40:8).

The purpose of the Bible: an autobiography of God, a book about you

Another reason is the purpose of the Bible itself. It is an autobiography of God's person and works. It is also a book about you—why you are here, what you should do about it, where you should be headed, and how you can be sure to arrive there. The purpose of the Bible is to help you find purpose for your life on earth and for your life beyond this earth.

The Bible is the blueprint of God's eternal plan, the big story

The Bible is also the blueprint of God's eternal plan. It reveals the part of his plan that spans human history. It tantalizes us with hints about the eons of time before Creation and the eons of time after consumma-tion. It pulls aside the curtain of divine mystery and lets us peek, ever

558

>

What
Everyone
Should
Know
about
the

Bible

so slightly, into the heavenlies. We see enough of this incredible place to want to be there forever, not merely because of its grandeur, but because of who is there. So what is the Bible all about? It's about the Who of heaven.

Of course, the Bible helps us to have a better life on earth for a few years, but life on earth is very short and eternity is very long. Job said, "My days fly faster than a weaver's shuttle. . . . My life is but a breath" (Job 7:6-7). James added a footnote about the brevity of life on earth: "Your life is like the morning fog—it's here a little while, then it's gone" (James 4:14). Every one of us has commented, perhaps just recently, about how fast the years pass us by. No, the world's stage is not the place for us, although it is our only route toward *the* place—our forever home.

Let's look at it this way. You're about to rent a motel room for one day as you prepare to move into your new house and live there for the next fifty years. How do your priorities relate to these two homes? Where is your heart? Where should your heart and its priorities be?

To understand the end of all things, we must first understand the beginning of all things. Alpha and Omega are always linked by an unbroken chain. We started this book with some perspective on the God who was never born and will never die, and who invested eons of time before Creation in planning that creation. He laid careful plans for every snowflake, every sunrise and sunset, every DNA map in billions of people. Creation took infinite planning.

He also spent much divine energy in planning the consummation of time and history as well as Creation. In the mind and heart of God, there formed a plan that reached far, far beyond the stage for human drama called Creation. Like the empires of the ancient world, and like our world today, the entire human drama will pass like the morning fog. It is fleeting, so don't count on this world for your forever home.

The consummation of time and history was fully planned before Creation began. The end and the beginning have always been inseparable. God has always seen the entire portrait of time and eternity.

The writer of Proverbs said, "The LORD formed me [wisdom] from the beginning, before he created anything else. I was appointed in ages past, at the very first, before the earth began. I was born before the oceans were created, before the springs bubbled forth their waters. Before the mountains were formed, before the hills, I was born—before he had made the earth and fields and the first handfuls of soil" (Proverbs 8:22-26). Profound! You and I were planned before the dawn of Creation. God knew your name, and he knew every moment of your formation in your mother's womb. He knew this before he started his work at Creation.

Since God's plans for each and every person—very small parts of the human drama—were planned before the first brushstroke of Creation, surely all of the intricate pieces of eternity's puzzle were also carefully planned before Creation began. Breathtaking! Awesome!

The sun, moon, stars, galaxies, black holes of space, and all the far-flung heavens are staggering. The sheer distance among all of these celestial bodies is beyond human comprehension. The intricacies of the microworld are equally awesome. It seems that we can't get telescopes powerful enough to reach the extremities outward, and we can't get microscopes powerful enough to reach the extremities inward.

Even more mind-boggling is that part of Creation that we see in the mirror each morning. Try to unravel your DNA and fully comprehend the iris prints of your eyes and the uniqueness of your fingerprints. Try to comprehend twelve billion people like you, each completely unique in all these ways, and in many other ways. Try to comprehend a million more evidences that we are "fearfully and wonderfully made," as some translations of Psalm 139:14 express it.

The psalmist said, "Thank you for making me so wonderfully complex! Your workmanship is marvelous—how well I know it. You watched me as I was being formed in utter seclusion, as I was woven together in the dark of the womb. You saw me before I was born. Every day of my life was recorded in your book. Every moment was laid out before a single day had passed" (Psalm 139:14-16).

Perspective and purpose

Since the purpose of the Bible is to give perspective and purpose to our lives, we can't linger with each breathtaking idea about God's eternal plans. We are searching for perspective. To use a sports analogy, the game of life was carefully planned before the kickoff of Creation. The game plan was carefully worked out before the whistle blew to start the human drama. The Bible was ultimately written as God's owner's manual to help us discover who we are, why we're here, and what we can do about it as we head toward our eternal home.

Before God put two pristine people in the Garden of Eden, he saw in his mind the ten thousand times ten thousands of people who would stand before his throne in the last days. He also saw the connecting link between the two people in a lovely garden and the millions of people who would gather before him in his eternal Eden. You and I are two small parts of that human drama, but in God's eyes we are of enormous significance, for he yearns for us to live with him forever in his home.

That yearning is God's majestic purpose beyond which there is nothing greater. In the plans and purposes of God, one truth rises like

>

What
Everyone
Should
Know
about
the

Bible

Mount Everest—the Creator of the universe loves us and yearns eagerly for us to live with him forever in his home called heaven.

Why not create us without the choice to sin?

If God yearns for everyone to live with him in heaven, why didn't he just make us without sin, or shield us from sin, and thereby set our feet toward heaven with no option to stray? He could have done it, so why didn't he? Did we have to have the capacity to sin? Why couldn't he simply mandate that we would love him and live with him forever?

Two words provide the answer: love and choice.

God wants us in his heavenly home only if we truly love him and choose to be there with him. Love is not love and choice is not choice if they are enforced or mandated. God could have said, "You *will* all go to heaven forever, like it or not!" Heaven would not be a very heavenly place with unwilling inhabitants who never wanted to be there. (That's what hell is like, isn't it?)

Perhaps you are married or about to be married. What if you were forced to marry a person you didn't love, a person you would never choose for your lifelong mate? What kind of marriage would that be? It certainly wouldn't be choice or love. That would be hell on earth. But if you chose that one special person because you loved him or her, and you worked at keeping that love alive, your marriage would be heaven on earth.

Choice suggests an alternative—of something else or something other. For example, we may think that we want something else more than we want heaven or the God who is at its center. But the only other alternative is sin, and the lifestyle and mind-set that come with it are the bitter offering of a fallen angel called Satan, who is a master of spin. He is so skilled at spin that he can make good look bad and bad look good. He spins a tapestry of evil from threads that look deceptively good but really are not.

It all boils down to this—we either want to go to heaven or we don't, and if we do, we are willing to meet the entrance requirements. Otherwise we just don't get in. We are faced with an alternative that may look enticing in the short run but becomes wretched in the long run—and heaven and hell are both definitely for the long run.

The entrance requirements to heaven

What are the entrance requirements to heaven? One day a man asked Jesus, "Of all the commandments, which is the most important?" (Mark 12:28). Jesus' answer, quoted from Deuteronomy 6:4-5, was clear: "'The LORD our God is the one and only LORD. And you must love the LORD your God with all your heart, all your soul, all your mind, and all your strength.' The second is equally important: 'Love your neighbor as your-self'" (Mark 12:29-31). That sums up the essence of loving God and choosing God above everything else.

There is one problem that needs to be solved before we can live in God's perfect heavenly home. Our spiritual clothes are dirty from sin. No matter how much God loves us and we love him, he has to clean us up before he can let us into his spotless heavenly home. Think of the mess we would bring into heaven if we carried all our spiritual garbage with us. "For everyone has sinned; we all fall short of God's glorious standard" (Romans 3:23).

God must wash our spirits, or souls. He must wash that sin away. How? "Without the shedding of blood, there is no forgiveness" (Hebrews 9:22). The Scriptures explain that "the blood of Christ will purify our consciences" and that "Christ offered himself to God as a perfect sacrifice for our sins" (Hebrews 9:14). We don't understand how or why, but we accept the Bible teaching that blood must be spilled to pay the price for sin. Under the Old Testament system, the blood of innocent lambs was offered in sacrifice again and again. The New Testament is based on the blood of the Lamb of God—Jesus—offered once and for all time for people who accept his sacrifice for their cleansing.

The book of Revelation

We come at last to Revelation, the final book in our Bible. It is a power-ful book with awesome imagery. John, a once-upon-a-time fisherman on the Sea of Galilee, is now a one-hundred-year-old apostle and church leader who has been banished to the lonely island of Patmos. John was very close to Jesus as one of the Twelve, probably closer than any of the others. He sat next to Jesus at the Last Supper, ran to the tomb with Peter to verify that Jesus had risen, was in the upper room when the risen Christ visited his disciples, and was the favored one whom Jesus chose to care for his mother, Mary, after he was gone.

John wrote the Gospel of John and the three epistles also bearing his name. Revelation was his masterpiece. Jesus drew aside the curtain of heaven and let his close friend peek in as much as he dared. John discov-ered that there are some sights too magnificent to communicate. Words simply are not big enough to carry the imagery of all that he saw.

How does one describe two hundred million angels armed for war against the principalities and powers of evil? How does one describe the final judgment of Satan as he is tossed into a great lake of fire? How does one describe God's great white throne, with the nations of the earth streaming before him for judgment? How does one describe the New Jerusalem, a heavenly city coming down to earth, sparkling like a precious gem and formed with crystal-clear gold and precious

562

>

What
Everyone
Should
Know
about
the

Bible

stones? How does one describe the nations of the world bringing their glory of the ages into the heavenly city to present it to Jesus? How does one describe the prayers of all the people of all the ages stored in great golden bowls, now released as a fragrance to permeate heaven?

How does one describe the nail prints in Jesus' hands and feet that are still visible as emblems of unimaginable honor, eternal reminders that "God loved the world so much that he gave his one and only Son, so that everyone who believes in him will not perish but have eternal life" (John 3:16). Every time we see those wounds throughout eternity, we will say thank you!

So from eons before Creation, God carefully laid his plans—for Creation and for consummation, for the beginning of the world as we know it until the end of the world as we know it, to be replaced at last by a new heaven and a new earth (Revelation 21:1). God carefully laid his plans—for you and for billions of others, each with a choice to accept his love or reject his love. Before Creation God carefully laid his plans for an eternal home—the new heaven and the new earth, where we may dwell with him forever if we choose to accept his love.

Significant Dates of This Time

Circa A.D. 95, John wrote Revelation while in exile on Patmos, approximately one hundred years after the birth of Jesus at Bethlehem.

What everyone should know about the book of Revelation

IF ONLY I COULD KNOW THE FUTURE

If only I knew the future, what a difference that would make! If I knew what the stock market would do next week, or even tomorrow, I could get rich. If I knew that my house would never burn down, think how much I could save on fire insurance. If I knew that I would never get sick, I could plan better for the future. If I knew when I would die, I could plan the rest of my life better. If only I knew . . .

But you and I don't know the future—only God does. In Old Testament times, God occasionally drew aside the curtain of time and showed a prophet such as Isaiah, Micah, or Daniel some things that were to come. Occasionally in New Testament times God revealed small video clips of the future to men such as Paul. But no place in the Bible draws aside the curtain of time and eternity so vividly as Revelation.

This is John's last writing as well as the last biblical writing. The apostle John had outlived all of the other twelve apostles. He had outlived Peter and Paul. He was the last of a select group who had seen Jesus and walked with him. John had even cared for Jesus' mother, Mary, after the Crucifixion.

John was now a one-hundred-year-old man, banished on the Island of Patmos. That is old even by today's standards, but it was almost unheard of then. Alone, near the end of life's journey, John waited for God to reveal something special. From heaven Jesus revealed the future to John (Revelation 1:1), and John tried to find words to describe what he saw.

Jesus directed John to send this letter to seven churches in Asia Minor, which is present-day Turkey. The letter is also for you and me.

Discovering My Purpose from God's Plan

1. *The Bible has endured longer than every empire or emperor.* It is eternal.
2. *The Bible is an autobiography of God.*
3. *The Bible is a blueprint for your life—now and forever.*
4. *The Bible is a map to heaven.*
5. *To understand the end of all things, we must understand the beginning of all things.* Alpha and Omega are linked with an unbroken chain.
6. *The consummation of time and history was fully planned before Creation began.*
7. *The macroworld and the microworld are without limit.* There is no microscope powerful enough to see to the absolute depths of the microworld and no telescope powerful enough to see to the outer limits of the macroworld.
8. *The purpose of the Bible, and this book, is to give perspective and purpose to your life.*
9. *The Creator of the universe yearns for us to live in his home in heaven—if we choose to do so.*
10. *Love is not love if it is enforced or mandated, and choice is not choice unless it is freely made.* Love is love only when it is a choice. Choice selects the best alternative when motivated by love.
11. *Jesus' wounds will remain throughout eternity, and every time we see them we will say thank you.*

INDEX

568

>

What
Everyone
Should
Know
about
the
Bible

570

>

What
Everyone
Should
Know
about
the

Bible

> What
Everyone
Should
Know
about
the

Bible

Dr. V. Gilbert Beers has written more than 150 books, of which more than one hundred are for children, including *The Toddlers Bible, My Bedtime Anytime Storybook, The One Year Bible for Children,* and *Tell Me the Story of Jesus.* His books have appeared more than one hundred times on the best-seller lists. More than forty of his books have been published in twenty-four languages. He also helped develop nine specialty Bibles, including *The Life Application Bible* and the *Touchpoint Bible.* His most recent works are the eight-volume *Family Bible Library* and *Character Building from the Life of Jesus.*

An avid photographer, Gil has published more than 2,500 photos with more than twenty publishers, especially as book covers. More than twenty thousand of his photos appear on the Internet site *www. christianimagelibrary.com,* an image subscription service.

Gil has two earned doctorates: a PhD in communications from Northwestern University and a ThD from Northern Baptist Theological Seminary. He is listed in *Who's Who in America, Who's Who in Biblical Studies and Archaeology, Contemporary Authors,* and several other compilations of leadership biographies.

Happily married for fifty-six years, Gil and his wife, Arlie, have five children and eleven grandchildren. Gil's passion in life is to help people of all ages love the Bible and become godly people in Christ Jesus. He says, "If we can help people *love to learn* the Bible, they will then *learn to love* the Bible."

Books in The Complete Book Popular Reference Series

The Complete Book of Bible Trivia contains more than 4,500 questions and answers about the Bible.

J. STEPHEN LANG

The Complete Book of Christian Heroes is an in-depth popular reference about those who have suffered for the cause of Christ throughout the world.

DAVE & NETA JACKSON

The Complete Book of When and Where in the Bible and throughout History focuses on more than 1,000 dates that illustrate how God has worked throughout history to do extraordinary things through ordinary people.

E. MICHAEL & SHARON RUSTEN

The Complete Book of Zingers is an alphabetized collection of one-sentence sermons.

CROFT M. PENTZ

The Complete Book of Who's Who in the Bible is your ultimate resource for learning about the people of the Bible.

PHILIP COMFORT
WALTER A. ELWELL

The Complete Book of Bible Basics identifies and defines the names, phrases, events, stories, and terms from the Bible and church history that are familiar to most Christians.

MARK D. TAYLOR

In **The Complete Book of Bible Secrets and Mysteries** Stephen Lang, an expert on the Bible, serves up secrets and mysteries of the Bible in a fun, entertaining way.

J. STEPHEN LANG

The Complete Book of Bible Trivia: Bad Guys Edition, an extension of Stephen Lang's best-selling book *The Complete Book of Bible Trivia,* focuses on facts about the "bad guys" in the Bible.

J. STEPHEN LANG

The Complete Book of Hymns is the largest collection of behind-the-scenes stories about the most popular hymns and praise songs.

WILLIAM J. PETERSEN
& ARDYTHE PETERSEN

The Complete Book of Wacky Wit is filled with more than 1,500 humorous sayings to live by.

VERNON McLELLAN